Documents Collection

THIRD EDITION

Henretta Brownlee Brody Ware Johnson

Documents Collection

America*'s History

Volume 1 TO 1877

Cathy Matson
University of Delaware

John K. Alexander
University of Cincinnati

Louis S. Gerteis
University of Missouri–St. Louis

Worth Publishers

Documents Collection by Cathy Matson, John K. Alexander,
and Louis S. Gerteis

to accompany
Henretta, Brownlee, Brody, Ware, and Johnson:
America's History, Volume 1 to 1877, Third Edition

ISBN: 1–57259–223–0

Printing: 3 4 5   Year: 01 00 99

Cover: William Britton, *Market Square, Germantown,* c. 1820. Oil on canvas,
12 1/4 × 19 7/8". Philadelphia Museum of Art: Collection of Edgar William
and Bernice Chrysler Garbisch. (Detail)

Most credits and acknowledgments appear with the documents. Some changes, however, appear in
"Credits and Acknowledgments," page 321. This listing constitutes a continuation of the copyright page.

Worth Publishers
33 Irving Place
New York, NY 10003

Preface

Volume 1 of the *Documents Collection* brings together over 160 primary source documents to enrich the study of *America's History*. In addition to key speeches, laws, contemporary accounts, letters, diaries, and other written documents, the collection includes political cartoons, engravings, and statistical tables that shed light on all aspects of political, social, economic, and cultural history.

The *Collection* follows the chapter organization of the textbook. The ten or so documents in each chapter are grouped into two or three sets corresponding to the main headings of the textbook chapter. Each set begins with an introduction that places that group of documents in their wider historical context. The individual documents follow, each with its own headnote and questions. The document set concludes with three Questions for Further Thought designed to help students to see connections among the documents and how the documents illustrate or exemplify larger themes.

The *Collection* has been designed for maximum flexibility of use. Because headnotes and questions accompany each document, instructors who want to focus on a particular document can do so, while those who wish to explore a section in depth can assign a complete document set. Some of the documents provide interesting comparisons and contrasts to specific American Voices excerpts in the textbook, for example.

For documents-based courses or courses with a special focus, the *Instructor's Resource Manual* to accompany *America's History* contains more than 100 *additional* documents that can be reproduced as student handouts. These collections of documents have been designed to help your students learn to read and interpret the rich diversity of source materials used in American history today.

Contents

P A R T **2**

The New Republic, 1775–1820

★   ★   ★

Documents Collection

CHAPTER 1

Worlds Collide: Europe and America 1450–1630

★ ★ ★

Native American Worlds

Until late in the fifteenth century unbreachable oceans bordered the Europeans' world. Totally unknown to them were the two continents of the Western Hemisphere with at least 40 million inhabitants. Those indigenous peoples were the descendants of Asian migrants who had traveled across the temporary land bridge spanning the Bering Strait during the last great Ice Age (see text pp. 4–5).

After 1492 contact with Europeans proved devastating to the inhabitants of the "New World." Lacking a natural immunity to European diseases such as smallpox, measles, and influenza, native Americans were powerless to resist them. Document 1-1 is a graph showing the precipitous decline in the American Indian population north of Mexico in the five centuries after contact with Europeans. From an estimated 5 million to 7 million people, the native American population shrank to about a quarter million by 1900.

Disease made it easier for the Spanish to conquer indigenous civilizations in Mesoamerica, but technological superiority was equally important. Document 1-2 presents excerpts from the classic eyewitness account of Bernal Díaz del Castillo.

Well before 1492 native Americans had developed civilizations and societies of great complexity and variety (see text pp. 4–11). As Document 1-3 shows, stories passed from generation to generation recorded many different beliefs in very distinctive tribes. Europeans were amazed—and often affronted—by the implacable cultural differences they encountered. One of those differences is highlighted in Document 1-4, a description of aspects of Iroquoian society that were utterly alien to Europeans.

1-1   Indian and Non-Indian Population Charts, 1492–1980

Two parabolic lines on the graphs below tell the story of North American population trends after 1492. One part of the story is tragic: the calamitous decline in native American numbers primarily as a result of the impact of European disease (see text pp. 21–22). The other part is celebratory: the startling increase in the population of non-Indian peoples, which was due primarily to high fertility rates and massive immigration. These graphs refer only to populations in what is now the United States. The combined native American population on the two continents of the Western Hemisphere at the time of Columbus has been estimated at more than 40 million; the overall decline is similar to that for the United States. This is the greatest known demographic catastrophe in human history.

Source: From *American Indian Holocaust and Survival: A Population History since 1492*, by Russell Thornton. Copyright © 1987 by the University of Oklahoma Press. Reprinted by permission.

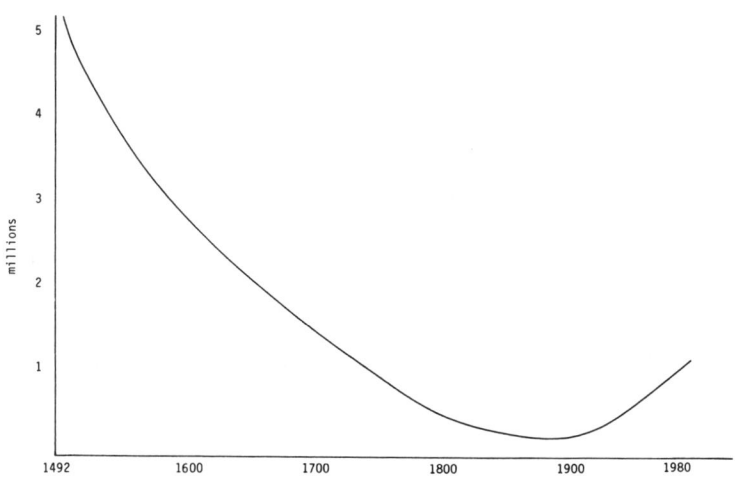

American Indian Population Decline and Recovery in the United States Area, 1492–1980

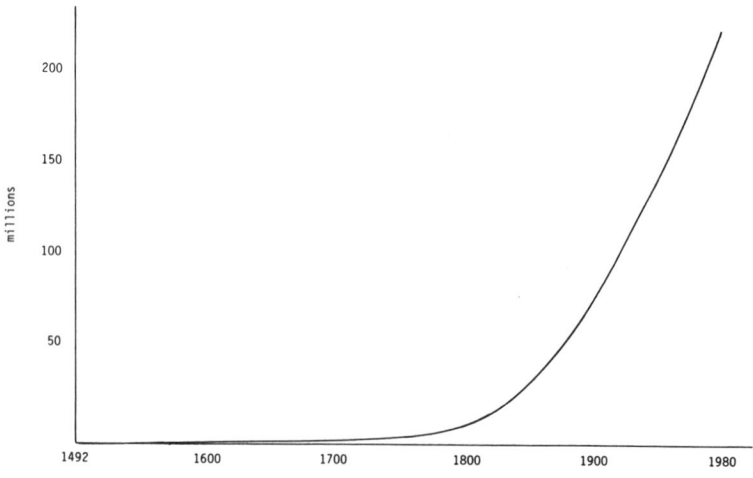

Non-Indian Population Growth in the United States Area, 1492–1980

Questions

1. Put this rate of decline in perspective by thinking about a family, a clan, or a tribe. Speculate about the social impact. Imagine a state—say, Wisconsin, with a population of about 5 million in 1990—losing 95 percent of its people. How would the survivors feel? How could they maintain their economic activities?
2. In which years were Indian and non-Indian populations even? Why did rapid Indian decline occur *before* the arrival of many non-Indians?
3. The non-Indian population rose dramatically after 1800, and the Indian population recovered after 1900. Why?

1-2   Díaz del Castillo's *Discovery and Conquest of Mexico*

Most of the precontact hieroglyphic writings of the Aztecs and Maya were destroyed by Spanish priests, and we have learned about these cultures mainly through European eyes. Bernal Díaz del Castillo, who was born in 1492, accompanied Hernando Cortés on the march to Tenochtitlán and the conquest of Mexico. His firsthand account offers many glimpses of Mexican customs and societies and fascinating hints about Cortés's military strategies. Most subsequent histories of the conquest employ Díaz's reminiscences (see text pp. 5–6, 20–21, and especially Map 1.3).

Cacique is a Caribbean term, adopted by the Spanish, meaning a native chief. For Díaz's "Montezuma" read "Moctezuma" (see text pp. 20–21).

Source: Excerpts from *The Discovery and Conquest of Mexico, 1517–1521*, by Bernal Díaz del Castillo, translated by A. P. Maudslay, pp. 102–105, 119, 156–157. Copyright © 1956 by Farrar, Straus & Cudahy. Copyright renewed © 1984 by Farrar, Straus & Giroux, Inc. Reprinted by permission of Farrar, Straus & Giroux, Inc.

We slept the night in those huts, and all the caciques bore us company all the way to our quarters in their town. They were really anxious that we should not leave their country, as they were fearful that Montezuma would send his warriors against them, and they said to Cortés that as we were already their friends, they would like to have us for brothers, and that it would be well that we should take from their daughters, so as to have children by them; and to cement our friendship, they brought eight damsels, all of them daughters of caciques, and gave one of these cacicas, who was the niece of the fat cacique, to Cortés; and one who was the daughter of another great cacique was given to Alonzo Hernández Puertocarrero. All eight of them were clothed in the rich garments of the country, beautifully ornamented as is their custom. Each one of them had a golden collar around her neck and golden earrings in her ears, and they came accompanied by other Indian girls who were to serve as their maids. When the fat cacique presented them, he said to Cortés: "Tecle (which in their language means Lord)—these seven women are for your captains, and this one, who is my niece, is for you, and she

is the señora of towns and vassals." Cortés received them with a cheerful countenance, and thanked the caciques for the gifts, but he said that before we could accept them and become brothers, they must get rid of those idols which they believed in and worshipped, and which kept them in darkness, and must no longer offer sacrifices to them, and that when he could see those cursed things thrown to the ground and an end put to sacrifices that then our bonds of brotherhood would be most firmly tied. He added that these damsels must become Christians before we could receive them. Every day we saw sacrificed before us three, four or five Indians whose hearts were offered to the idols and their blood plastered on the walls, and the feet, arms and legs of the victims were cut off and eaten, just as in our country we eat beef brought from the butchers. I even believe that they sell it by retail in the *tianguez* as they call their markets. Cortés told them that if they gave up these evil deeds and no longer practised them, not only would we be their friends, but we would make them lords over other provinces. All the caciques, priests and chiefs replied that it did not seem to them good to give up their idols and sacrifices and that these gods of theirs gave them health and good harvests and everything of which they had need. . . .

When the Caciques, priests, and chieftains were silenced, Cortés ordered all the idols which we had overthrown and broken to pieces to be taken out of sight and burned. Then eight priests who had charge of the idols came out of a chamber and carried them back to the house whence they had come, and burned them. These priests wore black cloaks like cassocks and long gowns reaching to their feet, and some had hoods like those worn by canons, and others had smaller hoods like those worn by Dominicans, and they wore their hair very long, down to the waist, with some even reaching down to the feet, covered with blood and so matted together that it could not be separated, and their ears were cut to pieces by way of sacrifice, and they stank like sulphur, and they had another bad smell like carrion, and as they said, and we learnt that it was true, these priests were the sons of chiefs and they abstained from women, and they fasted on certain days, and what I saw them eat was the pith of seeds of cotton when the cotton was being cleaned, but they may have eaten other things which I did not see. . . .

I remember that in the plaza where some of their oratories stood, there were piles of human skulls so regularly arranged that one could count them, and I estimated them at more than a hundred thousand. I repeat again that there were more than one hundred thousand of them. And in another part of the plaza there were so many piles of dead men's thigh bones that one could not count them; there was also a large number of skulls strung between beams of wood, and three priests who had charge of these bones and skulls were guarding them. We had occasion to see many such things later on as we penetrated into the country for the same custom we observed in all the towns, including those of Tlaxcala. . . .

Cortés then took these Caciques aside and questioned them very fully about Mexican affairs. Xicotenga, as he was the best informed and a great chieftain, took the lead in talking, and from time to time he was helped by Mase Escasi who was also a great chief.

He said that Montezuma had such great strength in warriors that when he wished to capture a great city or make a raid on a province, he could place a hundred and fifty thousand men in the field, and this they knew well from the experience of the wars and hostilities they had had with them for more than a hundred years past.

Cortés asked them how it was that with so many warriors as they said came down on them they had never been entirely conquered. They answered that although the Mexicans sometimes defeated them and killed them, and carried off many of their vassals for sacrifice, many of the enemy were also left dead on the field and others were made prisoners, and that they never could come so secretly that they did not get some warning, and that when they knew of their approach they mustered all their forces and with the help of the people of Huexotzingo they defended themselves and made counter attacks. That as all the provinces which had been raided by Montezuma and placed under his rule were ill disposed towards the Mexicans, and that as their inhabitants were carried off by force to the wars, they did not fight with good will; indeed, it was from these very men that they received warnings, and for this reason they had defended their country to the best of their ability.

The place from which the most continuous trouble came to them was a very great city a day's march distant, which is called Cholula, whose inhabitants were most treacherous. It was there that Montezuma secretly mustered his companies and, as it was near by, they made their raids by night. Moreover, Mase Escasi said that Montezuma kept garrisons of many warriors stationed in all the provinces in addition to the great force he could bring from the city, and that all the provinces paid tribute of gold and silver, feathers, stones, cloth and cotton, and Indian men and women for sacrifice and others for servants, that he [Montezuma] was such a great prince that he possessed everything he could desire, that the houses where he dwelt were full of riches and [precious] stones and chalchihuites which he had robbed and taken by force from those who would not give them willingly, and that all the wealth of the country was in his hands.

Then they spoke of the great fortifications of the city, and what the lake was like, and the depth of water, and about the causeways that gave access to the city, and the wooden bridges in each causeway, and how one can go in and out [by water] through the opening that there is in each bridge, and how when the bridges are raised one can be cut off between bridge and bridge and not be able to reach the city. How the greater part of the city was built in the lake, and that one could not pass from house to house except by draw-bridges and canoes which they had ready. That all the houses were flat-roofed and all the roofs were provided with parapets so that they could fight from them.

They brought us pictures of the battles they had fought with the Mexicans painted on large henequen cloths, showing their manner of fighting. . . .

Questions

1. What "unusual" customs or rituals did Díaz del Castillo observe?
2. Díaz del Castillo emphasizes the strange and the bizarre. Can you spot any similarities between the native American and Spanish cultures?

3. Do you think Cortés could have conquered Mexico without Indian allies? Why or why not?

1-3 Myths of Creation

The peoples of the eastern Northern American woodlands (see text pp. 10–11) recounted their origins and explained important aspects of their cultures through verbal storytelling. Some accounts of clan or language–group origins seemed strange and even unbelievable to Europeans in the sixteenth and seventeenth centuries. Yet there often were striking similarities between Indian stories and European folklore or biblical accounts of birth, natural disasters, and the significance of certain rituals. Corn, or maize, was the central object of many eastern and southeastern peoples' sacred and secular history. It was probably domesticated in the central plains of Mexico at least 8,000 years ago and was gradually transmitted and adapted to more northerly climates.

Source: The Iroquois account is a composite of Iroquois stories of their origins, adopted from Daniel Richter, *The Ordeal of the Longhouse: The Peoples of the Iroquois League in the Era of European Colonization* (Chapel Hill, N.C.: University of North Carolina Press, 1992), pp. 9–11; who adopted them from nineteenth century accounts, including that of J. N. B. Hewitt, ed., "Iroquoian Cosmology," part 2, *Annual Report*, 1899–1900 (Washington, D.C.: Bureau of American Ethnology, 1903), pp. 464–469. Corn Mother is a Penobscot myth taken from various tellings, especially Joseph Nicolar, *The Life and Traditions of the Red Man* (Bangor, Maine: C. H. Glass, 1893).

Iroquois Account of the Origins of Human Life

In a house in the Sky World, a man and a woman lived on opposite sides of a fireplace. The two had great spiritual power because each had been isolated from other people until the age of puberty. Everyday after the housemates went out to work, the woman crossed to the other side of the fire to comb the man's hair. Through mysterious means, she became pregnant and bore a daughter. Shortly thereafter, the man fell ill and announced that he would soon die. Because no one in the Sky World knew what death was, he had to explain to the woman what would happen to him and instruct her how to preserve his body. After he died, the woman's growing daughter endured fits of weeping that, despite the best efforts of village neighbors to comfort her, could be relieved only by visits to the preserved corpse of the deceased, whose spirit told her that he was her father and taught her many things.

When the daughter, whom the Iroquois called Sky Woman, reached adulthood, her father's spirit instructed her to take a dangerous journey to the village of a man destined to become her spouse. She brought her prospective husband loaves of bread baked with berries and then, enduring great travail, cooked him a potent soup that cured him of a long-troublesome ailment. In exchange, he sent her home with a burden of venison that nearly filled her family's house. After Sky Woman returned to her husband, the pair always slept on opposite sides of the fire and refrained from sexual intercourse. Nevertheless, she, like her mother before her, inexplicably became pregnant. Stricken by jealousy, the husband again became ill and dreamed that a great tree near his house must be uprooted so that he and his spouse could look down through the resulting hole to the world below. To cure his sickness, all the people of the village worked together to pull it up. When Sky Woman looked over the edge of the abyss, her husband pushed her down.

As Sky Woman fell toward the endless waters below, the spirit birds and animals of the sea held a council to decide how to rescue her, Ducks flew up to catch her on their wings and bring her safely down, and the Turtle agreed to provide a place for her to rest on his Back. Meantime, various animals tried to dive to the bottom of the lake and bring up earth on which the woman could walk; only the Muskrat succeeded. The material he placed on the Turtle's back grew, with Sky Woman's help, into the living dry land of North America. Soon the celestial visitor gave birth to a daughter, who in time became supernaturally pregnant by the spirit of the Turtle. In the younger woman's womb grew male twins, who began arguing over the best way to emerge from her body. The Good Twin (Upholder of the Heavens, or Sky Grasper) was born normally. The second, the Evil Twin, burst forth from his mother's side and thus killed her. When Sky Woman asked which of her grandsons had slain her daughter, they blamed each other, but the Evil Twin was the more persistent and persuasive. The Grandmother cherished him, and she turned the body and head of the boys' deceased mother into the sun and moon, respectively; and she threw the Good Twin out of her house, assuming he would die.

But he did not. Instead, with the aid of his father the Turtle, the Good Twin improved Iroquoia, making various animals, learning the secrets of cultivating maize and other crops, and bringing into existence mortal human beings. All of these things he did not create from nothingness; they grew through a process of transformation and infusion of supernatural power from the living earth and from a kind of spirit beings who dwelled in the Sky World and under the waters. With each new creation, however, Sky Woman and the Evil Twin partially undid the Good Twin's efforts in ways that forever after would make life difficult for humans. When the Good Twin constructed straight rivers for canoeing, with the water flowing in both ways at once, the Evil Twin threw in rocks and hills to twist the streams and make their waters fall in only one direction. When the Good Twin grew succulent ears of corn, Sky Woman threw ashes into his cooking pot and decreed that maize must be parched and ground before it could be eaten. When the good Twin made animals readily give themselves to humans as food, the Evil Twin sealed them all in a cave, from which Sky Grasper could rescue only a portion; the rest the Evil Twin turned into enemies of humans.

Finally, the two brothers also fought, and the Good Twin won. He could not, however, undo all the evil that his brother and Grandmother had left in the world. So he taught humans how to grow corn, and how to keep harm at bay with ceremonies of thanksgiving and peacekeeping with the spirits. Sky Grasper made these ceremonies easier by designating clans named after certain animals such as Wolf, Bear, Turtle. But he knew that mortals could never keep the ritual well enough. But Sky Grasper also predicted the time would come when all peoples would fall into great dispute and destroy one another. Good Twin went home, where he never died, but instead continually passed through stages of aging and then rejuvenating himself.

Corn Mother: A Penobscot Myth

When Kloskurbeh, the All-maker, lived on earth, there were no people yet. But one day when the sun was high, a youth appeared and called him "Uncle, brother of my mother." This young man was born from the foam of the waves, foam quickened by the wind and warmed by the sun. It was the motion of the wind, the moistness of water, and the sun's warmth, which gave him life. . . . And the young man lived with Kloskurbeh and became his chief helper.

Now, after these two powerful beings had created all manner of things, there came to them, as the sun was shin-

ing at high noon, a beautiful girl. She was born of the wonderful earth plant, and of the dew, and of warmth. Because a drop of dew fell on a leaf and was warmed by the sun, and the warming sun is life, this girl came into being from the green living plant, from moisture, and from warmth.

"I am love," said the maiden. "I am a strength giver, I am the nourisher, I am the provider of men and animals. They all love me."

Then Kloskurbeh thanked the Great Master Above for having sent them the maiden. The youth, the Great Nephew, married her, and the girl conceived and thus became First Mother. An Kloskurbeh, the Great Uncle, who teaches humans all they need to know, taught their children how to live. Then he went away to dwell in the north, from which he will return sometime when he is needed.

Now, the people increased and became numerous. They lived by hunting, and the more people there were, the less game they found. They were hunting it out, and as the animals decreased, starvation came upon the people. And First Mother pitied them.

The little children came to First Mother and said: "We are hungry. Feed us." But she had nothing to give them, and she wept. She told them: "Be patient. I will make some food. Then your little bellies will be full." But she kept weeping.

Her husband asked: "How can I make you smile? How can I make you happy?"

"There is only one thing that will stop my tears."

"What is it?" asked her husband.

"It is this: you must kill me."

"I could never do that."

"You must, or I will go on weeping and grieving forever."

The husband traveled far, to the end of the earth, to the north he went, to ask the Great Instructor, his uncle Kloskurbeh, what he should do.

"You must do what she wants. You must kill her," said Kloskurbeh. Then the young man went back to his home, and it was his turn to weep. But First Mother said: "Tomorrow at high noon you must do it. After you have killed me, let two of our sons take hold of my hair and drag my body over that empty patch of earth. Let them drag me back and forth, back and forth, over every part of the patch, until all my flesh has been torn from my body. Afterwards, take my bones, gather them up, and bury them in the middle of this clearing. Then leave that place."

She smiled and said, "Wait seven moons and then come back, and you will find my flesh there, flesh given out of love, and it will nourish and strengthen you forever and ever."

So it was done. The husband slew his wife and her sons, praying, dragged her body to and fro as she had commanded, until her flesh covered all the earth. Then they took up her bones and buried them in the middle of it. Weeping loudly, they went away.

When the husband and his children and his children's children came back to that place after seven moons had passed, they found the earth covered with tall, green, tasseled plants. The plants' fruit—corn—was First Mother's flesh, given so that people might live and flourish. And they partook of First Mother's flesh and found it sweet beyond words. Following her instructions, they did not eat all, but put many kernels back into the earth. In this way her flesh and spirit renewed themselves every seven months, generation after generation.

And at the spot where they had burned First Mother's bones, there grew another plant, broad-leafed and fragrant. It was First Mother's breath, and they heard her spirit talking: "Burn this up and smoke it. It is scared. It will clear your minds, help your prayers, and gladden your hearts."

And First Mother's husband called the first plant Skarmunal, corn, and the second plant utarmur-yayeh, tobacco.

"Remember," he told the people, "and take good care of First Mother's flesh, because it is her goodness become substance. Take good care of her breath, because it is her love turned into smoke. Remember her and think of her whenever you eat, whenever you smoke this sacred plant, because she has given her life that you might live. Yet she is not dead, she lives: in undying love she renews herself again and again."

Questions

1. What similarities are there between the Iroquois account of human origins and the way many Europeans understood how the world began?
2. What can one learn about the role of women and children in these cultures?
3. In what ways is a myth, as in these two examples, both a history and a moral lesson?

1-4 Charlevoix's Account of Huron Society

Pierre de Charlevoix, a Jesuit, came to New France as a French spy in 1720. He traveled up the Saint Lawrence River, through the Great Lakes, and down the Mississippi to New Orleans. During his travels he kept a journal, cast in the form of letters, that was first published in 1744. Charlevoix's careful observations reveal a structure that seemed extraordinary to Europeans (see text pp. 10–11). Among the Huron, he tells us, women played an important role in a democratic decision-making process. The historian James Axtell calls Huron society a "gynecocracy," or a government ruled by women.

Source: P[ierre] de Charlevoix, *Journal of a Voyage to North-America* (London, 1761), vol. 2, pp. 23–27. In James Axtell, *The Indian Peoples of Eastern America: A Documentary History of the Sexes.* (New York: Oxford University Press, 1981), pp. 150–153.

In the northern parts, and wherever the Algonquin tongue prevails, the dignity of chief is elective; and the whole ceremony of election and installation consists in some feasts, accompanied with dances and songs; the chief elect likewise never fails to make the panegyrick of his predecessor, and to invoke his genius. Amongst the Hurons, where this dignity is hereditary, the succession is continued through the women, so that at the death of a chief, it is not his own, but his sister's son who succeeds him; or, in default of which, his nearest relation in the female line. When the whole branch happens to be extinct, the noblest matron of the tribe or in the nation chuses the person she approves of most, and declares him chief. The person who is to govern must be come to years of maturity; and when the hereditary chief is not as yet arrived at this period, they appoint a regent, who has all the authority, but which he holds in name of the minor. These chiefs generally have no great marks of outward respect paid them, and if they are never disobeyed, it is because they know how to set bounds to their authority. It is true that they request or propose, rather than command; and never exceed the boundaries of that small share of authority with which they are vested. Thus it is properly reason which governs, and the government has so much the more influence, as obedience is founded in liberty; and that they are free from any apprehension of its degenerating into tyranny.

Nay more, each family has a right to chuse a counsellor of its own, and an assistant to the chief, who is to watch for their interest; and without whose consent the chief can undertake nothing. These counsellors are, above all things, to have an eye to the public treasury; and it is properly they who determine the uses it is to be put to. They are invested with this character in a general council, but they do not acquaint their allies with it, as they do at the elections and installations of their chief. Amongst the Huron nations, the women name the counsellors, and often chuse persons of their own sex.

This body of counsellors or assistants is the highest of all; the next is that of the elders, consisting of all those who have come to the years of maturity. I have not been able to find exactly what this age is. The last of all is that of the warriors; this comprehends all who are able to bear arms. This body has often at its head, the chief of the nation or town; but he must first have distinguished himself by some signal action of bravery; if not, he is obliged to serve as a subaltern, that is, as a single centinel; there being no degrees in the militia of the Indians.

In fact, a large body may have several chiefs, this title being given to all who ever commanded; but they are not therefore the less subject to him who leads the party; a kind of general, without character or real authority, who has power neither to reward nor punish, whom his soldiers are at liberty to abandon at pleasure and with impunity, and whose orders notwithstanding are scarce ever disputed: so true it is, that amongst a people who are guided by reason, and inspired with sentiments of honour and love for their country, independence is not destructive of subordination; and, that a free and voluntary obedience is that on which we can always rely with the greatest certainty. Moreover, the qualities requisite are, that he be fortunate, of undoubted courage, and perfectly disinterested. It is no miracle, that a person possessed of such eminent qualities should be obeyed.

The women have the chief authority amongst all the nations of the Huron language; if we except the Iroquois canton of Onneyouth [Oneida], in which it is in both sexes alternately. But if this be their lawful constitution, their practice is seldom agreeable to it. In fact, the men never tell the women any thing they would have to be kept secret; and rarely any affair of consequence is communicated to them, though all is done in their name, and the chiefs are no more than their lieutenants. . . . The real authority of the women is very small: I have been however assured, that they always deliberate first on whatever is proposed in council; and that they afterwards give the result of their deliberation to the chiefs, who make the report of it to the general council, composed of the elders; but in all probability this is done only for form's sake, and with the restrictions I have already mentioned. The warriors likewise consult together, on what relates to their particular province, but can conclude nothing of importance which concerns the nation or town; all being subject to the examination and controul of the council of elders, who judge in the last resource.

It must be acknowledged, that proceedings are carried on in these assemblies with a wisdom and a coolness, and a knowledge of affairs, and I may add generally with a probity, which would have done honour to the areopagus of Athens, or to the senate of Rome, in the most glorious days of those republics: the reason of this is, that nothing is resolved upon with precipitation; and that those violent passions, which have so much disgraced the politics even of Christians, have never prevailed amongst the Indians over the public good. Interested persons fail not, however, to set many springs in motion, and apply an address in the execution of their designs, we could hardly believe barbarians capable of; they also all of them possess, in the most sovereign degree, the art of concealing their real intentions: but generally speaking, the glory of the nation and motive of honour, are the chief movers in all enterprizes. What can never be excused in them is, that they often make honour consist in satiating a revenge which knows no bounds; a fault which Christianity alone is able to correct, and in which all our politeness and religion are often unsuccessful.

Each tribe has an orator in every town, which orators are the only persons who have a liberty to speak in the public councils and general assemblies: they always speak well and to the purpose. Besides this natural eloquence . . . they have a perfect knowledge of the interests of their employers, and an address in placing the best side of their own cause in the most advantageous light, which nothing can exceed. On some occasions, the women have an orator, who speaks in their name, or rather acts as their interpreter.

Questions

1. What role did women play in Huron decision making?
2. Was their power real or merely a mask for male supremacy?

3. Ideally, Hurons suppressed their "violent passions" for the sake of the public good. Would this be realistic in any society?

Questions for Further Thought

1. A demographic catastrophe and a brutal conquest of another culture: Should we pay more attention to American history before European settlement? Why or why not?

2. A demographic catastrophe and a brutal conquest of another culture: Is this the stuff of history, or should we feel moral outrage? Why or why not?

3. Can we learn profitable lessons by studying native American cultures? Why or why not?

Traditional European Society in 1450 and Europe and the World, 1450–1550

Even before 1450 "traditional" European society was growing and changing. The population increased, farming techniques improved, and towns and trade expanded. Europe flexed its muscles by looking outward to the Holy Land, which it sought to re-Christianize by conquest, and to new trade routes to Africa and the East. At the same time many Europeans worked toward the spiritual purification of the continent. Much still remained "traditional," including the ties of most people to the land and the supremacy of the Christian faith. Secular rulers rose and fell; wars and anarchy occurred frequently; famine and disease remained an omnipresent threat; and the Black Death, or bubonic plague (roughly 1347–1400), seemed to be an example of God's inexplicable ways. Social conditions changed everywhere, although not at the same time.

The Renaissance, which began early in the fourteenth century in Italy, transformed Europe, and a transformed Europe discovered America (text pp. 16–18). This "rebirth," or renewal of intellectual inquiry and human knowledge, offered limitless possibility for learning and creativity. Renaissance humanism liberated Europeans from the spiritual and hierarchical dogmas of the past. It celebrated secular and individual characteristics: willpower, activity, the unlimited potential of human nature, creative talent, and *virtù*. By *virtù*, Italian scholars meant the application of the "manly" powers in the secular pursuits of war, statecraft, and the arts.

Portugal, a small and remote European nation that for fifty years had set its sights on the East, paved the way for the discovery of America (see text p. 18). The Portuguese pioneered new navigational techniques that were eagerly studied by the young Christopher Columbus, who lived in Portugal from 1476 to 1485. Columbus was looking for a quick route to the East when he encountered the unknown American landmass in 1492. The Atlantic Ocean, long a barrier to Europeans, became a bridge to the New World.

Quickly Portugal and Spain began Europeanizing the globe, dividing the new lands between them. In 1498 Vasco Da Gama landed on the Malabar Coast of India, establishing an Asian empire of trade and commerce backed by sea power, war, and plunder (see text p. 18). Spain established sugar plantations in the Caribbean that soon were worked by African slaves. Cortés conquered the Aztecs in Mexico; Pizarro, the Incas in Peru (see text pp. 19–23).

The documents in this section explore both continuity and change from the eleventh century through the Renaissance. Document 1-5 recounts the recurring problem of famine. Document 1-6 reveals the goals of the Portuguese. Document 1-7 describes the moment of first contact between Europeans and native Americans.

1-5   Raoul Glaber's Account of Famine

Tens of thousands of people still die of famine in the modern world, and their stories often goad the machinery of international relief into action. Imagine a time when the causes of famine were almost wholly natural rather than political, no national or international support system existed, and people were left to their own devices (see text pp. 12–13). The monk Raoul Glaber was a member of the Cluniac monastic order in France. For leadership, the Cluniacs looked exclusively to the pope in Rome rather than to a secular ruler, but on this subject no leadership was forthcoming. Here Glaber describes the effects of the great European famine of 1032–1034.

Source: In Eugen Weber, *The Western Tradition,* 4th ed., vol. 1, *From the Ancient World to Louis XIV* (Lexington, Mass.: D. C. Heath, 1990), pp. 250–251. Reprinted by permission.

The famine started to spread its ravages and one could fear the disappearance of the human race almost whole. The weather became so bad that none could find the right time for any sowing and that, especially because of the floods, there was no way of harvesting. . . . Continual rains had steeped the whole earth to the extent that during three years one could not dig furrows that would harbor the seed. By harvest time weeds and inauspicious tares had covered all the surface of the fields. In those parts where it gave the best results, a hogshead of seed would produce a harvest of about twelve bushels [about one-fifth of the original seed], and this in turn produced hardly a handful. If by chance one found any food on sale, the seller could exact an excessive price at his will.

Meantime, when the savage beasts and the birds had been eaten, men began, under the empire of a devouring hunger, to gather in order to eat, all kinds of carrion and of things horrible to tell. Certain among them had recourse to escape from death to the roots of the forests and the weeds of the rivers. In the end one is seized by horror at the tale of perversions which then reigned over the human race. Alas! Oh, woe! A thing rarely heard of in the course of ages, a maddening hunger made that men devoured human flesh. Travellers were carried off by those stronger than they, their members cut up, cooked on the fire and devoured. Many of the people who were going from one place to another to flee the famine and who had found hospitality on the way, were slaughtered during the night and served as nourishment for those who had welcomed them. Many, by showing a fruit or an egg to children, lured them into isolated places, massacred and devoured them. The bodies of the dead were in many places torn from the earth and served equally to appease hunger.

There was then tried in the region of Macon an experiment which had not, to our knowledge, yet been attempted anywhere else. Many people drew from the ground a white soil similar to clay, mixed it with what they had of wheat or bran, and made of this mixture bread, on which they relied so as not to die of hunger. However this practice brought merely the hope of salvation and the illusion of relief. One saw only pale and emaciated faces: many presented a skin distended by swellings; the human voice itself became shrill, similar to the little cries of dying birds. The corpses of the dead, whose multitude forced the living to abandon them here and there without burial, served as pasture to wolves who continued for a long time thereafter to seek their pittance among men. And as one could not, as we said, bury everyone individually because of the great number of dead, in certain places the men, fearing God, dug what was commonly known as charnel houses, in which the bodies of the dead were thrown by the five hundreds and more as long as room remained, pell mell, half naked or without any covering. The cross roads, the edges of the fields, also served as cemeteries. If some heard say that they would be better if they moved to other regions, many were those who perished on the way for want of food.

Questions

1. What does this account tell us about the state of transportation and communication in eleventh-century Europe?
2. Short of outside aid, is there any possible human remedy for the situation described here?
3. Do you think the clay eaters were driven by physical or mental urges?

1-6   Prince Henry of Portugal

Prince Henry "the Navigator" (1394–1460) founded a center for exploration and the study of ocean navigation. He sent Portuguese vessels farther and farther south along the western coast of Africa, until in 1488 Bartolomew Diaz rounded the Cape of Good Hope and entered the Indian Ocean, an event comparable in its contemporary significance to Columbus's discovery of new islands in the Atlantic (see text p. 18). In this account Gomes Eannes de Azurara, the chronicler of Prince Henry's achievements, lists Henry's six principal motivations for exploration. "Lord Infant" is a translation of Prince Henry's Portuguese title, *Infante*, or "(royal) child."

Source: Gomes Eannes de Azurara, *The Chronicle of the Discovery and Conquest of Guinea*, trans. Charles Raymond Beazley and Edgar Prestage (London: Hakluyt Society, 1896), vol. 1, pp. 27–30.

We imagine that we know a matter when we are acquainted with the doer of it and the end for which he did it. And since in former chapters we have set forth the Lord Infant as the chief actor in these things . . . it is meet that in this present chapter we should know his purpose in doing them. And you should note well that the noble spirit of this Prince, by a sort of natural constraint, was ever urging him both to begin and to carry out very great deeds. For which reason, after the taking of Ceuta he always kept ships well armed against the Infidel, both for war, and because he had also a wish to know the land that lay beyond the isle of Canary and that Cape called Bojador, for that up to his time, neither by writings, nor by the memory of man, was known with any certainty the nature of the land beyond that Cape. . . . And because the said Lord Infant wished to know the truth of this,—since it seemed to him that if he or some other lord did not endeavour to gain that knowledge, no mariners or merchants would ever dare to attempt it— (for it is clear that none of them ever trouble themselves to sail to a place where there is not a sure and certain hope of profit)—and seeing also that no other prince took any pains in this matter, he sent out his own ships against those parts, to have manifest certainty of them all. And to this he was stirred up by his zeal for the service of God and of the King Edward his Lord and brother, who then reigned. And this was the first reason of his action.

The second reason was that if there chanced to be in those lands some population of Christians, or some havens, into which it would be possible to sail without peril, many kinds of merchandise might be brought to this realm, which would find a ready market, and reasonably so, because no other people of these parts traded with them, nor yet people of any other that were known; and also the products of this realm might be taken there, which traffic would bring great profit to our countrymen.

The third reason was that, as it was said that the power of the Moors in that land of Africa was very much greater than was commonly supposed, and that there were no Christians among them, nor any other race of men; and because every wise man is obliged by natural prudence to wish for a knowledge of the power of his enemy; therefore the said Lord Infant exerted himself to cause this to be fully discovered, and to make it known determinately how far the power of those infidels extended.

The fourth reason was because during the one and thirty years that he had warred against the Moors, he had never found a Christian king, nor a lord outside his land, who for the love of our Lord Jesus Christ would aid him in the said war. Therefore he sought to know if there were in those parts any Christian princes, in whom the charity and the love of Christ was so ingrained that they would aid him against those enemies of the faith.

The fifth reason was his great desire to make increase in the faith of our Lord Jesus Christ and to bring to him all the souls that should be saved, understanding that all the mystery of the Incarnation, Death, and Passion of our Lord Jesus Christ was for this sole end—namely the salvation of lost souls—whom the said Lord Infant by his travail and spending would fain bring into the true path. For he perceived that no better offering could be made unto the Lord than this; for if God promised to return one hundred goods for one, we may justly believe that for such great benefits, that is to say for so many souls as were saved by the efforts of this Lord, he will have so many hundreds of guerdons in the kingdom of God, by which his spirit may be glorified after this life in the celestial realm. For I that wrote this history saw so many men and women of those parts turned to the holy faith, that even if the Infant had been a heathen, their prayers would have been enough to have obtained his salvation. And not only did I see the first captives, but their children and grandchildren as true Christians as if the Divine grace breathed in them and imparted to them a clear knowledge of itself.

But over and above these five reasons I have a sixth that would seem to be the root from which all the others proceeded: and this is the inclination of the heavenly wheels. For, as I wrote not many days ago in a letter I sent to the Lord King, that although it be written that the wise man shall be Lord of the stars, and that the courses of the planets (according to the true estimate of the holy doctors) cannot cause the good man to stumble; yet it is manifest that they are bodies ordained in the secret counsels of our Lord God and run by a fixed measure, appointed to different ends, which are revealed to men by his grace, through whose influence bodies of the lower order are inclined to certain passions. And if it be a fact, speaking as a Catholic, that the contrary predestinations of the wheels of heaven can be avoided by natural judgment with the aid of a certain divine grace, much more does it stand to reason that those who are predestined to good fortune, by the help of this same grace, will not only follow their course but even add a far greater increase to themselves. But here I wish to tell you how by the constraint of the influence of nature this glorious Prince was inclined to those actions of his. [Here Azurara describes Prince Henry's horoscope.] And the fact of his being accompanied by the sun, as I said, and the sun being in the house of Jupiter, signified that all his traffick and his conquests would be loyally carried out, according to the good pleasure of his king and lord.

Questions

1. According to Azurara, what motivated Prince Henry to explore the African coast?
2. Was the prince a medieval or a modern figure? Explain your answer.
3. Were the prince's motives scientific or practical? Explain your answer.

1-7 Columbus's Landfall

In 1492 a Genoese mariner in the pay of Spain set out from Palos for the Canary Islands and thence for Asia (see text pp. 19–20). He had accepted early Renaissance miscalculations of the width of the Eurasian continent, the distance from China to Japan, and the length of a degree of longitude. At the end of his 3,000-mile voyage Columbus thought he had reached Asia; instead, he had landed in the Bahamas. However, great events are measured by their consequences. Christopher Columbus "discovered" America, and the world has never been the same since.

Columbus's journal is not original; it is the work of the Dominican missionary and historian Bartolomé de las Casas (see American Voices, text p. 23), who quoted parts of Columbus's log, paraphrased others, and inserted new information.

Source: Bartolomé de Las Casas, *The Journal of Christopher Columbus* (1847/1870), trans. Cecil Jane, rev. and annotated by L. A. Vigneras (London: Hakluyt Society, 1960), pp. 19–41.

Thursday, October 11th. He navigated to the west-southwest; they had a rougher sea than they had experienced during the whole voyage. They saw petrels and a green reed near the ship. Those in the caravel *Pinta* saw a cane and a stick, and they secured another small stick, carved, as it appeared, with iron, and a piece of cane, and other vegetation which grows on land, and a small board. Those in the caravel *Niña* also saw other indications of land and a stick loaded with barnacles. At these signs, all breathed again and rejoiced. On this day, to sunset, they went twenty-seven leagues. After sunset, he steered his former course to the west; they made twelve miles an hour, and up to two hours before midnight they had made ninety miles, which are twenty-two leagues and a half. And since the caravel *Pinta* was swifter and went ahead of the admiral, she found land and made the signals which the admiral had commanded. This land was first sighted by a sailor called Rodrigo de Triana, although the admiral, at ten o'clock in the night, being on the sterncastle, saw a light. It was, however, so obscured that he would not affirm that it was land, but called Perro Gutierrez, butler of the King's dais, and told him that there seemed to be a light, and that he should watch for it. He did so, and saw it. He said the same also to Rodrigo Sanchez de Segovia, whom the King and Queen had sent in the fleet as *veedor* [comptroller], and he saw nothing since he was not in a position from which it could be seen. After the admiral had so spoken, it was seen once or twice, and it was like a small wax candle, which was raised and lowered. Few thought that this was an indication of land, but the admiral was certain that they were near land. Accordingly, when they had said the *Salve*, which all sailors are accustomed to say and chant in their manner, and when they had all been gathered together, the admiral asked and urged them to keep a good look out from the forecastle and to watch carefully for land, and to him who should say first he saw land, he would give at once a silk doublet apart from the other rewards which the Sovereigns had promised, which were ten thousand maravedis annually to him who first sighted it. Two hours after midnight land appeared, at a distance of about two leagues from them. They took in all sail, remaining with the mainsail, which is the great sail without bonnets, and kept jogging, waiting for day, a Friday, on which they reached a small island of the Lucayos, which is called in the language of the Indians "Guanahaní." Immediately they saw naked people, and the admiral went ashore in the armed boat, and Martin Alonso Pinzón and Vicente Yañez, his brother, who was captain of the *Niña*. The admiral brought out the royal standard, and the captains went with two banners of the Green Cross, which the admiral flew on all the ships as a flag, with an F and a Y, and over each letter their crown, one being on one side of the   and the other on the other. When they had landed, they saw very green trees and much water and fruit of various kinds. The admiral called the two captains and the others who had landed, and Rodrigo de Escobedo, secretary of the whole fleet, and Rodrigo Sanchez de Segovia, and said that they should bear witness and testimony how he, before them all, took possession of the island, as in fact he did, for the King and Queen, his Sovereigns, making the declarations which are required, as is contained more at length in the testimonies which were there made in writing. Soon many people of the island gathered there. What follows are the actual words of the admiral, in his book of his first voyage and discovery of these Indies.

"I," he says, "in order that they might feel great amity towards us, because I knew that they were a people to be delivered and converted to our holy faith rather by love than by force, gave to some among them some red caps and some glass beads, which they hung round their necks, and many other things of little value. At this they were greatly pleased and became so entirely our friends that it was a wonder to see. Afterwards they came swimming to the ships' boats, where we were, and brought us parrots and cotton thread in balls, and spears and many other things, and we exchanged for them other things, such as small glass beads and hawks' bells, which we gave to them. In fact, they took all and gave all, such as they had, with good will, but it seemed to me that they were a people very deficient in everything. They all go naked as their mothers bore them, and the women also, although I saw only one very young girl. And all those whom I did see were youths, so that I did not see one who was over thirty years of age; they were very well built, with very handsome bodies and very good faces. Their hair is coarse almost like the hairs of a horse's tail and short; they wear their hair down over their eyebrows, except for a few strands behind, which they wear long and never cut. Some of them are painted black, and they are the colour of the people of the Canaries, neither black nor white, and some of them are painted white and some red and some in any colour that they find. Some of them paint their faces, some their whole bodies, some only the eyes, and some only the nose. They do not bear arms or know them, for I showed to them swords and they took them by the blade and cut themselves through ignorance. They have no iron. Their spears are certain reeds, without iron, and some of these have a fish tooth at the end, while others are pointed in various ways. They are all generally fairly tall, good looking and well proportioned. I saw some who bore marks of wounds on their bodies, and I made signs to them to ask how this came about, and they indicated to me that people came from other islands, which are near, and wished to capture them, and they defended themselves. And I believed and still believe that they come here from the mainland to take them for slaves. They should be good servants and of quick intelligence, since I see that they very soon say all that is said to them, and I believe that they would easily be made Christians, for it appeared to me that they had no creed. Our Lord willing, at the time of my departure I will bring back six of them to Your Highness, that they may learn to talk. I saw no beast of any kind in this island, except parrots." All these are the words of the admiral.

Questions

1. What personal characteristics of Christopher Columbus are revealed in this excerpt?
2. Why did Columbus believe he was in Asia?
3. Can you discover Columbus's motives for making his journey? What were they?

Questions for Further Thought

1. What characteristics of the Renaissance can be discerned in the European voyages of discovery (see Document 1-6)?
2. Was Europe in 1492 modern or medieval? Progressive or backward? Explain your answer.
3. We know that Columbus's landfall (Document 1-7) was disastrous for native Americans. Should we celebrate it? Why or why not?

The Protestant Reformation and the Rise of England, 1500–1630

In the sixteenth century Catholicism helped fuel the Spanish conquest of America, but the Protestant Reformation reshaped England and delayed that country's exploration of the New World. When Martin Luther published his Ninety-five Theses in 1517 (see text pp. 26–27), England was not prepared politically or economically to join the Iberian countries in the race for empire. John Calvin's emphasis on predestination and congregationalism (see text p. 27) appealed to many people in England and Scotland. When Henry VIII declared himself the head of the Church in England (see text p. 32), he inaugurated more than a half century of religious turmoil. During the long reign of Elizabeth I (1558–1603) the compromise later known as Anglicanism was hammered out, considerably Protestant in content but unacceptable to either Roman Catholics or ardent Calvinists (see text pp. 32–33). Many religious dissenters sought refuge in America.

Not only religion but also economics reshaped England. A series of economic changes, including a massive rise in inflation, the beginnings of capitalism, and the transition from a local to a national economy, affected the island (see text pp. 29–31). Spain imported vast amounts of gold from America, which it then spent in Europe.

The resulting inflation benefited merchants and landowners who were dependent on rents. Mercantilism brought an emphasis on payment in bullion and government aid to merchants (see text pp. 31–32). The English colonies became sources of raw materials, conveniently distant havens for political and religious dissenters, and markets for manufactured goods. England's new wealth made possible a military buildup that led to the defeat of a Spanish invasion in 1588 (see text p. 28).

Document 1-8 addresses the serious social difficulties created by enclosure in England. In Document 1-9 Separatists define their differences with the Anglican Church. Document 1-10 reproduces Richard Hakluyt's arguments in favor of colonization in America.

1-8   Objections against Enclosure (1548)

Two economic factors challenged sixteenth-century England: a dramatic rise in population and a shortage of agricultural jobs. England's population had shrunk drastically during the Black Death in the fourteenth century. By 1550 it had made good the loss; after that time, people increased their numbers faster than the economy was able to absorb them. The shortage of agricultural jobs was caused partly by enclosure, the large-scale conversion of arable land to sheep pasturage and the consequent eviction of tenant farmers (see text pp. 30–31). Modern scholarship has minimized the actual extent of enclosure, but to contemporaries it symbolized all the economic problems they had to endure. In 1548 John Hales, an opponent of enclosure, conducted a commission of inquiry in the Midlands (central England) and vented his wrath.

Source: J. Strype, *Ecclesiastical Memorials* (London, 1721), vol. 2, Appendix of Documents, Document Q. In G. R. Elton, *Renaissance and Reformation, 1300–1648* (New York: Macmillan, 1963).

As by natural experience we find it to be true that if any one part of man's body be grieved . . . it is a great pain to all the whole body . . . so ought we to consider and remember in the state of the body of the realm. If the poorest sort of the people, which be members of the same body as well as the rich, be not provided and cherished in their degree, it cannot but be a great trouble of the body and a decay of the strength of the realm. Surely, good people, methinks that if men would know how much this ungodly desire of worldly things, and the unlawful getting and heaping together of riches, were hated of God, how hurtful and dangerous for the commonwealth of the realm it is, and what a virtue the mean in all things is, these laws nor a great many more that be needed not. God's Word is full of threats and curses against these kind of greediness. . . . When men in a commonwealth go about to gather as much as they can, and to get it they care not how; not considering whether by their gain any hurt should come to their neighbours or to the commonwealth; not only others, but they themselves should shortly perish. What avails a man to have his house full of gold and be not able to keep it with his force against his enemies? So what shall all our goods avail us if we be not able to defend us from our enemies?

The force and puissance [power] of the realm consists not only in riches but chiefly in the multitude of people. But it appears, good people, that the people of this realm, our native country, is greatly decayed through the greediness of a few men in comparison, and by this ungodly means of gathering together goods, by pulling down towns and houses, which we ought all to lament. Where there were [a few years ago] ten or twelve thousand people, there be now scarce four thousand. Where there were a thousand, now scarce three hundred, and in many places, where there were very many able to defend our country from landing of our enemies, now almost none. Sheep and cattle, that were ordained to be eaten of men, has eaten up the men, not of their own nature but by the help of men. Is it not a pitiful case that there should be so little charity among men? Is it not a sorrowful hearing that one Englishman should be set to destroy his countrymen? The places where poor men dwelt clearly destroyed; lands improved to so great rents, . . . that the poor husbandman cannot live. All things at this present . . . be so dear as never they were—victual and other things that be necessary for man's use. And yet, as it is said, there was never more cattle, specially sheep, than there is at this present. But the cause of the dearth is that those have it that may choose whether they will sell it or not, and will not sell it but at their own prices. . . .

To declare unto you what is meant by this word, enclosures. It is not taken where a man does enclose and hedge in his own proper ground where no man has commons. For such enclosure is very beneficial to the commonwealth: it is a cause of great increase of wood. But it is meant thereby when any man has taken away and enclosed any other men's commons, or has pulled down houses of husbandry and converted the lands from tillage to pasture. This is the meaning of the word, and so we pray you remember it.

To defeat these statutes [laws banning enclosure] as we be informed, some have not pulled down their houses but maintain them; howbeit, no person dwells therein, or if there be it is but a shepherd or a milkmaid; and convert the lands from tillage to pasture. And some about one hundred acres of ground, or more or less, make a furrow and sow that, and the rest they till not but pasture with their sheep. And some take the lands from their houses and occupy them in husbandry, but let the houses out to beggars and old poor people. Some, to colour the multitude of their sheep father them on their children, kinsfolk and servants. All which be but only crafts and subtleties to defraud the laws, such as no man will use but rather abhor. . . .

Besides, it is not unlike but that these great fines for lands and improvement of rents shall abate, and all things wax better cheap—20 and 30 eggs for a penny, and the rest after the rate as has been in times past. And the poor craftsmen may live and set their wares at reasonable prices. And noblemen and gentlemen that have not improved nor enhanced their rents, nor were sheepmasters nor graziers but lived like noblemen and gentlemen, shall be the better able to keep good hospitality among you, and keep servants about them, as they have done in time past. . . .

Questions

1. In Hales's opinion, was enclosure a religious or an economic problem? Why?

2. Do you think moral strictures alone would have been sufficient to reverse the enclosure movement? Why or why not?

3. Does Hales elucidate any underlying economic reasons for enclosure? If so, what are those reasons?

1-9   The Separatists State Their Case

Two groups of Protestant dissenters were among the first English people to immigrate to the New World. The Separatists, who founded the Plymouth colony in 1620, sought total withdrawal from the Anglican Church to establish independent congregations. The non-Separatists wanted to reform the Church of England from within (see text p. 33). Non-Separatists (Puritans) founded a settlement at Massachusetts Bay in 1629.

In the 1580s a small group of Separatists left England for the Netherlands, where they could worship freely (see text p. 33). When James I succeeded Elizabeth I in 1603, the Amsterdam Separatists (Pilgrims) petitioned the new king for permission to return to England. Their unsuccessful petition spelled out fourteen points of difference between Separatism and Anglicanism.

Source: "The Points of Difference Between Congregationalism and the Church of England (1603)." In Williston Walker, *The Creeds and Platforms of Congregationalism* (Boston, 1893; reprint, Philadelphia and Boston: Pilgrim Press, 1960), pp. 75, 77–80.

THE POINTS OF DIFFERENCE.

1. That Christ the Lord hath by his last Testament given to his Church, and set therein, sufficient ordinary Offices, with the maner of calling or Entrance, Works, and Maintenance, for the administration of his holy things, and for the sufficient ordinary instruction guydance and service of his Church, to the end of the world.

2. That every particular Church hath like and full interest and power to enjoy and practise all the ordinances of Christ given by him to his Church to be observed therein perpetually.

3. That every true visible Church, is a company of people called and separated from the world by the word of God, and joyned together by voluntarie profession of the faith of Christ, in the fellowship of the Gospell. And that therfore no knowne Atheist, unbelever, Heretique, or wicked liver, be received or reteined a member in the Church of Christ, which is his body; God having in all ages appointed and made a separation of his people from the world, before the Law, under the Law, and now in the tyme of the Gospell.

4. That discreet, faithfull, and able men (though not yet in office of Ministerie) may be appointed to preach the gospell and whole truth of God, that men being first brought to knowledge, and converted to the Lord, may then be ioyned togeather in holy communion with Christ our head and one with another.

5. That being thus ioyned, every Church hath power in Christ to chuse and take unto themselves meet and sufficient persons, into the Offices and functions of Pastors, Teachers, Elders, Deacons and Helpers, as those which Christ hath appointed in his Testament, for the feeding, governing, serving, and building up of his Church. And that no Antichristia Hierarchie or Ministerie, of Popes, Arch-bishops, Lord-bishops, Suffraganes, Deanes, Archdeacons, Chauncellors, Parsons, Vicars, Priests, Dumbministers, nor any such like be set over the Spouse and Church of Christ, nor reteined therein.

6. That the Ministers aforesaid being lawfully called by the Church where they are to administer, ought to continew in their functions according to Gods ordinance, and carefully to feed the flock of Christ committed unto them, being not inioyned or suffered to beare Civill offices withall, neither burthened with the execution of Civill affaires, as the celebration of marriage, burying the dead etc. which things belong as well to those without as within the Church.

7. That the due maintenance of the Officers aforesaid, should be of the free and voluntarie contribution of the Church, that according to Christs ordinance, they which preach the Gospell may live of the Gospell: and not by Popish Lordships and Livings, or Iewish Tithes and Offerings. And that therefore the Lands and other like revenewes of the Prelats and Clergie yet remayning (being still also baits to allure the Iesuites and Seminaries into the Land, and incitements unto them to plott and prosecute their woonted evill courses, in hope to enioy them in tyme to come) may now by your Highnes be taken away, and converted to better use, as those of the Abbeyes and Nunneries have been heertofore by your Maiestyes worthie predecessors, to the honor of God and great good of the Realme.

8. That all particular Churches ought to be so constituted, as having their owne peculiar Officers, the whole body of every Church may meet togeather in one place, and iointly performe their duties to God and one towards another. And that the censures of admonition and excommunication be in due maner executed, for sinne, convicted, and obstinatly stood in. This power also to be in the body of the Church wherof the partyes so offending and persisting are members.

9. That the Church be not governed by Popish Canons, Courts, Classes, Customes, or any humane inventions, but by the lawes and rules which Christ hath appointed in his Testament. That no Apocrypha writings, but only the Canonicall scriptures be used in the Church. And that the Lord be worshipped and called upon in spirit and truth, according to that forme of praier given by the Lord Iesus, Math. 6. and after the Leitourgie of his owne Testament, not by any other framed or imposed by men, much lesse by one traslated from the Popish leitourgie, as the Book of common praier etc.

10. That the Sacraments, being seales of Gods covenant, ought to be administred only to the faithfull, and Baptisme to their seed or those under their governement. And that according to the simplicitie of the Gospell, without any Popish or other abuses, in either Sacrament.

11. That the Church be not urged to the observation of dayes and tymes, Iewish or Popish, save only to sanctify the Lords day: Neyther be laden in things indifferent, with rites and ceremonies, whatsoever invented by men; but that Christian libertie may be reteined: And what God hath left free, none to make bound.

12. That all monuments of Idolatry in garments or any other things, all Temples, Altars, Chappels, and other place, dedicated heertofore by the heathens or Antichristians to their false worship, ought by lawfull aucthoritie to be rased and abolished, not suffered to remayne, for nourishing superstition, much lesse imploied to the true worship of God.

13. That Popish degrees in Theologie, inforcement to single life in Colledges, abuse of the study of prophane heathen Writers, with other like corruptions in Schooles and Academies, should be remooved and redressed, that so they may be the welsprings and nurseries of true learning and godlinesse.

14. Finally that all Churches and people (without ex-

ception) are bound in Religion not only to receave and submit unto that constitution, Ministerie, Worship, and order, which Christ as Lord and King hath appointed unto his Church: and not to any other devised by Man whatsoever.

Questions

1. How did the Separatists define their religious beliefs and practices?

2. In what way was the Church of England too Catholic for Separatists? (Hint: Look for the word *Popish.)*

3. The Church of England was a *territorial* church; that is, all English subjects had to be members. How did the Separatists criticize this practice?

1-10　Richard Hakluyt Promotes Colonization

By the end of the sixteenth century England's economic and imperial aspirations had led inexorably to colonization. Explorers such as Martin Frobisher and Humphrey Gilbert had reconnoitered the Atlantic coast of North America. The first Roanoke voyage took place in 1584 (see text p. 31), the year in which Richard Hakluyt (1552–1616) issued his *Discourse Concerning Western Planting*. Hakluyt, a clergyman and travel writer (although he never traveled), was an effective pamphleteer and propagandist for colonization. The *Discourse* was written at the request of Sir Walter Raleigh and contains virtually every positive argument for settlement that would be advanced over the next century. Its purpose was to persuade Queen Elizabeth I to put the English state squarely behind American ventures.

Source: Richard Hakluyt, *A Discourse Concerning Western Planting.* In Charles Deane et al., eds., *Documentary History of the State of Maine* (Collections of the Maine Historical Society, 1869–1916), vol. 2, pp. 152–161.

Chapter XX. A brief collection of certain reasons to induce her Majesty and the state to take in hand the western voyage and the planting there.

1. The soil yields and may be made to yield all the several commodities of Europe. . . .

2. The passage thither and home is neither too long nor too short, but easy, and to be made twice in the year.

3. The passage cuts not near the trade of any prince, nor near any of their countries or territories, and is a safe passage, and not easy to be annoyed by prince or potentate whatsoever.

4. The passage is to be performed at all times of the year, and in that respect passes our trades in the Levant Seas within the Straits of Gibraltar, and the trades in the seas within the King of Denmark's Strait, and the trades to the ports of Norway and of Russia, etc. . . .

5. And where England now for certain hundred years last passed, by the peculiar commodity of wool, and of later years, by clothing of the same, has raised itself from meaner state to greater wealth and much higher honour, might, and power than before, to the equalling of the princes of the same to the greatest potentates of this part of the world; it comes now so to pass that by the great endeavour of the increase of the trade of wool in Spain and in the West Indies, now daily more and more multiplying, that the wool of England, and the cloth made of the same, will become base, and every day more base than [the] other; which, prudently weighed it behooves this realm, if it mean not to return to former old means and baseness, but to stand in present and late former honour, glory, and force, and not negligently and sleepingly to slide into beggary . . . were it not for anything else but for the hope of the sale of our wool. . . .

6. This enterprise may stay the Spanish king from

flowing over all the face of that waste firmament of America, if we seat and plant there in time. . . . And England possessing the purposed place of planting, her Majesty may, by the benefit of the seat, having won good and royal havens, have plenty of excellent trees for masts, of goodly timber to build ships and to make great navies, of pitch, tar, hemp, and all things incident for a navy royal, and that for no price, and without money or request. How easy a matter may it be to this realm, swarming at this day with valiant youths, rusting and hurtful by lack of employment, and having good makers of cable and of all sorts of cordage, and the best and most cunning shipwrights of the world, to be lords of all those seas, and to spoil Philip's Indian navy, and to deprive him of yearly passage of his treasure to Europe, and consequently to abate the pride of Spain and of the supporter of the great Anti-christ of Rome, and to pull him down in equality to his neighbour princes, and consequently to cut off the common mischiefs that come to all Europe by the peculiar abundance of his Indian treasure, and this without difficulty.

7. This voyage, albeit it may be accomplished by bark or smallest pinnace for advice or for a necessity, yet for the distance, for burden and gain in trade, the merchant will not for profit's sake use it but by ships of great burden; so as this realm shall have by that means ships of great burden and of great strength for the defence of this realm. . . .

8. This new navy of mighty new strong ships, so in trade to that Norumbega and to the coasts there, shall never be subject to arrest of any prince or potentate as the navy of this realm from time to time has been in the ports of the empire, in the ports of the Low Countries, in Spain, France, Portugal, etc., in the times of Charles the Emperor, Francis the French king, and others. . . .

9. The great mass of wealth of the realm embarked in the merchants' ships, carried out in this new course, shall not lightly, in so far distant a course from the coast of Europe, be driven by winds and tempests into ports of any foreign princes, as the Spanish ships of late years have been into our ports of the West countries, etc. . . .

10. No foreign commodity that comes into England comes without payment of custom once, twice, or thrice, before it comes into the realm, and so all foreign commodities become dearer to the subjects of this realm; and by this course to Norumbega foreign princes' customs are avoided; and the foreign commodities cheaply purchased, they become cheap to the subjects of England, to the common benefit of the people, and to the saving of great treasure in the realm; whereas now the realm becomes poor by the purchasing of foreign commodities in so great a mass at so excessive prices.

11. At the first traffic with the people of those parts, the subjects of this realm for many years shall change many cheap commodities of these parts for things of high value there not esteemed; and this to the great enriching of the realm, if common use fail not.

12. By the great plenty of those regions the merchants and their factors shall lie there cheap, buy and repair their ships cheap, and shall return at pleasure without stay or restraint of foreign prince; whereas upon stays and restraints the merchant raiseth his charge in sale over of his ware. . . .

13. By making of ships and by preparing of things for the same, by making of cables and cordage, by planting of vines and olive trees, and by making of wine and oil, by husbandry, and by thousands of things there to be done, infinite numbers of the English nation may be set on work, to the unburdening of the realm with many that now live chargeable to the state at home.

14. If the sea coast serve for making of salt, and the inland for wine, oils, oranges, lemons, figs, etc., and for making of iron, all which with much more is hoped, without sword drawn, we shall cut the comb of the French, of the Spanish, of the Portuguese, and of enemies, and of doubtful friends, to the abating of their wealth and force, and to the greater saving of the wealth of the realm.

15. The substances serving, we may out of those parts receive the mass of wrought wares that now we receive out of France, Flanders, Germany, etc.; and so we may daunt the pride of some enemies of this realm, or at the least in part purchase those wares, that now we buy dearly of the French and Flemish, better cheap; and in the end, for the part that this realm was wont to receive, drive them out of trade to idleness for the setting of our people on work.

16. We shall by planting there enlarge the glory of the gospel, and from England plant sincere religion, and provide a safe and a sure place to receive people from all parts of the world that are forced to flee for the truth of God's word.

17. If frontier wars there chance to arise, and if thereupon we shall fortify, it will occasion the training up of our youth in the discipline of war, and make a number fit for the service of the wars and for the defence of our people there and at home.

18. The Spaniards govern in the Indies with all pride and tyranny; and like as when people of contrary nature at sea enter into galleys, where men are tied as slaves, all yell and cry with one voice, *Liberta, liberta*, as desirous of liberty and freedom, so no doubt whensoever the Queen of England, a prince of such clemency, shall seat upon that firmament of America, and shall be reported throughout all that tract to use the natural people there with all humanity, courtesy, and freedom, they will yield themselves to her government, and revolt clean from the Spaniard. . . .

19. The present short trades cause the mariner to be cast off, and often to be idle, and so by poverty to fall to piracy. But this course to Norumbega being longer, and a continuance of the employment of the mariner, doth keep the mariner from idleness and from necessity; and so it cuts off the principal actions of piracy, and the rather because no rich prey for them to take comes directly in their course or anything near their course.

20. Many men of excellent wits and of diverse singular gifts, overthrown by suretyship, by sea, or by some folly of youth, that are not able to live in England, may there be raised again, and do their country good service; and many needful uses there may (to great purpose) require the saving of great numbers, that for trifles may otherwise be devoured by the gallows.

21. Many soldiers and servitors, in the end of the wars, that might be hurtful to this realm, may there be unladen, to the common profit and quiet of this realm, and to our foreign benefit there, as they may be employed.

22. The fry of the wandering beggars of England, that grow up idly, and hurtful and burdenous to this realm, may there be unladen, better bred up, and may people waste countries to the home and foreign benefit, and to their own more happy state.

23. If England cry out and affirm that there are so many in all trades that one cannot live for another, as in all places they do, this Norumbega (if it be thought so good) offers the remedy.

Questions

1. What are Hakluyt's arguments for colonization? Do they seem persuasive after 400 years? Why or why not?

2. Which of Hakluyt's arguments pertain to England's internal conditions? Which have an imperial cast?

3. Are Hakluyt's proposed colonies more important as sources of raw materials or as markets? Why?

Questions for Further Thought

1. In what ways did religious and economic motivations for colonization reinforce each other?

2. Were English colonists driven out of their country by adverse conditions, or were they drawn to America primarily by the promise of progress? Explain your answer.

3. Did England consider America a dumping ground for undesirables? Why or why not?

CHAPTER 2

Invasion and Settlement 1565–1675

★ ★ ★

Spanish, French, and Dutch Goals

Early Spanish efforts at colonization and exploration were centered in the Caribbean and Mesoamerica (Document 2-1; see text pp. 20–23). Only isolated expeditions penetrated North America, motivated mainly by the search for gold. A few mission settlements took hold (see text p. 38). Otherwise, most of North America was put on hold until the states of northwestern Europe began flexing their colonialist muscles (see Map 2-1 on text p. 39). The French explored the Saint Lawrence and Mississippi waterways in pursuit of furs. The English considered settlements along the Atlantic coast. The Dutch, in the most famous real estate transaction in American history, purchased Manhattan Island (Document 2-2) and established a commercial network along the Hudson River.

2-1 A Franciscan Monk Refutes Las Casas (1555)

In 1542 the Dominican Bishop Bartholomé de Las Casas indicted his countrymen for their brutal treatment of native peoples in the New World (see American Voices, text p. 23). Thirteen years later a Franciscan monk admonished Las Casas for impugning the Spanish and offered an alternative explanation for the demographic decline of native Americans. These opposing viewpoints have reverberated down through the centuries and now appear as bloodless arguments in history textbooks.

In the *encomienda* system the Franciscan refers to, Indian men were required to work on Spanish holdings for nine months of the year in order to enjoy even minimum civil rights under Spanish law (see text p. 40).

Source: Originally published in Madrid, 1864; this translation reprinted from James Lockhart and Enrique Otte, eds., *Letters and People of the Spanish Indies: Sixteenth Century.* Copyright © 1976 Cambridge University Press, pp. 220–222, 236, 239. Reprinted with permission of Cambridge University Press.

I saw and read a treatise that Las Casas composed on the subject of the Indians enslaved here in New Spain and on the islands, and another one concerning the opinion he rendered on putting the Indians in encomiendas. . . .

No human being of whatever nation, law or status could read them without feeling abhorrence and mortal hate and considering all the residents of New Spain as the most cruel, abominable and detestable people there are under the sun. . . .

May God pardon Las Casas for so gravely dishonoring and defaming, so terribly insulting and affronting these communities and the Spanish nation, its prince, councils, and all those who administer justice in your majesty's name in these realms. . . .

First I must tell your majesty that when the Spaniards entered New Spain here, it had not been ruled for very long from Mexico City, nor by the Mexica [Aztecs], and the Mexica themselves had won and usurped dominion through war. . . .

People suffered the cruelest of deaths, and our adversary the demon was very pleased with the greatest idolatries and most cruel homicides there ever were, because the predecessor of Moctezuma, lord of Mexico, called Ahuit-

zotzin, offered to the idols in a single temple and in one sacrifice that lasted three or four days, 80,400 men, whom they brought along four streets, in four lines, until they reached the sacrificial block before the idols. And at the time when the Christians entered New Spain, more than ever before there was sacrificing and killing of men before the idols in all the towns and provinces. . . .

Now these and many other abominations, sins, and offenses made publicly to God and neighbors have been prevented and removed, our holy Catholic faith implanted, the cross of Jesus Christ and the confession of his holy name raised everywhere, and God has brought about a great conversion of people, in which many souls have been saved and are being saved every day; and many churches and monasteries have been built, with more than fifty monasteries inhabited by Franciscan friars alone. . . .

During the last ten years the natives of this land have diminished greatly in number. The reason for it has not been bad treatment, rather the cause has been the great diseases and plagues that New Spain has had, so that the natives continue to decrease each day. God knows the cause; his judgements are many and hidden from us.

Questions

1. Compare and contrast the two broadsides. Where do the two authors agree, and where do they differ?
2. Is either statement more believable than the other? Who or why not?
3. When the Franciscan monk decries Aztec sacrifices and attributes epidemics to God's judgment, is he offering an excuse or an explanation for the Spaniards' activities?

2-2   The Dutch Buy Manhattan Island (1624)

Early in the seventeenth century the small country of Holland was the leading commercial power in Europe. This maritime empire almost monopolized the Atlantic slave trade with its "castles" on the Guinea coast of Africa and plantations in Brazil and the Caribbean (see text pp. 42-43). Also, there was money to be made from furs in North America. The river discovered by Henry Hudson offered the deepest navigable penetration of any coastal river, and the Dutch soon established trading posts at New Amsterdam and Albany. The Dutch treated the Indian people brutally during their brief period of occupancy, but they did negotiate for Manhattan. At sixty guilders, it was a steal.

Source: Pieter Jansen Schagen to the States-General at The Hague, November 5, 1626. In John A. Kouwenhoven, *The Columbia Historical Portrait of New York* (New York: Harper & Row, 1953), p. 29.

High Mighty Sirs:

Here arrived yesterday the ship The Arms of Amsterdam which sailed from New Netherland out of the Mauritius [Hudson] River on September 23; they report that our people there are of good courage, and live peaceably. Their women, also, have borne children there, they have bought the island Manhattes from the wild men for the value of sixty gilders, is 11,000 morgens in extent. They sowed all their grain in the middle of May, and harvested it the middle of August. Thereof being samples of summer grain, such as wheat, rye, barley, oats, buckwheat, canary seed, small beans, and flax. The cargo of the aforesaid ship is: 7246 beaver skins, 178½ otter [half-otter?] skins, 675 otter skins, 48 mink skins, 36 wild-cat skins, 33 mink, 34 rat skins. Many logs of oak and nut-wood. Herewith be ye High Mighty Sirs, commended to the Almighty's grace, In Amsterdam, November 5, Anno 1626.

Your High Might.'s Obedient,

P. Schagen

Questions

1. What can you tell about the economic bases of New Netherland from this brief report?
2. Are furs a "renewable resource"? Do these numbers indicate depletion?
3. The Dutch were good at picking sites for colonization. Why did New Amsterdam survive and thrive?

Questions for Further Thought

1. What can you discern about Spanish and Dutch moral principles and values from these two documents?
2. Native Americans played a very different role in the economy of New Spain than they did in those of New France and New Amsterdam. Did this make a difference to the native peoples in the short run? In the long run?
3. The European settlement of the Western Hemisphere has been called both a triumph and a tragedy. Which is closer to the truth? Can you envisage an alternative outcome to the European discovery of America?

Social Conflict in the Chesapeake

Seventeenth-century Virginia was not a happy place for English settlers or native Americans. The colony that would produce the revolutionary leadership of Patrick Henry, George Washington, and Thomas Jefferson had extremely troubled beginnings. The colony almost did not make it (see text pp. 44–45). People died at an astonishing rate: 80 percent in the first generation of settlement and 50 percent in the first half century (Document 2-3). England poured thousands of mostly male indentured servants into Virginia to raise the tobacco crop. Many died, few married, and increasingly, most were unable to obtain land of their own after completing a term of servitude (see text pp. 49–50). Document 2-4 is a list of items that John Smith recommended each colonist bring in order to overcome some of the difficulties in those earliest years.

Beginning around the mid-seventeenth century, a wave of affluent Englishmen arrived in Virginia, buying up land, securing political power, and supporting the Green Spring faction of Governor Sir William Berkeley (see text pp. 50–51). By the 1670s this elite leadership group was squeezing out newcomers, one of whom, Nathaniel Bacon, took advantage of hard economic times and recurring Indian attacks to mount a revolt against Berkeley (Document 2-5). Bacon's rebellion of 1676 was the most significant event in Virginia's formative era (see text pp. 51–52). It was the culmination of the instability of the early seventeenth century, rocking the colonies with the largest civil uprising in America before the Revolution. Bacon's Rebellion led to the development of aristocratic rule, a flourishing gentry culture, and African slavery in the Chesapeake region. The Old South was born.

2-3   "A True Relation of . . . Virginia" (1608)

John Smith

Governor John Smith (1580–1631) is white America's first authentic hero (see text p. 44). A soldier of fortune in Europe, he arrived in Jamestown in 1607 as one of its seven councillors. Over the next two and a half years he almost single-handedly saved the colony from starvation, served as its virtual dictator, explored and mapped the area, and was dramatically rescued from a death sentence by Pocahontas, the daughter of the Indian chief Powhatan. Smith wrote an account of events in the colony; the "True Relation" brought news of Virginia's early trials to England.

The English built a military fort at Jamestown; Smith described the log walls as "palisadoed." *Aqua vitae* ("water of life") is strong liquor—considered essential for good health.

Source: John Smith, *A True Relation of such occurrences and accidents of noate as hath happened in Virginia since the first planting of that Collony, which is now resident in the South part thereof, till the last returne from thence* (London, 1608). In Merrill Jensen, ed., *English Colonial Documents: American Colonial Documents to 1776* (New York: Oxford University Press, 1964), pp. 132–136. Reprinted by permission of Methuen Books, London.

Kind Sir, commendations remembered, etc. You shall understand that after many crosses in the downs by tempests, we arrived safely upon the south-west part of the great Canaries. Within four or five days after, we set sail for Dominica the 26 of April. The first land we made, we fell with Cape Henry, the very mouth of the Bay of Chesapeake, which at that present we little expected, having by a cruel storm been put to the northward.

Anchoring in this bay, twenty or thirty went ashore with the captain, and in coming aboard [on land], they were assaulted with certain Indians, which charged them within pistol shot, in which conflict Captain Archer and Matthew Morton were shot, whereupon Captain Newport seconding them, made a shot at them, which the Indians little respected, but having spent their arrows retired without harm. And in that place was the box opened wherein the Council for Virginia was nominated, and arriving at the place [Jamestown] where we are now seated, the Council was sworn and the President elected, which for that year was Master Edmund Maria Wingfield, where was made choice for our situation, a very fit place for the erecting of a great city, about which some contention passed betwixt Captain Wingfield and Captain Gosnold. Notwithstanding, all our provision was brought ashore, and with as much speed as might be we went about our fortification.

[On 22 May, Captain Newport, Smith, and several others set forth to explore the country up the James River. They returned on 27 May.] . . . the first we heard was that 400 Indians the day before [26 May] had assaulted the fort and surprised it. Had not God (beyond all their expectations) by means of the ships (at whom they shot with their ordnances and muskets) caused them to retire, they had entered the fort with our own men, which were then busied in setting corn, their arms being then in dry fats and few ready but certain gentlemen of their own, in which conflict most of the Council was hurt, a boy slain in the pinnace, and thirteen or fourteen more hurt.

With all speed we palisadoed our fort; each other day for six or seven days we had alarms by ambuscadoes, and four or five cruelly wounded by being abroad. The Indians' loss we know not, but as they report three were slain and divers hurt. . . .

The day before the ship's departure the king of Pamaunke [i.e. Opechancanough] sent the Indian that had met us before in our discovery, to assure us peace, our fort being then palisadoed round, and all our men in good health and comfort, albeit that through some discontented humours it did not so long continue. For the President and Captain Gosnold, with the rest of the Council, being for the most part discontented with one another, in so much that things were neither carried with that discretion nor any business effected in such good sort as wisdom would, nor our own good and safety required, whereby, and through the hard dealing of our President, the rest of the Council being diversely affected through his audacious command; and for Captain Martin, albeit very honest and wishing the best good, yet so sick and weak, and myself so disgraced through others' malice, through which disorder God (being angry with us) plagued us with such famine and sickness that the living were scarce able to bury the dead; our want of sufficient and good victuals, with continual watching four or five each night at three bulwarks, being the chief cause. Only of sturgeon we had great store,

whereon our men would so greedily surfeit as it cost many their lives; the sack, *aqua vitae*, and other preservatives for our health being kept only in the President's hands, for his own diet, and his few associates.

Shortly after Captain Gosnold fell sick, and within three weeks died. Captain Ratcliffe being then also very sick and weak, and myself having also tasted of the extremity thereof, but by God's assistance being well recovered. Kendall about this time, for divers reasons, deposed from being of the Council, and shortly after it pleased God in our extremity to move the Indians to bring us corn ere it was half ripe, to refresh us, when we rather expected when they would destroy us.

About the tenth of September there was about 46 of our men dead, at which time Captain Wingfield having ordered the affairs in such sort that he was generally hated of all, in which respect with one consent he was deposed from his presidency, and Captain Ratcliffe according to his course was elected.

Our provision being now within twenty days spent, the Indians brought us great store both of corn and bread ready made, and also there came such abundance of fowls into the rivers as greatly refreshed our weak estates, whereupon many of our weak men were presently able to go abroad.

As yet we had no houses to cover us, our tents were rotten, and our cabins worse than nought. Our best commodity was iron, which we made into little chisels.

The President's and Captain Martin's sickness constrained me to be cape merchant and yet to spare no pains in making houses for the company, who notwithstanding our misery, little ceased their malice, grudging, and muttering.

As at this time were most of our chiefest men either sick or discontented, the rest being in such despair as they would rather starve and rot with idleness than be persuaded to do anything for their own relief without constraint. Our victuals being now within eighteen days spent, and the Indian trade decreasing, I was sent to the mouth of the river to Kegquouhtan, an Indian town, to trade for corn, and try the river for fish, but our fishing we could not effect by reason of the stormy weather. The Indians, thinking us near famished, with careless kindness offered us little pieces of bread and small handfuls of beans or wheat for a hatchet or a piece of copper. In like manner I entertained their kindness and in like scorn offered them like commodities, but the children, or any that showed extraordinary kindness, I liberally contented with free gift of such trifles as well contented them. . . .

[In January 1608], by a mischance our fort was burned and the most of our apparel, lodging, and private provision. Many of our old men [became] diseased, and [many] of our new for want of lodging perished. . . .

[O]ur men being all or the most part well recovered, and we not willing to trifle away more time than necessity enforced us unto, we thought good for the better content of the adventurers, in some reasonable sort to freight home Master Nelson [of the ship *Phenix*, which had arrived on 20 April] with cedar wood. About which, our men going with willing minds, [it] was in very good time effected and the ship sent for England [on 2 June 1608]. We now remaining being in good health, all our men well contented, free from mutinies, in love one with another, and as we hope, in a continual peace with the Indians. Where we doubt not but by God's gracious assistance, and the adventurers' willing minds and speedy furtherance to so honourable an action, in after times to see our nation to enjoy a country not only exceeding pleasant for habitation, but also very profitable for commerce in general; no doubt pleasing to Almighty God, honourable to our gracious sovereign, and commodious generally to the whole kingdom.

Questions

1. Does the early experience at Jamestown support the arguments for colonization that had been offered earlier by Richard Hakluyt (see Document 1-10)?

2. Was there any discernible economic base in Smith's Virginia? Explain.

3. What does Smith tell us about Indian-white relations in the first year of the Jamestown colony?

4. Why did Smith feel that the settlers would "rather starve and rot with idleness than be persuaded to do anything for their own relief"?

2-4 *Check List for Virginia-Bound Colonists* (1624)

John Smith

When John Smith sat down to write his *Generall Historie* in 1624, he had already led Virginians through their "starving times" and the Indian massacre of 1622 (see text pp. 44–45). He also had helped the Virginians overcome their reluctance to work. But it was from London that he kept a keen eye on the colonization of the North Atlantic coastline, including the settlement of New England. Although there is no evidence that John Smith met John Winthrop, the leader of the Puritan exodus to Massachusetts, Winthrop probably was familiar with Smith's *Generall Historie*.

Source: Captain John Smith, *The Generall Historie* (1624); edited by Edward Arber and reprinted in his *Travels and Works of Captain John Smith* (Edinburgh: J. Grant, 1910), book 4.

A particular of such necessaries as either private families, or single persons, shall have cause to provide to go to Virginia, whereby greater numbers may in part conceive the better how to provide for themselves.

Apparel

A Monmouth cap.	1s.	10d.
3 falling bands [collars].	1s.	3d.
3 shirts.	7s.	6d.
1 waistcoat.	2s.	2d.
1 suit of canvas.	7s.	6d.
1 suit of frieze [coarse wool].	10s.	
1 suit of cloth.	15s.	
3 pair of Irish stockings.	4s.	
4 pair of shoes.	8s.	8d.
1 pair of garters.		10d.
1 dozen of points [for lacing clothes].		3d.
1 pair of canvas sheets.	8s.	
7 ells of canvas to make a bed and bolster, to be filled in Virginia, serving for two men.	8s.	
5 ells of coarse canvas to make a bed at sea for two men.	5s.	
1 coarse rug at sea for two men.	6s.	

Victual for a whole year for a man,
and so after the rate for more.

8 bushels of meal.	2£.		
2 bushels of peas.		6s.	
2 bushels of oatmeal.		9s.	
1 gallon of aqua vitae.		2s.	6d.
1 gallon of oil.		3s.	6d.
2 gallons of vinegar.		2s.	
	3£.	3s.	

Arms for a man; but if half
your men be armed it is well,
so all have swords and pieces.

1 armor complete, light.		17s.	
1 long piece five feet and a half, near musket bore.	1£.	2s.	
1 sword.		5s.	
1 belt.		1s.	
1 bandolier.		1s.	6d.
20 pound[s] of powder.		18s.	
60 pound[s] of shot or lead, pistol and goose shot.		5s.	
	3£.	9s.	6d.

Tools for a family of six persons,
and so after the rate for more.

5 broad hoes at 2s. apiece.	10s.	
5 narrow hoes at 16d. apiece.	6s.	8d.
2 broad axes at 3s. 8d. apiece.	7s.	4d.
5 felling axes at 18d. apiece.	7s.	6d.
2 steel handsaws at 16d. apiece.	2s.	8d.
2 two-handsaws at 5s. apiece.	10s.	
1 whipsaw, set and filed; with box, file and wrest [screw key].	10s.	
2 hammers [at] 12d. apiece.	2s.	
3 shovels at 18d. apiece.	4s.	6d.
2 spades at 18d. apiece.	3s.	
2 augers at 6d. apiece.	1s.	
6 chisels at 6d apiece.	3s.	

2 percers stocked [at] 4d apiece.			8d.
3 gimlets at 2d. apiece.			6d.
2 hatchets at 21d. apiece.		3s.	6d.
2 froes to cleave pale [make staves or shingles] [at] 18d. each.		3s.	
2 hand bills [at] 20d apiece.		3s.	4d.
1 grindstone.		4s.	
nails of all sorts to the value of	2£.		
2 pickaxes.		3s.	
	6£.	2s.	8d.

Household implements for a
family and six persons, and so
for more or less after the rate.

1 iron pot.		7s.	
1 kettle.		6s.	
1 large frying pan.		2s.	6d.
1 gridiron.		1s.	6d.
2 skillets.		5s.	
1 spit.		2s.	
platters, dishes, spoons of wood.		4s.	
	1£.	8s.	

For sugar, spice, and fruit, and at sea for six men. 12s.6d.

So the full charge after this rate for each person, will amount to about the sum of 12£.10s.10d.

The passage of each man is 6£.

The fraught of these provisions for a man, will be about half a ton, which is 1£.10s.

So the whole charge will amount to about 20£.

Now if the number be great; [not only] nets, hooks, and lines, but cheese, bacon, kine and goats must be added.

And this is the usual proportion the Virginia Company doe[s] bestow upon their tenants they send.

Questions

1. Can you tell from this list of necessary items what kind of colony Smith hoped Virginia would become?
2. What kind of life-style do you imagine early Virginians had?
3. What is missing from this list that colonists might obtain from Virginia's environment?

2-5 Nathaniel Bacon's "Manifesto" (1676)

Who was Nathaniel Bacon (1647–1676)? Early twentieth-century historiography, associated with the patrician Virginian Thomas Jefferson Wertenabaker, depicted him as a popular democratic leader leading a revolt of the have-nots against the privileged few. The historian Wilcomb Washburn later dismissed him as an Indian killer, whereas Edmund S. Morgan sees Bacon's Rebellion as a war of plunder. Evidence for all these views can be found in Bacon's words. This troubled young fop who was exiled from England by his own father may not deserve a heroic reputation, but his "Manifesto" tells us what was wrong in Governor Berkeley's Virginia (see text pp. 51–52).

Source: Nathaniel Bacon, "Manifesto Concerning the Troubles in Virginia." *The Virginia Magazine of History and Biography*, 1 (1894), pp. 56–61.

If virtue be a sin, if piety be guilt, all the principles of morality, goodness and justice be perverted, we must confess that those who are now called rebels may be in danger of those high imputations. Those loud and several bulls would affright innocents and render the defence of our brethren and the inquiry into our sad and heavy oppressions, treason. But if there be, as sure there is, a just God to appeal to; if religion and justice be a sanctuary here; if to plead the cause of the oppressed; if sincerely to aim at his Majesty's honour and the public good without any reservation or by interest; if to stand in the gap after so much blood of our dear brethren bought and sold; if after the loss of a great part of his Majesty's colony deserted and dispeopled, freely with our lives and estates to endeavour to save the remainders be treason; God Almighty judge and let guilty die. But since we cannot in our hearts find one single spot of rebellion or treason, or that we have in any manner aimed at the subverting the settled government or attempting of the person of any either magistrate or private man, notwithstanding the several reproaches and threats of some who for sinister ends were disaffected to us and censured our innocent and honest designs, and since all people in all places where we have yet been can attest our civil, quiet, peaceable behaviour far different from that of rebellion and tumultuous persons, let truth be bold and all the world know the real foundations of pretended guilt. We appeal to the country itself what and of what nature their oppressions have been, or by what cabal and mystery the designs of many of those whom we call great men have been transacted and carried on; but let us trace these men in authority and favour to whose hands the dispensation of the country's wealth has been committed. Let us observe the sudden rise of their estates composed with the quality in which they first entered this country, or the reputation they have held here amongst wise and discerning men. And let us see whether their extractions and education have not been vile, and by what pretence of learning and virtue they could so soon [come] into employments of so great trust and consequence. Let us consider their sudden advancement and let us also consider whether any public work for our safety and defence or for the advancement and propagation of trade, liberal arts, or sciences is here extant in any way adequate to our vast charge. Now let us compare these things together and see what sponges have sucked up the public treasure, and whether it has not been privately contrived away by unworthy favourites and juggling parasites whose tottering fortunes have been repaired and supported at the public charge. Now if it be so, judge what greater guilt can be than to offer to pry into these and to unriddle the mysterious wiles of a powerful cabal; let all people judge what can be of more dangerous import than to suspect the so long safe proceedings of some of our grandees, and whether people may with safety open their eyes in so nice a concern.

Another main article of our guilt is our open and manifest aversion of all, not only the foreign but the protected and darling Indians. This, we are informed, is rebellion of a deep dye for that both the governor and council are by Colonel Cole's assertion bound to defend the queen and the Appamatocks with their blood. Now, whereas we do declare and can prove that they have been for these many years enemies to the king and country, robbers and thieves and invaders of his Majesty's right and our interest and estates, but yet have by persons in authority been defended and protected even against his Majesty's loyal subjects, and that in so high a nature that even the complaints and oaths of his Majesty's most loyal subjects in a lawful manner proffered by them against those barbarous outlaws, have been by the right honourable governor rejected and the delinquents from his presence dismissed, not only with pardon and indemnity, but with all encouragement and favour; their firearms so destructful to us and by our laws prohibited, commanded to be restored them, and open declaration before witness made that they must have ammunition, although directly contrary to our law. Now what greater guilt can be than to oppose and endeavour the destruction of these honest, quiet neighbours of ours? . . .

THE DECLARATION OF THE PEOPLE

For having upon specious pretences of public works, raised unjust taxes upon the commonalty for the advancement of private favourites and other sinister ends, but no visible effects in any measure adequate.

For not having during the long time of his government in any measure advanced his hopeful colony, either by fortification, towns or trade.

For having abused and rendered contemptible the majesty of justice, of advancing to places of judicature scandalous and ignorant favourites.

For having wronged his Majesty's prerogative and interest by assuming the monopoly of the beaver trade.

By having in that unjust gain bartered and sold his Majesty's country and the lives of his loyal subjects to the barbarous heathen.

For having protected, favoured and emboldened the Indians against his Majesty's most loyal subjects, never contriving, requiring, or appointing any due or proper means of satisfaction for their many invasions, murders, and robberies committed upon us.

For having, when the army of the English was just upon the track of the Indians, which now in all places burn, spoil, and murder, and when we might with ease have destroyed them who then were in open hostility, for having expressly countermanded and sent back our army by passing his word for the peaceable demeanour of the said Indians, who immediately prosecuted their evil intentions, committing horrid murders and robberies in all places, being protected by the said engagement and word passed of him, the said Sir William Berkeley, having ruined and made desolate a great part of his Majesty's country, have now drawn themselves into such obscure and remote places and are by their successes so emboldened and confirmed, and by their confederacy so strengthened that the cries of blood are in all places, and the terror and consternation of the people so great, that they are now become not only a difficult, but a very formidable enemy who might with ease have been destroyed, etc. When upon the loud outcries of blood, the Assembly had with all care raised and framed an army for the prevention of future mischiefs and safeguard of his Majesty's colony.

For having with only the privacy of some few favourites, without acquainting the people, only by the alteration of a figure, forged a commission by we know not what hand, not only without but against the consent of the people, for raising and effecting of civil wars and distractions, which being happily and without bloodshed prevented.

For having the second time attempted the same thereby calling down our forces from the defence of the frontiers, and most weak exposed places, for the prevention of civil mischief and ruin amongst ourselves, whilst the barbarous enemy in all places did invade, murder, and spoil us, his Majesty's most faithful subjects.

Of these, the aforesaid articles, we accuse Sir William Berkeley, as guilty of each and every one of the same, and as one who has traitorously attempted, violated and injured his Majesty's interest here, by the loss of a great part of his colony, and many of his faithful and loyal subjects by him betrayed, and in a barbarous and shameful manner exposed to the incursions and murders of the heathen.

And we further declare these, the ensuing persons in this list, to have been his wicked, and pernicious counsellors, aiders and assisters against the commonalty in these our cruel commotions:

Sir Henry Chicherly, Knt.	Jos. Bridger
Col. Charles Wormley	Wm. Clabourne
Phil. Dalowell	Thos. Hawkins, Jr.
Robert Beverly	William Sherwood
Robert Lee	Jos. Page, Clerk
Thos. Ballard	Jo. Cliffe, „
William Cole	Hubberd Farrell
Richard Whitacre	John West
Nicholas Spencer	Thos. Reade
Mathew Kemp	

And we do further demand, that the said Sir William Berkeley, with all the persons in this list, be forthwith delivered up, or surrender themselves, within four days after the notice hereof, or otherwise we declare as followeth: that in whatsoever house, place, or ship any of the said persons shall reside, be hid, or protected, we do declare that the owners, masters, or inhabitants of the said places, to be confederates and traitors to the people, and the estates of them, as also of all the aforesaid persons, to be confiscated. This we, the commons of Virginia, do declare desiring a prime union amongst ourselves, that we may jointly, and with one accord defend ourselves against the common enemy. And let not the faults of the guilty be the reproach of the innocent, or the faults or crimes of the oppressors divide and separate us, who have suffered by their oppressions.

These are therefore in his Majesty's name, to command you forthwith to seize the persons above mentioned as traitors to the king and country, and them to bring to Middle Plantation, and there to secure them, till further order, and in case of opposition, if you want any other assistance, you are forthwith to demand it in the name of the people of all the counties of Virginia.

[signed]   NATH BACON, Gen'l.
                           By the Consent of the People.

Questions

1. Bacon's Rebellion was the first serious tax revolt in American history. What evidence can you find to support this statement in Bacon's "Manifesto"?
2. Did Indian assaults trigger the rebellion? Were the native Americans pawns in a larger dispute between Bacon and Berkeley? Explain why or why not.
3. Can you find evidence of "democracy" in Bacon's "Manifesto" and Declaration? Was Bacon a democrat?

Questions for Further Thought

1. The textbook (see p. 48) states that "tobacco and disease shaped the early history of Maryland and Virginia." What evidence for this assertion can you find in Documents 2-3 and 2-5?
2. Chesapeake society, one historian asserts, was "frighteningly turbulent, wracked by ugly tensions." Can you find any evidence of social instability in these documents?
3. Compare the depictions of Indian people in Smith's and Bacon's documents. Which is more favorable?

Puritan New England and *The Indians' New World*

If Virginia was founded primarily as a capitalistic money-making venture, New England was launched for religious purposes. Other kinds of colonies would sooner or later have appeared in the region, but the stamp of Puritanism came first. The Puritans, or non-Separatists (Puritans remained members of the Church of England), came to America to perfect a Protestant reformation, something that had been prevented at home by the Anglican Church (see text pp. 52–54). Most of their Calvinist theology had been worked out earlier in England. Puritans sought to achieve salvation, or God's grace, through a combination of clean living (works) and intense belief (faith). They believed in "predestination"; only a few—the elect—could expect God's redemption on Judgment Day.

In Massachusetts Bay the Puritans adopted two organizational departures from English precedent. First, they tightened membership standards in their congregations, requiring proof of morality and faith as evidence of conversion (see text p. 56). Second, they repudiated toleration and attempted to enforce religious conformity. The banishments to Rhode Island of Roger Williams and Anne Hutchinson (Document 2-6) demonstrated this hostility to dissent (see text pp. 57–58). Established in the 1630s, these twin pillars of Puritanism—the conversion test and enforced conformity—were modified over time but remained official practice until the Great Awakening of the 1740s (see text Chapter 4).

New England's early history is therefore religious, indeed theological, in nature. However, even a devout people must acquire land, earn a living, procreate, and establish a government (Document 2-7). Hardworking Calvinists turned the region into an economic and demographic success, and the Massachusetts Bay colony governed itself less as a colony of England than as an independent commonwealth (Document 2-8).

Puritan success brought conflict with the Pequot Indians in Connecticut (see text pp. 54–55). A bloody massacre induced submission and even persuaded a few native Americans to convert to Congregationalism. Puritan intolerance extended to native Americans, who were pushed out, exterminated by disease, or brutalized into servility. Ultimately, however, nearly every New England tribe rose in rebellion. Metacom's (King Philip's) War (see text pp. 63–65) was the bloodiest conflict in terms of per capita casualties in American history (Document 2-9).

2-6 The Examination of Anne Hutchinson (1637)

Anne Hutchinson (1591–1643) caused the worst internal crisis in the early theological history of Massachusetts (see text p. 58) by rejecting the Puritan belief that good works are a sign of God's grace. Instead, she believed in salvation by faith alone, a heresy the Puritans called antinomianism. Her "subversive" teachings undermined the authority of magistrates and ministers alike and called into question the traditional submissiveness of women. Tried in court for her opinions, Hutchinson admitted her differences with mainstream theology. She might have won a theological battle, but she lost the political war and was expelled from Massachusetts.

Note: Among Protestants, Jesuits were hated and feared because of the subtlety of their theological arguments.

Source: Thomas Hutchinson, *History of the Colony and Province of Massachusetts Bay* (Boston, 1767).

NOVEMBER 1637.

The Examination of Mrs. Ann Hutchinson at the court at Newtown.

Mr. Winthrop, governor. Mrs. Hutchinson, you are called here as one of those that have troubled the peace of the commonwealth and the churches here; you are known to be a woman that hath had a great share in the promoting and divulging of those opinions that are causes of this trouble, and to be nearly joined not only in affinity and affection with some of those the court had taken notice of and passed censure upon, but you have spoken divers things as we have been informed very prejudicial to the honour of the churches and ministers thereof, and you have maintained a meeting and an assembly in your house that hath been condemned by the general assembly as a thing not tolerable nor comely in the sight of God nor fitting for your sex, and notwithstanding that was cried down you have continued the same, therefore we have thought good to send for you to understand how things are, that if you be in an erroneous way we may reduce you

that so you may become a profitable member here among us, otherwise if you be obstinate in your course that then the court may take such course that you may trouble us no further, therefore I would intreat you to express whether you do not hold and assent in practice to those opinions and factions that have been handled in court already, that is to say, whether you do not justify Mr. Wheelwright's sermon and the petition. . . .

Mrs. H. . . . I shall not equivocate, there is a meeting of men and women, and there is a meeting only for women. . . .

Mr. Endicot. Who teaches in the men's meetings, none but men? Do not women sometimes?

Mrs. H. Never as I heard, not one. . . .

Deputy Gov. Now it appears by this woman's meeting that Mrs. Hutchinson hath so forestalled the minds of many by their resort to her meeting that now she hath a potent party in the country. Now if all these things have endangered us as from that foundation, and if she in particular hath disparaged all our ministers in the land that they have preached a covenant of works, . . . why this is not to be suffered. And therefore being driven to the foundation, and it being found that Mrs. Hutchinson is she that hath depraved all the ministers and hath been the cause of what is fallen out, why we must take away the foundation and the building will fall.

Mrs. H. I pray Sir prove it that I said they preached nothing but a covenant of works.

Deputy Gov. Nothing but a covenant of works, why a Jesuit may preach truth sometimes.

Mrs. H. Did I ever say they preached a covenant of works then?

Deputy Gov. If they do not preach a covenant of grace clearly, then they preach a covenant of works.

Mrs. H. No Sir, one may preach a covenant of grace more clearly than another, so I said.

Deputy Gov. We are not upon that now but upon position.

Mrs. H. Prove this then Sir that you say I said.

Deputy Gov. When they do preach a covenant of works do they preach truth?

Mrs. H. Yes Sir, but when they preach a covenant of works for salvation, that is not truth.

Deputy Gov. I do but ask you this, when the ministers do preach a covenant of works do they preach a way of salvation?

Mrs. H. I did not come hither to answer to questions of that sort.

Deputy Gov. Because you will deny the thing.

Mrs. H. Ey [Aye], but that is to be proved first.

Deputy Gov. I will make it plain that you did say that the ministers did preach a covenant of works.

Mrs. H. I deny that. . . . Now if you do condemn me for speaking what in my conscience I know to be truth I must commit myself unto the Lord.

Mr. Nowell. How do you know that that was the spirit?

Mrs. H. How did Abraham know that it was God that bid him offer his son, being a breach of the sixth commandment [Thou shalt not kill]?

Deputy Gov. By an immediate voice.

Mrs. H. So to me by an immediate revelation.

Deputy Gov. How! an immediate revelation.

Mrs. H. By the voice of his own spirit to my soul. . . .

Gov. The court hath already declared themselves satisfied concerning the things you hear, and concerning the troublesomeness of her spirit and the danger of her course amongst us, which is not to be suffered. Therefore if it be the mind of the court that Mrs. Hutchinson for these things that appear before us is unfit for our society, and if it be the mind of the court that she shall be banished out of our liberties and imprisoned till she be sent away, let them hold up their hands.

All but three. . . .

Mrs. Hutchinson, the sentence of the court you hear is that you are banished from out of our jurisdiction as being a woman not fit for our society, and are to be imprisoned till the court shall send you away.

Mrs. H. I desire to know wherefore I am banished?

Gov. Say no more, the court knows wherefore and is satisfied.

Questions

1. Why was Hutchinson's "immediate revelation" subversive?
2. Was this court stacked? Was there any way Hutchinson could have won?
3. Can you find evidence of sexism in this document?

2-7   The Mayflower Compact (1620)

The Mayflower Compact of 1620 (see text pp. 52–53) is one of the most important political statements in American history. In it a small band of Separatists agreed on how to govern themselves. The Separatists honored the king of England but not the Church of England; they came to America (greater Virginia) to effect a complete withdrawal from Anglicanism (see Document 1-9). These were the Pilgrims, who settled at Plymouth about a decade before the Massachusetts Bay colony was established. They governed Plymouth as a separate colony until it was absorbed into Massachusetts in 1691.

Source: In Francis N. Thorpe, ed., *The Federal and State Constitutions . . . of the United States* (Washington, D.C., U.S. Government Printing Office, 1909), vol. 3, p. 1841.

In the name of God, amen. We, whose names are underwritten, the Loyal Subjects of our dread Sovereign Lord King *James*, by the Grace of God, of *Great Britain, France,* and *Ireland*, King, *Defender of the Faith*, &c. Having undertaken for the Glory of God, and Advancement of the Christian Faith, and Honour of our King and Country, a Voyage to plant the first Colony in the northern Parts of *Virginia*; Do by these Presents, solemnly and mutually, in the Presence of God and one another, covenant and combine ourselves together into a civil Body Politick, for our better Ordering and Preservation, and Furtherance of the Ends aforesaid: And by Virtue hereof do enact, constitute, and frame, such just and equal Laws, Ordinances, Acts, Constitutions, and Officers, from time to time, as shall be thought most meet and convenient for the general Good of the Colony; unto which we promise all due Submission and Obedience. IN WITNESS whereof we have hereunto subscribed our names at *Cape-Cod* the eleventh of *November*, in the Reign of our Sovereign Lord King *James*, of *England, France,* and *Ireland*, the eighteenth, and of *Scotland*, the fifty-fourth, *Anno Domini*, 1620.

Questions

1. What reasons for colonization can you find in the Mayflower Compact?

2. Is the compact a democratic document? If so, how? If not, what kind of government does it imply?

3. How could the Separatists pledge allegiance to King James I, who was both a secular sovereign and the "Defender of the Faith" they abhorred?

2-8   Seal of the Massachusetts Bay Company (1629)

In 1628 English Puritans incorporated the Massachusetts Bay Company (see text pp. 53–54) for the purpose of colonizing America. One year later they transferred the administration of the company from London to Boston. Thus, the government of the company became the government of the colony, which was effectively removed from control by the king. The first truly American corporation governed itself as an independent commonwealth until its charter was vacated in 1684. The Latin inscription on the Seal of the Massachusetts Bay Company translates as "Seal [of the] Government and Society of Massachusetts Bay in New England."

Source: Courtesy of the Office of the Secretary of State, the Commonwealth of Massachusetts.

Questions

1. Are there any symbols on this seal which require an explanation?
2. What is the significance of using a native American as the centerpiece of the seal?
3. To whom is the Indian saying, "Come over and help us"? Is this an altruistic justification for the establishment of the colony?

2-9   Metacom's War: A Puritan Explanation (1675)

In June 1675, Metacom (see illustration on text p. 63), a Wampanoag Indian whom the English called King Philip, launched the most devastating Indian uprising in American colonial history (see text pp. 63–65). Lasting almost two years and threatening the very survival of New England, the rebellion called into question the colonies' religious underpinnings. The Massachusetts General Court responded with a mixture of piety and military preparation. On the one hand, the Puritans blamed themselves for straying from God's ways and calling down divine wrath. On the other hand, they intensified their military response.

Source: Nathaniel B. Shurtleff, ed., *Records of the Governor and Company of the Massachusetts Bay* (1853–1854), vol. 5, pp. 59–64.

WHEREAS the most wise & holy God, for severall yeares past, hath not only warned us by his word, but chastized us with his rods, inflicting upon us many generall (though lesser) judgments, but we have neither heard the word nor rod as wee ought, so as to be effectually humbled for our sinns to repent of them, reforme, and amend our wayes; hence it is the righteous God hath heightened our calamity, and given commission to the barbarous heathen to rise up against us, and to become a smart rod and severe scourge to us, in burning & depopulating severall hopefull plantations, murdering many of our people of all sorts, and seeming as it were to cast us off, and putting us to shame, and not going forth with our armies, heereby speaking aloud to us to search and try our wayes, and turne againe unto the Lord our God, from whom wee have departed with a great backsliding.

1. The Court, apprehending there is too great a neglect of discipline in the churches, and especially respecting those that are their children, through the non acknowledgment of them according to the order of the gospell; in watching over them, as well as chattechising of them, inquireing into theire spirittuall estates, that, being brought to take hold of the covenant, they may acknowledge & be acknowledged according to theire relations to God & to his church, and theire obligations to be the Lords, and to approove themselves so to be by a suiteable profession & conversation; and doe therefore solemnly recommend it unto the respective elders and brethren of the severall churches throughout this jurisdiction to take effectuall course for reformation herein.

2. Whereas there is manifest pride openly appearing amongst us in that long haire, like weomens haire, is worne by some men, either their owne or others haire made into perewiggs, and by some weomen wearing borders of haire, and theire cutting, curling, & immodest laying out theire haire, which practise doeth prevayle & increase, especially amongst the younger sort,—

This Court doeth declare against this ill custome as offencive to them, and divers sober christians amongst us, and therefore doe hereby exhort and advise all persons to use moderation in this respect; and further, doe impower all grand juries to present to the County Court such persons, whither male or female, whom they shall judge to exceede in the premisses; and the County Courts are hereby authorized to proceed against such delinquents either by admonition, fine, or correction, according to theire good discretion.

3. Notwithstanding the wholesome lawes already made by this Court for restreyning excesse in apparrell, yet through corruption in many, and neglect of due execution of those lawes, the evill of pride in apparrell, both for costlines in the poorer sort, & vaine, new, strainge fashions, both in poore & rich, with naked breasts and armes, or, as it were, pinioned with the addition of superstitious ribbons both on haire & apparrell; for redresse whereof, it is or-

dered by this Court, that the County Courts, from time to time, doe give strict charge to present all such persons as they shall judge to exceede in that kinde, and if the grand jury shall neglect theire duty herein, the County Court shall impose a fine upon them at their discretion.

And it is further ordered, that the County Court, single magistrate, Commissioners Court in Boston, have heereby power to summon all such persons so offending before them, and for the first offence to admonish them, and for each offence of that kinde afterwards to impose a fine of tenn shillings upon them, or, if unable to pay, to inflict such punishment as shall be by them thought most suiteable to the nature of the offence; and the same judges above named are heereby impowred to judge of and execute the lawes already extant against such excesse. . . .

5. Whereas there is so mutch profanes amongst us in persons turning their backs upon the publick worship before it be finished and the blessing pronounced,—

It is ordered by this Court, that the officers of the churches, or selectmen, shall take care to prevent such disorders, by appointing persons to shutt the meeting house doores, or any other meete way to attaine the end.

6. Whereas there is much disorder & rudenes in youth in many congregations in time of the worship of God, whereby sin & prophaness is greatly increased, for reformation whereof,—

It is ordered by this Court, that the select men doe appoint such place or places in the meeting house for children or youth to sit in where they may be most together and in publick veiw, and that the officers of the churches, or selectmen, doe appoint some grave & sober person or persons to take a particcular care of and inspection over them, who are heereby required to present a list of the names of such, who, by their owne observance or the information of others, shallbe found delinquent, to the next magistrate or Court, who are impowred for the first offence to admonish them, for the second offence to impose a fine of five shillings on theire parents or governors, or order the children to be whipt, and if incorrigible, to be whipt with ten stripes, or sent to the house of correction for three dayes.

7. Whereas the name of God is prophaned by common swearing and cursing in ordinary communication, which is a sin that growes amongst us, and many heare such oathes and curses, and conceales the same from authority, for reformation whereof, it is ordered by this Court, that the lawes already in force against this sin be vigorously prosecuted; and, as addition thereunto, it is further ordered, that all such persons who shall at any time heare prophane oathes and curses spoken by any person or persons, and shall neglect to disclose the same to some magistrate, commissioner, or constable, such persons shall incurr the same poenalty provided in that law against swearers.

8. Whereas the shamefull and scandelous sin of excessive drinking, tipling, & company keeping in tavernes, &c, ordinarys, grows upon us, for reformation whereof,—

It is commended to the care of the respective County Courts not to license any more publick houses then are absolutely necessary in any toune, and to take care that none be licenst but persons of approoved sobriety and fidelity to law and good order; and that licensed houses be regulated in theire improovement for the refreshing & enterteynment of travailers & strangers only, and all toune dwellers are heereby strictly enjoyned & required to forbeare spending their time or estates in such common houses of enterteynment, to drincke & tiple, upon poenalty of five shillings for every offence, or, if poore, to be whipt, at the discretion of the judge, not exceeding five stripes; and every ordinary keeper, permitting persons to transgress as above said, shall incurr the poenalty of five shillings for each offence in that kinde; and any magistrate, commissioner, or selectmen are impowred & required vigorously to putt the abovesaid law in execution.

And, ffurther, it is ordered, that all private, unlicensed houses of enterteinment be diligently searched out, and the poenalty of this law strictly imposed; and that all such houses may be the better discovered, the selectmen of every toune shall choose some sober and discreete persons, to be authorized from the County Court, each of whom shall take the charge of ten or twelve families of his neighbourhood, and shall diligently inspect them, and present the names of such persons so transgressing to the magistrate, commissioners, or selectmen of the toune, who shall returne the same to be proceeded with by the next County Court as the law directs; and the persons so chosen and authorized, and attending theire duty ffaithfully therein, shall have one third of the fines allowed them; but, if neglect of their duty, and shall be so judged by authority, they shall incurr the same poenalty provided against unlicensed houses.

9. Whereas there is a wofull breach of the fifth comandment [Honor thy father and thy mother] to be found amongst us, in contempt of authority, civil, ecclesiasticall, and domesticall, this Court doeth declare, that sin is highly provoaking to the Lord, against which he hath borne severe testimony in his word, . . . and therefore doe strictly require & comand all persons under this government to reforme so great an evil, least God from heaven punish offenders heerin by some remarkeable judgments. And it is further ordered, that all County Courts, magistrates, commissioners, selectmen, and grand jurors, according to theire severall capacities, doe take strict care that the lawes already made & provided in this case be duely executed, and particcularly that evil of inferiours absenting themselves out of the families whereunto they belong in the night, and meeting with corrupt company without leave, and against the minde & to the great greife of theire superiours, which evil practise is of a very perrillous nature, and the roote of much disorder.

It is therefore ordered by this Court, that whatever in-feriour shall be legally convicted of such an evil practise, such persons shall be punished with admonition for the first offence, with fine not exceeding ten shillings, or whipping not exceeding five stripes, for all offences of like nature afterwards.

10. Whereas the sin of idlenes (which is a sin of Sodom) doeth greatly increase, notwithstanding the wholesome lawes in force against the same, as an addition to that law,—

This Court doeth order, that the constable, with such other person or persons whom the selectmen shall appoint, shall inspect particcular families, and present a lyst of the names of all idle persons to the selectmen, who are heereby strictly required to proceed with them as already the law directs, and in case of obstinacy, by charging the constable with them, who shall convey them to some magistrate, by him to be committed to the house of correction. . . .

12. Whereas there is a loose & sinfull custome of going or riding from toune to toune, and that oft times men & weomen together, upon pretence of going to lecture, but it appeares to be meerely to drincke & revell in ordinarys & tavernes, which is in itself scandalous, and it is to be feared a notable meanes to debauch our youth and hazard the chastity of such as are draune forth thereunto, for prevention whereof,—

It is ordered by this Court, that all single persons who, meerly for their pleasure, take such journeyes, & frequent such ordinaryes, shall be reputed and accounted riotous & unsober persons, and of ill behaviour, and shall be liable to be summoned to appeare before any County Court, magistrate, or commissioner, & being therof convicted, shall give bond & sufficient sureties for the good behaviour in twenty pounds, and upon refusall so to doe, shall be committed to prison for ten days, or pay a fine of forty shillings for each offence.

It is ordered by this Court, that every toune in this jurisdiction shall provide, as an addition to their toune stocke of ammunition, six hundred of flints for one hundred of lysted souldiers, and so proportionably for a lesser or greater number, to be constantly mainteyned & fitted for publick service.

14. This Court, considering the great abuse & scandall that hath arisen by the license of trading houses with the Indians, whereby drunkenes and other crimes have binn, as it were, sold unto them,—

It is ordered by this Court, that all such trading houses, from the publication hereof, shall wholly cease, and none to presume to make any sale unto them, except in open shops and tounes where goods are sold unto the English, upon the poenalty of ten pounds for every conviction before laufall authority, one third to the informers, the remainder to the country, any law, usage, or custome to the contrary notwithstanding. . . .

Questions

1. List the causes of Metacom's War as indicated in this document. Do they make sense to you? Was there a direct relationship between Metacom's resistance and Puritan permissiveness?

2. Why and how would the reforms set forth in this legislation produce a more vigorous military effort? Is there a connection between internal cohesion and the prosecution of war?

3. Do you detect any generational differences among Puritans in this lament?

Questions for Further Thought

1. Considering that the Puritans fled persecution in England to seek religious freedom in America, why were they so intolerant of others' beliefs?

2. Was seventeenth-century New England attractive to emigrants? Would free-thinkers choose to live there?

3. What was the line between religion and government in Massachusetts? Was Anne Hutchinson (Documents 2-6) a theological or a political threat?

4. Did the English "come over and help" native Americans (see Document 2-8)?

CHAPTER 3

The British Empire in America 1660–1750

★   ★   ★

The Politics of Empire, 1660–1713

By 1660 England had established a series of colonies in America but did not have a system for controlling them. Over the next quarter century the Stuarts would tighten their control economically and politically. A generous and extravagant man, Charles II rewarded his supporters with millions of acres of land by creating proprietorships in New York, New Jersey, the Carolinas, and Pennsylvania (see text p. 70). For example, William Penn was granted land that became Pennsylvania in gratitude for the services of his father, Admiral Sir Thomas Penn, to the Stuarts. There he established a refuge for Quakers (see text pp. 71–72 and Document 3-1). Except for the requirement of broad conformity to the laws of England, the proprietors could do as they pleased with their vast domains.

Although the king doled out land liberally to pay his political and financial debts, he kept tight control over colonial trade, which was an important source of royal revenue. Following a pattern established by the Navigation Act of 1651, Charles II and several English governments enacted a series of measures designed to confer on England the full benefit of colonial trade while excluding the Dutch (Document 3-2; see also text pp. 72–73).

The new mercantilism constituted a successful trade policy but was resented as an intrusion into the colonies' internal affairs. The Stuart monarchs then went a step further to establish political control. With the accession to the throne of James II in 1685, the charters of Rhode Island and Connecticut were revoked and those colonies were merged with the Massachusetts Bay and Plymouth colonies to form a new royal province, the Dominion of New England (see text p. 73). Two years later New York and New Jersey were added to create a political unit extending from Maine to the Hudson River. The dominion represented a new kind of authoritarian administration that attacked local institutions by abolishing legislative assemblies and town meetings, levying arbitrary taxes, and challenging land titles under the original charters. The

Glorious Revolution of 1688 in England (see text p. 74) triggered a series of insurrections in the colonies (Document 3-3). Local differences, including ethnic rivalry in New York and Protestant-Catholic conflict in Maryland, influenced the causes and outcomes (see text pp. 74–75). But everywhere the rebellions marked a turning point in the history of the colonies, primarily an end to authoritarian rule, a new level of political stability, and an imperial presence limited mainly to the supervision of colonial trade (see text pp. 77–78).

3-1 Preface to the Frame of Government for Pennsylvania (1682)

William Penn

The charter for the settlement of Pennsylvania (see text p. 71) as a Quaker colony was granted in 1681 to William Penn by Charles II, "having regard to the memory and merits of his late father." The preface, a bold statement of intent, was enacted in the 1682 Charter of Privileges and its subsequent revisions. Penn regarded the founding of the colony as an opportunity to carry out a "Holy Experiment": a colony devoted to the ideal of religious toleration. The development of the government of the colony was an experimental process in which Penn showed no fixed convictions in regard to political forms except for the principle of political participation by the governed.

Source: Minutes of the Provincial Council of Pennsylvania (Philadelphia and Harrisburg, 1852–1853), vol. 1, pp. 29–32.

. . . Government seems to me a part of religion itself, a thing sacred in its institution and end. For, if it does not directly remove the cause, it crushes the effects of evil, and is as such an emanation of the same Divine Power that is both author and object of pure religion; the difference being that the one is more free and mental, the other more corporal and compulsive in its operations. But that is only to evildoers; government itself being otherwise as capable of kindness, goodness, and charity as a more private society. . . .

I know what is said by the several admirers of monarchy, aristocracy, and democracy, which are the rule of one, a few, and many, and are the three common ideas of government. But I choose to solve the controversy with this small distinction, and it applies to all three: Any government is free to the people under it (whatever be the frame) where the laws rule, and the people participate in making those laws, and more than this is tyranny, oligarchy, or confusion. . . .

I know some say let us have good laws, and no matter for the men that execute them; but let them consider that though good laws do well, good men do better; for good men will never lack good laws, nor submit to ill ones. That, therefore, which makes a good constitution must keep it, namely: men of wisdom and virtue, qualities that—because they descend not with worldly inheritances—must be carefully propagated by a virtuous education of youth. . . . The great end of all government, namely: to support power in reverence with the people, and to secure the people from the abuse of power; that they may be free by their just obedience, and the magistrates honorable, for their just administration; for liberty without obedience is confusion, and obedience without liberty is slavery. To carry this balance is partly owing to the constitution, and partly to the magistracy. Where either of these fail, government will be subject to convulsions; but where both are lacking, it must be totally subverted; then where both meet, the government is likely to endure. Which I humbly pray and hope God will please to make the destiny of Pennsylvania. Amen.

Questions

1. Why does Penn feel that government is "a part of religion itself"?
2. In Penn's view, why are good laws not enough to guarantee good government? What else is needed?

3. According to Penn, what is the "great end of all government"? What can cause a government to fail?

3-2 The Navigation Act of 1660

The Acts of Trade and Navigation (see Table 3.2, text p. 72) were designed to further the mercantilist aims of the British empire. The first was enacted by Parliament in 1651. The Act of 1660 strengthened the original act's intent of blocking Holland from all trade with England and its colonies. But it also made more specific the provisions requiring the colonies to produce raw products only and ship them directly to England in English or colonial ships.

Source: Statutes at Large, ed. D. Pickering (1762–1807), vol. 7, pp. 452–454, 459–460.

For the increase of shipping and encouragement of the navigation of this nation wherein, under the good providence and protection of God, the wealth, safety, and strength of this kingdom is so much concerned; . . . (2) be it enacted . . . from thence forward, no goods or commodities whatsoever shall be imported into or exported out of any lands, islands, plantations, or territories to his Majesty belonging or in his possession . . . in Asia, Africa, or America, in any other ship or ships, vessel or vessels whatsoever, but in such ships or vessels as do . . . belong only to the people of England or Ireland, dominion of Wales . . . or are of the build of and belonging to any the said lands, islands, plantations, or territories, as the proprietors and right owner thereof, and whereof the master and three fourths of the mariners at least are English. . . .

III. And it is further enacted . . . that no goods or commodities whatsoever, of the growth, production or manufacture of Africa, Asia, or America, or of any part thereof . . . be imported into England, Ireland, or Wales . . . in any other ship or ships vessel or vessels whatsoever, but in such as do . . . belong only to the people of England or Ireland, dominion of Wales . . . or of the lands, islands, plantations or territories in Asia, Africa, or America, to his Majesty belonging. . . .

XVIII. And it is further enacted . . . that . . . no sugars, tobacco, cotton-wool, indigoes, ginger, fustic, or other dyeing wood, of the growth, production, or manufacture of any English plantations in America, Asia, or Africa, shall be . . . transported from any of the said English plantations to any land . . . other than to such other English plantations as do belong to his Majesty. . . .

XIX. And be it further enacted . . . that for every ship or vessel which . . . shall set sail out of or from England, Ireland, Wales . . . for any English plantation in America, Asia, or Africa, sufficient bond shall be given with one surety . . . that the same commodities shall be by the said ship brought to some port . . . and shall there unload. . . .

Questions

1. What was the stated purpose of the Navigation Act of 1660?
2. What limits did the act place on colonial trade?
3. How did the act define an "English" ship?

3-3   The Glorious Revolution in Massachusetts (1689)

When the Protestants William and Mary replaced James II as England's monarchs (see text p. 74), New Englanders rebelled against Governor Edmund Andros, an unpopular governor who had been appointed by James II. The author of the following account, Thomas Danforth, had been a leading participant in the uprising. Although he seems to have been apprehensive about prosecution, none of the participants were punished. Danforth's correspondent, Increase Mather, had been sent to London to plead with James II for restoration of the colony's charter; he stayed on to negotiate a new charter with William and Mary.

Source: Thomas Danforth to the Rev. Increase Mather, July 30, 1689. In Thomas Hutchinson, *A Collection of Original Papers Relative to the History of the Colony of Massachusetts-Bay* (Boston, 1769), pp. 567–571.

It is now fourteen weeks since the revolution of the government here. Future consequences we are ignorant of, yet we know that, at present, we are eased of those great oppressions that we groaned under, by the exercise of an arbitrary and illegal commission.

The business [i.e., the seizure of Governor Andros] was acted by the soldiers that came armed into Boston from all parts, being greatly animated by the Prince's [William of Orange] declarations, which about that time came into the country, and heightened by the oppressions of the governor, judges, and the most wicked extortion of their debauched officers. The ancient magistrates and elders, although they had strenuously advised to further waiting for orders from England, were compelled to assist with their presence and counsels for the prevention of bloodshed, which had most certainly been the result if prudent counsel had not been given to both parties. . . .

I am deeply sensible that we have a wolf by the ears. I do therefore earnestly entreat of you to procure the best advice you can in this matter that, if possible, the good intents of the people and their loyalty to the Crown of England may not turn to their prejudice. The example of England, the declarations put forth by the Prince of Orange, now our King, the alteration of the government in England

making the arbitrary commission of Sir Edmund [Andros] null and void in the law; these considerations, in conjunction with the great oppressions the people lay under, were so far prevalent in the minds of all, that although some could not advise to the enterprise, yet are hopeful that we shall not be greatly blamed, but shall have a pardon granted for any error the law will charge us with in this matter.

We do crave that the circumstances of our case and condition in all respects may be considered. Nature has taught us self-preservation. God commands it as being the rule of charity toward our neighbor. Our great remoteness from England denies us the opportunity of direction for the regulation of ourselves in all emergencies, nor have we means to know the laws and customs of our nation. These things are our great disadvantage. We have always endeavored to prove ourselves loyal to the Crown of England. And we have also labored to attend the directions of our charter, under which were laid by our fathers the foundation of this His Majesty's colony; and we are not without hopes but that we shall receive from Their Royal Majesties the confirmation of our charter, with such addition of privileges as may advance the revenue of the Crown, and be an encouragement to Their Majesties' subjects here.

Questions

1. What justification does Danforth give for the rebellion?
2. What problems does Danforth fear may result from the rebellion?
3. What does Danforth hope the rebellion will achieve?

Questions for Further Thought

1. How did the Navigation Acts (Document 3-2) both help and hinder the colonial economy? Judging from Danforth's letter (Document 3-3), how do you think the colonists, especially in New England, felt about the acts?

2. Do you think William Penn's concept and design of government for Pennsylvania (Document 3-1) would have met with the approval of the inhabitants of Massachusetts?

3. In *Two Treatises on Government* (1690), the English philosopher John Locke set forth a theory of government that justified the Glorious Revolution (see text p. 74). What precursors of Locke's argument can you find in the writings of Penn and Danforth (Documents 3-1 and 3-3)?

The Imperial Slave Economy

The creation of a new agricultural system in America profoundly affected the history of four continents (see text pp. 80–81). Lands seized from Indians in North and South America were used to raise sugar, tobacco, and other crops. These lands were worked by millions of slaves from Africa and triggered a commercial revolution in Europe. The impact on western Africa and parts of eastern Africa was tragic as 10 million to 12 million people were transplanted, draining Africa of its population and lowering its standard of living (see text p. 81). The spiritual cost may have been higher, disrupting lives, encouraging tribal violence in a struggle to control the slave trade, and transforming African political structures (Document 3-4).

Although there were a few Africans in Virginia as early as 1619, they were not fully defined as slaves until, beginning in the 1660s, new statutes began to gradually designate them as chattel bound for life. Blackness was becoming a mark of inferiority. In the Chesapeake as in the West Indies and later the Carolinas, the English built an economy based on slave labor (see text pp. 82–84 and Documents 3-5 and 3-6).

Slavery was a brutal experience from the initial capture in Africa, to the middle passage (see American Voices, text p. 82), to a degrading life of labor in America. Sugar growing in the West Indies was the worst killer; the loss of life from disease and oppressive labor was staggering. The Chesapeake was less deadly to slaves. The cultivation of tobacco was less physically demanding and only modestly profitable, so that planters did not have to replace their labor force constantly. In South Carolina, however, the death rate was high and the reproduction rate was low, so planters imported large numbers of Africans (see text p. 85). Throughout the southern colonies staple export crops turned slavery into a central feature of the economic and social systems (Documents 3-7 and 3-8).

Many Africans adopted Christianity. Even within the restrictions of slavery some found ways to overcome the limits placed on their education and self-expression (Document 3-8).

3-4   An African Prince Sold into Slavery

James Albert Ukawsaw Gronniosaw was sold into slavery when he was about fifteen. The narrative of his enslavement provides some insight into the intrigue and culture shock produced in West Africa by the slave trade (see text pp. 79–80). Eventually Gronniosaw was freed when his master died. After serving as a sailor in the French and Indian War, he left New York, where he had settled when he gained his freedom, and went to England. There he and his family fell on hard times. One purpose of this narrative was to raise money to help him get out of debt.

Source: Ukawsaw Gronniosaw, *A Narrative of the Most Remarkable Particulars in the Life of James Albert Ukawsaw Gronniosaw, An African Prince* (Bath, 1780?), pp. 7–17.

I was born in the city of Bournou; my mother was the eldest daughter of the reigning King there. . . . I had, from my infancy, a curious turn of mind; was more grave and reserved, in my disposition, than either of my brothers and sisters. . . . 'Twas certain that I was, at times, very unhappy in myself: It being strongly impressed on my mind that there was some GREAT MAN of power, which resided above the sun, moon and stars, the objects of our worship. My dear indulgent mother would bear more with me than any of my friends beside. I often raised my hands to heaven, and asked her who lived there? . . . I was frequently lost in wonder at the works of the creation: Was afraid, and uneasy, and restless, but could not tell for what. I wanted to be informed of things that no person could tell me; and was always dissatisfied. . . .

To this moment I grew more and more uneasy every day, insomuch that one Saturday (which is the day on which we keep our sabbath) I labored under anxieties and fears that cannot be expressed; and, what is more extraordinary, I could not give a reason for it. I rose, as our custom is, about three o'clock (as we are obliged to be at our place of worship an hour before the sunrise). We say nothing in our worship, but continue on our knees with our hands held up, observing a strict silence till the sun is at a certain height. . . . When, at a certain sign made by the Priest, we get Up (our duty being over) and disperse to our different houses. Our place of meeting is under a large palm tree; we divide ourselves into many congregations. . . .

About this time there came a merchant from the Gold Coast (the third city in GUINEA). He traded with the inhabitants of our country in ivory, etc. He took great notice of my unhappy situation, and inquired into the cause; he expressed vast concern for me, and said, if my parents would part with me for a little while, and let him take me home with him, it would be of more service to me than any thing they could do for me. He told me that if I would go with him, I should see houses with Wings to them walk upon the water, and should also see the white folks; and

that he had many sons of my age, which should be my companions; and he added to all this that he would bring me safe back again soon. I was highly pleased with the account of this strange place, and was very desirous of going. I seemed sensible of a secret impulse upon my mind, which I could not resist, that seemed to tell me I must go. When my dear mother saw that I was willing to leave them, she spoke to my father and grandfather and the rest of my relations, who all agreed that I should accompany the merchant to the Gold Coast. . . . Indeed if I could have known when I left my friends and country, that I should never return to them again my misery on that occasion would have been inexpressible. . . .

I had a very unhappy and discontented journey, being in continual fear that the people I was with would murder me. I often reflected with extreme regret on the kind friends I had left, and the idea of my dear mother frequently drew tears from my eyes. I cannot recollect how long we were in going from Bournou to the Gold Coast; but as there is no shipping nearer to Bournou than that city, it was tedious in travelling so far by land, being upwards of a thousand miles. I was heartily rejoiced when we arrived at the end of our journey: I now vainly imagined that all my troubles and inquietudes would terminate here; but could I have looked into futurity, I should have perceived that I had much more to suffer than I had before experienced, and that they had as yet but barely commenced.

I was now more than a thousand miles from home, without a friend or means to procure one. . . . I was mightily pleased with sounds so entirely new to me, and was very inquisitive to know the cause of this rejoicing, and asked many questions concerning it; I was answered that it was meant as a compliment to me, because I was grandson to the King of Bournou.

This account gave me a secret pleasure; but I was not suffered long to enjoy this satisfaction, for, in the evening of the same day, two of the merchant's sons (boys about my own age) came running to me, and told me, that the next day I was to die, for the King intended to behead me.

I reply'd that I was sure it could not be true, for that I came there to play with them, and to see houses walk upon the water with wings to them, and the white folks; but I was soon informed that their King imagined I was sent by my father as a spy, and would make such discoveries, at my return home, that would enable them to make war with greater advantage to ourselves; and for these reasons he had resolved I should never return to my native country. When I heard this, I suffered misery that cannot be described. I wished, a thousand times, that I had never left my friends and country, but still the Almighty was pleased to work miracles for me.

The morning I was to die, I was washed and all my gold ornaments made bright and shining, and then carried to the palace, where the King was to behead me himself (as is the custom of the place). . . . I went with an undaunted courage, and it pleased God to melt the heart of the King, who sat with his scymitar in his hand ready to behead me; yet, being himself so affected, he dropped it out of his hand, and took me upon his knee and wept over me. I put my right hand round his neck, and prest him to my heart. He set me down and blest me; and added, that he would not kill me, and that I should not go home, but be sold for a slave, so then I was conducted back again to the merchant's house. . . .

A few days after a Dutch ship came into the harbour, and they carried me on board, in hopes that the captain would purchase me. As they went, I heard them agree, that, if they could not sell me then, they would throw me overboard. I was in extreme agonies when I heard this; and as soon as ever I saw the Dutch Captain, I ran to him, and put my arms round him, and said, "Father save me;" (for I knew that if he did not buy me, I should be treated very ill, or, possibly murdered.) And though he did not understand my language, yet it pleased the Almighty to influence him in my behalf, and he bought me for two yards of check [checkered cloth], which is of more value there, than in England. . . .

I was now washed and clothed in the Dutch or English manner. My master grew very fond of me, and I loved him exceedingly. . . . He used to read prayers in public to the ship's crew every sabbath day; and when first I saw him read, I was never so surprised in my whole life as when I saw the book talk to my master; for I thought it did, as I observed him to look upon it, and move his lips. I wished it would do so to me. As soon as my master had done reading I follow'd him to the place where he put the book, being mightily delighted with it, and when nobody saw me, I open'd it and put my ear down close upon it, in great hope that it would say something to me; but was very sorry and greatly disappointed when I found it would not speak, this thought immediately presented itself to me, that every body and every thing despised me because I was black.

Questions

1. Why did Gronniosaw leave his native Bournou?
2. Why was he enslaved?
3. What were his first impressions of being enslaved? How did enslavement affect his self-image?

3-5   Slavery and Prejudice: "An Act for the Better Order and Government of Negroes and Slaves," South Carolina (1712)

Until the early 1700s most legislation involving African-Americans was concerned with the personal status of slaves and was motivated primarily by racial prejudice. Subsequently, another element came into play: fear of their growing numbers. The presence of a servile but potentially rebellious population made it seem necessary to adopt measures of control (see text pp. 91–92). The act passed by South Carolina served as a model for slave codes in the colonial South and later in the southern states.

Source: Statutes at Large of South Carolina, ed. Thomas Cooper and David J. McCord (1836–1841), vol. 7, pp. 352–357.

WHEREAS, the plantations and estates of this Province cannot be well and sufficiently managed and brought into use, without the labor and service of negroes and other slaves [i.e., Indians]; and forasmuch as the said negroes and other slaves brought unto the people of this Province for that purpose, are of barbarous, wild, savage natures, and such as renders them wholly unqualified to be governed by the laws, customs, and practices of this Province; but that it is absolutely necessary, that such other constitutions, laws and orders, should in this Province be made and enacted, for the good regulating and ordering of them, as may restrain the disorders, rapines and inhumanity, to which they are naturally prone and inclined, and may also tend to the safety and security of the people of this Province and their estates; to which purpose, . . .

II. . . . That no master, mistress, overseer, or other person whatsoever . . . shall give their negroes and other slaves leave . . . to go out of their plantations, except such negro or other slave as usually wait upon them at home or abroad, or wearing a livery; and every other negro or slave that shall be taken hereafter out of his master's plantation, without a ticket, or leave in writing, from his master or mistress, or some other person by his or her appointment, or some white person in the company of such slave, to give an account of his business, shall be whipped; and every person who shall not (when in his power) apprehend every negro or other slave which he shall see out of his master's plantation, without leave as aforesaid, and after apprehended, shall neglect to punish him by moderate whipping, shall forfeit twenty shillings. . . . And for the better security of all such persons that shall endeavor to take any runaway, or shall examine any slave for his ticket, passing to and from his master's plantation, it is hereby declared lawful for any white person to beat, maim or assault, and if such negro or slave cannot otherwise be taken, to kill him, who shall refuse to shew his ticket, or, by running away or resistance, shall endeavor to avoid being apprehended or taken.

III. And be it further enacted by the authority aforesaid, That every master, mistress or overseer of a family in this Province, shall cause all his negro houses to be searched diligently and effectually, once every fourteen days, for fugitive and runaway slaves, guns, swords, clubs, and any other mischievous weapons, and finding any, to take them away, and cause them to be secured. . . .

VI. And be it further enacted . . . That every master or head of any family, shall keep all his guns and other arms, when out of use, in the most private and least frequented room in the house, upon the penalty of being convicted of neglect therein, to forfeit three pounds.

IX. And be it further enacted by the authority aforesaid, That upon complaint made to any justice of the peace, of any heinous or grievous crime, committed by any slave or slaves, as murder, burglary, robbery, burning of houses, or any lesser crimes, as killing or stealing any meat or other cattle, maiming one the other, stealing of fowls, provisions, or such like trespasses or injuries, the said justice shall issue out his warrant for apprehending the offender or offenders, . . . he shall commit him or them to prison, or immediately proceed to tryal of the said slave or slaves . . . [and if] they shall find such negro or other slave or slaves guilty thereof, they shall give sentence of death, if the crime by law deserve the same. . . .

X. And in regard great mischiefs daily happen by petty larcenies committed by negroes and slaves of this Province, Be it further enacted by the authority aforesaid, That if any negro or other slave shall hereafter steal or destroy any goods, chattels, or provisions whatsoever, of any other person than his master or mistress . . . [if] adjudged [guilty is] to be publicly and severely whipped, not exceeding forty lashes; and if such negro or other slave punished as aforesaid, be afterwards, by two justices of the peace, found guilty of the like crimes, he or they, for such his or their second offence, shall either have one of his ears cut off, or be branded in the forehead with a hot iron, that the mark thereof may remain; and if after such punishment, such negro or slave for his third offence, shall have his nose slit; and if such negro or other slave, after the third time as aforesaid, be accused of petty larceny, or of any of the offences before mentioned, such negro or other slave shall be tried in such manner as those accused of murder, burglary, etc. are before by this Act provided for to be tried, and in case they shall be found guilty a fourth time of any the offences before mentioned, then such negro or other slave shall be adjudged to suffer death, or other punishment, as the said justices shall think fitting. . . .

XII. And It is Further enacted by the authority aforesaid, That if any negroes or other slaves shall make mutiny or insurrection . . . the offenders shall be tried by two justices of the peace and three freeholders . . . who are hereby empowered and required to . . . inflict death, or any other punishment, upon the offenders . . . if the Governor and council of this Province shall think fitting . . . that only one or more of the said criminals should suffer death as exemplary, and the rest to be returned to the owners. . . .

Questions

1. What is the assumption of this act concerning the cultural level of the slave population?
2. What are the responsibilities and duties of slave owners in regard to governing their slaves?

3. What does the willingness of white South Carolinians to carry out sentences of death or mutilation on slaves, who represented a capital investment, imply about race relations at that time?

3-6   Early Protests against Slavery: The Mennonites (1688)

As laws began to define the condition of African servants and slaves and to distinguish slavery from other forms of labor in the colonies, a few voices were raised against the institution (see text p. 90). Among the earliest protests were those of Quakers and Mennonites. The following document is a Mennonite statement that dates from 1688, about the time of the Glorious Revolution in England and the beginning of the extensive importation of slaves into the Chesapeake area.

Source: Source Book and Bibliographical Guide for American Church History (1921; reprint, edited by P. G. Mode, Boston: J. S. Canner, 1964, pp. 552–553).

This is to the monthly meeting held at Richard Worrell's:

These are the reasons why we are against the traffic of men-body, as followeth: Is there any that would be done or handled in this manner? viz., to be sold or made a slave for all the time of his life? How fearful and faint-hearted are many at sea, when they see a strange vessel, being afraid it should be a Turk, and they should be taken, and sold for slaves into Turkey. Now, what is *this* better done, than Turks do? Yea, rather it is worse for them, which say they are Christians; for we hear that the most part of such negers are brought hither against their will and consent, and that many of them are stolen. Now, though they are black, we cannot conceive there is more liberty to have them slaves, as it is to have other white ones. There is a saying, that we should do to all men like as we will be done ourselves; making no difference of what generation, descent, or colour they are. And those who steal or rob men, and those who buy or purchase them, are they not all alike? Here is liberty of conscience, which is right and reasonable; here ought to be likewise liberty of the body, except of evil-doers, which is another case. But to bring men hither, or to rob and sell them against their will, we stand against. In Europe there are many oppressed for conscience-sake; and here there are those oppressed which are of a black colour. . . . Ah! do consider well this thing, you who do it, if you would be done at this manner—and if it is done according to Christianity! You surpass Holland and Germany in this thing. This makes an ill report in all those countries of Europe, where they hear of [it], that the Quakers do here handel men as they handel there the cattle. And for that reason some have no mind or inclination to come hither. And who shall maintain this your cause, or plead for it? Truly, we cannot do so, except you shall inform us better hereof, viz.: that Christians have liberty to practice these things. Pray, what thing in the world can be done worse towards us, than if men should rob or steal us away and sell us for slaves to strange countries; separating husbands from their wives and children. Being now this is not done in the manner we would be done at; therefore, we contradict, and are against this traffic of men-body. . . .

If once these slaves (which they say are so wicked and stubborn men) should join themselves—fight for their freedom, and handel their masters and mistresses, as they did handel them before; will these masters and mistresses take the sword at hand and war against these poor slaves, like, as we are able to believe, some will not refuse to do? Or, have these poor negers not as much right to fight for their freedom, as you have to keep them slaves? . . .

Questions

1. What are the grounds on which this congregation of Mennonites protests against slavery?
2. Why does the document make reference to the Turks?

3. Are the arguments against slavery in this passage different from the reasons that were offered later in the colonial era and into the nineteenth century?

3-7   Conflicts between Masters and Slaves: Maryland in the Mid-Seventeenth Century

Almost from the beginning of Maryland and Virginia's slave history, as the first legislation defined the lifelong condition of slavery, colonists imposed harsher punishments against laborers of African descent than against white servants. Masters could, for example, whip a slave naked without breaking the law, and there were no laws requiring that food and clothing be provided to slaves (see text p. 91). But there were limits to punishment and daily mistreatment of slaves, as the following case outlines. In the end, however, the case was referred to a higher court, where testimony was given that the slave, Tony, was a rogue and persistent runaway. At that point the court acquitted Overzee for cruelty against the slave.

Source: "Att a Provincial Court Held att St. Clement's Manor December 2, 1658," Provincial Court Proceedings, *Archives of Maryland* (Baltimore: Maryland Historical Society, 1941), vol. 41, pp. 190–191.

Att a Provincial Court Held att St. Clement's Manor December 2, 1658

Attorney General v. [Symon] Overzee

Mr. William Barton informes the court against Mr. Symon Overzee, for that the said Overzee correcting his negro servant the said negro dyed under his said correction.

The examination of Hannah Littleworth aged 27 yeares or thereabouts taken the 27th of November 1658, before Philip Calvert, Esq.

This Examinant sayth that sometime (as shee conseives) in September was two yeares, Mr. Overzee commanded a negro (commonly called Tony) formerly chayned up for some misdemeanors by the command of Mr. Overzee (Mr. Overzee being then abroad) to be lett loose, and ordered him to goe to worke, but instead of goeing to worke the said negro layd himselfe downe and would not stirre. Whereupon Mr. Overzee beate him with some peare tree wands or tweiggs to the bigness of man's finger att the biggest end, which hee held in his hand, and upon the stubberness of the negro caused his dublett to be taken of, and whip'd him upon his bare back, and the negro still remayned in his stubbernes, and feyned himselfe in fitts, as hee used att former times to doe. Whereuppon Mr. Overzee commanded this examinant to heate a fyre shovel, and to bring him some lard, which shee did and sayth that the said fyre shovel was hott enough to melt the lard, but not soe hot as to blister anyone, and that it did not blister the negro, on whom Mr. Overzee powr'd it. Immediately

thereuppon the negro rose up, and Mr. Overzee commanded him to be tyed to a Ladder standing on the foreside of the dwelling howse, which was accordingly done by an Indian slve, who tyed him by the wrist, with a piece of dryed hide, and (as she remembers but cannot justly say) that hee did stand uppong the grownd. And still the negro remayned mute or stubborne, and made noe signs of conforming himselfe to his masters will or command. And about a quarter of an howre after, or less, Mr. Overzee and Mrs. Overzee went from home, and [she] doth not know of any order Mr. Overzee gave concerning the said negro. And that while Mr. Overzee beate the negro and powred the lard on him, there was nobody by, save only Mr. Mathew Stone, and Mrs. Overzee now deceased. And that from the time of Mr. Overzee and his wife going from hime, till the negro was dead, there was nobody about the howse but only the said Mr. Mathew Stone, William hewes, and this examinant, and a negro woman in the quartering house, who never stir'd out. And that after Mr. Overzee was gone, upon the relation of Mr. Mathew Stone, in the presence of William Hewes that the negro was dying, this examinant desyred Mr. Mathew Stone to cutt the negro downe, and hee refused to doe it, William Hewes also bidding him let him alone and within lesse then halfe a howre after the negro dyed, the wind comming up att northwest soone after hee was soe tyed, and hee was tyed up betweene three and fowre o'clock in the afternoone, and dyed about six or seaven. . . .

William Hewes sworne in upon court sayth that hee

was present, att the time when Mr. Overzee beate the negro, and saw him allso powre lard upon him, and that as hee conceaves and remembers, he saw noe blood drawne of the negro, and this deponent being willing to help the negro from the grownd, Mr. Overzee haveing his knife in his hand, cutting the twigs, threatened him to runne his knife in him (or words to that effect) if he molested him, and that the negro (as he think, but cannot justly say) stood upon the grownd, and sayth further that the negro did commonly use to runne away, and absent himselfe from his Mr. Overzees service. . . .

Questions

1. What was Symon Overzee tried for? What were the excuses he gave, according to the witnesses?
2. Do the witnesses offer unambiguous testimony, or did you develop doubts about their memories of details?
3. What is the tone of the testimony given? What might Tony have offered as a defense of his behavior?

3-8 Desire for Freedom: Poems by Phillis Wheatley

Born in Africa about 1753, Phillis Wheatley was brought as a young girl to Boston. She was purchased by Susannah Wheatley, the wife of a prosperous tailor, who took her into her family. There Wheatley learned to read and write, showing a remarkable aptitude for study and reflection. She was freed after her mistress's death. The first poem below, composed in 1770, reflects her new Christian identity in a white world but still affirms her "sable race." The second, written in 1772, expresses the connection between her personal history, her blackness, and her devotion to the Anglo-American controversy. Although she was already published in Boston, her fame spread with the publication of a volume of her poems in London at the age of twenty, only the third book of verse published by a woman in colonial America. The work would be republished twice in England and seven times in America during the nineteenth century.

Source: Phillis Wheatley, *Poems on Various Subjects, Religious and Moral* (London: A. Bell, 1773), pp. 18, 74.

ON BEING BROUGHT FROM AFRICA TO AMERICA

'Twas mercy brought me from my Pagan land,
Taught my benighted soul to understand
That there's a God, that there's a Saviour too:
Once I redemption neither sought nor knew.

Some view our sable race with scornful eye,
"Their colour is a diabolic die."
Remember, Christians, Negroes, black as Cain,
May be refin'd, and join th'angelic train.

TO THE RIGHT HONORABLE WILLIAM, EARL OF DARTMOUTH,
HIS MAJESTY'S SECRETARY OF STATE FOR NORTH AMERICA, ETC.

Hail, Happy day, when, smiling like the morn,
Fair Freedom rose New-England to adorn.
No more America, in mournful strain
Of wrongs, and grievance unredress'd complain,
No longer shall thou dread the iron chain,
Which wanton Tyranny with lawless hand
Had made, and with it meant t'enslave the land.
Should you, my lord, while you peruse my song,
Wonder from whence my love of Freedom sprung,

Whence flow these wishes for the common good,
By feeling hearts alone best understood,
I, young in life, by seeming cruel fate
Was snatch'd from Afric's fancy'd happy seat:
What pangs excruciating must molest,
What sorrows labour in my parent's breast?
Steel'd was that soul and by no misery mov'd
That from a father seiz'd his babe belov'd:
Such, such my case. And can I then but pray
Others may never feel tyrannic sway?

Questions

1. These two poems were written two years apart. How do the author's attitudes and self-image change from the earlier to the later poem?
2. What is Wheatley's attitude toward Christianity? Toward her African background?
3. How does she explain her love of freedom to Lord Dartmouth?

Questions for Further Thought

1. Does Gronniosaw's literacy (Document 3-4) suggest that his experiences were not typical of those of most slaves in North America? Compare his writing to the evidence of slaves' attitudes given in other documents in this section.
2. How did the slave codes reflect the political and economic goals of slave owners and their social attitudes toward slaves?
3. What differences are there between moral statements such as the Mennonite one (Document 3-6) and the testimony of people in courts of law (Document 3-7)?

The New Politics of Empire, 1713–1750

Before 1689 the English government ruled most colonies with authoritarian statutes and in accordance with authoritarian principles (Document 3-2; see text p. 95). After the Glorious Revolution and Queen Anne's War the tremendous success of colonization drew support from the imperial center. Colonial assemblies gained greater autonomy from governors and royal placemen. In addition, there was a growing colonial interest in defining political liberties, some of which colonists perceived to be different from the deference and patronage of "the English system" of rule (see text pp. 96–97; Document 3-9). In everyday business and trade colonists began to challenge the core of mercantilist tenets; as Document 3-10 shows, the impending Molasses Act of 1733 (see text p. 99) gave rise to concern about continuing colonial prosperity. The colonies had reached a high level of maturity and independence, which they sought to protect as the eighteenth century progressed.

3-9   Increasing Liberties: The Case of Pennsylvania (1701)

From 1682 to 1692 Pennsylvanians lived under a cumbersome Frame of Government worked out by Willian Penn (Document 3-1). In 1692 Parliament placed the colony under the authority of New York's governor, Benjamin Fletcher, thereby making it a royal colony. Over the following years, however, Pennsylvanians demanded more privileges than this relationship allowed, and slowly enlarged the powers of their own colonial Assembly. The Assembly's powers grew at the expense of the Governor's council, until the latter became no more than an advisory committee. Finally, colonists adopted a new plan of government in 1701, also worked out by William Penn, which became the basis for embodying Assembly privileges and lasted until the American Revolution.

Source: In Francis N. Thorpe, ed., *The Federal and State Constitutions . . . of the United States* (Washington, D.C.: U.S. Government Printing Office, 1909), vol. 5, pp. 3076–3077.

. . . for the further Well-being and good Government of the said Province, and Territories and in Pursuance of the Rights and Powers before-mentioned, I the said William Penn do declare, grant and confirm, unto all the Freemen, Planters and Adventurers, and other Inhabitants of this Province and Territories, these following Liberties, Franchises and Privileges. . . .

First

Because no People can be truly happy, though under the greatest Enjoyment of Civil Liberties, if abridged of the Freedom of their Consciences, as to their Religious Profession and Worship: And Almighty God being the only Lord of Conscience, Father of Lights and Spirits; and the Author as well as Object of all divine Knowledge, Faith and Worship, who only doth enlighten the Minds, and persuade and convince the Understandings of People, I do hereby grant and declare, That no Person or Persons, inhabiting in this province or Territories, who shall confess and acknowledge *One* almighty God, the Creator, Upholder and Ruler of the World; and profess him or themselves obliged to live quietly under the Civil Government, shall be in any Case molested or prejudiced, in his or their Person or Estate, because of his or their conscientious Persuasion or Practice, nor be compelled to frequent or maintain any religious Worship, Place or Ministry, contrary to his or their Mind, or to do or suffer any other Act or Thing, contrary to their religious Persuasion.

And that all Persons who also profess to believe in *Jesus Christ*, the Saviour of the World, shall be capable . . . to serve this Government in any Capacity, both legislatively and executively, he or they solemnly promising, when lawfully required, Allegiance to the King as Sovereign, and Fidelity to the Proprietary and Governor. . . .

For the well government of this Province and Territories, there shall be an Assembly yearly chosen, by the Freemen thereof, to consist of Four Persons out of each County, of most Note for Virtue, Wisdom and Ability . . . Which Assembly shall have Power to chuse a Speaker and other their Officers; and shall be Judges of the Qualifications and Elections of their own Members; sit upon their own Adjournments; appoint Committees; prepare Bills in order to pass into Laws; impeach Criminals, and redress Grievances; and shall have all other Powers and Privileges of an Assembly, according to the Rights of the free-born Subjects of *England*, and as is usual in any of the King's Plantations in *America*. . . .

That the Freemen in each respective County, at the Time and Place of Meeting for Electing their Representatives to serve in Assembly, may as often as there shall be Occasions, chuse a double Number of Persons to present to the Governor for Sheriffs and Coroners to serve for *Three* Years, if so long they behave themselves well. . . .

And that the Justices of the respective Counties shall or may nominate and present to the Governor *Three* Persons, to serve for Clerk of the Peace for the said County, when there is a Vacancy, one of which the Governor shall commissionate within *Ten* Days after such Presentment, or else the *First* nominated shall serve in the said Office during good Behavior.

That the Laws of this Government shall be in the Stile, viz. *By the Governor, with the Consent and Approbation of the Freemen in General Assembly met*; and shall be, after Confirmation by the Governor, forthwith recorded in the Rolls Office, and kept at *Philadelphia*, unless the Governor and Assembly shall agree to appoint another Place.

That all Criminals shall have the same Privileges of Witnesses and Council as their Prosecutors.

That no Person or Persons shall or may, at any Time hereafter, be obliged to answer any Complaint, matter or Thing whatsoever, relating to Property, before the Governor and Council, or in any other Place, but in ordinary Course of Justice, unless Appeals thereunto shall be hereafter by Law appointed.

That no Person within this Government, shall be licensed by the Governor to keep an Ordinary, Tavern or House of Public Entertainment, but such who are first recommended to him, . . . [and] Justices are and shall be hereby impowered, to suppress and forbid any Person, keeping such Public-House as aforesaid, upon their Misbehavior, on such Penalties as the Law doth or shall direct. . .

Questions

1. What different offices does this charter create, and what powers are conferred on the major branches of the government?
2. Are the privileges and obligations discussed in this document similar to those you recognize in American government today? In what ways?
3. The liberty of conscience professed in this document applied to a great number of Pennsylvanians, but some groups would be permitted to live in the colony yet would be excluded from officeholding. Who is included, and who is excluded?

3-10   The Necessity of the West Indies Trade (1732)

When news reached the colonies that Parliament was considering passing what would later be known as the Molasses Act (see text p. 99), few colonists favored its provisions. Even in England international traders and captains familiar with the profitable commerce in the West Indies raised their voices against the new restrictions on colonial transport of Caribbean commodities. One of the many protests heard in a long Parliamentary investigation about the effects of new mercantile regulations was delivered in a speech by Captain Fayrer Hall in 1732.

Source: The New York Gazette, July 17, 24, 31, 1732.

Capt. Fayrer Hall's Evidence before a Committee of the whole House of Commons, in relation to the Trade carried on between our Plantations and the Foreign Colonies. . . .

Capt. Fayrer Hall, you will acquaint the Committee whether you know the Trade between the West-Indies and Northern Colonies?

I have lived in and traded for twenty Years past to the West-Indies, and the Northern Colonies. . . .

What Quantities of Lumber do the French take off [from the northern colonies]?

Martineco, Gardaloupa, Grand-terre, Marigalant & Granada, these Islands all together, I believe, may take off as much, or more than [the British-owned islands] do. . . .

Is there a sufficient Quantity of Molasses made at our [British] Sugar Islands to supply the Northern Colonies?

No, they have a Demand for a much greater Quantity than they can make, for they take all that is made at our own [British] islands, and, if I am rightly informed, as much or more from the foreign Settlements; ever since I remember our People have taken Molasses from [Dutch] Suranam, I believe near as much as they did from all our [British] Islands; and the Demand is so much increased, that the Northern People could use and vend more, if they knew where to get more, even nothwithstanding what they have from the French. . . .

Have our [British] Sugar Islands a demand for all their [northern colonial] Lumber & Horses?

It is impossible; I have known many losing Voyages [from the northern colonies] by sending of Lumber and Horses, and they the [British] Islanders have sent [the unsold portions of the goods] to other Islands. The Northern Colonies are capable of selling and sending a thousand Times as much [as the British islands can buy]; the District of Land is larger than all Europe.

Supposing they were confined only to sell their Lumber and Horses to our [British] Islands?

It would destroy the Employment of three hundred sail of Ships and Vessels; we have three sail to one of any other Nation's. It is not long ago that the Dutch . . . had ten to our one, but the Act of Navigation put an end to that; we are now what the Dutch were at that Time, we have three sail to one, we are the Carriers as they used to be; but if this [Molasses] Act passes, the French will have the far greater Number of Ships, as we have now. There is no more Difficulty in going to Mississipi, than to our Northern Colonies, and the Passage there will be gained in a quarter of the time; now if we were to suppose that the Passage from Mississippi or Mobile, were to be near twice as long from thence to Martineco, as from Boston to Martineco, the French would be, in all Respects, in a much better Case. And there is no other Reason that they are not supplied from their own [French] Settlements [on the Mississippi River] than that we have got the [business from them first], and at present sell cheaper [goods from the northern colonies]; that is the only Reason the french have not [diverted their trade]. . . .

How is the Ballance [of Payments] in regard to the Northern Colonies? Do they take more Goods [from English merchants] than they send us [from the colonies]?

Yes, they have no other way of paying [English merchants] but by the Remittance of Money which they have from the Dutch & French [trade in the West Indies]. . . .

Supposing the Northern Colonies are not suffered to take their Molasses, will not that put a Stop to the Trade of their Lumber and Horses?

Yes. . . . We receive Money from [the French] now, and we never got so much from any of our own [British] Islands; besides, they produce more Sugar, Rum, and Molasses lately, then they used to do, and Barbados is not so good, it is almost worn out . . . the French have the Advantage of us in their having better Ground, as well as better Management.

Questions

1. What goods did the northern colonists send to the Caribbean, and what did they get in return that was essential for their trade with England? Why would the Molasses Act upset that set of relationships?
2. Why did English authorities fear the trade of northern colonists with foreign islands?
3. What was the significance of the lower Mississippi River trade?

Questions for Further Thought

1. Given the evidence in the documents in this section and in the textbook, were the colonists growing apart from English ways or growing toward them?
2. Which elements of English culture and economy did the colonists adopt deliberately? Which ones do you believe they adopted unwittingly? Which ones did they reject outright or challenge?
3. What was the extent of colonists' exposure to the cultures and political systems of other empires in the early eighteenth century?

CHAPTER 4

Growth and Crisis in American Society 1720–1765

★   ★   ★

Freehold Society in New England and *The Mid-Atlantic: Toward a New Society, 1720–1765*

After 1720 the population and economies of the mainland British colonies grew dramatically, and those colonies developed distinctively American characteristics. In New England that distinctiveness was characterized by the maintenance of communities of independent property owners. In Great Britain 75 percent of the land was owned by the gentry and nobility; in New England 70 percent was owned by freeholding families. Strategies for maintaining this system varied (Document 4-1; see text pp. 106–107).

Although the pattern of land ownership was distinctive, the place of women in rural New England was close to that in Britain. Women were socialized to accept a subordinate role; their marriage portions were smaller than those of their brothers, and they received no land. Women also had few property rights (see text pp. 104–106). Although a woman had the right to use a third of the family estate after her husband died, it legally belonged to her children. The expectation was that a woman would be deferential toward and work hard to help her father and then her husband. Her work usually included a broad spectrum of household tasks along with the bearing and raising of children (Documents 4-2 and 4-3).

The stability of the system depended on the ability of parents to provide land for their children, but the very success of that system created a crisis (see text pp. 107–108 and Table 4.1 on text p. 107). A population of 100,000 in 1700 grew to 400,000 by 1750, and even though the average birth rate of five to seven children declined to four after 1750, many parents could no longer provide land for their children. Farm communities responded to this crisis in ways that preserved a freehold society: many towns created new communities in frontier areas, and the people who remained increased productivity by introducing new crops and helping one another.

Unlike New England, the middle colonies of New York, New Jersey, and Pennsylvania had a mixture of peoples with diverse religious and ethnic backgrounds (see text pp. 111–114). Quakers were the dominant group in Pennsylvania and were highly influential in New Jersey. In the eighteenth century they were followed by three waves of Germans and large numbers of Scots-Irish. Land was available for the Pennsylvania newcomers. In contrast, the more recent German and Irish immigrants to New York found a scarcity of freehold land and were forced to become tenants on large estates (Document 4-5). Land in New York was dominated by the long-established Dutch patroonships in the Hudson River Valley as well as a few families that held large tracts that had been granted by the first English governors.

The middle colonies prospered because of a growing demand for wheat in Western Europe; however, by midcentury this prosperity had turned an early equality into a system with increasing social divisions (see text p. 110 and Figure 4.2 on text p. 110). Tensions continued and could sometimes be traumatic, but many ethnic and religious groups developed self-governing churches and created an increasingly open and competitive political system. This religious, ethnic, and political pluralism was a distinctively American phenomenon (Document 4-4; see text pp. 114–115).

4-1 A New Hampshire Will (1763)

This document is illustrative of the New England system of inheritance (see text pp. 106–107). The colonial woman's most important legal right was her dower right: under common law a man had to leave his wife at least a life interest in one-third of his real estate, which after her death or remarriage would go to his heirs. At the same time the husband's will was intended to perpetuate the pattern of independent property holding.

Source: The will of Nicholas Dudley, 1763. In Dean Dudley, *The History of the Dudley Family* (Montrose, Mass., 1894), vol. I, pp. 242–247.

I Nicholas Dudley give and bequeath to my well-beloved wife Elizabeth Dudley the use and improvement of all my lands in Brentwood called my home place, with the buildings thereon, and also the use and improvement of all my stock of cattle, sheep, swine, and horses, and my quarter part of Deer Hill saw mill, so long as she remains my widow. . . .

I give and bequeath to my son Nicholas Dudley all my right in Deer Hill mill pond during his natural life, and also the improvements of the same to Abigail Dudley, his wife, if she should survive him, so long as she remains his widow. And then the said right in the said mill pond I give, devise, and bequeath to my grandson Nicholas Dudley, son of Trueworthy Dudley, deceased, to be at his disposal forever.

I give to my son John Dudley twenty shillings . . . he having received his portion of my estate.

I give to my son Byley Dudley twenty shillings . . . he having received his portion of my estate.

I give to my son Joseph Dudley and to his four sons . . . all my land in the parish of Epping, called my common right, excepting the fifty acres I sold to Nicholas Gilman.

I give, devise, and bequeath to my daughters Sarah Robinson and Betty Hill, and to my grandson John Dudley, son of Trueworthy Dudley, deceased, their heirs and assigns, forever, after the decease or second marriage of my wife aforesaid all my lands in Brentwood, called my home place, except the mill pond aforesaid, with the buildings thereon, my stock of cattle, sheep, swine, and horses, excepting one cow and also all my out-door moveables after the decease or second marriage of my wife aforesaid. . . .

Questions

1. What actions did Nicholas Dudley take to protect the livelihood of his widow? Why do you think he took those actions?
2. Does he treat his male heirs equally? If your answer is no, why do you think he treats them differently?
3. Does he treat his daughters as beneficiaries?

4-2   The Obligations of a Wife (1712)

This selection comes from a Puritan marriage manual in which the author is attempting to define the duties and obligations of each member of the family, particularly the husband and the wife. It is a good example of what was expected of a deferential wife (see text pp. 104–105).

Source: Benjamin Wadsworth, *The Well-Ordered Family, or Relative Duties* (Boston, 1712), pp. 22–47.

Wives are part of the House and Family, and ought to be under the Husband's Government: they should Obey their own Husbands. Though the Husband is to rule his Family and his Wife yet his Government of his Wife should not be with rigour, haughtiness, harshness, severity; but with the greatest love, gentleness, kindness, tenderness that may be. Though he governs her, he must not treat her as a Servant, but as his own flesh: he must love her as himself. He should make his government of her, as easie and gentle as possible; and strive more to be lov'd than fear'd; though neither is to be excluded. On the other hand, Wives ought readily and cheerfully to obey their Husbands. Wives submit your selves to your own Husbands, be in subjection to them.

Those Husbands are much to blame, who dont carry it [behave] lovingly and kindly to their Wives. O man, if thy Wife be not so young, beautiful, healthy, well temper'd and qualify'd as thou couldst wish; if she brought not so much Estate to thee, or cannot do so much for thee, as some other women brought to or have done for their Husbands; nay, if she does not carry it so well to thee as she should yet she is thy Wife, and the Great God Commands thee to love her, not to be bitter, but kind to her. What can be more plain and express than that? Let every one of you in particular, so love his Wife even as himself. . . . Those Wives are much to blame who dont carry it lovingly and obediently to their own Husbands. O Woman, if thy Husband be not so young, beautiful, healthy, so well temper'd and qualified as thee couldst wish; if he has not such abilities, riches, honours, as some others have; if he does not carry it so well as he should; yet he's thy Husband, and the Great God Commands thee to love, honour and obey him. Yea, though possibly thou hast greater abilities of mind than he has, wast of some high birth, and he of a more mean Extract, or didst bring more Estate at Marriage than he did; yet since he is thy Husband, God has made him thy Head, and set him above thee, and made it thy duty to love and reverence him. . . .

Questions

1. How is a husband expected to behave toward his wife?
2. How is a wife expected to behave toward her husband?
3. Does higher birth, intelligence, or estate alter a wife's obligation to her husband? Why or why not?

4-3   Letter on the Birth of Her Son (March 26, 1756)

Esther Edwards Burr

Esther Edwards Burr (1732–1758) was the daughter of the famed Great Awakening minister Jonathan Edwards (see American Lives, text pp. 120–121) and the wife of the Reverend Aaron Burr, a Presbyterian minister and the president of the College of New Jersey (Princeton). Here she describes the trials of childbirth faced by all colonial women regardless of wealth or social position. Her son was Aaron Burr, Jr., later to be vice-president of the United States.

Source: In Nancy Woloch, ed., *Early American Women: Documentary History, 1600–1900* (Belmont, Calif.: Wadsworth, 1992), pp. 52–53.

I am my dear Fidelia yet alive and allowed to tell you so. . . . I was unexpectedly delivered of a Son the sixth of Febry. Had a fine time altho' it pleased God in infinite wisdome so to order it that Mr Burr was from home. . . . It seemed very gloomy when I found I was actually in Labour to think that I was, as it were, destitute of Earthly friends—No Mother—No Husband and none of my petecular [*sic*] friends that belong to this Town, they happening to be out of Town—but O my dear God was all these relations and more then [*sic*] all to me in the Hour of my dis-

tre[ss]. . . . I had a very quick and good time—A very good laying in till about 3 weeks, then I had the Canker [an infection of the mouth] very bad, and before I had recovered of that my little Aaron (for so we call him) was taken very sick so that for some days we did not expect his life—he has never been so well since tho' he is comfortable at present. I have my self got a very bad Cold and very soar Eyes which makes it very difficult [*sic*] for me to write atall. Some times I am almost blind.

Questions

1. Given this description, how could Burr describe the birth as a "fine time"?
2. What does she seem to regard as the most serious problems in the process?
3. Why do you think she refers to her husband as Mr. Burr?

4-4   A Description of Philadelphia (1748)

Probably the most striking features of the British middle colonies of North America were their prosperity, diverse ethnic makeup, and multiplicity of religious forms (see text pp. 111–114). The following selection consists of the observations of Peter Kalm, a Swedish naturalist who toured the colonies from 1748 to 1751. During his visit to Philadelphia in 1748 Kalm noted the town's abundance and religious and ethnic diversity.

Source: Peter Kalm, *Travels in North America,* trans. John Reinhold Forester (London, 1770), vol. 1, pp. 36–43, 58–60.

The town is now quite filled with inhabitants, which in regard to their country, religion, and trade, are very different from each other. You meet with excellent masters in all trades, and many things are made here full as well as in England. Yet no manufactures, especially for making fine cloth, are established. Perhaps the reason is, that it can be got with so little difficulty from England, and that the breed of sheep which is brought over, degenerates in process of time, and affords but a coarse wool.

Here is great plenty of provisions, and their prices are very moderate. There are no examples of an extraordinary dearth. Every one who acknowledges God to be the Creator, preserver, and ruler of all things, and teaches or undertakes nothing against the state, or against the common peace, is at liberty to settle, stay, and carry on his trade here, be his religious principles ever so strange. No one is here molested on account of the erroneous principles of the doctrine which he follows, if he does not exceed the abovementioned bounds. And he is so well secured by the laws in his person and property, and enjoys such liberties, that a citizen of Philadelphia may in a manner be said to live in his house like a king.

On a careful consideration of what I have already said, it will be easy to conceive how this city should rise so suddenly from nothing, into such grandeur and perfection, without supposing any powerful monarch's contributing to it, either by punishing the wicked, or by giving great supplies in money. And yet its fine appearance, good regulations, agreeable situation, natural advantages, trade, riches and power, are by no means inferior to those of any, even of the most ancient towns in Europe. It has not been necessary to force people to come and settle here; on the contrary, foreigners of different languages have left their country, houses, property, and relations, and ventured over wide and stormy seas, in order to come hither. Other countries, which have been peopled for a long space of time, complain of the small number of their inhabitants. But Pennsylvania, which was no better than a desert in the year 1681, and hardly contained five hundred people, now vies with several kingdoms in Europe in number of inhabitants. It has received numbers of people, which other countries, to their infinite loss, have either neglected or expelled.

Questions

1. What factors does Kalm believe were the most significant in accounting for Philadelphia's rapid rise to prominence?
2. What is Kalm's perception of the religious environment in Philadelphia?
3. In Kalm's view, has the immigration to Philadelphia of people neglected in or expelled from other colonies and countries had a positive effect? Why or why not?

4-5   Class Structure in New York (1765)

Cadwallader Colden, lieutenant governor of New York from 1761 to 1776, lived in America for fifty-six years. Merchant, writer, scientist, philosopher, and politician, he was a perceptive observer of colonial life. Colden's attitudes can be discerned in this description of the class structure in New York. Unlike observers such as Crèvecoeur (see text pp. 273–274), Colden did not view America as a classless society.

Source: Cadwallader Colden, "State of the Province of New York" (1765). In *Collections of the New-York Historical Society* (1878), vol. 10, pp. 68–69.

The people of New York are properly Distinguished into different Ranks.

1. The Proprietors of the large Tracts of Land, who include within their claims from 100,000 acres to above one Million of acres under one Grant. Some of these remain in one single Family. Others are, by Devises and Purchases claim'd in common by considerable numbers of Persons.

2. The Gentlemen of the Law make the second class in which properly are included both the Bench and the Bar. Both of them act on the same Principles, and are of the most distinguished Rank in the Policy of the Province.

3. The Merchants make the third class. Many of them

have rose suddenly from the lowest Rank of the People to considerable Fortunes, and chiefly by illicit Trade in the last War [French and Indian War]. They abhor every limitation of Trade and Duty on it, and therefore gladly go into every Measure whereby they hope to have Trade free.

4. In the last Rank may be placed the Farmers and Mechanics. Tho' the Farmers hold their Lands in fee simple, they are as to condition of Life in no way superior to the common Farmers in England; and the Mechanics such only as are necessary in Domestic Life. This last Rank comprehends the bulk of the People, and in them consists the strength of the Province. They are the most useful and the most Morall, but allwise made the Dupes of the former; and often are ignorantly made their Tools for the worst purposes.

Questions

1. What factors determined the distinctions of rank in Colden's New York?
2. According to Colden, which rank is the most "useful" to the province? Why?
3. For which rank does Colden have the least regard? Why?

Questions for Further Thought

1. Based on Documents 4-1 through 4-3, how would you describe the status and circumstances of women in eighteenth-century America?

2. After reading the text and these documents, how would you describe the organization of the New England family unit—husband, wife, and children? What impact did it have on the structure of the community?

3. In what ways were the societies of eighteenth-century New England and the middle colonies similar and different?

The Enlightenment and the Great Awakening, 1740–1765

As the societies of British North America were transformed from relatively simple frontier communities to complex but distinctive extensions of Europe, they began to participate in the religious and intellectual movements of the larger European world. Two powerful Continental movements in particular transformed the cultural and intellectual life of the colonies. The Enlightenment emphasized the power of human reason and had its roots in the scientific revolution of the seventeenth century (see text pp. 116-118). If any single individual epitomized the American Enlightenment, it was Benjamin Franklin (Document 4-6). If any single place was its center, it was Franklin's Philadelphia.

As some Americans were abandoning, or at least revising, an older religious world view, many more were embracing a new one. Pietism came to America from Europe with German immigrants in the 1720s and led to religious revivals throughout the colonies (see text pp. 118–122). Little concerned with formal theology, it emphasized moral behavior and a mystical union with God.

Charismatic preachers such as Theodore Jacob Freylinghuysen, William and Gilbert Tennent, and Jonathan Edwards played a key role in the revivals (see text p. 118 and American Lives, text pp. 120–121). No individual had a greater impact on the spread of revivalism than did the British evangelist George Whitefield (Document 4-7). From 1739 to 1741 Whitefield preached to huge audiences throughout the colonies, transforming local revivals into a Great Awakening (see text p. 118).

The Great Awakening was a social upheaval that created controversy and split churches, leading to the creation of new ones. It also led to a questioning of religious taxes, the idea of an established church, the authority of ministers, and the morality of economic competition (Document 4-8).

4-6 The American Enlightenment (1749)

Benjamin Franklin

Benjamin Franklin was one of colonial America's outstanding examples of the influence of Enlightenment ideas (see text p. 117). In the document that follows Franklin proposes methods for the education of colonial youth that departed dramatically from the founding generations' more modest attention to training in the "domestic arts" or a trade. Franklin's proposal resulted in the creation of an academy in Philadelphia in 1751.

Source: Benjamin Franklin, *Proposals Relating to the Education of Youth in Pensilvania, Philadelphia* (1749; facsimile reprint, edited by William Pepper, Philadelphia: University of Pennsylvania, 1931).

"Proposals Relating to the Education of Youth in Pensilvania, Philadelphia," 1749.

It has long been regretted as a Misfortune to the Youth of this Province, that we have no Academy, in which they might receive the Accomplishments of a regular Education . . . the Sentiments and Advice of Men of Learning, Understanding, and Experience. . . .

The good Education of Youth has been esteemed by wise Men in all Ages, as the surest Foundation of the Happiness both of private Families and of Commonwealths. Almost all Governments have therefore made it a principal Object of their Attention, to establish and endow with proper Revenues, such Seminaries of Learning, as might supply the succeeding Age with Men qualified to serve the Publick with Honour to themselves, and to their Country. . . .

It is propos'd

That some Persons of Leisure and publick Spirit apply for a Charter, by which they may be incorporated, with Power to erect an Academy for the Education of Youth, to govern the same, provideMasters, make Rules, receive Donations, purchase Lands, etc., and to add to their Number, from Time to Time such other Persons as they shall judge suitable.

That the Members of the Corporation make it their Pleasure and in some Degree their Business, to visit the Academy often, . . . advance the Usefulness and Reputation of the Design; that they look on the Students as in some Sort their Children, treat them with Familiarity and Affection. . . .

That a House be provided for the Academy, if not in the Town, not many Miles from it . . . having a Garden, Orchard, Meadow, and a Field or two.

That the House be furnished with a Library . . . with Maps of all Countries, Globes, some mathematical Instruments, an Apparatus for experiments in Natural Philosophy, and for Mechanics; Prints, of all Kinds, Prospects, Buildings, Machines, etc.

That the Rector be a Man of good Understanding, good Morals, diligent and patient, learn'd in the Languages and Sciences, and a correct Speaker and Writer of the English Tongue; to have such Tutors under him as shall be necessary. . . .

As to their Studies, it would be well if they could be taught every Thing that is useful, and every Thing that is ornamental: But Art is long, and their Time is short. It is therefore propos'd that they learn those Things that are likely to be most useful and most ornamental. . . . All should be taught to write a fair Hand, and swift . . . Drawing . . . Arithmetick, Accounts . . . Geometry and Astronomy.

The English Language might be taught by Grammar;

in which some of our best Writers, as Tillotson, Addison, Pope, Algernoon Sidney, Cato's Letters, etc. should be Classicks. . . .

Antient Customs, religious and civil . . . Morality, be descanting and making continual Observations on the Causes of the Rise or Fall of any Man's Character, Fortune, Power etc. . . . the Advantages of Temperance, Order, Frugality, Industry, Perseverance etc. . . .

While they are reading Natural History, might not a little Gardening, Planting, Grafting, inoculating, etc., be taught and practised; and now and then Excursions made to the neighbouring Plantations of the best Farmers. . . .

The History of Commerce, of the Invention of Arts, Rise of Manufactures, Progress of Trade, Change of its Seats . . . will be useful to all. And this, with the Accounts in other History of . . . Engines and Machines used in War, will naturally introduce a Desire to be instructed in Mechanicks, and to be inform'd of the Principles of that Art by which weak Men perform such Wonders, Labour is sav'd, Manufactures expedited, etc. . . .

With the whole should be constantly inculcated and cultivated, that Benignity of Mind, shich shows itself in . . . Good Breeding; highly useful to the Possessor, and most agreeable to all. . . .

Questions

1. According to Franklin, why should young colonial men attend school when there are many practical reasons not to?
2. What are the things young Pennsylvanians should be learning?
3. How does Franklin reconcile public service, the benefits of classical learning, and the necessity of practical training for young people in the colony?

4-7 The Great Awakening in Charles Town, South Carolina (1740)

The Anglican cleric George Whitefield was a leading proponent of the Great Awakening and its most celebrated itinerant preacher (see text p. 118). In this document Whitefield recounts his visit to and work in Charles Town (as it was called before the Revolution), which was famous as a wealthy playground for South Carolina's planter and merchant aristocracy. He went there to spread the gospel and raise funds for his orphanage in Georgia.

Source: George Whitefield, *A Continuation of the Reverend Mr. Whitefield's Journal . . .* (Philadelphia, 1740), pp. 14–21.

Friday, March 14. Arrived last night at Charles Town. . . . Waited on the Commissary [official representative of the Bishop of London]. . . . He charged me with Enthusiasm and Pride [i.e., with being too harsh], for speaking against the Generality of the Clergy. . . . I told him, I thought I had already; but, as yet, I had scarce begun with them. He then asked me, Wherein were the Clergy so much to blame? I answered, they did not preach up Justification by Faith alone. . . . He charged me with breaking the Canons and Ordination vow; . . . in a great rage he told me, if I preached in any publick church in that Province, he would suspend me. I replied, "I shall regard that as much as I would a Pope's Bull [papal decree].["] . . . [I said to him,]

"But if you will make an application to yourself, be pleased, Sir, to let me ask you one Question: have you delivered your Soul by exclaiming against the Assemblies and Balls here?" "What, Sir," says he, "must you come to catechise me? No, I have not exclaim'd against them; I think there is no Harm in them." "Then, Sir," said I, "I shall think it my Duty to exclaim against you." "Then, Sir," replied he, (in a very great Rage) "get you out of my House." Upon which I made my Bow, and, with my Friends took my leave, pitying the Commissary, who I really tho't was more noble than to give such Treatment. . . .

Saturday, March 15. Preached in the Baptist Meeting-House. . . . I was led out to shew the utter Inability of Man to save himself, and the absolute Necessity of his depending on the rich and sovereign Grace of God in Christ Jesus, in order to be restored to his primitive Dignity. Some, I observ'd, were put under concern, and most seem'd willing to know, whether those Things were so. In the Evening I preach'd again in the Independent Meeting-House, to a more attentive Auditory [audience] than ever; And had the Pleasure afterwards of Finding that a Gentlewoman, whose Family has been carried away for some time with Deistical Principles [see text p. 193], began now to be unhinged, and to see that there was no Rest in such a Scheme, for a fallen Creature to rely on. . . .

Sunday, March 16. Preached at Eight in the Morning at the Scotch Meeting-House, . . . heard the Commissary represent me under the Character of the Pharisee, who came to the Temple, saying, "God, I thank thee that I am not as other Men are." But whether I do what I do out of a Principle of Pride, or Duty, the Searcher of Hearts will discover 'ere long, before Men and Angels. . . .

Monday, March 17. Preach'd in the Morning at the Independent Meeting-House, and was more explicit than ever, in exclaiming against Balls and Assemblies, to which the People seem'd to hearken with much Attention.

Preached again in the Evening, and being excited thereto by some of the Inhabitants, spoke on Behalf of my poor Orphans. God was pleased to give it his Blessing, and I collected upwards of Seventy Pounds Sterling for them, the largest Collection I ever yet made on that Occasion. . . .

Tuesday, March 18. Preached twice again today, and took an affectionate Leave of, and gave Thanks to, my Hearers for their great Liberality. Many wept, and my own Heart yearn'd much towards them. For I believe a good Work is begun in many Souls. . . . The Congregations grew larger on the Week Days, and many Things concurred to induce us to think that God intended to visit some in Charlestown with his Salvation.

Questions

1. What evidence in this document suggests that Whitefield might pose a threat to the political and religious establishment and to established social mores?
2. What evidence suggests that Whitefield was more concerned with saving souls than with promoting a particular denomination?
3. What theological doctrines does Whitefield emphasize?

4-8   Reaction against the Great Awakening (1742)

Though at first welcoming the Great Awakening, Old Light ministers began denouncing a movement that was, it seemed to them, unhinging reason and order (see text p. 119). A leader of the Old Light reaction was Charles Chauncy, a Congregational minister of the First Church in Boston (see text p. 119). Chauncy's religious views, as revealed in the following excerpt from one of his sermons, were strongly influenced by the Enlightenment and in many respects resembled those of Benjamin Franklin. His attack on religious enthusiasm reflects an educated gentleman's disgust at the New Lights' attacks on the rational learning of the orthodox clergy and an intellectual conservative's suspicion of the emotional hysteria of the lower classes, the divisive effect of revivalism on churches and communities, and challenges to authority.

Source: Charles Chauncy, *Enthusiasm Describ'd and Caution'd against* (Boston, 1742), pp. 3–7.

[The] Enthusiast is one who has a conceit of himself as a person favored with the extraordinary presence of the Deity. He mistakes the workings of his own passions for divine communications, and fancies himself immediately inspired by the Spirit of God, when all the while, he is under no other influence than that of an overheated imagination.

The cause of this enthusiasm is a bad temperament of the blood and spirits; 'tis properly a disease, a sort of madness, and there are few, perhaps none at all, but are subject to it; though none are so much in danger of it as those in whom melancholy is the prevailing ingredient in their constitution. . . .

And various are the ways in which their enthusiasm discovers itself. Sometimes, it may be seen in their countenance. A certain wildness is discernable in their look and air, especially when their imaginations are moved and fired. Sometimes, it strangely loosens their tongues and gives them such an energy, as well as fluency and volubility in speaking, as they themselves, by their utmost efforts, can't so much as imitate, when they are not under the enthusiastic influence. . . . Sometimes, it appears in their imaginary peculiar intimacy with heaven. They are, in their own opinion, the special favorites of God, have more familiar converse with Him than other good men, and receive immediate, extraordinary communications from Him. . . . And what extravagances, in this temper of mind, are they not capable of, and under the specious pretext, too, of paying obedience to the authority of God? . . . But in nothing does the enthusiasm of these persons discover itself more than in the disregard they express to the dictates of reason. They are above the force of argument. . . . And in vain will you endeavor to convince such persons of any mistakes they are fallen into. . . .

Questions

1. According to Chauncy, what are the causes of religious enthusiasm?
2. Which manifestations of that enthusiasm does Chauncy find disturbing? Why do you think they upset him?
3. As a minister, why is Chauncy so disturbed by the revivalist belief in direct contact with God?

Questions for Further Thought

1. Based on Documents 4-6 and 4-8, do you think Franklin and Chauncy would have agreed in their assessments of reason, science, revivalism, and the meaning of the Enlightenment? How would they have differed?
2. Is it possible that after reading Whitefield's account of his stay in Charles Town (Document 4-7), Franklin and Chauncy could have found areas of agreement with the evangelist? Why or why not?
3. Both the Enlightenment and the Great Awakening profoundly influenced American ideas and popular attitudes in the Revolutionary Era and beyond. How do you think individual Americans reconciled the secular outlook of Franklin with the intense religious emotionalism of revivalism?

The Midcentury Challenge: War, Trade, and Land

In the years 1740–1765 the British empire in North America was redefined by three sets of events: the French and Indian War, an expansion of transatlantic trade that increased prosperity but raised colonial debt, and a great westward movement.

In the late 1740s a shortage of land and the influx of immigrants into the middle and southern colonies brought pressure for expansion and led to a clash between

Britain and France for the interior of North America. At first the war in America went badly for the British side. When William Pitt became first minister in 1757, he devised a strategy that turned the conflict into a Great War for Empire (see Map 4.5, text p. 127). The turning point in North America was the British capture of Quebec in 1759; the war ended with the reduction of the French empire in North America to a handful of islands (see text pp. 124–128).

As the colonial population continued to expand, serious land shortages led to conflicts over land rights, Indian policy, law and order, and political representation. For example, Connecticut fought with Pennsylvania over settlement in the Wyoming Valley. In Pennsylvania conflicts between Scots-Irish migrants along the frontier and the Quaker political establishment stirred violence and nearly led to civil war (Document 4-10). Such conflict also led to frontier rebellions in North Carolina and South Carolina (see text pp. 130–133).

4-9 George Washington's Report to Governor Robert Dinwiddie of Virginia on the Defeat of General Braddock (1755)

The French and Indian War began in the Ohio Valley in 1754 when Robert Dinwiddie, Virginia's royal governor, dispatched a force of militiamen under the command of Colonel George Washington to secure British claims. Britain then sent Sir Edward Braddock and two regiments of troops to America. In May 1755 a small force of French and Indians launched an attack and killed Braddock and half his men. The following account by Washington, the commander of the Virginia militia, describes this disastrous defeat of combined British-Virginian forces (see text pp. 124–126). Washington's original spelling and punctuation have been preserved.

Source: In W. W. Abbot, ed., *The Papers of George Washington, I: Colonial Series, 1748–August 1755* (Charlottesville: University of Virginia Press, 1983), pp. 339–340.

As I am favour'd with an oppertunity, I should think myself inexcusable, was I to omit givg you some acct of our late Engagemt with the French on the Monongahela the 9th Inst.

We continued our March from Fort Cumberland to Frazer's (which is within 7 Miles of Duquisne) witht meetg any extraordinary event, havg only a stragler or two picked Up by the French Indians. When we came to this place, we were attackd, (very unexpectedly) by abt 300 French and Indns; Our number's consisted of abt 1300 well armd Men, chiefly regular's, who were immediately struck with such a Panick, that nothing but confusion and disobedience of order's prevaild amongst them: The Officer's in genl behavd with incomparable bravery, for which they greatly sufferd, there being near 60 killd and woundd A large proportion out of the number we had! The Virginian behavd like Men, and died like Soldier's; for I believe out of 3 Companys that were that Day, scarce 30 were left alive: Captn Peyrouny and all his Officer's down to a Corporal, were killd; Captn Polson shard almost as hard a Fate, for only one of his Escap'd: In short the dastardly behaviour of the Regular Troops exposd all those who were inclin'd to do their duty, to almost certai[n] death; and at length, in despight of every effort to the contrary, broke & run as Sheep before Hounds, leavg the Artillery, Ammunition, Provisions, Baggage & in short every thing a prey to the Enemy; and when we endeavourd to rally them in hopes of regaining the ground and what we had left upon it was with as little success as if we had attempted to have stopd the wild Bears of the Mountains or rivulets with our feet, for they wd break by in spite of the every effort that could be made to prevent it.

The Genl was wounded in the Shoulder, & the Breast; of wch he died three days after; his two Aids de Camp were both wounded, but are in a fair way of Recovering; Colo Burton and Sir Jno St Clair are also wounded, and I hope will get over it; Sir Peter Halket, with many other brave Officers were killd in the Field; [I luckily escapd with a wound, tho I had four Bullets through my Coat and two Horses shot under me:] It is supposed that we had 300 or more killed in the Field; abt that number we brought of wounded; and it is conjectured (I believe with much truth) that two thirds of both receiv'd their shott from our own

cowardly Regulars, who gatherd themselves into a body contrary to orders 10 or 12 deep, woud then level, Fire, & shoot down the Men before them.

I Tremble at the consequences that this defeat may have upon our back setlers, who I suppose will all leave their habitation's unless their are proper measures taken for their security.

Questions

1. To what factors does Washington attribute the shattering defeat of the Anglo-Virginian force?
2. What is Washington's assessment of the performance of the British regulars? Of the Virginia militia?
3. What consequences does Washington predict will result from this defeat?

4-10 Protests on the Frontier

Even before the French and Indian War began, settlers were spreading far out into the wilderness. By the close of the war, when the Proclamation Line of 1763 defined the extent of English jurisdiction on the frontier, thousands of new farms and villages dotted the countryside of Pennsylvania, Virgina, North Carolina, and South Carolina. Many of these people had just arrived from Scotland, Wales, and Germany, although a significant number also came from the older coastal settlements because they needed land. Everywhere on this developing frontier, people struggled to define political institutions or challenged the dominant elites of the coastline. Sometimes this strife erupted into violence between the judges, sheriffs, and tax collectors who attempted to enforce imperial laws and the frontier settlers who rejected them. In North Carolina, the Regulators fought against authorities for many years and demanded to be represented in colonial government (see text pp. 132–133). When the Revolution came, most Regulators fought with the British or became neutral because their old enemies on the coastline had become Patriot leaders.

Source: "To the INHABITANTS of the Province of North-Carolina," Salisbury, North Carolina, September 14, 1769. In William K. Boyd, ed., *Some Eighteenth Century Tracts Concerning North Carolina* (Raleigh, N.C.: Edwards & Broughton Company, 1927), pp. 301–304.

"To the INHABITANTS of the Province of *North-Carolina*"

Dear Brethren,

Nothing is more common than for Persons who look upon themselves to be injured than to resent and complain. These are sounded aloud, and plain in Proportion to the Apprehension of it. Our Fearfulness too, frequently augment our real as well as apparent Dangers. Let us adjust our Complaints or Resentments to the Reality as well as the Nature of the Injury received.

Excess in any Matter breeds Contempt; whereas strict Propriety obtains the Suffrage of every Class. The Oppression of inferior Individuals must only demand Tutelage of superiors; and in civil Matters our Cries should reach the authorative Ear, when the Weight that crusheth from the higher Powers. —But when imposed by the Populace, to the Populace our complaints must extend. —When therefore the Cry of any City, Province or Nation is general, it must be generally directed to the Source from whence the Cry is caused.

The late Commotions and crying Dissatisfactions among the common People of this Province, is not unknown nor unfelt by any thinking Person. —No Person among you could be at a Loss to find out the true Cause. —I dare venture to assert you [are] all advised to the Application of the Public Money; —these you saw misapplied to the enriching of Individuals, or at least embezzled in some way without defraying the publick Expenses. Have not your Purses been pillaged by the exorbitant and unlawful Fees taken by Officers, Clerks, &c. —I need not mention the intolerable expensive Method of Recovery by Law, occasioned by the narrow Limits of the inferior Court's Jurisdiction. —Have you not been grieved to find the Power of our County Courts so curtailed, that scarce the Shadow of Power is left. This Body, however respectable, is intrusted with little more than might pertain to the Jurisdiction of a single Magistrate, or at least two or three Justices of the Peace in Conjunction. —In Consequence of this, very small Sums drags us to Superior Courts. —These must be attended with all our Evidences, altho many at the Distance of 150 Miles. Add to this a double Fee to all Officers; Hence we are made feelingly sensible, that our necessary Expenses, with the additional Costs, are equal, if not surpass the original Sum.

For what End was the Jurisdiction of the Courts reduced to such narrow Limits? Is it not to fill the Superior Houses with Business? Why has the Authority fallen upon this wonderful Expedient? Is it not evident, that this was calculated for the Emolument of Lawyers, Clerks, &c. What other Reason can be assigned for this amazing Scheme? —none Brethren, none! . . .

The Exorbitant, not to say unlawful Fees, required and assumed by Officers, —the unnecessary, not to say destructive Abridgement of a Court's Jurisdiction, —the enormous Encrease of the provincial tax unnecessary; these are Evils of which no Person can be insensible, and which I doubt not has been lamented by each of you. It must have obliged you to examine from what Quarter Relief might be found against these sad Calamities —In Vain will you search for a Remedy until you find out the Disease.

Many are accusing the Legislative Body as the Source of all those woful Calamities. —These, it must be confessed, are the instrumental Cause; they can, yea do impose some of these heavy Burdens. —But whence received they this Power? Is not their Power delegated from the Populace? The original principal Cause is our own blind stupid Conduct.

If it be queried, How doth our Conduct contribute to this? Answer presents itself—we have chosen Persons to represent us to make Laws, &c. whose former Conduct and Circumstance might have given us the highest Reason to expect they would sacrifice the true Interest of their Country to Avarice, or Ambition, or both.

I need not inform you, that a Majority of our Assembly is composed of Lawyers, Clerks, and others in Connection with them, while by our own Voice we have excluded the Planter. —Is it not evident their own private Interest is, designed in the whole Train of our Laws? —We have not the least Reason to expect the Good of the Farmer, and consequently of the Community, will be consulted, by those who hang on Favour, or depend on the Intricacies of the Laws. —What can be expected from those who have ever discovered a Want of good Principles, and whose highest Study is the Promotion of their Wealth; and with whom the Interest of the Publick, when it comes in Competition with their private Advantages, is suffered to sink? —nothing less than the Ruin of the Publick. . . . Doth not Reason declare we might expect such cringing Vassals would readily sacrifice the Interest of the Community to the Idol Self? . . . .

But you will say, what is the Remedy against this malignant Disease?

I will venture to prescribe a sovereign one if duly applied; that is, as you have now a fit Opportunity, choose for your Respresentatives or Burgesses such Men as have given you the strongest Reason to believe they are truly honest: Such as are disinterested, publick spirited, who will not allow their private Advantage once to stand in Competition with the publick Good. . . . Let your Judgment be formed on their past Conduct; let them be such as have been unblamable in Life, independent in their Fortunes, without Expectations from others; let them be such as enjoy no Places of Benefit under the Government; such as do not depend upon Favour for their Living, nor do derive Profit or Advantage from the intricate Perplexity of the Law. In short, let them be Men whose private Interest neither doth nor can clash with the Interest or special Good of their Country.

Are you not sensible, Brethren, that we have too long groaned in Secret under the Weight of these crushing Mischiefs? How long will ye in this servile Manner subject yourselves to Slavery? Now shew yourselves to be Freemen, and for once assert your Liberty and maintain your Rights—This, this Election let us exert ourselves, and show, that we will not through Fear, Favour or Affection, bow and subject ourselves to those who, under the Mask of Friendship, have long drawn Calamities upon us. . . .

Have they not monopolized your Properties; and what is wanting but Time to draw from you the last Farthing? Who that has the Spirit of a Man could endure this? Who that has the least Spark of Love to his Country or to himself would bear the Delusion?

In a special Manner then, let us, at this Election, rose all our Powers to act like free publick spirited Men, knowing that he that betrays the Cause now betrays his Country, and must sink in the general Ruin . . . .

Salisbury, [North Carolina], September 14, 1769

Questions

1. What are the Regulators' major grievance? Do they sound anything like the grievances colonists express against imperial authorities during the Revolutionary crisis?

2. What kind of people do the Regulators oppose—what kind of character do they have, what kind of occupations do they have, and what makes them so different from the frontiersmen writing this document?

3. What do the Regulators mean when they write about a "public good"? What do they mean by "self interest"?

Questions for Further Thought

1. Documents 4-9 and 4-10 raise many issues that will not be resolved during the 1750s and 1760s and will become part of the imperial crisis that leads colonists toward the Revolution. What are those issues?

2. Do you find similarities between the complaints of the soldiers on the frontier against the British regulars and the complaints of the Regulators against their colonial rulers on the East Coast? What are they?

3. Both groups of colonists writing Documents 4-9 and 4-10 identify serious consequences if authorities do not correct the problems they identify. What are those consequences? What "lessons" do you believe colonists might have learned from both military fighting on the frontier and Regulator demands from their government that they later carried with them into the Revolution?

CHAPTER 5

Toward Independence: Years of Decision 1763–1775

★   ★   ★

The Reform Movement, 1763–1765, and The Dynamics of Rebellion, 1765–1766

In 1763 the British empire, which included almost forty colonies, was magnificent in its scope and potential (see Map 5.1 on text p. 138). However, as the textbook (pp. 138–140) shows, the empire had problems. British statesmen were aware that the established mainland colonies of North America had a history of circumventing British regulation and control. With the mother country deeply in debt, it was evident that imperial reform was required and that Britain's New World colonists would have to pay more of the cost of running the empire (see text pp. 140–141). Document 5-1, Jared Ingersoll's report on British attitudes and the debate in Parliament over the passage of the Stamp Act, reveals what British politicians believed about the logic of taxing the colonists and about the issue of their constitutional right do so.

The other documents in this section illustrate the nature of the colonial response to the Stamp Act. As is demonstrated in the textbook (pp. 144–146), crowd actions played a crucial role in the colonists' attack on the Stamp Act. Indeed, Thomas Hutchinson's account of his confrontation with such a crowd (Document 5-2) and the report of the riot in Rhode Island (see American Voices, text p. 146) remind us that significant crowd actions occurred even before the Stamp Act was scheduled to take effect. Such actions, which occurred throughout the colonies in 1765, effectively blocked the implementation of the Stamp Act—for the moment.

The colonists' ultimate goal was to have Parliament repeal the new revenue laws. To achieve that end, their weapon of choice was the economic boycott (see text pp. 149–150). The agreement signed in New York (Document 5-3) describes how the boycott was organized. The resolutions of the Norfolk, Virginia, Sons of Liberty (Document 5-4) describe some of the measures that were employed to get the Stamp Act repealed (see text pp. 145–146). To further their cause, the colonial governments, which were notorious for quarreling with each other, held an intercolonial congress (see text p. 148). The "Declarations" of the Stamp Act Congress (Document 5-5) enunciated the colonists' essential position on both the Stamp Act and the issue of imperial reform. The "Declarations" also clearly reflect the roots of the colonists' ideology (see text pp. 146–148).

5-1   Jared Ingersoll's Report on the Debates in Parliament

Jared Ingersoll, a Connecticut lawyer who was in Great Britain on business, accepted a commission from his home colony to do what he could to oppose the Stamp Act, which it appeared Parliament would soon pass (see text pp. 143–144). By communicating with Thomas Whately, who played a central role in the drafting of the bill, Ingersoll obtained a few minor modifications. However, he could not persuade British officials to abandon the idea of passing a Stamp Act for America.

As part of his effort to oppose the Stamp Act, Ingersoll attended the debates on the proposed legislation in Parliament. On February 11, 1765, he sent a lengthy report on those debates to Thomas Fitch, the governor of Connecticut. The sections of that letter reprinted here describe the general British attitude and the attitudes of different segments of Parliament toward the Stamp Act.

Source: New Haven Colonial Historical Society, *Papers* (1918), vol. 9, pp. 306–315, *passim*. The entry has been modernized to the extent that *&* is changed to *and* and *&c* is changed to *etc.*

The principal Attention has been to the Stamp bill that has been preparing to Lay before Parliament for taxing America. The Point of the Authority of Parliament to impose such Tax I found on my Arrival here was so fully and Universally yielded, that there was not the least hopes of making any impressions that way. Indeed it has appeared since that the House would not suffer to be brought in, nor would any one Member Undertake to Offer to the House, any Petition from the Colonies that held forth the Contrary of that Doctrine. I own I advised the Agents if possible to get that point Canvassed that so the Americans might at least have the Satisfaction of having the point Decided upon a full Debate, but I found it could not be done, and here before I proceed to acquaint you with the Steps that have been taken, in this Matter, I beg leave to give you a Summary of the Arguments which are made Use of in favour of such Authority.

The House of Commons, say they, is a branch of the supreme legislature of the Nation, and which in its Nature is supposed to represent, or rather to stand in the place of, the Commons, that is, of the great body of the people, who are below the dignity of peers; that this house of Commons Consists of a certain number of Men Chosen by certain people of certain places, which Electors, by the Way, they

Insist, are not a tenth part of the people, and that the Laws, rules and Methods by which their number is ascertained have arose by degrees and from various Causes and Occasions, and that this house of Commons, therefore, is now fixt and ascertained and is a part of the Supreme unlimited power of the Nation, as in every State there must be some unlimited Power and Authority; and that when it is said they represent the Commons of England, it cannot mean that they do so because those Commons choose them, for in fact by far the greater part do not, but because by their Constitution they must themselves be Commoners, and not Peers, and so the Equals, or of the same Class of Subjects, with the Commons of the Kingdom. They further urge, that the only reason why America has not been heretofore taxed in the fullest Manner, has been merely on Account of their Infancy and Inability; that there have been, however, not wanting Instances of the Exercise of this Power, in the various regulations of the American trade, the Establishment of the post Office etc., and they deny any Distinction between what is called an internal and external Tax as to the point of the Authority imposing such taxes. And as to the Charters in the few provinces where there are any, they say, in the first place, the King cannot grant any that shall exempt them from the Authority of one of the branches of the great body of Legislation, and in the second place say the King has not done, or attempted to do it. In that of Pensilvania the Authority of Parliament to impose taxes is expressly mentioned and reserved; in ours tis said, our powers are generally such as are *According to the Course of other Corporations in England* (both which Instances by way of Sample were mentioned and referred to by Mr. Grenville in the House); in short they say a Power to tax is a necessary part of every Supreme Legislative Authority, and that if they have not that Power over America, they have none, and then America is at once a Kingdom of itself.

On the other hand those who oppose the bill say, it is true the Parliament have a supreme unlimited Authority over every Part and Branch of the Kings dominions and as well over Ireland as any other place, yet we believe a British parliament will never think it prudent to tax Ireland. Tis true they say, that the Commons of England and of the british Empire are all represented in and by the house of Commons, but this representation is confessedly on all hands by Construction and Virtually only as to those who have no hand in choosing the representatives, and that the Effects of this implied Representation here and in America must be infinitely different in the Article of Taxation. Here in England the Member of Parliament is equally known to the Neighbour who elects and to him who does not; the Friendships, the Connections, the Influences are spread through the whole. If by any Mistake an act of Parliament is made that prove injurious and hard the Member of Parliament here sees with his own Eyes and is moreover very accessible to the people, not only so, but the taxes are laid equally by one Rule and fall as well on the Member himself as on the people. But as to America, from the great distance in point of Situation, from the almost total unacquaintedness, Especially in the more northern Colonies, with the Members of Parliament, and they with them, or with the particular Ability and Circumstances of one another, from the Nature of this very tax laid upon others not Equally and in Common with ourselves, but with express purpose to Ease ourselves, we think, say they, that it will be only to lay a foundation of great Jealousy and Continual Uneasiness, and that to no purpose, as we already by the Regulations upon their trade draw from the Americans all that they can spare, at least they say this Step should not take place untill or unless the Americans are allowed to send Members to Parliament; for *who of you*, said Coll Rarre Nobly in his Speech in the house upon this Occasion, *who of you reasoning upon this Subject feels warmly from the Heart* (putting his hand to his own breast) *for the Americans as they would for themselves or as you would for the people of your own native Country?* and to this point Mr. Jackson produced Copies of two Acts of Parliament granting the priviledge of having Members to the County Palitine of Chester and the Bishoprick of Durham upon Petitions preferred for that purpose in the Reign of

King Henry the Eighth and Charles the first, the preamble of which Statutes counts upon the Petitions from those places as setting forth that being in their general Civil Jurisdiction Exempted from the Common Law Courts etc., yet being Subject to the general authority of Parliament, were taxed in Common with the rest of the Kingdom, which taxes by reason of their having no Members in Parliament to represent their Affairs, often proved hard and injurious etc. and upon that ground they had the priviledge of sending Members granted them—and if this, say they, could be a reason in the case of Chester and Durham, how much more so in the case of America.

Thus I have given you, I think, the Substance of the Arguments on both sides of that great and important Question of the right and also of the Expediency of taxing America by Authority of Parliament. I cannot, however, Content myself without giving you a Sketch of what the aforementioned Mr. Barre said in Answer to some remarks made by Mr. Ch. Townsend in a Speech of his upon this Subject. I ought here to tell you that the Debate upon the American Stamp bill came on before the house for the first time last Wednesday, when the same was open'd by Mr. Grenville the Chanceller of the Exchequer, in a pretty lengthy Speech, and in a very able and I think in a very candid manner he opened the Nature of the Tax, Urged the Necessity of it, Endeavoured to obviate all Objections to it—and took Occasion to desire the house to give the bill a most Serious and Cool Consideration and not suffer themselves to be influenced by any resentments which might have been kindled from any thing they might have heard out of doors—alluding I suppose to the N. York and Boston Assemblys' Speeches and Votes—that this was a matter of revenue which was of all things the most interesting to the Subject etc. The Argument was taken up by several who opposed the bill (viz) by Alderman Beckford, who, and who only, seemed to deny the Authority of Parliament, by Col. Barre, Mr. Jackson, Sir William Meredith and some others. Mr. Barre, who by the way I think, and I find I am not alone in my Opinion, is one of the finest Speakers that the House can boast of, having been some time in America as an Officer in the Army, and having while there, as I had known before, contracted many Friendships with American Gentlemen, and I believe Entertained much more favourable Opinions of them than some of his profession have done, Delivered a very handsome and moving Speech upon the bill and against the same, Concluding by saying that he was very sure that Most who Should hold up their hands to the Bill must be under a Necessity of acting very much in the dark, but added, perhaps as well in the Dark as any way.

After him Mr. Charles Townsend spoke in favour of the Bill—took Notice of several things Mr. Barre had said, and concluded with the following or like Words:—And now will these Americans, Children planted by our Care, nourished up by our Indulgence untill they are grown to a

Degree of Strength and Opulence, and protected by our Arms, will they grudge to contribute their mite to releive us from the heavy weight of that burden which we lie under? When he had done, Mr. Barre rose and having explained something which he had before said and which Mr Townsend had been remarking upon, he then took up the beforementioned Concluding words of Mr. Townsend, and in a most spirited and I thought an almost inimitable manner, said—

"They planted by your Care? No! your Oppressions planted em in America. They fled from your Tyranny to a then uncultivated and unhospitable Country—where they exposed themselves to almost all the hardships to which human Nature is liable, and among others to the Cruelties of a Savage foe, the most subtle and I take upon me to say the most formidable of any People upon the face of Gods Earth. And yet, actuated by Principles of true english Lyberty, they met all these hardships with pleasure, compared with those they suffered in their own Country, from the hands of those who should have been their Friends.

"They nourished up by *your* indulgence? they grew by your neglect of Em:—as soon as you began to care about Em, that Care was Excercised in sending persons to rule over Em, in one Department and another, who were perhaps the Deputies of Deputies to some Member of this house—sent to Spy out their Lyberty, to misrepresent their Actions and to prey upon Em; men whose behavior on many Occasions has caused the Blood of those Sons of Liberty to recoil within them; men promoted to the highest Seats of Justice, some, who to my knowledge were glad by going to a foreign Country to Escape being brought to the Bar of a Court of Justice in their own.

"They protected by *your* Arms? they have nobly taken up Arms in your defence, have Exerted a Valour amidst their constant and Laborious industry for the defence of a Country, whose frontier, while drench'd in blood, its interior Parts have yielded all its little Savings to your Emolument. And believe me, remember I this Day told you so, that same Spirit of freedom which actuated that people at first, will accompany them still.—But prudence forbids me to explain myself further. God knows I do not at this Time speak from motives of party Heat, what I deliver are the genuine Sentiments of my heart; however superiour to me in general knowledge and Experience the reputable body of this house may be, yet I claim to know more of America than most of you, having seen and been conversant in that Country. The People I believe are as truly Loyal as any Subjects the King has, but a people Jealous of their Lyberties and who will vindicate them, if ever they should be violated—but the Subject is too delicate and I will say no more."

These Sentiments were thrown out so intirely without premeditation, so forceably and so firmly, and the breaking off so beautifully abrupt, that the whole house sat awhile as Amazed, intently Looking and without answering a Word.

I own I felt Emotions that I never felt before and went the next Morning and thank'd Coll Barre in behalf of my Country for his noble and spirited Speech.

However, Sir after all that was said, upon a Division of the house upon the Question, there was about 250 to about 50 in favour of the Bill. . . .

The Merchants in London are alarmed at these things; they have had a meeting with the Agents and are about to petition Parliament upon the Acts that respect the trade of North America.

What the Event of these things will be I dont know. . . .

Your Most Obedient Humble Servant.

J: Ingersoll.

Questions

1. On the basis of Ingersoll's observations, how sympathetic were British politicians and the British people to the colonists' view that Parliament did not have the right to tax them?
2. Do the members of Parliament seem well informed about the situation in the mainland colonies of North America? Why or why not?
3. Do the members of Parliament believe that they rather than the colonists are acting to preserve essential British rights? Why or why not?

5-2   Thomas Hutchinson's Account of a Crowd Action (1765)

Thomas Hutchinson, a descendant of Anne Hutchinson, was born in Boston in 1711. In 1765 he held a number of appointed political offices. In addition to serving, as he had since 1749, on the Governor's Council, Hutchinson was both the chief justice and the lieutenant governor of Massachusetts. He served as the colony's acting governor from 1769 to 1771 and then as its governor until he moved to Great Britain in 1774. He died in Britain in 1780.

Hutchinson was a leading and wealthy conservative, and many colonists saw him as a symbol of British imperial rule. These factors made him an appealing target during the Stamp Act controversy, and as the letter he wrote on August 30, 1765, indicates, Hutchinson personally experienced the fury of the Boston crowds (see text p. 144). Ironically, Hutchinson had opposed the Stamp Act and had tried to convince the Grenville administration that enacting it would be a mistake.

Source: Thomas Hutchinson to Richard Jackson, August 30, 1765, *Massachusetts Archives,* vol. 26, pp. 146–147.

Boston, August 30, 1765

My Dear Sir

I came from my [country] house at Milton with my family the 26th in the morning. After dinner it was whispered in town there would be a mob at night and that Paxtons Hallowell, and the custom-house and admiralty officers houses would be attacked but my friends assured me the rabble were satisfied with the insult I had received and that I was become rather Popular. In the evening whilst I was at supper and my children round me somebody ran in and said the mob were coming. I directed my children to fly to a secure Place and shut up my house as I had done before intending not to quit it but my eldest daughter repented her leaving me and hastened back and protested she would not quit the house unless I did. I could not stand against this and withdrew with her to a neighbouring house where I had been but a few minutes before the hellish crew fell upon my house with the Rage of devils and in a moment with axes split down the doors and entred my son being in the great entry heard them cry damn him he is upstairs we'll have him. Some ran immediately as high as the top of the house others filled the rooms below and cellars and others Remained without the house to be employed there. Messages soon came one after another to the house where I was to inform me the mob were coming in Pursuit of me and I was obliged to retire thro yards and gardens to a house more remote where I remained until 4 o'clock by which time one of the best finished houses in the Province had nothing remaining but the bare walls and floors. Not contented with tearing off all the wainscot and hangings and splitting the doors to pieces they beat down the Partition walls and altho that alone cost them near two hours they cut down the cupola or lanthern and they began to take the slate and boards from the roof and were prevented only by the approaching daylight from a total demolition of the building. The garden fence was laid flat and all my trees etc. broke down to the ground. Such ruins were never seen in America. Besides my Plate and family Pictures houshold furniture of every kind my own my children and servants apparel they carried off about £900 sterling in money and emptied the house of every thing whatsoever except a part of the kitchen furniture not leaving a single book or paper in it and have scattered or destroyed all the manuscripts and other papers I had been collecting for 30 years together besides a great number of Publick Papers in my custody. The evening being warm I had undressed me and slipt on a thin camlet surtout over my wastcoat, the next morning the weather being changed I had not cloaths enough in my possession to defend me from the cold and was obliged to borrow from my host. Many articles of clothing and good part of my Plate have since been picked up in different quarters of the town but the Furniture in general was cut to pieces before it was thrown out of the house and most of the beds cut open and the feathers thrown out of the windows. The next evening I intended with my children to Milton but meeting two or three small Parties of the Ruffians who I suppose had concealed themselves in the country and my coachman hearing one of them say there he is, my daughters were terrified and said they should never be safe and I was forced to shelter them that night at the castle.

The encouragers of the first mob never intended matters should go this length and the people in general express the utmost detestation of this unparalleled outrage and I wish they could be convinced what infinite hazard there is of the most terrible consequences from such daemons where they are let loose in a government where there is not constant authority at hand sufficient to suppress them.

I am told the government here will make me a compensation for my own and my family's loss which I think cannot be much less than £3000 sterling. I am not sure that they will. If they should not it will be too heavy for me and I must humbly apply to his Majesty in whose service I am a sufferer but this and a much greater sum would be an insufficient compensation for the constant distress and anxiety of mind I have felt for some time past and must feel for months to come. You cannot conceive the wretched state we are in. Such is the resentment of the people against the stamp duty that there can be no dependence upon the general court to take any steps to enforce or rather advise the payment of it. On the other hand, such will be the effects of not submitting to it that all trade must cease all courts fall and all authority be at an end. Must not the ministry be extremely embarrassed. On the one hand it will be said if concessions be made the Parliament endanger the loss of their authority over the colonies on the other hand if external force should be used there seems to be danger of a total lasting alienation of affection. Is there no alternative? May the infinitely wise God direct you. I am with the greatest esteem

Sir Your most faithful humble servant

Questions

1. Considering the damage done to Hutchinson's property and the time and effort it took to inflict that damage, is Hutchinson's use of the word *mob* misleading? Why or why not?
2. Does it appear that Hutchinson was attacked *both* because he was a symbol of British rule *and* because he was a member of the Massachusetts economic elite? Why or why not?
3. Faced with the threat of crowd action, did Hutchinson display personal courage? Do you find his report of the incident believable? Why or why not?

5-3 New York Merchant Boycott Agreement (1765)

Crowd actions prevented the Stamp Act from being enforced when it was scheduled to take effect on November 1, 1765 (see text p. 145). As shown in the textbook (p. 149), members of Parliament were outraged by those actions. Thus, it seemed unlikely that crowds could achieve the colonists' ultimate goal: getting the Stamp Act repealed. Realizing that economic pressure might impel British merchants to lobby for repeal, Patriots in many locations entered into formal agreements to boycott British goods. The article reprinted below, which first appeared in the *Pennsylvania Gazette* on November 7, 1765, describes an agreement entered into and signed by more than 200 of the "principal Merchants" of New York (see text p. 145).

Source: Pennsylvania Gazette, November 7, 1765.

At a general Meeting of the Merchants of the City of New-York, trading to Great-Britain, at the House of Mr. George Burns, of the said City, Innholder, to consider what was necessary to be done in the present Situation of Affairs, with respect to the STAMP ACT, and the melancholy State of the North-American Commerce, so greatly restricted by the Impositions and Duties established by the late Acts of Trade: They came to the following Resolutions, viz.

FIRST, That in all Orders they send out to Great-Britain, for Goods or Merchandize, of any Nature, Kind or Quality whatsover, usually imported from Great-Britain, they will direct their Correspondents not to ship them, unless the STAMP ACT be repealed: It is nevertheless agreed, that all such Merchants as are Owners of, and have Vessels already gone, and now cleared out for Great-Britain, shall be at Liberty to bring back in them, on their own Accounts, Crates and Casks of Earthen Ware, Grindstones, Pipes, and such other bulky Articles, as Owners usually fill up their Vessels with.

SECONDLY, It is further unanimously agreed, that all Orders already sent Home, shall be countermanded by the very first Conveyance; and the Goods and Merchandize thereby ordered, not to be sent, unless upon the Condition mentioned in the foregoing Resolution.

THIRDLY, It is further unanimously agreed, that no Merchant will vend any Goods or Merchandize sent upon

Commission from Great-Britain, that shall be shipped from thence after the first Day of January next, unless upon the Condition mentioned in the first Resolution.

FOURTHLY. It is further unanimously agreed, that the foregoing Resolutions shall be binding until the same are abrogated at a general Meeting hereafter to be held for that Purpose.

In Witness whereof we have hereunto respectively subscribed our Names. [*This was subscribed by upwards of Two Hundred principal Merchants.*]

Questions

1. How clearly, if at all, do the merchants spell out the basic rights they believe they are defending?
2. Do the merchants seem as concerned about not losing money as about defending basic British constitutional rights? Why or why not?
3. To what extent do the merchants seem to be concerned about creating an effective way to enforce the boycott? Do they recommend fair and effective means for achieving this purpose? Explain.

5-4 Norfolk Sons of Liberty Pronouncement (1766)

Having instituted a boycott movement, the Patriots needed an apparatus to ensure that it would not be violated. Taking their name from the phrase used by Colonel Barré in his speech against the Stamp Act (Document 5-1), Patriots calling themselves Sons of Liberty formed committees and organizations to enforce the boycott against the Stamp Act (see text pp. 144–146). While doing this, the Patriots routinely emphasized their loyalty to George III and their commitment to the rule of law. The statement issued by the Norfolk, Virginia, Sons of Liberty, which is reprinted from the *Pennsylvania Journal* of April 17, 1766, describes both the philosophy and the enforcement measures typically espoused by the Sons of Liberty.

Source: Pennsylvania Gazette, April 17, 1766.

At a meeting of a considerable number of inhabitants of the town and county of Norfolk, and others, SONS OF LIBERTY, *at the Court House of the said county, in the colony of Virginia, on Monday the 31st of March, 1766.*

Having taken into consideration the evil tendency of that oppressive and unconstitutional act of parliament commonly called the Stamp Act, and being desirous that our sentiments should be known to posterity, and recollecting that we are a part of the colony, who first, in General Assembly, openly expressed their detestation to the said act, which is pregnant with ruin, and productive of the most pernicious consequences; and unwilling to rivet the

shackles of slavery and oppression on ourselves, and millions yet unborn, have unanimously come to the following resolutions:

I. Resolved, That we acknowledge our sovereign Lord King George III to be our rightful and lawful King, and that we will at all times, to the utmost of our power and ability, support and defend his most sacred person, crown, and dignity; and will be always ready, when constitutionally called upon, to assist his Majesty with our lives and fortunes, and defend all his just rights and prerogatives.

II. Resolved, That we will by all lawful ways and means, which divine providence hath put into our hands, defend ourselves in the full enjoyment of, and preserve inviolate to posterity, those inestimable privileges of all free-born British subjects, of being taxed by none but representatives of their own choosing, and of being tried only by a jury of their own Peers; for, if we quietly submit to the execution of the said Stamp Act, all our claims to civil liberty will be lost, and we and our posterity become absolute slaves.

III. Resolved, That we will, on any future occasion, sacrifice our lives and fortunes, in concurrence with the other Sons of Liberty in the American provinces, to defend and preserve those invaluable blessings transmitted us by our ancestors.

IV. Resolved, That whoever is concerned, directly or indirectly, in using, or causing to be used, in any way or manner whatever, within this colony, unless authorized by the General Assembly thereof, those detestable papers called the Stamps, shall be deemed, to all intents and purposes, an enemy to his country, and by the Sons of Liberty treated accordingly.

V. Resolved, That a committee be appointed to present the thanks of the Sons of Liberty to Colonel Richard Bland, for his treatise entitled "An Inquiry into the Rights of the British Colonies."

VI. Resolved, That a committee be appointed, who shall make public the above resolutions, and correspond as they shall see occasion, with the associated Sons and Friends of Liberty in the other British colonies in America.

Questions

1. How clearly, if at all, do the Sons of Liberty spell out the basic rights they believe they are defending?
2. Do the Sons of Liberty seem as concerned about not losing money as about defending basic British constitutional rights? Why or why not?
3. To what extent do the Sons of Liberty seem to be concerned about creating an effective way to enforce the boycott? Do they recommend fair and effective means for enforcing the boycott? Explain.

5-5 "Declarations" of the Stamp Act Congress (1765)

Boston was the scene of the first major crowd actions against the Stamp Act. Those actions and others effectively blocked the implementation of the act (see text p. 144). Also, it was Massachusetts that suggested that each colony send delegates to a special intercolonial congress that would formulate a unified response to the detested British legislation (see text p. 148). The colonies of Virginia, North Carolina, and Georgia could not attend because their governors refused to convene their assemblies; New Hampshire chose not to send delegates. However, twenty-seven delegates representing the other colonies met in New York on October 7, 1765. During twelve days of deliberations the members of the Stamp Act Congress prepared a petition to the king, a memorial to the House of Lords, a petition to the House of Commons, and a series of "Declarations . . . respecting the most Essential Rights and Liberties of the Colonists." The "Declarations" of the Stamp Act Congress provide the clearest statement of the pragmatic and philosophical positions of the colonists on the Stamp Act and the efforts of the British government to institute general imperial reform (see the analysis in the text, pp. 146–148).

Source: Proceedings of the Congress at New-York (1766), pp. 15–16.

The Members of this Congress, sincerely devoted, with the warmest Sentiments of Affection and Duty to his Majesty's Person and Government, inviolably attached to the present happy Establishment of the Protestant Succession, and with Minds deeply impressed by a Sense of the present and impending Misfortunes of the *British* Colonies on this Continent; having considered as maturely as Time will permit, the Circumstances of the said Colonies, esteem it our indispensable Duty, to make the following Declarations of our humble Opinion, respecting the most Essential Rights and Liberties of the Colonists, and of the Grievances under which they labour, by Reason of several late Acts of Parliament.

I. That his Majesty's Subjects in these Colonies, owe the same Allegiance to the Crown of *Great-Britain*, that is owing from his Subjects born within the Realm, and all due Subordination to that August Body the Parliament of *Great-Britain*.

II. That his Majesty's Liege Subjects in these Colonies, are entitled to all the inherent Rights and Liberties of his Natural born Subjects, within the Kingdom of *Great-Britain*.

III. That is is inseparably essential to the Freedom of a People, and the undoubted Right of *Englishmen*, that no Taxes be imposed on them, but with their own Consent, given personally, or by their Representatives.

IV. That the People of these Colonies are not, and from their local Circumstances cannot be, Represented in the House of Commons in *Great-Britain*.

V. That the only Representatives of the People of these Colonies, are Persons chosen therein by themselves, and that no Taxes ever have been, or can be Constitutionally imposed on them, but by their respective Legislature.

VI. That all Supplies to the Crown, being free Gifts of the People, it is unreasonable and inconsistent with the Principles and Spirit of the *British* Constitution, for the People of *Great-Britain*, to grant to his Majesty the Property of the Colonists.

VII. That Trial by Jury, is the inherent and invaluable Right of every *British* Subject in these Colonies.

VIII. That the late Act of Parliament, entitled, *An Act for granting and applying certain Stamp Duties, and other Duties, in the* British *Colonies and Plantations* in America, etc. by imposing Taxes on the Inhabitants of these Colonies, and the said Act, and several other Acts, by extending the Jurisdiction of the Courts of Admiralty beyond its ancient Limits, have a manifest Tendency to subvert the Rights and Liberties of the Colonists.

IX. That the Duties imposed by several late Acts of Parliament, from the peculiar Circumstances of these Colonies, will be extremely Burthensome and Grievous; and from the scarcity of Specie, the Payment of them absolutely impracticable.

X. That as the Profits of the Trade of these Colonies ultimately center in *Great-Britain*, to pay for the Manufactures which they are obliged to take from thence, they eventually contribute very largely to all Supplies granted there to the Crown.

XI. That the Restrictions imposed by several late Acts of Parliament, on the Trade of these Colonies, will render them unable to purchase the Manufactures of *Great-Britain*.

XII. That the Increase, Prosperity, and Happiness of these Colonies, depend on the full and free Enjoyment of their Rights and Liberties, and an Intercourse with *Great-Britain* mutually Affectionate and Advantageous.

XIII. That it is the Right of the *British* Subjects in these Colonies, to Petition the King, or either House of Parliament.

Lastly, That it is the indispensable Duty of these Colonies, to the best of Sovereigns, to the Mother Country, and to themselves, to endeavour by a loyal and dutiful Address to his Majesty, and humble Applications to both Houses of Parliament, to procure the Repeal of the Act for granting and applying certain Stamp Duties, of all Clauses of any other Acts of Parliament, whereby the Jurisdiction of the Admiralty is extended as aforesaid, and of the other late Acts for the Restriction of *American* Commerce.

Questions

1. Does it appear that the members of the Stamp Act Congress are determined to demonstrate that they are not rebels but loyal British subjects? Why or why not?
2. According to the Congress, what basic constitutional rights do the colonists have?
3. In what ways does the Congress emphasize pragmatic as well as philosophical arguments against British imperial reforms?
4. Considering the British ideas about the mother country's rights explained in Document 5-1, how convincing is the case the Congress makes against the Stamp Act?

Questions for Further Thought

1. What principal rights did the colonists claim they were defending in opposing the Sugar and Stamp acts?
2. To what extent do these documents suggest that on the issue of taxation the colonists were as determined to oppose the supremacy of Parliament as Parliament was to assert it?
3. Does it appear that the colonists were concerned more with evading their responsibilities as members of the British empire than with defending basic British constitutional rights? Why or why not?
4. Would British politicians have agreed with colonists who suggested that something more than money was at stake in the British effort at imperial reform? What, if any, vital noneconomic considerations were at issue in the fight over the Sugar and Stamp acts?

The Growing Confrontation, 1767–1770

As chancellor of the exchequer Charles Townshend was as determined as George Grenville had been to tax the colonists and rein in their representative political institutions. He hoped that the duties placed on paper, paint, glass, and tea imported into the colonies in the Townshend Act of 1767, which came to be called the Townshend duties, could be slipped by the colonists (see text pp. 150–151). The duties were small, and the colonists supposedly drew a distinction between internal taxes such as the Stamp Act and external taxes such as the Townshend duties. However, as shown in the textbook (p. 151) and revealed in the arguments of John Dickinson (Document 5-6), the colonists did not make that a distinction. Equally important, Dickinson forcefully explored the issue of what the colonists had to do to defend their claim that they could not legally be taxed by Parliament.

To oppose the Townshend duties, colonists turned to the tactic that had won repeal of the Stamp Act: an economic boycott of British goods (see text pp. 151–154). The imposition of organized and ongoing boycotts drew women into the political process on a scale unprecedented in the colonies (see text p. 152). Because of their traditional role as managers of the home, women were essential to the success of the boycott. Document 5-7, the boycott agreements entered into by a large number of Boston women in 1770, illustrates how that was done.

Believing that colonial opposition to imperial reform would wilt if more pressure were applied, the British government escalated the confrontation. An important illustration of that escalation was the placing of troops in Boston, a hotbed of opposition to the reform measures (see text pp. 153–154). The growing confrontation of the late 1760s scared many colonists, especially those who eventually joined the ranks of the Loyalists (see text pp. 155–156). Peter Oliver, the author of Document 5-8, shared that fear. His judgments on the breadth and depth of the growing opposition to British policy reflect the view held by many future Loyalists and the great majority of politicians in Britain. Captain Thomas Preston's account of the "Boston Massacre" (Document 5-9) relates how the conflict, fueled by the determination of British officials and of most colonists to protect what each group saw as its basic rights, turned shockingly bloody in 1770.

5-6   John Dickinson's Letter VII from "A Farmer"

John Dickinson, who was born in Maryland in 1732, studied law in London and returned to Philadelphia in 1757. He began publishing attacks on British reforms in a 1765 pamphlet, *The Late Regulations Respecting the British Colonies*. In that work Dickinson argued that the Sugar and Stamp acts would be detrimental to the British mercantile system. Writing anonymously under the pen name "A Farmer," this sophisticated lawyer won fame and popularity with a series of twelve essays attacking the Townshend duties (see text pp. 150–151). These essays appeared in the *Pennsylvania Chronicle* between December 1767 and February 1768 and were then issued in pamphlet form as *Letters from a Farmer in Pennsylvania to the Inhabitants of the British Colonies* (1768). Letter VII was first published on January 11, 1768. The essays were so popular that other authors soon could simply refer to "The Farmer" or "The Farmer's Letters" and expect readers to recognize the reference.

Source: Pennsylvania Chronicle and Universal Advertiser, January 11, 1768.

There are two ways of laying taxes. One is, by imposing a certain sum on particular kinds of property, to be paid by the *user* or *consumer*, or by rating the *person* at a certain sum. The other is, by imposing a certain sum on particular kinds of property, to be paid by the *seller*.

When a man pays the first sort of tax, he *knows with certainty* that he pays so much money *for a tax*. The *consideration* for which he pays it, is remote, and, it may be, does not occur to him. He is sensible too, that he is *commanded and obliged* to pay it *as a tax*; and therefore people are apt to be displeased with this sort of tax.

The other sort of tax is submitted to in a very different manner. The purchaser of an article, very seldom reflects that the seller raises his price, so as to indemnify himself for the tax *he* has paid. He knows that the prices of things are continually fluctuating, and if he thinks about the tax, he thinks at the same time, in all probability, that he *might* have paid as much, if the article he buys had not been taxed. He gets something *visible* and *agreeable* for his money; and tax and price are so confounded together, that he cannot separate, or does not chuse to take the trouble of separating them.

This mode of taxation therefore is the mode suited to arbitrary and oppressive governments. The love of liberty is so natural to the human heart, that unfeeling tyrants think themselves obliged to accommodate their schemes as much as they can to the appearance of justice and reason, and to deceive those whom they resolve to destroy, or oppress, by presenting to them a miserable picture of freedom, when the inestimable original is lost.

I shall now apply these observations to the late act of parliament. Certain duties are thereby imposed on paper and glass, etc. imported into these colonies. By the laws of *Great-Britain* we are prohibited to get these articles from any other part of the world. We cannot at present, nor for many years to come, tho' we should apply ourselves to these manufactures with the utmost industry, make enough ourselves for our own use. That paper and glass are not only convenient, but absolutely necessary for us, I imagine very few will contend. Some perhaps, who think mankind grew wicked and luxurious, as soon as they found out another way of communicating their sentiments than by speech, and another way of dwelling than in caves, may advance so whimsical an opinion. But I presume no body will take the unnecessary trouble of refuting them.

From these remarks I think it evident, that we *must* use paper and glass; that what we use *must* be *British*; and that we *must* pay the duties imposed, unless those who sell these articles, are so generous as to make us presents of the duties they pay.

Some persons may think this act of no consequence, because the duties are so *small*. A fatal error. *That* is the very circumstance most alarming to me. For I am convinced, that the authors of this law would never have obtained an act to raise so trifling a sum as it must do, had they not intended by *it* to establish a *precedent* for future use. To console ourselves with the *smallness* of the duties, is to walk deliberately into the snare that is set for us, praising the *neatness* of the workmanship. Suppose the duties imposed by the late act could be paid by these distressed colonies with the utmost ease, and that the purposes to which they are to be applied, were the most reasonable and equitable that can be conceived, the contrary of which I hope to demonstrate before these letters are concluded; yet even in such a supposed case, these colonies ought to regard the act with abhorrence. For WHO ARE A FREE PEOPLE? Not *those*, over whom government is reasonably and equitably exercised, but *those*, who live under a government *so constitutionally checked and controuled*, that proper provision is made against its being otherwise exercised.

The late act is founded on the destruction of this constitutional security. If the parliament have a right to lay a duty of Four Shillings and Eight-pence on a hundred weight of glass, or a ream of paper, they have a right to lay a duty of any other sum on either. They may raise the duty, as the author before quoted says has been done in some countries, till it "exceeds seventeen or eighteen times the value of the commodity." In short, if they have a right *to* levy a tax of *one penny* upon us, they have a right to levy a *million* upon us: For where does their right stop? At any given number of Pence, Shillings or Pounds? To attempt to limit their right, after granting it to exist at all, is as con-

trary to reason—as granting it to exist at all, is contrary to justice. If *they* have any right to tax *us*—then, whether *our own money* shall continue in *our own pockets* or not, depends no longer on *us*, but on *them*. [As Lord Cambden said,] "There is nothing which" we can call our own; or, to use the words of Mr. *Locke*—"WHAT PROPERTY HAVE WE IN THAT, WHICH ANOTHER MAY, BY RIGHT, TAKE, WHEN HE PLEASES, TO HIMSELF?"

These duties, which will inevitably be levied upon us—which are now levying upon us—are *expressly* laid FOR THE SOLE PURPOSES OF TAKING MONEY. This is the true definition of "*taxes*." They are therefore *taxes*. This money is to be taken from *us*. We are therefore taxed. *Those* who are *taxed* without their own consent, given by themselves or their representatives, are slaves. *We are taxed* without our own consent, expressed by ourselves or our representatives. We are therefore—I speak it with grief—I speak it with indignation—We are SLAVES. . . .

A FARMER.

Questions

1. Would Dickinson agree with those who stated that British politicians were sincerely concerned about the needs and concerns of the colonists? Why or why not?
2. According to Dickinson, why did colonists have to refuse to pay the small Townshend duties?
3. Would you describe Dickinson's argument as an emotional appeal or a pragmatic appeal? Why?

5-7 The Boycott Agreements of Women in Boston (1770)

Women, who in accordance with the standards of the day were not permitted to vote, were traditionally excluded from participating in the hurly-burly of politics (see text p. 152). However, because of their role in the management of households, unless women actively participated, the boycott against the Townshend duties would fail. While never intending that women be allowed to participate in electoral politics, the men who organized the boycott urged them to support liberty by joining the boycott. As the following reports show, women gave positive demonstrations of their ability to organize in support of the boycott.

Source: Boston Evening-Post, February 12, 1770; Boston Gazette, February 19, 1770, as reprinted in Pennsylvania Gazette, March 8, 1770.

The following Agreement has lately been come into by upwards of 300 Mistresses of Families in this Town; in which

Number the Ladies of the highest Rank and Influence, that could be waited upon in so short a Time, are included.

Boston, January 31, 1770.

["]At a Time when our invaluable Rights and Privileges are attacked in an unconstitutional and most alarming Manner, and as we find we are reproached for not being so ready as could be desired, to lend our Assistance, we think it our Duty perfectly to concur with the true Friends of Liberty, in all the Measures they have taken to save this abused Country from Ruin and Slavery: And particularly, we join with the very respectable Body of Merchants, and other Inhabitants of this Town, who met in Faneuil-Hall the 23d of this Instant, in their Resolutions, *totally* to abstain from the Use of TEA: And as the greatest Part of the Revenue arising by Virtue of the late Acts, is produced from the Duty paid upon Tea, which Revenue is wholly expended to support the American Board of Commissioners, We the Subscribers do strictly engage, that we will *totally* abstain from the Use of that Article (Sickness excepted) not only in our respective Families; but that we will absolutely refuse it, if it should be offered to us upon any Occasion whatsoever. This Agreement we chearfully come into, as we believe the very distressed Situation of our Country requires it, and we do hereby oblige ourselves religiously to observe it, till the late Revenue Acts are repealed."

The following is a Copy of the Agreement of the young Ladies of this Town against drinking foreign TEA.
Boston, February 12, 1770.
["]We the Daughters of those Patriots who have, and now do appear for the public Interest, and in *that* principally for *us* their Posterity; *we*, as such, do with Pleasure engage with them, in denying ourselves the drinking of foreign Tea, in Hopes to frustrate a Plan that tends to deprive the whole Community of their *All* that is valuable in Life."
To the above Agreement 126 young Ladies have already signed. In Addition to the List of Mistresses of Families, who signed the Agreement against drinking foreign Tea, 110 have been added the Week past.

Questions

1. Do the women who made these agreements appear to be leaders of the boycott movement, or do they appear to be responding to the actions of others?
2. To what extent, if any, do the signers of the agreements spell out the basic rights they believe they are supporting?
3. Does it appear that the specifics of the agreements, including any provisions for their enforcement, will help make the tea boycott effective? Why or why not?

5-8   Peter Oliver's "Origin & Progress of the American Rebellion"

Peter Oliver, who was born in Boston in 1713 and educated at Harvard, detested protests against the reform of British imperial policy. A wealthy member of the legal profession, Oliver was a part of that system: beginning in 1756, he served as a judge of the superior court of Massachusetts. In addition, the first great Stamp Act crowd action (August 14, 1765, in Boston) was directed against the property of Andrew Oliver, his brother (see text p. 144). Once the Revolution broke out, Oliver went to Britain, fully expecting to return to Massachusetts once the "rebellion" had been put down. However, Oliver never returned; he died in Britain in 1791. He expressed his thoughts about the causes of the Revolution in his "Origin & Progress of the American Rebellion." This work, written in the early 1780s, was not published until the twentieth century.

Source: Reprinted with the permission of the Henry E. Huntington Library from Douglas Adair and John A. Schutz, eds., *Peter Oliver's Origin & Progress of the American Rebellion: A Tory View*, rev. ed. (Stanford, Calif.: Stanford University Press, 1967), pp. 60–65 *passim*. The entry has been modernized to the extent that *&* is changed to *and* and *ye* is changed to *the*.

I am now come to the Year 1767, a Year fraught with Occurrences, as extraordinary as 1765, but of a different Texture. Notwithstanding the Warnings that the Colonies had repeatedly given, of their determined Resolution to throw off the Supremacy of the british Parliament, yet the then Ministry chose to make another Trial of Skill; never adverting to the ill Success of former Attempts. They might have known, that the Contest had reached so great an Heighth, that the Colonists would never descend one Step untill they had first ascended the last Round of the Ladder. . . . It required no great Degree of second Sight to calculate Consequences. But the Ministry confiding in their own good Intentions, and placing too much Confidence in the Gratitude of the Colonists to the parent State (which by the Way they did not possess a Spark of, neither is it to be but seldom Expected to find it inhabit any where but in the private Breast, and too seldom there; to the Disgrace of human Nature), they procured a new Act to be passed, laying Duties upon *Tea, Glass, Paper, and Painters Colours.* This Act was not more unreasonable than many other Acts which had been submitted to for many Years past, and which, even at this Time, they made no Objection to. But the Colonists had succeeded in their first Experiment of Opposition, and their new Allies in Parliament increased their Importance.

As to the *Glass* in particular, the Duty was so trifling, that it would not have enhanced the Price of it to the Purchaser; for there were so many Sellers who aimed at a Market for their Commodities, and the Merchants had so great a Profit upon their Goods, that they could render the Duty of little or no Importance in their Sales; and this was actually the Case. For the Glass, during the Continuance of the Act, was sold at the same Price which it commanded before the Commencement of the Act. The true Reason of Opposition was this. The Inhabitants of the Colonies were a Race of Smugglers. . . .

The Smugglers then, who were the prevailing Part of the Traders in the Capitals of the several Provinces, found it necessary for their Interest, to unite in defeating the Operation of the Act; and *Boston* appeared in the Front of the Battle. Accordingly they beat to Arms, and manœuvred in a new invented Mode. They entred into nonimportation Agreements. A Subscription Paper was handed about, enumerating a great Variety of Articles not to be imported from *England*, which they supposed would muster the Manufacturers in *England* into a national Mob to support their Interests. Among the various prohibited Articles, were *Silks, Velvets, clocks, Watches, Coaches and Chariots*; and it was highly diverting, to see the names and marks, to the Subscription, of Porters and Washing Women. But every mean and dirty Art was used to compass all their bad Designs. One of those who handed about a Subscription Paper being asked, whether it could be imagined that such Tricks would effectuate their Purposes? He replied "Yes! It would do to scare them in England:"

and perhaps there never was a Nation so easy to be affrighted: witness the preceding Repeal of the Stamp Act.

In order to effectuate their Purposes to have this Act repealed also, they formed many Plans of Operation. Associations were convened to prevent the Importation of Goods from *Great Britain*, and to oblige all those who had already sent for them, to reship them after their arrival. This was such an Attack upon the mercantile Interest, that it was necessary to use private evasive Arts to decieve the Vulgar. Accordingly, when the Goods arrived, they were to be in Warehouses, which were to be guarded by a publick Key, at the same Time the Owners of the Stores and Goods had a Key of their Own. This amused the Rabble, whom the Merchants had set to mobbing; and such were the blessed Effects of some of those Merchants Villainy, that Bales and Trunks were disgorged of their Contents and refilled with Shavings, Brickbats, Legs of Bacon and other Things, and shipped for *England*; where some of them were opened on the King's Wharves or Quays, and the Fraud discovered. Many of those Merchants also continued to import the prohibited Goods, in Disguise; of which a bold Printer of *Boston* detected them in his publick Papers; for which they, out of Revenge, in 1768, attempted to murder him; but narrowly escaping with his Life he fled to *England*, as the civil Power of the Country was not sufficient to protect any one who was obnoxious to the Leaders of the Faction. . . .

Mr. [James] *Otis's* black Regiment, the dissenting Clergy, were also set to Work, to preach up Manufactures instead of Gospel. They preached about it and about it; untill the Women and Children, both within Doors and without, set their Spinning Wheels a whirling in Defiance of *Great Britain*. The female Spinners kept on spinning for 6 Days of the Week; and on the seventh, the Parsons took their Turns and spun out their Prayers and Sermons to a long Thread of Politicks, and to much better Profit than the other Spinners; for they generally cloathed the Parson and his Family with the Produce of their Labor. This was a new Species of Enthusiasm, and might be justly termed, the Enthusiasm of the Spinning Wheel.

An *American* is an adept in the Arts of Shrewdness. In these he is *generally* an Overmatch for a *Briton*, although he may sometimes fail in the Execution. As an Instance of each, take the following Anecdote of a Deacon of one [of] the dissenting Congregations in *Boston*, who imported large Quantities of Woolens from *England*. *Hogarth* drew his Line of Beauty for the Leg of a Chair; so this Person had sat so long in a Deacon's Seat, that the Muscles of his Face were so contracted into the Line of Sanctity, that he passed himself upon the World as a Man of great Reputation for Honesty. He was also a great Stickler for the Manufactures of *America*; and in the Heighth of his pious Zeal for the good old Cause, wrote to his Correspondent in *London* about american Grievances; and informed him, that unless they were redressed, they not only could, but they would redress them their selves by making Cloths from their own Produce. As a Proof that they could do it, he sent Patterns of fine broad Cloths, which he said were manufactured in *America*. His Correspondent was surprized on seeing the Patterns, and shewed them to the Manufacturer of whom he had bought them. He also was surprized; but, on examination, told the Merchant that those were the very Cloths he had sold him to ship to *America*—such are the blessed Effects of Cant and Hypocrisy. . . .

All this Struggle and Uproar arose from the selfish Designs of the Merchants. They disguised their Private Views by mouthing it for Liberty. The Magick of this Sound echoed through the interior Parts of the Country, and the deluded Vulgar were charmed with it—like the poor harmless *Squirrel* that runs into the Mouth of the *Rattlesnake,* the Fascination in the Word *Liberty* threw the People into the harpy Claws of their Destroyers; and for what? But to gratifie the artfull Smugglers in carrying on their contraband Tea Trade with the Dutch, to make their deluded Consumers purchase at their Prices who were the Venders; for the act of Parliament had reduced the Duties upon it from 12 d p [Pence per] Pound to three Pence, with a View

to prevent Smugling; which would effectually have prevented it, had the Act been in Force a few Years, and would have broke up the Nests of those worse than Highway Men; who, for many Years, had kept the Province in a Ferment, and created Uneasiness in the parent State.

As for the People in general, they were like the Mobility of all Countries, perfect Machines, wound up by any Hand who might first take the Winch; they were like the poor Negro Boy, who, in the Time of the late Stamp Act, was bid by his Master, in the Evening, to fetch something from his Barn; but did not move at the command. His Master spoke to him with Severity, and asked him why he did not go as he was bid? The poor Wretch replied, with Tears in his Eyes, "me fraid Massah Tamp Act he catch me." Thus the common People had had that Act, and all the Acts of Parliament since, dressed up by their seditious Leaders, either with raw Head and bloody Bones, or with Horns, Tails, and cloven Feet, which were sufficient to affright their weak Followers. And as for Men of Sense, who could see through the Delusion, it would have been imprudent for them to have interposed; for the Government was in the Hands of the Mob, both in Form and Substance, and it was in vain to combat a Whirlwind or a Hurricane.

Questions

1. What, if any, significance can you discern in the fact that Oliver referred to his study as the "Origin & Progress of the American Rebellion" rather than the "Origin & Progress of the American Revolution"?
2. Judging from this excerpt, is it accurate to say that Oliver was a philosophical conservative? Why or why not?
3. On the basis of this excerpt, is it accurate to say that Oliver respected ordinary people? Why or why not?

5-9 Captain Thomas Preston's Account of the "Boston Massacre"

When the British escalated the growing confrontation by placing troops in Boston as a kind of police force to enforce imperial reform measures (see text p. 155), many colonists considered this another step on the road to political slavery. Bostonians' horror at being "occupied" by a standing army in peacetime was only part of the problem. Because off-duty soldiers were allowed to take civilian employment, they competed, often successfully, for jobs that were essential to many in Boston's lower classes. Tensions mounted, and many claimed that Boston would see more dramatic events. The infamous "Boston Massacre" of March 5, 1770, proved them right. The following description of the event was written by Captain Thomas Preston, who was in command of the British troops directly involved in the massacre. Preston was tried for murder and acquitted.

Source: "Historical Chronicle," *Gentlemen's Magazine* 40 (April 1770), p. 189.

Saturday, 28 April, 1770. The Representation of the Affairs at Boston ["the Massacre," March 5] by the Town Committee, having been inserted in the beginning of the Magazine, the case of Capt. Preston here epitomized, will serve to show the other side of the question.

It is a matter of too great notoriety to need proofs, that the arrival of his majesty's troops in Boston was extremely obnoxious to its inhabitants. They have ever used all means in their power to weaken the regiments, and to bring them into contempt, by promoting desertions, and by grossly and falsely propagating untruths concerning them. On the arrival of the 64th and 65th, their ardour seemingly began to abate; it being too expensive to buy off so many. But the same spirit revived immediately on its being known that those regiments were ordered for Halifax. After their embarkation, one of their justices, from the seat of justice, declared, "that the soldiers must now take care of themselves, nor trust too much to their arms, for they were but a handful." This was an alarming circumstance to the soldiery, since which several disputes have happened between the towns-people and the soldiers of both regiments. In general such disputes have been kept too secret from the officers. On the 2d instant, two of the 29th going through one Gray's Rope Walk, the rope-makers insultingly asked them if they would empty a vault. This unfortunately had the desired effect by provoking the soldiers, and from words they went to blows. Both parties suffered in this affray, and finally, the soldiers retired to their quarters. The insolence, as well as utter hatred of the inhabitants to the troops increased daily; insomuch, that Monday and Tuesday, the 5th and 6th instant, were privately agreed on for a general engagement; in consequence of which, several of the militia came from the country, armed, to join their friends, menacing to destroy any who should oppose them. This plan has since been discovered.

On Monday night about eight o'clock, two soldiers were attacked and beat. About nine some of the guard informed me, the town inhabitants were assembling to attack the troops, and that the bells were ringing as a signal, and not for fire, and the Beacon intended to be fired to bring in the distant people of the country. Being captain of the day, I repaired immediately to the main guard. In my way, I saw the people in great commotion. In a few minutes about 100 people passed and went toward the cus-

tom-house, where the King's money is lodged. They immediately surrounded the sentinel posted there, and with clubs and other weapons threatened to execute their vengeance on him. A Townsman assured me he heard the mob declare they would murder him. I fearing their plundering the King's chest, immediately sent a non-commissioned officer and 12 men to protect both the sentinel and the King's money, and very soon followed myself, to prevent disorder. The troops rushed thro' the people, and, by charging their bayonets in half circle, kept them at a distance. So far was I from intending death, that the troops went to the spot where the unhappy affair took place, without loading their pieces.

The mob still increased, and were more outrageous, striking bludgeons one against another, and calling out, "Come on, you Rascals, you bloody backs, you lobster scoundrels; fire if you dare; G—d damn you, fire and be damned; we know you dare not;" and much more such language was used. They advanced to the points of the bayonets, stuck some of them, and even the muzzles of the pieces, and seemed to be endeavouring to close with the soldiers. Some well-behaved persons asked me if their guns were charged? I replied, yes. If I intended to order the men to fire? I answered no. While I was speaking, a soldier having received a severe blow with a stick, instantly fired. On reprimanding him, I was struck with a club on my arm, so violent a blow, that had it fallen on my head, probably it would have destroyed me. A general attack was then made on the men by heaving clubs, and snow balls, by which all our lives were in imminent danger; some persons from behind called out, "Damn your bloods, why don't you fire?" Instantly three or four of the soldiers fired, one after another, and directly after, three more in the same confusion and hurry.

The mob than ran away, except three unhappy men who instantly expired. . . . The whole of this melancholy affair was transacted in almost 20 minutes. . . .

On examination before the justices they have sworn, that I used the word fire, and so bitter and inveterate are the malcontents against the officers and troops, that I am, though perfectly innocent, under most unhappy circumstances, having nothing in reason to expect but the loss of life in a very ignominious manner, without the interposition of his majesty's royal goodness.

Questions

1. According to Captain Preston, did the Bostonians have legitimate reasons for being unhappy about the fact that British troops were stationed in their city?

2. Judging from Preston's account, does the term *Boston Massacre* seem accurate? Why or why not?

3. Since Preston would naturally be inclined to present his actions and the actions of his men in the best light, how believable is his account of what happened?

Questions for Further Thought

1. Considering the fact that the British government was eager to raise significant sums by taxing the colonists, why were the Townshend duties so small?
2. Compare the boycott agreement entered into in New York against the Stamp Act (Document 5-3) with the agreements by Boston women in 1770 to oppose the Townshend duties (Document 5-7). Do the differences reflect the experience that the colonists had gained between 1765 and 1770 or the fact that the New York document was produced by men and the Boston agreements were produced by women?
3. According to Peter Oliver (Document 5-8), why was there a dangerous and growing confrontation between the colonies and Britain? Is his view of the situation convincing? Why or why not?
4. On the basis of these documents, do you think British politicians or the colonists were more to blame for the confrontations of 1767–1770? Or were both groups equally to blame? (Is *blame* the wrong word? Should one instead try to assess "responsibility"?)

The Road to War, 1771–1775

At the time of the "Boston Massacre," the colonists did not know that the British government, beset by troubles at home, was again ready to an succumb to an economic boycott (see text pp. 154–156). Ironically, Parliament debated repeal on the very day of the Massacre and formally rescinded all the Townshend duties except that on tea in April 1770. In response to the Massacre itself, the British pulled their troops out of Boston proper. As the relatively quiet period that developed after the traumatic events of 1770 revealed, the British government seemed willing, at least temporarily, to stop escalating the confrontation with the colonists (see text p. 156). But when Parliament passed the Tea Act of 1773, it raised a new threat of economic monopoly. Colonists looked again to the tactics they had used against the Stamp Act; they also tried newer techniques, such as the threat of tar and feathering. Once again Boston became the scene of vigorous action (see text pp. 156–157). Document 5-10, a participant's account of the Boston Tea Party of 1773 (see text pp. 156–157), illustrates the degree of organization and the effectiveness of that crowd operation. Not surprisingly, the Patriots also turned again to an economic boycott. The agreement signed by fifty-one women of Edenton, North Carolina (Document 5-11 and the illustration on text p. 163) demonstrates their commitment to the Patriot cause.

When news of the Boston Tea Party reached Parliament, the members expressed outrage over the destruction of private property. Determined to punish Boston—which had become known as "the Metropolis of Sedition"—the British government passed the infamous Coercive Acts (see text pp. 157, 160). As they had done in response to the Stamp Act, the colonists called an intercolonial congress (see text pp. 160–161). This Continental Congress, which opened in Philadelphia on September 5, 1774, deliberated until late October. As the textbook authors note, "men of 'loyal principles'" at the Continental Congress supported a plan to create a new structure of empire (see text p. 160). That plan (Document 5-12) was not adopted, and the Continental Congress became a milestone in the ongoing and organized opposition to Britain's renewed efforts to exert control over the colonies. The Congress's Plan of Association (Document 5-13) shows the detailed program advanced by the Congress to counter the Coercive Acts and the British imperial reform effort (see text pp. 160–161).

5-10 George Robert Twelve Hewes's Account of the Boston Tea Party of 1773

Boston was the site of many crowd actions that marked the growing confrontation and the march toward the War of Independence. On the night of December 16, 1773, Bostonians staged the Boston Tea Party to show their opposition to the Tea Act of 1773 (see text pp. 156–157). George Robert Twelve Hewes, the Boston shoemaker whose life story is given in the textbook (see American Lives, text pp. 158–159), was one of the participants. Late in his long life, Hewes provided the following description of what occurred in Boston's harbor that December night in 1773.

Source: James Hawkes, *A Retrospect of the Boston Tea-Party, with a Memoir of George R. T. Hewes, a Survivor of the Little Band of Patriots Who Drowned the Tea in Boston Harbour in 1773* (1834), pp. 37–41.

The tea destroyed was contained in three ships, laying near each other, at what was called at that time Griffin's wharf, and were surrounded by armed ships of war; the commanders of which had publicly declared, that if the rebels, as they were pleased to style the Bostonians, should not withdraw their opposition to the landing of the tea before a certain day, the 17th day of December, 1773, they should on that day force it on shore, under the cover of their cannon's mouth. On the day preceding the seventeenth, there was a meeting of the citizens of the county of Suffolk, convened at one of the churches in Boston, for the purpose of consulting on what measures might be considered expedient to prevent the landing of the tea, or secure the people from the collection of the duty. At that meeting a committee was appointed to wait on Governor Hutchinson, and request him to inform them whether he would take any measures to satisfy the people on the object of the meeting. To the first application of this committee, the governor told them he would give them a definite answer by five o'clock in the afternoon. At the hour appointed, the committee again repaired to the governor's house, and on inquiry found he had gone to his country seat at Milton, a distance of about six miles. When the committee returned and informed the meeting of the absence of the governor, there was a confused murmur among the members, and the meeting was

immediately dissolved, many of them crying out, Let every man do his duty, and be true to his country; and there was a general huzza for Griffin's wharf. It was now evening, and I immediately dressed myself in the costume of an Indian, equipped with a small hatchet, which I and my associates denominated the tomahawk, with which, and a club, after having painted my face and hands with coal dust in the shop of a blacksmith, I repaired to Griffin's wharf, where the ships lay that contained the tea. When I first appeared in the street, after being thus disguised, I fell in with many who were dressed, equipped and painted as I as, and who fell in with me, and marched in order to the place of our destination. When we arrived at the wharf, there were three of our number who assumed the authority to direct our operations, to which we readily submitted. They divided us into three parties, for the purpose of boarding the three ships which contained the tea at the same time. The name of him who commanded the division to which I was assigned, was Leonard Pitt. The names of the other commanders I never knew. We were immediately ordered by the respective commanders to board all the ships at the same time, which we promptly obeyed. The commander of the division to which I belonged, as soon as we were on board the ship, appointed me boatswain, and ordered me to go to the captain and demand of him the keys to the hatches and a dozen candles. I made the demand accordingly, and the captain promptly replied, and delivered the articles; but requested me at the same time to do no damage to the ship or rigging. We then were ordered by our commander to open the hatches, and take out all the chests of tea and throw them overboard, and we immediately proceeded to execute his orders; first cutting and splitting the chests with our tomahawks, so as thoroughly to expose them to the effects of the water. In about three hours from the time we went on board, we had thus broken and thrown overboard every tea chest to be found in the ship; while those in the other ships were disposing of the tea in the same way, at the same time. We were surrounded by British armed ships, but no attempt was made to resist us. We then quietly retired to our several places of residence, without having any conversation with each other, or taking any measures to discover who were our associates; nor do I recollect of our having had the knowledge of the name of a single individual concerned in the affair, except that of Leonard Pitt, the commander of my division, who I have mentioned. There appeared to be an understanding that each individual should volunteer his services, keep his own secret, and risk the consequences for himself. No disorder took place during the transaction, and it was observed at that time, that the stillest night ensued that Boston had enjoyed for many months.

During the time we were throwing the tea overboard, there were several attempts made by some of the citizens of Boston and its vicinity, to carry off small quantities of it for their family use. To effect that object, they would watch their opportunity to snatch up a handful from the deck, where it became plentifully scattered, and put it into their pockets. One Captain O'Conner, whom I well knew, came on board for that purpose, and when he supposed he was not noticed, filled his pockets, and also the lining of his coat. But I had detected him, and gave information to the captain of what he was doing. We were ordered to take him into custody, and just as he was stepping from the vessel, I seized him by the skirt of his coat, and in attempting to pull him back, I tore it off; but springing forward, by a rapid effort, he made his escape. He had however to run the gauntlet through the crowd upon the wharf; each one, as he passed, giving him a kick or a stroke.

The next day we nailed the skirt of his coat, which I had pulled off, to the whipping post in Charlestown, the place of his residence, with a label upon it, commemorative of the occasion which had thus subjected the proprietor to the popular indignation.

Another attempt was made to save a little tea from the ruins of the cargo, by a tall aged man, who wore a large cocked hat and white wig, which was fashionable at that time. He had slightly slipped a little into his pocket, but being detected, they seized him, and taking his hat and wig from his head, threw them, together with the tea, of which they had emptied his pockets, into the water. In consideration of his advanced age, he was permitted to escape, with now and then a slight kick.

The next morning, after we had cleared the ships of the tea, it was discovered that very considerable quantities of it was floating upon the surface of the water; and to prevent the possibility of any of its being saved for use, a number of small boats were manned by sailors and citizens, who rowed them into those parts of the harbour wherever the tea was visible, and by beating it with oars and paddles, so thoroughly drenched it, as to render its entire destruction inevitable.

Questions

1. How thorough was the planning for the Boston Tea Party?
2. Were the participants eager to have their names known? Why or why not?
3. What, if any, specific rights does Hewes claim that he was trying to support by participating in the Boston Tea Party?

5-11 The Edenton, North Carolina, Boycott Agreement (1774)

When colonists decided to attack the Tea Act of 1773 by boycotting British goods, they were using a tried and heretofore effective means of countering British legislation (see text pp. 149–150, 152–154). Over the years many colonists had signed various boycott agreements. And, as Document 5-7 shows, women had done so before, at least in Boston in 1770. But the agreement that the women of Edenton, North Carolina, signed on October 25, 1774, in response to the action taken by North Carolina Patriots, struck contemporaries as particularly unusual. Indeed, the women's action was judged so extraordinary that a British print reproduced in the textbook (p. 163), was issued to ridicule it.

Source: In Peter Force, ed., *American Archives*, 4th ser. (1837), vol. 1, pp. 891–892.

ASSOCIATION SIGNED BY LADIES OF EDENTON, NORTH CAROLINA, OCTOBER 25, 1774

As we cannot be indifferent on any occasion that appears to affect the peace and happiness of our country; and as it has been thought necessary for the publick good to enter into several particular Resolves by a meeting of Members of Deputies from the whole Province, it is a duty that we owe not only to our near and dear relations and connexions, but to ourselves, who are essentially interested in their welfare, to do every thing as far as lies in our power to testify our sincere adherence to the same; and we do therefore accordingly subscribe this paper as a witness of our fixed intention and solemn determination to do so.

Signed by fifty-one Ladies

Questions

1. Do the women who entered into this agreement appear to be leaders of the boycott movement, or do they appear to be responding to the actions of others?
2. To what extent, if any, do the signers of the agreement clearly spell out the basic rights they believed they were supporting?
3. Does it appear that the specifics of the agreement, including any provisions for its enforcement, would help make the boycott effective?
4. If you compare this document with the agreements signed by Boston women in 1770 (Document 5-7), would you say that what the Edenton women did was much more radical than what the Boston women had done? Why or why not?

5-12   Joseph Galloway's Plan of Union (1774)

Despite the British reform efforts that produced such conflict and hostility between colonists and the British government, Americans moved toward independence reluctantly and cautiously (see text pp. 154–156). Indeed, as the authors of the textbook note, "support for the Patriot cause . . . was far from unanimous" (text p. 162). Joseph Galloway of Pennsylvania took a leading role among those members of the Continental Congress who, as the textbook authors note, considered themselves "men of 'loyal principles'"(text p. 160). Galloway offered the following plan, briefly described in the text (p. 160), in the hope that it would allow America and Britain to end the growing confrontation. But the Congress rejected Galloway's plan. When the colonists declared their independence, Galloway cast his lot with Great Britain, moved to England in 1778, and lived out his life as an exile from his native land.

Source: In W. C. Ford, ed., *Journals of the Continental Congress* (Washington, D.C.: U.S. Government Printing Office, 1904), vol. 1, pp. 49–51.

[28 September, 1774]

Resolution submitted by Joseph Galloway:

Resolved, That the Congress will apply to his Majesty for a redress of grievances under which his faithful subjects in America labour; and assure him, that the Colonies hold in abhorrence the idea of being considered independent communities on the British government, and most ardently desire the establishment of a Political Union, not only among themselves, but with the Mother State, upon those principles of safety and freedom which are essential in the constitution of all free governments, and particularly that of the British Legislature; and as the Colonies from their local circumstances, cannot be represented in the Parliament of Great-Britain, they will humbly propose to his Majesty and his two Houses of Parliament, the following plan, under which the strength of the whole Empire may be drawn together on any emergency, the interest of both countries advanced, and the rights and liberties of America secured.

A Plan of a proposed Union between Great Britain and the Colonies.

That a British and American legislature, for regulating the administration of the general affairs of America, be proposed and established in America, including all the said colonies; within, and under which government, each colony shall retain its present constitution, and powers of regulating and governing its own internal police, in all cases what[so]ever.

That the said government be administered by a President General, to be appointed by the King, and a grand Council, to be chosen by the Representatives of the people of the several colonies, in their respective assemblies, once in every three years.

That the several assemblies shall choose members for the grand council. . . .

Who shall meet at the city of   for the first time, being called by the President-General, as soon as conveniently may be after his appointment.

That there shall be a new election of members for the Grand Council every three years; and on the death, removal or resignation of any member, his place shall be supplied by a new choice, at the next sitting of Assembly of the Colony he represented.

That the Grand Council shall meet once in every year, if they shall think it necessary, and oftener, if occasions shall require, at such time and place as they shall adjourn to, at the last preceding meeting, or as they shall be called to meet at, by the President-General, on any emergency.

That the grand Council shall have power to choose their Speaker, and shall hold and exercise all the like rights, liberties and privileges, as are held and exercised by and in the House of Commons of Great-Britain.

That the President-General shall hold his office during the pleasure of the King, and his assent shall be requisite to all acts of the Grand Council, and it shall be his office and duty to cause them to be carried into execution.

That the President-General, by and with the advice and consent of the Grand-Council, hold and exercise all the legislative rights, powers, and authorities, necessary for regulating and administering all the general police and affairs of the colonies, in which Great-Britain and the colonies, or any of them, the colonies in general, or more than one colony, are in any manner concerned, as well civil and criminal as commercial.

That the said President-General and the Grand Council, be an inferior and distinct branch of the British legislature, united and incorporated with it, for the aforesaid general purposes; and that any of the said general regulations may originate and be formed and digested, either in the Parliament of Great Britain, or in the said Grand Council, and being prepared, transmitted to the other for their approbation or dissent; and that the assent of both shall be requisite to the validity of all such general acts or statutes.

That in time of war, all bills for granting aid to the crown, prepared by the Grand Council, and approved by the President General, shall be valid and passed into a law, without the assent of the British Parliament.

Questions

1. As the authors of the textbook indicate, the colonists had staunchly resisted British efforts to tax them without their consent. Under Galloway's plan, would Parliament be able to tax the colonies? Why or why not?

2. As the authors of the textbook indicate, Benjamin Franklin and Thomas Hutchinson had sharply differing views about the issue of sovereignty and the British empire (text p. 155). Considering the basic features of the Galloway plan, does it seem closer to the view of Franklin or to Hutchinson's views. Why?

3. If the Continental Congress hadbeen willing to support Galloway's plan, do you believe the British government would have been willing to endorse and implement the plan? Why or why not? (*Hint*: In addition to considering the material in the text, it might be helpful to review Document 5-1).

5-13　The Continental Congress Creates the Association (1774)

As described in the textbook (pp. 157, 160), the harsh British response to the Boston Tea Party spurred the colonists to create a Continental Congress to coordinate opposition to British imperial reform measures, especially the Coercive Acts. The Congress began deliberations in Philadelphia on September 5, 1774, and adjourned on October 26, 1774. As part of its general effort to defend colonial rights (see text pp. 160–161), the Congress created a Plan of Association. The Association, as it was called, outlined actions that the Congress and the people would take to try to force Britain into rescinding the measures that the colonists believed threatened their basic rights. The Association was passed on October 18; the formal copy was signed two days later.

Source: Journals of the Continental Congress, 1774–1789 (1904), vol. 1, pp. 75–80.

We, his majesty's most loyal subjects, the delegates of the several colonies of New-Hampshire, Massachusetts-Bay, Rhode-Island, Connecticut, New-York, New-Jersey, Pennsylvania, the three lower counties of New-Castle, Kent and Sussex, on Delaware, Maryland, Virginia, North-Carolina, and South-Carolina, deputed to represent them in a continental Congress, held in the city of Philadelphia, on the 5th day of September, 1774, avowing our allegiance to his majesty, our affection and regard for our fellow-subjects in Great-Britain and elsewhere, affected with the deepest anxiety, and most alarming apprehensions, at those grievances and distresses, with which his Majesty's American subjects are oppressed; and having taken under our most serious deliberation, the state of the whole continent, find, that the present unhappy situation of our affairs is occasioned by a ruinous system of colony administration, adopted by the British ministry about the year 1763, evidently calculated for inslaving these colonies, and, with them, the British empire. In prosecution of which system, various acts of parliament have been passed, for raising a revenue in America, for depriving the American subjects, in many instances, of the constitutional trial by jury, exposing their lives to danger, by directing a new and illegal trial beyond the seas, for crimes alleged to have been committed in America: and in prosecution of the same system, several late, cruel, and oppressive acts have been passed, respecting the town of Boston and the Massachusetts-Bay, and also an act for extending the province of Quebec, so as to border on the western frontiers of these colonies, establishing an arbitrary government therein, and discouraging the settlement of British subjects in that wide extended country; thus, by the influence of civil principles and ancient prejudices, to dispose the inhabitants to act with hostility against the free Protestant colonies, whenever a wicked ministry shall chuse so to direct them.

To obtain redress of these grievances, which threaten destruction to the lives, liberty, and property of his majesty's subjects, in North America, we are of opinion, that a non-importation, non-consumption, and non-exportation agreement, faithfully adhered to, will prove the most speedy, effectual, and peaceable measure: and, therefore, we do, for ourselves, and the inhabitants of the several colonies, whom we represent, firmly agree and associate, under the sacred ties of virtue, honour and love of our country, as follows:

1. That from and after the first day of December next, we will not import, into British America, from Great-Britain or Ireland, any goods, wares, or merchandise whatsoever, or from any other place, any such goods, wares, or merchandise, as shall have been exported from Great-Britain or Ireland; nor will we, after that day, import any East-India tea from any part of the world; nor any molasses, syrups, paneles, coffee, or pimento, from the British plantations or from Dominica; nor wines from Madeira, or the Western Islands; nor foreign indigo.

2. We will neither import nor purchase, any slave imported after the first day of December next; after which time, we will wholly discontinue the slave trade, and will neither be concerned in it ourselves, nor will we hire our vessels, nor sell our commodities or manufactures to those who are concerned in it.

3. As a non-consumption agreement, strictly adhered to, will be an effectual security for the observation of the non-importation, we, as above, solemnly agree and associate, that, from this day, we will not purchase or use any tea, imported on account of the East-India company, or any on which a duty hath been or shall be paid; and from and after the first day of March next, we will not purchase or use any East-India tea whatever; nor will we, nor shall any person for or under us, purchase or use any of those goods, wares, or merchandise, we have agreed not to import, which we shall know, or have cause to suspect, were imported after the first day of December, except such as come under the rules and directions of the tenth article hereafter mentioned.

4. The earnest desire we have, not to injure our fellow-

subjects in Great-Britain, Ireland, or the West-Indies, induces us to suspend a non-exportation, until the tenth day of September, 1775; at which time, if the said acts and parts of acts of the British parliament herein after mentioned are not repealed, we will not, directly or indirectly, export any merchandise or commodity whatsoever to Great-Britain, Ireland, or the West-Indies, except rice to Europe.

5. Such as are merchants, and use the British and Irish trade, will give orders, as soon as possible, to their factors, agents and correspondents, in Great-Britain and Ireland, not to ship any goods to them, on any pretence whatsoever, as they cannot be received in America; and if any merchant, residing in Great-Britain or Ireland, shall directly or indirectly ship any goods, wares or merchandise, for America, in order to break the said non-importation agreement, or in any manner contravene the same, on such unworthy conduct being well attested, it ought to be made public; and on the same being so done, we will not, from thenceforth, have any commercial connexion with such merchant.

6. That such as are owners of vessels will give positive orders to their captains, or masters, not to receive on board their vessels any goods prohibited by the said non-importation agreement, on pain of immediate dismission from their service.

7. We will use our utmost endeavours to improve the breed of sheep, and increase their number to the greatest extent; and to that end, we will kill them as seldom as may be, especially those of the most profitable kind; nor will we export any to the West-Indies or elsewhere; and those of us, who are or may become overstocked with, or can conveniently spare any sheep, will dispose of them to our neighbours, especially to the poorer sort, on moderate terms.

8. We will, in our several stations, encourage frugality, economy, and industry, and promote agriculture, arts and the manufactures of this country, especially that of wool; and will discountenance and discourage every species of extravagance and dissipation, especially all horse-racing, and all kinds of gaming, cock-fighting, exhibitions of shews, plays, and other expensive diversions and entertainments; and on the death of any relation or friend, none of us, or any of our families, will go into any further mourning-dress, than a black crape or ribbon on the arm or hat, for gentlemen, and a black ribbon and necklace for ladies, and we will discontinue the giving of gloves and scarves at funerals.

9. Such as are venders of goods or merchandise will not take advantage of the scarcity of goods, that may be occasioned by this association, but will sell the same at the rates we have been respectively accustomed to do, for twelve months last past.—And if any vender of goods or merchandise shall sell any such goods on higher terms, or shall, in any manner, or by any device whatsoever violate

or depart from this agreement, no person ought, nor will any of us deal with any such person, or his or her factor or agent, any any time thereafter, for any commodity whatever.

10. In case any merchant, trader, or other person, shall import any goods or merchandise, after the first day of December, and before the first day of February next, the same ought forthwith, at the election of the owner, to be either re-shipped or delivered up to the committee of the county or town, wherein they shall be imported, to be stored at the risque of the importer, until the non-importation agreement shall cease, or be sold under the direction of the committee aforesaid; and in the last-mentioned case, the owner or owners of such goods shall be reimbursed out of the sales, the first cost and charges, the profit, if any, to be applied towards relieving and employing such poor inhabitants of the town of Boston, as are immediate sufferers by the Boston port-bill; and a particular account of all goods so returned, stored, or sold, to be inserted in the public papers; and if any goods or merchandises shall be imported after the said first day of February, the same ought forthwith to be sent back again, without breaking any of the packages thereof.

11. That a committee be chosen in every county, city, and town, by those who are qualified to vote for representatives in the legislature, whose business it shall be attentively to observe the conduct of all persons touching this association; and when it shall be made to appear, to the satisfaction of a majority of any such committee, that any person within the limits of their appointment has violated this association, that such majority do forthwith cause the truth of the case to be published in the gazette; to the end, that all such foes to the rights of British-America may be publicly known, and universally contemned as the enemies of American liberty; and thenceforth we respectively will break off all dealings with him or her.

12. That the committee of correspondence, in the respective colonies, do frequently inspect the entries of their custom-houses, and inform each other, from time to time, of the true state thereof, and of every other material circumstance that may occur relative to this association.

13. That all manufactures of this country be sold at reasonable prices, so that no undue advantage be taken of a future scarcity of goods.

14. And we do further agree and resolve, that we will have no trade, commerce, dealings or intercourse whatsoever, with any colony or province, in North-America, which shall not accede to, or which shall hereafter violate this association, but will hold them as unworthy of the rights of freemen, and as inimical to the liberties of their country.

And we do solemnly bind ourselves and our constituents, under the ties aforesaid, to adhere to this association, until such parts of the several acts of parliament passed since the close of the last war, as impose or continue duties on tea, wine, molasses, syrups, paneles, coffee, sugar, pimento, indigo, foreign paper, glass, and painters' colours, imported into America, and extend the powers of the admiralty courts beyond their ancient limits, deprive the American subject of trial by jury, authorize the judge's certificate to indemnify the prosecutor from damages, that he might otherwise be liable to from a trial by his peers, require oppressive security from a claimant of ships or goods seized, before he shall be allowed to defend his property, are repealed.—And until that part of the act of the 12 G. 3. ch. 24, entitled "An act for the better securing his majesty's dock-yards, magazines, ships, ammunition, and stores," by which any persons charged with committing any of the offences therein described, in America, may be tried in any shire or county within the realm, is repealed—and until the

four acts, passed the last session of parliament, viz. that for stopping the port and blocking up the harbour of Boston—that for altering the charter and government of the Massachusetts-Bay—and that which is entitled "An act for the better administration of justice, &c."—and that "for extending the limits of Quebec, &c." are repealed. And we recommend it to the provincial conventions, and to the committees in the respective colonies, to establish such farther regulations as they may think proper, for carrying into execution this association.

The foregoing association being determined upon by the Congress, was ordered to be subscribed by the several members thereof; and thereupon, we have hereunto set our respective names accordingly.

IN CONGRESS, PHILADELPHIA, *October 20, 1774*

Questions

1. What essential tool did the Congress hope to use to get Britain to rescind its imperial reforms? Does it appear that the Congress was well versed in the use of that tool?
2. How fully and forcefully, if at all, does the Association state what the Congress considered to be the essential basic rights of the colonists?
3. What measures did the Congress propose to ensure that its dictates were followed? Would you expect those measures to be effective? Why or why not?
4. Judging from the Association, what kind of imperial policies did the Continental Congress want the British government to follow? What would the British government have to do to restore harmony?
5. What insights does the document give you into the principal economic activities of the American colonies at that time?

Questions for Further Thought

1. On the basis of these documents, what basic political rights did the Patriots believe they were supporting?
2. In what ways are the statements about basic rights in these documents similar or dissimilar to those advanced in Documents 5-3 through 5-5?
3. Did the colonists who opposed British imperial policies seem more concerned about basic political rights or about avoiding taxes?
4. Considering the positions taken and the arguments advanced by the Patriots in the period after the "Boston Massacre," what would the British government have had to do to restore harmony and stop the process that led to war in April 1775?

CHAPTER 6

War and Revolution 1775–1783

★   ★   ★

Toward Independence, 1775–1776

Many troubles beset the American colonists when they went to war against Great Britain, the greatest imperial power in the world. One problem was that the movement toward war and the opening of hostilities produced a sharpening of the social divisions among Americans (see text pp. 170–171). With the coming of war, the possibility emerged that artisans and people even lower on the socioeconomic ladder would gain more power (see text pp. 171–172). As Gouverneur Morris's observations (Document 6–1) show, some upper-class Patriots were bothered that less politically influential lower-class Patriots would use the revolutionary crisis to increase their power. Document 6-2 shows that the quest for greater autonomy or freedom by the less powerful could raise the specter of a race war sparked by a British promise of freedom for American slaves (see text pp. 170–171, 181). Such daunting problems made it harder for the Patriots to embrace the idea of declaring independence.

It was also difficult to declare independence because the colonists had consistently stated that they loved the British monarchy and that George III was a noble monarch. Thus, Patriots believed that their fight was with Parliament, not with the king (see text pp. 171–172). With the publication of Thomas Paine's stunningly popular *Common Sense* (Document 6-3), those issues were addressed directly and forcefully (see text pp. 171–172). When the Continental Congress finally declared independence on July 2, 1776, and then explained its reasons for doing so in the Declaration of Independence approved two days later, attacks on George III became the order of the day. Document 6-4, a section of Thomas Jefferson's draft of the Declaration of Independence, reveals that, in declaring independence, the members of the Congress were confronted with yet another of the problems that slavery posed for the fledgling republic.

6-1 Gouverneur Morris on the "Poor Reptiles" (1774)

Gouverneur Morris, who came from an established and wealthy New York family, was not a leading revolutionary Patriot in 1774 (see text p. 204). He had been graduated from King's College at the age of sixteen in 1768; six years later he was on the verge of starting his career as one of the leaders of the Revolution. Morris's service culminated in his appointment as a delegate to the U.S. Constitutional Convention. In a letter he wrote to Thomas Penn on May 20, 1774, Morris offered his judgment on how the movement toward independence might transform America's political society. In doing so, he illustrates, as the authors of the textbook show (pp. 170–171), that social divisions were sharpened during the era of the War of Independence.

Source: In Peter Force, ed., *American Archives*, 4th ser. (1837), vol. 1 , pp. 342–343.

DEAR SIR:

You have heard, and you will hear a great deal about politics, and in the heap of chaff you may find some grains of good sense. Believe me, sir, freedom and religion are only watchwords. We have appointed a committee, or rather we have nominated one. Let me give you the history of it. It is needless to premise that the lower orders of mankind are more easily led by specious appearances than those of a more exalted station. This, and many similar propositions, you know better than your humble servant.

The troubles in America during Grenville's administration put our gentry upon this finesse. They stimulated some daring coxcombs to rouse the mob into an attack upon the bounds of order and decency. These fellows became the Jack Cades of the day, the leaders in all the riots, the bell-wethers of the flock. The reason of the manœuvre in those who wished to keep fair with the government, and at the same time to receive the incense of popular applause, you will readily perceive. On the whole, the shepherds were not much to blame in a politic point of view. The bell-wethers jingled merrily and roared out liberty and property, and religion, and a multitude of cant terms which everyone thought he understood, and was egregiously mistaken. For you must know the shepherds kept the dictionary of the day, and like the mysteries of the ancient mythology, it was not for profane eyes or ears. This answered many purposes; the simple flock put themselves entirely under the protection of these most excellent shepherds. By and by, behold a great metamorphosis without the help of Ovid or his divinities, but entirely effectuated by two modern Genii, the god of Ambition and the goddess of Faction. The first of these prompted the shepherds to shear some of their flock, and then in conjunction with the other, converted the bell-wethers into shepherds. That we have been in hot water with the British Parliament ever since everybody knows. Consequently these new shepherds had their hands full of employment. The old ones kept themselves least in sight, and a want of confidence in each other was

not the least evil which followed. The port of Boston has been shut up. These sheep, simple as they are, cannot be gulled as heretofore. In short, there is no ruling them, and now, to leave the metaphor, the heads of the mobility grow dangerous to the gentry, and how to keep them down is the question. While they correspond with the other colonies, call and dismiss popular assemblies, make resolves to bind the consciences of the rest of mankind, bully poor printers, and exert with full force all their other tribunitial powers, it is impossible to curb them.

But art sometimes goes farther than force, and therefore, to trick them handsomely a committee of patricians was to be nominated, and into their hands was to be committed the majesty of the people, and the highest trust was to be reposed in them by a mandate that they should take care, that the republic should not suffer injury. The tribunes, through the want of good legerdemain in the senatorial order, perceived the finesse; and yesterday I was present at a grand division of the city, and there I beheld my fellow-citizens very accurately counting all their chickens, not only before any of them were hatched, but before above one half of the eggs were laid. In short, they fairly contended about the future forms of our government, whether it should be founded upon aristocratic or democratic principles.

I stood in the balcony, and on my right hand were ranged all the people of property, with some few poor dependents, and on the other all the tradesmen, etc., who thought it worth their while to leave daily labour for the good of the country. The spirit of the English constitution has yet a little influence left, and but a little. The remains of it, however, will give the wealthy people a superiority this time, but would they secure it they must banish all schoolmasters and confine all knowledge to themselves. This cannot be. The mob begin to think and to reason. Poor reptiles! It is with them a vernal morning; they are struggling to cast off their winter's slough, they bask in the sunshine, and ere noon they will bite, depend upon it. The gentry begin to fear this. Their committee will be appointed, they will deceive the people and again forfeit a share of their confidence. And if these instances of what with one side is policy, with the other perfidy, shall continue to increase and become more frequent, farewell aristocracy. I see, and I see it with fear and trembling, that if the disputes with Great Britain continue, we shall be under the worst of all possible dominions; we shall be under the domination of a riotous mob.

It is the interest of all men, therefore, to seek for reunion with the parent state. . . .

Questions

1. What vital change in the American political system does Morris think is occurring?
2. Does he approve of that change? Why or why not?
3. When Morris talks of the "bell-wethers of the flock," he is talking about the leaders (the bellwethers) of sheep (the flock). What does this image tell you about his view of the average person?
4. In what ways, if any, do Morris's judgments remind you of the Loyalist Peter Oliver's pronouncements (Document 5-8)?

6-2   The Dangers of Race War within a War for Independence (December 1775)

In 1775 approximately one-fifth of the residents of the British mainland colonies were African-American slaves. Realizing that those slaves might be useful in defeating the rebels, Lord Dunmore, the royal governor of Virginia, took decisive action. On November 7, 1775, he issued a proclamation addressed to every slave or indentured servant who belonged to a rebel. Dunmore offered freedom to those slaves and indentured servants *if* they joined the Loyalist cause and fought for the king (see text p. 170; see also text pp. 180–181, 190). By December 1, Dunmore had 300 slaves in uniforms that carried the inscription "Liberty to Slaves." He called this force "Lord Dunmore's Ethiopian Regiment." The following report from the *Pennsylvania Evening Post* of December 14, 1775, about a Philadelphia African-American illustrates the type of powerful response Lord Dunmore's proclamation could stimulate.

Source: Pennsylvania Evening Post, December 14, 1775.

PHILADELPHIA, December 14, 1775

Late last night a gentlewoman, going along Second-street, was insulted by a Negro, near Christ church. And upon her reprimanding him for his rude behaviour, the fellow replied, "Stay, you d—d white bitch, till Lord Dunmore and his black regiment come, and then we will see who is to take the wall." Two gentlemen coming up, and hearing his reply, they endeavoured to secure him, but the fellow escaped, the lamps not being lighted.

Questions

1. Is it significant that word of Dunmore's proclamation had reached at least some Philadelphians by mid-December? Why or why not?

2. Considering the social standards of that day, how bold were the words of the African-American?

3. If you were a Patriot, how might this news story influence your attitude toward seeking reconciliation with Britain? Why would it have that influence?

6-3 Thomas Paine, *Common Sense* (1776)

As the authors of the textbook emphasize (pp. 171–172) and as Documents 5-3, 5-4, and 5-5 illustrate, throughout the movement toward independence, the Patriots proclaimed their loyalty to the British monarch. Members of Parliament seemed to be the villains; they were the ones who supposedly wanted to strip the colonists of their fundamental rights. Reverence for the king had to be undermined if independence was to be declared. Thomas Paine did that and much more with his powerful and broadly popular *Common Sense* (see text pp. 171–172), which was first published on January 9, 1776. The selections reprinted here come from the expanded "NEW EDITION," which was dated February 14, 1776.

Source: Thomas Paine, *Common Sense; Addressed to the Inhabitants of America, . . . A New Edition* (1776), *passim.*

OF MONARCHY AND HEREDITARY SUCCESSION

There is something exceedingly ridiculous in the composition of monarchy; it first excludes a man from the means of information, yet empowers him to act in cases where the highest judgment is required. The state of a king shuts him from the world, yet the business of a king requires him to know it thoroughly; wherefore the different parts, by unnaturally opposing and destroying each other, prove the whole character to be absurd and useless. . . .

In the early ages of the world, according to the scripture chronology, there were no kings; the consequence of which was, there were no wars; it is the pride of kings which throw mankind into confusion. . . .

As the exalting one man so greatly above the rest cannot be justified on the equal rights of nature, so neither can it be defended on the authority of scripture; for the will of the Almighty, as declared by Gideon and the prophet Samuel, expressly disapproves of government by kings. All antimonarchical parts of scripture have been very smoothly glossed over in monarchical governments. . . .

To the evil of monarchy we have added that of hereditary succession; and as the first is a degradation and lessening of ourselves, so the second, claimed as a matter of right, is an insult and an imposition on posterity. For all men being originally equals, no *one* by *birth* could have a right to set up his own family in perpetual preference to all others for ever, and though himself might deserve *some* decent degree of honors of his contemporaries, yet his descendants might be far too unworthy to inherit them. One

of the strongest *natural* proofs of the folly of hereditary right in kings, is, that nature disapproves it, otherwise she would not so frequently turn it into ridicule by giving mankind an *Ass for a Lion.* . . .

Most wise men, in their private sentiments, have ever treated hereditary right with contempt; yet it is one of those evils, which when once established is not easily removed; many submit from fear, others from superstition, and the more powerful part shares with the king the plunder of the rest. . . .

In short, monarchy and succession have laid (not this or that kingdom only) but the world in blood and ashes. 'Tis a form of government which the word of God bears testimony against, and blood will attend it.

In England a king hath little more to do than to make war and give away places; which in plain terms, is to impoverish the nation and set it together by the ears. A pretty business indeed for a man to be allowed eight hundred thousand sterling a year for, and worshipped into the bargain! Of more worth is one honest man to society and in the sight of God, than all the crowned ruffians that ever lived.

THOUGHTS ON THE PRESENT STATE OF AMERICAN AFFAIRS

In the following pages I offer nothing more than simple facts, plain arguments, and common sense; and have no other preliminaries to settle with the reader, than that he will divest himself of prejudice and prepossession, and suffer his reason and his feelings to determine for themselves; that he will put *on*, or rather that he will not put *off* the true character of a man, and generously enlarge his views beyond the present day.

Volumes have been written on the subject of the struggle between England and America. Men of all ranks have embarked in the controversy, from different motives, and with various designs; but all have been ineffectual, and the period of debate is closed. Arms, as the last resource, decide the contest; the appeal was the choice of the king, and the continent hath accepted the challenge. . . .

The sun never shined on a cause of greater worth. 'Tis not the affair of a city, a county, a province, or a kingdom, but of a continent—of at least one eighth part of the habitable globe. 'Tis not the concern of a day, a year, or an age; posterity are virtually involved in the contest, and will be more or less affected, even to the end of time, by the proceedings now. Now is the seed-time of continental union, faith and honor. The least fracture now will be like a name engraved with the point of a pin on the tender rind of a young oak; the wound will enlarge with the tree, and posterity read it in full grown characters.

By referring the matter from argument to arms, a new æra for politics is struck; a new method of thinking hath arisen. . . .

As much hath been said of the advantages of reconciliation, which, like an agreeable dream, hath passed away and left us as we were, it is but right, that we should examine the contrary side of the argument, and inquire into some of the many material injuries which these colonies sustain, and always will sustain, by being connected with, and dependant on Great-Britain: To examine that connexion and dependance, on the principles of nature and common sense, to see what we have to trust to, if separated, and what we are to expect, if dependant.

I have heard it asserted by some, that as America hath flourished under her former connexion with Great-Britain, that the same connexion is necessary towards her future happiness, and will always have the same effect. Nothing can be more fallacious than this kind of argument. We may as well assert that because a child has thrived upon milk, that it is never to have meat, or that the first twenty years of our lives is to become a precedent for the next twenty. But even this is admitting more than is true, for I answer roundly, that America would have flourished as much, and probably much more, had no European power had any thing to do with her. The commerce, by which she hath enriched herself, are the necessaries of life, and will always have a market while eating is the custom of Europe.

But she has protected us, say some. That she has engrossed us is true, and defended the continent at our expence as well as her own is admitted, and she would have defended Turkey from the same motive, viz. the sake of trade and dominion.

Alas, we have been long led away by ancient prejudices, and made large sacrifices to superstition. We have boasted the protection of Great-Britain, without considering, that her motive was *interest* not *attachment*; that she did not protect us from *our enemies* on *our account*, but from *her enemies* on *her own account*, from those who had no quarrel with us on any *other account*, and who will always be our enemies on the *same account*. . . .

France and Spain never were, nor perhaps ever will be our enemies as *Americans*, but as our being the *subjects of Great-Britain*.

But Britain is the parent country, say some. Then the more shame upon her conduct. Even brutes do not devour their young, nor savages make war upon their families; wherefore the assertion, if true, turns to her reproach; but it happens not to be true, or only partly so, and the phrase *parent* or *mother country* hath been jesuitically adopted by the king and his parasites, with a low papistical design of gaining an unfair bias on the credulous weakness of our minds. Europe, and not England, is the parent country of America. This new world hath been the asylum for the persecuted lovers of civil and religious liberty from *every part* of Europe. Hither have they fled, not from the tender embraces of the mother, but from the cruelty of the monster; and it is so far true of England, that the same tyranny which drove the first emigrants from home, pursues their descendants still.

In this extensive quarter of the globe, we forget the narrow limits of three hundred and sixty miles (the extent of England) and carry our friendship on a larger scale; we claim brotherhood with every European Christian, and triumph in the generosity of the sentiment.

It is pleasant to observe by what regular gradations we surmount the force of local prejudice, as we enlarge our acquaintance with the world. A man born in any town in England divided into parishes, will naturally associate most with his fellow-parishioners (because their interests in many cases will be common) and distinguish him by the name of *neighbour*; if he meet him but a few miles from home, he drops the narrow idea of a street, and salutes him by the name of *townsman*; if he travel out of the county, and meet him in any other, he forgets the minor divisions of street and town, and calls him *countryman*, i. e. *countyman*; but if in their foreign excursions they should associate in France or any other part of *Europe*, their local remembrance would be enlarged into that of *Englishmen*. And by a just parity of reasoning, all Europeans meeting in America, or any other quarter of the globe, are *countrymen*; for England, Holland, Germany, or Sweden, when compared with the whole, stand in the same places on the larger scale, which the divisions of street, town, and county do on the smaller ones; distinctions too limited for continental minds. Not one third of the inhabitants, even of this province, are of English descent. Wherefore I reprobate the phrase of parent or mother country applied to

England only, as being false, selfish, narrow and ungenerous. . . .

As to government matters, it is not in the power of Britain to do this continent justice: The business of it will soon be too weighty, and intricate, to be managed with any tolerable degree of convenience, by a power so distant from us, and so very ignorant of us; for if they cannot conquer us, they cannot govern us. To be always running three or four thousand miles with a tale or a petition, waiting four or five months for an answer, which when obtained requires five or six more to explain it in, will in a few years be looked upon as folly and childishness—There was a time when it was proper, and there is a proper time for it to cease.

Small islands not capable of protecting themselves, are the proper objects for kingdoms to take under their care; but there is something very absurd, in supposing a continent to be perpetually governed by an island. In no instance hath nature made the satellite larger than its primary planet, and as England and America, with respect to each other, reverses the common order of nature, it is evident they belong to different systems; England to Europe, America to itself. . . .

But where, says some, is the King of America? I'll tell you. Friend, he reigns above, and doth not make havoc of mankind like the Royal Brute of Britain. Yet that we may not appear to be defective even in earthly honors, let a day be solemnly set apart for proclaiming the charter; let it be brought forth placed on the divine law, the word of God; let a crown be placed thereon, by which the world may know, that so far we approve of monarchy, that in America THE LAW IS KING. For as in absolute governments the King is law, so in free countries the law *ought* to be King; and there ought to be no other. But lest any ill use should afterwards arise, let the crown at the conclusion of the ceremony, be demolished, and scattered among the people whose right it is.

A government of our own is our natural right: And when a man seriously reflects on the precariousness of human affairs, he will become convinced, that it is infinitely wiser and safer, to form a constitution of our own in a cool deliberate manner, while we have it in our power, than to trust such an interesting event to time and chance. . . .

O ye that love mankind! Ye that dare oppose, not only the tyranny, but the tyrant, stand forth! Every spot of the old world is overrun with oppression. Freedom hath been hunted round the globe. Asia, and Africa, have long expelled her—Europe regards her like a stranger, and England hath given her warning to depart. O! receive the fugitive, and prepare in time an asylum for mankind.

Questions

1. What essential arguments against the institution of monarchy does Paine develop?
2. What pragmatic arguments for declaring independence does Paine advance? How logical and convincing are those arguments?
3. Does Paine suggest that an independent America would have a special mission in the world? If so, what would that mission be?

6-4 Thomas Jefferson Attacks the King on the Issue of Slavery (1776)

As the full text of the Declaration of Independence reveals (see text pp. D1–D2), Thomas Jefferson, the principal author, prepared a lengthy and varied bill of indictment against George III (see text pp. 172–173). However, not all the charges Jefferson drew up gained the approval of the Continental Congress. Indeed, the Congress totally expunged from its records what would have been the longest section in Jefferson's list of charges against the king. Congress took that extraordinary action because the Georgia and South Carolina delegations had said that they would not sign the Declaration unless that section was eliminated. The "missing" section is reprinted here.

Source: In Julian P. Boyd, ed., *The Papers of Thomas Jefferson,* vol. 1, p. 426. Copyright © 1950 by Princeton University Press. Reprinted by permission of Princeton University Press.

He [the king] has waged cruel war against human nature itself, violating it's most sacred rights of life & liberty in the persons of a distant people who never offended him, captivating & carrying them into slavery in another hemisphere, or to incur miserable death in their transportation thither. this piratical warfare, the opprobrium of *infidel* powers, is the warfare of the CHRISTIAN king of Great Britain. determined to keep open a market where MEN should be bought & sold, he has prostituted his negative for suppressing every legislative attempt to prohibit or to restrain this execrable commerce: and that this assemblage of horrors might want no fact of distinguished die, he is now exciting those very people to rise in arms among us, and to purchase that liberty of which *he* has deprived them, by murdering the people upon whom *he* also obtruded them; thus paying off former crimes committed against the *liberties* of one people, with crimes which he urges them to commit against the *lives* of another.

Questions

1. Comparing this section with the pronouncement in the Declaration of Independence that "all men are created equal" (see text p. D-1), is it accurate to say that as Jefferson uses it, the term *men* stands for both men and women?
2. Is Jefferson saying that slavery is wrong or just that the slave trade is wrong? Why or why not?
3. Must the colonists share the blame for allowing the evils Jefferson denounces? Why or why not?

Questions for Further Thought

1. Do these documents help explain why the colonists waited more than a year after the fighting had begun to declare independence? Why or why not?
2. In what ways do these documents suggest that the War for Independence profoundly sharpened social divisions in America? Explain.
3. Although Gouverneur Morris, Thomas Paine, and Thomas Jefferson all actively championed American independence, they differed on many points. On the basis of these documents, what political label—conservative, liberal, or radical—would you give to each man? Why did you assign those labels?

The Perils of War and Finance, 1776–1778, and The Path to Victory, 1778–1783

Despite some heroic achievements, the rebel forces fared poorly in the military conflict in 1775–1776 (see text pp. 173–174). Thomas Paine's famous commentary on the "times that try men's souls" (Document 6-5) illustrates some of the many difficulties the Patriots faced. Document 6-6 illustrates, as the text authors note, the vital impact of the Patriot victory at Trenton, New Jersey, late in 1776 (see text p. 174). Document 6-7 reminds us, as the text stresses (pp. 175, 188–189), that women as well as men took an active and vital part in winning independence. Others, who often were numbered among the less powerful segments of society (see text pp. 175–176), also joined the Patriot cause. Jacob Francis's account (Document 6-8) reminds us that even though large numbers of African-Americans cast their lot with the British (Document 6-2), some fought to win independence for America.

Winning independence proved to be a long and difficult task. As a group, Documents 6-7 through 6-11 illustrate the nature of the military conflict that ranged broadly across and even beyond the area of settlement. They reveal that the fighting could be especially vicious when Patriots opposed Loyalists or native Americans (see text pp. 170, 180–183). For some persons, fighting ended when they were captured and became prisoners of war (POWs). As these documents show, the experiences of POWs varied. The selections from the diary of Charles Herbert (Document 6-10) demonstrate that even as POWs held in Great Britain, Patriots could attempt to support the war effort.

The text authors (pp. 179–180) forcefully prove that brilliant Patriot diplomacy helped bring the French into the war and turn military victories into diplomatic triumphs. Moreover, the final major military triumph was, as the authors of the text stress, "the Franco-American victory at Yorktown" (p. 183). French troops and a French fleet were instrumental in achieving that great victory. Sarah Osborn (Document 6-7) and Major Ebenezer Denny (Document 6-11) participated in the Battle of Yorktown. Their accounts convey a sense of the battle that, as far as the British empire was concerned, turned the world upside down.

The British imperial reform effort, which was organically linked to economic considerations, thus produced revolutionary results that the British could only rue. As the authors of the textbook (pp. 178–179) emphasize, financial problems also bedeviled the revolutionaries. The Patriots' economic difficulties often became intertwined with the issue of republicanism in action (see text pp. 187–189). Accordingly, Documents 6-12 and 6-13, which are reprinted in the next set of documents, illustrate some of the ramifications of the Patriots' financial difficulties.

6-5 Thomas Paine, Number I of "The American Crisis" (December 1776)

Thomas Paine's literary contributions to the cause of American independence did not end with the publication of the many editions of *Common Sense* (Document 6-3). In the bleak days of December 1776 Paine, who was then serving in the army, published an essay in the *Pennsylvania Journal* (December 19, 1776) that echoed the sense of travail that permeated rebel thought (see text pp. 173–174). This was the first essay in a series Paine called "The American Crisis"; he wrote a dozen more essays in the series by April 19, 1783. On December 9, 1783, he published what an editor of his papers called "A Supernumerary Crisis." In that work Paine discussed the question of American trade with the British. The essays that form what is commonly referred to as "The Crisis" reveal Paine's ability to put words together in powerful and memorable ways. That is especially true of the first installment of "The American Crisis," sections of which are reprinted here.

Source: Pennsylvania Journal, December 19, 1776.

THESE are the times that try men's souls. The summer soldier and the sunshine patriot will, in this crisis, shrink from the service of their country; but he that stands it *now*, deserves the love and thanks of man and woman. Tyranny, like hell, is not easily conquered; yet we have this consolation with us, that the harder the conflict, the more glorious the triumph. What we obtain too cheap, we esteem too lightly: it is dearness only that gives every thing its value. Heaven knows how to put a proper price upon its goods; and it would be strange indeed if so celestial an article as

FREEDOM should not be highly rated. Britain, with an army to enforce her tyranny, has declared that she has a right (*not only to* TAX) but "to BIND us in ALL CASES WHATSOEVER," and if being *bound in that manner,* is not slavery, then is there not such a thing as slavery upon earth. Even the expression is impious; for so unlimited a power can belong only to God. . . .

I have as little superstition in me as any man living, but my secret opinion has ever been, and still is, that God Almighty will not give up a people to military destruction, or leave them unsupportedly to perish, who have so earnestly and so repeatedly sought to avoid the calamities of war, by every decent method which wisdom could invent. Neither have I so much of the infidel in me, as to suppose that He has relinquished the government of the world, and given us up to the care of devils; and as I do not, I cannot see on what grounds the king of Britain can look up to heaven for help against us: a common murderer, a highwayman, or a house-breaker, has as good a pretence as he.

'Tis surprising to see how rapidly a panic will sometimes run through a country. All nations and ages have been subject to them: Britain has trembled like an ague at the report of a French fleet of flat bottomed boats; and in the fourteenth [fifteenth] century the whole English army, after ravaging the kingdom of France, was driven back like men petrified with fear; and this brave exploit was performed by a few broken forces collected and headed by a woman, Joan of Arc. Would that heaven might inspire some Jersey maid to spirit up her countrymen, and save her fair fellow sufferers from ravage and ravishment! Yet panics, in some cases, have their uses; they produce as much good as hurt. Their duration is always short; the mind soon grows through them, and acquires a firmer habit than before. But their peculiar advantage is, that they are the touchstones of sincerity and hypocrisy, and bring things and men to light, which might otherwise have lain forever undiscovered. In fact, they have the same effect on secret traitors, which an imaginary apparition would have upon a private murderer. They sift out the hidden thoughts of man, and hold them up in public to the world. . . .

I shall conclude this paper with some miscellaneous remarks on the state of our affairs; and shall begin with asking the following question, Why is it that the enemy have left the New-England provinces, and made these middle ones the seat of war? The answer is easy: New-England is not infested with tories, and we are. I have been tender in raising the cry against these men, and used numberless arguments to show them their danger, but it will not do to sacrifice a world either to their folly or their baseness. The period is now arrived, in which either they or we must change our sentiments, or one or both must fall. And what is a tory? Good God! what is he? I should not be afraid to go with a hundred whigs against a thousand tories, were they to attempt to get into arms. Every tory is a coward; for servile, slavish, self-interested fear is the foundation of toryism; and a man under such influence, though he may be cruel, never can be brave.

But, before the line of irrecoverable separation be drawn between us, let us reason the matter together: Your conduct is an invitation to the enemy, yet not one in a thousand of you has heart enough to join him. Howe is as much deceived by you as the American cause is injured by you. He expects you will all take up arms, and flock to his standard, with muskets on your shoulders. Your opinions are of no use to him, unless you support him personally, for 'tis soldiers, and not tories, that he wants.

I once felt all that kind of anger, which a man ought to feel, against the mean principles that are held by the tories: a noted one, who kept a tavern at Amboy, was standing at his door, with as pretty a child in his hand, about eight or nine years old, as I ever saw, and after speaking his mind as freely as he thought was prudent, finished with this unfatherly expression, *"Well! give me peace in my day."* Not a man lives on the continent but fully believes that a separation must some time or other finally take place, and a generous parent should have said, *"If there must be trouble, let it be in my day, that my child may have peace;"* and this single reflection, well applied, is sufficient to awaken every man to duty. Not a place upon earth might be so happy as America. Her situation is remote from all the wrangling world, and she has nothing to do but to trade with them. A man can distinguish himself between temper and principle, and I am as confident, as I am that Good governs the world, that America will never be happy till she gets clear of foreign dominion. Wars, without ceasing, will break out till that period arrives, and the continent must in the end be conqueror; for though the flame of liberty may sometimes cease to shine, the coal can never expire.

Quitting this class of men, I turn with the warm ardor of a friend to those who have nobly stood, and are yet determined to stand the matter out: I call not upon a few, but upon all: not on *this* state or *that* state, but on *every* state: up and help us; lay your shoulders to the wheel; better have too much force than too little, when so great an object is at stake. Let it be told to the future world, that in the depth of winter, when nothing but hope and virtue could survive, that the city and the country, alarmed at one common danger, came forth to meet and to repulse it. Say not that thousands are gone, turn out your tens of thousands; throw not the burden of the day upon Providence, but *"show your faith by your works,"* that God may bless you. It matters not where you live, or what rank of life you hold, the evil or the blessing will reach you all. The far and the near, the home counties and the back, the rich and the poor, will suffer or rejoice alike. The heart that feels not now, is dead: the blood of his children will curse his cowardice, who shrinks back at a time when a little might have saved the whole, and made *them* happy. I love the man that can smile in trouble, that can gather strength from distress, and grow brave by reflection. 'Tis the business of little minds to shrink; but he whose heart is firm, and whose conscience approves his conduct, will pursue his principles unto death. . . .

I thank God, that I fear not. I see no real cause for fear. I know our situation well, and can see the way out of it. While our army was collected, Howe dared not risk a battle; and it is no credit to him that he decamped from the White Plains, and waited a mean opportunity to ravage the defenceless Jerseys; but it is great credit to us, that, with a handful of men, we sustained an orderly retreat for near an hundred miles, brought off our ammunition, all our field pieces, the greatest part of our stores, and had four rivers to pass. None can say that our retreat was precipitate, for we were near three weeks in performing it, that the country might have time to come in. Twice we marched back to meet the enemy, and remained out till dark. The sign of fear was not seen in our camp, and had not some of the cowardly and disaffected inhabitants spread false alarms through the country, the Jerseys had never been ravaged. Once more we are again collected and collecting; our new army at both ends of the continent is recruiting fast, and we shall be able to open the next campaign with sixty thousand men, well armed and clothed. This is our situation, and who will may know it. By perseverance and fortitude we have the prospect of a glorious issue; by cowardice and submission, the sad choice of a variety of evils—a ravaged country—a depopulated city—habitations without safety, and slavery without hope—our homes turned into barracks and bawdy-houses for Hessians, and a future race to provide for, whose fathers we shall doubt of. Look on this picture and weep over it! and if there yet remains one thoughtless wretch who believes it not, let him suffer it unlamented.

COMMON SENSE.

Questions

1. According to Paine, what major problems did the Patriots face?
2. In *Common Sense* (Document 6-3) Paine spoke idealistically about what an independent America could mean to future generations and to the world. Does he effectively adopt the same approach in Number I of "The Crisis"? Why or why not?
3. Do you agree that sections of this essay are especially powerful and memorable? If your answer is no, why not? If it is yes, what lines or sections strike you as especially powerful and memorable? Why?

6-6 A Loyal Englishman Assesses the Importance of the American Victory at Trenton (1776–1777)

Nicholas Cresswell, the son of a prosperous landowner, was born in England in 1750. In 1774 Cresswell journeyed to Virginia to scout out the land. He planned to locate good yet inexpensive land, after which he would return home and, as he put it, prevail upon friends to give him something to begin life with. He arrived in Virginia in May 1774, just in time to get caught up in the rush toward revolution. Cresswell adamantly opposed the Patriots and took to describing the most ardent Patriots with his own special epithet: they were *Slebers*. The following entries from his journal reveal the impact the Patriot victory at Trenton had on his thinking (see text p. 174). Cresswell returned to Britain in 1777.

Source: Nicholas Cresswell, *The Journal of Nicholas Cresswell* (New York: Dial Press, 1924), pp. 176, 179–180.

Saturday, December 14th, 1776. News that General Howe is at Trenton in the Jerseys, from Philadelphia. It is certain the Congress has left Philadelphia and are now at Baltimore. Great numbers of recruiting parties are out to raise men, but can scarcely get a man by any means, tho' their bounty is 12£. None will enlist that can avoid it. They get some servants and convicts which are purchased from their Masters, these will desert the first opportunity. The violent *Slebers* are much dispirited. The Politicians (or rather timid Whigs) give all up for lost. And the Torys begin to exult. The time is out that the Flying Camp was enlisted for, and it is said that they refuse to serve any longer, tho' they have been solicited in the strongest terms. This will make a great deficiency in their Army, the loss of Ten Thousand men. I am convinced that if General Howe will push to Philadelphia the day is his own. . . .

Monday, Jan. 6th, 1777. News that Washington had taken 760 Hessian prisoners at Trenton in the Jerseys. Hope it is a lie. This afternoon hear he has likewise taken six pieces of Brass Cannon. *Tuesday, Jan. 7th, 1777.* The news is confirmed. The minds of the people are much altered. A few days ago they had given up the cause for lost. Their late successes have turned the scale and now they are all liberty mad again. Their Recruiting parties could not get a man (except he bought him from his master) no longer since than last week, and now the men are coming in by companies. Confound the turncoat scoundrels and the cowardly Hessians together. This has given them new spirits, got them fresh succours and will prolong the War, perhaps for two years. They have recovered their panic and it will not be an easy matter to throw them into that confusion again. Volunteer Companies are collecting in every County on the Continent and in a few months the rascals will be stronger than ever. Even the parsons, some of them, have turned out as Volunteers and Pulpit Drums or Thunder, which you please to call it, summoning all to arms in this cursed babble. D— them all.

Questions

1. Compare the ideas of the Patriot Thomas Paine (Document 6-5) with what Cresswell thought late in 1776. Did the Patriot and the Loyalist agree or disagree about the situation the Patriot war effort faced?

2. Does Cresswell seem as adamant in his Loyalism as Paine (Document 6-5) was in his support for the Revolution? Why or why not?

3. According to Cresswell, was the Patriot victory at Trenton only a minor setback for the British war effort? Why or why not?

6-7 Sarah Osborn's Account of Life with the Army

In colonial America women had been almost totally excluded from a role in public politics. However, as Documents 5-7 and 5-11 demonstrate, women were drawn into some of the political conflicts that marked the movement toward independence. Also, as the textbook emphasizes (pp. 188–189), during the war women actively participated in the Patriots' efforts at a number of levels. Sarah Osborn was one of the women who traveled with the army (see text p. 175). We know about her activities because in 1832 Congress passed what the historian John C. Dann describes as the first comprehensive pension act for veterans and the widows of veterans of the American Revolution. Under that and subsequent legislation, the applicant had to provide a statement to prove his or her right to a pension. Osborn prepared her account in 1837. It was given in the legal deposition form, which is why Osborn is referred to as "deponent." Osborn was eighty-one in 1837, but her powerful memory had not dimmed; her account, as far as it can be verified, is accurate. The section reprinted here describes her activities as the spouse of Aaron Osborn, a soldier she married in January 1780. Professor Dann, whose work with the pension records led him to edit the insightful collection of accounts entitled *The Revolution Remembered* (Chicago: University of Chicago

Press, 1980), notes that Sarah Osborn's deposition may be the only extant autobiographical account of a woman who traveled with the army (*The Revolution Remembered*, p. 240).

Source: Sarah Osborn's application for a pension, Record Group 15 of the Records of the Veterans Administration, National Archives. In John C. Dann, ed., *The Revolution Remembered: Eyewitness Accounts of the War for Independence* (Chicago: University of Chicago Press, 1980), pp. 242–250 *passim*.

After deponent had married said [Aaron] Osborn, he informed her that he was returned during the war, and that he desired deponent to go with him. Deponent declined until she was informed by Captain Gregg that her husband should be put on the commissary guard, and that she should have the means of conveyance either in a wagon or on horseback. That deponent then in the same winter season in sleighs accompanied her husband and the forces under command of Captain Gregg on the east side of the Hudson river to Fishkill, then crossed the river and went down to West Point. There remained till the river opened in the spring, when they returned to Albany. Captain Gregg's company was along, and she thinks Captain Parsons, Lieutenant Forman, and Colonel Van Schaick, but is not positive.

Deponent, accompanied by her said husband and the same forces, returned during the same season to West Point. Deponent recollects no other females in company but the wife of Lieutenant Forman and of Sergeant Lamberson. . . .

Deponent further says that she and her husband remained at West Point till the departure of the army for the South, a term of perhaps one year and a half, but she cannot be positive as to the length of time. While at West Point, deponent lived at Lieutenant Foot's, who kept a boardinghouse. Deponent was employed in washing and sewing for the soldiers. Her said husband was employed about the camp. . . .

When the army were about to leave West Point and go south, they crossed over the river to Robinson's Farms and remained there for a length of time to induce the belief, as deponent understood, that they were going to take up quarters there, whereas they recrossed the river in the nighttime into the Jerseys and traveled all night in a direct course for Philadelphia. Deponent was part of the time on horseback and part of the time in a wagon. Deponent's said husband was still serving as one of the commissary's guard. . . . They continued their march to Philadelphia, deponent on horseback through the streets, and arrived at a place towards the Schuylkill where the British had burnt some houses, where they encamped for the afternoon and night. Being out of bread, deponent was employed in baking the afternoon and evening. Deponent recollects no females but Sergeant Lamberson's and Lieutenant Forman's wives and a colored woman by the name of Letta. The Quaker ladies who came round urged deponent to stay,

but her said husband said, "No, he could not leave her behind." Accordingly, next day they continued their march from day to day till they arrived at Baltimore, where deponent and her said husband and the forces under command of General Clinton, Captain Gregg, and several other officers, all of whom she does not recollect, embarked on board a vessel and sailed down the Chesapeake. . . .They continued sail until they had got up the St. James River as far as the tide would carry them, about twelve miles from the mouth, and then landed, and the tide being spent, they had a fine time catching sea lobsters, which they ate.

They, however, marched immediately for a place called Williamsburg, as she thinks, deponent alternately on horseback and on foot. There arrived, they remained two days till the army all came in by land and then marched for Yorktown, or Little York as it was then called. The York troops were posted at the right, the Connecticut troops next, and the French to the left. In about one day or less than a day, they reached the place of encampment about one mile from Yorktown. Deponent was on foot and the other females above named and her said husband still on the commissary's guard. . . . Deponent took her stand just back of the American tents, say about a mile from the town, and busied herself washing, mending, and cooking for the soldiers, in which she was assisted by the other females; some men washed their own clothing. She heard the roar of the artillery for a number of days, and the last night the Americans threw up entrenchments, it was a misty, foggy night, rather wet but not rainy. Every soldier threw up for himself, as she understood, and she afterwards saw and went into the entrenchments. Deponent's said husband was there throwing up entrenchments, and deponent cooked and carried in beef, and bread, and coffee (in a gallon pot) to the soldiers in the entrenchment.

On one occasion when deponent was thus employed carrying in provisions, she met General Washington, who asked her if she "was not afraid of the cannonballs?"

She replied, "No, the bullets would not cheat the gallows," that "It would not do for the men to fight and starve too."

They dug entrenchments nearer and nearer to Yorktown every night or two till the last. While digging that, the enemy fired very heavy till about nine o'clock next morning, then stopped, and the drums from the enemy beat excessively. Deponent was a little way off in Colonel Van Schaick's or the officers' marquee and a number of officers were present, among whom was Captain Gregg, who, on account of infirmities, did not go out much to do duty.

The drums continued beating, and all at once the officers hurrahed and swung their hats, and deponent asked them, "What is the matter now?"

One of them replied, "Are not you soldier enough to know what it means?"

Deponent replied, "No."

They then replied, "The British have surrendered."

Deponent, having provisions ready, carried the same down to the entrenchments that morning, and four of the soldiers whom she was in the habit of cooking for ate their breakfasts.

Deponent stood on one side of the road and the American officers upon the other side when the British officers came out of the town and rode up to the American officers and delivered up [their swords, which the deponent] thinks were returned again, and the British officers rode right on before the army, who marched out beating and playing a melancholy tune, their drums covered with black handkerchiefs and their fifes with black ribbands tied around them, into an old field and there grounded their arms and then returned into town again to await their destiny. Deponent recollects seeing a great many American officers, some on horseback and some on foot, but cannot call them all by name. Washington, Lafayette, And Clinton were among the number. The British general at the head of the army was a large, portly man, full face, and the tears rolled down his cheeks as he passed along. She does not recollect his name, but it was not Cornwallis. She saw the latter afterwards and noticed his being a man of diminutive appearance and having cross eyes. . . .

After two or three days, deponent and her husband, Captain Gregg, and others who were sick or complaining embarked on board a vessel from Yorktown, not the same they came down in, and set sail up the Chesapeake Bay and continued to the Head of Elk, where they landed. The main body of the army remained behind but came on soon afterwards. Deponent and her husband proceeded with the commissary's teams from the Head of Elk, leaving Philadelphia to the right, and continued day after day till they arrived at Pompton Plains in New Jersey. Deponent does not recollect the county. They were joined by the main body of the army under General Clinton's command, and they set down for winter quarters. Deponent and her husband lived a part of the time in a tent made of logs but covered with cloth, and a part of the time at a Mr. Manuel's near Pompton Meetinghouse. She busied herself during the winter in cooking and sewing as usual. Her said husband was on duty among the rest of the army and held the station of corporal from the time he left West Point.

In the opening of spring, they marched to West Point and remained there during the summer, her said husband still with her. In the fall they came up a little back of Newburgh to a place called New Windsor and put up huts on Ellis's lands and again sat down for winter quarters, her said husband still along and on duty. The York troops and Connecticut troops were there. In the following spring or autumn they were all discharged. Deponent and her said husband remained in New Windsor in a log house built by the army until the spring following. Some of the soldiers boarded at their house and worked round among the farmers, as did her said husband also.

Deponent and her said husband spent certainly more than three years in the service, for she recollects a part of one winter at West Point and the whole of another winter there, another winter at Pompton Plains, and another at New Windsor. And her husband was the whole time under the command of Captain Gregg as an enlisted soldier holding the station of corporal to the best of her knowledge.

In the winter before the army were disbanded at New Windsor, on the twentieth of February, deponent had a child by the name of Phebe Osborn, of whom the said Aaron Osborn was the father. A year and five months afterwards, on the ninth day of August at the same place, she had another child by the name of Aaron Osborn, Jr., of whom the said husband was the father. . . .

About three months after the birth of her last child, Aaron Osborn, Jr., she last saw her said husband, who then left her at New Windsor and never returned. He had been absent at intervals before this from deponent, and at one time deponent understood he was married again to a girl by the name of Polly Sloat above Newburgh about fifteen or sixteen miles. Deponent got a horse and rode up to inquire into the truth of the story. She arrived at the girl's father's and there found her said husband, and Polly Sloat, and her parents. Deponent was kindly treated by the inmates of the house but ascertained for a truth that her husband was married to said girl. After remaining overnight, deponent determined to return home and abandon her said husband forever, as she found he had conducted in such a way as to leave no hope of reclaiming him. About two weeks afterwards, her said husband came to see deponent in New Windsor and offered to take deponent and her children to the northward, but deponent declined going, under a firm belief that he would conduct no better, and her said husband the same night absconded with two others, crossed the river at Newburgh, and she never saw him afterwards. This was about a year and a half after his discharge. . . .

After deponent was thus left by Osborn, she removed from New Windsor to Blooming Grove, Orange County, New York, about fifty years ago, where she had been born and brought up, and, having married Mr. [John] Benjamin . . . she continued to reside there perhaps thirty-five years, when she and her husband Benjamin removed to Pleasant Mount, Wayne County, Pennsylvania, and there she has resided to this day. Her said husband, John Benjamin, died there ten years ago last April, from which time she has continued to be and is now a widow.

Questions

1. What motivated Sarah Osborn to serve in what was at least a quasi-military capacity?
2. Does it appear that the officers and men understood the value of Osborn's support of the war effort? Why or why not?
3. Does her account strike you as believable? Why or why not?

6-8   Jacob Francis's Account of His War Service

The evidence suggests that for the reasons illustrated in Document 6-2, African-Americans were more likely to join the British than join the rebels. However, African-Americans fought on both sides in the Revolution (see text pp. 190–191). As in the case of Sarah Osborn, we know about the actions of the African-American Jacob Francis because he applied for a federal pension (see Document 6-7). Francis was born to a slave woman in New Jersey in 1754 but apparently was treated as an indentured servant rather than a slave. That interpretation is supported by the fact that he gained his freedom in January 1775, when he turned twenty-one. At that time twenty-one was the standard age at which men who had been bound to service as youngsters achieved their freedom. Francis completed a number of tours of duty and fought in several engagements. The sections of his 1836 deposition reprinted here recount his service in the war in the North in 1776 (see text pp. 173–174).

Source: Jacob Francis's application for a pension, Record Group 15 of the Records of the Veterans Administration, National Archives. In John C. Dann, ed., *The Revolution Remembered: Eyewitness Accounts of the War for Independence* (Chicago: University of Chicago Press, 1980), pp. 391–396 *passim.*

[I arrived in Salem, Massachusetts, about November 1769.] I lived and served in Salem until my time was out, which was in January 1775. I lived in Salem and worked for different persons till the fall of 1775. In the spring of that year the war had commenced, and the battles of Bunker Hill and Lexington had taken place. About the last of October, I enlisted as a soldier in the United States service for one year. I was told they were enlisting men to serve one year from the first of January, 1776, but I should receive pay from the time I enlisted, and I enlisted and entered the service about the last of October and received two months' pay for my service up to 1 January 1776. I enlisted at Cambridge . . . in Col. Paul Dudley Sergeant's regiment. . . . At the time I was enlisted, the British army lay in Boston. After that, I remained with the regiment at Cambridge and in the neighborhood of Boston until the British were driven out of Boston. . . .

In 1776, after the British left Boston, the army, with our regiment and myself along with them, marched by way of Roxbury (that way we could go by land) over a causeway into Boston and lay over two or three days, then were ordered out to Bunker Hill. We marched out and en-

camped there and lay there some time. Then our regiment was ordered to an island at that time called Castle William. . . . Then we left the island and was ordered to New York from the island. . . . [At] a place called Hell Gate, on the north side of the East River, . . . we threw up breastworks, and the British threw up breastworks on Long Island on the opposite side of the East River and used to fire across. We lay there some time.

While we lay there, the Battle of Long Island took place. There was a number of men detailed from our regiment, so many from each company, to go over and join the American army, perhaps two hundred men. I was one. We crossed the river at Hell Gate and marched on to the island in the direction we was ordered, but did not get to join the army till the battle had commenced and our army was on the retreat. We had to cross a creek to get to our army, who had engaged the enemy on the other side, but before we got to that creek our army was repulsed and retreating, and many of them were driven into the creek and some drowned. The British came in sight, and the balls flew round us, and our officers, finding we could do no good, ordered us to retreat, which we did under the fire of the enemy. We retreated back to Hell Gate and recrossed to our fortifications. Soon after that, we had orders to leave that place and marched to Westchester by way of Kingsbridge. We lay there some time, and every night we had a guard stationed out two or three miles from where the regiment lay at a place called Morrisania. I mounted guard there every time it came to my turn. There was an island near there. The tide made up round it. The British had a station on the island, and a British ship lay there. In an attack on the island one night, Colonel Jackson was wounded. After some time, we were ordered to march to the White Plains. We marched there and there joined General Washington's army.

We lay some time at the White Plains. While we lay there, the British landed and attacked some of our troops and had a brush there. Our regiment and I with them marched by General Washington's orders toward a hill where the engagement was, but the British got possession of the hill, and we retreated back to the camp. The British established a garrison on that hill. I stood sentinel that night in a thicket between the American camp and the hill, so near the British lines that I could hear the Hessians in the garrison, which was between one-quarter and one-half mile from me. The British lay there awhile and then left that place, and our regiments marched after them about three or four miles farther east. Then we received orders and marched to Peekskill on the North River. We halted a day and night a little distance from the river and there crossed at Peekskill to the west side of the river. From thence we marched on, and I do not recollect the names of places we passed through till we got to Morristown, New Jersey. We lay there one night, then marched down near to Baskingridge and lay there the next night. That night General Lee was taken in or about Baskingridge. I heard the guns firing. The next morning we continued our march across Jersey to the Delaware and crossed over to Easton. From thence we marched down the Pennsylvania side into Bucks County.

It was then cold weather, and we were billeted about in houses. Our company lay off from the river a few miles below Coryell's Ferry and above Howell's Ferry. We lay there a week or two; then we received orders to march and, Christmas night, crossed the river and marched down to Trenton early in the morning. . . . We marched down the street from the River Road into the town to the corner

where it crosses the street running up towards the Scotch Road and turned up that street. General Washington was at the head of that street coming down towards us and some of the Hessians between us and them. We had the fight. . . . After about half an hour the firing ceased, and some officers, among whom I recollect was General Lord Stirling, rode up to Colonel Sergeant and conversed with him. Then we were ordered to follow them, and with these officers and Colonel Sergeant at our head, we marched down through the town toward Assanpink and up the Assanpink on the north side of it and to the east of the town, where we were formed in line and in view of the Hessians, who were paraded on the south side of the Assanpink and grounded their arms and left them there and marched down to the old ferry below the Assanpink, between Trenton and Lamberton.

Soon after that, a number of men from our regiment were detailed to go down and ferry the Hessians across to Pennsylvania. I went as one, and about noon it began to rain and rained very hard. We were engaged all the afternoon ferrying them across till it was quite dark, when we quit. I slept that night in an old millhouse above the ferry on Pennsylvania side. The next morning I joined my regiment where I had left them the day before up the Assanpink, east of Trenton. We lay there a day or two, and then the time of the year's men was out, and our regiment received part of their pay and were permitted to return home. I did not get a discharge. At that time I had seven and a half months' pay due to me, and I believe others had the same. I received three months' pay, and all the rest of the regiment received the same, and we were ordered after a certain time to come to Peekskill on the North River, and then we should receive our pay and get our discharges. I was with the regiment and in service from the time of enlistment till that time about fourteen months and never left it until I had received the three months' pay and had permission to return to the place of my nativity in Amwell, about fifteen miles from Trenton. I immediately returned to Amwell and found my mother living, but in ill health. I remained with her, and when the time came to go to Peekskill for my pay and discharge, I gave up going and never received either my pay or a discharge in writing. That pay, four and one-half months at forty shillings a month (nine pounds proclamation money equal to twenty-four dollars), is yet due to me from the United States.

Questions

1. On the basis of his account, what do you believe motivated Francis to serve in the military?
2. Does his account strike you as believable? Why or why not?
3. Does Francis's account support or challenge the views of Peter Oliver (Document 5-8) about the ordinary people of America? Why or why not?

6-9   John Struthers's Account of War on the Frontier

As the textbook authors indicate (pp. 176, 182–183 and see the illustration on p. 176), the long-running battle between British colonists and native Americans for control of the land carried over into the War of Independence. John Struthers, who was born in Maryland in 1759 and moved to Pennsylvania in 1775, was one of the many frontier colonists who became involved in that ongoing conflict. In 1841 Struthers, as many others had, applied for a federal pension for his service (see Documents 6-7 and 6-8). However, as was the case with most of those who asked for pensions on the basis of service on the frontier, his request was denied. The sections of his application reprinted here reveal the nature of the conflict between native Americans and colonists.

Source: John Struthers's application for a pension, Record Group 15 of the Records of the Veterans Administration, National Archives. In John C. Dann, ed., *The Revolution Remembered: Eyewitness Accounts of the War for Independence* (Chicago: University of Chicago Press, 1980), pp. 253–258 *passim.*

The summer of 1777 was a season of great alarm, and the whole settlement from Fort Pitt to Kentucky was broken up. A number of families assembled at the house of my father in order to erect a fort, but, hearing that families had collected at Hoagland's and Beelor's, eight or ten miles nearer to the Ohio, for the same purpose, they only repaired the cabins as well as they could to resist an attack and remained in them during the summer. The others went on and built forts.

It was early resolved to raise a small company of volunteers to act as spies and wood rangers. Capt. James Scott, a brave and experienced officer, offered his services and appointed a place of rendezvous, and in a few days had upwards of twenty, of whom I was one, enrolled and ready to march with as much provision as we could conveniently carry. We started about the first of May, as nearly as I can now state, and I state it accordingly to be on that day. The country traversed was from a few miles below Fort Pitt, down the Ohio, crossing Raccoon Creek, Traver's and Tomlinson's Runs, Cross Creek, King's and Heoman's creeks, near their junction with the Ohio, passing on our way down Reardon's and Holliday's stations, where we occasionally drew provisions. From Holliday's Cove, we traversed the country backward and forward, carefully watching the Indian warpaths until we arrived at some one of the forts or stations on the headwaters of some of the streams above mentioned, in the vicinity of which most of our company resided, where we remained a day or two to get washing and mending done and a recruit of provisions, and at every station would spend an hour or two in the exercise of the tomahawk and rifle, not only for our own improvement in the use of these weapons of warfare but also to alarm the savages if they should be lurking in the neighborhood.

In the latter part of the season, the alarm was still kept up and increased by the attack (as was reported at the time) of two or three hundred Indians on Wheeling Fort, and in this stage of alarm many others volunteered to protect the frontier, and so effactually was the country scoured from Holliday's Cove to Fort Pitt, that, though we had no triumphs in battle to record nor defeats to lament, yet not an individual was massacred by the savages in that region during this year.

In the spring of 1778 the Indians broke out earlier than usual and committed several murders on Ten Mile Creek, which was then considered an interior settlement and, although not within the range of my excursions the preceding year, was within ten or twelve miles of my father's dwelling. I believe it was in March, and the whole settlement, from Wheeling upwards, was broken up and retired into forts, of which there was now perhaps too many, as from the paucity of males in each they could spare none to act as spies or wood rangers and scarce enough to defend the forts if they should be attacked. On my return from an ineffectual scout in pursuit of the savages who had committed these barbarities, though we passed two men whom they had murdered and scalped and who were not yet cold, yet they escaped punishment. On my return from this scout, which lasted but three or four days, a request was sent me from Hoagland's Fort to turn out with as many volunteers as I could collect. I did so and, referring to my previous acquaintance with the woods and Indian warpaths, was (though among the youngest) elected to head about fifteen or sixteen active and brave men and continued during the greater part of the season, that is, from March to November with short intervals to obtain ammunition, clothing, etc., on the same route as in the preceding year but not quite so extensive. The result, however, was that no Indian depredations were committed in that settlement during the whole season. . . .

In March 1779 I entered a volunteer in Capt. David Vance's company of mounted men, in General McIntosh's campaign to Fort Laurens on Tuscarawas. . . . I returned home in April and spent the remainder of the Indian season on the same route and in the same manner as during the two preceding summers. And during this season, according to the best of my knowledge and belief, I served at least six months.

Early in the spring of 1780 intelligence was received, I do not remember how, that a large body of Indians were on their march to devastate the whole country from Wheeling to Fort Pitt. This news was either not believed or at least not heeded until a party of them, crossing below Wheeling, had penetrated nearly halfway from the Ohio to Catfish Camp, now the seat of justice for Washington County, Pennsylvania. They had taken a number of prisoners but, becoming alarmed, speedily retraced their steps to the Ohio and murdered all their male prisoners on the way. The main body of those who were expected to have ravaged Raccoon Settlement, it was supposed, never crossed the Ohio, but sent two of their warriors to reconnoiter, who, approaching Dillow's Fort late in the evening, spied two boys at play and tomahawked and scalped them within two hundred yards of the fort and escaped. And it was supposed that their report was rather unfavorable, and that they immediately commenced their retrograde march, as no other mischief was done by them this season. Colonel Broadhead commanded at Fort Pitt, and this was the summer of his campaigns to the Muncee towns up the Allegheny River and to Coshocton at the forks of Muskingum, at which two places he was supposed to have destroyed five hundred acres of corn. . . .

Early in the year 1781 the Indians made an incursion into the upper settlements of Buffalo Creek and, notwithstanding the vigilance and bravery of Col. David Williamson and his party, cruelly murdered several persons in his immediate neighborhood and took others prisoners. This caused a general alarm through all the settlements, and the people crowded into the forts, but still their great dependence for safety was on the volunteer spies and wood rangers; so I spent from April till November, at least five months, in scouting the frontier and watching the Indian crossing places and warpaths.

In the fall of this year too was the first expedition of Colonel Williamson to the Moravian Towns on the Tuscarawas, in which I (at the risk of my popularity as a soldier) declined taking a part. In the latter part of February 1782, the Indians invaded the settlement of Raccoon and murdered the family of a Mr. Wallace and took John Carpenter prisoner and took his two horses. He, however, soon made his escape and brought his horses with him.

In March, another expedition under Colonel Williamson started to the Moravian Towns and destroyed them with the inhabitants, amounting to nearly a hundred of all ages and sexes. In this, also, I refused to be concerned. These occurrences were considered by the settlers as harbingers of great distress and suffering during the summer. Yet such was the vigilance of the settlers and spies that no other mischief was done, save in one instance, and they paid dearly for their temerity. Six Indians had crawled up ten or twelve miles into the settlement and captured an old lone man of the name of William Jackson and plundered his cabin and retreated; but, so instant was the pursuit, they were overtaken at the river before they had time to embark, and a skirmish ensued wherein five Indians were killed and the other wounded in the abdomen. . . . This was the only skirmish that I recollect took place in that region during the Revolutionary War.

In the spring of this year I was elected to the command of a militia company, and my attention to the duties of that office caused necessarily a relaxation of my excursions on the frontiers; yet I spent at least two months in that service during the season, which, added to the services heretofore listed, will amount to two years and seven months. Although from the lapse of so many years and the absence of other data than memory it is impossible to specify correctly the weeks and months spent as a volunteer on the frontier during the Revolutionary War, yet I believe the statement several months less than the services really performed. I am the more confirmed in this opinion by this, that in frequent conversations with several young men, my neighbors, who had listed for three years and returned at the close of the war, it was admitted by all that I and my companions had actually served longer and endured more fatigue and hardship than they had. These conversations it is probable would not now be thought of, but that they were sometimes carried on with a considerable degree of acrimony, the regulars affecting to consider the volunteers as an inferior class, and these retorting on those as a worthless set, not daring to set heads outside the gates but under the protection of volunteers and so on.

The regular soldier performs only during the summer and then retires to winter quarters, receiving pay and clothing and rations for the whole year. The volunteers, to whom I belonged, performed at least an equal amount of service and retired home during the winter, not receiving either pay or rations and not even clothing for any part of the time, with the trifling exception of a little flour obtained now and then at the posts, or stations, and furnishing their own ammunition. Justice therefore requires that these volunteers, on applying for pensions, should have their time calculated in the same rule as the regulars. The few regulars stationed along the Ohio, from Pitt to Wheeling, and I here speak of them only, the only reliance placed on them was to defend the forts should they be attacked. Indeed, it was admitted by everyone at the time that the only security of the people along the river and adjacent settlements was the vigilance of the volunteers in watching their crossing places and warpaths and ferreting them out of their lurking places near the stations, and that by their means, principally, was the settlement saved from savage vengeances.

Questions

1. On the basis of his account, what do you believe motivated Struthers to serve in the military?
2. Does his account strike you as believable? Why or why not?
3. Does Struthers's account support or challenge the views of Peter Oliver (Document 5-8) about the ordinary people of America? Why or why not?
4. To what extent does Struthers's account explain why the fighting between Americans on the frontier and native Americans was so vicious?

6-10   Charles Herbert's Prisoner of War Diary

As Document 6-9 and the American Voices entry for Moses Hall (see text p. 177) illustrate, those captured in land battles could meet a horrible fate. The rebel seamen captured at sea and taken to Great Britain were not treated so harshly. However, the British considered them pirates, not POWs, and the seamen were put in prison camps ostensibly to await trial—and possible execution—on the charge of piracy.

As the authors of the textbook note (p. 179), public support wavered as the war dragged on. The following passages from Charles Herbert's prison diary show us how POWs responded to their incarceration. Herbert, who was born in Massachusetts in 1757, was a crewman on the American ship *Dolton* when it was captured on December 24, 1776. He was incarcerated in Mill Prison, Plymouth, for almost two years and then was released under a prisoner exchange arrangement.

Source: Richard Livsey, ed., *A Relic of the Revolution . . . by Charles H. Herbert* (1847), pp. 68–173 *passim*.

MILL PRISON AT PLYMOUTH, ENGLAND

1777

[October] 18. We learn by those who came to prison last, that Dr. Franklin has written to the English ambassador, concerning an exchange of prisoners.

[October] 19. Sunday. This morning we found out that one of our company, confederate with a black man, had stolen, last night, an allowance of bread and cheese from those who came last to prison,—for which they made him run the gantlet up one side of the prison and down the other, one hundred and thirty feet, through a double file of men armed each with a nettle.

[October] 27. Last night two prisoners, Cutter and Morris, made their escape from the prison hospital; also to-day another prisoner ran the gantlet for stealing a penny loaf from one of the prisoners.

[November] 15. It is twelve months to-day since we sailed from Newburyport. I hope the Lord in whom we ought to trust, will, in his own good time, deliver us out of

the hands of our enemies, and return us to a free country,—which would be a day of good fortune, a day of agreeable surprise and great joy. Then would I say—

> Thrice happy youth, though destitute and poor,
> These are my restoration days;
> The Lord, who brought me out, I'm sure
> Can teach me how his name to praise.

December 3. This morning the guard discovered another hole which we begun to dig yesterday. I think we have been very diligent and careful to improve every opportunity to make our escape, but the guard is so very strict with us, that I think it almost impossible to succeed, and we have reason to think that there are some traitors amongst us, who give information of every thing of the kind which we undertake.

[December] 8. To-day we were all mustered, and after this was over, the [British] agent informed us that he had received a letter . . . to put all in this prison on half allowance, for breaking orders and attempting to make our escape, until the transgressor should be found out. But as we all, with one voice joined in one cause, we thought it inhuman to pitch upon any one man; therefore, by way of contribution, we raised money enough to hire one man to own the same and suffer for all, so that we are obliged to support him while on half allowance and make him amends for his sufferings.

[December] 9. To-day the man delivered himself up, to go to the Black-hole, and the agent allows him every indulgence consistent with his orders, which is a very uncommon thing for him.

[December] 11. There have been various reports for several days past, but I thought them not worthy of observation, because they did not come from so good authority as I could wish they might; but to-day [we] have a very authentic account from Captain Henry Johnston's brother, who is lately from London, that General Burgoyne and his army are totally routed, many killed, and taken to a man; and as I do not doubt the truth of it, it gives me more satisfaction than any news I have heard since I have been a prisoner. . . .

[December] 12. I purchased a book called the "American Crisis," on purpose to lend it to a friend without. We are told that the generality of the people in England are very much disaffected at the proceedings of the ministry.

[December] 25. Christmas. . . . I must confess I have a very agreeable expectation, if my life is spared and the Lord pleases to permit me, to sit down at my father's table next Christmas.

1778

[January] 24. I have heard little or no news, for this week past, and indeed no news is the best news for us; for if there is any thing against us, they are ready enough to tell us.

[March] 12. We are informed that General Howe has written home for a reinforcement immediately, or he must inevitably share the fate of Burgoyne; this inspires us with fresh courage. . . . I hope our days of trouble are nearly at an end, and after we have borne them with a spirit of manly fortitude, we shall be returned to a free country to enjoy our just rights and privileges, for which we have been so long contending. This will make ample satisfaction for all our sufferings.

[June] 5. . . . It is twelve months to-day since I came to prison. I believe four months ago it was the opinion of every one within these walls, that we should be out before this day, but I believe now, most of us despair of being exchanged this summer, unless General Burgoyne's coming home should be of advantage to us. He is able to represent the case as it is, for we hear that the Congress told him, before he left America, to go home and take his seat in Parliament, and speak the truth, for the truth could not hurt them.

Twelve months in prison we have spent,—
This judgment for our sins was sent,
To awake us from our carnal sleep,
And teach us God's commands to keep.

[June] 25. According to the newspapers, General Burgoyne gives the American troops a brave name; he says that the troops he had at his command were as good as double the number of any other troops the King has, and that the American troops were as good as his, and would fight as well.

[July] 3. As it is two years to-morrow since the Declaration of Independence in America, we are resolved, although we are prisoners, to bear it in remembrance; and for that end, several of us have employed ourselves to-day in making cockades. They were drawn on a piece of paper, cut in the form of a half-moon, with the thirteen stripes, a union, and thirteen stars, painted out, and upon the top is printed in large capital letters, "Independence," and at the bottom "Liberty or Death," or some appeal to Heaven.

[July] 4. This morning when we were let out, we all hoisted the American flag upon our hats, except about five or six, who did not choose to wear them. The agent, seeing us all with those papers on our hats, asked for one to look at, which was sent him, and it happened to be one which had "Independence" written upon the top, and at the bottom, "Liberty or Death." He, not knowing the meaning of it, and thinking we were going to force the guard, directly ordered a double sentry at the gate. Nothing happened till one o'clock; we then drew up in thirteen divisions, and each division gave three cheers, till it came to the last, when we all cheered together, all of which was conducted with the greatest regularity. We kept our colors hoisted till sunset, and then took them down.

July 17. There are a number of very quarrelsome, lawless men in prison, who have been the occasion of a great deal of mutiny and disturbance amongst us, which has obtained for us the ill-will of our friends; and we have been informed that unless there is an alteration among us, our donations [from kindly Britons] will be stopped; so that we thought it proper to have Articles among ourselves. These were drawn up to-day; they forbid all gambling, and blackguarding, which have caused great disturbance in the yard, and occasioned much fighting. They also forbid any improper language to any officer or soldier, who are now, or may hereafter be, appointed to preside over us. These articles were read in the yard before all the prisoners, and then stuck up in prison, and two men out of each ship's company were appointed to see them put into execution.

[July] 23. Most of this day the prison has been in an uproar, occasioned by a few men that will not be conformable to the rules and articles that we have amongst ourselves, but threaten to take them down and destroy them.

[July] 24. This morning we found that our articles were abused, and we took three of the before-mentioned men and tied them up to a post in the prison, and poured cold water down their arms and neck, for the space of half an hour. One of the three was afterwards complained of to the agent, who ordered him to be put in irons, and separated from us.

[August] 18. This afternoon there were five Americans brought to prison. They were all taken in different vessels. Some of them belonged to armed ships, others to merchantmen. Some of them have been taken this six months, and have been hurried about from ship to ship, and used scandalously. They had a bounty offered them to go on board this fleet, now lying in the Sound, but they, like brave Americans, refused, and chose rather to come to prison. They were sent here without being examined, or committed by any justice of the peace.

[October] 4. Sunday. This forenoon a gentleman came with a pardon for thirty-three men that petitioned to go on board the men-of-war, which was nearly as follows:

"His Majesty has been graciously pleased to grant a free pardon to thirty-three men, by name—, resident in this prison, upon condition that they will serve, and continue to serve in His Majesty's Navy." This gentleman said that these men are to be taken out of prison to-morrow, but one of the thirty-three has lately made his escape, and we have heard since that he is on board a man-of-war. He also said that those whose names are not on the list, but wish to enter on board the men-of-war, if they would petition, the same course would be taken, and he had no doubt it would be answered to their satisfaction. Accordingly, this afternoon a petition was written, and about fourteen signed it.

[October] 6. Last night there was but very little sleep in this prison, for the men who went on board the men-of-war this morning, were so overjoyed at the thought of being released from prison, that they could not, or would not, sleep the fore part of the night, but ran about the prison, hallooing, and stamping, and singing, like madmen, till they were tired out, and then went to bed; but the rest in prison were resolved, as they would not let us sleep the first part of the night, we would not let them sleep the latter; accordingly, we all turned out, and had an Indian Pow-wow, and as solid as the prison is, we made it shake. In this manner we spent the night, and in the morning early the men were called out, twenty of whom were immediately carried on board the Russel ship-of-war, now lying in the Sound. The other twelve were taken out about eleven o'clock, and sent on board the Royal George, now lying in Plymouth dock. As they went out, they gave us three cheers; we returned it, for in joy we parted. Among those who went to-day were about a dozen Americans, but they were chiefly inconsiderate youths. This is a move that I have long wished to see, but it came now very unexpectedly. For my own part, to enter on board a ship of war is the last thing I would do. I would undergo every thing but death before I would think of such a thing. This prison has been a little hell upon earth, but I prefer it as much before a man-of-war, as I would a palace before a dungeon. Ten days ago there were 330 prisoners here, now there are only 294.

[October] 6. There is a great alteration to be seen in this prison since those men went away, and I make no doubt that after another draft, we shall have peace and tranquillity, and live in harmony, and make ourselves happy, considering our situation, to what we have been for months past.

Questions

1. On the basis of these selections from Herbert's diary, what was likely to raise prisoners' morale and what was likely to lower it?
2. Did the prisoners show a talent for governing themselves? Why or why not?
3. What did Herbert hope to gain from American independence?
4. Does Herbert's diary support or challenge the views of Peter Oliver (Document 5-8) about the ordinary people of America? Why or why not?

6-11 Ebenezer Denny Describes the Victory at Yorktown (1781)

The Battle of Yorktown in 1781 convinced the British, who were also being isolated diplomatically from the rest of Europe, that the war was lost (see text pp. 182–183). Skillful American diplomats knew how to turn that situation into a diplomatic triumph (see text pp. 186–187). Sarah Osborn (Document 6-7) provides a valuable but brief description of some aspects of the Battle of Yorktown. Ebenezer Denny, a major in the

Continental army who was born in Pennsylvania in 1761, left a much more extensive description of that famous battle. His account, which helps us see the importance of George Washington's leadership (see text pp. 173–174, 183, 186), includes a revealing description of Denny's personal response to combat. Moreover, his observations, which offer specific examples of the value of the French alliance (see text pp. 179–180), illustrate why the textbook emphasizes that this crucial triumph was actually a Franco-American victory (see text p. 183).

Source: William H. Denny, ed., "Military Journal of Major Ebenezer Denny," *Memoirs of the Historical Society of Pennsylvania* (1860), vol. 7, pp. 239–249 *passim.*

[1781] *June* 18*th*.—Joined the troops under command of Lafayette. The Marquis had marched two or three days to meet us. His men look as if they were fit for business. They are chiefly all light infantry, dressed in frocks and over-alls of linen. One day spent in washing and refreshing—in fixing arms, carriages, etc., and served out ammunition. Move toward Richmond, where Lord Cornwallis with the British army lay. . . .

This was a severe march for me—found myself asleep more than once on the route. . . . After a variety of marching and counter-marching, . . . a smart skirmish takes place. . . . Here for the first time saw wounded men; feelings not very agreeable; endeavor to conquer this disposition or weakness; the sight sickened me. This little engagement within six miles of Williamsburg, where the enemy were encamped. Pennsylvania troops retreat—advance again. See the Marquis' light troops but seldom—know they are not far off. Kept constantly on the move. Hear that the enemy have decamped and preparing to cross James river at Jamestown. Our brigade move down; lay on arms all night about nine miles from the enemy. At daylight move on; middle of the afternoon of the 6th of July firing ahead. Our advance drove in the enemy's pickets, marching at this time by companies, in open order. . . . When perhaps within one hundred and fifty yards of the enemy, we closed column and displayed; advanced in battalion until the firing commenced, and ran along the whole line. A regiment or more of the light infantry and three pieces of artillery were in the line. Saw the British light infantry, distinctly, advancing at arm's-length distance, and their second line in close order, with shouldered musket, just in front of their camp—their infantry only engaged. The main body were discovered filing off to the right and left, when orders were given us to retreat. My captain, Montgomery, received a shot in his foot and had hopped back in the rear; Lieutenant Bluer being absent, the charge of the company devolved on me; young and inexperienced, exhausted with hunger and fatigue, had like to have disgraced myself—had eat nothing all day but a few blackberries—was faint, and with difficulty kept my place; once or twice was about to throw away my arms (a very heavy espontoon). The company were almost all old soldiers. Kept compact and close to our leading company, and con-

tinued running until out of reach of the fire. The enemy advanced no farther than to the ground we left. We could not have been engaged longer than about three or four minutes, but at the distance of sixty yards only. Our loss is said to be upward of one hundred killed and wounded. . . . Retreated two miles to very commanding ground, where we met the Marquis with our main body; halted and had some Indian meal served out, the wounded dressed, etc., and before day changed our ground and encamped about five miles from the field.

July 7*th*.—Our wounded who were prisoners, had been properly treated. The British moved from Jamestown. . . . Kept at a respectful distance from the enemy; rather between them and the route to North Carolina. Some idea of their design to return to the southward. Report going of a French fleet below. This news confirmed—great joy—army on the alert.

Sept. 1*st*.—Army encamped on the bank of James river—part of French fleet, with troops on board, in view. Recrossed James river and encamped at Williamsburg. Army in high spirits—reinforcements coming on.

14*th*.—General Washington arrived; our brigade was paraded to receive him; he rode along the line—quarters in Williamsburg.

15*th*.—Officers all pay their respects to the Commander-in-chief; go in a body; those who are not personally known, their names given by General Hand and General Wayne. He stands in the door, takes every man by the hand—the officers all pass in, receiving his salute and shake. This the first time I had seen the General. . . .

The presence of so many general officers, and the arrival of new corps, seem to give additional life to everything; discipline the order of the day. In all directions troops seen exercising and manœuvring. Baron Steuben, our great military oracle. The guards attend the grand parade at an early hour, where the Baron is always found waiting with one or two aids on horseback. These men are exercised and put through various evolutions and military experiments for two hours—many officers and spectators present; excellent school, this. At length the duty of the parade comes on. The guards are told off; officers take their posts, wheel by platoons to the right; fine corps of music detailed for this duty, which strikes up; the whole march off, saluting the Baron and field officer of the day, as they pass. Pennsylvania brigade almost all old soldiers, and well disciplined when compared with those of Maryland and Virginia. But the troops from the eastward far superior to either.

25th.—Joined by the last of their troops from the eastward. French encamped a few miles on the right; busy in getting cannon and military stores from on board the vessels.

28th.—The whole army moved in three divisions toward the enemy, who were strongly posted at York, about twelve miles distant. Their pickets and light troops retire. We encamped about three miles off—change ground and take a position within one mile of York; rising ground (covered with tall handsome pines) called Pigeon Hill, separates us from a view of the town. Enemy keep possession of Pigeon Hill. York on a high, sandy plain, on a deep navigable river of same name. Americans on the right; French on the left, extending on both sides of the river; preparations for a siege. One-third of the army on fatigue every day, engaged in various duties, making gabions, fascines, saucissons, etc., and great exertions and labor in getting on the heavy artillery. Strong covering parties (whole regiments) moved from camp as soon as dark, and lay all night upon their arms between us and the enemy. Our regiment, when on this duty, were under cover, and secured from the shot by Pigeon Hill; now and then a heavy shot from the enemy's works reached our camp. Our patrols, and those of the British, met occasionally in the dark, sometimes a few shot were exchanged—would generally retire. . . .

At length, everything in readiness, a division of the army broke ground on the night of the 6th of October, and opened the first parallel about six hundred yards from the works of the enemy. Every exertion to annoy our men, who were necessarily obliged to be exposed about the works; however, the business went on, and on the 9th our cannon and mortars began to play. The scene viewed from the camp now was grand, particularly after dark—a number of shells from the works of both parties passing high in the air, and descending in a curve, each with a long train of fire, exhibited a brilliant spectacle. Troops in three divisions manned the lines alternately. We were two nights in camp and one in the lines; relieved about ten o'clock. Passed and repassed by a covert way leading to the parallel.

Oct. 11th.—Second parallel thrown up within three hundred yards of the main works of the enemy; new batteries erected, and additional number of cannon brought forward—some twenty-four pounders and heavy mortars and howitzers. A tremendous fire now opened from all the new works, French and American. The heavy cannon directed against the embrasures and guns of the enemy. Their pieces were soon silenced, broke and dismantled. Shells from behind their works still kept up. Two redoubts advanced of their lines, and within rifle shot of our second parallel, much in the way. These forts or redoubts were well secured by a ditch and picket, sufficiently high parapet, and within were divisions made by rows of casks ranged upon end and filled with earth and sand. On tops of parapet were ranged bags filled with sand—a deep narrow ditch communicating with their main lines. On the night of the 14th, shortly after dark, these redoubts were taken by storm; the one on our right, by the Marquis, with part of his light infantry—the other, more to our left, but partly opposite the centre of the British lines, by the French. Our batteries had kept a constant fire upon the redoubts through the day. Belonged this evening to a command detailed for the purpose of supporting the Marquis. The night was dark and favorable. Our batteries had ceased—there appeared to be a dead calm; we followed the infantry and halted about half way—kept a few minutes in suspense, when we were ordered to advance. The business was over, not a gun was fired by the assailants; the bayonet only was used; ten or twelve of the infantry were killed. French had to contend with a post of more force—their loss was considerable. Colonel Hamilton led the Marquis' advance; the British sentries hailed them—no answer made. They also hailed the French, "Who comes there?" were answered, "French grenadiers." Colonel Walter Stewart commanded the regiment of reserve which accompanied the Marquis; they were immediately employed in connecting, by a ditch and parapet, the two redoubts, and completing and connecting the same with our second parallel. The British were soon alarmed; some from each of the redoubts made their escape. The whole enemy were under arms—much firing round all their lines, but particularly toward our regiment, where the men were at work; the shot passed over. In about three quarters of an hour we were under cover. Easy digging; light sandy ground.

15th.—Heavy fire from our batteries all day. A shell from one of the French mortars set fire to a British frigate; she burnt to the water's edge, and blew up—made the earth shake. Shot and shell raked the town in every direction. Bomb-proofs the only place of safety.

16th.—Just before day the enemy made a sortie, spiked the guns in two batteries and retired. Our troops in the parallel scarcely knew of their approach until they were off; the thing was done silently and in an instant. The batteries stood in advance of the lines, and none within but artillery. This day, the 16th, our division manned the lines—firing continued without intermission. Pretty strong detachments posted in each battery over night.

17th.—In the morning, before relief came, had the pleasure of seeing a drummer mount the enemy's parapet, and beat a parley, and immediately an officer, holding up a white handkerchief, made his appearance outside their works; the drummer accompanied him, beating. Our batteries ceased. An officer from our lines ran and met the other, and tied the handkerchief over his eyes. The drummer sent back, and the British officer conducted to a house in rear of our lines. Firing ceased totally.

18th.—Several flags pass and repass now even without

the drum. Had we not seen the drummer in his red coat when he first mounted, he might have beat away till doomsday. The constant firing was too much for the sound of a single drum; but when the firing ceased, I thought I never heard a drum equal to it—the most delightful music to us all.

19th.—Our division man the lines again. All is quiet. Articles of capitulation signed; detachments of French and Americans take possession of British forts. Major Hamilton commanded a battalion which took possession of a fort immediately opposite our right and on the bank of York river. I carried the standard of our regiment on this occasion. On entering the fort, Baron Steuben, who accompanied us, took the standard from me and planted it himself. The British army parade and march out with their colors furled; drums beat as if they did not care how. Grounded their arms and returned to town. Much confusion and riot among the British through the day; many of the soldiers were intoxicated; several attempts in course of the night to break open stores; an American sentinel killed by a British soldier with a bayonet; our patrols kept busy. . . . Returns of British soldiers, prisoners six thousand, and seamen about one thousand. Lord Cornwallis excused himself from marching out with the troops; they were conducted by General O'Hara. Our loss said to be about three hundred; that of the enemy said not more than five hundred and fifty. Fine supply of stores and merchandise had; articles suitable for clothing were taken for the use of the army. A portion furnished each officer to the amount of sixty dollars.

Questions

1. Is Denny's account of his actions during the fighting believable? Why or why not?
2. According to Denny's account, would he agree that French aid was crucial to achieving victory at Yorktown? Why or why not?
3. Does Denny's account support or challenge the views of Peter Oliver (Document 5-8) about the ordinary people of America? Why or why not?

Questions for Further Thought

1. Assume for the sake of discussion that you are an African-American slave owned by a Virginia Patriot. Based on the documents in this set, would you support the rebels or the British? Why would you choose that side?
2. Assume for the sake of discussion that you are a native American who lives near the frontier of colonial settlement. On the basis of the documents in this set, would you support the rebels or the British? Why?
3. On the basis of these documents, how accurate is it to describe the War of Independence as "a people's war"?
4. On the basis of these documents and the material in the textbook, what do you believe were the most difficult obstacles the Patriots had to overcome to achieve victory?
5. Based on these documents and the material in the textbook, what do you consider the most important factors that explain why the rebels won the war?

Republicanism Defined and Challenged

The American Revolution did more than transform the British Empire; under the pressure of republicanism in action (see text pp. 187–193), society and politics also underwent transformations. The bold action by Boston women (Document 6-12) in support of price regulation, when linked with Sarah Osborn's activities in support of the army (Document 6-7), highlights an important point: women took an active role in the transformation of American society (see text pp. 188–189). Document 6-12 also illustrates the fight between virtue and self-interest that marked the war years and led to numerous attempts to regulate prices. The memorial prepared by Philadelphia militiamen in 1779 (Document 6-13) touches on the same themes and also provides graphic testimony about the role the militia played in the war. In addition, it suggests how war service caused the militiamen to arrive at a new sense of their role in the developing republicanism of America (see text pp. 187–189). The militiamen's memorial also helps us appreciate the bitterness that Patriots felt, not only toward Loyalists but also toward those who did not actively support the Revolution (see text pp. 189–190). As the authors of the textbook indicate (pp. 192–193), American religious institutions were dramatically transformed during the Revolutionary era. The famous Virginia statute of religious freedom (Document 6-14) provides an important example of the increasing religious freedom that emerged from the republicanism in action of the American Revolution.

6-12   Boston Women Support Price Control (1777)

Financing the Patriots' war effort produced a range of problems including disagreements over how to control prices and thus prevent greedy self-interest from overwhelming public virtue (see text pp. 178–179, 187–189). Given the active role women had played in earlier economic boycotts (Documents 5-7 and 5-11) and were taking in the war effort (Document 6-7 and text pp. 188–189), it seems logical that women would have participated in any program to regulate prices. Such an effort occurred in Massachusetts in 1777 (see text pp. 187–188). As the following letter of July 31, 1777, from Abigail Adams to her husband, John, shows, what some Boston women did to achieve price regulation proved most intriguing.

Source: Charles F. Adams, ed., *Letters of Mrs. Adams, the Wife of John Adams*, 4th ed. (Boston, 1848), pp. 84–85.

31 July, 1777

I have nothing new to entertain you with, unless it is an account of a new set of mobility, which has lately taken the lead in Boston. You must know that there is a great scarcity of sugar and coffee, articles which the female part of the state is very loth to give up, especially whilst they consider the scarcity occasioned by the merchants having secreted a large quantity. There had been much rout and noise in the town for several weeks. Some stores had been opened by a number of people, and the coffee and sugar carried into the market, and dealt out by pounds. It was rumored that an eminent, wealthy, stingy merchant (who is a bachelor) had a hogshead of coffee in his store, which he refused to sell to the committee under six shillings per pound. A number of females, some say a hundred, some say more, assembled with a cart and trucks, marched down to the warehouse, and demanded the keys, which he refused to deliver. Upon which, one of them seized him by his neck, and tossed him into the cart. Upon his finding no quarter, he delivered the keys, when they tipped up the cart and discharged him; then opened the warehouse, hoisted out the coffee themselves, put it into the truck, and drove off.

It was reported, that he had personal chastisement among them; but this, I believe was not true. A large concourse of men stood amazed, silent spectators of the whole transaction.

Questions

1. What exactly did these women do, and did they do it on their own?
2. Would Gouverneur Morris (Document 6-1) have been surprised by what happened in Boston? Why or why not?
3. Compare the actions these Boston women took with the actions described in Documents 5-7, 5-11, and 6-7. Does it appear that as the Patriot movement progressed into war, women acted more independently? Why or why not?

6-13 Philadelphia Militiamen Seek to Protect Their Rights (1779)

The militiamen of the American Revolution often justifiably complained that they were not being supported adequately (see text pp. 174, 178–179). Just as Continental troops were not always willing merely to accept their plight (see text pp. 187–188), militiamen could demand that they and their families be treated fairly. Militiamen certainly did so in Philadelphia in 1779 during their campaign to regulate prices and to deal with persons who were less than fully committed to the war. As part of their campaign to support the war and receive economic justice, in May 1779 a Philadelphia militia company sent the following memorial to Pennsylvania's president and the Supreme Executive Council (the council was the equivalent of the governor in other states).

Source: In Samuel Hazard, ed., *Pennsylvania Archives*, 1st ser. (Philadelphia, 1853), vol. 7, pp. 392–394.

The Memorial and Petition of the first company of Philadelphia Militia Artillery. . . .

To His Excellency Joseph Reed, Esquire, President, and the Honorable Supreme Executive Council of the Commonwealth of Pennsylvania.

Humbly Sheweth,

That your Petitioners and Memorialists, again call'd out in defence of this State, being ever willing to exert ourselves in behalf of the United States, and this in particular, and to support as much as in us lies, the Virtuous Cause of Freedom and Independency, have once more chearfully stepped forth in obedience to the Laws of our Country, to act in a Military Capacity.

Nevertheless, we humbly beg leave to represent to your Excellency and this Honorable Board, the Circumstances and Grievances attending ourselves and many of our worthy fellow Countreymen, who having uniformly conducted themselves hitherto, are with us, Still determined to exert their utmost Efforts.

In the Month of July, 1776, We were first call'd forth to . . . endeavor to repel the force of a formidable British and Hessian Army then landed, or landing, on Staten Island. We chearfully attended the call, and associated to stem the Current of their violent Determinations to destroy and ravage this Country; at the same time leaving our families at every risque of distress and hardships, and at the mercy of the disaffected, Inimical, or self Interested; and, we might presume to say, the most Obnoxious part of the Community. Upon the return of most of us, (for some died, were killed by accident, or taken prisoners) We found every necessary and convenience of life greatly enhanced in price, and ourselves Caluminated and despised; as having justly merited our loss of Business, etc., by being too forward in takeing an Active part, and bearing Arms. But it was at that time borne with patience, in expectation of redress.

In the month of December following, when the British Army were attempting by crossing the Jersey State to take possession of this City, we were exhorted . . . to turn out again and support the Army of his Excellency, General Washington, with the most Solemn assurance that those who turn'd out might expect to receive satisfaction and redress in the premises, and Delinquents proportionally pay for their refusal. We, with a number of virtuous Citizens and Countrymen, rushed forth, notwithstanding the Inclemency of the Season, and the Services then perform'd, thro' the Assistance of Divine Providence, and the abilities of our Excellent Commander in Chief in the Defeat of the

British and Hessian forces at Trenton and Princeton, are too recent to be recapitulated, and will remain a lasting Memorial of Virtue, Prudence, and Success.

After a Series of Hardships unusual to Citizens in private life, and not common to Soldiers in the Field, we return'd, and found those persons we left behind had again taken Advantage of our Absence, and enormously advanced the prices on every thing; this was encreasing the distress of the Associators [i.e. militia], who were treated at the same time with Indignity and Contempt. We had Arms in our hands, and knew the use of them; but instead of avenging ourselves, or retaliating on our Innate and Worse of Enemies, we patiently waited the Interference of the Legislative Authority. We were amused by the promises of Fines, Penalties, etc., on the Delinquents and that the Virtuous, Voluntary Militia would be put on a respectable Footing; but we cannot help observing, that the Militia are Viewed in the most disrespectful light, and few of the Fines then mentioned, or afterwards enacted, but what were artfully evaded so as not to comply with the true End and Intention of such Imposition.

The Spring, and part of the Summer in the year 1777, pass'd without any Material Circumstances respecting the Militia, except the Law in that Clause provided whereby it was enacted, that Substitutes might be allow'd in Case the rightful Persons did not appear. By this Law, the Designing or disaffected Secur'd themselves by hiring Substitutes, many of whom were not worthy of the Charge as not being Citizens; others deserted, whilst their Employers, by staying behind, were reaping advantage at our Expence, and amassing Fortunes.

Your Petitioners, apart of the Sufferers, (and some of them among the foremost) were, in September and part of October, in the year 1777, in public Service as Militia, station'd at Billingsport, while many of our wives and families were in this City, then in possession of the Enemy. Several have lost their All; and when we return'd (as we

thought) happily to the City last year, Shortly every Article of life or Convenience was rais'd upon us, Eight, ten, or twelve fold at least; and many of us are at a loss to this day what Course or Station of Life to adopt to Support ourselves and Families.

The Honorable House of Assembly during their last session, have been pleas'd to Enact a Supplement to the Militia Law impowering heavy Fines upon Delinquents not forming in Militia, or, when call'd out on service, which we are Convinced was expected to answer the purpose Intended; but when we consider that Men in these Exorbitant Times can acquire more by Monopolizeing, or by an under Trade, in one Day, than will defray all their Expences of Fines or Penalties in a whole year, We humbly presume the Midling and poor will still bear the Burden, and either be totally ruin'd by heavy Fines, or Risque the starving of their Families, whilst themselves are fighting the Battles of those who are Avariciously intent on Amassing Wealth by the Destruction of the more virtuous part of the Community.

These weighty Circumstances being duly considered, Your Petitioners most humbly pray your Excellency and this Honorable Board to state the Facts, and use your Interest with the Honorable House of Assembly at their next Session; either to enact a Law whereby every Delinquent, not turning out in Militia when Legally call'd forth, may be fined in proportion to his Estate; or, otherwise, take of[f] all the Fines and Penalties, and leave it to the Militia who obey the Call to Compell every able bodied Man to join them in some Station, lest when the Militia are call'd forth, by leaving such numbers of Disaffected in their Rear, they, by pursuing their usual Methods, render our Situation worse than making us prisoners of War.

And your Petitioners and Memorialists, as in Duty Bound, will Ever Pray.

Signed at Fort Mifflin, May 12th, 1779.

Questions

1. What rights did the militiamen believe they had?
2. How accurate is it to say that the militiamen embraced the republican ideal as it is described in the textbook (p. 187)?
3. Does the memorial support the analysis and predictions that Gouverneur Morris (Document 6-1) made in 1774? Why or why not?
4. Does the memorial support or challenge the views of Peter Oliver (Document 5-8) about the ordinary people of America? Why or why not?

6-14   Virginia Statute of Religious Freedom (1786)

As the Patriots waged war against Britain to attain political freedom as a nation, they had, as many of the documents in this set illustrate, to deal with the fact that some

Patriots wanted greater freedom at home. This quest for greater freedom could be seen clearly where religion was concerned (see text pp. 192–193). One of the landmarks on the road to true religious freedom in the republic was the Virginia statute of religious liberty, which is reprinted in full here. Thomas Jefferson, who authored the law, considered its enactment one of the three principal achievements of his life.

Source: In William W. Hening, ed., *The Statutes at Large of Virginia*, vol. 12, pp. 84–86.

I. WHEREAS Almighty God hath created the mind free; that all attempts to influence it by temporal punishments or burthens, or by civil incapacitations, tend only to beget habits of hypocrisy and meanness, and are a departure from the plan of the Holy author of our religion, who being Lord both of body and mind, yet chose not to propagate it by coercions on either, as was in his Almighty power to do; that the impious presumption of legislators and rulers, civil as well as ecclesiastical, who being themselves but fallible and uninspired men, have assumed dominion over the faith of others, setting up their own opinions and modes of thinking as the only true and infallible, and as such endeavouring to impose them on others, hath established and maintained false religions over the greatest part of the world, and through all time; that to compel a man to furnish contributions of money for the propagation of opinions which he disbelieves, is sinful and tyrannical; that even the forcing him to support this or that teacher of his own religious persuasion, is depriving him of the comfortable liberty of giving his contributions to the particular pastor, whose morals he would make his pattern, and whose powers he feels most persuasive to righteousness, and is withdrawing from the ministry those temporary rewards, which proceeding from an approbation of their personal conduct, are all additional incitement to earnest and unremitting labours for the instruction of mankind; that our civil rights have no dependence on our religious opinions, any more than our opinions in physics or geometry; that therefore the proscribing any citizen as unworthy the public confidence by laying upon him an incapacity of being called to offices of trust and emolument, unless he profess or renounce this or that religious opinion, is depriving him injuriously of those privileges and advantages to which in common with his fellow-citizens he has a natural right; that it tends only to corrupt the principles of that religion it is meant to encourage, by bribing with a monopoly of worldly honours and emoluments, those who will externally profess and conform to it; that though indeed these are criminal who do not withstand such temptation, yet neither are those innocent who lay the bait in their way; that to suffer the civil magistrate to intrude his powers into the field of opinion, and to restrain the profession or propagation of principles on supposition of their ill tendency, is a dangerous fallacy, which at once destroys all religious liberty, because he being of course judge of that tendency will make his opinions the rule of judgment, and approve or condemn the sentiments of others only as they shall square with or differ from his own; that it is time enough for the rightful purposes of civil government, for its officers to interfere when principles break out into overt acts against peace and good order; and finally, that truth is great and will prevail if left to herself, that she is the proper and sufficient antagonist to error, and has nothing to fear from the conflict, unless by human interposition disarmed of her natural weapons, free argument and debate, errors ceasing to be dangerous when it is permitted freely to contradict them:

II. *Be it enacted by the General Assembly,* That no man shall be compelled to frequent or support any religious worship, place, or ministry whatsoever, nor shall be enforced, restrained, molested, or burthened in his body or goods, nor shall otherwise suffer on account of his religious opinions or belief; but that all men shall be free to profess, and by argument to maintain, their opinion in matters of religion, and that the same shall in no wise diminish, enlarge, or affect their civil capacities.

III. And though we well know that this assembly elected by the people for the ordinary purposes of legislation only, have no power to restrain the acts of succeeding assemblies, constituted with powers equal to our own, and that therefore to declare this act to be irrevocable would be of no effect in law; yet we are free to declare, and do declare, that the rights hereby asserted are of the natural rights of mankind, and that if any act shall be hereafter passed to repeal the present, or to narrow its operation, such act will be an infringement on natural right.

Questions

1. Does the wording of this statute truly guarantee absolute religious freedom? Why or why not?
2. Does this statute echo the Declaration of Independence in any important ways? If so, how?

Questions for Further Thought

1. On the basis of these documents, is it accurate to say that the War of Independence caused major social transformations to occur? Why or why not?
2. Do these documents suggest that Americans truly were trying to make America live up to the philosophical ideals enunciated in the Declaration of Independence? Why or why not?
3. Compare—which also means contrast—what Thomas Paine (Documents 6-3 and 6-5) and Gouverneur Morris (Document 6-1) probably would have said about the actions and developments described in this set of documents. On what would Paine and Morris have agreed? On what would they have disagreed? Why?

CHAPTER 7

The New Political Order 1776–1800

★ ★ ★

Creating New Institutions, 1776–1787

As the authors of the textbook indicate (p. 198), the American Revolution involved two struggles. One was the struggle to win independence from Great Britain; the other was the struggle over who should, and would, build and control America's new political institutions. The inhabitants of Concord, Massachusetts (Document 7-1), made an important contribution to the theory of how a republican constitution should be built. For Patriots who argued that America should put more real power into the hands of the common people (see text pp. 198–200), the Virginia Declaration of Rights (Document 7-2) took on special importance. Not all Patriots had faith in the people. John Adams, as the authors of the textbook stress (pp. 198–200), was one of the influential revolutionary leaders who were not eager to have the common man gain political power. Adams wanted to win independence but did not want to jettison the theory of mixed government in the process. The fight over "who should rule at home" (see text p. 198) was waged almost exclusively by men such as John Adams and the authors of the Virginia Declaration of Rights. However, a few intrepid women stepped forward to argue for or claim what they believed were their rights (see text pp. 200–201). One of those women was Abigail Adams, the wife of John Adams. Although she did so in private letters rather than public pronouncements, Abigail Adams was as willing as John to offer political analysis. In doing so, she explained why she believed that women deserved more rights (see text p. 200 for portraits and an analysis of Abigail and John Adams; see also text p. 201). Document 7-3 gives the spirited exchange between these two American Patriots on the question of women's rights.

The struggle over the establishment of new political institutions extended to creating a central government and deciding how the new nation would govern its western territory. Despite its many problems, the Articles of Confederation government developed an effective system for opening the western United States to settlement (see text pp. 202–203). However, as Document 7-4 illustrates, the opening of this segment of the West came at the expense of native Americans.

7-1 The Concord Town Meeting's Observations on Constitution Making (1776)

Each colony that rebeled against Great Britain faced the question: How they should we go about formulating a constitution for our state (see text p. 198)? In Massachusetts, the house of representatives called for all free males twenty-one and older to meet in their townships to determine whether they wanted to have the state legislature produce a constitution for the new state. While the great majority of townships approved of the plan, a few rejected the idea by calling for a special constitutional convention to create the state's new frame of government. Concord was among that small minority, and its town meeting spelled out the reasons why the convention process should be adopted. Over time, the idea of creating constitutions though special conventions became a hallmark of the American system of government.

Source: The manuscript copy is in Massachusetts Archives, vol. 156, p. 182. This text is from a facsimile copy in the Massachusetts Commission to Compile Information . . . ., *Manual of the Constitutional Convention of 1917* (Boston: 1917).

At a meeting of the Inhabitants of the Town of Concord being free & twenty one years of age and upward, met by adjournment on the twenty first Day of october 1776 to take into Consideration a Resolve of the Honourable house of Representatives of this State on the 17th of September Last the Town Resolved as followes—

Resolve 1st: That this State being at Present destitute of a Properly established form of Government, it is absolutely necessary that one should be emmediatly formed and established.

Resolved 2. That the Supreme Legislative, either in their Proper Capacity or in Joint Committee, are by no means a body proper to form & Establish a Constitution or form of Government; for Reasons following. first Because we Conceive that a Constitution in its Proper Idea intends a System of Principles Established to Secure the Subject in the Possession & enjoyment of their Rights & Privileges, against any Encroachments of the Governing Part. 2—Because the Same Body that forms a Constitution have of Consequence a power to alter it. 3—because a Constitution alterable by the Supreme Legislative is no Security at all to the Subject against any Encroachment of the Governing part on any, or on all of their Rights and priviliges.

Resolved 3d. That it appears to this Town highly necessary & Expedient that a Convention, or Congress be immediately Chosen, to form & establish a Constitution, by the inhabitants of the Respective Towns in this State, being free & of twenty-one years of age and upward, in Proportion as the Representatives of this State formerly were Chosen: the Convention or Congress not to Consist of a greater number than the house of assembly of this State heretofore might Consist of, Except that each Town & District shall have the Liberty to Send one Representative, or otherwise as Shall appear meet to the Inhabitants of this State in General.

Resolve 4th. that when the Convention or Congress have formed a Consitution they adjourn for a Short time and Publish their Proposed Constitution for the Inspection and Remarks of the Inhabitants of this State.

Resolved 5ly. that the honourable house of assembly of this State be Desired to Recommend it to the Inhabitants of the State to Proceed to Chuse a Convention or Congress for the Purpas abovesaid as soon as Possable.

CONCORD, October the 22d, 1776.

Questions

1. The Concord town meeting that formulated this response was not limited to those who could meet the normal property requirements to vote, but the town meeting stated that those requirements should continue to apply in the constitution-making process. Does this seem to match the philosophy of governments "deriving their just powers from the consent of the governed" stated in the Declaration of Independence (p. D-1)?
2. Do the arguments advanced by Concord's town meeting suggest that the inhabitants believed they should defer to their political leaders? Why or why not?
3. According to the town meeting, what specifically is a constitution designed to do? Do you agree with that view? Why or why not?
4. Would the Concord town meeting have approved of the way the national Constitution of 1787 was ratified (see text pp. 210–213)? Why or why not?

7-2   The Virginia Declaration of Rights (1776)

The people of Great Britain and its colonies could look back to the Magna Charta of 1215 as an example of a written guarantee of basic political rights. Moreover, England adopted a Bill of Rights in 1689, and many of the colonies passed laws that amounted to bills of rights. Thus, it was logical that a number of the new Patriot-led governments would formulate statements of what they considered basic rights. The fifth Virginia revolutionary convention was the first to act. Its Declaration of Rights, which was written principally by George Mason and was issued on June 12, 1776, offered a bold vision of how Virginia's—and America's—political system should be built and what that system should do. The democratically inclined men among those who drafted new state constitutions (see text pp. 198–200) often copied sections of this declaration verbatim.

Source: In Francis N. Thorpe, ed., *The Federal and State Constitutions . . . of the United States* (Washington, D.C., U.S. Government Printing Office, 1909), vol. 7, pp. 3812–3814.

A declaration of rights made by the representatives of the good people of Virginia, assembled in full and free convention; which rights do pertain to them and their posterity, as the basis and foundation of government.

SECTION 1. That all men are by nature equally free and independent, and have certain inherent rights, of which, when they enter into a state of society, they cannot, by any compact, deprive or divest their posterity; namely, the enjoyment of life and liberty, with the means of acquiring and possessing property, and pursuing and obtaining happiness and safety.

SEC. 2. That all power is vested in, and consequently derived from, the people; that magistrates are their trustees and servants, and at all times amenable to them.

SEC. 3. That government is, or ought to be, instituted for the common benefit, protection, and security of the people, nation, or community; of all the various modes and forms of government, that is best which is capable of producing the greatest degree of happiness and safety, and is most effectually secured against the danger of maladministration; and that, when any government shall be found inadequate or contrary to these purposes, a majority of the community hath an indubitable, inalienable, and indefeasible right to reform, alter, or abolish it, in such manner as shall be judged most conducive to the public weal.

SEC. 4. That no man, or set of men, are entitled to exclusive or separate emoluments or privileges from the community, but in consideration of public services; which, not being descendible, neither ought the offices of magistrate, legislator, or judge to be hereditary.

SEC. 5 That the legislative and executive powers of the State should be separate and distinct from the judiciary;

and that the members of the two first may be restrained from oppression, by feeling and participating the burdens of the people, they should, at fixed periods, be reduced to a private station, return into that body from which they were originally taken, and the vacancies be supplied by frequent, certain, and regular elections, in which all, or any part of the former members, to be again eligible, or ineligible, as the laws shall direct.

SEC. 6. That elections of members to serve as representatives of the people, in assembly, ought to be free; and that all men, having sufficient evidence of permanent common interest with, and attachment to, the community, have the right of suffrage, and cannot be taxed or deprived of their property for public uses, without their own consent, or that of their representives so elected, nor bound by any law to which they have not, in like manner, assembled, for the public good.

SEC. 7. That all power of suspending laws, or the execution of laws, by any authority, without consent of the representatives of the people, is injurious to their rights, and ought not to be exercised.

SEC. 8. That in all capital or criminal prosecutions a man hath a right to demand the cause and nature of his accusation, to be confronted with the accusers and witnesses, to call for evidence in his favor, and to a speedy trial by an impartial jury of twelve men of his vicinage, without whose unanimous consent he cannot be found guilty; nor can he be compelled to give evidence against himself; that no man be deprived of his liberty, except by the law of the land or the judgment of his peers.

SEC. 9. That excessive bail ought not to be required, nor excessive fines imposed, nor cruel and unusual punishments inflicted.

SEC 10. That general warrants, whereby an officer or messenger may be commanded to search suspected places without evidence of a fact committed, or to seize any person or persons not named, or whose offence is not particularly described and supported by evidence, are grievous and oppressive, and ought not to be granted.

SEC. 11. That in controversies respecting property, and in suits between man and man, the ancient trial by jury is preferable to any other, and ought to be held sacred.

SEC. 12. That the freedom of the press is one of the great bulwarks of liberty, and can never be restrained but by despotic governments.

SEC. 13. That a well-regulated militia, composed of the body of the people, trained to arms, is the proper, natural, and safe defence of a free State; that standing armies, in time of peace, should be avoided, as dangerous to liberty; and that in all cases the military should be under strict subordination to, and governed by, the civil power.

SEC. 14. That the people have a right to uniform government; and, therefore, that no government separate from, or independent of the government of Virginia, ought to be erected or established within the limits thereof.

SEC. 15. That no free government, or the blessings of liberty, can be preserved to any people, but by a firm adherence to justice, moderation, temperance, frugality, and virtue, and by frequent recurrence to fundamental principles.

SEC. 16. That religion, or the duty which we owe to our Creator, and the manner of discharging it, can be directed only by reason and conviction, not by force or violence; and therefore all men are equally entitled to the free exercise of religion, according to the dictates of conscience; and that it is the mutual duty of all to practice Christian forbearance, love, and charity towards each other.

Questions

1. According to the Virginia Declaration of Rights, where does legitimate power come from?
2. According to this declaration, what responsibilities does government have?
3. Compare the Virginia Declaration of Rights with the American Declaration of Independence (see text pp. D-1–D-2). To what extent did Thomas Jefferson draw upon the Virginia Declaration as he framed the American Declaration?

7-3   Abigail and John Adams Debate the Rights of Women (1776)

As the authors of the textbook indicate (p. 200), John Adams was not the only member of the Adams family who thought about the nature of people as well as that of governments. Abigail Adams, the wife of John Adams, was an active Patriot in her own right and kept the family functioning while John was serving in Congress. The two exchanged letters regularly. The following selections are from their correspondence, sections of which are quoted in the textbook to illustrate the issue of women and republicanism (p. 200). These letters reveal Abigail's and John's differing attitudes about the possibility of expanding the rights of women.

Source: In L. H. Butterfield, ed., *Adams Family Correspondence,* 4 vols. (Cambridge, Mass.: Harvard University Press, 1963), vol. 1, pp. 370, 382–383, 402–403; vol. 2, p. 94.

ABIGAIL ADAMS TO JOHN ADAMS, MARCH 31, 1776

I long to hear that you have declared an independency—and by the way in the new Code of Laws which I suppose it will be necessary for you to make I desire you would Remember the Ladies, and be more generous and favourable to them than your ancestors. Do not put such unlimited power into the hands of the Husbands. Remember all Men would be tyrants if they could. If perticuliar care and attention is not paid to the Laidies we are determined to foment a Rebelion, and will not hold ourselves bound by any Laws in which we have no voice, or Representation.

That your Sex are Naturally Tyrannical is a Truth so thoroughly established as to admit of no dispute, but such of you as wish to be happy willingly give up the harsh title of Master for the more tender and endearing one of Friend. Why then, not put it out of the power of the vicious and the Lawless to use us with cruelty and indignity with impunity. Men of Sense in all Ages abhor those customs which treat us only as the vassals of your Sex. Regard us then as Beings placed by providence under your protection and in immitation of the Supreem Being make use of that power only for our happiness. . . .

JOHN ADAMS TO ABIGAIL ADAMS, APRIL 14, 1776

As to your extraordinary Code of Laws, I cannot but laugh. We have been told that our Struggle has loosened the bands of Government every where. That Children and Apprentices were disobedient—that schools and Colledges were grown turbulent—that Indians slighted their Guardians and Negroes grew insolent to their Masters. But your Letter was the first Intimation that another Tribe more numerous and powerfull than all the rest were grown discontented—This is rather too coarse a Compliment but you are so saucy, I wont blot it out.

Depend upon it, We know better than to repeal our Masculine systems. Altho they are in full Force, you know they are little more than Theory. We dare not exert our Power in its full Latitude. We are obliged to go fair, and softly, and in Practice you know We are the subjects. We have only the Name of Masters, and rather than give up this, which would compleatly subject Us to the Despotism of the Peticoat, I hope General Washington, and all our brave Heroes would fight. I am sure every good Politician would plot, as long as he would against Despotism, Empire, Monarchy, Aristocracy, Oligarchy, or Ochlocracy. A

fine Story indeed. I begin to think the Ministry as deep as they are wicked. After stirring up Tories, Landjobbers, Trimmers, Bigots, Canadians, Indians, Negroes, Hanoverians, Hessians, Russians, Irish Roman Catholicks, Scotch Renegadoes, at last they have stimulated the . . . [Ladies?] to demand new Priviledges and threaten to rebell.

ABIGAIL ADAMS TO JOHN ADAMS, MAY 7, 1776

I can not say that I think you very generous to the Ladies, for whilst you are proclaiming peace and good will to Men, Emancipating all Nations, you insist upon retaining an absolute power over Wives. But you must remember that Arbitary power is like most other things which are very hard, very liable to be broken—and notwithstanding all your wise Laws and Maxims we have it in our power not only to free ourselves but to subdue our Masters, and without violence throw both your natural and legal authority at our feet—

"Charm by accepting, by submitting sway
Yet have our Humour most when we obey."

I thank you for several Letters which I have received since I wrote Last. They alleviate a tedious absence, and I long earnestly for a Saturday Evening, and experience a similar pleasure to that which I used to find in the return of my Friend upon that day after a weeks absence. The Idea of a year dissolves all my Phylosophy.

Our Little ones whom you so often recommend to my care and instruction shall not be deficient in virtue or probity if the precepts of a Mother have their desired Effect, but they would be doubly inforced could they be indulged with the example of a Father constantly before them; I often point them to their Sire

"engaged in a corrupted State
Wrestling with vice and faction."

ABIGAIL ADAMS TO JOHN ADAMS, AUGUST 14, 1776

If you complain of neglect of Education in sons, What shall I say with regard to daughters, who every day experience the want of it. With regard to the Education of my own children, I find myself soon out of my debth, and destitute and deficient in every part of Education.

I most sincerely wish that some more liberal plan might be laid and executed for the Benefit of the rising

Generation, and that our new constitution may be distinguished for Learning and Virtue. If we mean to have Heroes, Statesmen and Philosophers, we should have learned women. The world perhaps would laugh at me, and accuse me of vanity, But you I know have a mind too enlarged and liberal to disregard the Sentiment. If much depends as is allowed upon the early Education of youth and the first principals which are instilld take the deepest root, great benifit must arise from litirary accomplishments in women.

Questions

1. Scholars disagree about whether Abigail Adams in the material reprinted here argued that women should have the vote. Do you believe that she said that women should have the vote? What caused you to reach your decision?
2. What specific rights does Abigail Adams argue that women should have?
3. What pragmatic arguments does Abigail Adams advance to support the idea that women should have greater rights? How convincing are her arguments?
4. Does John Adams treat Abigail Adams's suggestions seriously? Why or why not?

7-4   Pachgantschihilas Warns about "The Long Knives" (1781)

John Heckewelder, a Moravian, was born in England in 1743 and moved with his parents to Pennsylvania when he was eleven. As an adult he became an evangelist to the native Americans. In 1818, a year after his death, his *An Account of the History, Manners, and Customs of the Indian Nations* was published. In it he recounted and quoted the close of a 1781 speech delivered by Pachgantschihilas, a noted war chief of the Delaware. Pachgantschihilas was addressing a group of native Americans living in western Pennsylvania who had embraced Christianity and were called Moravian Indians.

When Pachgantschihilas spoke of the *long knives*, he used the term to refer to white people because some white soldiers used swords—literally, long knives. Heckewelder's account of Pachgantschihilas's thoughts and of subsequent events is reprinted here and should be compared with the ideals for western development described in the text (pp. 202–203).

Source: Memoirs of the Historical Society of Pennsylvania (1876), vol. 12, pp. 80–81.

I have given here only a brief specimen of the charges which they exhibit against the white people. There are men among them, who have by heart the whole history of what took place between the whites and the Indians, since the former first came into their country; and relate the whole with ease and with an eloquence not to be imitated. On the tablets of their memories they preserve this record for posterity. I, at one time, in April, 1781, was astonished when I heard one of their orators, a great chief of the Delaware nation, go over this ground, recapitulating the most extraordinary events which had before happened, and concluding in these words: "I admit that there are good white men, but they bear no proportion to the bad; the bad must be the strongest, for they rule. They do what they please. They enslave those who are not of their colour, although created by the same Great Spirit who created us. They would make slaves of us if they could, but as they cannot do it, they kill us! There is no faith to be placed in their words. They are not like the Indians, who are only enemies, while at war, and are friends in peace. They will say to an Indian, 'my friend! my brother!' They will take him by the hand, and at the same moment destroy him. And so you (addressing himself to the Christian Indians) will also be treated by them before long. Remember! that this day I have warned you to beware of such friends as these. I know the *long knives*; they are not to be trusted."

Eleven months after this speech was delivered by this prophetic chief, ninety-six of the same Christian Indians, about sixty of them women and children, were murdered at the place where these very words had been spoken, by the same men he had alluded to, and in the same manner that he had described.

Questions

1. Does Heckewelder seem interested in assuring that the native Americans receive justice? Why or why not?
2. Would Pachgantschihilas say that the Americans believe that the ideals expressed in the Virginia Declaration of Rights (Document 7-2) apply to native Americans? Why or why not?
3. Would Pachgantschihilas say that the Americans believe that the ideals expressed in the Declaration of Independence about the people's equality and "unalienable rights" (see text p. D–1) apply to native Americans? Why or why not?
4. Given Pachgantschihilas's analysis, in what ways, if at all, were native Americans involved in what Carl Becker has called the conflict over "who should rule at home" (see text p. 198)?

Questions for Further Thought

1. The Declaration of Independence proclaims that all people "are created equal." As a group, do the documents in this section suggest that the Patriots believed that all people are created equal? Why or why not?
2. Do the authors of these documents express faith that the average person can be trusted with political power? Why or why not?
3. Considering these documents as a group, what factors do the authors or speakers consider most likely to divide people socially?
4. Considering these documents as a group, what factors do the authors or speakers consider most likely to divide people politically?

The Constitution of 1787

As the textbook indicates (pp. 201–202), the deficiencies of the Articles of Confederation government, which was based on the nation's first federal constitution, were quickly exposed. Despite the achievements of the Confederation Congress in dealing with western lands (see text pp. 202–203), most American analysts agreed that the Articles had to be modified. One of the problems of the Confederation government, as shown most dramatically in Shays's Rebellion in Massachusetts (see text pp. 206–207), was its inability to preserve domestic tranquillity. In Document 7-5, Elbridge Gerry, a Massachusetts delegate to the Constitutional Convention of 1787, explained to his fellow delegates how Shays's Rebellion had influenced his political views. As the authors of the text emphasize (pp. 207–210), because the delegates to the Constitutional Convention differed sharply over many substantive issues, they had to struggle to reach compromises on a number of important points. At the convention Benjamin Franklin, the oldest and one of the most respected members, assessed both the importance of that spirit of compromise and what it might mean for the nation (Document 7-6).

James Madison, the chief architect of the Constitution of 1787 (see text pp. 208–209), joined in the public effort to explain and defend that document when he became one of the major authors of the series of essays called *The Federalist* (see text p. 211). As indicated in the text (p. 211), it was in *The Federalist*, No. 10, that Madison spelled out why the Constitution would work in a large republic. That essay, the most frequently cited one in *The Federalist*, is reprinted in its entirety as Document 7-7. Madison and his political allies did not have an easy task getting the Constitution adopted. As the authors of the textbook stress (pp. 210–213), the Constitution was a controversial document; a firestorm of protest erupted because it lacked a Bill of Rights. The Constitution barely won approval, and the promise that a guarantee of rights would be added to it was essential to gaining that approval. Document 7-8 shows why the question of a Bill of Rights proved so important and indicates the kinds of changes Antifederalists wanted to make in the Constitution itself.

7-5   Elbridge Gerry Warns the Delegates about Leveling (1787)

Shays's Rebellion (see text pp. 206–207) horrified most Americans. It seemed to demonstrate how impotent the federal government was and how easily the Union might slip into chaos. However, for many Americans Shays's Rebellion also signaled the need to reassess the nature of the American experiment with democracy. That certainly was the case for Elbridge Gerry, a delegate from Massachusetts to the Constitutional Convention. Gerry, a prominent Massachusetts Patriot, had signed the Declaration of Independence and served in the Confederation Congress. On May 31, 1787, during the Constitutional Convention's deliberations about allowing the people to elect members of the U. S. Senate directly, Gerry told his fellow delegates what Shays's Rebellion meant to him.

Source: In Max Farrand, ed., *The Records of the Federal Convention of 1787*, rev. ed., vol. 1, pp. 48, 50. Copyright © 1911 by Yale University Press. Reprinted by permission.

Mr Gerry. The evils we experience flow from the excess of democracy. The people do not want virtue; but are the dupes of pretended patriots. In Massts. it has been fully confirmed by experience that they are daily misled into the most baneful measures and opinions by the false reports circulated by designing men, and which no one on the spot can refute. One principal evil arises from the want of due provision for those employed in the administration of Governnt. It would seem to be a maxim of democracy to starve the public servants. He mentioned the popular clamour in Massts. for the reduction of salaries and the attack made on that of the Govr. though secured by the spirit of the Constitution itself. He had he said been too republican

heretofore: he was still however republican, but had been taught by experience the danger of the levilling spirit. . . .

Mr Gerry [said he] did not like the election by the people. The maxims taken from the British constitution were often fallacious when applied to our situation which was extremely different. Experience he said had shewn that the State Legislatures drawn immediately from the people did not always possess their confidence. He had no objection however to an election by the people if it were so qualified that men of honor and character might not be unwilling to be joined in the appointments. He seemed to think the people might nominate a certain number out of which the State legislatures should be bound to choose.

Questions

1. According to Gerry, what kind of problems produced the dissatisfaction that burst forth in Shays's Rebellion?

2. According to Gerry, who caused Shays's Rebellion?
3. If one defines democracy as allowing the average person to exercise real political power, would you describe Gerry as a supporter of democracy? Why or why not?

7-6 Benjamin Franklin on Compromise and the Future (1787)

Because of partisan wrangling in Pennsylvania, Benjamin Franklin was not originally selected to attend the Constitutional Convention. His addition to the state's delegation added luster to it and to the convention. At age eighty-one Franklin was the oldest delegate and was recognized as a symbol of American virtue. Franklin attended the convention regularly but rarely spoke during the debates. Many of the major provisions he wanted—a single legislative chamber, an executive board, and no salaries for executives of the government—did not find their way into the Constitution drafted in Philadelphia. Therefore, when he addressed the issue of compromise on September 17, 1787, the last day of the convention, Franklin had good reasons for doing so. Later that day he commented on the nation's prospects for success under the proposed new government (see text p. 210). The following account of Franklin's views comes from the record kept by James Madison.

Source: In Max Farrand, ed., *The Records of the Federal Convention of 1787*, rev. ed., vol. 2, pp. 641–643, 648. Copyright © 1911 by Yale University Press. Reprinted by permission.

MONDAY SEPR. 17. 1787. IN CONVENTION

The engrossed Constitution being read,

Docr. Franklin rose with a speech in his hand, which he had reduced to writing for his own conveniency, and which Mr. Wilson read in the words following.

Mr President

I confess that there are several parts of this constitution which I do not at present approve, but I am not sure I shall never approve them: For having lived long, I have experienced many instances of being obliged by better information or fuller consideration, to change opinions even on important subjects, which I once thought right, but found to be otherwise. It is therefore that the older I grow, the more apt I am to doubt my own judgment, and to pay more respect to the judgment of others. Most men indeed as well as most sects in Religion, think themselves in possession of all truth, and that whereever others differ from them it is so far error. Steele, a Protestant in a Dedication tells the Pope, that the only difference between our Churches in their opinions of the certainty of their doctrines is, the Church of Rome is infallible and the Church of England is never in the wrong. But though many private persons think almost as highly of their own infallibility as of that of their sect, few express it so naturally as a certain french lady, who in a dispute with her sister, said "I don't know how it happens, Sister but I meet with no body but myself, that's always in the right"—*Il n'y a que moi qui a toujours raison."*

In these sentiments, Sir, I agree to this Constitution with all its faults, if they are such; because I think a general Government necessary for us, and there is no form of Government but what may be a blessing to the people if well administered, and believe farther that this is likely to be well administered for a course of years, and can only end in Despotism, as other forms have done before it, when the people shall become so corrupted as to need despotic Government, being incapable of any other. I doubt too whether any other Convention we can obtain may be able to make a better Constitution. For when you assemble a number of men to have the advantage of their joint wisdom, you inevitably assemble with those men, all their prejudices, their passions, their errors of opinion, their local interests, and their selfish views. From such an Assembly can a perfect production be expected? It therefore astonishes me, Sir, to find this system approaching so near to perfection as it does; and I think it will astonish our enemies, who are waiting with confidence to hear that our councils are confounded like those of the Builders of Babel; and that our States are on the point of separation, only to meet hereafter for the purpose of cutting one another's throats. Thus I consent, Sir, to this Constitution because I expect no better, and because I am not sure, that it is not the best. The opinions I have had of its errors, I sacrifice to the public good— I have never whispered a syllable of them abroad— Within these walls they were born, and here they shall die— If every one of us in returning to our Constituents were to report the objections he has had to it, and endeavor to gain partizans in support of them, we might prevent its being generally received, and thereby lose all the salutary effects and great advantages resulting naturally in our favor among foreign Nations as well as among ourselves, from our real or apparent unanimity. Much of the strength and efficiency of any Government in procuring and securing happiness to the people, depends on opinion, on the general opinion of the goodness of the Government, as well . . . as of the wisdom and integrity of its Governors. I hope therefore that for our own sakes as a part of the people, and for the sake of posterity, we shall act heartily and unanimously in recommending this Constitution (if approved by Congress and confirmed by the Conventions) wherever our influence may extend, and turn our future thoughts and endeavors to the means of having it well administered.

On the whole, Sir, I cannot help expressing a wish that every member of the Convention who may still have objections to it, would with me, on this occasion doubt a little of his own infallibility—and to make manifest our unanimity, put his name to this instrument.

[Later, as the members were signing the Constitution, said Madison, the following occurred.]

Whilst the last members were signing it Doctr. Franklin looking towards the Presidents Chair, at the back of which a rising sun happened to be painted, observed to a few members near him, that Painters had found it difficult to distinguish in their art a rising from a setting sun. I have, said he, often and often in the course of the Session, and the vicissitudes of my hopes and fears as to its issue, looked at that behind the President without being able to tell whether it was rising or setting: But now at length I have the happiness to know that it is a rising and not a setting Sun.

Questions

1. What reasons did Franklin give for asking the delegates to vote for the Constitution?
2. Do you find Franklin's reasons for voting for the Constitution convincing? Why or why not?
3. Do you find Franklin's reference to the movements of the sun powerful image? Why or why not?

7-7   James Madison, *The Federalist*, No. 10 (1787)

Having compromised enough to produce a new Constitution in 1787 (see text pp. 208–210), its advocates had to persuade the American people to adopt it. That proved difficult (see text pp. 210–213). As part of the effort to win support for the Constitution in the crucial state of New York, James Madison, Alexander Hamilton, and John Jay wrote a series of essays published between October 27, 1787, and May 28, 1788 (see text p. 211). Scholars now generally agree that these essays, collectively known as *The Federalist*, probably did not play a significant role in persuading New Yorkers to accept the Constitution. Nevertheless, scholars also agree that *The Federalist* is essential for those who want to understand the thinking of the men who wrote the Constitution (see text p. 211). Madison, obviously one of the most important of the framers (see text pp. 208–209), penned *The Federalist*, No. 10, the most widely cited essay in the series. This essay is reprinted here in its entirety.

Source: New-York Daily Advertiser, November 22, 1787.

THE FEDERALIST. NO. X.

To the People of the State of New-York.

Among the numerous advantages promised by a well constructed Union, none deserves to be more accurately developed than its tendency to break and control the violence of faction. The friend of popular governments, never finds himself so much alarmed for their character and fate, as when he contemplates their propensity to this dangerous vice. He will not fail therefore to set a due value on any plan which, without violating the principles to which he is attached, provides a proper cure for it. The instability, injustice and confusion introduced into the public councils, have in truth been the mortal diseases under which popular governments have every where perished; as they continue to be the favorite and fruitful topics from which the adversaries to liberty derive their most specious declamations. The valuable improvements made by the American Constitutions on the popular models, both ancient and modern, cannot certainly be too much admired; but it would be an unwarrantable partiality, to contend that they have as effectually obviated the danger on this side as was wished and expected. Complaints are every where heard from our most considerate and virtuous citizens, equally the friends of public and private faith, and of public and personal liberty; that our governments are too unstable; that the public good is disregarded in the conflicts of rival parties; and that measures are too often decided, not according to the rules of justice, and the rights of the minor party; but by the superior force of an interested and overbearing majority. However anxiously we may wish that these complaints had no foundation, the evidence of known facts will not permit us to deny that they are in some degree true. It will be found indeed, on a candid review of our situation, that some of the distresses under which we labor, have been erroneously charged on the operation of our governments; but it will be found, at the same time, that other causes will not alone account for many of our heaviest misfortunes; and particularly, for that prevailing and increasing distrust of public engagements, and alarm for private rights, which are echoed from one end of the continent to the other. These must be chiefly, if not wholly, effects of the unsteadiness and injustice, with which a factious spirit has tainted our public administration.

By a faction I understand a number of citizens, whether amounting to a majority or minority of the whole, who are united and actuated by some common impulse of passion, or of interest, adverse to the rights of other citizens, or to the permanent and aggregate interests of the community.

There are two methods of curing the mischiefs of faction: the one, by removing its causes; the other, by controlling its effects.

There are again two methods of removing the causes of faction: the one by destroying the liberty which is essential to its existence; the other, by giving to every citizen the same opinions, the same passions, and the same interests.

It could never be more truly said than of the first remedy, that it is worse than the disease. Liberty is to faction, what air is to fire, an aliment without which it instantly expires. But it could not be a less folly to abolish liberty, which is essential to political life, because it nourishes faction, than it would be to wish the annihilation of air, which is essential to animal life, because it imparts to fire its destructive agency.

The second expedient is as impracticable, as the first would be unwise. As long as the reason of man continues fallible, and he is at liberty to exercise it, different opinions will be formed. As long as the connection subsists between his reason and his self-love, his opinions and his passions will have a reciprocal influence on each other; and the former will be objects to which the latter will attach themselves. The diversity in the faculties of men from which the rights of property originate, is not less an insuperable obstacle to a uniformity of interests. The protection of these faculties is the first object of Government. From the protection of different and unequal faculties of acquiring property, the possession of different degrees and kinds of property immediately results: and from the influence of these on the sentiments and views of the respective proprietors, ensues a division of the society into different interests and parties.

The latent causes of faction are thus sown in the nature of man; and we see them every where brought into different degrees of activity, according to the different circumstances of civil society. A zeal for different opinions concerning religion, concerning Government, and many other points, as well of speculation as of practice; an attachment to different leaders ambitiously contending for pre-eminence and power; or to persons of other descriptions whose fortunes have been interesting to the human passions, have in turn divided mankind into parties, inflamed them with mutual animosity, and rendered them much more disposed to vex and oppress each other, than to co-operate for their common good. So strong is this propensity of mankind to fall into mutual animosities, that where no substantial occasion presents itself, the most frivolous and fanciful distinctions have been sufficient to kindle their unfriendly passions, and excite their most violent conflicts. But the most common and durable source of factions, has been the various and unequal distribution of property. Those who hold, and those who are without property, have ever formed distinct interests in society. Those who are creditors, and those who are debtors, fall under a like discrimination. A landed interest, a manufacturing interest, a mercantile interest, a monied interest, with many lesser interests, grow up of necessity in civilized nations, and divide them into different classes, actuated by different sentiments and views. The regulation of these various and interfering interests forms the principal task of modern Legislation, and involves the spirit of party and faction in the necessary and ordinary operations of Government.

No man is allowed to be a judge in his own cause; because his interest would certainly bias his judgment, and, not improbably, corrupt his integrity. With equal, nay with greater reason, a body of men, are unfit to be both judges and parties, at the same time; yet, what are many of the most important acts of legislation, but so many judicial determinations, not indeed concerning the rights of single persons, but concerning the rights of large bodies of citizens; and what are the different classes of legislators, but advocates and parties to the causes which they determine? Is a law proposed concerning private debts? It is a question to which the creditors are parties on one side, and the debtors on the other. Justice ought to hold the balance between them. Yet the parties are and must be themselves the judges; and the most numerous party, or, in other words, the most powerful faction must be expected to prevail. Shall domestic manufactures be encouraged, and in what degree, by restrictions on foreign manufactures? are questions which would be differently decided by the landed and the manufacturing classes; and probably by neither, with a sole regard to justice and the public good. The apportionment of taxes on the various descriptions of property, is an act which seems to require the most exact impartiality; yet there is perhaps no legislative act in which greater opportunity and temptation are given to a predominant party, to trample on the rules of justice. Every shilling with which they over-burden the inferior number, is a shilling saved to their own pockets.

It is in vain to say, that enlightened statesmen will be able to adjust these clashing interests, and render them all subservient to the public good. Enlightened statesmen will not always be at the helm: Nor, in many cases, can such an adjustment be made at all, without taking into view indirect and remote considerations, which will rarely prevail over the immediate interest which one party may find in disregarding the rights of another, or the good of the whole.

The inference to which we are brought, is, that the *causes* of faction cannot be removed; and that relief is only to be sought in the means of controling its *effects*.

If a faction consists of less than a majority, relief is supplied by the republican principle, which enables the majority to defeat its sinister views by regular vote: It may clog the administration, it may convulse the society; but it will be unable to execute and mask its violence under the forms of the Constitution. When a majority is included in a faction, the form of popular government on the other hand enables it to sacrifice to its ruling passion or interest, both the public good and the rights of other citizens. To secure the public good, and private rights, against the danger of such a faction, and at the same time to preserve the spirit and the form of popular government, is then the great object to which our enquiries are directed: Let me add that it is the great desideratum, by which alone this form of government can be rescued from the opprobrium under which it has so long labored, and be recommended to the esteem and adoption of mankind.

By what means is this object attainable? Evidently by one of two only. Either the existence of the same passion or interest in a majority at the same time, must be prevented; or the majority, having such co-existent passion or interest, must be rendered, by their number and local situation, unable to concert and carry into effect schemes of oppression. If the impulse and the opportunity be suffered to coincide, we well know that neither moral nor religious motives can be relied on as an adequate control. They are not found to be such on the injustice and violence of individuals, and lose their efficacy in proportion to the number combined together; that is, in proportion as their efficacy becomes needful.

From this view of the subject, it may be concluded, that a pure Democracy, by which I mean, a Society, consisting of a small number of citizens, who assemble and administer the Government in person, can admit of no cure for the mischiefs of faction. A common passion or interest will, in almost every case, be felt by a majority of the whole; a communication and concert results from the form of Government itself; and there is nothing to check the inducements to sacrifice the weaker party, or an obnoxious individual. Hence it is, that such Democracies have ever been spectacles of turbulence and contention; have ever been found incompatible with personal security, or the rights of property; and have in general been as short in their lives, as they have been violent in their deaths. Theoretic politicians, who have patronized this species of Government, have erroneously supposed, that by reducing mankind to a perfect equality in their political rights, they would, at the same time, be perfectly equalized and assimilated in their possessions, their opinions, and their passions.

A Republic, by which I mean a Government in which the scheme of representation takes place, opens a different prospect, and promises the cure for which we are seeking. Let us examine the points in which it varies from pure Democracy, and we shall comprehend both the nature of the cure, and the efficacy which it must derive from the Union.

The two great points of difference between a Democracy and a Republic are, first, the delegation of the Government, in the latter, to a small number of citizens elected by the rest: secondly, the greater number of citizens, and greater sphere of country, over which the latter may be extended.

The effect of the first difference is, on the one hand to refine and enlarge the public views, by passing them through the medium of a chosen body of citizens, whose wisdom may best discern the true interest of their country, and whose patriotism and love of justice, will be least likely to sacrifice it to temporary or partial considerations. Under such a regulation, it may well happen that the public voice pronounced by the representatives of the people, will be more consonant to the public good, than if pronounced by the people themselves convened for the purpose. On the other hand, the effect may be inverted. Men of factious tempers, of local prejudices, or of sinister designs, may by intrigue, by corruption or by other means, first obtain the suffrages, and then betray the interests of the people. The question resulting is, whether small or extensive Republics are most favorable to the election of proper guardians of the public weal; and it is clearly decided in favor of the latter by two obvious considerations.

In the first place it is to be remarked that however small the Republic may be, the Representatives must be raised to a certain number, in order to guard against the cabals of a few; and that however large it may be, they must be limited to a certain number, in order to guard against the confusion of a multitude. Hence the number of Representatives in the two cases, not being in proportion to that of the Constituents, and being proportionally greatest in the small Republic, it follows, that if the proportion of fit characters, be not less, in the large than in the small Republic, the former will present a greater option, and consequently a greater probability of a fit choice.

In the next place, as each Representative will be chosen by a greater number of citizens in the large than in the small Republic, it will be more difficult for unworthy candidates to practise with success the vicious arts, by which elections are too often carried; and the suffrages of the people being more free, will be more likely to centre on men who possess the most attractive merit, and the most diffusive and established characters.

It must be confessed, that in this, as in most other cases, there is a mean, on both sides of which inconveniencies will be found to lie. By enlarging too much the number of electors, you render the representative too little acquainted with all their local circumstances and lesser interests; as by reducing it too much, you render him unduly attached to these, and too little fit to comprehend and pursue great and national objects. The Federal Constitution forms a happy combination in this respect; the great and aggregate interests being referred to the national, the local and particular, to the state legislatures.

The other point of difference is, the greater number of citizens and extent of territory which may be brought within the compass of Republican, than of Democratic Government; and it is this circumstance principally which renders factious combinations less to be dreaded in the former, than in the latter. The smaller the society, the fewer probably will be the distinct parties and interests composing it; the fewer the distinct parties and interests, the more frequently will a majority be found of the same party; and the smaller the number of individuals composing a majority, and the smaller the compass within which they are placed, the more easily will they concert and execute their plans of oppression. Extend the sphere, and you take in a greater variety of parties and interests; you make it less probable that a majority of the whole will have a common motive to invade the rights of other citizens; or if such a common motive exists, it will be more difficult for all who feel it to discover their own strength, and to act in unison with each other. Besides other impediments, it may be remarked, that where there is a consciousness of unjust or dishonorable purposes, communication is always checked by distrust, in proportion to the number whose concurrence is necessary.

Hence it clearly appears, that the same advantage, which a Republic has over a Democracy, in controling the effects of faction, is enjoyed by a large over a small Republic—is enjoyed by the Union over the States composing it. Does this advantage consist in the substitution of Representatives, whose enlightened views and virtuous sentiments render them superior to local prejudices, and to schemes of injustice? It will not be denied, that the Representation of the Union will be most likely to possess these requisite endowments. Does it consist in the greater security afforded by a greater variety of parties, against the event of any one party being able to outnumber and oppress the rest? In an equal degree does the encreased variety of parties, comprised within the Union, encrease this security. Does it, in fine, consist in the greater obstacles opposed to the concert and accomplishment of the secret wishes of an unjust and interested majority? Here, again, the extent of the Union gives it the most palpable advantage.

The influence of factious leaders may kindle a flame within their particular States, but will be unable to spread a general conflagration through the other States: a religious sect, may degenerate into a political faction in a part of the Confederacy; but the variety of sects dispersed over the entire face of it, must secure the national Councils against any danger from that source: a rage for paper money, for an abolition of debts, for an equal division of property, or for any other improper or wicked project, will be less apt to pervade the whole body of the Union, than a particular member of it; in the same proportion as such a malady is more likely to taint a particular county or district, than an entire State.

In the extent and proper structure of the Union, therefore, we behold a Republican remedy for the diseases most incident to Republican Government. And according to the degree of pleasure and pride, we feel in being Republicans, ought to be our zeal in cherishing the spirit, and supporting the character of Federalists.

Questions

1. According to Madison, what causes "factions" to develop?
2. According to Madison, why are factions dangerous?
3. Given his assessment of how factions develop, can Madison be called an economic determinist? Why or why not?
4. If one believes in a democratic-style republic, why, according to Madison, is it logical to want to have a physically large nation? Do you agree or disagree? Why?
5. On the basis of *The Federalist*, No. 10, would you describe Madison as a democrat? Why or why not?

7-8 Virginia Proposes Amendments to the Constitution (1788)

As indicated in the textbook (pp. 210–211), Americans who opposed the Constitution created in 1787 were afraid that it was designed to produce rule by the elite and that the elite would establish a tyranny. Opponents of the proposed Constitution, who were cleverly and misleadingly labeled "Antifederalists" by its supporters (see text pp. 210–211), considered the fact that the proposed Constitution lacked a Bill of Rights an especially dangerous sign. In the hard-fought battles that ended in the adoption of the Constitution, persons who styled themselves Federalists were able to succeed only by promising to amend the document to include a Bill of Rights (see text pp. 211–213). The following statement issued by the Virginia Ratifying Convention on June 27, 1788, explains the rationale of advocates for a Bill of Rights. It also provides the fullest single list of the kinds of changes—amendments—most Antifederalists wanted.

Source: In Jonathan Elliot, ed., *Debates in the Several State Conventions on the Adoption of the Federal Constitution . . . in 1787*, 2d. ed. (1881), vol. 3, pp. 657–661.

Mr. WYTHE reported, from the committee appointed, such *amendments* to the proposed Constitution of government for the United States as were by them deemed necessary to be recommended to the consideration of the Congress which shall first assemble under the said Constitution, to be acted upon according to the mode prescribed in the 5th article thereof; and he read the same in his place, and afterwards delivered them in at the clerk's table, where the same were again read, and are as follows:

—"That there be a declaration or bill of rights asserting, and securing from encroachment, the essential and unalienable rights of the people, in some such manner as the following:—

"1st. That there are certain natural rights, of which men, when they form a social compact, cannot deprive or divest their posterity; among which are the enjoyment of life and liberty, with the means of acquiring, possessing, and protecting property, and pursuing and obtaining happiness and safety.

"2d. That all power is naturally invested in, and consequently derived from, the people; that magistrates therefore are their *trustees* and *agents,* at all times amenable to them.

"3d. That government ought to be instituted for the common benefit, protection, and security of the people; and that the doctrine of non-resistance against arbitrary power and oppression is absurd, slavish, and destructive to the good and happiness of mankind.

"4th. That no man or set of men are entitled to separate or exclusive public emoluments or privileges from the community, but in consideration of public services, which not being descendible, neither ought the offices of magistrate, legislator, or judge, or any other public office, to be hereditary.

"5th. That the legislative, executive, and judicial powers of government should be separate and distinct; and, that the members of the two first may be restrained from oppression by feeling and participating the public burdens, they should, at fixed periods, be reduced to a private station, return into the mass of the people, and the vacancies be supplied by certain and regular elections, in which all or any part of the former members to be eligible or ineligible, as the rules of the Constitution of government, and the laws, shall direct.

"6th. That the elections of representatives in the legislature ought to be free and frequent, and all men having sufficient evidence of permanent common interest with, and attachment to, the community, ought to have the right of suffrage; and no aid, charge, tax, or fee, can be set, rated, or levied, upon the people without their own consent, or that of their representatives, so elected; nor can they be bound by any law to which they have not, in like manner, assented, for the public good.

"7th. That all power of suspending laws, or the execution of laws, by any authority, without the consent of the representatives of the people in the legislature, is injurious to their rights, and ought not to be exercised.

"8th. That, in all criminal and capital prosecutions, a man hath a right to demand the cause and nature of his accusation, to be confronted with the accusers and witnesses, to call for evidence, and be allowed counsel in his favor, and to a fair and speedy trial by an impartial jury of his vicinage, without whose unanimous consent he cannot be found guilty, (except in the government of the land and naval forces;) nor can he be compelled to give evidence against himself.

"9th. That no freeman ought to be taken, imprisoned, or disseized of his freehold, liberties, privileges, or franchises, or outlawed, or exiled, or in any manner destroyed, or deprived of his life, liberty, or property, but by the law of the land.

"10th. That every freeman restrained of his liberty is entitled to a remedy, to inquire into the lawfulness thereof, and to remove the same, if unlawful, and that such remedy ought not to be denied nor delayed.

"11th. That, in controversies respecting property, and in suits between man and man, the ancient trial by jury is one of the greatest securities to the rights of the people, and to remain sacred and inviolable.

"12th. That every freeman ought to find a certain remedy, by recourse to the laws, for all injuries and wrongs he may receive in his person, property, or character. He ought to obtain right and justice freely, without sale, completely and without denial, promptly and without delay; and that all establishments or regulations contravening these rights are oppressive and unjust.

"13th. That excessive bail ought not to be required, nor excessive fines imposed, nor cruel and unusual punishments inflicted.

"14th. That every freeman has a right to be secure from all unreasonable searches and seizures of his person, his papers, and property; all warrants, therefore, to search suspected places, or seize any freeman, his papers, or property, without information on oath (or affirmation of a person religiously scrupulous of taking an oath) of legal and sufficient cause, are grievous and oppressive; and all general warrants to search suspected places, or to apprehend any suspected person, without specially naming or describing the place or person, are dangerous, and ought not to be granted.

"15th. That the people have a right peaceably to assemble together to consult for the common good, or to instruct their representatives; and that every freeman has a right to petition or apply to the legislature for redress of grievances.

"16th. That the people have a right to freedom of speech, and of writing and publishing their sentiments; that the freedom of the press is one of the greatest bulwarks of liberty, and ought not to be violated.

"17th. That the people have a right to keep and bear arms; that a well-regulated militia, composed of the body of the people trained to arms, is the proper, natural, and safe defence of a free state; that standing armies, in time of peace, are dangerous to liberty, and therefore ought to be avoided, as far as the circumstances and protection of the community will admit; and that, in all cases, the military should be under strict subordination to, and governed by, the civil power.

"18th. That no soldier in time of peace ought to be quartered in any house without the consent of the owner, and in time of war in such manner only as the law directs.

"19th. That any person religiously scrupulous of bearing arms ought to be exempted, upon payment of an equivalent to employ another to bear arms in his stead.

"20th. That religion, or the duty which we owe to our Creator, and the manner of discharging it, can be directed only by reason and conviction, not by force or violence; and therefore all men have an equal, natural, and unalienable right to the free exercise of religion, according to the dictates of conscience, and that no particular religious sect or society ought to be favored or established, by law, in preference to others."

AMENDMENTS TO THE CONSTITUTION

"1st. That each state in the Union shall respectively retain every power, jurisdiction, and right, which is not by this Constitution delegated to the Congress of the United States, or to the departments of the federal government.

"2d. That there shall be one representative for every thirty thousand, according to the enumeration or census mentioned in the Constitution, until the whole number of representatives amounts to two hundred; after which, that number shall be continued or increased, as Congress shall direct, upon the principles fixed in the Constitution, by apportioning the representatives of each state to some greater number of people, from time to time, as population increases.

"3d. When the Congress shall lay direct taxes or excises, they shall immediately inform the executive power of each state, of the quota of such state, according to the census herein directed, which is proposed to be thereby raised; and if the legislature of any state shall pass a law which shall be effectual for raising such quota at the time required by Congress, the taxes and excises laid by Congress shall not be collected in such state.

"4th. That the members of the Senate and House of Representatives shall be ineligible to, and incapable of holding, any civil office under the authority of the United States, during the time for which they shall respectively be elected.

"5th. That the journals of the proceedings of the Senate and House of Representatives shall be published at least once in every year, except such parts thereof, relating to treaties, alliances, or military operations, as in their judgment, require secrecy.

"6th. That a regular statement and account of the receipts and expenditures of public money shall be published at least once a year.

"7th. That no commercial treaty shall be ratified without the concurrence of two thirds of the whole number of the members of the Senate; and no treaty ceding, contracting, restraining, or suspending, the territorial rights or claims of the United States, or any of them, or their, or any of their rights or claims to fishing in the American seas, or navigating the American rivers, shall be made, but in cases of the most urgent and extreme necessity; nor shall any such treaty be ratified without the concurrence of three fourths of the whole number of the members of both houses respectively.

"8th. That no navigation law, or law regulating commerce, shall be passed without the consent of two thirds of the members present, in both houses.

"9th. That no standing army, or regular troops, shall be raised, or kept up, in time of peace, without the consent of two thirds of the members present, in both houses.

"10th. That no soldier shall be enlisted for any longer term than four years, except in time of war, and then for no longer term than the continuance of the war.

"11th. That each state respectively shall have the power to provide for organizing, arming, and disciplining its own militia, whensoever Congress shall omit or neglect to provide for the same. That the militia shall not be subject to martial law, except when in actual service, in time of war, invasion, or rebellion; and when not in the actual service of the United States, shall be subject only to such fines, penalties, and punishments, as shall be directed or inflicted by the laws of its own state.

"12th. That the exclusive power of legislation given to Congress over the federal town and its adjacent district, and other places, purchased or to be purchased by Congress of any of the states, shall extend only to such regulations as respect the police and good government thereof.

"13th. That no person shall be capable of being President of the United States for more than eight years in any term of sixteen years.

"14th. That the judicial power of the United States

shall be vested in one Supreme Court, and in such courts of admiralty as Congress may from time to time ordain and establish in any of the different states. The judicial power shall extend to all cases in law and equity arising under treaties made, or which shall be made, under the authority of the United States; to all cases affecting ambassadors, other foreign ministers, and consuls; to all cases of admiralty and maritime jurisdiction; to controversies to which the United States shall be a party; to controversies between two or more states, and between parties claiming lands under the grants of different states. In all cases affecting ambassadors, other foreign ministers, and consuls, and those in which a state shall be a party, the Supreme Court shall have original jurisdiction; in all other cases before mentioned, the Supreme Court shall have appellate jurisdiction, as to matters of law only, except in cases of equity, and of admiralty, and maritime jurisdiction, in which the Supreme Court shall have appellate jurisdiction both as to law and fact, with such exceptions and under such regulations as the Congress shall make: but the judicial power of the United States shall extend to no case where the cause of action shall have originated before the ratification of the Constitution, except in disputes between states about their territory, disputes between persons claiming lands under the grants of different states, and suits for debts due to the United States.

"15th. That, in criminal prosecutions no man shall be restrained in the exercise of the usual and accustomed right of challenging or excepting to the jury.

"16th. That Congress shall not alter, modify, or interfere in the times, places, or manner of holding elections for senators and representatives, or either of them, except when the legislature of any state shall neglect, refuse, or be disabled, by invasion or rebellion, to prescribe the same.

"17th. That those clauses which declare that Congress shall not exercise certain powers, be not interpreted, in any manner whatsoever, to extend the powers of Congress; but that they be construed either as making exceptions to the specified powers where this shall be the case, or otherwise, as inserted merely for greater caution.

"18th. That the laws ascertaining the compensation of senators and representatives for their services, be postponed, in their operation, until after the election of representatives immediately succeeding the passing thereof; that excepted which shall first be passed on the subject.

"19th. That some tribunal other than the Senate be provided for trying impeachments of senators.

"20th. That the salary of a judge shall not be increased or diminished during his continuance in office, otherwise than by general regulations of salary, which may take place on a revision of the subject at stated periods of not less than seven years, to commence from the time such salaries shall be first ascertained by Congress."

Questions

1. Do the Virginia Convention's proposed amendments show that that state was trying to live up to the Virginia Declaration of Rights (Document 7-2)? Why or why not?

2. Compare these proposed amendments with the Bill of Rights adopted in 1791 (see text pp. D-12–D-13). If Virginia's proposed amendments had been adopted, would the Constitution have been radically different? Why or why not?

3. Given what you know from Documents 7-5 through 7-7 and from the textbook (especially pp. 201–202, 206–210), which of the amendments would the Federalists have fairly readily accepted? Why?

4. Given what you know from Documents 7-5 through 7-7 and from the textbook (especially, pp. 201–202, 206–210), which of the amendments would the Federalists have adamantly refused to accept? Why?

Questions for Further Thought

1. Do these documents demonstrate that the Articles of Confederation government was so defective that it had to be replaced rather than revised? Why or why not?

2. As a group, do these documents suggest that fear of democracy was an important force in the movement for and creation of the 1787 Constitution? Why or why not?

3. As Documents 6-3 and 6-5 illustrate, Thomas Paine invoked idealism in championing the drive for American independence. Do these documents also emphasize idealism? Why or why not?

4. Based on these documents, is it accurate to depict the framers of the Constitution as like-minded political thinkers? Why or why not?

The Political Crisis of the 1790s

With the adoption of the Constitution and the addition of a Bill of Rights (see text p. 214), America's political problems changed but did not disappear. The financial difficulties that had bedeviled the Confederation government still existed. Alexander Hamilton—talented, ambitious, and aristocratically inclined—was determined to confront those problems boldly (see text pp. 214–218). As the authors of the text indicate (pp. 214–218), Hamilton successfully worked to restore the public credit in a way that benefited financial speculators and "monied men". Document 7-9 does not cover the intricacies of Hamilton's financial program; instead, it presents his rationale for restoring national credit and his assessment of the significance of a national debt. Having gotten his way on public credit, Hamilton strove to create the Bank of the United States as a national financial institution. In so doing, he argued for a "loose" interpretation of the Constitution that would greatly increase the national government's power. As is indicated in the textbook (p. 217), Thomas Jefferson fought the bank proposal and presented an argument that advocated a "strict" interpretation of the Constitution. These positions reflected fundamentally different visions of what America was and should become (see text pp. 214–220). As the fight over the course the government should follow became more heated, it extended into foreign policy and deepened political divisions (see text pp. 220–223). George Washington (Document 7-10) tried to point the way toward a foreign policy that would match the nation's needs. His analysis did not, however, stop the bickering that reflected the rise of political parties and that later touched Washington himself (see text pp. 223–224). These political battles reached a crisis in the years 1798–1800 as the Federalist party, itself rent by factions, desperately attempted to hold on to political power. Document 7-11, the Sedition Act of 1798, illustrates the lengths to which the Federalists were willing to go. The Federalists, however, could not prevail; they lost the election of 1800. However, chance and political machinations kept the final election result in doubt almost until inauguration day (see text pp. 224–225). In the end Thomas Jefferson, the victor in the 1800 contest, was able to take the oath of office on the legally mandated date, March 4, 1801. Document 7-12 presents the complete text of what the authors of the textbook (p. 225) emphasize was a significant inaugural address.

7-9   Alexander Hamilton's *Report on Public Credit* (1790)

As early as 1781, Alexander Hamilton, demonstrating his admiration for British institutions and economic policies, said that "a national debt if it is not excessive will be to us a national blessing, it will be [a] powerfull cement of our union." When he became the nation's first secretary of the treasury in 1789, he tried to implement his ideals by devising innovative financial policies to overcome the fiscal problems that had helped undermine the Confederation government (see text p. 215). The intricacies of those policies are clearly analyzed in the textbook (pp. 215–218). Document 7-9, which consists of sections of Hamilton's "Report on Public Credit" (1790), explains his view on public credit, including his position concerning a national debt.

Source: In Harold C. Syrett, ed., *The Papers of Alexander Hamilton* (New York: Columbia University Press, 1962), vol. 6, pp. 65–71, 106.

Treasury Department, January 9, 1790.
[Communicated on January 14, 1790]
[To the Speaker of the House of Representatives]
The Secretary of the Treasury, in obedience to the resolution of the House of Representatives . . . has . . . applied himself to the consideration of a proper plan for the support of the Public Credit, with all the attention which was due to the authority of the House, and to the magnitude of the object.

In the discharge of this duty, he has felt . . . a deep and solemn conviction of the momentous nature of the truth contained in the resolution under which his investigations have been conducted, "That an *adequate* provision for the

support of the Public Credit, is a matter of high importance to the honor and prosperity of the United States."

With an ardent desire that his well-meant endeavors may be conducive to the real advantage of the nation, and with the utmost deference to the superior judgment of the House, he now respectfully submits the result of his enquiries and reflections, to their indulgent construction.

In the opinion of the Secretary, the wisdom of the House, in giving their explicit sanction to the proposition which has been stated, cannot but be applauded by all, who will seriously consider, and trace through their obvious consequences, these plain and undeniable truths.

That exigencies are to be expected to occur, in the affairs of nations, in which there will be a necessity for borrowing.

That loans in times of public danger, especially from foreign war, are found an indispensable resource, even to the wealthiest of them.

And that in a country, which, like this, is possessed of little active wealth, or in other words, little monied capital, the necessity for that resource, must, in such emergencies, be proportionably urgent.

And as on the one hand, the necessity for borrowing in particular emergencies cannot be doubted, so on the other, it is equally evident, that to be able to borrow upon *good terms*, it is essential that the credit of a nation should be well established.

For when the credit of a country is in any degree questionable, it never fails to give an extravagant premium, in one shape or another, upon all the loans it has occasion to make. Nor does the evil end here; the same disadvantage must be sustained upon whatever is to be bought on terms of future payment.

From this constant necessity of *borrowing* and *buying dear*, it is easy to conceive how immensely the expences of a nation, in a course of time, will be augmented by an unsound state of the public credit.

To attempt to enumerate the complicated variety of mischiefs in the whole system of the social œconomy, which proceed from a neglect of the maxims that uphold public credit, and justify the solicitude manifested by the House on this point, would be an improper intrusion on their time and patience.

In so strong a light nevertheless do they appear to the Secretary, that on their due observance at the present critical juncture, materially depends, in his judgment, the individual and aggregate prosperity of the citizens of the United States; their relief from the embarrassments they now experience; their character as a People; the cause of good government.

If the maintenance of public credit, then, be truly so important, the next enquiry which suggests itself is, by what means it is to be effected? The ready answer to which question is, by good faith, by a punctual performance of contracts. States, like individuals, who observe their engagements, are respected and trusted: while the reverse is the fate of those, who pursue an opposite conduct. . . .

While the observance of that good faith, which is the basis of public credit, is recommended by the strongest inducements of political expediency, it is enforced by considerations of still greater authority. There are arguments for it, which rest on the immutable principles of moral obligation. And in proportion as the mind is disposed to contemplate, in the order of Providence, an intimate connection between public virtue and public happiness, will be its repugnancy to a violation of those principles.

This reflection derives additional strength from the nature of the debt of the United States. It was the price of liberty. The faith of America has been repeatedly pledged for it, and with solemnities, that give peculiar force to the obligation. There is indeed reason to regret that it has not hitherto been kept; that the necessities of the war, conspiring with inexperience in the subjects of finance, produced direct infractions; and that the subsequent period has been a continued scene of negative violation, or non-compliance. But a diminution of this regret arises from the reflection, that the last seven years have exhibited an earnest and uniform effort, on the part of the government of the union, to retrieve the national credit, by doing justice to the creditors of the nation; and that the embarrassments of a defective constitution, which defeated this laudable effort, have ceased.

From this evidence of a favorable disposition, given by the former government, the institution of a new one, cloathed with powers competent to calling forth the resources of the community, has excited correspondent expectations. A general belief, accordingly, prevails, that the credit of the United States will quickly be established on the firm foundation of an effectual provision for the existing debt. . . .

It cannot but merit particular attention, that among ourselves the most enlightened friends of good government are those, whose expectations are the highest.

To justify and preserve their confidence; to promote the encreasing respectability of the American name; to answer the calls of justice; to restore landed property to its due value; to furnish new resources both to agriculture and commerce; to cement more closely the union of the states; to add to their security against foreign attack; to establish public order on the basis of an upright and liberal policy. These are the great and invaluable ends to be secured, by a proper and adequate provision, at the present period, for the support of public credit.

To this provision we are invited, not only by the general considerations, which have been noticed, but by others of a more particular nature. It will procure to every class of the community some important advantages, and remove some no less important disadvantages. . . .

But these good effects of a public debt are only to be looked for, when, by being well funded, it has acquired an *adequate* and *stable* value. Till then, it has rather a contrary tendency. The fluctuation and insecurity incident to it in an unfunded state, render it a mere commodity, and a precarious one. As such, being only an object of occasional and particular speculation, all the money applied to it is so much diverted from the more useful channels of circulation, for which the thing itself affords no substitute: So that, in fact, one serious inconvenience of an unfunded debt is, that it contributes to the scarcity of money.

This distinction which has been little if at all attended to, is of the greatest moment. It involves a question immediately interesting to every part of the community; which is no other than this—Whether the public debt, by a provision for it on true principles, shall be rendered a *substitute* for money; or whether, by being left as it is, or by being provided for in such a manner as will wound those principles, and destroy confidence, it shall be suffered to continue, as it is, a pernicious drain of our cash from the channels of productive industry. . . .

Persuaded as the Secretary is, that the proper funding of the present debt, will render it a national blessing: Yet he is so far from acceding to the position, in the latitude in which it is sometimes laid down, that "public debts are public benefits," a position inviting to prodigality, and li-

able to dangerous abuse,—that he ardently wishes to see it incorporated, as a fundamental maxim, in the system of public credit of the United States, that the creation of debt should always be accompanied with the means of extinguishment. This he regards as the true secret for rendering public credit immortal. And he presumes, that it is difficult to conceive a situation, in which there may not be an adherence to the maxim. At least he feels an unfeigned solicitude, that this may be attempted by the United States, and that they may commence their measures for the establishment of credit, with the observance of it.

Questions

1. According to Hamilton, why is it essential for a nation to have good public credit?
2. According to Hamilton, what has to be done to ensure that the United States will have sound public credit?
3. Hamilton makes an open appeal to patriotism. Do you find it effective? Why or why not?

7-10   George Washington's Farewell Address (1796)

As Document 6-11 illustrates, foreign aid, especially the direct military aid that resulted from the French Alliance, proved essential to winning American independence. That alliance, however, was made when France was still a monarchy. When the French Revolution transformed France into a republic and then plunged that nation into war, the U. S. government faced a dilemma. Should the United States, a weak nation, honor its alliance with a France that was fundamentally different from the country that had entered into the Alliance of 1778? As the textbook authors indicate (pp. 220–223), the country split over the issue, and President Washington and the Federalist-dominated Congress chose to embrace neutrality (see text p. 220). In taking that position, President Washington revealed his Federalist party leanings (see text p. 224). Still, his emphasis on keeping America out of harm's way also reflected his view on the foreign policy guidelines that the young, still militarily weak nation should follow. In his Farewell Address of 1796, which also included extensive comments on "the baneful effects of the spirit of [political] parties," President Washington clearly spelled out his views on foreign policy.

Source: In James D. Richardson, ed., *A Compilation of the Messages and Papers of the Presidents* (Washington, D.C.: U. S. Government Printing Office, 1896–1899), vol. 1, pp. 205–216 *passim.*

Observe good faith and justice toward all nations. Cultivate peace and harmony with all. Religion and morality enjoin this conduct. And can it be that good policy does not equally enjoin it? It will be worthy of a free, enlightened, and at no distant period a great nation to give to mankind the magnanimous and too novel example of a people always guided by an exalted justice and benevolence. Who can doubt that in the course of time and things

the fruits of such a plan would richly repay any temporary advantages which might be lost by a steady adherence to it? . . .

In the execution of such a plan nothing is more essential than that permanent, inveterate antipathies against particular nations and passionate attachments for others should be excluded, and that in place of them just and amicable feelings toward all should be cultivated. The nation which indulges toward another an habitual hatred or an habitual fondness is in some degree a slave. It is a slave to its animosity or to its affection, either of which is sufficient to lead it astray from its duty and its interest. . . .

As avenues to foreign influence in innumerable ways, such attachments are particularly alarming to the truly enlightened and independent patriot. How many opportunities do they afford to tamper with domestic factions, to practice the arts of seduction, to mislead public opinion, to influence or awe the public councils! Such an attachment of a small or weak toward a great and powerful nation dooms the former to be the satellite of the latter. Against the insidious wiles of foreign influence (I conjure you to believe me, fellow-citizens) the jealousy of a free people ought to be *constantly* awake, since history and experience prove that foreign influence is one of the most baneful foes of republican government. But that jealousy, to be useful, must be impartial, else it becomes the instrument of the very influence to be avoided, instead of a defense against it. Excessive partiality for one foreign nation and excessive dislike of another cause those whom they actuate to see danger only on one side, and serve to veil and even second the arts of influence on the other. Real patriots who may resist the intrigues of the favorite are liable to become suspected and odious, while its tools and dupes usurp the applause and confidence of the people to surrender their interests.

The great rule of conduct for us in regard to foreign nations is, in extending our commercial relations to have with them as little *political* connection as possible. So far as we have already formed engagements let them be fulfilled with perfect good faith. Here let us stop.

Europe has a set of primary interests which to us have none or a very remote relation. Hence she must be engaged in frequent controversies, the causes of which are essentially foreign to our concerns. Hence, therefore, it must be unwise in us to implicate ourselves by artificial ties in the ordinary vicissitudes of her politics or the ordinary combinations and collisions of her friendships or enmities.

Our detached and distant situation invites and enables us to pursue a different course. If we remain one people, under an efficient government, the period is not far off when we may defy material injury from external annoyance; when we may take such an attitude as will cause the neutrality we may at any time resolve upon to be scrupulously respected; when belligerent nations, under the impossibility of making acquisitions upon us, will not lightly hazard the giving us provocation; when we may choose peace of war, as our interest, guided by justice, shall counsel.

Why forego the advantages of so peculiar a situation? Why quit our own to stand upon foreign ground? Why, by interweaving our destiny with that of any part of Europe, entangle our peace and prosperity in the toils of European ambition, rivalship, interest, humor, or caprice?

It is our true policy to steer clear of permanent alliances with any portion of the foreign world, so far, I mean, as we are now at liberty to do it; for let me not be understood as capable of patronizing infidelity to existing engagements. I hold the maxim no less applicable to public than to private affairs that honesty is always the best policy. I repeat, therefore, let those engagements be observed in their genuine sense. But in my opinion it is unnecessary and would be unwise to extend them.

Taking care always to keep ourselves by suitable establishments on a respectable defensive posture, we may safely trust to temporary alliances for extraordinary emergencies.

Harmony, liberal intercourse with all nations are recommended by policy, humanity, and interest. But even our commercial policy should hold an equal and impartial hand, neither seeking nor granting exclusive favors or preferences; consulting the natural course of things; diffusing and diversifying by gentle means the streams of commerce, but forcing nothing; establishing with powers so disposed, in order to give trade a stable course, to define the rights of our merchants, and to enable the Government to support them, conventional rules of intercourse, the best that present circumstances and mutual opinion will permit, but temporary and liable to be from time to time abandoned or varied as experience and circumstances shall dictate; constantly keeping in view that it is folly in one nation to look for disinterested favors from another; that it must pay with a portion of its independence for whatever it may accept under that character; that by such acceptance it may place itself in the condition of having given equivalents for nominal favors, and yet of being reproached with ingratitude for not giving more. There can be no greater error than to expect or calculate upon real favors from nation to nation. It is an illusion which experience must cure, which a just pride ought to discard.

In offering to you, my countrymen, these counsels of an old and affectionate friend I dare not hope they will make the strong and lasting impression I could wish—that they will control the usual current of the passions or prevent our nation from running the course which has hitherto marked the destiny of nations. But if I may even flatter myself that they may be productive of some partial benefit, some occasional good—that they may now and then recur to moderate the fury of party spirit, to warn against the mischiefs of foreign intrigue, to guard against the impostures of pretended patriotism—this hope will be a full recompense for the solicitude for your welfare by which they have been dictated.

How far in the discharge of my official duties I have been guided by the principles which have been delineated the public records and other evidences of my conduct must witness to you and to the world. To myself, the assurance of my own conscience is that I have at least believed myself to be guided by them.

In relation to the still subsisting war in Europe my proclamation of the 22d of April, 1793, is the index to my plan. Sanctioned by your approving voice and by that of your representatives in both Houses of Congress, the spirit of that measure has continually governed me, uninfluenced by any attempts to deter or divert me from it.

After deliberate examination, with the aid of the best lights I could obtain, I was well satisfied that our country, under all the circumstances of the case, had a right to take, and was bound in duty and interest to take, a neutral position. Having taken it, I determined as far as should depend upon me to maintain it with moderation, perseverance, and firmness. . . .

The inducements of interest for observing that conduct will best be referred to your own reflections and experience. With me a predominant motive has been to endeavor to gain time to our country to settle and mature its yet recent institutions, and to progress without interruption to that degree of strength and consistency which is necessary to give it, humanly speaking, the command of its own fortunes. . . .

Questions

1. What foreign policy guidelines does President Washington recommend for the United States?
2. Are Washington's reasons for following those guidelines convincing? Why or why not?
3. What does Washington mean when he says that "a free people ought to be *constantly* awake"? Do you agree or disagree with his assertion? If your answer is yes, is his advice on this point as applicable today as it was in 1796? Why or why not?

7-11   The Sedition Act (1798)

As the analysis in the textbook makes clear (pp. 223-225), President Washington was in some measure undoubtedly correct when he spoke of "the baneful effects of the spirit of [political] parties." One baneful effect was the way in which the Federalist party responded to its declining popularity in the late 1790s, when it was faced with the prospect of becoming a minority party. In an effort to retain power, leading Federalists trampled on the rights of their political opponents and precipitated a major political crisis. This crisis was evidenced and symbolized by the passage of the Alien and Sedition Acts of 1798. As indicated in the textbook (pp. 224–225), the Sedition Act, which is reprinted here, was seen as a direct assault on the Bill of Rights and thus provoked a sharp response.

Source: United States, *Statutes at Large*, vol. 1, pp. 596–597.

An Act in addition to the act, entitled "An act for the punishment of certain crimes against the United States."
SEC. 1. *Be it enacted . . .* , That if any persons shall unlawfully combine or conspire together, with intent to oppose any measure or measures of the government of the United States, which are or shall be directed by proper authority, or to impede the operation of any law of the United States, or to intimidate or prevent any person holding a place or office in or under the government of the United States, from undertaking, performing or executing his trust or duty; and if any person or persons, with intent as aforesaid, shall counsel, advise or attempt to procure any insurrection, riot, unlawful assembly, or combination, whether such conspiracy, threatening, counsel, advice, or attempt shall have the proposed effect or not, he or they shall be deemed guilty of a high misdemeanor, and on conviction, before any court of the United States having jurisdiction thereof, shall be punished by a fine not exceeding five thousand dollars, and by imprisonment during a term not less than six months nor exceeding five years; and further,

at the discretion of the court may be holden to find sureties for his good behaviour in such sum, and for such time, as the said court may direct.

Sec. 2. That if any person shall write, print, utter, or publish, or shall cause or procure to be written, printed, uttered or published, or shall knowingly and willingly assist or aid in writing, printing, uttering or publishing any false, scandalous and malicious writing or writings against the government of the United States, or either house of the Congress of the United States, or the President of the United States, with intent to defame the said government, or either house of the said Congress, or the said President or to bring them, or either of them, into contempt or disrepute; or to excite against them, or either or any of them, the hatred of the good people of the United States, or to stir up sedition within the United States, or to excite any unlawful combinations therein, for opposing or resisting any law of the United States, or any act of the President of the United States, done in pursuance of any such law, or of the powers in him vested by the constitution of the United States, or to resist, oppose, or defeat any such law or act, or to aid, encourage or abet any hostile designs of any foreign nation against the United States, their people or government, then such person, being thereof convicted before any court of the United States having jurisdiction thereof, shall be punished by a fine not exceeding two thousand dollars, and by imprisonment not exceeding two years.

Sec. 3. That if any person shall be prosecuted under this act, for the writing or publishing any libel aforesaid, it shall be lawful for the defendant, upon the trial of the cause, to give in evidence in his defence, the truth of the matter contained in the publication charged as a libel. And the jury who shall try the cause, shall have a right to determine the law and the fact, under the direction of the court, as in other cases.

Sec. 4. That this act shall continue to be in force until March 3, 1801, and no longer. . . .

Questions

1. Compare the Sedition Act with the First Amendment to the Constitution (see text p. D-12). Does the Sedition Act violate the First Amendment? Why or why not?
2. Does Section 3 of the Sedition Act offer special protection for those who comment on politics? Why or why not?
3. What is the significance of the fact that the Sedition Act passed by a Federalist-dominated Congress would expire on March 3, 1801? (*Hint:* Read the headnote to Document 7-12.) What does this tell you about the Federalists who championed the Sedition Act?

7-12 Thomas Jefferson's First Inaugural Address (1801)

The 1800 presidential election was the first one marked by especially vicious mudslinging (see text pp. 224–225). However, by that time it was clear that the vision associated with the Republican party headed by Thomas Jefferson had gained ascendancy. The Federalist party was in fact disintegrating (see text pp. 214, 218–220, 223–225). Ironically, when a mix-up among the Republicans unexpectedly threw the election into the House of Representatives, Alexander Hamilton championed Thomas Jefferson, his longtime rival, rather than let Aaron Burr become president. Hamilton opposed Burr in part because he considered Burr a scoundrel (see text p. 225). However, Hamilton also supported Jefferson because he believed that Jefferson as president would follow a more moderate course than would Jefferson as Republican party leader. The first proof of how perceptive Hamilton was became clear on March 4, 1801, when Jefferson delivered his stunning First Inaugural Address, which is reprinted here in full. As the textbook emphasizes (p. 225): "In 1801, as in the Declaration of Independence of 1776, he [Jefferson] defined the American republic as a government based on both majority rule and minority rights, with laws that treated citizens equally and respected their liberty."

Source: In James D. Richardson, ed., *A Compilation of the Messages and Papers of the Presidents* (Washington, D.C.: U.S. Government Printing Office, 1913), vol. 1, pp. 309–312.

Friends and Fellow-Citizens.

Called upon to undertake the duties of the first executive office of our country, I avail myself of the presence of that portion of my fellow-citizens which is here assembled to express my grateful thanks for the favor with which they have been pleased to look toward me, to declare a sincere consciousness that the task is above my talents, and that I approach it with those anxious and awful presentiments which the greatness of the charge and the weakness of my powers so justly inspire. A rising nation, spread over a wide and fruitful land, traversing all the seas with the rich productions of their industry, engaged in commerce with nations who feel power and forget right, advancing rapidly to destinies beyond the reach of mortal eye—when I contemplate these transcendent objects, and see the honor, the happiness, and the hopes of this beloved country committed to the issue and the auspices of this day, I shrink from the contemplation, and humble myself before the magnitude of the undertaking. Utterly, indeed, should I despair did not the presence of many whom I here see remind me that in the other high authorities provided by our Constitution I shall find resources of wisdom, of virtue, and of zeal on which to rely under all difficulties. To you, then, gentlemen, who are charged with the sovereign functions of legislation, and to those associated with you, I look with encouragement for that guidance and support which may enable us to steer with safety the vessel in which we are all embarked amidst the conflicting elements of a troubled world.

During the contest of opinion through which we have passed the animation of discussions and of exertions has sometimes worn an aspect which might impose on strangers unused to think freely and to speak and to write what they think; but this being now decided by the voice of the nation, announced according to the rules of the Constitution, all will, of course, arrange themselves under the will of the law, and unite in common efforts for the common good. All, too, will bear in mind this sacred principle, that though the will of the majority is in all cases to prevail, that will to be rightful must be reasonable; that the minority possess their equal rights, which equal law must protect, and to violate would be oppression. Let us, then, fellow-citizens, unite with one heart and one mind. Let us restore to social intercourse that harmony and affection without which liberty and even life itself are but dreary things. And let us reflect that, having banished from our land that religious intolerance under which mankind so long bled and suffered, we have yet gained little if we countenance a political intolerance as despotic, as wicked, and capable of as bitter and bloody persecutions. During the throes and convulsions of the ancient world, during the agonizing spasms of infuriated man, seeking through blood and slaughter his long-lost liberty, it was not wonderful that the agitation of the billows should reach even this distant and peaceful shore; that this should be more

felt and feared by some and less by others, and should divide opinions as to measures of safety. But every difference of opinion is not a difference of principle. We have called by different names brethren of the same principle. We are all Republicans, we are all Federalists. If there be any among us who would wish to dissolve this Union or to change its republican form, let them stand undisturbed as monuments of the safety with which error of opinion may be tolerated where reason is left free to combat it. I know, indeed, that some honest men fear that a republican government can not be strong, that this Government is not strong enough; but would the honest patriot, in the full tide of successful experiment, abandon a government which has so far kept us free and firm on the theoretic and visionary fear that this Government, the world's best hope, may by possibility want energy to preserve itself? I trust not. I believe this, on the contrary, the strongest Government on earth. I believe it the only one where every man, at the call of the law, would fly to the standard of the law, and would meet invasions of the public order as his own personal concern. Sometimes it is said that man can not be trusted with the government of himself. Can he, then, be trusted with the government of others? Or have we found angels in the forms of kings to govern him? Let history answer this question.

Let us, then, with courage and confidence pursue our own Federal and Republican principles, our attachment to union and representative government. Kindly separated by nature and a wide ocean from the exterminating havoc of one quarter of the globe; too high-minded to endure the degradations of the others; possessing a chosen country, with room enough for our descendants to the thousandth and thousandth generation; entertaining a due sense of our equal right to the use of our own faculties, to the acquisitions of our own industry, to honor and confidence from our fellow-citizens, resulting not from birth, but from our actions and their sense of them; enlightened by a benign religion, professed, indeed, and practiced in various forms, yet all of them inculcating honesty, truth, temperance, gratitude, and the love of man; acknowledging and adoring an overruling Providence, which by all its dispensations proves that it delights in the happiness of man here and his greater happiness hereafter—with all these blessings, what more is necessary to make us a happy and a prosperous people? Still one thing more, fellow-citizens—a wise and frugal Government, which shall restrain men from injuring one another, shall leave them otherwise free to regulate their own pursuits of industry and improvement, and shall not take from the mouth of labor the bread it has earned. This is the sum of good government, and this is necessary to close the circle of our felicities.

About to enter, fellow-citizens, on the exercise of duties which comprehend everything dear and valuable to you, it is proper you should understand what I deem the essential principles of our Government, and consequently those which ought to shape its Administration. I will compress them within the narrowest compass they will bear, stating the general principle, but not all its limitations. Equal and exact justice to all men, of whatever state or persuasion, religious or political; peace, commerce, and honest friendship with all nations, entangling alliances with none; the support of the State governments in all their rights, as the most competent administrations for our domestic concerns and the surest bulwarks against antirepublican tendencies; the preservation of the General Government in its whole constitutional vigor, as the sheet anchor of our peace at home and safety abroad; a jealous care of the right of election by the people—a mild and safe corrective of abuses which are lopped by the sword of revolution where peaceable remedies are unprovided; absolute acquiescence in the decisions of the majority, the vital principle of republics, from which is no appeal but to force, the vital principle and immediate parent of despotism; a well-disciplined militia, our best reliance in peace and for the first moments of war, till regulars may relieve them; the supremacy of the civil over the military authority; economy in the public expense, that labor may be lightly burthened; the honest payment of our debts and sacred preservation of the public faith; encouragement of agriculture, and of commerce as its handmaid; the diffusion of information and arraignment of all abuses at the bar of the public reason; freedom of religion; freedom of the press, and freedom of person under the protection of the habeas corpus, and trial by juries impartially selected. These principles form the bright constellation which has gone before us and guided our steps through an age of revolution and reformation. The wisdom of our sages and blood of our heroes have been devoted to their attainment. They should be the creed of our political faith, the text of civic instruction, the touchstone by which to try the services of those we trust;

and should we wander from them in moments of error or of alarm, let us hasten to retrace our steps and to regain the road which alone leads to peace, liberty, and safety.

I repair, then, fellow-citizens, to the post you have assigned me. With experience enough in subordinate offices to have seen the difficulties of this the greatest of all, I have learnt to expect that it will rarely fall to the lot of imperfect man to retire from this station with the reputation and the favor which bring him into it. Without pretensions to that high confidence you reposed in our first and greatest revolutionary character, whose preeminent services had entitled him to the first place in his country's love and destined for him the fairest page in the volume of faithful history, I ask so much confidence only as may give firmness and effect to the legal administration of your affairs. I shall often go wrong through defect of judgment. When right, I shall often be thought wrong by those whose positions will not command a view of the whole ground. I ask your indulgence for my own errors, which will never be intentional, and your support against the errors of others, who may condemn what they would not if seen in all its parts. The approbation implied by your suffrage is a great consolation to me for the past, and my future solicitude will be to retain the good opinion of those who have bestowed it in advance, to conciliate that of others by doing them all the good in my power, and to be instrumental to the happiness and freedom of all.

Relying, then, on the patronage of your good will, I advance with obedience to the work, ready to retire from it whenever you become sensible how much better choice it is in your power to make. And may that Infinite Power which rules the destinies of the universe lead our councils to what is best, and give them a favorable issue for your peace and prosperity.

Questions

1. According to Jefferson, why might some observers misread the presidential election of 1800? Do you agree with his observations? Why or why not?
2. According to Jefferson, what is the "sacred principle" of American constitutional government?
3. Did the members of the Federalist party have good reason to applaud Jefferson for his proclamation of that sacred principle? Why or why not?
4. According to Jefferson, what were "the essential principles of our Government"? Would Alexander Hamilton (Document 7-9) generally agree or disagree with Jefferson's assertions? Why or why not?

Question for Further Thought

1. Do these documents support or challenge the analysis offered by James Madison in *The Federalist*, No. 10 (Document 7-7)? Why or why not?

2. On the basis of the documents produced by Hamilton (7-9), Jefferson (7-12), and Washington (7-10), what description—political ideologue or political pragmatist—would you apply to each of these men? Why did you assign those terms?

3. On the basis of the documents produced by Hamilton (7-9), Jefferson (7-12), and Washington (7-10), would you call any of those men a political idealist? Why or why not?

4. For this question, on the basis of your father's occupation, translate your socio-economic status into its 1790s American equivalent. (Remember that in the United States of the 1790s virtually all married women managed a household or otherwise worked in the home, in the fields, or at the same occupation as their spouses.) Considering the information and arguments presented in these documents, would you, if you had lived in the America of the 1790s, have supported a loose or a strict interpretation of the Constitution? Why?

CHAPTER **8**

Toward a Continental Nation 1790–1820

★   ★   ★

Western Expansion

From its inception, the United States controlled vast territories stretching westward to the Mississippi River. By 1790 farming settlements extended into western New York, western Pennsylvania, and western Georgia, crossing or skirting the Appalachian Mountains (see Map 8.1, text p. 231). The lure of the West was strong among land speculators and farmer-settlers (see text pp. 232–234), but powerful forces restrained the expansion of the farming frontier until the 1830s. Indian nations west of the Appalachians—the Miami, Shawnee, Chickasaw, Cherokee, and Choctaw, among others—remained strong and resisted American encroachment. As military efforts to drive the native Americans from their lands stalled (see text pp. 230–232), President Thomas Jefferson inaugurated a more sophisticated and eventually more successful policy to promote Indian removal (Document 8-1).

As farmer-settlers streamed into the West, the role played by the federal government in western expansion became a matter for partisan political debate. Federalists generally favored the slow, regulated settlement of the western lands (see text p. 236). In their view, the nation's economic policy should be focused on commerce and the expansion of manufacturing. Those goals could best be met by policies that kept land prices relatively high and provided for the sale of large units of land; such policies favored speculators over farmer-settlers. By the mid-1790s, however, the Federalist plan for western development faced serious opposition as farmer-settlers' demands for affordable land began to influence Congressional legislation (Document 8-2). After that time, the virtues of western settlement became a principal theme in American democratic politics.

Farming settlements in the West initially were clustered along routes carved by rivers and large streams. Overland transportation remained arduous and expensive (see text pp. 234–235). Moreover, rivers and streams were separated by hills and mountains and were made impassable by falls and rapids. Transportation bottlenecks fragmented and slowed the settlement of the trans-Appalachian West (Document 8-3). Gradually roads and then canals extended from rivers and streams into the interior, and the process of settlement steadily advanced. Nine new states joined the nation in the period 1791–1819.

8-1 Message to Congress (January 18, 1803)

Thomas Jefferson

Thomas Jefferson (1743–1826), the third president of the United States, was one of the leading intellectual figures in the early republic. Jefferson's republican belief in the United States as a nation of independent yeomen farmers called for new lands for settlement (see text pp. 236–240). He shared the prevailing view that the barrier represented by native Americans had to be removed one way or another. In the following message to Congress Jefferson described the peaceful means by which he hoped to induce the Indians to sell their lands to the United States.

Source: In James D. Richardson, ed., *A Compilation of the Messages and Papers of the Presidents* (Washington, D.C.: U.S. Government Printing Office, 1908), vol. 1, pp. 352–353.

The Indian tribes residing within the limits of the United States have for a considerable time been growing more and more uneasy at the constant diminution of the territory they occupy. . . . and the policy has long been gaining strength with them of refusing absolutely all further sale on any condition. . . . In order peaceably to counteract this policy of theirs and to provide an extension of territory which the rapid increase of our numbers will call for, two measures are deemed expedient. First. To encourage them to abandon hunting, to apply [themselves] to the raising [of] stock, to agriculture, and domestic manufacture, and thereby prove to themselves that less land and labor will maintain them . . . better than in their former mode of living. The extensive forests necessary in the hunting life will then become useless, and they will see advantage in exchanging them for the means of improving their farms and of increasing their domestic comforts. Secondly. To multiply trading houses among them, and place within their reach those things which will contribute more to their domestic comfort than the possession of extensive but uncultivated wilds. . . . In leading them thus to agriculture, to manufactures, and civilization; in bringing together their and our sentiments, and in preparing them ultimately to

participate in the benefits of our Government, I trust and believe we are acting for their greatest good. . . . In one quarter this is particularly interesting . . . on the Mississippi . . . it is [desirable] to possess a respectable breadth of country . . . so that we may present as firm a front on that as on our eastern border. We possess what is below the Yazoo, and can probably acquire a certain breadth from the Illinois and Wabash to the Ohio; but between the Ohio and Yazoo the country all belongs to the Chickasaws, the most friendly tribe within our limits, but the most decided against the alienation of lands. The portion of their country most important for us is exactly that which they do not inhabit. Their settlements are not on the Mississippi, but in the interior country. They have lately shown a desire to become agricultural, and this leads to the desire of buying implements and comforts. In the strengthening and gratifying of these wants I see the only prospect of planting on the Mississippi itself the means of its own safety. Duty has required me to submit these views to the judgment of the Legislature, but as their disclosure might embarrass and defeat their effect, they are committed to the special confidence of the two Houses.

Questions

1. The United States claimed sovereignty over the native American nations but recognized the Indians' ownership of the lands they traditionally occupied. How did Jefferson propose to overcome this difficulty?

2. Why did Jefferson believe that native Americans would be better off with less land?
3. Why did Jefferson want his plans for the Indians—plans he said were "for their greatest good"—kept secret?

8-2 From Albany, New York, to Frankfort, Kentucky, in 1815

Noah M. Ludlow

Noah M. Ludlow (1795–1886) was born in New York City and took an early interest in the theater. He made his first stage appearance in Albany in 1813 with a traveling theatrical troupe, and two years later he joined a touring company formed by Samuel Drake, a pioneering theatrical manager in the West. The troupe had ample opportunity to experience the transportation bottlenecks of that era (see text pp. 234–235). In his memoirs, Ludlow described his first trip to the West.

Source: Noah M. Ludlow, *Dramatic Life as I Found It* (St. Louis: G. I. Jones and Company, 1880), pp. 5–14, 17–21, 76–78.

With the commencement of the year 1815, Mr. [Samuel] Drake was looking around for some actors and actresses bold and adventurous enough to risk their lives and fortunes in a Western wilderness, as Kentucky was then popularly supposed to be. . . . His course was to travel northwest in the State of New York, until he should reach Canandaigua; then to deflect to the south-west, strike the head waters of the Allegheny river, descend by boat to Pittsburgh, and perform there until the assembling of the State Legislature of Kentucky, early in December. . . .

Sometime about the latter part of July, 1815, our party started from Canandaigua for the head waters of the Allegheny River. Our means of transportation were a road-wagon, drawn by two horses, owned by Mr. Drake, and a light spring-wagon . . . drawn by one horse, and used for the convenience and comfort of his wife . . . the other portions of the company . . . were expected to walk the greater part of the way . . . and in this way we started for Olean, a settlement on the Allegheny . . . about one hundred and fifty miles south-west . . . through what was then almost a wilderness. . . .

Olean, in the summer of 1815, was a wild-looking place . . . Mr. Drake immediately made a trade, disposing of his wagons and horses, and purchasing a flat-bottomed boat, known in those days as an "Ark," or "Broad-horn." It was about twenty-five feet long by fifteen wide, boarded up at the sides, and covered with an elliptical roof about high enough to allow a man of medium stature to stand erect beneath the centre. It was quadrangular, and intended to be a kind of floating house. . . . In one end of this boat were two rooms, partitioned off as bed-rooms, one for Mr.

Lewis and wife; the other for the three single young ladies. . . . The men . . . were expected to "rough it," and rough it we did. . . . For awhile . . . the good "Broad-horns" [*sic*] wended her slow but steady way wherever it pleased the current of old Allegheny to carry her. But the repose . . . was suddenly disturbed by . . . an alarming cry that the boat was going over a waterfall. . . . Looking . . . ahead . . . I saw a "mill-dam" made across the portion of the river we were on . . . five . . . plunged into the river . . . and . . . succeeded in getting the boat safely to shore. . . .

After resting a little, we set to work to retrace the course we had come, until we should reach that point at which . . . the boat had taken the wrong "chute," or fork of the river. This we effected with much labor, by passing a rope to the shore . . . those on shore pulled it along, while the manager, Mr. Drake, kept it from the shore with a large steering-oar; and thus, by . . . this way of "cordelling," practiced on the rivers of the West in those days . . . we . . . got out of our unpleasant situation. . . .

[At Pittsburgh] another "broad-horn" boat had been purchased, larger and more conveniently arranged than our former one . . . and . . . near the middle of November . . . we commenced our voyage down the Ohio. . . .

There was a great sameness in this water journey of about four hundred miles. . . . The point at which Mr. Drake proposed to disembark was known as Limestone and afterwards as Maysville, on the Kentucky side of the river. . . . This point we reached . . . about a week from the time we left Pittsburgh. After landing . . . I was requested by Mr. Drake to go up into the village . . . to procure a large wagon, that might be engaged to transport our trunks . . . to Frankfort . . . less than a hundred miles. . . .

I do not recollect how many days we were journeying to Frankfort, but it was not a disagreeable trip, except from being a very slow method of travelling. We did not make more than from twenty to twenty-five miles each day. . . . We found no "inns," except in one or two villages we passed through; yet we never had any difficulty in finding "houses of entertainment," as they were called, which simply were . . . farmers' houses, who would take you in, and feed you and your horse with such as they had, and only make a trifling charge.

Questions

1. Ludlow's account illustrates the relative ease of river travel downstream and the arduousness of travel upstream. What implications did this have for commerce west of the Appalachian Mountains?
2. Where did the bottlenecks occur in Ludlow's trip? How might they have been alleviated?
3. Ludlow's party was able to secure boats, wagons, and lodging with relative ease. What does that suggest about travel at that time?

8-3 Congressional Resolution on Western Lands (1800)

Wealthy speculators and poor farmer-settlers competed for control of western lands. Because speculators tended to be comfortable with the political processes through which land sales took place, they held the upper hand in this competition (see text pp. 232–234). But the demands of yeomen farmers for access to western lands created political pressure that could not be ignored by eastern politicians. As a groundswell of popular support built for Thomas Jefferson and his Democratic-Republican party, Congress passed the Land Act of 1800, which sharply reduced the minimum acreage offered for sale and provided liberal credit terms for the purchase of land (see text p. 238). In a series of resolutions Congress authorized the drafting of a new land act.

Source: Annals of the Congress of the United States, 1789–1824 (Washington, D.C.: U.S. Government Printing Office, 1799–1800), 6th Cong., 1st sess., pp. 537–538.

The House resolved itself into a Committee of the Whole . . . to inquire whether any, and, if any, what, alterations are necessary in the laws providing for the sale of the lands of the United States Northwest of the Ohio; and, after some time spent therein, the Committee rose and reported several resolutions . . . as follows:

Resolved, That all the townships directed to be sold, either in quarter townships or in tracts of one mile square, by the act "providing for the sale of the lands of the United States, in the Territory Northwest of the river Ohio, and above the mouth of Kentucky river," shall be subdivided into half sections, containing, as nearly as may be, three hundred and twenty acres each: the additional expense of surveying to be paid by the purchasers, at the rate of three dollars per tract.

Resolved, That all the said lands shall be offered for sale at public sale, in tracts of three hun[d]red and twenty acres as above directed: *Provided,* That the same shall not be sold under the price of two dollars per acre, and that the sale shall be at the following places, to wit:

All the lands contained in the seven first ranges of townships, and north of the same, shall be offered for sale at Pittsburg[h].

All the lands contained in the eight next ranges of townships, shall be offered for sale at Marietta.

All the lands lying west of the fifteen first ranges of townships, and east of the Sciota river, shall be offered for sale at Chilicothe.

All the lands lying below the Great Miami shall be offered for sale at Cincinnati.

Resolved, That one or more land offices shall be opened in the Northwestern Territory, and that every person be permitted to locate and purchase at the rate of two dollars per acre, one or more of the half sections that shall not have been sold at public sale.

Resolved, That the payments for lands purchased either at public or private sale . . . shall be made in the following manner, and under the following conditions, viz:

1st. At the time of purchase, every purchaser shall deposit one-twentieth part of the amount of purchase money; to be forfeited, if, within three months, one-fourth of the purchase-money, including the said twentieth part, is not paid.

2d. One-fourth of the purchase-money to be paid as aforesaid, within three months, and the other three-fourths in three equal payments, within two, three, and four years, respectively, after the date of purchase.

3d. No interest to be charged in case of punctual pay-

ment; but interest at the rate of six per cent, a year, to be charged from the date of purchase, on any part of the purchase-money which shall not have been paid at the times, respectively, when the same shall have become due.

4th. A discount at the rate of eight per cent. a year, to be allowed on any of the three last payments, which shall be paid before the same shall have become due.

5th. If any tract shall not be completely paid [for] within one year after the date of the last payment, the tract to be sold in such manner as shall be provided by law; and after paying the balance due to the United States, including interest, the surplus, if any, to be returned to the original purchaser.

Ordered, That a bill or bills be brought in pursuant to the said resolutions. . . .

Questions

1. How much money did a farmer need to buy a farm under the terms of this proposed legislation?
2. Did some parts of the proposed legislation clearly favor speculators? Explain why.
3. Why did Congress specify the locations for all land sales? Whose interest did this provision serve?

Questions for Further Thought

1. The West and westward expansion profoundly influenced America's sense of its national character. How did Americans relate the idea of the West to the ideal of democracy?
2. Summarize the Federalist and Jeffersonian views of western land policy. Which policy or combination of policies do you think would have served the nation best? Explain why.
3. Westward expansion resulted in the extinction or displacement of almost all native Americans east of the Mississippi River. At that time, most white Americans viewed this process as the inevitable result of progress. What alternative historical course can you imagine?

Republican Policy and Diplomacy

After the Democratic-Republican tide swept Thomas Jefferson to victory in the presidential election of 1800, the United States entered a new era of continental conquest

In his *Notes on the State of Virginia* (1785) Jefferson described "Those who labor in the earth" as "the chosen people of God," referring to the independent yeomen who were the source of civic virtue in a republic. Civic virtue required simplicity, and simplicity began in government, which in Jefferson's view should function to protect independent farmers from the "dependence" and "subservience" he associated with commerce and manufacturing. The best government governed the least, Jefferson argued, and he endeavored to demonstrate as president how a truly simple government could ease the burden of domestic taxation (Document 8-4)

The purchase of the Louisiana Territory during Jefferson's first administration (see text pp. 238–240) ensured that Americans would continue to have land to labor on for a very long time, but it also raised problems of jurisdiction and control. Jefferson's decentralized agrarian republic would flourish only if the United States could exercise sovereignty over its vast North American territories. To do this, however, the nation had to enter an international competition for empire. It was vital that the United States control the transportation (and invasion) routes into the interior of the continent: the Ohio, Mississippi, and Missouri river valleys. To that end, Jefferson directed his personal secretary, Meriwether Lewis, and the army officer William Clark to explore the Missouri Valley and form alliances with Indian tribes beyond the reach of American military control. The detailed journals of Lewis and Clark reveal how closely intertwined the motives of conquest and scientific inquiry were (Document 8-5).

Throughout the West the British use of Indian allies (see text p. 242) challenged American control, and it became the policy of the United States to destroy or remove the native American population east of the Mississippi River. Preoccupation with western expansion and conflicts with Great Britain culminated in the War of 1812 and produced deep and bitter divisions in the eastern United States. When war came, American forces defeated the Indians in the West (Document 8-6). In the East, however, the British navy faced little opposition as it attacked American shipping and seaports, and a British army easily captured the new U. S. capital city and burned its public buildings (see text p. 244)

The extraordinary victory over the British in the Battle of New Orleans (see text pp. 244–245) enabled most Americans to respond to the frustrations, divisions, and ambiguities of the War of 1812 with a postwar outpouring of national enthusiasm. The new spirit of nationalism expressed the sense that a distinctive American national character had been shaped by the conquest of the West. For the next generation westerners and Indian fighters, most notably William Henry Harrison and Andrew Jackson, emerged as the political heroes of American democracy (Document 8-7).

8-4   Second Inaugural Address (March 4, 1805)

Thomas Jefferson

Thomas Jefferson served as secretary of state in George Washington's first administration and became a leading critic of Treasury Secretary Alexander Hamilton's plans for national economic development and a strong central government. As President Washington came to rely increasingly on Hamilton's advice, Jefferson resigned from the cabinet in 1793 and with his fellow Virginian James Madison formed the Democratic-Republican party to oppose the Hamilton-Washington Federalist party. Narrowly beaten by the Federalist candidate John Adams in the election of 1796, Jefferson won decisively in the "Revolution of 1800."

Jefferson's "revolution," which swept Federalists from federal office, left many of the accomplishments of the Federalist era intact, including the Bank of the United States (see text p. 236). But Jefferson's firm belief in limited government produced significant changes in the income and expenditures of the federal government. After his sweeping victory in 1804 (with only token Federalist opposition) Jefferson reviewed in his second inaugural address the success of his first administration in eliminating internal taxes and explained why, even with the prospect of a budget surplus, he believed that a tax on imports should be maintained.

Source: In James D. Richardson, ed., *A Compilation of the Messages and Papers of the Presidents, 1789–1908* (Washington, D.C.: U.S. Government Printing Office, 1908), vol. 1, pp. 378–382.

At home, fellow-citizens, you best know whether we have done well or ill. The suppression of unnecessary offices, of useless establishments and expenses, enabled us to discontinue our internal taxes. These, covering our land with officers and opening our doors to their intrusions, had already begun that process of domiciliary vexation which once entered is scarcely to be restrained from reaching successively every article of property and produce. . . .

The remaining revenue on the consumption of foreign articles is paid chiefly by those who can afford to add foreign luxuries to domestic comforts, being collected on our seaboard and frontiers only, and incorporated with the transactions of our mercantile citizens, it may be the pleasure and the pride of an American to ask, What farmer, what mechanic, what laborer ever sees a tax gatherer of the United States? These contributions enable us to support the current expenses of the Government, to fulfill contracts with foreign nations, to extinguish the native right of soil [to buy Indian lands] within our limits, to extend those limits, and to apply such a surplus to our public debts as places at a short day their final redemption, and that redemption once effected the revenue thereby liberated may, by a just repartition of it among the States and a corresponding amendment of the Constitution, be applied *in time of peace* to rivers, canals, roads, arts, manufactures, education, and other great objects within each State. . . .

Contemplating the union of sentiment now manifested so generally as auguring harmony and happiness to our future course, I offer to our country sincere congratulations. With those, too, not yet rallied to the same point the disposition to do so is gaining strength; facts are piercing through the veil drawn over them, and our doubting brethren will at length see that the mass of their fellow-citizens with whom they can not yet resolve to act as to principles and measures, think as they think and desire what they desire; that our wish as well as theirs is that the public efforts may be directed honestly to the public good, that peace be cultivated, civil and religious liberty unassailed, law and order preserved, equality of rights maintained, and that state of property, equal or unequal, which results to every man from his own industry or that of his father's. When satisfied of these views it is not in human nature that they should not approve and support them. In the meantime let us cherish them with patient affection, let us do them justice, and more than justice, in all competitions of interest, and we need not doubt that truth, reason, and their own interest will at length prevail, will gather them into the fold of their country, and will complete that entire union of opinion which gives to a nation the blessing of harmony and the benefit of all its strength.

Questions

1. Describe Jefferson's distinction between "internal taxes" and tariff duties on "foreign luxuries." Why did he consider the first bad and the second good?
2. When the national debt was paid off, Jefferson proposed to maintain the tariff on foreign luxuries—for what purposes?
3. Who were Jefferson's "doubting brethren," and why did he think they needed to be reassured that he would maintain "that state of property, equal or unequal, which results to every man from his own industry or that of his father's"?

8-5 Journals of the Lewis and Clark Expedition (1804–1806)

Shortly after completing the Louisiana Purchase, President Jefferson commissioned two army captains, William Clark (the younger brother of the Revolutionary War hero

George Rogers Clark) and Meriwether Lewis (Jefferson's personal secretary), to explore the new American territory (see text p 240). In the spring of 1804 Lewis and Clark led an expedition of twenty-five men up the Missouri River to present-day central North Dakota. In the spring of 1805 they followed the Missouri and Columbia rivers west to the Pacific. The following spring they returned to their point of departure at St. Louis. In their journals they recorded a journey of discoveries as they encountered new flora, fauna, and a rich variety of native American cultures. In the following passages Clark and Lewis observe their surroundings as they travel west on the Missouri from the Yellowstone to the Musselshell River.

Source: Reuben Gold Thwaites, ed., *Original Journals of the Lewis and Clark Expedition, 1804–1806* (New York: Dodd, Mead and Company, 1904–1905; facsimile reprint, New York: Arno Press, 1969), vol. 1, pp. 359–360.

William Clark, May 1, Wednesday 1805
We set out at sun rise under a stiff Breeze from the East, the morning cool & cloudy. . . . One of the men . . . shot a gull or pleaver [plover], which is about the size of an Indian hen, with a sharp pointed bill turned up & four inches long, the head and neck of a light brown, the breast, the under feathers of the 2nd and 3rd joint of the wings, the short feathers of the upper part of the 3rd joint of the wings, down the back, the back, the rump & tail white. The large feathers of the 1st joints of the wing, the upper feathers of the 2nd joints of the wings, on the body on the joints of the wing and the bill is black. The legs long and of a sky blue. The feet webbed &c. This fowl may be properly styled the Missouri Pleaver [probably a Hudsonian or marbled godwit in migration and between its winter and summer plumage]. The wind became very hard and we put to on the l.[eeward] side, as the wind continued with some degree of violence and the waves too high for the canoes; we were obliged to stay all day.

Meriwether Lewis, Thursday May 2, 1805
The wind continued violent all night nor did it abate much of its violence this morning, when at daylight it was attended with snow which continued to fall until about 10 a.m. Being about one inch deep, it formed a singular contrast with the vegetation which was considerably advanced. Some flowers had put forth in the plains, and the leaves of the cottonwood were as large as a dollar. Sent out some hunters who killed two deer, three elk, and several buffalo; on our way this evening we also shot three beaver along the shore. These animals in consequence of not being hunted are extremely gentle; where they are hunted they never leave their lodges in the day. The flesh of the beaver is esteemed a delicacy among us; I think the tail a most delicious morsal; when boiled it resembles in flavor . . . fresh . . . codfish, and is usually sufficiently large to afford a plentiful meal for two men. . . . One of the hunters who was out today found several yards of scarlet cloth which had been suspended on the bough of a tree near an old indian hunting camp, where it had been left as a sacrifice to the deity by the indians . . . it being a custom with . . . all the nations inhabiting the waters of the Missouri so far as they are known to us, to offer or sacrifice in this manner to the deity whatever they may be possessed of which they think most acceptable to him, and very honestly making their own feelings the test of those of the deity, [they] offer him the article which they most prize themselves. This being the most usual method of worshipping the great spirit as they term the deity, is practiced on interesting occasions, or to produce the happy eventuation of the important occurances incident to human nature, such as relief from hunger or malady, protection from their enemies, or the delivering [to] them into their hands, and with such as cultivate, to prevent the river's overflowing and destroying their crops &c. Sacrifices of a similar kind are also made to the deceased by their friends and relatives. The air was vary piercing this evening. The [water] friezed [*sic*] on the oars as they rowed. The wind dying at 5 p.m. we set out.

Questions

1. In your opinion, are Clark and Lewis describing a "wilderness"? Explain why or why not.
2. Why do Clark and Lewis describe these particular experiences in such detail?
3. What do the descriptions of the Missouri plover, the beaver tail, and Indian sacrifice reveal about Lewis and Clark's view of the place of native Americans in the natural world?

8-6   Speech to Tecumseh and the Prophet (1811) and Report to the Secretary of War (1814)

William Henry Harrison

William Henry Harrison would be elected president of the United States in 1840 largely because of his reputation as an Indian fighter. His nickname, "Tippecanoe," celebrated his victory over the followers of chief Tecumseh and his brother Tenskwatawa (the Prophet) at the Battle of Tippecanoe on November 7, 1811 (see text p. 242). As governor of the Indiana Territory, Harrison carried out the Democratic-Republican policy of divesting native Americans of their land (see Document 8-1). Tecumseh and Tenskwatawa formed a coalition to resist this policy of piecemeal dispossession. As Harrison warned in his speech to Tecumseh and the Prophet, he had assembled an army of seasoned Indian fighters. He soon moved them to Tippecanoe Creek near the hostile Indian encampment called Prophetstown. Convinced by the Prophet that they were invincible, the Indians swept into the American camp in the predawn darkness. But Harrison's men held their ground, formed a defensive line, and soon turned the Indians back with heavy losses.

Tecumseh's people abandoned Prophetstown (which Harrison subsequently burned) and, fighting in small bands, made war on settlers across the Northwest. During the War of 1812 Tecumseh joined forces with the British. At the Battle of the Thames on October 5, 1813 (see text p. 244), Harrison's forces decisively defeated the Indians and their British allies and killed Tecumseh. In his letter to the secretary of war Harrison summarized the Democratic-Republican Indian policy and his successes in implementing it.

Source: Benjamin Drake, *Life of Tecumseh* (Cincinnati: E. Morgan & Co., 1841; facsimile reprint, New York: Arno Press and New York Times, 1969).

Harrison to Tecumseh and the Prophet, June 24, 1811:
Brothers,—Listen to me. I speak to you about matters of importance, both to the white people and yourselves; open your ears, therefore, and attend to what I shall say.

Brothers, this is the third year that all the white people in this country have been alarmed at your proceedings; you threaten us with war, you invite all the tribes in the north and west of you to join against us. . . .

Brothers, our citizens are alarmed, and my warriors are preparing themselves; not to strike you, but to defend themselves and their women and children. You shall not surprise us as you expect to do; you are about to undertake a vary rash act; as a friend, I advise you to consider well of it. . . . Do you really think that the handful of men that you have about you, are able to contend with the Seventeen Fires [the seventeen states then composing the United States], or even that the whole of the tribes united, could contend against the Kentucky Fire alone?

Brothers, I am myself of the long knife fire; as soon as they hear my voice, you will see them pouring forth their swarms of hunting shirt men, as numerous as the musquetoes [*sic*] on the shores of the Wabash; brothers, take care of their stings.

Harrison to the Secretary of War March 22, 1814:
I received instruction from President Jefferson, shortly after his first election, to make efforts for extinguishing the Indian claims upon the Ohio, below the mouth of the Kentucky river, and to such other tracts as were necessary to connect and consolidate our settlements. It was at once determined, that the community of interests in the lands among the Indian tribes, which seemed to be recognized by the treaty of Greenville, should be objected to. . . . Care was taken . . . to place the title to such tracts as might be desireable to purchase . . . upon a footing that would facilitate the procuring of them, by getting the tribes who had no claim themselves, and who might probably interfere, to recognize the titles of those who were ascertained to posses [*sic*] them.

This was particularly the case with regard to the lands watered by the Wabash, which were declared to be the property of the Miamis, with the exception of the tract occupied by the Delawares on White river, which was to be considered the joint property of them and the Miamis. This arrangement was very much disliked by Tecumseh, and the banditti that he had assembled at Tippecanoe. He complained loudly, as well of the sales that had been made, as of the principle of considering a particular tribe as the exclusive proprietors of any part of the country, which he said the Great Spirit had given to all his red children. . . .

The question of the title to the lands south of the Wabash, has been thoroughly examined; every opportunity

was afforded to Tecumseh and his party to exhibit their pretensions [land claims], and they were found to rest upon no other basis than that of their being the common property of all the Indians.

Questions

1. Why did Harrison expect his image of "swarms of hunting shirt men" to intimidate Tecumseh and the Prophet?
2. By what means did Harrison intend to extinguish native American land claims along the Ohio River?
3. Why did Tecumseh protest against these methods and organize resistance to them?

8-7 "The Hunters of Kentucky"

**Samuel Woodworth and
Noah Ludlow**

In New Orleans in 1822 Noah Ludlow (Document 8-2) put to music the poem "The Hunters of Kentucky" by Samuel Woodworth and first performed what soon became an enormously popular song. The song celebrated Andrew Jackson's victory over the British at the Battle of New Orleans in 1815 (see text pp. 244–245). The victory had been a stunning one: the Americans emerged from battle virtually unscathed, whereas the British were nearly destroyed with hundreds dead and more than a thousand wounded or missing. As the historian John William Ward observed, the standard infantryman's weapon was the smooth bore musket. Riflemen in Jackson's army functioned as sharpshooters and played a minor role in the battle. Nevertheless, the prowess of the Kentucky riflemen became an essential part of popular representations of Jackson's victory; the success of Ludlow's song demonstrated the legend's popular appeal. The third verse refers to the British major general Sir Edward Pakenham, who died in the battle.

Source: Samuel Woodworth and Noah Ludlow, "The Hunters of Kentucky" (1882). In John William Ward, *Andrew Jackson: Symbol for an Age* (New York: Oxford University Press, 1953), pp. 217–218.

---

1. Ye gentlemen and ladies fair,
      Who grace this famous city,
    Just listen if you've time to spare,
      While I rehearse a ditty;
    And for the opportunity
      Conceive yourselves quite lucky,
    For 'tis not often that you see
      A hunter from Kentucky
    O Kentucky, the hunters of Kentucky!
    O Kentucky, the hunters of Kentucky!

2. We are a hardy, free-born race,
      Each man to fear a stranger;

Whate'er the game we join in chase,
  Despising toil and danger,
And if a daring foe annoys,
  Whate'er his strength and forces,
We'll show him that Kentucky boys
  Are alligator horses.
      Oh Kentucky, etc.

3. I s'pose you've read it in the prints,
      How Packenham attempted
    To make Old Hickory Jackson wince,
      But soon his scheme repented;
    For we with rifles ready cock'd,

Thought such occasion lucky,
    And soon around the gen'ral flock'd
The Hunters of Kentucky.
        Oh Kentucky, etc.

4. You've heard, I s'pose how New-Orleans
        Is fam'd for wealth and beauty,
    There's girls of ev'ry hue it seems,
        From snowy white to sooty.
    So Packenham he made his brags,
        If he in fight was lucky,
    He'd have their girls and cotton bags,
        In spite of old Kentucky.
            Oh Kentucky, etc.

5. But Jackson he was wide awake,
        And was not scar'd at trifles,
    For well he knew what aim we take
        With our Kentucky rifles.
    So he led us down to Cypress swamp,
        The ground was low and mucky,
    There stood John Bull in martial pomp
        And here was old Kentucky.
            Oh Kentucky, etc.

6. A bank was rais'd to hide our breasts,
        Not that we thought of dying,

But that we always like to rest,
    Unless the game is flying.
Behind it stood our little force,
    None wished it to be greater,
For ev'ry man was half a horse,
    And half an alligator.
        Oh Kentucky, etc.

7. They did not let our patience tire,
        Before they showed their faces;
    We did not choose to waste our fire,
        So snugly kept our places.
    But when so near we saw them wink,
        We thought it time to stop 'em,
    And 'twould have done you good I think,
        To see Kentuckians drop 'em.
            Oh Kentucky, etc.

8. They found, at last, 'twas vain to fight,
        Where *lead* was all the *booty*,
    And so they wisely took to flight,
        And left *us* all our *beauty*.
    And now if danger e'er annoys,
        Remember what our trade is,
    Just send for us Kentucky boys,
        And we'll protect ye, ladies.
            Oh Kentucky, etc.

Questions

1. According to the song's lyrics, what attributes did the hunters of Kentucky possess that accounted for Jackson's victory?
2. Ludlow stated in his reminiscences, *Dramatic Life as I Found It*, that he made the fifth verse the dramatic focus of his performance. Why did he choose that particular verse?
3. Contrast the American victory at New Orleans as it was celebrated in Ludlow's song with the humiliating British capture of Washington, D. C. How were regional sources of patriotism expressed in the lyrics of "The Hunters of Kentucky"?

Questions for Further Thought

1. Compare and contrast the requirements for Jefferson's ideal of a decentralized agrarian republican with the interests of the United States as it laid claim to a continental empire.
2. In popular expressions of patriotism (Document 8-7 is a good example) the West shaped a heroic national character. Identify the principal elements of that character and consider what needs or uncertainties it was formed to meet.
3. In Jeffersonian thought republican equality required only the security, simplicity, and independence of yeomen farmers. Yet heroic themes soon dominated popular expressions of patriotism. Were those themes compatible with Jefferson's republican ideal?

Regional Diversity and National Identity

As the seaboard culture of the United States expanded westward, a new sense of an American continental empire emerged. With that vision came conflicts over the shape and character of the empire. Slavery emerged as a central divisive issue (see text pp. 249–251). As white settlers from the Chesapeake and Carolinian cultures migrated west, they brought black slaves with them. East of the Mississippi River the antislavery provision of the Northwest Ordinance made the Ohio River the de facto dividing line between free states to the north and slave states to the south. After the Louisiana Purchase, however, the presence of slaves in the trans-Mississippi West raised troubling questions about the status of slavery in western territories and new states (see text pp. 250–251). The debate over slavery in Missouri brought those questions to the fore-front of national politics, and the resolution of the slavery issue in the Missouri Compromise settled the matter for the next thirty years.

The debate over slavery in Missouri revealed the close connection of slavery to the political and economic issues that would distinguish the North and the South. One such issue had to do with the relationship between the enslavement of African-Americans and equality among whites, who were by definition nonslaves. On one side of this debate were northerners who defended free wage labor as the moral foundation of the nation's economy. The other side was represented by Senator Richard M. Johnson of Kentucky during the Missouri controversy, when he insisted that black slavery sustained white equality (Document 8-8).

As the debate over slavery continued, the forced westward migration of southern slaves disrupted the lives of thousands of African-Americans and established new plantation-based slave communities from western Georgia across the Gulf Plains to Louisiana (see text p. 249). The western expansion of slavery also transformed established slave communities in the Chesapeake and Carolinian cultures. In religion, language, architecture, dress, music, dance, and labor systems African-American cultures continued to influence the regional cultures of the South. Especially in the South Carolina lowland slave communities, a degree of autonomy and cultural distinctiveness contrasted sharply with the situation in the plantations of the West and with the developing northern antislavery view that chattel slavery denied slaves all control over their lives and labor (Document 8-9).

The vision of a continental empire partially overcame the clash of regional cultures that accompanied westward expansion (Document 8-10). Americans found common elements of national pride and identity in territorial expansion, population growth, and a transportation revolution that knitted the regions and the western hinterlands together with roads and canal-improved river systems. But visions of the continental empire varied and ultimately came into conflict as the ideal of an agrarian (and slave-holding) republic clashed with the expanding influence of the commercial centers of the Northeast.

8-8   The Benefits of Slavery in Missouri

Richard Mentor Johnson

Richard Mentor Johnson (1780–1850) was born in a frontier settlement on the Ohio River that became the site of Louisville, Kentucky. He studied law at Transylvania College, was admitted to the bar in 1802, and won election to the Kentucky state legislature in 1804. From 1807 to 1819 he served in the U.S. House of Representatives as an ardent Jeffersonian.

In 1819 the Kentucky legislature elected Johnson to the U.S. Senate, where he served for the next decade. He warmly supported Andrew Jackson in the presidential election of 1828. Largely as a result of Jackson's support, Johnson served as vice-president in Van Buren's administration. Never married, he was the father of two daughters born to a slave mistress whom he had inherited from his father.

In 1819 and 1820 the question of admitting Missouri as a slave state touched off a heated debate that produced the Missouri Compromise of 1820 (see text pp. 250–251). The focal point of the Missouri debates was a proposal for the gradual abolition of slavery in Missouri. In his speech on the Missouri question Senator Johnson explained why he believed slavery was not an evil but a blessing to the American republic.

Source: Annals of the Congress of the United States, 1789–1824 (Washington, D.C.: U.S. Government Printing Office, 1819–1820), 16th Cong., 1st sess., pp. 345–359.

. . . Can gentlemen sincerely believe that the cause of humanity will be promoted by still confining this population [i.e., slaves] within such limits, as that their relative numbers will oppose everlasting obstacles to their emancipation? Upon the most extensive principles of philanthropy, I say, let them spread forth with the growing extent of our nation. I am sure I plead the cause of humanity. I advocate the best interests of the sons of bondage, when I entreat you to give them room to be happy; and so disperse them as that, under the auspices of Providence, they may one day enjoy the rights of man, without convulsing the empire or endangering society. . . .

There is no just cause for irritation on this subject. We should suppress our feelings, when they threaten to transport us beyond the bounds of reason. Early habits beget strong prejudices, and under a heavy burden of them we all labor. But it becomes us to bring them to one common altar, and consume them together. Before we compel our brother to pluck the mote from his eye, it will be wise to take the beam from our own. On this occasion I cannot omit to mention my own feelings on a former occurrence. When I first came to Congress, it was with mingled emotions of horror and surprise that I saw citizens from the non-slaveholding States, as they are called—yes, and both branches of our National Legislature—riding in a coach and four, with a white servant seated before, managing the reins, another standing behind the coach, and both of these white servants in livery. Is this, said I to myself, the degraded condition of the citizen, on whose voice the liberties of a nation may depend? I could not reconcile it with my ideas of freedom; because, in the State where I received my first impressions, slaves alone were servile. All white men there are on an equality, and every citizen feels his independence. We have no classes—no patrician or plebeian rank. Honesty and honor form all the distinctions that are felt or known. Whatever may be the condition of a citizen with us, you must treat him as an equal. This I find is not so in every part of the non-slaveholding States, especially in your populous cities, where ranks and distinctions, the precursors of aristocracy, already begin to exist. They whose business it is to perform menial offices in other States, are as servile as our slaves in the West. Where is the great difference betwixt the conditions of him who keeps your stable, who blacks your boots, who holds your stirrups, or mounts behind your coach when you ride, and the slave who obeys the command of his master? There may be a nominal difference; but it would be difficult to describe its reality. In the one case it is called voluntary, because it is imposed by its own necessity, and in the other involuntary, because imposed by the will of another. Whatever difference there may be in the principle, the effects upon society are the same. The condition, in some respects, is in favor of the slave. He is supplied with food and clothing; and in the hour of sickness he finds relief. No anxious cares, in relation to age and infirmity, invade his breast. He fears no duns [demands for payment]: careless of the pressure of the times, he dreads not the coercion of payment, nor feels the cruelty of that code which confines the white servant in prison, because the iron hand of poverty has wrested from him the means of support for his family. Though slavery still must be confessed a bitter draught, yet where the stamp of nature marks the distinction, and when the mind, from early habit, is moulded to the condition, the slave often finds less bitterness in the cup of life than most white servants. What is the condition of many, who are continually saluting our ears with cries of want, even in this city? Men, women, boys, girls, from infancy to old age, craving relief from every passenger. Are they slaves? No. Among the slaves are no beggars; no vagrants; none idle for want of employ, or crying for want of bread. Every condition of life has its evils; and most evils have some palliative; though perhaps none less than those of white menials. Yet, sir, none are more lavish of their censures against slaveholders than those lordlings with livery servants of their own complexion. . . .

I never could stand having white servants dressed in livery. No, sir, when the honest laborer, the mechanic, however poor, or whatever his employment, visits my house, it matters not what company is there, he must sit with me at my board, and receive the same treatment as the most distinguished guest; because in him I recognise a fellow citizen and an equal.

The condition of the slave is but little understood by those who are not the eye-witnesses of his treatment. His sufferings are greatly aggravated in their apprehension. The general character of the slaveholding community can no more be determined, nor should they be any more stigmatized, by a particular instance of cruelty to a slave, than the character of the non-slaveholding community by a particular instance of cruelty in a parent towards his child, a guardian to his ward, or a master to his apprentice. No man among us can be cruel to his slave without incurring the execration of the whole community.

Questions

1. What does Johnson mean when he suggests that the westward extension of slavery might encourage its demise?
2. According to Johnson, in what ways did the enslavement of blacks encourage equality among whites?
3. On what did Johnson base his claim that slaves found "less bitterness in the cup of life than most white servants"?

8-9   Life on a South Carolina Cotton and Rice Plantation

Charles Ball

Charles Ball (1780–?) was born a slave in eastern Maryland. There he worked as a farmhand and for two years was hired out as a shipyard worker in Washington, D.C. Shortly after marrying and starting a family, he was sold to a South Carolina cotton planter. He was then sold to a planter in the Georgia upcountry. Eventually he managed to escape and settled near Philadelphia, where he told his story to Isaac Fisher, who later wrote Ball's slave narrative. In the following passage Ball describes aspects of life among a community of slaves in the South Carolina lowlands (see text p. 252) in about 1800.

Source: Isaac Fisher, *Slavery in the United States: A Narrative of the Life and Adventures of Charles Ball, A Black Man. . .* (New York: John S. Taylor, 1837), pp. 164–167, 187.

At the time I first went to Carolina, there were a great many African slaves in the country, and they continued to come in for several years afterwards. I became intimately acquainted with some of these men. Many of them believed there were several gods; some of whom were good, and others evil, and they prayed as much to the latter as to the former. I knew several who must have been, from what I have since learned, Mohamedans [Muslims]; though at that time, I had never heard of the religion of Mohamed.

There was one man on this plantation, who prayed five times every day, always turning his face to the east, when in the performance of his devotion.

There is, in general, very little sense of religious obligation, or duty, amongst the slaves on the cotton plantations; and Christianity cannot be, with propriety, called the religion of these people. They are universally subject to the grossest and most abject superstition; and uniformly believe in witchcraft, conjuration [conjuring—summoning the devil or spirits by incantation], and the agency of evil spirits in the affairs of human life. . . .

They have not the slightest religious regard for the Sabbath-day, and their masters make no efforts to impress them with the least respect for this sacred institution. My first Sunday on this plantation was but a prelude to all that followed; and I shall here give an account of it.

At the time I rose . . . a large number of the men, as well as some of the women, had already quitted the quarter, and gone about the business of the day. That is, they had gone to work for wages for themselves—in this manner: our overseer had, about two miles off, a field of near twenty acres, planted in cotton, on his own account. He was the owner of this land; but as he had no slaves, he was

obliged to hire people to work it for him, or let it lie waste. . . . About twenty of our people went to work for him today, for which he gave them fifty cents each. . . .

On every plantation, with which I ever had any acquaintance, the people are allowed to make patches, as they are called—that is, gardens, in some remote and unprofitable part of the estate, generally in the woods, in which they plant corn, potatoes, pumpkins, melons, &c. for themselves.

These patches they must cultivate on Sunday, or let them go uncultivated. I think, that on this estate, there were about thirty of these patches. . . .

The vegetables that grew in these patches, were always consumed in the families of the owners [of the patches]; and the money that was earned by hiring out, was spent . . . sometimes for clothes, sometimes for better food . . . and sometimes for rum; but those who drank rum, had to do it by stealth. . . .

As I had nothing to do for myself, I went with Lydia, whose husband was still sick, to help her to work in her patch. . . . She had onions, cabbages, cucumbers, melons, and many other things in her garden.

In the evening, as we returned home, we were joined by the man who prayed five times a day; and at the going down of the sun, he stopped and prayed aloud in our hearing, in a language I did not understand. . . .

I must here observe, that when the slaves go out to work for wages on Sunday, their employers never flog them; and so far as I know never give them abusive language. . . . I worked faithfully, because I knew that if I did not, I could not expect payment; and those who hired me, knew that if I did not work well, they need not employ me.

Questions

1. Why were the African "superstition" and language Ball encountered in South Carolina strange to him?
2. Why might it have been in the interests of South Carolina slave owners to allow their slaves to cultivate garden plots on their own or to labor for others for wages?
3. Ball implies that men worked better for wages than they did as slaves. If the slaveholders had replaced slave labor with wage labor, what would they have lost?

8-10   "Eagle Map of the United States"

The 1819 treaty with Spain negotiated by Secretary of State John Quincy Adams (see text p. 261) extended American sovereignty over Florida and secured American control of the Gulf Coast (after prolonged guerrilla warfare against renegade native Americans and escaped slaves in Florida). The treaty also established a western boundary between the American Louisiana Territory and the Spanish empire in North America. Using the symbol of federal union and sovereignty adopted in the early national period, the "Eagle Map" (see facing page) was drawn to display the new western border from the Gulf Coast north and west across the Great Divide.

Source: Courtesy of the University of Pittsburgh Libraries Special Collections. Photograph by Dereich, Pittsburgh, PA.

Questions

1. What do the eagle's features suggest to you about the regional sources of national ambitions in the 1820s?
2. Follow the eagle's wings westward and consider how the "Eagle Map" encouraged a seaboard nation to begin conceiving of itself as a continental empire. What elements of that continental vision were not yet in place when the "Eagle Map" was drawn?
3. Compare the "Eagle Map" with Map 8.5 (see text p. 251). Where is there room for the expansion of slavery? What do the eagle's wings suggest will be the role of slavery in the West?

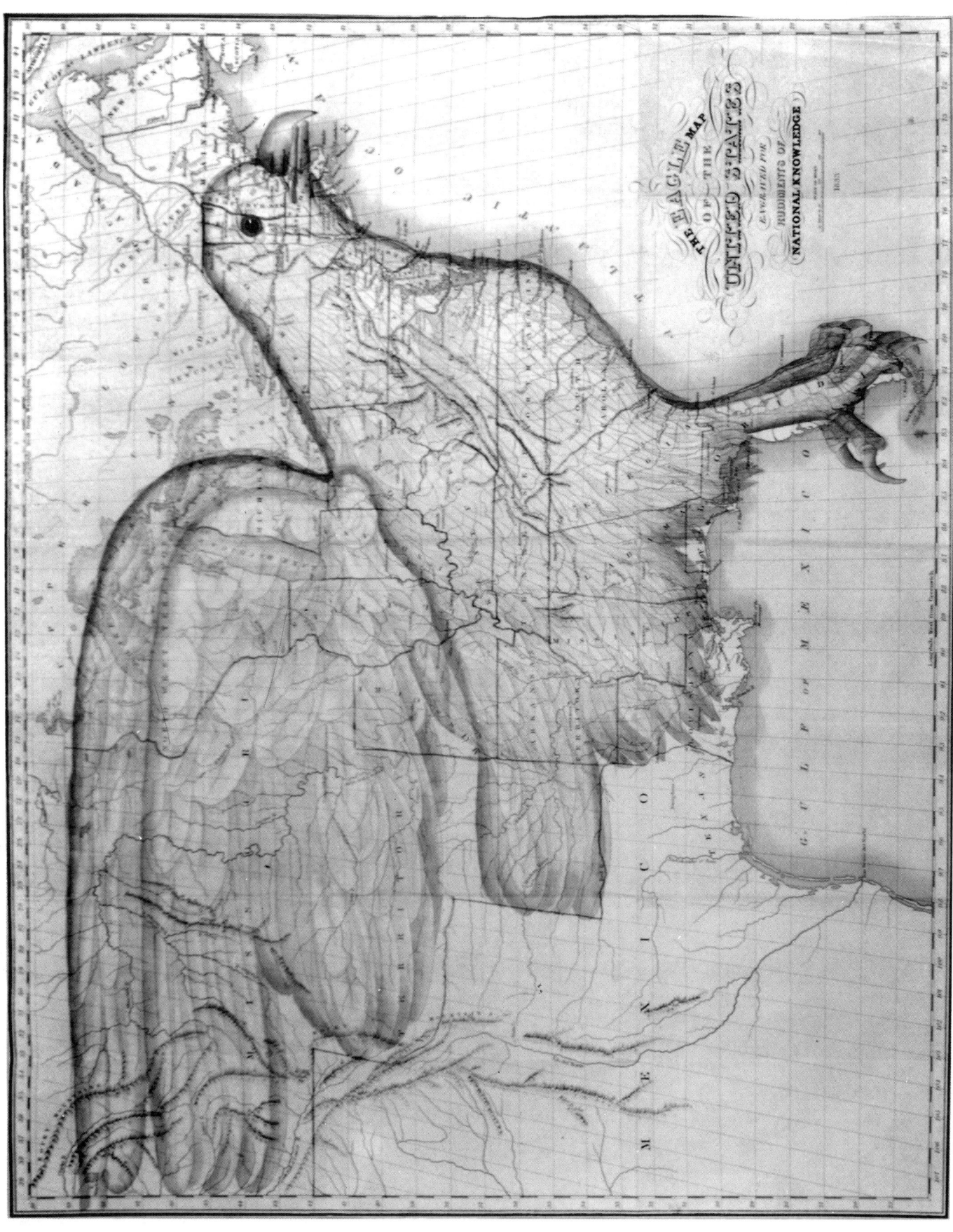

Questions for Further Thought

1. Do you agree with Richard Johnson (Document 8-8) that there was only a "nominal difference" between a free white servant and a black slave? How might an antislavery proponent have responded to the issue, raised in Johnson's speech, of social inequality in the free states?

2. The "Eagle Map" (Document 8-10) emphasized westward expansion and a specific vision of national unity. However, the Missouri debates underscored the idea that westward expansion could also promote disunity. In what ways did the creation of a continental empire promote unity and disunity in the expanding United States?

3. An important feature in the creation of the American continental empire was the forced westward migration of thousands of African-American slaves (see text pp. 249–251). Using Charles Ball's description (Document 8-9) of a South Carolina slave community as a starting point, consider why slaves feared and resisted removal to the West.

CHAPTER 9

Toward a Capitalist Protestant Republic 1790–1820

★   ★   ★

Political Economy: The Capitalist Commonwealth

In the early Industrial Revolution an American society based on household manufacturing and independent artisan producers was replaced by one based on wages paid by employers for "outwork" and labor in factories and central shops (Document 9-1). In response to this transformation, the debate between Federalists and Democratic-Republicans focused on the role of government in the economy and the virtues of democracy in political life. Federalists looked to the national government, particularly the national judiciary, to protect property rights (see text pp. 272–273). Federalists also distrusted the rising tide of democracy in the states. By contrast, Democratic-Republicans championed the legislative will of the people over static jurisprudence and allied themselves with the movement toward widening political democracy in the states. Despite these ideological divisions, few people disagreed with the idea that the absence of aristocratic privilege in America was a great blessing and that it was the object of public policy to promote the common good—the *commonwealth* (see text pp. 270–271). In this spirit, Americans rallied beneath the banner of nationalism to promote internal improvements, expand manufacturing, and improve fortifications, all with the intent of securing the independence of the American commonwealth from British credit and manufactured goods (Document 9-2).

This partisan political debate reflected a confrontation between traditional and new property interests. Federalists generally favored protecting traditional property interests; Democratic-Republicans frequently promoted change. Traditional property interests had been well served by the policies of state mercantilism, in which state charters were granted to individuals and groups to provide communities with bridges, tunnels, turnpikes, mills, and canals. Similar charters established banks and granted mining and manufacturing rights. Underlying these charters was the idea that a state grant of exclusive privilege benefited the entire community (see text pp. 269–270). Over time these traditional interests became the object of hostility from aspiring groups. Exclusive privileges, it was argued, retarded the growth of communities by denying them new bridges and mills and by promoting monopoly at the expense of equal rights.

Competing interests produced conflicting views about the meaning of contracts and the status of property. Traditional interests held tenaciously to the principles of common law, which were derived from traditional usage and defined and applied by judges (see text p. 270). Aspiring interests turned to positive law (see text p. 271), which was defined by statute to represent the legislative will of the electorate. Those interests argued that charters granted by the state could be revised or modified by the state to serve the changing needs of society. Traditional interests argued that charters, like contracts, established property rights and that the protection of property rights was fundamental to republican liberty and the authority of the federal constitution (Document 9-3).

The debate over property rights raised far-reaching sectional issues in conjunction with several Supreme Court decisions issued during John Marshall's tenure as chief justice (see text pp. 271–273). Marshall defended traditional property rights against encroachments by aspiring interests in a manner that broadened the power of the federal judiciary over state courts and legislatures (Document 9-4). This represented a victory for traditional property rights that would stand for nearly twenty years.

9-1   Cotton Cultivation and Textile Factories (1810)

Tench Coxe

A native of Philadelphia, Tench Coxe (1755–1824) studied at the College of Philadelphia (which later became the University of Pennsylvania) before working in his father's countinghouse. A strong supporter of the Constitution, Coxe held a number of minor government offices during the presidencies of George Washington and Thomas Jefferson. He had his greatest influence, however, as a writer on economics. Coxe emphasized what he viewed as a harmony of interests between a small but growing manufacturing sector and the dominant agricultural interest. He advocated a modest tariff on imported manufactures and firmly opposed commercial restrictions between states. Coxe was also one of the first to see the full economic implications of the cotton gin and increased cultivation of cotton in the South (see text p. 220). In a report drafted for Jefferson's treasury secretary, Albert Gallatin (see text p. 268), Coxe noted the emergence of a cotton textile industry in the Northeast and tied its future growth to the cultivation of cotton on southern plantations.

Source: A Statement of the Arts and Manufactures of the United States of America, for the Year 1810: Digested and Prepared by Tench Coxe, Esquire, of Philadelphia (Philadelphia: A. Cornman, 1814).

It is a fact of great importance. . . . on the subject of the relation of manufactures to the landed interest, that none of the productions of the earth, whether of *natural growth* or *the fruits of cultivation*, in the middle, northern and eastern states, which can be considered as "raw materials," are now exported in an *unmanufactured* condition to foreign markets. . . .

Until the late revolution in the cultivation of cotton, by which it was converted, through the strenuous excitements of the friends of manufactures, from a petty object in little fields and gardens, into an article of extensive cultivation among the planters and farmers, there was no redundant [surplus] raw materials for the manufacture of cloths and stuffs, for apparel and furniture, in the United States. There is at this time no other redundant raw material.

The green seed cotton was the best adapted to the general quality and situation, and to the climate of the southern states. But its cultivation, though perfectly pleasant and easy, was very much restrained by the extraordinary difficulty of separating it from the seeds. This operation required so much manual industry, as greatly to impede the manufacture, and of course, for the time, to prevent an extensive cultivation. In the year 1793 *the invaluable . . . gin* was invented by a citizen of the United States [in a note Coxe identified "Mr. Eli Whitney, of Connecticut"], and was so improved and perfected, as to render it easy, it is said to separate the seeds from one hundred million of pounds weight of cotton wool by the employment of three or four hundred persons, although it is alleged that it would require three hundred thousand persons to effect the same by hand. . . . By employing this machinery, every vicinity can easily and expeditiously prepare its cotton for the manufacturing cards . . . to any extent, that the world could require, were it to clothe itself entirely in cotton manufactures. Thus has been added, by our own invention, to the machinery *to facilitate the manufacture of a staple production of our soil*, a single improvement movable by water, steam, cattle or hand, which has set loose these immense powers of agriculture, *to produce cotton wool. . . .*

The water spinners of cotton, in one of the states, have represented . . . that they can make eighty-two pounds and one half of yarn by each spindle in every year. But the owners of other spinning mills deem it unsafe to calculate upon more than fifty-two pounds of yarn per annum for each spindle. . . . At the lowest of the rates, the United States, had they 1,160,000 spindles, could work up into yarn the sixty-four millions of pounds weight of cotton, which are the maximum of our exportation, in a single year. . . . Sixty-four millions of pounds of cotton . . . would produce about 50,000,000 pounds of cotton yarn, and with the labor . . . of about 58,000 persons . . . one eighth part ought to be adult males. The remaining seven eighths, might be women and children. This employment of less than *an hundredth part of* our white population of 1810

would be no inconvenience to agriculture or commerce. . . . If the weaving of this be executed, as may be done with perfect ease, by the employment of 100,000 women (less than one sixth of our adult females) with *the fly shuttle*, during *one half* of each working day in the year, the quantity of cloth by the Rhode Island rule of four yards for every pound, would amount to about 200,000,000 of yards. This quantity of cotton cloth, at one third of a dollar per yard, would be worth about 67,000,000 dollars.

There is yet another operation, which can be effected by labor-saving means, and by a process superceding the labor of many hands. Machinery is now in actual operation in the United States, for printing cotton and linen cloths, by engraving rollers of copper, moved by water. Ten thousand yards have been printed, with ease in a single day, by one man and two boys, with these rollers. . . . Similar means are in constant use for staining and dying cotton and linen cloths of one colour, in the same expeditious manner, so as to make them fit for a greater variety of apparel and furniture. Were these operations to be performed, upon the whole quantity of cotton goods estimated in this statement, they would add seven or eight millions to their value, and would require but 50 or 60,000 men and children. . . . The total addition to the original value of our cotton crop alone would be at a rate, far exceeding the value of our exports of American growth. . . . A quantity of cotton wool equal to all that is now produced by the civilized and uncivilized nations of the world, could be raised on a very small portion of our southern soil.

Such are the benefits, which agriculture and the country at large may derive from the manufacture of *our only redundant raw material*. The states of Rhode Island and Massachusetts have expelled all doubts about the practicability of the cotton operations. With the smallest territory in the United States, Rhode Island has already attained and introduced into her vicinity a cotton branch of our manufactures as valuable, as the cotton branch of any country in Europe was, at the time of the formation of our present constitution.

Questions

1. Coxe wanted the United States to spin, weave, and print the cotton it cultivated rather than export it raw. Why?
2. From Coxe's perspective, why was it important that manufactures be linked to the "landed interest"?
3. Why did Coxe emphasize that cotton manufacturers needed to employ relatively few men and that cotton cultivation required only a small amount of southern land?

9-2 John C. Calhoun's Speech on the Tariff Bill (April 4, 1816)

John C. Calhoun (1782–1850) was born in South Carolina and became that state's most prominent political figure. First elected to Congress as a War Hawk in 1810, Calhoun began his political career as a strident nationalist and defender of capitalism as the foundation for a self-sufficient and unified nation (see text pp. 266–269). His early nationalism faded in the 1830s, however, as he came to believe that slaveholding interests were threatened by the manufacturing and commercial interests of the North. In the following speech delivered in the House of Representatives (and reported in the third person), Calhoun's nationalism was still unruffled as he warned against the dangers of disunion and strongly supported a protective tariff to encourage domestic manufactures and strengthen the American commonwealth.

Source: Annals of the Congress of the United States, 1789–1824 (Washington, D.C.: U.S. Government Printing Office), 14th Cong., 1st sess., 1816, pp. 1326–1336.

He regretted much his want of preparation. . . . But whatever his arguments might want on that account in weight, he hoped might be made up in the disinterestedness of his situation. He was no manufacturer; he was not from that portion of our country supposed to be peculiarly interested. Coming, as he did, from the South, having, in common with his immediate constituents, no interest, but in the cultivation of the soil, in selling its products high, and buying cheap the wants and conveniences of life, no motive could be attributed to him, but such as were disinterested. . . . It is certainly a great political evil, incident to the character of the industry of this country, that, however prosperous our situation when at peace, with an uninterrupted commerce, . . . the moment that we were involved in war the whole is reversed. . . . The result of a war in the present state of our naval power is the blockade of our coast, and consequent destruction of our trade. . . .

To this distressing state of things there were two remedies, and only two; one is in our power immediately, the other requiring much time and exertion; but both constituting, in his opinion, the essential policy of this country; he meant the navy, and domestic manufactures. . . . Had we the means of attaining an immediate naval ascendancy, he acknowledged that the policy recommended by this bill, would be very questionable; but as that is not the fact . . . it became the duty of this House to resort . . . to the only remaining remedy . . . objection had been made . . . that capital employed in manufacturing produced a greater dependency on the part of the employed, than in commerce, navigation or agriculture. It is certainly an evil and to be regretted; but he did not think it a decisive objection to the system especially when it had incidental political advantages which in his opinion more than counterpoised it. It produced an interest strictly American, as much so as agriculture. . . . The country will from this [national interest in manufacturing] derive much advantage. Again, it is calculated to bind together more closely our widely-spread Republic. It will greatly increase our mutual dependence and intercourse; and will as a necessary consequence, excite an increased attention to internal improvement, a subject every way so intimately connected with the ultimate attainment of national strength and the perfection of our political institutions. He regarded the fact that it would make the parts adhere more closely, that it would form a new and most powerful cement, far out-weighing any political objections that might be urged against the system. In his opinion the *liberty* and the *union* of this country were inseparably united! That as the destruction of the latter would most certainly involve the former; so its maintenance will with equal certainty preserve it. He did not speak lightly. He had often and long revolved it in his mind; and he had critically examined into the causes that destroyed the liberty of other states. There are none that apply to us, or apply with a force to alarm. The basis of our Republic is too broad and its structure too strong to be shaken by them . . . but let it be deeply impressed on the heart of this House and country, that while they guarded against the old they exposed us to a new and terrible danger, disunion. This single word comprehended almost the sum of our political dangers; and against it we ought to be perpetually guarded.

Questions

1. What factors made Calhoun's views on the tariff "disinterested"?
2. How did Calhoun associate domestic manufacturing with national security?

3. In Calhoun's view, how did the encouragement of manufacturing protect the nation against "disunion"?

9-3 John Marshall's Decision in *Fletcher v. Peck* (1810)

In January 1801, in one of his last acts as president, John Adams appointed the staunchly Federalist John Marshall of Virginia Chief Justice of the United States. Marshall presided over the Supreme Court for the next thirty-four years, until his death in 1835. Marshall's significance is difficult to overemphasize (see text pp. 271–273): he shaped the direction of the Supreme Court as the guarantor of national capitalism. The fact that he did so in the era of the Democratic-Republican "Virginia Dynasty"—that is, during the presidencies of Thomas Jefferson, James Madison, and James Monroe—makes this achievement truly remarkable. During most of Marshall's tenure he presided over a Court majority that had been appointed by Jefferson, Madison, and Monroe. Eventually Marshall was the only remaining Federalist appointee. Nevertheless, Marshall shaped the direction of the Court, repeatedly carrying a majority of the justices with him in a series of landmark decisions, including *Fletcher v. Peck* (1810) (see text pp. 272–273). In his decision, Marshall acknowledged the corruption that tainted a Georgia land grant, but he relied on a strict construction of Article I, section 10, of the Constitution (protecting "obligation of Contracts") to strike down a law passed by the state of Georgia.

Source: Fletcher v. Peck, 6 Cranch 87 (1810). In Joseph P. Cotton, Jr., ed. *The Constitutional Decisions of John Marshall* (New York: P. D. Commanger, 1905; facsimile reprint, New York: Da Capo Press, 1969), vol. 1, pp. 243–250.

In this case the [Georgia] legislature may have had ample proof that the original grant was obtained by practices which can never be too much reprobated, and which would have justified its abrogation so far as respected those to whom crime was imputable. But the grant, when issued, conveyed an estate in fee-simple to the grantee, clothed with all the solemnities which law can bestow. This estate was transferable; and those who purchased parts of it were not stained by that guilt which infected the original transaction. . . . Their situation was the same, their title was the same, with that of every other member of the community who holds land by regular conveyances from the original patentee. . . .

The validity of this rescinding act [by the Georgia legislature] . . . might well be doubted, were Georgia a single sovereign power. But Georgia cannot be viewed as a single unconnected, sovereign power, on whose legislature no other restrictions are imposed than may be found in its own constitution. She is a part of a large empire; she is a member of the American Union; and that Union has a constitution the supremacy of which all acknowledge, and which imposes limits to the legislatures of the several states, which none claim a right to pass. The constitution of the United States declares that no state shall pass any bill of attainder, *ex post facto* law, or law impairing the obligation of contracts.

Does the case now under consideration come within this prohibitory section of the constitution? . . .

Since . . . in fact, a grant is a contract executed, the obligation of which still continues, and since the constitution uses the general term contract . . . it must be construed to comprehend the latter as well as the former. . . .

Whatever respect might have been felt for the state sovereignties, it is not to be disguised that the framers of the constitution viewed, with some apprehension, the violent acts which might grow out of the feelings of the moment; and that the people of the United States, in adopting that instrument, have manifested a determination to shield themselves and their property from the effects of those sudden and strong passions to which men are exposed. The restrictions on the legislative power of the states are obviously founded in this sentiment; and the constitution of the United States contains what may be deemed a bill of rights for the people of each state. . . .

It is, then, the unanimous opinion of the court, that, in this case, the estate having passed into the hands of a purchaser for a valuable consideration, without notice, the state of Georgia was restrained, either by general principles, which are common to our free institutions, or by the particular provisions of the constitution of the United States, from passing a law whereby the estate of the plaintiff in the premises so purchased could be constitutionally and legally impaired and rendered null and void.

Questions

1. In Marshall's view, why did the framers of the Constitution place restrictions on state legislatures?
2. The passage of the Constitution cited by Marshall appears in Article I, section 10. Locate that passage in the Constitution (see text p. D-9). Do you agree with Marshall's interpretation of its meaning?
3. How did Marshall's decision help lay the foundation for national capitalism?

9-4 Argument for the Plaintiff in *Dartmouth College v. Woodward* (1818)

Daniel Webster

In addition to his distinguished political career, Daniel Webster (1782–1852) established himself as an influential and financially successful constitutional lawyer. When the New Hampshire legislature circumvented a colonial charter establishing Dartmouth College by attempting to make the college a state institution, Webster defended his alma mater (and the inviolability of contracts) before the Supreme Court (see text p. 273). The Court agreed with Webster, endorsing a static view of property that protected established property rights for the next two decades. In this case, Dartmouth College was the plaintiff and William Woodward (the college's treasurer, who had been directed by state law to report to a new board of trustees) was the defendant.

Source: In Rev. B. F. Tefft, ed., *The Speeches of Daniel Webster* (New York: Lincoln Centenary Association, n.d. [186?]), pp. 11–59, passim.

The charter of 1769 created and established a corporation, to consist of twelve persons, and no more; to be called the "Trustees of Dartmouth College." . . . The charter, or letters patent, then proceed to create such a corporation . . . to have perpetual existence, as such corporation, and with power to hold and dispose of lands and goods, for the use of the college with all the ordinary powers of corporations. They are in their discretion to apply the funds and property of the college to the support of the president, tutors, ministers, and other officers of the college. . . .

No funds are given to the college by this charter. A corporate existence and capacity are given to the trustees, with the privileges and immunities which have been mentioned, to enable the founder and his associates the better to manage the funds which they themselves had con-

tributed, and such others as they might afterwards obtain.

After the institution thus created and constituted had existed, uninterruptedly and usefully, nearly fifty years, the legislature of New Hampshire passed the acts in question.

The first act makes the twelve trustees under the charter, and nine other individuals, to be appointed by the governor and council, a corporation, by a new name; and to this new corporation transfers all the *property, rights, powers, liberties, and privileges* of the old corporation; with further power to establish new colleges and an institute, and to apply all or any part of the funds to these purposes; subject to the power and control of a board of twenty-five overseers, to be appointed by the governor and council.

The second act makes further provisions for executing

the objects of the first, and the last act authorizes the defendant, the treasurer of the plaintiffs, to retain and hold their property, against their will.

If these acts are valid, the old corporation is abolished, and a new one created. . . . It will be contended by the plaintiffs, that these acts are not valid . . . because they are repugnant . . . to the tenth section of the first article of the constitution of the United States. The material words of that section are: "No state shall pass any bill of attainder, *ex post facto* law, or law impairing the obligation of contracts."

The object of these most important provisions in the national constitution has often been discussed. . . . It has already been decided in this court, that a *grant* is a contract, within the meaning of this provision; and that a grant by a state is also a contract, as much as the grant of an individual. In Fletcher *v.* Peck, this court says: ". . . A grant, in its own nature, amounts to an extinguishment of the right of the grantor, and implies a contract not to reassert that right. . . . The restrictions on the legislative power of the states are obviously founded in this sentiment; and the constitution of the United States contains what may be deemed a bill of rights for the people of each state."

It has also been decided that a grant by a state before the revolution is as much to be protected as a grant since. . . . This court, then, does not admit the doctrine that a legislature can repeal statutes creating private corporations. . . . And because charters of incorporation are of the nature of contracts, they cannot be altered or varied but by consent of the original parties. . . .

The case before the court is not of ordinary importance, or of every-day occurrence. It affects not this college only, but every college. . . . They have all a common principle of existence, the inviolability of their charters. It will be a dangerous, a most dangerous experiment, to hold these institutions subject to the rise and fall of popular parties, and the fluctuations of political opinions. If the franchise may be at any time taken away, or impaired, the property, also, may be taken away, or its use perverted. . . . Party and faction will be cherished in the places consecrated to piety and learning. These consequences are neither remote nor possible only. They are certain and immediate.

Questions

1. In what ways did the New Hampshire legislature change Dartmouth College's charter?
2. What constitutional argument did Webster employ to defend the original charter?
3. In Webster's view, why should colleges such as Dartmouth be privately controlled and therefore beyond the reach of "party and faction"?

Questions for Further Thought

1. In what ways did Webster's argument in the *Dartmouth College* case (Document 9-4) help secure traditional property rights?
2. In what ways did state actions involving the creation and destruction of property rights threaten the national capitalism envisioned by Coxe, Webster, and Marshall?
3. Evaluate Marshall's decision in *Fletcher v. Peck* (Document 9-3) from the perspective of aspiring economic interests. How might established property rights be viewed as entrenched privilege?

Visions of a Republican Social Order

The extension of voting rights to white men of all socioeconomic classes represented a major advancement of democracy in the early nineteenth century (see text pp. 274–276). In the political sphere, legislation granting universal (or nearly universal) white male suffrage was enacted in most of the nation (Document 9-5). But the eradication of property qualifications for voting presented a severe challenge to a republican tradition rooted in the ideal of civic virtue. If the virtue of a republican citizen was no longer tied to that citizen's interests as a property owner, what would the republic's foundation be? The answer lay in the social sphere, where urban America in particular, driven by the aspirations of a burgeoning middle class, saw far-reaching changes in the roles of men and women in marriage and in family life (see text pp. 277–278).

These changes in conjugal life did not affect all strata of society and did not spread uniformly across the country. But they did create a powerful new sensibility, a new sense of propriety, and a new sense of social responsibility that established new standards of social harmony and equity. The new standards had a social authority that reached beyond the middle class. From the perspective of the urban middle class a new era of human fulfillment had begun. The republican pursuit of happiness extended to the domestic sphere, where women challenged the traditions of patriarchy and began to claim a measure of equality with men (see text pp. 277–278). Happiness in marriage and family life required the cultivation of moral sentiments, placing women on a par with men (Documents 9-6 and 9-7).

9-5   Martin Van Buren against Unrestricted Male Suffrage (1821)

Martin Van Buren (1782–1862), born to a family of Dutch descent in upstate New York, became the leader of a powerful Jeffersonian political organization known as the Albany Regency. Van Buren played a leading role in the convention that redrafted the New York constitution in 1821 (see text p. 276). The convention embraced the principle of universal white manhood suffrage but increased the property qualifications for black men. Van Buren initially favored maintaining a minimal property qualification, suggesting in the following remarks that unrestricted manhood suffrage threatened to sweep aside distinctions of race as well as those of class.

Source: In The Votes and Speeches of Martin Van Buren . . . In the Convention of the State of New-York (Assembled to Amend the Constitution in 1821) (Albany, N.Y.: T. Weed, 1840), pp. 15–17.

Mr. Van Buren . . . observed, that it was evident, and indeed some gentlemen did not seem disposed to disguise it, that the amendment proposed . . . contemplated nothing short of universal suffrage. Mr. V. B. did not believe that there were twenty members . . . who, were the bare naked question of universal suffrage put to them, would vote in its favor; and he was very sure that its adoption was not expected, and would not meet the views of their constituents. . . .

One word on the main question. . . . We had already reached the verge of universal suffrage. There was but one step beyond. And are gentlemen prepared to take that step? We were cheapening this invaluable right. He was disposed to go as far as any man in the extension of rational liberty; but he could not consent to undervalue this

precious privilege, so far as to confer it with an undiscriminating hand upon every one, black or white, who would be kind enough to condescend to accept it. . . .

Mr. Van Buren said . . . he felt it a duty to make a brief explanation of the motives which governed him. The qualifications reported [for consideration] . . . were of three kinds, viz: the payment of a money tax—the performance of military duty, and working on the highway. The two former had met with his decided approbation; to the latter, he wished to add the additional qualification, that the elector [voter] should, if he paid no tax, performed no military duty, but offered his vote on the sole ground that he had labored on the highways, also be a *house-holder*. . . . The question then recurred [of] . . . abandoning all qualifications, and throwing open the ballot-boxes to every body—

demolishing at one blow, the distinctive character of an elector, the proudest and most invaluable attribute of freemen[.]

Mr. Van Buren said, he had, . . . this day hinted at the numerous objections which he had . . . in regard to the right of suffrage: objections which he intended to make . . . to convince every member . . . of the dangerous and alarming tendency of that precipitate and unexpected prostration of all qualifications. At this moment, he would only say, that among the evils which would flow from a wholly unrestricted suffrage, the following would be the most injurious, viz. . . . That the character of the increased number of votes would be such as would render . . . elections rather a curse than a blessing; which would drive from the polls all sober minded people. . . .

Questions

1. What reasons did Van Buren give for wanting to maintain a minimal property qualification for voting?
2. What did Van Buren mean when he referred to "rational liberty"?
3. Why did Van Buren refer to race when he opposed conferring the right to vote "with an undiscriminating hand"?

9-6 *The Mother's Book*

Lydia Maria Child

Lydia Maria Child (1802–1880) was born in Medford, Massachusetts, and married a prominent Boston lawyer. She was best known as a leading abolitionist agitator, but she also enjoyed a successful career as a writer of fiction, juvenile literature, and works on domestic economy. Her most widely read work, *The Mother's Book* (1831), explained to women in middle-class households how the mother's role in child rearing had assumed vast new meaning and significance. In Child's view, an internalized sense of self-restraint represented the central object of the "affectionate rationalist" approach to child rearing (see text pp. 280–281): children should not be whipped into obedience, they should be instructed in a manner that encouraged them to wish to be obedient. In this passage, Child explored the means by which this moral education could be accomplished.

Source: Lydia Maria Child, *The Mother's Book* (Boston: Carter and Hendee, 1831).

I once saw a mother laugh very heartily at the distressed face of a kitten, which a child of two years old was pulling backward by the tail. At last, the kitten, in self-defense, turned and scratched the boy. He screamed, and his mother ran to him, kissed the wound, and beat the poor kitten, saying all the time, "Naughty kitten, to scratch John!" . . .

This little incident, trifling as it seems, no doubt had important effects on the character of the child. . . .

In the first place, the child was encouraged in cruelty, by seeing that it gave his mother amusement. . . .

In the next place, the kitten was struck for defending herself; this was injustice to the injured animal, and a lesson of tyranny to the boy. In the third place, striking the kitten because she had scratched him, was teaching him retaliation . . . the influence upon him is, that it is right to injure when we are injured. . . .

The mind of a child is not like that of a grown person . . . it is a vessel empty and pure—always ready to receive, and always receiving.

Every look, every movement, every expression, does something toward forming the character of the little heir to immortal life. . . .

The rule, then, for developing good affections in a

child is, that he never be allowed to see or feel the influence of bad passions, even in the most trifling things; and in order to effect this, you must drive evil passions from your own heart. Nothing can be real that has not its home *within* us. The only sure way, as well as the easiest, to *appear* good, is to *be* good.

It is not possible to indulge anger, or any other wrong feeling, and conceal it entirely. If not expressed in words, a child *feels* the baneful influence. Evil enters into his soul, as the imperceptible atmosphere he breathes enters into his lungs: and the beautiful little image of God is removed farther and farther from his home in heaven.

Questions

1. What moral lessons were drawn from the "trifling" incident of the child pulling the cat's tail?
2. Do you agree with Child's premise that a child's mind is "a vessel empty and pure"?
3. Consider the new authority and responsibility of the middle-class mother. How, in Child's view, should a mother develop "good affections" in a child's mind?

9-7 Mercy Otis Warren and the Writing of American History (1805)

Mercy Otis Warren (1728–1814) lived most of her life in Plymouth, Massachusetts. Through her brother (James Otis) and husband (James Warren) she knew many of the leaders of the American Revolution. She took upon herself the role of poet and historian of the Patriot cause; her *History of the Rise, Progress, and Termination of the American Revolution* appeared in three volumes in 1805 (see text p. 282). John Adams, a Revolutionary Era leader and the second president of the United States, felt that Warren's history did not do him justice and engaged in a lengthy correspondence with the author. After five years of private arguing, the two reestablished a public cordiality, although Adams confided sourly to a friend that "History is not the Providence of the Ladies." In the introduction to her *History*, Warren publicly confronted this male sense of propriety.

Source: Mrs. Mercy Warren, *History of the Rise, Progress, and Termination of the American Revolution* (Boston: 1805; facsimile reprint, New York: AMS Press, 1970), pp. iii–viii.

At a period when every manly arm was occupied, and every trait of talent or activity engaged, either in the cabinet or the field, apprehensive, that amidst the sudden convulsions, crowded scenes, and rapid changes, that flowed in quick succession, many circumstances might escape the more busy and active members of society [i.e., men], I have been induced to improve the leisure Providence had lent, to record as they passed, in the following pages, the new and unexperienced events exhibited in a land previously blessed with peace, liberty, simplicity, and virtue. . . .

Connected by nature, friendship, and every social tie, with many of the first patriots, and most influential characters on the continent; in the habits of confidential and epistolary intercourse with several gentlemen employed abroad in the most distinguished stations, and with others since elevated to the highest grades of rank and distinction, I had the best means of information, through a long period that the colonies were in suspense, waiting the operation of foreign courts, and the success of their own enterprising spirit.

The solemnity that covered every countenance, when contemplating the sword uplifted, and the horrors of civil war rushing to habitations not inured to scenes of rapine and misery; even to he quiet cottage, where only concord and affection had reigned; stimulated to observation a mind that had not yielded to the assertion, that all political attentions lay out of the road of female life.

It is true there are certain appropriate duties assigned

to each sex; and doubtless it is the more peculiar province of masculine strength, not only to repel the bold invader of the rights of his country and of mankind, but in the nervous style of manly eloquence, to describe the blood-stained field, and relate the story of slaughtered armies.

Sensible of this, the trembling heart has recoiled at the magnitude of the undertaking, and the hand often shrunk back from the task; yet, recollecting that every domestic enjoyment depends on the unimpaired possession of civil and religious liberty, that a concern for the welfare of society ought equally to flow in every human breast, the work was not relinquished. The most interesting circumstances were collected, active characters portrayed, the principles of the times developed, and the changes marked; nor need it cause a blush to acknowledge, a detail was preserved with a view of transmitting it to the rising youth of my country, some of them in infancy, others in the European world, while the most interesting events lowered over their native land. . . .

The state of the public mind, appears at present to be prepared to weigh these reflections with solemnity, and to receive with pleasure an effort to trace the origin of the American revolution, to review the characters that effected it, and to justify the principles of the defection and final separation from the parent state. With an expanded heart, beating with high hopes of the continued freedom and prosperity of America, the writer indulges a modest expectation, that the following pages will be perused with kindness and candor: this she claims, both in consideration of her sex, the uprightness of her intentions, and the fervency of her wishes for the happiness of all the human race.

Questions

1. What justification did Warren offer for having a woman write American history?
2. In what specific ways did her undertaking challenge the pre-Revolutionary understanding of women's civil capacities?
3. Explore the links between the republican principles of the Revolution and Warren's assertion that politics did not "lay out of the road of female life."

Questions for Further Thought

1. How did broadening the franchise promote change in American republican culture? Why were women and children central to this change?
2. Compare these documents with the illustrations on pages 280 and 286 of the text. What new opportunities and limitations did women and men face in the new conjugal family?
3. How did the new moral role of women affect women's traditionally subordinate social sphere?

Protestant Christianity and Women's Lives

In the early decades of the nineteenth century the national character was shaped by westward expansion, capitalist development, democratic politics, and evangelical Protestantism (see text pp. 282–284). In a country without a monarchy, aristocracy, or established church, majority rule and conformity mitigated the atomizing effects of individualism. Waves of revivalism collectively known as the Second Great Awakening (see text pp. 282–285) challenged ecclesiastical authority while generating intense religious awakenings and promoting the growth of evangelical Protestant denominations (Document 9-8).

The individual conversion experience revealed to believers the divine presence that heralded the perfection of human society and the Second Coming of Christ. Material and moral progress advanced society toward the state of perfection that would mark the beginning of Christ's thousand-year reign on earth. The Second Great Awakening emphasized the individual's capacity for immediate reformation and the society's capacity, through the perfection of the individual, to advance toward the millennium (Document 9-9). Just as political democracy included the individual citizen within the workings of majority rule, revivalism sought the conversion of individual souls to Christ within the collective advance of a Christian society toward the millennium. The forms of Old World authority had been rejected in America, where individualism shaped a mass culture that was liberating in its rejection of traditional social hierarchy but constraining in its capacity to enforce conformity.

The rejection of traditional social hierarchy also encouraged men and women to marry as loving companions and to nurture in themselves and their children the affections that were deemed central to the conjugal and family bond. For many urban middle-class families the nurturing family was a significantly smaller one (see text p. 279). With the economic incentive for having large families gone, husbands and wives used abstinence and birth control to limit family size. Women, bearing fewer children over a shorter period, lived longer and engaged in new activities. As the moral stewards of their families and the nurturers of their children, women sustained the republic. As Americans considered the social implications of their republican experiment, the education of women became a topic of concern (see text p. 287 and Document 9-10).

9-8 The Formation of the American Home Missionary Society (1826)

The American Home Missionary Society (see text p. 285) was founded in New York City in 1826 as a product of a "Plan of Union" that united Congregationalists and Presbyterians in an effort to send ministers west with the growing stream of settlers. Although national in its aspirations, the society focused its efforts in western New York State. Along the course of the Erie Canal, eastern merchants and capitalists transformed towns such as Utica, Syracuse, and Rochester into manufacturing centers while evangelical ministers fanned the flames of revivalism during the Second Great Awakening. In the following passage the founders of the American Home Missionary Society set out their society's mission.

Source: Address of the American Home Missionary Society to the Christian Public (New York: Vanderpool, 1826).

Since the commencement of the present century . . . Christians of different names have been brought under a practical conviction—that in their design to preach the gospel to every creature, there is a need of extended co-operation. Sectional partialities have accordingly been overcome, the great brotherhood of the churches has been recognized, and distant portions of Christendom have consented to commune together. . . .

In the midst of the progress of this state of things, the American Home Missionary Society has had its origins. . . .

Composed . . . as it is of those who are united in their belief of essential doctrines, and who do not greatly differ in their views of church government, and the qualifications for admission to the sacraments of Christianity, it is to be expected . . . that [the Society] . . . will assist in the support of only such ministers as hold a regular standing in the several ecclesiastical connexions represented in the Society, or are in doctrinal agreement and friendly correspondence with the same. By the employment of such missionaries, it is the object of this Society to occupy . . . the ground that otherwise would remain destitute of an evangelical ministry, and to assist feeble congregations in all parts of the

United States, which, on these principles, shall desire its aid in the support of settled pastors. . . .

In connexion with this national object, let it be considered that the Congregationalists, and Presbyterians of different names, who are already represented in this Society, are probably the largest denominations of Christians in the United States.—Let it be considered also that other denominations may hereafter make this Society the channel through which to convey their contributions to the destitute, and its founders can hardly be charged with presumption in having given to it the style of *National Institution*. . . .

It remains only to state, that the location of this Society has been chosen in reference to the great national object which it contemplates. The city of New-York possesses peculiar advantages as the seat of this Institution. Its site is central, in that portion of the country which at present will be expected to furnish the principal resources of the Society, and its intercourse with all parts of the United States is constant. Here the necessary means can be more conveniently collected, and information more readily received, than in any other place. It is the heart of the land; and the God of nature seems to have designed that the channels through which this city derives its wealth from every line of the continent, should in return, be channels of mercy, through which the knowledge that saves is to be conveyed to the farthest limits of the nation.

Questions

1. How did the founders of the American Home Missionary Society propose to advance the evangelical goals of the Second Great Awakening?
2. Refer to Map 9.2 (see text p. 283). Why did the founders of the society seek a "national" organization that could overcome "sectional partialities"?
3. Why did the society's founders make New York City their headquarters? What did they mean when they said that God intended the channels of commerce to serve also as "channels of mercy"?

9-9　*The Duty of Christian Freemen to Elect Christian Rulers* (1828)

Ezra Stiles Ely

A Presbyterian clergyman in Philadelphia, Ezra Stiles Ely (1786–1861) strongly supported the Sabbatarian reforms of the Second Great Awakening, which urged Americans to respect the Sabbath by opposing all secular activities on Sundays. When the Pennsylvania state senate refused to grant an act of incorporation to the American Sunday School Union, an interdenominational society devoted to the Sabbatarian movement, Ely published extracts from a sermon he had delivered the previous Fourth of July calling on Christians to unite to elect devout Christians to public office (see text p. 285).

Source: Ezra Stiles Ely, *The Duty of Christian Freemen to Elect Christian Rulers* (Philadelphia: W. F. Gettes, 1828), pp. 6–14.

God, my hearers, requires a Christian faith, a Christian profession, and a Christian practice of all our public men; and we as Christian citizens ought, by the publication of our opinions, to require the same.

. . . . Since it is the duty of all our rulers to serve the Lord and kiss the Son of God, it must be most manifestly the duty of all our Christian fellow-citizens to honour the Lord Jesus Christ and promote christianity by electing and supporting as public officers the friends of our blessed Saviour. Let it only be granted, that Christians have the same rights and privileges in exercising the elective franchise, which are here accorded to Jews and Infidels, and we ask no other evidence to show, that those who prefer a Christian ruler, may unite in supporting him, in preference to any one of a different character. It shall cheerfully be granted, that every citizen is eligible to every office, whatever may be his religious opinions and moral character; and that every one may constitutionally support any person whom he may *choose*; but it will not hence follow, that he is without accountability to his Divine Master for his choice; or that he may lay aside all his Christian principles and feelings when he selects his ticket and presents it at the polls. "*In all* thy ways acknowledge him," is a maxim which should dwell in a Christian's mind on the day of a public election as much as on the Sabbath; and which should govern him when conspiring with others to honour Christ, either at the Lord's table, or in the election of a Chief Magistrate. In elucidating the duty of private Christians in relation to the choice of their civil rulers, it seems to me necessary to remark,

That every Christian who has the right and the opportunity of exercising the elective franchise ought to do it. Many pious people feel so much disgust at the manner in which elections are conducted, from the first nomination to the closing of the polls, that they relinquish their right of voting for years together. But if all *pious* people were to conduct thus, then our rulers would be wholly elected by the *impious*. If all *good men* are to absent themselves from elections, then the *bad* will have the entire transaction of our public business. . . .

I propose, fellow-citizens, a new sort of union, or, if you please, a *Christian party in politics,* which I am exceedingly desirous all good men in our country should join: not by *subscribing a constitution* and the formation of a new society, to be added to the scores which now exist; but by adopting, avowing, and determining to act upon, truly religious principles in all civil matters. I am aware that the true Christians of our country are divided into many different denominations; who have, alas! too many points of jealousy and collision; still, a union to a very great extent, and for the most valuable purposes is not impracticable. For,

All Christians, of all denominations, may, and ought to, agree in determining, that they will never wittingly support for any public office, any person whom they know or believe to sustain, at the time of his proposed election, a bad moral character. In this, thousands of moralists, who profess no experimental acquaintance with Christianity, might unite and co-operate with *our Christian party.* And surely, it is not impossible, nor unreasonable for all classes of Christians to say within themselves, no man that we have reason to think is a liar, thief, gambler, murderer, debauchee, spendthrift, or openly immoral person in any way, shall have our support at any election. REFORMATION should not only be allowed, but encouraged; for it would be requiring too much to insist upon it, that a candidate for office *shall always have sustained an unblemished moral character*, and it would be unchristian not to forgive and support one who has proved his repentance by recantation and a considerable course of new obedience.

Some of the best men were once vile; but they have been washed from their sins. Present good moral character should be considered as essential to every candidate for the post of honour. In this affair I know we are very much dependent on testimony, and that we may be deceived; especially in those controverted elections in which all manner of falsehoods are invented and vended, wholesale and retail, against some of the most distinguished men of our country: but after all, we must exercise our candour and best discretion, as we do in other matters of belief. We must weigh evidence, and depend most on those who appear the most competent and credible witnesses. It will be natural for us to believe a man's neighbours and acquaintances in preference to strangers. When we have employed the lights afforded us for the illumination of our minds, we shall feel peace of conscience, if we withhold our vote from every one whom we believe to be an immoral man.

Come then, fellow Christians, and friends of good morals in society, let us determine thus far to unite; for thus far we may, and ought to, and shall unite, if we duly weigh the importance of a good moral character in a ruler. Let no love of *the integrity of a party* prevent you from striking out the name of every dishonest and base man from your ticket. You have a right to choose, and you glory in your freedom: make then your own election: and when all good *men* act on this principle it will not be a vain thing. Candidates then, must be moral men, or seem to be, or they will not secure an election. . . .

All who profess to be Christians of any denomination ought to agree that they will support no man as a candidate for any office, who is not professedly friendly to Christianity, and a believer in divine Revelation. We do not say that true or even pretended Christianity shall be made a constitutional test of admission to office; but we do affirm that Christians may in their elections lawfully prefer the avowed friends of the Christian religion to Turks, Jews, and Infidels. . . . While every religious system is tolerated in our country, and no one is established by law, it is still possible for me to think, that the friend of Christianity will make a much better governor of this commonwealth or President of the United States, than the advocate of Theism or Polytheism. . . . If three or four of the most numerous denominations of Christians in the United States, the Presbyterians, the Baptists, the Methodists and Congregationalists for instance, should act upon this principle, our country would never be dishonoured with an *avowed infidel* in her national cabinet or capitol. . . . Let a man be of good moral character, and let him profess to believe in and advocate the Christian religion, and we can all support him. At one time he will be a Baptist, at another an Episcopalian, at another a Methodist, at another a Presbyterian of the American, Scotch, Irish, Dutch, or German stamp, and always a friend to our common Christianity. . . .

Let us elect men who dare to acknowledge the Lord Jesus Christ for their Lord in their public documents. Which of our Presidents has ever done this? It would pick no infidel's pocket, and break no Jew's neck, if our President should be so singular as to let it be known, that he is a *Christian* by his Messages, and an advocate for the Deity of Christ by his personal preference. . . .

We are a Christian nation: we have a right to demand that all our rulers in their conduct shall conform to Christian morality; and if they do not, it is the duty and privilege of Christian freemen to make a new and a better election.

May the Lord Jesus Christ for ever reign in and over these United States, and call them peculiarly his own. *Amen.*

Questions

1. How does Ely define a "good moral character"?
2. In Ely's view, what were the limitations of the existing system of party politics? How could voters determine a candidate's moral character?
3. How did Ely deal with the First Amendment's separation of church and state?

9-10   The Education of Republican Women (1798)

Benjamin Rush

Benjamin Rush (1745–1813) studied medicine in Philadelphia and the University of Edinburgh. He returned to Philadelphia in 1769 to practice medicine and advance American republican values. For Rush, republicanism implied a host of social and moral reforms as Americans distinguished their society from that of monarchical Great Britain. Here he advocates improved education for young women to prepare them to be republican mothers (see text p. 286). Rush addressed his remarks on female education to "The Visitors of the Young Ladies' Academy in Philadelphia, 28th July, 1787." The essay was first published in 1798.

Source: Benjamin Rush, *Essays Literary, Moral, and Philosophical* (Philadelphia, 1798; reprint, Schenectady, N.Y.: Union College Press, 1988), pp. 44–54.

The first remark that I shall make upon this subject, is, that female education should be accommodated to the state of society, manners, and government of the country, in which it is conducted.

This remark leads me at once to add, that the education of young ladies, in this country, should be conducted upon principles very different from what it is in Great Britain, and in some respects, different from what it was when we were part of a monarchical empire.

There are several circumstances in the situation, employments, and duties of women in America, which require a peculiar mode of education. . . .

The equal share that every citizen has in the liberty, and the possible share he may have in the government of our country, make it necessary that our ladies should be qualified to a certain degree by a peculiar and suitable education, to concur in instructing their sons in the principles of liberty and government. . . .

Vocal music should never be neglected, in the education of a young lady, in this country. Besides preparing her to join in that part of public worship which consists in psalmody, it will enable her to soothe the cares of domestic life. The distress and vexation of a husband—the noise of a nursery, and, even, the sorrows that will sometimes intrude into her own bosom, may all be relieved by a song, where sound and sentiment unite to act upon the mind. . . .

The attention of our young ladies should be directed, as soon as they are prepared for it, to the reading of history—travels—poetry—and moral essays. These studies are accommodated, in a peculiar manner, to the present state of society in America, and when a relish is excited for them, in early life, they subdue that passion for reading novels, which so generally prevails among the fair sex. . . . As yet the intrigues of a British novel, are . . . foreign to our manners. . . . Let it not be said, that the tales of distress, which fill modern novels, have a tendency to soften the female heart into acts of humanity. The fact is the reverse of this. The abortive sympathy which is excited by the recital of imaginary distress, blunts the heart to that which is real; and, hence, we sometimes see instances of young ladies, who weep away a whole forenoon over the criminal sorrows of a fictitious Charlotte . . . turning with disdain at three o'clock from the sight of a beggar, who solicits in feeble accents or signs, a small portion only of the crumbs which fall from their fathers' tables. . . .

It should not surprise [*sic*] us that British customs, with respect to female education have been transplanted into our American schools and families. . . . It is high time to awake from this servility—to study our own character—to examine the age of our country—and to adopt manners in every thing, that shall be accommodated to our state of society, and to the forms of our government. In particular it is incumbent upon us to make ornamental accomplishments yield to principles and knowledge, in the education of our women. . . . The influence of female education would be still more extensive and useful in domestic life. The obligations of gentlemen to qualify themselves by knowledge and industry to discharge the duties of benevolence, would be encreased [*sic*] by marriage; and the patriot—the hero—and the legislator, would find the sweetest regard of their toils, in the approbation and applause of their wives. Children would discover the marks of maternal prudence and wisdom in every station of life; for it has been remarked that there have been few great or good men who have not been blessed with wise and prudent mothers. . . . I know that the elevation of the female mind, by means of moral, physical and religious truth, is considered by some men as unfriendly to the domestic character of a woman. But this is a prejudice of little minds, and springs from the same spirit which opposes the general diffusion of knowledge among the citizens of our republic. If men believe that ignorance is favourable to the government of the female sex, they are certainly deceived; for a weak and ignorant woman will always be governed with the greatest difficulty. . . . It will be in our power, LADIES, to correct the mistakes and practice of our sex upon these subjects, by demonstrating, that the female temper can only be governed by reason, and that the cultivation of reason in women, is alike friendly to the order of nature, and to private as well as public happiness.

Questions

1. Why did Rush want to discourage young American women from reading novels?
2. What did he mean when he insisted that "ornamental accomplishments" must "yield to principles and knowledge"?
3. In what ways would the proper education of women promote republican virtue?

Questions for Further Thought

1. Religious revivalism promoted both social conformity and radical individualism. What were the secular consequences of that dynamic?
2. How could the process of moral reformation championed by Ely (Document 9-9) promote the social status of women (see text pp. 285–287)?
3. In the absence of central authority, how were power and authority established in early nineteenth-century America?

CHAPTER 10

The Industrial Revolution 1820–1840

★   ★   ★

The Rise of Northeastern Manufacturing

The word *revolution* in the term *Industrial Revolution* refers to the fundamental nature of the changes that occurred as household manufacturing was displaced by shops and factories. Centralized production increased productivity and generated wealth, but it also changed the lives of owners and workers alike. These changes, beginning in the Northeast with the emergence of the textile industry (see text p. 297) in the 1820s, gradually altered the social relations of many Americans.

The emergence of the textile industry (see text pp. 297–299) depended on several factors: entrepreneurs with access to capital, an abundant supply of cheap labor, and a reliable source of energy. Competition with British manufactures added to the difficulties American businessmen faced in bringing these factors of production together (Document 10-1). But in New England, Francis Cabot Lowell and Nathan Appleton successfully invested in a number of textile factories that were powered by water wheels and employed young women from neighboring farms. The Lowell and Appleton ventures came to be called the Waltham plan (see text p. 300). That system solved the American problem of high labor costs while offering young farm women freedom from the drudgery of farm labor, good wages, and well-supervised living conditions (Document 10-2). The paternalism of the Waltham plan also seemed to offer an American alternative to the specter of pauper labor that haunted industrial Great Britain (Document 10-3).

The changes wrought by the Industrial Revolution were not all positive, but in the early phase of social transformation the promise of technological innovation seemed limitless. The establishment of the Franklin Institute in Philadelphia (see text p. 302) and similar mechanics' institutes elsewhere in the country made a virtue of technological innovations and linked progress in production with the democratic aspirations of workers (Document 10-4).

10-1   A Textile Manufacturer Discusses His Enterprise (1832)

In 1832 Secretary of the Treasury Louis McLane, responding to a Congressional resolution, asked manufacturers a series of questions about their businesses. The purpose of the inquiry was to determine their attitudes toward the protective tariff (see text p. 299). Jacob Pusey owned and operated a cotton textile mill in Delaware. His answers illustrate the precariousness of the American textile industry forty years after the opening of Samuel Slater's mill (see text pp. 297–298). The new law enacted in July 1832 responded to Pusey's concerns by retaining a 50 percent tariff on imported cotton cloth.

Source: U.S. Treasury Department, *Documents Relative to the Manufactures in the United States* (1833), vol. 3, pp. 800–802, 224–226. In *Reprints of Economic Classics* (New York: Augustus M. Kelly, 1969), vol. 2, pp. 663–666, 224–225.

QUESTIONS.

1. State and county in which the manufactory is situated?

2. Kind or description of the manufactory; and whether water, steam, or other power?

3. When established; and whether a joint stock concern?

4. Capital invested in ground and buildings, and water power, and in machinery?

5. Average amount in materials, and in cash for the purchase of materials and payment of wages?

6. Annual rate of profit on the capital invested since the establishment of the manufactory; distinguishing between the rate of profit upon that portion of the capital which is borrowed, after providing for the interest upon it, and the rate of profit upon that portion which is not borrowed?

7. Cause of the increase, (or decrease, as the case may be,) of profit?

8. Rates of profit on capital otherwise employed in the same State and county?

9. Amount of articles annually manufactured since the establishment of the manufactory? Description, quality, and value of each kind?

ANSWERS.

1. Delaware State, Newcastle county.

2. Cotton spinning, by water power.

3. In the year 1814; private property.

4. $30,000 [$423,000 in 1990 dollars].

5. Variable. When in full operation about $10,000 must be afloat in materials and manufactures on hand, with provision for payment of wages.

6. The first seven years sunk all the capital invested, and the last ten years have recovered about two-thirds of it; though some of the last ten were years of loss: my books will not distinguish between the two kinds of capital.

7. Frequently by competition in the home market the profits are reduced to cost and charges; sometimes (when the business would not have been affected by home competition,) the profits are reduced to nothing, by overimportation of other descriptions of goods causing such a press for money in seaports as to put down the price of yarn when the stock in market was not greater than ordinary; and vice versa for increased profits.

8. Not known to the writer.

9. From 70,000 to 100,000 lbs. cotton yarn per annum; the quantity varying in the year according to the demand in some measure. It is difficult to ascertain the value, as the price has varied since the commencement from sixty-four cents in 1814, to eighteen cents per lb. in 1830.

QUESTIONS.

10. Quantity and value of different kinds of raw materials used, distinguishing between foreign products and domestic products?

11. Cost in the United States of similar articles of manufacture imported from abroad, and from what countries?

12. Number of men, women, and children employed, and average wages of each class?

13. How many hours a day employed; and what portion of the year?

14. Rate of wages of similar classes otherwise employed in the same State and county, in other States, and in foreign countries?

15. Number of horses or other animals employed?

16. Whether the manufactures find a market at the manufactory? If not, how far they are sent to a market?

17. Whether foreign articles of the like kinds enter into competition with them at such place of sale; and to what extent?

18. Where are the manufactures consumed?

19. Whether any of the manufactures are exported to foreign countries? and if so, where?

20. Whether the manufacture is sold by the manufacturer for cash? and if on credit, at what credit? if bartered, for what?

21. Whether the cost of the manufactured article (to the manufacturer) has increased or decreased; and how much in each year, from the establishment of the manufactory; and whether the increase has been in the materials or the labor, and at what rate?

22. The prices at which the manufactures have been sold by the manufacturer since the establishment?

23. What rate of duty [i.e., tariff] is necessary to enable the manufacturer to enter into competition in the home market with similar articles imported?

25. What has been the rate of your profits, annually, for the last three years? . . .

26. What portion of the cost of your manufactures consists of the price of the raw material, what portion of the wages of labor, and what portion of the profits of capital?

27. What amount of the agricultural productions of the country is consumed in your establishment, and what amount of other domestic productions?

28. What quantity or amount of manufactures, such as you make, are produced in the United States; and what amount in your own State?

ANSWERS.

10. 350 bales of cotton, valued for 1831, at $10,500; all the produce of the United States.

11. Very little, if any; cotton yarn is imported of the degree of coarseness which is manufactured at this mill.

12. 6 men, average $6 each per week; 12 women, average $2 each per week; 25 children, average $1.25 per week.

13. 11 hours per day, exclusive of meals, and about 50 weeks in the year.

14. Not known to the writer.

15. Seven.

16. A small portion sold at the factory; the remainder sent 40 miles by land and water conveyance.

17. No foreign article of like kind is imported that I know of in latter years; domestic competition has settled that in the reduced price.

18. In Pennsylvania and the southern and western States.

19. None of this kind exported, known to the writer, until woven.

20. Much the largest part is sold on a credit, generally 6 months, after having lain in store sometimes three or four months.

21. The cost has decreased both in the material and labor; rather more in the material; have not sufficient data to answer more particularly; the labor has been rather higher since 1824; material has fluctuated, having been sold some years at 10 to 15 cents, and others at 25 to 30 cents.

22. In 1814 sixty-four cents per lb.; gradually declining till 1820, it was twenty-eight cents; then advancing till 1822, it was 34 or 35 cents; then gradually declining till 1831, it was 18 cents, (except excited prices in 1825, a few months.)

23. Not known.

25. Less than four per cent, after providing for necessary proportion of repairs.

26. About $\frac{1}{2}$ for raw material; $\frac{1}{4}$ for labor in the factory; 1-20, or sometimes 1-15, might be profit; the balance is made up by contingent expenses, wastage, etc., etc.

27. About $2,000 in value of agricultural and vegetable productions; $1,000 in domestic dry goods and groceries.

28. No data to answer from as respects the United States; upwards of 20,000 lbs. of cotton yarn are produced in this county in one week; (no other county in this State manufactures cotton.)

QUESTIONS.

29. If the duty upon the foreign manufacture of the kind of goods which you make were reduced to 12 $\frac{1}{2}$ per cent, with a corresponding reduction on all the imports, would it cause you to abandon your business, or would you manufacture at reduced prices?

30. If it would cause you to abandon your business, in what way would you employ your capital?

31. Is there any pursuit in which you could engage, from which you could derive greater profits, even after a reduction of the import duties to 12 $\frac{1}{2}$ per cent?

Newcastle, March 10th, 1832.

ANSWERS.

29. There can be no question but a *present* abandonment of business would be the consequence, as manufacturing at reduced prices would soon destroy the capital. All who could hold their property a few years would do an excellent business under such prices, both for raw material and manufactured goods, *as British monopoly would then dictate*, taken in connexion with the then low prices for bread, and meat, and labor.

30. Under such circumstances, I should have no capital, as purchasers for such property could not be found at any price; but, admitting a very small amount could be realized, agriculture or merchandizing would be the next business, in order to get bread, though both branches are well filled.

31. Certain loss would result, and total ruin would follow such an import duty; and twenty-five cents per day for my manual labor would be better than that; the effect (of such a change in the duties) on agriculture or other business might be to deter a man from engaging in them without the necessary experience, which he could not have if his time had been spent in manufacturing.

JACOB PUSEY, *Cotton Spinner*

Questions

1. To what degree and in what areas could Pusey be flexible in responding to changing business conditions?
2. What did Pusey need to make his manufacturing enterprise more stable?
3. What consequences did he foresee if the protective tariff was abandoned?

10-2 A Mill Worker Describes Her Work and Life (1844)

A majority of the workers in the early years of the textile industry were young women from New England farm families (see text p. 300). The women mill hands in Lowell, Massachusetts, published their own poetry and other compositions in *The Lowell Offering*. The following letters, written by a worker identified only as "Susan," were published in 1844.

Source: The Lowell Offering, June and August 1844, pp. 169–172, 237–240. In Stanley I. Kutler, ed., *Looking for America: The People's History*, 2d ed. (New York: Norton, 1979), vol. 1, pp. 260–265.

Dear Mary:

In my last I told you I would write again, and say more of my life here; and this I will now attempt to do.

I went into the mill to work a few days after I wrote to you. It looked very pleasant at first, the rooms were so

light, spacious, and clean, the girls so pretty and neatly dressed, and the machinery so brightly polished or nicely painted. The plants in the windows, or on the overseer's bench or desk, gave a pleasant aspect to things. You will wish to know what work I am doing. I will tell you of the different kinds of work.

There is, first, the carding-room, where the cotton flies most, and the girls get the dirtiest. But this is easy, and the females are allowed time to go out at night before the bell rings—on Saturday night at least, if not on all other nights. Then there is the spinning-room, which is very neat and pretty. In this room are the spinners and doffers. The spinners watch the frames; keep them clean, and the threads mended if they break. The doffers take off the full bobbins, and put on the empty ones. They have nothing to do in the long intervals when the frames are in motion, and can go out to their boarding-houses, or do any thing else that they like. In some of the factories the spinners do their own doffing, and when this is the case they work no harder than the weavers. These last have the hardest time of all— or can have, if they choose to take charge of three or four looms, instead of the one pair which is the allotment. And they are the most constantly confined. The spinners and dressers have but the weavers to keep supplied, and then their work can stop. The dressers never work before breakfast, and they stay out a great deal in the afternoons. The drawers-in, or girls who draw the threads through the harnesses, also work in the dressing-room, and they all have very good wages—better than the weavers who have but the usual work. The dressing-rooms are very neat, and the frames move with a gentle undulating motion which is really graceful. But these rooms are kept very warm, and are disagreeably scented with the "sizing," or starch, which stiffens the "beams," or unwoven webs. There are many plants in these rooms, and it is really a good green-house for them. The dressers are generally quite tall girls, and must have pretty tall minds too, as their work requires much care and attention.

I could have had work in the dressing-room, but chose to be a weaver; and I will tell you why. I disliked the closer air of the dressing-room, though I might have become accustomed to that. I could not learn to dress so quickly as I could to weave, nor have work of my own so soon, and should have had to stay with Mrs. C. two or three weeks before I could go in at all, and I did not like to be "lying upon my oars" so long. And, more than this, when I get well learned I can have extra work, and make double wages, which you know is quite an inducement with some.

Well, I went into the mill, and was put to learn with a very patient girl—a clever old maid. I should be willing to be one myself if I could be as good as she is. You cannot think how odd every thing seemed to me. I wanted to laugh at every thing, but did not know what to make sport of first. They set me to threading shuttles, and tying weaver's knots, and such things, and now I have improved so that I can take care of one loom. I could take care of two if I only had eyes in the back part of my head, but I have not got used to "looking two ways of a Sunday" yet.

At first the hours seemed very long, but I was so interested in learning that I endured it very well; and when I went out at night, the sound of the mill was in my ears, as of crickets, frogs, and jewsharps [small musical instrument; it twangs], all mingled together in strange discord. After that it seemed as though cotton-wool was in my ears, but now I do not mind it at all. You know that people learn to sleep with the thunder of Niagara in their ears, and a cotton mill is no worse, though you wonder that we do not have to hold our breath in such a noise.

It makes my feet ache and swell to stand so much, but I suppose I shall get accustomed to that too. The girls generally wear old shoes about their work, and you know nothing is easier; but they almost all say that when they have worked here a year or two they have to procure shoes a size or two larger than before they came. The right hand, which is the one used in stopping and starting the loom, becomes larger than the left; but in other respects the factory is not detrimental to a young girl's appearance. Here they look delicate, but not sickly; they laugh at those who are much exposed, and get pretty brown; but I, for one, had rather be brown than pure white. I never saw so many pretty looking girls as there are here. Though the number of men is small in proportion there are many marriages here, and a great deal of courting. I will tell you of this last sometime.

You wish to know minutely of our hours of labor. We go in at five o'clock; at seven we come out to breakfast; at half-past seven we return to our work, and stay until half-past twelve. At one, or quarter-past one four months in the year, we return to our work, and stay until seven at night. Then the evening is all our own, which is more than some laboring girls can say, who think nothing is more tedious than a factory life.

When I first came here, which was the last of February, the girls ate their breakfast before they went to their work. The first of March they came out at the present breakfast hour, and the twentieth of March they ceased to "light up" the rooms, and come out between six and seven o'clock.

You ask if the girls are contented here: I ask you, if you know of *any one* who is perfectly contented. Do you remember the old story of the philosopher, who offered a field to the person who was contented with his lot; and when one claimed it, he asked him why, if he was so perfectly satisfied, he wanted his field. The girls here are not contented; and there is no disadvantage in their situation which they do not perceive as quickly, and lament as loudly, as the sternest opponents of the factory system do. They would scorn to say they were contented, if asked the question; for it would compromise their Yankee spirit— their pride, penetration, independence, and love of "freedom and equality" to say that they were *contented* with such a life as this. Yet, withal, they are cheerful. I never saw a happier set of beings. They appear blithe in the mill, and out of it. If you see one of them, with a very long face, you may be sure that it is because she has heard bad news from home, or because her beau has vexed her. But, if it is a Lowell trouble, it is because she has failed in getting off as many "sets" or "pieces" as she intended to have done; or because she had a sad "break-out," or "break-down," in her work, or something of that sort.

You ask if the work is not disagreeable. Not when one is accustomed to it. It tried my patience sadly at first, and does now when it does not run well; but, in general, I like it very much. It is easy to do, and does not require very violent exertion, as much of our farm work does.

You also ask how I get along with the girls here. Very well indeed. . . .

Dear Mary: . . .

The mill girls are the prettiest in the city. You wonder how they can keep neat. Why not? There are no restrictions as to the number of pieces to be washed in the boarding-house. And, as there is plenty of water in the mill, the girls can wash their laces and muslins and other nice things themselves, and no boarding woman ever refuses the conveniences for starching and ironing. You say too that you do not see how we can have so many conveniences and comforts at the price we pay for board. You must remember that the boarding-houses belong to the companies, and are let to the tenants far below the usual city rent—sometimes the rent is remitted. Then there are large families, so that there are the profits of many individuals. The country farmers are quite in the habit of bringing their produce to the boarding-houses for sale, thus reducing the price by the omission of the market-man's profit. So you see there are many ways by which we get along so well.

You ask me how the girls behave in the mill, and what are the punishments. They behave very well while about their work, and I have never heard of punishments, or scoldings, or anything of that sort. Sometimes an overseer finds fault, and sometimes offends a girl by refusing to let her stay out of the mill, or some deprivation like that; and then, perhaps, there are tears and pouts on her part, but, in

general, the tone of intercourse between the girls and overseers is very good—pleasant, yet respectful. When the latter are fatherly sort of men the girls frequently resort to them for advice and assistance about other affairs than their work. Very seldom is this confidence abused; but, among the thousands of overseers who have lived in Lowell, and the tens of thousands of girls who have in time been here, there are legends still told of wrong suffered and committed. "To err is human," and when the frailties of humanity are exhibited by a factory girl it is thought of for worse than are the errors of any other persons.

The only punishment among the girls is dismission from their places. They do not, as many think, withhold their wages; and as for corporal punishment—mercy on me! To strike a female would cost any overseer his place. If the superintendents did not take the affair into consideration the girls would turn out [go on strike], as they did at the Temperance celebration, "Independent day;" and if they didn't look as pretty, I am sure they would produce as deep an impression. . . .

Do you wish to hear anything more about the overseers? Once for all, then, there are many very likely intelligent public-spirited men among them. They are interested in the good movements of the day; teachers in the Sabbath schools; and some have represented the city in the State Legislature. They usually marry among the factory girls, and do not connect themselves with their inferiors either. Indeed, in almost all the matches here the female is superior in education and manner, if not in intellect, to her partner.

The overseers have good salaries, and their families live very prettily. I observe that in almost all cases the mill girls make excellent wives. They are good managers, orderly in their households, and "neat as waxwork." It seems as though they were so delighted to have houses of their own to take care of, that they would never weary of the labor and the care. . . .

Questions

1. What appears to be the purpose of Susan's letters to Mary?
2. How does Susan describe the work environment?
3. What does she consider the advantages and disadvantages of working in the mill?

10-3 Harriet Martineau on "Morals of Manufactures" (1837)

Harriet Martineau (1802–1876) joined a steady stream of British and European visitors to the United States in the early nineteenth century. She published her observations about society in America after a two-year stay from 1834 to 1836. Martineau enthusiastically embraced the radical social implications of the Industrial Revolution and saw in the United States a brave social experiment in human equality. An ardent feminist and abolitionist, Martineau noted that the subordination of women and slaves in the United States contradicted the egalitarian principles enunciated in the Declaration of Independence. But she saw signs of future progress emerging in New England's new industrial order. The Waltham plan (see text p. 300) offered young American women of modest means an alternative to domestic service; the factory system also suggested to Martineau the manner in which the United States could protect itself from the ills of poverty that infected industrial society in Britain.

Source: Harriet Martineau, *Society in America* (London: Saunders and Otley, 1837; reprint, New York: AMS Press, 1966), vol. 2, pp. 355–358.

The morals of the female factory population may be expected to be good when it is considered of what class it is composed. Many of the girls are in the factories because they have too much pride for domestic service. Girls who are too proud for domestic service as it is in America, can hardly be low enough for any gross immorality; or to need watching; or not to be trusted to avoid the contagion of evil example. To a stranger, their pride seems to take a mistaken direction, and they appear to deprive themselves of a respectable home and station, and many benefits, by their dislike of service: but this is altogether their own affair. They must choose for themselves their way of life. But the reasons of their choice indicate a state of mind superior to the grossest dangers of their position.

I saw a bill fixed up in the Waltham mill which bore a warning that no young lady who attended dancing-school that winter should be employed: and that the corporation had given directions to the overseer to dismiss any one who should be found to dance at the school. I asked the meaning of this; and the overseer's answer was, "Why, we had some trouble last winter about the dancing-school. It must, of course, he held in the evening, as the young folks are in the mill all day. They are very young, many of them; and they forget the time, and everything but the amusement, and dance away till two or three in the morning. They are unfit for their work the next day; or, if they get properly through their work, it is at the expense of their health. So we have forbidden the dancing-school; but, to make up for it, I have promised them that, as soon as the great new room at the hotel is finished, we will have a dance once a-fortnight. We shall meet and break up early; and my wife and I will dance; and we will all dance together."

I was sorry to see one bad and very unnecessary arrangement, in all the manufacturing establishments. In England, the best friends of the poor are accustomed to think it the crowning hardship of their condition that solitude is wholly forbidden to them. It is impossible that any human being should pass his life as well as he might do who is never alone. . . . The silence, freedom and collectedness of solitude are absolutely essential to the health of the mind. . . . In the dwellings of the English poor, parents and children are crowded into one room. . . . All wise parents above the rank of poor, make it a primary consideration so to arrange their families as that each member may, at some hour have some place where he may enter in, and shut his door, and feel himself alone. If possible, the sleeping places are so ordered. In America, where space is of far less consequence . . . these same girls have no private apartments, and sometimes sleep six or eight in a room, and even three in a bed. This is very bad. . . .

Now are the days when these gregarious habits should be broken through. . . . If the change be not soon made, the American factory population, with all its advantages of education and of pecuniary sufficiency, will be found, as its numbers increase, to have been irreparably injured by its subjection to a grievance . . . to which poverty exposes artisans in old countries.

Questions

1. Why did the young women at Waltham prefer factory work to domestic service?
2. Why is Martineau concerned about the "morals" of industrial employment?
3. What social dangers does Martineau think will result from the absence of solitude in the new industrial order?

10-4   The Educational Purpose of the Franklin Institute (1826)

Mathew Carey   Born in Dublin, Ireland, Mathew Carey (1760–1839) immigrated to the United States, fleeing British persecution for his defense of the Catholic cause. Carey settled in Philadelphia, where he became a prominent editor and publisher and a writer on economic matters. Carey was a champion of internal improvements and manufactures in the United States and supported strong protective tariffs to insulate the economy from British manufactures, which he insisted were the product of pauper labor. Carey also championed universal education and played a leading role in the establishment of the Franklin Institute in 1824 (see text p. 302). The institute embodied the ideals and tensions of American republicanism. Its founders believed that the tyranny of the Old World had rested on the suppression of knowledge among the masses. It followed that in a republic access to knowledge should be unrestricted; a republican society also needed to be free from craft traditions shaped by the tyranny of the past. In America the "scientific mechanic" would integrate theory with practice and transcend the secrecy and exclusivity of the guild system. But how much emphasis should be placed on theory, and how much on practical experience? In this area distinctions of class generated social tensions. When the Franklin Institute opened a school for apprentices, the members of the institute disagreed sharply about its curriculum. Some envisioned a school that would offer a classical education and allow the brightest young artisans to attend a university. Carey argued in favor of the curriculum originally adopted by the institute because it provided a practical education that remained close to the experiences of apprentices.

Source: Mathew Carey, *Reflections on the Proposed Plan for Establishing a College in Philadelphia* (Philadelphia: M. C. Carey and I. Lea, 1826).

A valuable plan has been digested by a public spirited citizen, which promises to produce as much substantial good to a numerous and most useful class of the rising generation as any project ever carried into operation in this country. It is to facilitate, to those who for a future support are destined to learn trades or occupations, to which they are apprenticed . . . the means of acquiring a more solid knowledge of the sciences, and the most useful modern languages, and on more economical terms, than can be effected by the present system of education. . . .

Had I been reflecting for a month, I should never, in the wildest range of conjecture, have anticipated a denunciation of this plan on the ground of its aristocratical tendency. . . . I should as soon have expected the system of universal suffrage to be denounced for its aristocratical tendency as the contemplated college. . . .

From the decided opposition made to this plan it would almost appear that those who had not well considered the subject, that it was intended to produce, and would, if successful, produce, a rejection of the learned languages from education altogether. Nothing can be more foreign from the fact. The plan is grounded on the idea that youth who are bound apprentices to trades at 13, 14, 15, or even 16, cannot acquire the Latin and Greek without a sacrifice of branches of knowledge far more useful in their career through life. Every avenue at present open to the acquisition of those languages will remain open, whatever may be the success of the undertaking. . . .

It cannot be improper to state distinctly the views of the citizens who have engaged in the promotion of the proposed college. They generally believe that every young man intended for the learned professions . . . every one whose parent's wealth renders it unnecessary for him to apply to any profession or trade, and those whose education may be prolonged to seventeen or eighteen years of age, ought to acquire those languages. To such persons they will be not only ornamental but useful, and a source of great intellectual enjoyment. But they believe that it is highly absurd, and a deplorable waste of precious time, for those destined for the trades . . . or any vocation requiring a five or six years apprenticeship, to spend years learning those languages, to the utter neglect of knowledge which could be turned to good account almost every day of their future lives. I am happy to be able to adduce the testimony of the great [John] Locke on this subject . . . "Latin I look upon *as absolutely necessary to a 'gentleman'*" [Carey's note: "The word '*gentleman*' is used here in contradistinction to tradesman. Like the word '*lady*,' it had formerly a much more limited significance that it has at present. By courtesy almost every man is now considered *a gentleman*—and almost every woman a *lady*."]. . . .

It is asserted that it is impossible to write or speak the English language correctly without a knowledge of the Latin and Greek. This is a gratuitous assertion, wholly unfounded. . . . Dr. Franklin's case bears strongly on this point. He was very slenderly educated; for at ten years old, he was obliged to assist his father in his business of soap boiler and tallow chandler. . . . At 27 years, he began to learn the French—then the Italian—then the Spanish. He

afterwards began, probably at 30 years old, to study the Latin. . . . But this study took place while he was obliged to labour as a journeyman printer, to earn a livelihood, and, of course, could not devote much time to Latin. But where is the Latin or Greek scholar whose writings have commanded more universal attention in the new and old world?

We are told with great gravity, that this system is pernicious, because some of the young men educated under it, may in process of time become members of congress—heads of departments—and even presidents of the United States—for which stations, it is implied, the want of knowledge of the dead languages would disqualify them! . . . I might rest the question on the strong and unanswerable case of Dr. Franklin.

Questions

1. In Carey's view, why were the educational needs of workingmen different from those of people entering the "learned professions'?
2. Would you characterize Carey's argument as democratic or, as some of his opponents charged, "aristocratical"? Explain your characterization.
3. Did the class distinctions identified by Carey contradict the republican ideal?

Questions for Further Thought

1. What new experiences—for example, in widening markets and in the centralized workplace—did the Industrial Revolution create for employers and wage earners?
2. In what ways did those new experiences challenge or transform the traditional social relations associated with household production?
3. Were the changes wrought by the Industrial Revolution compatible with the American ideal of republican government? Why or why not?

The Expansion of Markets

The developing factory system made possible, and drew strength from, an expanding national market (see text pp. 303, 306). Trade expanded first within regions and then, more gradually, between regions as the regions competed for customers in the national market. Along the fall line in the Northeast new mill towns appeared, processing grain and lumber as well as manufacturing textiles (see text p. 306). In those towns American manufacturers enjoyed a substantial advantage over their British competitors. Water power was inexpensive and readily available and permitted centralized production without the use of steam power (Document 10-5). The American Industrial Revolution exploited the abundance of natural resources in a thinly populated land. The rise in manufacturing and the growth of cities and towns increased the demand for surplus agricultural produce, and farmers responded by abandoning less productive lands in the East for fertile virgin lands in the West. The westward migration of American farmers (Document 10-6) perpetuated the Jeffersonian ideal of an agricultural republic at the same time that it encouraged the development of regional and national agricultural markets (see text pp. 308–309), bringing flour and meat to cities and towns.

The expansion of markets progressed unevenly, however. In the South, where the plantation economy discouraged the development of towns and cities, the transportation infrastructure lagged far behind the North's. Document 10-7 describes the increasingly primitive transportation system travelers encountered as they moved southward from the well-developed city of Philadelphia to the isolated Sea Islands region of Georgia.

10-5 Typical Section of a Power Train

The plentiful supply of water power along the fall line in the northeastern United States (see text p. 306) was a boon to American manufactures, whose labor and transportation costs were generally higher than those of their British competitors. Water power provided Americans with a significant advantage and largely determined the location of mills and textile factories. This drawing of a typical power train in a textile factory illustrates the advantages water power offered manufacturers and suggests the discipline required of factory workers as they tended the machinery.

Source: Drawing by Robert Howard; from *Rockdale: The Growth of an American Village in the Early Industrial Revolution* by Anthony F. C. Wallace, pp. 132–133. Copyright © 1972 by Anthony F. C. Wallace. Reprinted by permission of Alfred A. Knopf Inc.

Questions

1. What controlled the pace of work in this textile factory?
2. How did that pace differ from household spinning and weaving?
3. What social implications can you discern in the transition from household to factory in the manufacture of textiles?

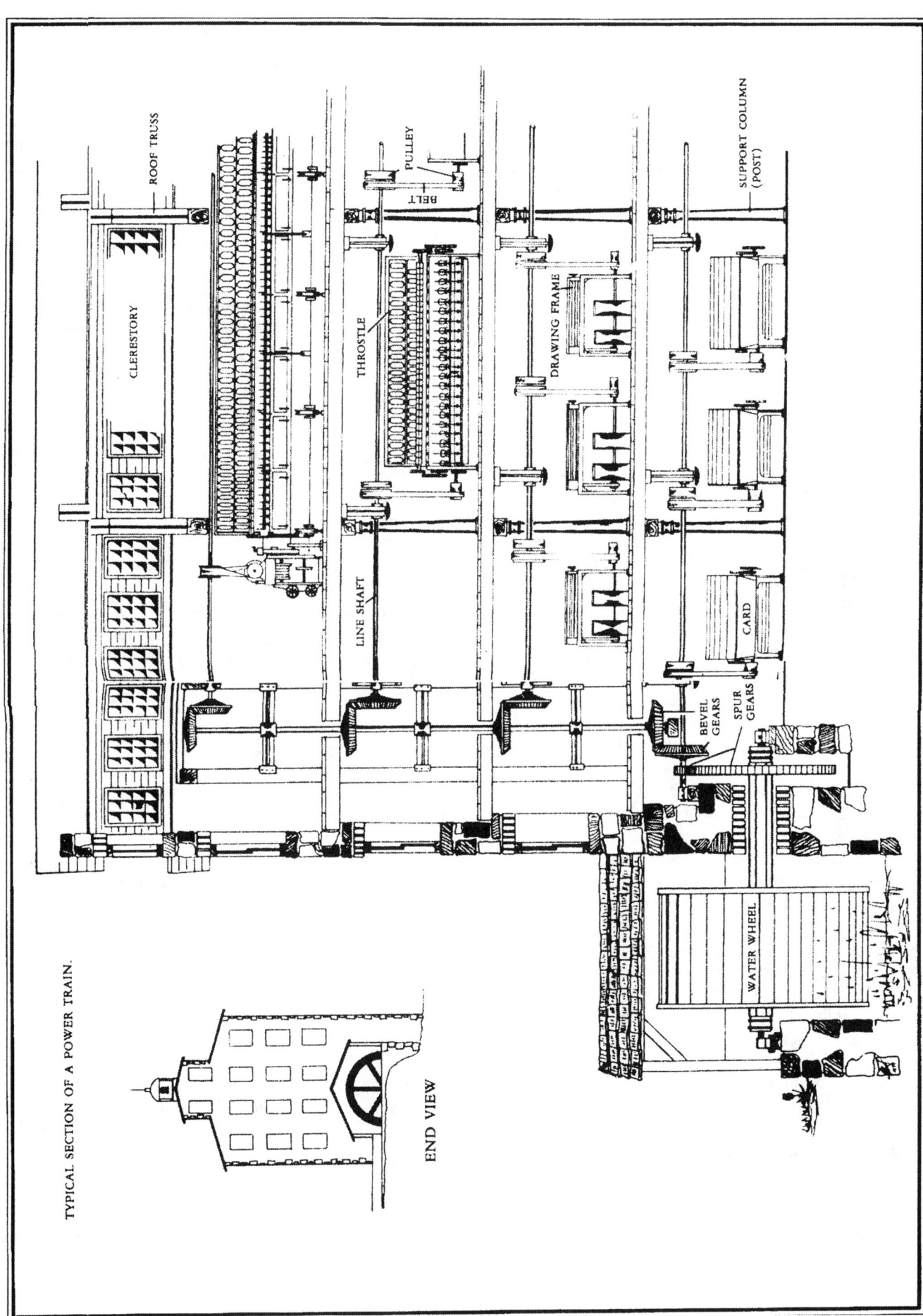

ROOF TRUSS

PULLEY

CLERESTORY

BELT

THROSTLE

DRAWING FRAME

LINE SHAFT

SUPPORT COLUMN (POST)

CARD

BEVEL GEARS

SPUR GEARS

WATER WHEEL

TYPICAL SECTION OF A POWER TRAIN.

END VIEW

10-6   From New Jersey to Illinois by Covered Wagon (1847)

Jane Voorhees Lewis

Neighbors of the Voorhees family moved from Hopewell, New Jersey, to Illinois. When they reported great pleasure in the new country, the Voorhees family decided to follow. Jane Voorhees Lewis was twenty-three years old and recently married when the family set out. The party traveled in two covered wagons about a thousand miles from Hopewell to White Hall, Illinois (see text pp. 308–309). The trip took forty-four days, and Jane Voorhees Lewis kept a journal.

Source: Excerpted from "The Journal of Jane Voorhees Lewis," *Proceedings of the New Jersey Historical Society* 65 (January 1947), pp. 83–92. Courtesy of the New Jersey Historical Society.

April 29th 1847 we started and went by Trenton there crossed the Delaware took dinner on the Pennsylvania shore then went 9 miles to a beautiful village called Milford where we staid all night   we staid under a shed   we all slept in the wagons and did not feel afraid

April 30th started this morning before sunrise and come 3 miles when we stopt and took breakfast   we have a good road and passed the finest farms and buildings I ever saw   arrived in Philadelphia at 3 oclock and came 4 miles this side and stopped for the night in a woods   the wind blows hard and it is not very pleasant as the people are passing continualy   I do not feel like sleeping so I sit writing   all the rest have gone to bed and I sit on the bed with my paper on the pillow and the candle hangs by a wire from the hoops

May 1st   we got our breakfast by sunrise and started   we have come 27 miles today   the roads are fine   we keep off the pike to save the toll   the roads are very hilly   every thing looks a month earlier than in Jersey   the grain looks fine and the blossoms is all out   22 miles from Philadelphia we passed through West Chester   it is a village as large as Princeton and as pretty a place   we pass through so many vilages I can not mention them   I am writing in the wagon by candle light . . .

May 3rd Slept in a tavern last night and took breakfast there   it was a verry nice place   we have come 20 miles today through fine country   they build very fine barns   the buildings are all stone or brick and fence 7 or 8 rails high   I could content myself here if we owned one of those farms

May 4th   We have a very good place to stay tonight and clever people to deal with   we have found clever people yet all along   they look as if they are rich here   they are many of them dutch [German] and we can hardly understand them   passed through Lancaster 40 miles from West Chester   that is a town larger than Trenton and is a prettier place the water is taken out of the Canistoga river it is a beautiful place where it comes up   11 miles from

Lancaster we passed through Columbia   the railroad and canal and susquehana river goes through here   this river is the is the [*sic*] largest I ever saw   it has a courious bridge and heavy toll   our toll was 1 dol 25 cts for both wagons . . .

May 6th   We have crossed some large hills   today we crossed south mountain   the road is cut along the side of it and looks dangerous   saw some beautiful flowers some trees of wild flowers look like peach blossons only prettier I gathered some   we keep off the pike all we can   the toll is high and the road is laid with small stones and it does not ride very good in these wagons it is a continual jar   we cannot walk much   the horses walk so fast we cannot keep up to them   Mother and me tried to walk today crossing these mountains for we was afraid to ride   it made my head turn to look down but the sun shone so hot and could get no air we had to ride

May 7th   We got over the mountains last night and put up in a wood   Mother wrote a letter to Jersey and put it in the ofice at Hagerstown   it looks better around this town we get on the national road here the road is good the toll is high   we have stopped for the night along Cumberland mountain   it is lonesome here among the pines and the owls screaming continualy

May 8th   Come through a poor mountainous country nothing but log houses and the people look rough land poor   it is difficult to get food for our horses   our provisions is getting scarse and have a great trouble to get more here . . .

May 11th   We have came to the alleganies   they are not as steep as the Cumberland mountains but longer   it has stormed all day   the roads are muddy on the top but the mud cant get deep   the road is full of stages and cart wagons and droves of fat cattle and hogs   they drive them from the west to Baltimore 3 and 400 in a drove

May 12th   Come only 14 miles today   Father's horses are both foundered and are very stiff . . .

May 16th   Come through Washington today   a large

town   it is 25 miles from Pitsburg and 31 to Wheling   we expect to get there tomorrow

May 17th   We come 20 miles today through a beautiful country   we have stoped for the night along a brook a beautiful place on the green grass under the large elm trees the corn is up so high you can see it over the fields and things in the gardens look almost fit to eat   there is a butonwood tree along this brook cut down it is hollow Jaques can stand strait in it 6 feet from the bottom   it looks like a house inside   we talk of putting our horses in for a stable there is coal mines in abundance along this road   we have traveled in Pennsylvania, Virginia and Maryland we are 1 miles from Wheeling   Father has traded brown for a 4 year old colt and gave 25 dls [dollars] to boot   he made a good trade . . .

May 18th   We arrived in Wheeling this morning and waited till this afternoon for a boat but the water is low and there was no boats there large enough to take us   we crossed the Ohio on a flat   we got across very good mother did not know the boat was moving until we got half over Wheeling is a large town but it is not pleasant it is under a hill along the river they all burn coal and it is black of the smoke   there is a great business done here   I was glad to set my feet on the shores of Ohio . . .

May 23rd   I am sitting on a log in the thick woods writing   there is wood each side of the road as far as you can see and the road is as strait as it can be   it is a beautiful evening   our horses are turned out   the pasture is good they do not go far from the wagons and if they hear a noise they all come running back   we look like an indian camp with our furnace smoking   our dogs lay as if they are dead they are so tired   Jaques bought a violin at Philadelphia and he is playing on that and the rest sits on the logs doing nothing   we would rather sleep in a woods than a house we crossed the muskingum river at Zanesville   it is a large town and very pretty   yesterday we come through Columbus the capitol of Ohio there is not a prettier town in Jersey there is some of the finest building in this town I ever saw   we see movers every day many going and some coming back

May 24th   Come through springfield   there is a railroad here and every thing high   there is a pike goes from here to Dayton   we kept the national road   there was no toll on that and they said the movers go that way   we went 6 mile and then we come to an end   their was a top Bridge used for a barn and nothing but a foot path but there was a road laid across to the pike and that ended the National road . . .

May 26th   Today we crossed the line and now are in Indiana and came through Richmond a beautiful village it is very wet here and the roads bad   we did not stick fast but many did   it beats every thing to see the movers   every time we stop there has been some there before us   sometimes there is a large fire burning against a log   we meet

some coming back and they look very pittiful and try to persuade us to go back but we would have to hear more than we have to sicken us for it looks better yet than we expected   the buildings are finer than I expected   we do not see as many log houses as we did in Pennsylvania . . . I like Indiana better than Ohio so far

June 1st   Came through Indianapolis the Capitol there is a fine state house here and they are building a lunatic asylum   it is very large   masons wages are 1 1/2 dol a day and boarded   we turned off the national road to go by Clinton   The national road goes to Terre Haute   we have to put up before night along walnut creek it is so high we cannot cross it will swim a horse and runs swift   they are fixing the bodies of the wagons on blocks to cross in the morning

June 2nd   We got over the creek very well Mother was so afraid she laid on the bed she said if she must drown she would not look   I sat up on the bed and looked out   I could not feel afraid for laughing to see her.

June 3rd   Today we crossed the wabash river at Clinton in a ferry boat   I was more afraid than I have been at all   the river is deep and was very high and an old concern of a Boat . . .

June 7th   we got off that prairie and come through woodland and beautiful places   we are now in Illinois we got in yesterday   we have come to another Prairie and have to stay on it all night it is 14 miles the nearest way over   their is nothing to be seen but the sky and ground not a tree or bush or house as far as you can see and as level as a floor   it is very green grass and beautiful flowers but we cannot get any water for ourselves or horses in the morning   we hardly know which way to go we are so turned around   the road does very well some bad wet places and then very good again   the broadest Prairie we crossed is 16 miles and not a house to be seen

June 8th we have good roads now and pleasant country   the prairies are smaller and all settled   their is not many log houses and fine peach and apple orchards   their is nothing wanting here but wood   there is plenty of game here   they shot two duck today and had a good dinner on them   we see plenty of deer and turkeys and geese and Prairie chickens but have not shot any   we had not time to stop long enough to shoot . . .

June 9th we come through Springfield Today   it was some out of our way but we wanted to see the place   it is a beautiful place and fine buildings   it is on a Prairie   The State house is very fine   It is built of Cut stone looks like Marble   The Bank and Court House is Built the same there is a great many stores   The Streets are wide and very shady large locust trees around the house there is very fine farms around Springfield the largest fields I have ever seen with corn knee high   Some are breaking up the Prairie and planting corn   we saw one man plowing with 4 yoke of oxen today and they drop the corn in the furrow and cover the plough   they do not do any thing to it the first year and raise 25 bushel to the acre

June 10th we expect to get to Manchester today   we like this part of the State the best   it is better divided with timber and prairie   the grain looks well   the people are very Clever   we get a great deal give to us milk and radishes and lettuce some try to take advantage of movers and charge high

June 11th we arrived at William Strykers the one that wrote to us to come and was received with a hearty welcome   they are very fine people and appear like relation we feel very much at home here   it is a pretty place   they are very well off and they have told us to make their house our home until we can suit ourselves better[.] . . .

Questions

1. How do the people and the countryside change as the party moves westward?
2. Why was the National Road advantageous to the Voorhees family?
3. Why does Lewis like Illinois?

10-7   A Railroad Journey South from Philadelphia in 1838

Frances Anne Kemble

Frances Anne (Fanny) Kemble (1809–1893) was born into a family of famous English actors. When Kemble was twenty, she made her reluctant debut as Juliet in Shakespeare's *Romeo and Juliet* and was an instant success. In 1832, accompanied by her father, she came to the United States for an American tour and delighted everyone from theater audiences to New England intellectuals. Kemble abandoned her stage career rather suddenly when she married Pierce Butler, a well-to-do American, in 1834. In December 1838 Fanny, her husband, a small daughter, a baby, and an Irish servant left Philadelphia by train on a trip that would take them to a family-owned slave plantation on the Georgia coast. In these excerpts from a letter to her friend Harriet St. Leger, Kemble describes the trip as far as North Carolina.

Source: Frances Kemble, *Records of Later Life* (London, 1882), vol. 1, pp. 170–172, 174, 178–179, 181–183.

Dearest Harriet,

On Friday morning [December 21, 1838] we started from Philadelphia, by railroad, for Baltimore. It is a curious fact enough, that half the routes that are traveled in America are either temporary or unfinished—one reason, among several, for the multitudinous accidents which befall wayfarers. At the very outset of our journey, and within scarce a mile of Philadelphia, we crossed the Schuylkill, over a bridge, one of the principal piers of which is yet incomplete, and the whole building (a covered wooden one, of handsome dimensions) filled with workmen, yet occupied about its construction. But the Americans are impetuous in the way of improvement, and have all the impatience of children about the trying of a new thing, often greatly retarding their own progress by hurrying unduly the completion of their works, or using them in a perilous state of incompleteness. Our road lay for a considerable length of time through flat low meadows that skirt the Delaware, which at this season of the year, covered with snow and bare of vegetation, presented a most dreary aspect. We passed through Wilmington . . . , and crossed a small stream called the Brandywine, the scenery along the banks of which is very beautiful. For its historical associations I refer you to the life of Washington. I cannot say that the aspect of the town of Wilmington, as viewed from the railroad cars, presented any very exquisite points of beauty; I shall therefore indulge in a few observations upon these same railroad cars just here.

And first, I cannot but think that it would be infinitely more consonant with comfort, convenience, and common sense, if persons obliged to travel during the intense cold of an American winter (in the Northern states), were to clothe themselves according to the exigency of the weather, and so do away with the present deleterious custom of warming close and crowded carriages with sheet iron stoves, heated with anthracite coal. No words can describe the foulness of the atmosphere, thus robbed of all vitality by the vicious properties of that dreadful combustible, and tainted besides with the poison emitted at every respiration from so many pairs of human lungs. These are facts which the merest tyro [beginner] in physiological science knows, and the utter disregard of which on the part of the Americans renders them the amazement of every traveler from countries where the preservation of health is considered worth the care of a rational creature. I once traveled to Harrisburg in a railroad car, fitted up to carry sixty-four persons, in the midst of which glowed a large stove. The trip was certainly a delectable one. Nor is there any remedy for this: an attempt to open a window is met by a universal scowl and shudder; and indeed it is but incurring the risk of one's death of cold, instead of one's death of heat. The windows, in fact, form the walls on each side of the carriage, which looks like a long greenhouse upon wheels; the seats, which each contain two persons (a pretty tight fit too), are placed down the whole length of the vehicle, one behind the other, leaving a species of aisle in the middle for the uneasy (a large portion of the traveling community here) to fidget up and down, for the tobacco chewers to spit in, and for a whole tribe of little itinerant fruit and cake sellers to rush through, distributing their wares at every place where the train stops. Of course nobody can well sit immediately in the opening of a window when the thermometer is twelve degrees below zero; yet this, or suffocation in foul air, is the only alternative. I generally prefer being half frozen to death to the latter mode of martyrdom.

Attached to the Baltimore cars was a separate apartment for women. It was of comfortable dimensions, and without a stove; and here I betook myself with my children, escaping from the pestilential atmosphere of the other compartment, and performing our journey with ease enough. My only trial here was one which I have to encounter in whatever direction I travel in America, and which, though apparently a trivial matter in itself, has caused me infinite trouble, and no little compassion for the rising generation of the United States—I allude to the ignorant and fatal practice of the women of stuffing their children from morning till night with every species of trash [food] which comes to hand. . . .

We pursued our way from Wilmington to Havre de Grace on the railroad, and crossed one or two inlets from the Chesapeake, of considerable width, upon bridges of a most perilous construction, and which, indeed, have given way once or twice in various parts already. They consist merely of wooden piles driven into the river, across which the iron rails are laid, only just raising the train above the level of the water. To traverse with an immense train, at full steam-speed, one of these creeks, nearly a mile in width, is far from agreeable, let one be never so little nervous; and it was with infinite cordiality each time that I greeted the first bush that hung over the water, indicating our approach to *terra firma*. At Havre de Grace we crossed the Susquehanna in a steamboat, which cut its way through the ice an inch in thickness with marvelous ease and swiftness, and landed us on the other side, where we again entered the railroad carriages to pursue our road. . . .

Toward four o'clock, as we approached the Roanoke, the appearance of the land improved; there was a good deal of fine soil well farmed, and the river, where we crossed it, although in all the naked unadornment of wintry banks, looked very picturesque and refreshing as it gushed along, broken by rocks and small islands into rapid reaches and currents. Immediately after crossing it, we stopped at a small knot of houses, which, although christened Weldon, and therefore pretending to be a place, was rather the place where a place was intended to be. Two or three rough pine warerooms, or station houses, belonging to the railroad; a few miserable dwellings, which might be either not half built up, or not quite fallen down, on the banks of a large millpond; one exceedingly dirty-looking old wooden house, whither we directed our steps as to the inn; but we did not take our ease in it, though we tried as much as we could. . . .

My poor little children, overcome with fatigue and sleep, were carried, and we walked from the *hotel* at Weldon to the railroad, and by good fortune obtained a compartment to ourselves.

It was now between eight and nine o'clock, and perfectly dark. The carriages were furnished with lamps, however, and, by the rapid glance they cast upon the objects which we passed, I endeavored in vain to guess at the nature of the country through which we were traveling; but, except the tall shafts of the ever-lasting pine trees which still pursued us, I could descry nothing, and resigned myself to the amusing contemplation of the attitudes of my companions, who were all fast asleep.

Between twelve and one o'clock [in the early morning of Sunday, December 23, 1838], the engine stopped, and it was announced to us that we had traveled as far upon the railroad as it was yet completed, and that we must transfer ourselves to stagecoaches; so in the dead middle of the night we crept out of the train, and taking our children in our arms, walked a few yards into an open space in the woods, where three four-horse coaches stood waiting to receive us. . . .

The horrors of that night's journey I shall not easily forget. The road lay almost the whole way through swamps, and was frequently itself under water. It was made of logs of wood (a corduroy road), and so dreadfully rough and unequal, that the drawing a coach over it at all seemed perfectly miraculous. I expected every moment that we must be overturned into the marsh, through which we splashed, with hardly any intermission, the whole night long. Their drivers in this part of the country deserve infinite praise both for skill and care; but the roadmakers, I think, are beyond all praise for their noble confidence in what skill and care can accomplish.

You will readily imagine how thankfully I saw the first whitening of daylight in the sky. I do not know that any morning was ever more welcome to me than that which found us still surrounded by the pine swamps of North Carolina, which, brightened by the morning sun, and breathed through by the morning air, lost something of their dreary desolateness to my senses. . . .

Questions

1. According to Kemble, why was it so dangerous to travel on American railroads?
2. What "American" characteristics does the transportation system suggest to Kemble?
3. What does the journey reveal about regional differences in transportation networks?

Questions for Further Thought

1. Compare and contrast the experiences and expectations of a young Illinois farm woman (Document 10-6) and a young female operative in a northeastern textile mill (Document 10-2). Would you choose one form of labor over the other? Why?
2. Trace Lewis's and Kemble's journeys (Documents 10-6 and 10-7) on Map 10.4 (see text p. 312) and Map 13.3 (see text p. 405). How direct were their routes? Then, using a modern highway map, estimate how long it would take to drive the two trips today.
3. Would you judge from Kemble's account that the railroad would soon become the nation's most important form of interior transportation? Why or why not?

Social Structure in an Industrializing Society

The Industrial Revolution reshaped the social structure and social values of the northeastern United States. The emergence of a business class and a wage-earning class revealed a striking and, to many, disturbing gap between the rich and the poor (see text pp. 314–317). For the business class it seemed clear that the expending American economy offered a wide field of opportunity for those with the discipline and diligence to work hard. Benjamin Franklin's *Autobiography*, which was widely read by the business class after its initial publication in 1818 (see text p. 319), offered wit and wisdom to guide the industrious to success (Document 10-8).

The gap between the rich (and the moderately well off) and the laboring poor also revealed social problems that were troubling to the business class. Workingmen no longer lived in the household and under the supervision of a master. These masterless men increasingly lived in neighborhoods separate from the residential areas occupied by the business class (see text p. 318). Workingmen also frequented saloons that catered to their class exclusively (see text p. 317). The question of how to assure social stability in a newly fragmented society was the era's major problem; this was an unwanted and potentially dangerous consequence of economic progress. Through benevolent reform and an evangelical Protestantism that stressed the individual conversion experience (Document 10-9) the business class worked to erect new standards of social order compatible with the individual autonomy that was characteristic of industrial society. Of all of the era's moral reforms, temperance (Document 10-10) reached the widest audience and achieved the greatest success across class lines (see text pp. 322–323).

10-8   *The Autobiography of Benjamin Franklin* (1818)

A native of Boston, Benjamin Franklin (1706–1790) established himself at an early age as a printer in Philadelphia and quickly rose to prominence in colonial politics. He also became famous in America, Britain, and Europe as a natural philosopher keenly interested in the scientific concerns of the day, notably electricity. As an American proud of the practicality of his countrymen, Franklin focused his scientific inquiry on practical applications: after demonstrating the electrical nature of lightning, for example, he invented the lightning rod. Bifocal eyeglasses and the Franklin stove also originated from his inventive genius. In the nineteenth century Franklin would be remembered as a mechanical genius whose wit and wisdom expressed the practical idealism of the American democrat (see text p. 319). In the following passage Franklin describes his efforts to achieve moral perfection.

Source: The Autobiography of Benjamin Franklin (1818; reprint, New York: Airmont Publishing, 1965, pp. 79–86).

. . . I conceived the bold and arduous project of arriving at *moral perfection.* I wished to live without committing any fault at any time, and to conquer all that either natural inclination, custom, or company might lead me into. As I knew, or thought I knew, what was right and wrong, I did not see why I might not *always* do the one and avoid the other. But I soon found I had undertaken a task of more difficulty than I had imagined. While my attention was taken up, and employed in guarding against one fault, I was often surprised by another. . . . I concluded, at length, that the mere speculative conviction that it was our interest to be completely virtuous, was not sufficient to prevent our slipping; and that the contrary habits must be broken, and good ones acquired and established, before we can have any dependence on a steady, uniform rectitude of conduct. For this purpose I therefore tried the following method. . . .

I made a little book, in which I allotted a page for each of the virtues. I ruled each page with red ink, so as it have seven columns, one for each day of the week, marking each column with a letter for the day. I crossed these columns with thirteen red lines, marking the beginning of each line with the first letter of one of the virtues [T for Temperance, S for Silence, etc.], on which line, and in its proper column, I might mark, by a little black spot, every fault I found upon examination to have been committed respecting that virtue upon that day.

I determined to give a week's strict attention to each of the virtues successively. Thus, in the first week, my great guard was to avoid every least offense against *Temperance,* leaving the other virtues to their ordinary chance, only marking every evening the faults of the day. Thus, if in the first week I could keep my first line, market T, clear of spots, I supposed the habit of that virtue so much strengthened, and its opposite weakened, that I might venture extending my attention to include the next, and for the following week both lines clear of spots. . . .

I entered upon the execution of this plan for self-examination, and continued it with occasional intermissions for some time. I was surprised to find myself so much fuller of faults than I had imagined; but I had the satisfaction of seeing them diminish. . . . I always carried my little book with me.

. . . [The virtue] *Order* gave me the most trouble . . . and my faults in it vexed me so much, and I made so little progress in amendment, and had such frequent relapses, that I was almost ready to give up the attempt, and content myself with a faulty character in that respect, like the man who, in buying an ax of a smith . . . desired to have the whole of its surface as bright as the edge. The smith consented to grind it bright for him if he would turn the wheel; he turned, while the smith pressed the broad face of the ax hard and heavily on the stone, which made the turning of it very fatiguing. The man came every now and then from the wheel to see how the work went on, and at length would take his ax as it was, without further grinding. "No," said the smith, "turn on, turn on, we shall have it bright by-and-by; as yet, it is only speckled." "Yes," said the man, "but *I think I like a speckled ax best.*". . . . for something, that pretended to be reason, was every now and then suggesting to me that such extreme nicety as I exacted of myself might be a kind of foppery in morals, which, if it were known, would make me ridiculous; that a perfect character might be attended with the inconvenience of being envied and hated; and that a benovelent man should allow a few faults in himself, to keep his friends in countenance. . . .

In reality, there is, perhaps, no one of our natural passions so hard to subdue as *pride.* Disguise it, struggle with it, stifle it, mortify it as much as one pleases, it is still alive, and will every now and then peep out and show itself; you will see it, perhaps, often in this history; for, even if I could conceive that I had completely overcome it, I should prob-

Questions

1. What does Franklin mean when he speaks of "foppery in morals"?
2. If in the end moral perfection is unattainable, why did Franklin offer such a detailed account of his pursuit of perfection?
3. In what ways did Franklin's wit and wisdom appeal to the new business class of the early nineteenth century?

10-9   Charles Grandison Finney Experiences Conversion (1821)

Charles Grandison Finney (1792–1875) (see text pp. 320–322) was the leading revivalist of the early nineteenth century. He was born in Connecticut, but his family moved westward to Oneida County, New York, where Finney grew up. The religious experience he describes here ended his career as a lawyer and inspired his work as a revivalist. Finney's dramatic preaching stressed the importance of the immediate acceptance of God's grace through Jesus Christ. He emphasized the individual's need to assume moral responsibility for himself or herself. Those who flocked to Finney's revivals hoped to experience God's regenerating grace in essentially the same way Finney had.

Source: Used with permission from *The Autobiography of Charles G. Finney*, condensed and edited by Helen Wessel, pp. 13–25. Published by Bethany House Publishers, Minneapolis. Copyrighted 1977. All rights reserved.

On a Sunday evening in the autumn of 1821 I made up my mind that I would settle the question of my soul's salvation at once, that if it were possible I would make my peace with God. . . .

During Monday and Tuesday my convictions increased, but still it seemed as if my heart grew harder. I could not shed a tear. I could not pray. . . .

Tuesday night I had become very nervous, and in the night a strange feeling came over me as if I were about to die. I knew that if I did I would sink down to hell, but I quieted myself as best I could until morning.

At an early hour I started for the office. But just before I arrived at the office, it seemed as if an inward voice confronted me with questions like these: "What are you waiting for? Did you not promise to give your heart to God? And what are you trying to do? Are you endeavoring to work out a righteousness of your own?"

Just at this point the whole question of Gospel salvation opened to my mind in a manner most marvelous. I think I then saw, as clearly as I ever have in my life, the reality and fullness of the atonement of Christ. I saw that his work was a finished work, and that instead of having, or needing, any righteousness of my own to recommend me to God, I had to submit to the righteousness of God through Christ. Gospel salvation seemed to be an offer to be accepted, and that it was full and complete. All that was necessary on my part was my own consent to give up my sins and accept Christ. Salvation was not achieved by my own works, but was to be found entirely in the Lord Jesus Christ, who presented himself before me as my God and my Savior.

Without being distinctly aware of it, I had stopped in the street right where the inward voice seemed to arrest me. How long I remained in that position I cannot say. But after this distinct revelation had stood for some little time before my mind, the question seemed to be, "Will you accept it now, today?"

I replied, "Yes, I will accept it today, or I will die in the attempt." . . .

The thought was pressing me of the rashness of my promise that I would give my heart to God that day or die in the attempt. It seemed to me as if that was binding upon my soul, and yet I was going to break my vow. A great sinking and discouragement came over me, and I felt almost too weak to stand upon my knees.

Just at this moment I again thought I heard someone approach me, and I opened my eyes to see whether it were so. But right there the revelation of my pride was distinctly shown to me as the great difficulty that stood in the way. An overwhelming sense of my wickedness in being ashamed to have a human being see me on my knees before God took such powerful possession of me that I cried at the top of my voice and exclaimed that I would not leave that place if all the men on earth and all the devils in hell surrounded me. "What!" I said, "such a degraded sinner as I am, on my knees confessing my sins to the great and holy God, ashamed to have any human being find me on my knees endeavoring to make my peace with my offended God!" The sin appeared awful, infinite. It broke me down before the Lord.

Just at that point this passage of scripture seemed to drop into my mind with a flood of light: "Then shall you go and pray unto me, and I will hearken to you. Then shall you seek me and find me, when you shall search for me with all your heart."

I instantly seized hold of this with my heart. I had intellectually believed the Bible before, but never had the truth been in my mind that faith was a voluntary trust instead of an intellectual state. I was as conscious of trusting at that moment in God's truthfulness as I was of my own existence. Somehow I knew that that was a passage of scripture, though I do not think I had ever read it. I knew that it was God's word, and God's voice, as it were, that spoke to me.

I cried to him, "Lord, I take Thee at Thy word. Now Thou knowest that I do search for Thee with all my heart, and that I have come here to pray to Thee; and Thou hast promised to hear me." . . .

But how was I to account for the quiet of my mind? I tried to recall my convictions, to get back again the load of sin under which I had been laboring. But all sense of sin, all consciousness of present sin or guilt, had departed from me. I said to myself, "What is this, that I cannot arouse any sense of guilt in my soul, as great a sinner as I am?" I tried in vain to make myself anxious about my present state. I was so quiet and peaceful that I tried to feel concerned about that, lest it should be a result of my having grieved the Spirit away. But take any view of it I would, I could not be anxious at all about my soul and about my spiritual state. The repose of my mind was unspeakably great. I cannot describe it in words. The thought of God was sweet to my mind, and the most profound spiritual tranquillity had taken full possession of me. This was a great mystery, but it did not distress or perplex me. . . .

[That evening] There was no fire and no light in this back room; nevertheless it appeared to me as if it were perfectly light. As I went in and shut the door after me, it seemed as if I met the Lord Jesus Christ face to face. It seemed to me that I saw him as I would see any other man. He said nothing, but looked at me in such a manner as to break me right down at his feet. It seemed to me a reality that he stood before me, and I fell down at his feet and poured out my soul to him. I wept aloud like a child and made such confessions as I could with my choked words. It

seemed to me that I bathed his feet with my tears, and yet I had no distinct impression that I touched him.

I must have continued in this state for a good while, but my mind was too much absorbed with the interview to remember anything that I said. As soon as my mind became calm enough I returned to the front office and found that the fire I had made of large wood was nearly burned out. But as I turned and was about to take a seat by the fire, I received a mighty baptism of the Holy Spirit. Without any expectation of it, without ever having the thought in my mind that there was any such thing for me, without any memory of ever hearing the thing mentioned by any person in the world, the Holy Spirit descended upon me in a manner that seemed to go through me, body and soul. I could feel the impression, like a wave of electricity, going through and through me. Indeed it seemed to come in waves of liquid love, for I could not express it in any other way. It seemed like the very breath of God. I can remember distinctly that it seemed to fan me, like immense wings.

No words can express the wonderful love that was spread abroad in my heart. I wept aloud with joy and love. I literally bellowed out the unspeakable overflow of my heart. These waves came over me, and over me, and over me, one after the other, until I remember crying out, "I shall die if these waves continue to pass over me." I said, "Lord, I cannot bear any more," yet I had no fear of death. . . .

In this state I was taught the doctrine of justification by faith as a present experience. That doctrine had never taken possession of my mind. I had never viewed it distinctly as a fundamental doctrine of the Gospel. Indeed, I did not know at all what it meant in the proper sense. But I could now see and understand what was meant by the passage, "Being justified by faith, we have peace with God through our Lord Jesus Christ." I could see that the moment I believed, while up in the woods, all sense of condemnation had entirely dropped out of my mind, and that from that moment I could not feel a sense of guilt or condemnation by any effort I could make. My sense of guilt was gone, my sins were gone, and I do not think I felt any more sense of guilt than if I never had sinned.

This was just the revelation I needed. I felt myself justified by faith, and, so far as I could see, I was in a state in which I did not sin. Instead of feeling that I was sinning all the time, my heart was so full of love that it overflowed. My cup ran over with blessing and with love. I could not feel that I was sinning against God, nor could I recover the least sense of guilt for my past sins. Of this experience of justification I said nothing to anybody at the time.

Questions

1. What does Finney mean by "salvation" and "faith"?

2. What physical and psychological changes does he undergo?

3. What does the conversion experience teach him, and how is he different after it?

10-10   The Beginning of the Temperance Movement (1812)

Lyman Beecher

Lyman Beecher (1775–1863) was a pastor in both Congregational and Presbyterian churches and founded one of America's most remarkable families. A graduate of Yale College, he led parishes in New York, Connecticut, Massachusetts, and Ohio. Many of his eleven children achieved distinction, including sons Henry Ward and Edward and daughters Catharine and Harriet Beecher Stowe (see American Lives, Chapter 13, text pp. 400–401). He composed his autobiography by dictating it to several of his children. This selection describes his commitment to temperance reform (see text pp. 322–323) soon after he became pastor of the Congregational Church in Litchfield, Connecticut.

Source: From *The Autobiography of Lyman Beecher*, edited by Barbara M. Cross, vol. 1, pp. 179–182. Copyright © 1961 by the President and Fellows of Harvard College. Reprinted by permission of Harvard University Press.

Soon after my arrival at Litchfield I was called to attend the ordination at Plymouth of Mr. Heart, ever after that my very special friend. I loved him as he did me. He said to me one day, "Beecher, if you had made the least effort to govern us young men, you would have had a swarm of bees about you; but, as you have come and mixed among us, you can do with us what you will."

Well, at the ordination at Plymouth, the preparation for our creature comforts, in the sitting-room of Mr. Heart's house, besides food, was a broad sideboard covered with decanters and bottles, and sugar, and pitchers of water. There we found all the various kinds of liquors then in vogue. The drinking was apparently universal. This preparation was made by the society as a matter of course. When the Consociation [of ministers] arrived, they always took something to drink round; also before public services, and always on their return. As they could not all drink at once, they were obliged to stand and wait as people do when they go to mill.

There was a decanter of spirits also on the dinner-table, to help digestion, and gentlemen partook of it through the afternoon and evening as they felt the need, some more and some less; and the sideboard, with the spillings of water, and sugar, and liquor, looked and smelled like the bar of a very active grog-shop. None of the Consociation were drunk; but that there was not, at times, a considerable amount of exhilaration, I can not affirm.

When they had all done drinking, and had taken pipes and tobacco, in less than fifteen minutes there was such a smoke you couldn't see. And the noise I can not describe; it was the maximum of hilarity. They told their stories, and were at the height of jocose talk. They were not old-fashioned Puritans. They had been run down. Great deal of spirituality on Sabbath, and not much when they got where there was something good to drink.

I think I recollect some animadversions [criticisms] were made at that time by the people on the amount of liquor drank, for the tide was swelling in the drinking habits of society.

The next ordination was of Mr. Harvey, in Goshen, and there was the same preparation, and the same scenes acted over, and then afterward still louder murmurs from the society at the quantity and expense of liquor consumed.

These two meetings were near together, and in both my alarm, and shame, and indignation were intense. 'Twas that that woke me up for the war. And silently I took an oath before God that I would never attend another ordination of that kind. I was full. My heart kindles up at the thoughts of it now.

There had been already so much alarm on the subject, that at the General Association [of ministers] at Fairfield in 1811, a committee of three had been appointed to make inquiries and report measures to remedy the evil. A committee was also appointed by the General Association of Massachusetts for the same purpose that same month, and to confer with other bodies.

I was a member of General Association which met in the year following at Sharon, June, 1812, when said committee reported. They said they had attended to the subject committed to their care; that intemperance had been for some time increasing in a most alarming manner; but that, after the most faithful and prayerful inquiry, they were obliged to confess they did not perceive that any thing could be done.

The blood started through my heart when I heard this, and I rose instanter, and moved that a committee of three be appointed immediately, to report at this meeting the ways and means of arresting the tide of intemperance.

The committee was named and appointed. I was chairman, and on the following day brought in a report, the most important paper that ever I wrote.

ABSTRACT OF REPORT.

The General Association of Connecticut, taking into consideration the undue consumption of ardent spirits, the enormous sacrifice of property resulting, the alarming increase of intemperance, the deadly effect on health, intellect, the family, society, civil and religious institutions, and especially in nullifying the means of grace and destroying souls, recommend,

1. Appropriate discourses on the subject by all ministers of Association.

2. That District Associations abstain from the use of ardent spirits at ecclesiastical meetings.

3. That members of Churches abstain from the unlawful vending, or purchase and use of ardent spirits where unlawfully sold; exercise vigilant discipline, and cease to consider the production of ardent spirits a part of hospitable entertainment in social visits.

4. That parents cease from the ordinary use of ardent spirits in the family, and warn their children of the evils and dangers of intemperance.

5. That farmers, mechanics, and manufacturers substitute palatable and nutritious drinks, and give additional compensation, if necessary, to those in their employ. . . .

Immense evils, we are persuaded, afflict communities, not because they are incurable, but because they are tolerated; and great good remains often unaccomplished merely because it is not attempted.

Questions

1. What does this account reveal about the social uses of alcohol before the beginning of the temperance campaign?

2. Why was Beecher offended by the two ordination meetings he described?

3. According to the "Abstract," what was the problem and what measures were proposed to deal with it?

Questions for Further Thought

1. In what specific ways did Franklin (Document 10-8), Finney (Document 10-9), and Beecher (Document 10-10) promote internalized self-restraint?

2. Why did reformers in the early nineteenth century prefer self-restraint to legislation that would make undesirable behavior illegal?

3. What wider social purposes did the self-restrained individual serve?

CHAPTER 11

A Democratic Revolution 1820–1844

★   ★   ★

Democratizing Politics, 1820–1829

The triumph of universal white male suffrage early in the nineteenth century (see Document 9-5) ended a political system that had reflected a hierarchical social order sustained by a property qualification for voters (see text p. 328). Property qualifications differed from state to state, but the idea that property ownership determined suffrage permitted men with modest property holdings to vote for candidates for, say, the lower house of the state legislature and the federal House of Representatives, whereas only those with substantial property holdings could vote for the state senate and for governor. Federalists and others favoring property qualifications argued that men with extensive property could be expected to cast their votes prudently and wisely because they had much to lose. By the same logic, men without property could not be trusted with the vote (Document 11-1).

This political order rested on two conditions: a geographically fixed population and a broad distribution of property. Both conditions quickly changed with the beginning of the Industrial Revolution. Improvements in transportation and new economic opportunities encouraged geographical mobility at the same time that a growing population of laborers and journeyman wage earners swelled the ranks of the propertyless poor. The extension of the franchise by men who were substantial property owners promoted a peaceful democratic revolution characterized by broad political participation. Except in Rhode Island (where the struggle for universal white male suffrage almost resulted in civil war), men of property, after debating the issue, eventually promoted or accepted change to preserve political stability (see Map 9.1, text p. 276).

In the new democratic political system, expanded commercial and manufacturing activity generated new political interests and alignments that could no longer be contained within the Democratic-Republican party structure. The debate over the federal tariff became the focus of conflicting sectional and economic interests and the rise of new political parties (Document 11-2). The advocates of Henry Clay's American System argued in nationalistic terms for a protective tariff to encourage American manufacturing and promote economic self-sufficiency (see text pp. 329–330). But an alliance of farmers of the South and West and artisans in the North denounced the American System, especially the protective tariff, as an unjust tax on the common man. It was to these interests that the emerging Jacksonian democracy appealed (Document 11-3).

11-1   James Kent Argues against Universal Suffrage (1821)

Thomas Jefferson's characterization of John Quincy Adams's presidential policies as the "splendid government of an aristocracy" and Adams's criticism of democracy (see text pp. 329–330) illustrate the divergence of political ideology that was central to the age of democratic revolution. In an increasingly commercial society the agricultural simplicity of the early republic faded, and critics of democracy warned that the foundations of republican liberty could be eroded by poor men seeking equality with the wealthy. James Kent (1763–1847), a New York Federalist, was a leading jurist and the author of the most influential treatise on American law in the nineteenth century. Kent expressed the antidemocratic point of view with striking clarity at the New York Constitutional Convention of 1821.

Source: Reports of the Proceedings and Debates of the Convention of 1821 Assembled for the Purpose of Amending the Constitution of the State of New York (Albany: E. and E. Hosford, 1821).

[W]e propose . . . to bow before the idol of universal suffrage. That extreme democratic principle . . . has been regarded with terror by the wise men of every age because, in every European republic, ancient and modern, in which it has been tried, it has terminated disastrously and been productive of corruption, injustice, violence, and tyranny. And dare we flatter ourselves that we are a peculiar people . . . exempted from the passions which have disturbed and corrupted the rest of mankind? . . . I wish those who have an interest in the soil to retain the exclusive possession of a branch in the legislature as a stronghold in which they may find safety through all the vicissitudes which the state may be destined . . . to experience. I wish them to be always enabled to say that their freeholds cannot be taxed without their consent. The men of no property, together with the crowds of dependents connected with great manufacturing and commercial establishments, and the motley and undefinable population of crowded ports, may, perhaps, at some future day, under skilful management, predominate in the assembly, and yet we should be perfectly safe if no

laws could pass without the free consent of the owners of the soil. . . .

The apprehended danger from the experiment of universal suffrage applied to the whole legislative department is no dream of the imagination. . . . The tendency of universal suffrage is to jeopardize the rights of property and the principles of liberty. There is a constant tendency . . . in the poor to covet and to share the plunder of the rich; in the debtor to relax or avoid the obligation of contracts; in the majority to tyrannize over the minority and trample down their rights; in the indolent and the profligate to cast the whole burdens of society upon the industrious and the virtuous. . . . We are no longer to remain plain and simple republics of farmers. . . . We are fast becoming a great nation, with great commerce, manufactures, population, wealth, luxuries, and with the vices and miseries that they engender. . . . [W]e have to apprehend the establishment of unequal and, consequently, unjust systems of taxation and all the mischiefs of a crude and mutable legislation.

Questions

1. In Kent's view, how did property qualifications protect America against "corruption, injustice, violence, and tyranny"?
2. What dangers did Kent see as the nation ceased to be composed of "simple republics of farmers"?
3. If Kent's view had prevailed, how might representative government have been structured in New York?

11-2 Speech on the Tariff (March 30–31, 1824)

Henry Clay

A native of Virginia, Henry Clay (1777–1852) migrated to Kentucky, where he established himself as a substantial slaveholding planter and lawyer. A strong nationalist and War Hawk, Clay won election to the House of Representatives in 1810 and became Speaker the following year. A candidate for president in 1824, Clay advocated what he called the "American System" (see text p. 329) and later played a leading role in building the Whig opposition to Andrew Jackson.

Clay's American System envisioned an integrated national economy in which a protective tariff would encourage domestic manufacturing while it generated revenues to support federally financed harbors, canals, and other major internal improvements. Clay was largely successful in his immediate aim: the Tariff of 1824 (see text p. 330), raising rates, passed. But his larger goal of harnessing the federal government to the development of the national economy fell victim to sectional rivalry and to a democratic critique of the special privilege enjoyed by established elites in the mainstream of economic development.

In the following extracts from Clay's two-day-long speech of March 1824 in the House of Representatives he explained why he believed it was in the nation's interest to impose a tariff on imports to protect domestic manufacturing.

Source: Annals of the Congress of the United States, 1789–1824 (Washington, D.C.: U.S. Government Printing Office), 18th Cong., 1st sess. (1824), pp. 1962–2001.

And what is this tariff? It seems to have been regarded as a sort of monster, huge and deformed; a wild beast, endowed with tremendous powers of destruction, about to be let loose among our people, if not to devour them, at least to consume their substance. But let us calm our passions, and deliberately survey this alarming, this terrific being. The sole object of the tariff is to tax the produce of foreign industry, with the view of promoting American industry. The tax is exclusively levelled at foreign industry. . . .

It has been treated as an imposition of burthens upon one part of the community by design for the benefit of another; as if, in fact, money were taken from the pockets of one portion of the people and put into the pockets of another. But, is that a fair representation of it? No man pays the duty assessed on the foreign article by compulsion, but voluntarily; and this voluntary duty, if paid, goes into the common exchequer, for the common benefit of all. . . . According to the opponents of the domestic policy, the proposed system will force capital and labor into new and reluctant employments; we are not prepared, in consequence of the high price of wages, for the successful establishment of manufactures, and we must fail in the experiment. We have seen that the existing occupations of our society, those of agriculture, commerce, navigation, and the learned professions, are overflowing with competitors, and that the want of employment is severely felt. Now what does this bill propose? To open a new and extensive field of business, in which all that choose may enter. There is no compulsion upon any one to engage in it. An option only is given to industry, to continue in the present unprofitable pursuits, or to embark in a new and promising one. The effect will be to lessen the competition in the old branches of business and to multiply our resources for increasing our comforts and augmenting the national wealth. The alleged fact of the high price of wages is not admitted. The truth is, that no class of society suffers more, in the present stagnation of business, than the laboring class. That is a necessary effect of the depression of agriculture, the principal business of the community. The wages of able-bodied men vary from five to eight dollars per month; and such has been the want of employment, in some parts of the Union, that instances have not been unfrequent, of men working merely for the means of present subsistence. . . . We are now, and ever will be, essentially, an agricultural people. Without a material change in the fixed habits of the country, the friends of this measure desire to draw to it, as a powerful auxiliary to its industry, the manufacturing arts. The difference between a nation with, and without the arts, may be conceived, by the difference between a keel-boat and a steam-boat, combatting the rapid torrent of the Mississippi. How slow does the former ascend, hugging the sinuosities of the shore, pushed on by her hardy and exposed crew, now throwing themselves in vigorous concert on their oars, and then seizing the pendant boughs of over-hanging trees: she seems hardly to move; and her scanty cargo is scarcely worth the transportation! With what ease is she not passed by the steam-boat, laden with the riches of all quarters of the world, with a crowd of gay, cheerful, and protected passengers, now dashing into the midst of the current, or gliding through the eddies near the shore. . . . The adoption of the restrictive system, on the part of the United States, by excluding the produce of foreign labor, would extend the consumption of American produce, unable, in the infancy and unprotected state of the arts, to sustain a competition with foreign fabrics. Let our arts breathe under the shade of protection; let them be perfected as they are in England, and we shall then be ready, as England now is said to be, to put aside protection, and to enter upon the freest exchanges. . . .

Other and animating considerations invite us to adopt the policy of this system. Its importance, in connexion with the general defence in time of war, cannot fail to be duly estimated. Need I recal [*sic*] to our painful recollection the sufferings, for the want of an adequate supply of absolute necessaries, to which the defenders of their country's rights and our entire population were subjected during the late war [the War of 1812]? Or to remind the committee of the great advantage of a steady and unfailing source of supply, unaffected alike in war and in peace? Its importance, in reference to the stability of our Union, that paramount and greatest of all our interests, cannot fail warmly to recommend it, or at least to conciliate the forbearance of every patriot bosom. Now our people present the spectacle of a vast assemblage of jealous rivals, all eagerly rushing to the sea-board, jostling each other in their way, to hurry off to glutted foreign markets the perishable produce of their labor. The tendency of that policy, in conformity to which this bill is prepared, is to transform these competitors into friends and mutual customers; and, by the reciprocal exchanges of their respective productions, to place the confederacy upon the most solid of all foundations, the basis of common interest. . . .

Even if the benefits of the policy were limited to certain sections of our country, would it not be satisfactory to behold American industry, wherever situated, active, animated, and thrifty, rather than persevere in a course which renders us subservient to foreign industry? But these benefits are twofold, direct, and collateral, and in the one shape or the other, they will diffuse themselves throughout the Union. All parts of the Union will participate, more or less, in both. As to the direct benefit, it is probable that the North and the East will enjoy the largest share. But the West and the South will also participate in them. . . . And where the direct benefit does not accrue, that will be enjoyed of supplying the raw material and provisions for the consumption of artisans. . . . I appeal to the South—to the high-minded, generous, and patriotic South—with which I have so often co-operated. . . . Of what does it complain? A possible temporary enhancement [i.e., price increase] in the objects of consumption. Of what do we complain? A total incapacity, produced by the foreign policy, to purchase, at any price, necessary foreign objects of consumption. In such an alternative, inconvenient only to it, ruinous to us, can we expect too much from Southern magnanimity? . . .

Questions

1. How does Clay explain the importance to an agricultural nation of the "manufacturing arts"?

2. According to Clay, how would a protective tariff promote a "common interest" across the nation?

3. How did Clay answer the South's complaint that the benefits of the tariff went primarily to the manufacturing sector in the Northeast?

11-3   The Beginnings of Grass-Roots Democracy (1830)

Amos Kendall (1789–1869) was born on a poor farm in western Massachusetts. With the support his family could offer and his own ambitious efforts he was graduated from Dartmouth College in 1811, studied law, and in 1814 sought brighter prospects in the West. Kendall settled in Kentucky, where he briefly tutored the sons of Henry Clay before establishing himself as a lawyer and newspaper editor. In 1816 he moved to the state capital, Frankfort, to take charge of the influential *Argus of Western America* and was soon joined by coeditor Francis P. Blair (see text p. 332 and Document 11-10). Kendall and Blair supported Clay in the presidential election of 1824 but helped carry Kentucky for Jackson in 1828. After Jackson's victory, Kendall moved to Washington and became one of the most influential of the new president's informal "Kitchen Cabinet"; Kendall was the principal author of Jackson's Bank Veto Message (see Document 11-4). In 1830, with Jackson's political support, Kendall founded the Washington, D.C., *Globe* and called Blair east to be its editor. Sustained by a patronage position in the Treasury Department, Kendall became a powerful dispenser of Democratic patronage as postmaster general (1835–1840). In the following extracts from private letters written by Kendall in Washington to Blair in Kentucky, Kendall examines the altered political landscape that produced Jackson's victory and assesses its significance for the future.

Source: Francis P. Blair Papers, Princeton University, Princeton, New Jersey.

AMOS KENDALL TO FRANCIS P. BLAIR,
JANUARY 28, 1830:

The Democratic ascendancy in our state can only be maintained by diminishing the power of lawyers. I can think of no way so effectual to do that as to induce our farmers and mechanics to take a part in the *nomination* of candidates as well as their election. Now, our lawyers, big and little, thrust themselves out and forestall the field, and no modest farmer or mechanic dare come in competition with their pretentions. If the people could be made sensible of the wrong and injury done them by these upstarts, they would be ready to apply the remedy. . . . Let meetings of the democratic Jackson men be called in each militia company of the county on the same day. . . . By such means, the people would take the government into their own hands and send to the Legislature sounder men and better politicians. The Lawyers would not attend all these company meetings and an entire class of politicians would spring up opposed to them. . . .

By this plan the town aristocracies and the influence of rich men in the country would be measurably disarmed.

AMOS KENDALL TO FRANCIS P. BLAIR,
AUGUST 27, 1830:

There is to be a new paper here entitled the "American Statesman and Workingmen's Advocate" devoted to Mr. [Henry] Clay. It will be a poor concern; but the factious object is seen by the title. . . I am not sorry to see the efforts made to organize the workingmen. If Mr. Clay shall succeed in teaching them their strength, they will hurl him and all the factious lawyers out of power and almost out of sight. They are whetting a razor to cut their own throat. I would rejoice to see the *real* workingmen take a decisive stand in politics and place more of themselves in public office. Besides, their notions in relation to the U.S. Bank and many other matters are not very congenial to the objects of H. Clay. I know his only object is to *use* them; but he ought to remember the old proverb—"Do not meddle with edge-tools."

Questions

1. Why did Kendall (himself a lawyer) think it was important for farmers and mechanics to take part in the *nomination* as well as the election of political candidates?

2. In Kendall's view, how would this grass roots involvement displace the "town aristocracies"?
3. Why did Kendall feel confident that Clay's efforts to "*use*" the workingmen would backfire?

Questions for Further Thought

1. Kent (Document 11-1) and Clay (Document 11-2) were both responding to the rising importance of manufactures in the United States. Based on these documents, what were the political implications of that impact?
2. Kent's elitist views, like the Federalist party, had to make way for the democratic revolution described by Kendall (Document 11-3). Compare the tone and content of Kent's and Clay's speeches. In what ways was Clay better equipped than Kent to meet the demands of that revolution?
3. Consider the relationship between politics and economic interest. In what ways would you expect Kendall's description of grass-roots democratic politics to affect Clay's comprehensive economic agenda?

The Jacksonian Presidency, 1829–1837

Andrew Jackson (see text pp. 332–342) became president in 1829 determined to use the power of the presidency to attack what he viewed as corruption in commercial relations. This attack soon focused on the nation's monetary system—the "paper system" as the Jacksonians derisively called it—and culminated in Jackson's veto of a bill to recharter the National Bank (Document 11-4). Jackson triumphed in the 1832 election (see text pp. 333–334) by making the National Bank the symbol of aristocracy, special privilege, and monopoly—that is, the enemy of democracy and equal rights (Document 11-5).

As a westerner and an expansionist, Jackson personally welcomed the declaration of independence of the Texas Republic in the last year of his presidency (see text pp. 340–342). Like many in his party he thought that the Rio Grande, not the Sabine River, was the proper southwestern border of the United States. But the Texas uprising also presented problems that Jackson did not welcome. A vast slaveholding territory, Texas raised the vexing issue of slavery once more. With memories of the nullification crisis still fresh, Jackson welcomed the events in Texas cautiously (Document 11-6).

11-4   Bank Veto Message (1832)

Andrew Jackson

The first Bank of the United States had been established at the behest of President Washington's treasury secretary, Alexander Hamilton, and was rechartered for a twenty-year period in 1816 during the Era of Good Feeling. The bank had become a political issue after the Panic of 1819, when the question of the country's monetary policy suddenly became associated with financial collapse and economic depression. The bank issue had for some years generated factional political divisions at the state level, and Jackson entered the presidency opposed to the existing structure and policies of the Second Bank of the United States. He also found himself in an intense personal struggle with the bank's president, Nicholas Biddle. When Congress approved an extended charter for Biddle's bank, Jackson vetoed the legislation (see text p. 333). Jackson made his veto message the opening shot in a campaign to destroy the bank, a war that became the defining event of his presidency (see text p. 334). In the following extracts from his veto message Jackson explains why he viewed the Bank as an undemocratic concentration of economic power and a threat to the republic.

Source: In James D. Richardson, ed., *A Compilation of the Message and Papers of the Presidents* (Washington, D.C.: U.S. Government Printing Office, 1896–1899), vol. 2, pp. 576–591.

The bill "to modify and continue" the act entitled "An act to incorporate the subscribers to the Bank of the United States" was presented to me on the 4th July instant. Having considered it with that solemn regard to the principles of the Constitution which the day was calculated to inspire, and come to the conclusion that it ought not to become a law, I herewith return it to the Senate, in which it originated, with my objections.

A bank of the United States is in many respects convenient for the Government and useful to the people. Entertaining this opinion, and deeply impressed with the belief that some of the powers and privileges possessed by the existing bank are unauthorized by the Constitution, subversive of the rights of the States, and dangerous to the liberties of the people, I felt it my duty at an early period of my Administration to call the attention of Congress to the practicability of organizing an institution combining all its advantages and obviating these objections. I sincerely regret that in the act before me I can perceive none of these modifications of the bank charter which are necessary, in my opinion, to make it compatible with justice, with sound policy, or with the Constitution of our country. . . .

But this act does not permit competition in the purchase of this monopoly [the bank]. It seems to be predicated on the erroneous idea that the present stockholders have a prescriptive right not only to the favor but to the bounty of Government. It appears that more than a fourth part of the stock is held by foreigners and the residue is held by a few hundred of our own citizens, chiefly of the richest class. For their benefit does this act exclude the whole American people from competition in the purchase of this monopoly and dispose of it for many millions less than it is worth. This seems the less excusable because some of our citizens not now stockholders petitioned that the door of competition might be opened, and offered to take a charter on terms much more favorable to the Government and country. . . .

It is to be regretted that the rich and powerful too often bend the acts of government to their selfish purposes. Distinctions in society will always exist under every just government. Equality of talents, of education, or of wealth can not be produced by human institutions. In the full enjoyment of the gifts of Heaven and the fruits of superior industry, economy, and virtue, every man is equally entitled to protection by law; but when the laws undertake to add to these natural and just advantages artificial distinction, to grant titles, gratuities, and exclusive privileges, to make the rich richer and the potent more powerful, the humble members of society—the farmers, mechanics, and laborers—who have neither the time nor the means of securing like favors to themselves, have a right to complain of the injustice of their Government. There are no necessary evils in government. Its evils exist only in its abuses. If it would confine itself to equal protection, and, as Heaven does its rains, shower its favors alike on the high and the low, the rich and the poor, it would be an unqualified blessing. In the act before me there seems to be a wide and unnecessary departure from these just principles. . . .

Many of our rich men have not been content with equal protection and equal benefits, but have besought us to make them richer by act of Congress. By attempting to gratify their desires we have in the results of our legislation arrayed section against section, interest against interest, and man against man, in a fearful commotion which threatens to shake the foundations of our Union. If we can not at once, in justice to interests vested under improvident legislation, make our Government what it ought to be, we can at least take a stand against all new grants of monopolies and exclusive privileges, against any prostitution of our Government to the advancement of the few at the expense of the many, and in favor of compromise and gradual reform in our code of laws and system of political economy. . . .

Questions

1. In his veto message, Jackson did not question the ability of the bank to regulate currency and credit. What public policy objectives does his message attempt to advance?

2. Despite the Supreme Court's decision in *McCulloch v. Maryland* (1819), Jackson insisted in his veto message that some of the "powers and privileges possessed by the existing bank are unauthorized by the Constitution." What reasons does he give for that judgment?
3. What did the "humbler members of society" rightly complain about, in Jackson's view?

11-5 Opposition to Banks and Monopoly (c. 1832)

William Leggett (1801–1839) was perhaps the most insightful political writer in the Jacksonian camp. He was born in New York City and briefly lived a frontier life with his parents in Illinois. In 1829 Leggett became joint owner and editor (with William Cullen Bryant) of the New York *Evening Post*. An enthusiastic and sophisticated supporter of Jackson's war against the Second Bank of the United States (see text pp. 332–334), Leggett developed the theoretical implications of Jacksonian antimonopoly and equal rights rhetoric. In the following editorial Leggett offers a practical description of the operations of unregulated banks and explains how bank-sponsored speculation entraps the unwary and makes honest producers the victims of financial corruption.

Source: In Theodore Sedgwick, Jr., ed., *A Collection of the Political Writings of William Leggett* (New York, 1840), vol. 1, pp. 97–101.

Our primary ground of opposition to banks as they at present exist is that they are a species of monopoly. All corporations are liable to the objection that whatever powers or privileges are given to them, are so much taken from the government of the people. Though a state legislature may possess a constitutional right to create bank incorporations, yet it seems very clear to our apprehension that the doing so is an invasion of the grand republican principle of Equal Rights—a principle which lies at the bottom of our constitution, and which, in truth, is the corner-stone of our national government. . . .

Let us trace the progress of a new banking institution. Let us imagine a knot of speculators to have possessed themselves, by certain acts of collusion, bribery, and political management, of a bank charter; and let us suppose them commencing operations under their corporate privileges. They begin by lending their capital. After that, if commercial business is active, and the demand for money urgent, they take care to put as many of their notes in circulation as possible. For awhile this does very well and the Bank realizes large profits. Every thing seems to flourish; merchants extend their operations. . . . Others, in the meanwhile, stimulated by the same appearance of commercial prosperity, borrow money (that is notes) from the bank, and embark in enterprises of a different nature. They purchase lots, build houses, set railway and canal projects on foot, and every thing goes on swimmingly. The demand for labour is abundant, property of all kinds rises in price, and speculators meet each other in the streets, and exult in their anticipated fortunes.

But by and by things take a different turn. . . . The bank now perceives that it has extended itself too far. Its notes, which, until now, circulated currently enough, begin to return in upon it in demand for specie; while, at the same time, the merchants, whom it has been all along eager to serve, now call for increased accommodations. But the bank cannot accommodate them any longer. Instead of increasing its loans, it is obliged to require payment of those which it had previously made. . . . The merchants, unable to get the amount of accommodation necessary to sustain their operations, are forced to suspend payment. . . . Then follows wider derangement. One commercial house after another becomes bankrupt, and finally the bank itself, by these repeated losses forced to discontinue its business, closes its doors, and hands over its affairs for the benefit of its creditors. . . . On investigation it is discovered, most likely, that the whole capital of the institution has been absorbed by its losses. The enormous profits which it made during the first part of its career, had been regularly withdrawn by the stockholders, and the deluded creditor has nothing but a worthless bit of engraved paper to show for the valuable consideration which he parted with for what he foolishly imagined [to be] money.

Questions

1. How does Leggett define a monopoly?
2. In Leggett's view, why do banks inevitably tend toward corruption?
3. Consider the implications of Leggett's remarks. How might the Jacksonians have protected the people from the mischief of what they "foolishly imagined money"?

11-6　Texas Declares Its Independence (1836)

The Adams-Onis Treaty (1819) established the Sabine River as the southwestern border between the United States and the Spanish territories in North America. Many Americans in the South and the West believed that Secretary of State John Quincy Adams, a New Englander, had conceded too much to Spain. They looked farther south to the Rio Grande and welcomed Mexican independence from Spain in 1822 because it potentially opened the Southwest to American settlers. Negotiating with Stephen Austin, Mexican authorities initially admitted about 2,000 families of American settlers. But relations between the Americans and the Mexican government were tense from the outset (see text p. 340). In October 1832 and again in April 1833 the Texans held conventions that called on Mexico to reform its governance of the region. Unresolved grievances led to fighting and, in March 1836, to the Texas Declaration of Independence.

Source: In Francis N. Thorpe, ed., *The Federal and State Constitutions . . . of the United States* (Washington, D.C.: U.S. Government Printing Office, 1909), vol. 6, p. 3528.

When a government has ceased to protect the lives liberty and property of its people, from whom its legitimate powers are derived, and for the advancement of whose happiness it was instituted, and so far from being a guarantee for the enjoyment of those inestimable and inalienable rights, becomes an instrument in the hands of evil rulers for their oppression: When the Federal Republican Constitution of their country [Mexico], which they have sworn to support, no longer has a substantial existence, and the whole nature of their government has been forcibly changed without their consent, from a restricted federative republic, composed of sovereign states to a consolidated central military despotism in which every interest is disregarded but that of the army and the priesthood—both the eternal enemies of civil liberty, the every-ready minions of power, and the usual instruments of tyrants: . . . the inherent and unalienable right of the people to appeal to first principles and take their political affairs into their own hands in extreme cases enjoins it as a right towards themselves and a sacred obligation to their posterity to abolish such government and create another in its stead, calculated to rescue them from impending dangers, and to secure their future welfare and happiness. . . .

The Mexican government, by its colonization laws, invited and induced the Anglo-American population of Texas to colonize its wilderness under the pledged faith of a written constitution that they should continue to enjoy that constitutional liberty and republican government to which they had been habituated in the land of their birth, the United States of America. In this expectation they have been cruelly disappointed, in as much as the Mexican nation had acquiesced in the late changes made in the government by General Antonio Lopez de Santa Anna, who, having overturned the constitution of his country, now offers as the cruel alternative either to abandon our homes, acquired by so many privations, or submit to the most intolerable of all tyranny, the combined despotism of the sword and the priesthood. . . .

It has suffered the military commandants stationed among us to exercise arbitrary acts of oppression and tyranny; thus trampling upon the most sacred rights of the citizen and rendering the military superior to the civil power. . . .

It denies us the right of worshiping the Almighty according to the dictates of our own conscience, by the support of a national religion calculated to promote the temporal interest of its human functionaries rather than the glory of the true and living God.

It has demanded us to deliver up our arms, which are essential to our defence, the rightful property of freemen, and formidable only to tyrannical governments. . . .

These, and other grievances, were patiently borne by the people of Texas until they reached the point at which forbearance ceases to be a virtue. We then took up arms in defence of the national constitution. We appealed to our Mexican brethren for assistance. Our appeal has been made in vain. Though months have elapsed, no sympathetic response has yet been heard from the interior. We are, therefore, forced to the melancholy conclusion that the Mexican people have acquiesced in the destruction of their liberty and the substitution therefore of a Military Government—that they are unfit to be free and incapable of self-government. . . .

We therefore, the delegates with plenary powers, of the people of Texas, in solemn convention assembled, appealing to a candid world for the necessities of our condition, do hereby resolve and declare that our political connections with the Mexican Nation has forever ended; and that the people of Texas do now constitute a free sovereign and independent republic. . . .

Questions

1. Compare the Texas Declaration of Independence with the United States Declaration of Independence (see text pp. D-1–D-2). How are they similar? Where do they differ?
2. Texans complained of the "combined despotism of the sword and the priesthood." What did they mean?
3. Did the Americans in Texas see their revolution as one which would liberate the Mexicans from oppression? Explain why.

Questions for Further Thought

1. Jackson's claim that the presidency represented the democratic will of the people had far-ranging consequences. How did Jackson's claim to a popular mandate affect his attitude toward the exercise of presidential power? Did his presidency alter the balance of power in the federal system?
2. If the presidency represented the collective will of the people, it followed that presidential candidates should appeal directly to the sentiments and affections of the people. What evidence can you find in Jackson's message that he was appealing beyond his immediate audience to the nation at large? Do you see any dangers in such popular appeals?
3. What alternatives did Jackson face when Texas declared its independence from Mexico? Why did he choose not to act?

The Early Labor Movement, 1794–1836, and Democrats and Whigs: The Second Party System, 1836–1844

The Industrial Revolution transferred manufacturing from the household to central shops and factories. This shift in the location of production profoundly altered the traditional role of the head of the household as well as the traditional relationship between master artisans, apprentices, and journeymen. As some masters became employers, as in the manufacture of shoes, the apprentice system collapsed and journeymen (and many masters) became permanent wage earners. Workingmen responded to these changes with outrage and resolve. Their outrage stemmed from their increasingly dependent condition and prompted them to band together in associations and societies (see text pp. 342–343); their resolve arose from a sense of collective power in politics and the workplace (Document 11-7). Wage earners banded together to bring their collective strength to bear against a small but powerful employer class. At stake was the process by which wages, hours, and working conditions would be set. The tradition of the independent artisan producer prompted collective activities that produced some victories amid the defeats (Document 11-8).

As the Industrial Revolution reshaped the workplace, Andrew Jackson made partisan political combativeness a democratic virtue, a lesson the Whigs soon learned. In 1836 and again in 1840 the Whigs united behind William Henry Harrison, a westerner and Indian fighter like Jackson. The Whigs depicted Jackson's successor, Martin Van Buren of New York, as an "aristocratic" easterner (Document 11-9). With the Whig presidential victory in 1840 (see text pp. 352–353) the Second Party System had become a political institution.

In important respects the workingmen's movement paralleled the course of Jacksonian democracy. The Jacksonians embraced the cause of the independent producer and celebrated the "healthy mechanic" as the natural ally of farmers and planters in the South and the West. The Jacksonian war against the Second Bank also paralleled the workingmen's hostility toward capitalists who profited by manipulating stocks and currency. The Jacksonians were quick to associate the regimentation of the factory system with the friends of the Second Bank and with the American System generally (Document 11-10). Responding to the workingmen's movement, Jackson set a ten-hour day at the Philadelphia navy yard in 1836, and in 1840 Martin Van Buren extended the ten-hour day to all federal employees and all federally sponsored construction projects (see text pp. 351–352).

11-7 Address to the Working Men of New England (1832)

Seth Luther

Seth Luther (1817?–1846), who probably was born in Providence, Rhode Island, became a strong voice for workingmen in Jacksonian America. A carpenter by trade, Luther had little formal education, but he was an avid reader of newspapers and books and became a leading figure in the fight for the ten-hour day (see text pp. 342–343). In the following speech, delivered to a gathering of workingmen, Luther described an "American System" dedicated not to expanding manufactures (see Document 11-2) but to securing the equality of men.

Source: The Globe (Washington, D.C.), May 13, 1832.

I would ask if persons not possessing one hundred and thirty four dollars in soil, are permitted to address this meeting. If so, I wish to make a few remarks. This community seems to be divided into two parties. Not Jackson men and Clay men . . . but the Aristocracy and Democracy. The term Aristocracy denotes a privileged class. Although the Constitution of the United States acknowledges no hereditary right, yet there exists among us a class well deserving the name of Aristocrats. I will mention some of their privi-leges. . . . Sir, this aristocracy of wealth claims the right to shut up in the Cotton Mill the almost infant child for . . . 13 or 14 hours per diem, with only 20 or 30 minutes for each meal . . . thereby depriving them of the best of all earthly good, an education. . . . Sir, we are in favor of an American System that will benefit all interests. But we are not satisfied with *the* System, whatever it may be, which enables a favored few to accumulate mountains of wealth, at the expense of our dearest interests. . . . We hear the philanthropist moaning over the fate of the Southern slave, when there are thousands of children in this State as truly slaves as the blacks of the South. . . .

Sir, we find the aristocracy in all countries, using their efforts, either directly or indirectly, to hold the poorer classes in ignorance; that they may rivet the chains of oppression more effectually. Where, Sir, is the difference in the effect between Southern measures, and measures now practiced by the Manufacturer, to accomplish this dreadful object?

Much, Sir, have we heard respecting the happiness of a manufacturing population. The Hon. H.[enry] Clay . . . draws a most beautiful picture. He has seen *one* Cotton Mill in Cincinnati. . . . He exclaims, " 'Tis a paradise!"— But . . . one of my friends remarked, if a *Cotton Mill* is paradise, it is "Paradise Lost." . . . we would presume to advise the Hon. Senator from Kentucky to . . . see . . . instead of rosy cheeks, the *pale*, the *sickly*, the *haggard*, countenance of the ragged child from six to twelve years of age. Haggard from the worse than slavish confinement in the cotton mill.

Questions

1. What does Luther mean by the "aristocracy of wealth"?
2. Why is Luther not moved by a philanthropic concern for southern slaves?
3. What is it about the factory system that Luther opposes?

11-8   Acquittal of Cordwainers of Hudson, New York, in *People v. Cooper* (1836)

In 1836 leading members of the United Society of the Journeymen Cordwainers of the City of Hudson in New York were tried by the state for engaging in a conspiracy against their employers for the purpose of demanding higher wages (see text p. 343). The following account of the trial, *People v. Cooper* (1836), was reported by the attorneys in the case.

Source: In John R. Commons et al., eds., *A Documentary History of American Industrial Society* (New York, Russell & Russell, 1958), vol. 4, pp. 277–312.

The defendants were indicted under the statute for a combination and conspiracy to raise their wages, etc., to "the great injury of trade and commerce." They were indicted at the instance of Eli Mosier, a boss shoemaker, of the city of Hudson. . . .

The first count charges, "that the defendants, not being content to work for the usual prices, but combining to increase their wages, and the wages of other journeymen . . . did on the 15th of September, 1835, combine together with other workmen, and agree that none of them, would after that day, work at any lower prices than those mentioned in the list, to the great damage of the boss shoemakers, and the injury of trade and commerce, and against the statute."

The second count charges, "that the defendants . . . did thereby agree . . . that any member who should work for less, should be expelled from the society and . . . that any boss who should refuse to pay their rates of wages should be fined, and no member of the society would work for him until he paid his fine. . . ."

SOLOMON SHATTOCK, sworn. I am a boss shoemaker. Several of the members of the society . . . left my employ because I would not give them the wages on their list. None but Defries left the first time—the rest did not leave until afterwards. Several members of the society . . . said that if I did not pay the fine they would leave me. . . . At the time Defries left me, I was paying the prices on their list to him—but in consequence of my not giving the full price to the other men Defries left me. . . .

His Hon. Judge Wilcoxon then charged the Jury in substance as follows: . . .

If the journeymen shoemakers of the city of Hudson had a right to combine, then the Journeymen [everywhere] . . . had a right to combine and to control the labor of every mechanical State in the Union. The question for consideration was whether the controlling the labor of the country in this manner had a tendency to injure trade. For instance, in a manufacturing establishment where there were a hundred hands, and where contracts had to be performed in a given time, would not a sudden combination and refusal to work, cause the ruin of the individual? . . .

The cause was then committed to the Jury. . . . The Jury were together about 209 minutes. . . . The next morning they delivered in Court the following verdict: The Jurors find the Prisoners Not Guilty.

Questions

1. Summarize the charges brought against the journeymen cordwainers.
2. Since Defries received the wage rate demanded by the journeymen, what motivated him to leave Shattock's employ?
3. In the view of the presiding judge, why were associations of journeymen dangerous?

11-9 "Set-To between the Champion Old Tip and the Swell Dutchman of Kinderhook" (1836)

Edward C. Clay

Andrew Jackson's direct appeal to voters in the presidential elections of 1824, 1828, and 1832 ended the reign of "King Caucus" and left a legacy of sharply contested partisan contests for the presidency (see text pp. 329, 330–331, 333–334). In this Whig cartoon (p. 217), the election of 1836 (see text p. 349) is depicted as a fistfight between Martin Van Buren and one of his Whig opponents, William Henry Harrison of Ohio. Van Buren won in 1836 but would be defeated by Harrison in 1840. Supporting Van Buren in the cartoon are a timorous and tipsy "Amos" Kendall (see Document 11-3) and an anxious Andrew Jackson. Backing Harrison are Davy Crockett and a war veteran holding Harrison's whiskey bottle.

Source: Library of Congress, Washington, D.C.

The words in the balloons, from left to right, are as follows:

"Amos" [Kendall] character:
I begin to tremble for Matty [Martin Van Buren].
There appears to be a Surplus Fund [a surplus of federal
    revenue from land sales distributed to the states during
    the 1836 campaign]
in this Bottle, so I'll een [var. of "even"]
take a pull to raise my spirits
Oh dear.

Andrew Jackson character:
By the Eternal! what a severe
counterhit! It's bunged up Matty's
peeper, and if he don't keep his other eye
Open he'll get a Cross buttock [a wrestling move to throw
    an opponent with the thrust of a hip or buttock] He
begins to be a little queerish already
D——n his *Dutch* courage [bravery induced by drinking]!
    Amos
where's the Bottle? after this
Round put some more into him

Martin Van Buren character:
Stand by me Old Hickory
or I'm a gone chicken!

William Henry Harrison character:
Look out for your bread-basket
Matty, I'll remove the deposits
for you

Davy Crockett character:
Whoop! wake snakes! Go it
Old Tip! by the Immortals he
puts it into him as fast as a
streak of greased lightning
through a gooseberry bush
That *Cold Blooded* Kinderhooker [Van Buren's nickname:
    "Red Fox of Kinderhook" (Kinderhook, New York)]
will be rowed up Salt river or I'm a nigger!

War veteran character:
Thank Heaven
the people have a
Champion at last
who will support the
Constitution and laws
that we fought and bled
to obtain Huzza for my
old Comrade

SET-TO BETWEEN THE CHAMPION OLD TIP & THE SWELL DUTCHMAN OF KINDERHOOK—1836

Questions

1. This cartoon suggests that Americans had come to view the election of a president as a rough-and-tumble fight. Why would a Whig want to depict the contest in this way?

2. Examine the cartoon for its symbolic meanings. What messages are the characters meant to convey?

3. Evaluate the cartoon from the perspective of the debate over the extension of the franchise (see Documents 11-1 and 11-3). Did this depiction of electoral politics express the fears of those who opposed the eradication of property qualifications?

11-10   Protecting "Domestic Industry" (1842)

Francis P. Blair (1791–1876) was born in Abington, Virginia, and settled in Frankfort, Kentucky, after graduating from Transylvania University. A coeditor of the Frankfort *Argus of the West*, Blair played a leading role in carrying Kentucky for Andrew Jackson in 1828. In 1830 Blair moved to the nation's capital to join Jackson's Kitchen Cabinet (see text p. 332) and to edit the staunchly Jacksonian Washington, D.C., *Globe*. Blair played a leading role in developing the Jacksonians' political appeal to southern and western planters, yeomen farmers, and workingmen in the urban North (see text p. 331). In the January 11, 1842, edition of the *Globe*, during the administration of John Tyler (see text p. 353), Blair attacked a Whig tariff proposal to protect "domestic industry" and commented on the changed meaning of the term.

Source: The Globe (Washington, D.C.), January 11, 1842.

In the good old days of the Republic, when every man minded his own business and left others to take care of their own; when dependence was placed on personal exertion alone, and people did not look up to HERCULES Congress to get them out of the slough into which they had plunged by their own folly and improvidence; in those times, domestic industry was a different thing from what it is now. If we are to believe the assertions of members of Congress advocating a protective tariff, there is no other domestic industry than that employed in our great manufactories. According to their definition, tending spinning jennies in a stupendous brick building, six or seven stories high, some ten or twenty miles from home, surrounded by hundreds of strapping "operatives," from all quarters of the world, with tremendous whiskers, is your only domestic industry for the young and blooming daughters of the land.

"DOMESTIC INDUSTRY" is no longer represented by the ruddy matron sitting at her own fireside in her own home, turning the spinning wheel with one foot and rocking a chubby bantling with the other, while singing it to sleep with lullabies. . . .

"DOMESTIC INDUSTRY," according to the tariff definition, is not that of the healthy mechanic or artisan, who works for himself at his own shop, or if he goes abroad, returns home to his meals every day, and sleeps under his own roof every night; whose earnings are regulated by the wants of the community at large, not by the discretion of a penurious master; whose hours of labor depend on universal custom; who, when the sun goes down, is a freeman until he rises again; who can eat his meals in comfort, and sleep as long as nature requires. . . . Domestic industry is nothing but bondage in its most oppressive form, labor in its utmost extremity of degradation.

"DOMESTIC INDUSTRY," according to the protective tariff cant, is that which separates wives, husbands, parents and children; annihilates every domestic tie and association, and renders all domestic duties subservient to the will, not of a husband or parent, but that of an unfeeling taskmaster, to whom the sacrifice of every moment of time, and every comfort of life, is wealth and prosperity.

Questions

1. What was the meaning of "domestic industry" in tariff legislation (see Document 11-2)?
2. What ironic meanings did Blair find in the term *domestic industry*?
3. How did Blair define the "healthy mechanic"? In his view, why was the mechanic's "health" in jeopardy?

Questions for Further Thought

1. From the traditional perspective of the independent artisan producer, consider the implications of a widening sphere of wage labor. Why, from this perspective, did the dangers of the Industrial Revolution often seem to overshadow its benefits?
2. In what ways was Blair's praise of the "healthy mechanic" (Document 11-10) a political appeal to workingmen? How might the views expressed by Blair have influenced the jury in *People v. Cooper* (Document 11-8)?
3. What were the strengths and weaknesses of the early labor movement? Why was the depression after the Panic of 1837 a devastating blow to that movement? Use the journeymen shoemakers of Hudson, New York, as an example.

CHAPTER 12

Freedom's Crusaders 1820–1860

★   ★   ★

Transcendentalists and Utopians

The Industrial Revolution weakened old social restraints and obligations and encouraged new visions of an ideal social order. To the era's social reformers, who characteristically were middle-class beneficiaries of what seemed to be limitless economic opportunity, the restraints and obligations of the past seemed artificial and contrived (see text pp. 358–359). They searched for society's "natural" foundations that at once would secure the autonomy of the individual and define the individual's social responsibility in terms of his or her highest interests (Document 12-1). This search for the natural foundations of society spawned a wide variety of social reforms and utopian experiments (Document 12-2), some of which were too eccentric or extreme to attract attention or challenge the established social order (see text pp. 363–367). But certain themes connected these enthusiasms and crusades and suggest the ways in which these expressions of middle-class radicalism reshaped society in industrializing America.

The individualism and self-restraint these reformers preached stood in sharp contrast to the forms of deference and coercion they associated with a rapidly fading age of barbarism. Individualism and self-restraint required self-reliance and a capacity to distinguish what was necessary and good from all that was frivolous and distracting. Individualism also strongly implied (and to many required) the equality of men and women and led to radical assaults on male domination and female subordination in public life and in marriage. Celibate Shaker communities ended marriage altogether and looked to their founder, Mother Ann Lee, as the embodiment of the female nature of God that was both male and female (see text pp. 364–365 and Document 12-3). More broadly in society, the self-restrained individual sought to free women from the dangers of unwanted pregnancies and to cultivate human love and affection in ways that united femininity and masculinity (Document 12-4). The social reforms of industrializing America altered and broadened the meaning of liberty and equality and challenged the authority of the state, the community, and the majority.

12-1 *Walden* (1854)

Henry David Thoreau

Henry David Thoreau (1817–1862) was born and lived most of his life in Concord, Massachusetts. A graduate of Harvard, he taught for a time in Concord but soon devoted himself to the transcendentalist movement (see text p. 359). His most famous works, an account of his residence at Walden Pond and the essay "On Civil Disobedience," although not widely read in his day, have become an enduring legacy of transcendentalism (see text p. 359). In contrast to Emerson (see text pp. 358–359), whose romantic individualism stayed aloof from material conditions, Thoreau offered a subversive twist to a principal tenet of liberal capitalism: the proposition that individuals exchange labor for leisure to promote future pleasure. If the highest sphere of individual pleasure is transcendental contemplation, Thoreau reasoned, an individual should strive to exchange the least labor for the most leisure.

Source: Henry David Thoreau, *Walden or, Life in the Woods and On the Duty of Civil Disobedience* (Boston, 1854; reprint, New York: NAL Penguin, 1960).

ECONOMY

When I wrote the following pages, or rather the bulk of them, I lived alone, in the woods, a mile from any neighbor, in a house which I had built myself, on the shore of Walden Pond, in Concord, Massachusetts, and earned my living by the labor of my hands only. I lived there two years and two months. At present I am a sojourner in civilized life again. . . . It would be some advantage to live a primitive and frontier life, though in the midst of an outward civilization, if only to learn what are the gross necessaries of life and what methods have been taken to obtain them. . . . By the words, *necessary of life,* I mean whatever, of all that man obtains by his own exertions, had been from the first, or from long use has become, so important to human life that few, if any whether from savageness, or poverty, or philosophy, ever attempt to do without it. . . .

Though we are not so degenerate but that we might possibly live in a cave or a wigwam or wear skins to-day, it certainly is better to accept the advantages, though so dearly bought, which the invention and industry of mankind offer. In such a neighborhood as this, boards and shingles, lime and bricks, are cheaper and more easily obtained than suitable caves. . . .

Near the end of March, 1845, I borrowed an axe and went down to the woods by Walden Pond. . . . It is difficult to begin without borrowing, but perhaps it is the most generous course thus to permit your fellow-men to have an interest in your enterprise. . . .

I hewed the main timbers six inches square, most of the studs on two sides only, and the rafters and floor timbers on one side, leaving the rest of the bark on, so that they were just as straight and much stronger than sawed ones. Each stick was carefully mortised or tenoned by its stump, for I had borrowed other tools by this time. . . .

By the middle of April, for I made no haste in my work, but rather made the most of it, my house was framed and ready for raising. . . . At length, in the beginning of May, with the help of some of my acquaintances, rather to improve so good an occasion for neighborliness than from any necessity, I set up the frame of my house. . . . Before winter I built a chimney, and shingled the sides of my house. . . . I have thus a tight shingled and plastered house, ten feet wide by fifteen long, and eight-feet posts, with a garret and a closet, a large window on each side. . . .

One says to me, "I wonder that you do not lay up money; you love to travel." . . . But I am wiser than that. . . . I say to my friend, Suppose we try who will get there first. The distance is thirty miles; the fare ninety cents. That is almost a day's wages. . . . Well, I start now on foot, and get there before night. . . . You will in the meanwhile have earned your fare, and arrive there some time to-morrow, or possibly this evening, if you are lucky enough to get a job in season. . . .

Such is the universal law, which no man can ever outwit, and with regard to the railroad even we may say it is as broad as it is long. To make a railroad round the world available to all mankind is equivalent to grading the whole surface of the planet. Men have an indistinct notion that if they keep up this activity of joint stocks and spades long enough all will at length ride somewhere, in next to no time, and for nothing; but though a crowd rushes to the depot, and the conductor shouts "All aboard!" when the smoke is blown away and the vapor condensed, it will be perceived that a few are riding, but the rest are run over,— and it will be called, and will be, "A melancholy accident." . . .

For more than five years I maintained myself thus solely by the labor of my hands, and I found that, by working about six weeks in a year, I could meet all the expenses of living. The whole of my winters, as well as most of my summers, I had free and clear for study. . . .

As I preferred some things to others, and especially valued my freedom. . . . I did not wish to spend my time in earning rich carpets or other fine furniture, or delicate cookery, or a house in the Grecian or the Gothic style just yet. . . . In short, I am convinced, both by faith and experience that to maintain one's self on this earth is not a hardship but a pastime, if we live simply and wisely. . . .

Questions

1. Thoreau lived alone at Walden Pond, but was he isolated from society?
2. What was the purpose of Thoreau's exercise in self-sufficiency?
3. What did Thoreau mean when he wrote that railroads would produce "a melancholy accident"? Analyze this passage as a critique of industrialization.

12-2 *The Blithedale Romance* (1852)

Nathaniel Hawthorne

Nathaniel Hawthorne (1804–1864), a native of Salem, Massachusetts, and a graduate of Bowdoin College, lived for a year at Brook Farm. He drew on this experience and on the themes of moral reform and feminism to write the novel *The Blithedale Romance*. With Herman Melville (the two writers admired each other's work) Hawthorne explored the human isolation of individualism and the destructive capacity of moral crusades. While most reformers identified with the antislavery movement, Hawthorne and Melville distanced themselves from the certitude of moral reform (see text pp. 360–361). In the following passage from *The Blithedale Romance* the narrator describes the romantic idealism of the Brook Farm community and the sense of moral isolation that followed its demise.

Source: Nathaniel Hawthorne, *The Blithedale Romance* (Boston, 1852).

If ever men might lawfully dream awake, and give utterance to their wildest visions, without dread of laughter or scorn on the part of the audience—yes, and speak of earthly happiness, for themselves and mankind, as an object to be hopefully striven for, and probably attained—we . . . were those very men. We had left the rusty iron framework of society behind us. We had broken through many hindrances that are powerful enough to keep most people on the weary tread-mill of the established system, even while they feel its irksomeness almost as intolerable as we did. . . . It was our purpose—a generous one, certainly, and absurd, no doubt, in full proportion with its generosity—to give up whatever we had theretofore attained, for the sake of showing mankind the example of a life governed by other than the false and cruel principles, on which human society has all along been based. . . . We meant to lessen the laboring man's great burthen of toil, by performing our due share of it. . . . We sought our profit by mutual aid, instead of wresting it by the strong hand from an enemy, or filching it craftily from those less shrewd than ourselves. . . .

The experiment, so far as its original projectors were concerned, proved long ago a failure, first leaping into Fourierism [see text pp. 363–364], and dying, as it well deserved, for this infidelity to its own higher spirit. . . .

My subsequent life has passed—I was going to say, happily—but, at all events, tolerably enough. I am now at middle-age—well, well, a step or two beyond the midmost point. . . . I live very much at my ease, and fare sumptuously every day. . . . As regards human progress . . . let them believe in it who can, and aid in it who choose! . . . I lack a purpose. . . . I by no means wish to die. Yet, were there any cause, in this whole chaos of human struggle, worth a sane man's dying for, and which my death would benefit, then—provided, however, the effort did not involve an unreasonable amount of trouble—methinks I might be bold to offer my life. . . . Farther than that, I should be loth to pledge myself.

Questions

1. Why do you think Hawthorne chose the word *Blithedale* for his fictionalized account of Brook Farm? Do you agree with the observation of the narrator (the character Miles Coverdale) that utopian reform was "absurd . . . in full proportion with its generosity"?
2. How would you answer the question posed by Miles Coverdale in the final paragraph: In a self-interested world is there "any cause . . . worth . . . dying for"?
3. Judging from this excerpt, what do you think Hawthorne missed most about Brook Farm?

12-3 The Shakers

Rebecca Cox Jackson

Rebecca Cox Jackson (1795–1871) was a free African-American woman who renounced a relatively secure life with her husband in Philadelphia to become an itinerant Methodist preacher. During the 1830s she traveled throughout the countryside, accompanied by a younger disciple, Rebecca Perot. In 1843 the "two Rebeccas" became committed Shakers, eventually settling in the community of Watervliet, near Albany, New York (see text pp. 364–365). They remained ambiguous about Shaker isolation, however, and in 1851 they resumed their ministry in the free black community. In 1858 Jackson founded her own Shaker family in Philadelphia. In the 1840s, Jackson began to write a memoir of her religious experiences, including powerful dreams and visions.

In these passages Jackson expressed three key elements of the Shaker faith: that they received the direct guidance of the Holy Ghost; that Mother Ann Lee (the movement's founder) represented the female embodiment of a God comprising both male and female attributes; and that the millennium (the end of human time) was near at hand.

Source: Excerpted from Jean McMahon Humez, ed., *Gifts of Power: The Writings of Rebecca Jackson, Black Visionary, Shaker Eldress* (Amherst: University of Massachusetts Press, 1981), pp. 220–221.

Monday evening, February 18, 1850. I was instructed concerning the atmosphere and its bounds. I saw its form—it is like the sea, which has her bounds. . . . It covered land and sea, so far above all moving things, and yet so far beneath the starry heavens. Its face is like the face of the sea, smooth and gentle when undisturbed by the wind. So is the atmosphere, when undisturbed by the power of the sun and moon. When agitated by these, it rages like the sea and sends forth its storms upon the earth. Nothing can live above it. A bird could no more live or fly above its face, than a fish can live or swim out of the water. It is always calm and serene between its face and the starry heaven. The sight, to me, was beautiful.

March 1, 1850. . . . Prayer given to me by Mother Ann Lee: "Oh God, my Everlasting Father, to Thee do I lift up my soul in prayer and thanksgiving for the gift of Thy dear Son, our Blessed Savior, who has begotten to us a living hope. And to Thee, Holy Mother Wisdom, do I lift up my soul in prayer and thanksgiving, for the gift of Thy Holy Daughter, whose blessed Spirit has led me and instructed me in this, the holy way of God, lo! these many years, and has borne with my infirmities and many shortcomings. And lo! Thou hast comforted me in all my sorrows and Thy blessed Spirit comforts me today."

Then I saw our Heavenly Parents look on me and smile, and Mother Ann gave me sweet counsel. And I was greatly strengthened in the way of God.

March 15, 1850. After I came to Watervliet . . . and saw how the Believers seemed to be gathered to themselves, in praying for themselves and not for the world, which lay in midnight darkness, I wondered how the world was to be saved, if Shakers were the only people of God on earth, and they seemed to be busy in their own concerns, which were mostly temporal. . . .

Then seeing these at ease in Zion, I cried in the name of Christ and Mother that He in mercy would do something for the helpless world. At that time, it seemed as if the whole world rested upon me. I cried to the Lord both day and night, for many months, that God would make a way that the world might hear the Gospel—that God would send spirits and angels to administer to their understanding, that they might be saved in the present tense, for I knew by revelation, that it was God's will that they should be.

Questions

1. What significance do you think Jackson attached to her vision of the atmosphere and the heavens?
2. Examine the prayer given to Jackson by Mother Ann Lee. In what ways does it deviate from the language of patriarchal religion?
3. How did Jackson's millenarianism affect her attitude toward the Shakers at Watervliet?

12-4 *Male Continence* (1872)

John Humphrey Noyes

John Humphrey Noyes (1811–1886) was born in Brattleboro, Vermont. After graduation from Dartmouth College he was drawn to the revivalist ministry. Noyes carried the logic of moral perfectionism (the belief that people, while living, could achieve the perfection of Christ) in a new direction, arguing that Christ had returned to earth in A.D. 70 and had established the one true Christian church. When he announced his own state of moral perfection in 1834, he broke his ties with established religion and society and began a spiritual journey that would lead him to the Christian communist and free love community he founded at Oneida (see text p. 365). In the treatise *Male Continence* he explained his theory of controlled propagation and complex marriage.

Source: John Humphrey Noyes, *Male Continence* (Oneida, N.Y., 1872).

I was married in 1838, and lived in the usual routine of matrimony till 1846. It was during this period of eight years that I studied the subject of sexual intercourse in connection with my matrimonial experience, and discovered the principle of Male Continence. And the discovery was occasioned and even forced upon me by very sorrowful experience. In the course of six years my wife went through the agonies of five births. Four of them were premature. Only one child lived. . . . After our last disappointment, I pledged my word to my wife that I would never again expose her to such fruitless suffering. I made up my mind to live apart from her, rather than break this promise. This was the situation in the summer of 1844. At that time I conceived the idea that the sexual organs have a social function which is distinct from the propagative function; and that these functions may be separated practically. I experimented on this idea, and found that the self-control which it requires is not difficult; also that my enjoyment was increased; also that my wife's experience was very satisfactory, as it had never been before; also that we have escaped the horrors and the fear of involuntary propagation. This was a great deliverance. It made a happy household. . . . In 1848, soon after our removal to Oneida, I published the new theory in a pamphlet. . . .

The pamphlet referred to embraced a general exhibition of the principles of the kingdom of heaven promised in the Bible, and for this reason it was entitled *The Bible Argument;* but the most important chapter of it was that which undertook to show *"How the sexual function is to be redeemed and true relations between the sexes are to be restored."* . . . I will now venture to reprint that notable chapter.

FROM THE BIBLE ARGUMENT, PRINTED IN 1848

The amative and propagative functions of the sexual organs are distinct from each other, and may be separated practically. . . . If amativeness is the first and noblest of the social affections, and if the propagative part of the sexual relation was originally secondary, and became paramount by the subversion of order in the fall [as had previously been shown], we are bound to raise the amative office of the sexual organs into a distinct and paramount function. . . . We insist, then, that the amative function—that which consists in a simple union of persons, making "of twain one flesh," and giving a medium of magnetic and spiritual interchange—is a distinct and independent function, as superior to the reproductive as we have shown amativeness to be to propagation. . . .

The method of controlling propagation which results from our argument is natural, healthy, favorable to amativeness, and effectual.

First, it is *natural*. The useless expenditure of seed certainly is not natural. . . . Our method simply proposes the subordination of the flesh to the spirit, teaching men to seek principally the elevated spiritual pleasures of sexual connection, and to be content with them in their general intercourse with women, restricting the more sensual part to its proper occasions. . . .

The separation of the amative from the propagative, places amative sexual intercourse on the same footing with other ordinary forms of social interchange. . . . In society trained in these principles . . . amative intercourse will have place among the "fine arts" . . . when sexual intercourse becomes an honored method of innocent and useful communion, and each is married to all.

Questions

1. How did Noyes change the "usual routine of matrimony"? How did he separate, "practically," amative from propagative sexual intercourse?
2. Assuming that amative and propagative sexual intercourse can be distinguished, how and why do you think Noyes concluded that amative intercourse would become indistinguishable from "ordinary forms of social interchange"?
3. Does sexuality separated from procreation and marriage promote equality between women and men? Why or why not?

Questions for Further Thought

1. For Thoreau and Noyes (Documents 12-1 and 12-4) and for Hawthorne in his Brook Farm days (Document 12-2) an ideal social order consisted of the free and mutually beneficial interaction of autonomous, self-restrained individuals. Under what conditions, if any, could such a society exist? What would become of the national state?
2. A central concern in these documents is the proper relationship of the individual to society. Examine each document from this perspective and consider what processes industrialization set in motion that generated this concern.
3. The word *utopian* is often used to mean "impractical." Consider, however, the significance of utopian thought and action in the transformation of social norms. Did the utopian thinkers of the nineteenth century influence the social norms of this century? In what way?

The Women's Movement

In the female-centered middle-class home women were insulated from the workplace, but their new role as the moral stewards of their families suggested new responsibilities and authority (see text p. 367). The moral reform movements of the early nineteenth century (see text p. 368) provided these women with a forum for the advancement of their rights as individuals and opportunities to assert equality with men in discussions of public policy. The antislavery movement projected a striking analogy between the dominion of master over slave and the dominion of man over woman (Document 12-5). As women reformers noted, all the evils of the former applied to the latter. Masterless women, like masterless men, searched for the natural foundations of gender roles. Just as individualism implied female and male equality, gender equality required a rethinking of the meaning of masculinity and femininity (Document 12-6). The participation of women in public discussions of government policy implied that women deserved the full rights of citizenship, most prominently property rights and the right to vote (Document 12-7). Women made significant progress in acquiring property rights (see text p. 372), but woman suffrage proved far more elusive. Even in reform circles the agitation for women's rights produced deep divisions. The assertion of female equality in the American Anti-Slavery Society, for example, contributed to a major schism in the ranks of abolitionists in 1840 (see text pp. 368–369). Many male reformers, and a number of female reformers as well, who embraced the equality of the races as a moral principle turned a deaf ear to advocates for women's rights. Nevertheless, perceptions of women's proper place changed fundamentally if haltingly.

12-5   Breaking Out of Women's "Separate Sphere"

Angelina E. Grimké

Angelina E. Grimké (1805–1879) was born in Charleston, South Carolina, and raised in a wealthy, aristocratic, conservative family. Deeply influenced by her older sister, Angelina soon rejected Charleston society, converted from the Episcopalianism to Quakerism during a visit to Philadelphia, and quickly embraced moral reform (see text pp. 368–369). In 1835, she wrote to William Lloyd Garrison to express her support for abolitionism. When Garrison published the letter in his newspaper, *The Liberator*, her public reform career began. Criticism of Grimké's public opposition to slavery soon led her to advocate women's rights in conjunction with abolitionism. One of Grimké's principal opponents was Catharine Beecher (1800–1878), the daughter of a prominent Congregationalist minister. Beecher was an early advocate of education for women but was also a formative figure in defining the female domestic sphere. Defending this sphere from the public activity of abolitionist women, Beecher published *An Essay on Slavery and Abolitionism, with Reference to the Duty of American Females* (1837). The following extracts are taken from Grimké's reply to Beecher.

Source: Angelina E. Grimké, *Letters to Catharine E. Beecher, in Reply to an Essay on Slavery and Abolitionism, Addressed to A. E. Grimké* (Boston, 1838; facsimile reprint, New York: Arno Press, 1969), pp. 103–113.

I come now to that part of thy book, which is, of all others, the most important to the women of this country; thy "general views in relation to the place woman is appointed to fill by the dispensations of heaven." . . .

Thou sayest, "Heaven has appointed to one sex the *superior*, and to the other the *subordinate* station. . . ." This is an assertion without proof. Thou further sayest, that "it was designed that the mode of faining influence and exercising power should be *altogether different and peculiar.*" Does the Bible teach this? . . . Did Jesus . . . give a different rule of action to men and women? . . . I read in the Bible, that Miriam, and Deborah, and Huldah, were called to fill *public stations* in Church and State. I find Anna, the prophetess, speaking in the temple "unto all them that looked for redemption in Jerusalem." . . . I see them even standing on Mount Calvary, around his cross . . . but he never *rebuked* them; He never told them it was unbecoming *their sphere of life* to mingle in the crowds which followed his footsteps. . . .

Thou sayest . . . "make no claims, and maintain no rights, but what are the gifts of honor, rectitude and love." From whom does woman receive her *rights*? From God, or from man? . . . I understand . . . her *rights* are an integral part of her moral being; they cannot be withdrawn; they must live with her forever. Her rights lie at the foundation of all her duties; and, so long as the divine commands are binding upon her, so long must her rights continue. . . .

Thou sayest, "In this country, petitions to Congress, in reference to official duties of legislators, seem IN ALL CASES, to fall entirely without the sphere of female duty. Men are the proper persons to make appeals to the rulers whom they appoint," etc. Here I entirely dissent from thee. The fact that women are denied the right of voting for members of Congress, is but a poor reason why they should also be deprived of the right of petition. If their numbers are counted to swell the number of Representatives in our State and National Legislatures, the *very least* that can be done is to give them the right of petition in all cases whatsoever. . . . If not, they are mere slaves, known only through their masters."

Questions

1. What arguments does Grimké use to link moral reform with women's rights and political action?
2. The campaign to collect signatures on antislavery petitions to Congress was an important aspect of the abolitionist movement in the 1830s. How did that campaign raise women's rights issues?
3. How does Grimké differ with Beecher on the issue of women's rights? How does Grimké define the relationship between rights and duties?

12-6 Margaret Fuller Meets George Sand

Massachusetts-born Margaret Fuller (1810–1850) (see American Voices, text p. 362), the leading woman in the transcendentalist movement, perhaps came closer than any woman of her day to achieving in her personal life the independence and equality she championed for all women. Her death in a shipwreck at the age of forty (see text p. 361) brought an untimely end to a remarkable life. An intelligent, nervous child, she was raised by a ruthlessly strict father who insisted that she receive a man's education. Fuller entered the world of New England transcendentalism with a sensitive temperament that seemed dark to some and luminous to others. Her intellectual powers and extraordinary education in literature and history enabled her to earn her own income as a critic and foreign correspondent for Horace Greeley's New York *Tribune*. In its pages she expressed her admiration for the radical French feminist George Sand, a figure widely reviled in America for her rejection of marriage. In Paris, Fuller visited the French novelist and recorded her impressions in a letter home.

Source: R. W. Emerson, W. H. Channing, and J. F. Clarke, *Memoirs of Margaret Fuller Ossoli,* (1884; facsimile reprint, New York: Burt Franklin, 1972), vol. 2, pp. 193–199.

You wished to hear of George Sand, or, as they say in Paris "Madame Sand." I find that all we had heard of her was true in the outline; I had supposed it might be exaggerated. She had every reason to leave her husband,—a stupid, brutal man, who insulted and neglected her. . . . But the love for which she left him lasted not well, and she has had a series of lovers, and I am told has one now, with whom she lives on the footing of combined means, independent friendship! But she takes rank in society like a man, for the weight of her thoughts, and has just given her daughter in marriage. . . . I went to see her at her house, Place d'Orleans. I found it a handsome modern residence. She had not answered my letter, written about a week before, and I felt a little anxious lest she should not receive me; for she is too much the mark of impertinent curiosity, as well as too busy, to be easily accessible to strangers. I am by no means timid, but I have suffered, for the first time in France, some of the torments of *mauvaise honte*, enough to see what they must be to many. . . . I speak very bad French; only lately have I sufficient command of it to infuse some of my natural spirit in my discourse. This has been a great trial to me, who am eloquent and free in my own tongue, to be forced to feel my thoughts struggling in vain for utterance.

The servant who admitted me was in the picturesque costume of a peasant. . . . She announced me . . . and returned into the ante-room to tell me, "*Madame says she does not know you.*" I began to think I was doomed to a rebuff, among the crowd who deserve it. However, to make assurance sure, I said, "Ask if she has not received a letter from me." As I spoke Madame S. opened the door, and stood looking at me an instant. Our eyes met. I never shall forget her at that moment. The doorway made a frame for her figure; she is large, but well-formed. She was dressed in a robe of dark violet silk, with a black mantle on her shoulders, her beautiful hair dressed with the greatest taste, her whole appearance and attitude, in its simple lady-like dignity, presenting an almost ludicrous contrast to the vulgar caricature idea of George Sand. . . . All these details I saw at a glance; but what fixed my attention was the expression of *goodness*, nobleness, and power that pervaded the whole,—the truly human heart and nature that shone in her eyes. As our eyes met, she . . . held out her hand. I took it, and went into her little study . . . it made me very happy to see such a woman, so large and so developed a character, and everything that *is* good in it so *really* good. I loved, shall always love her. . . . She was very much pressed for time, as she was then preparing copy for the printer, and, having just returned, there were many applications to see her, but she wanted me to stay then, saying, "It is better to throw things aside, and seize the present moment." I staid [*sic*] a good part of the day, and was very glad afterwards, for I did not see her again uninterrupted. . . .

Her way of talking is just like her writing,—lively, picturesque, with an undertone of deep feeling, and the same skill in striking a nail on the head every now and then with a blow.

We did not talk at all of personal or private matters. I saw, as one sees in her writings, the want of an independent, interior life, but I did not feel it as a fault, there is so much in her of her kind. I heartily enjoyed the sense of so rich, so prolific, so ardent a genius. I liked the woman in her, too, very much; I never liked a woman better. . . . She has that purity in her soul, for she knows well how to love and prize its beauty; but she herself is quite another sort of person. She needs no defense, but only to be understood, for she has bravely acted out her nature, and always with good intentions. She might have loved one man permanently, if she could have found one contemporary with her would could interest and command her throughout her range; but there was hardly a possibility of that, for such a person. Thus she has naturally changed the objects of her affection, and several times. Also, there may have been something of the Bacchante [female follower of Bacchus] in her life, and of the love of night and storm, and the free raptures amid which roamed on the mountain-tops the followers of Cybele [goddess of nature], the great goddess, the great mother. But she was never course, never gross, and I am sure her generous heart has not failed to draw some rich drops from every kind of wine-press. When she has done with an intimacy, she likes to break it off suddenly, and this has happened often, both with men and women. Many calumnies upon her are traceable to this cause.

I forgot to mention, that, while talking, she *does* smoke all the time her little cigarette. This is now a common practice among ladies abroad, but I believe it originated with her.

For the rest, she holds her place in the literary and social world of France like a man, and seems full of energy and courage in it. I suppose she has suffered much, but she has also enjoyed and done much, and her expression is one of calmness and happiness. . . .

Afterwards I saw [Frederic Francois] Chopin, not with her, although he lives with her and has for the last twelve years. I went to see him in his room with one of his friends. He is always ill, and as frail as a snow-drop, but an exquisite genius. He played to me, and I liked his talking scarcely less. Madame S. loved [Franz] Liszt before him; she has thus been intimate with the two opposite sides of the musical world. . . . It is said there, that Madame S. has long had only a friendship for Chopin, who, perhaps, on his side prefers to be a lover, and a jealous lover; but she does not leave him, because he needs her care so much, when sick and suffering.

Questions

1. What traits of character did Fuller admire in Sand?
2. Why did Fuller believe that conventional marriage was not appropriate for Sand?
3. Why did Fuller believe that Sand's behavior required no defense?

12-7 "Declaration of Sentiments" and Resolutions (1848)

Elizabeth Cady Stanton

Elizabeth Cady Stanton (1815–1902) and Lucretia Mott (1793–1880) met in London at the World's Anti-Slavery Convention in 1840 (see text p. 369). Stanton attended with her husband, the abolitionist Henry B. Stanton. Mott, a Quaker minister, attended as a delegate for the American Anti-Slavery Society. The convention's decision to deny recognition to women consigned Stanton and Mott to the gallery as observers, and they resolved to link the struggle against slavery with a struggle for women's rights. In 1848 they convened the first women's rights convention at Seneca Falls, New York, and Stanton drafted its famous "Declaration of Sentiments" and Resolutions, using the Declaration of Independence as a model (see text pp. 369, 372).

Source: In Elizabeth Cady Stanton, Susan B. Anthony, and Matilda Joslyn Gage, *History of Woman Suffrage* (1881–1922; reprint, New York: Arno Press and New York Times, 1969), vol. 1, pp. 70–73.

When, in the course of human events, it becomes necessary for one portion of the family of man to assume among the people of the earth a position different from that which they have hitherto occupied, but one to which the laws of nature and nature's God entitle them, a decent respect to the opinions of mankind requires that they should declare the causes that impel them to such a course.

We hold these truths to be self-evident: that all men and women are created equal; that they are endowed by their Creator with certain inalienable rights. . . . Whenever any form of government becomes destructive of these ends, it is the right of those who suffer from it to refuse allegiance to it, and to insist upon the institution of a new government. . . .

The history of mankind is a history of repeated injuries and usurpations on the part of man toward woman, having in direct object the establishment of an absolute tyranny over her. To prove this, let facts be submitted to a candid world.

He has never permitted her to exercise her inalienable right to the elective franchise. . . .

He has withheld from her rights which are given to the most ignorant and degraded men—both natives and foreigners. . . .

He has made her, if married, in the eye of the law, civilly dead.

He has taken from her all right in property, even to the wages she earns. . . .

After depriving her of all rights as a married woman, if single, and the owner of property, he has taxed her to support a government which recognizes her only when her property can be made profitable to it. . . .

He has denied her the facilities for obtaining a thorough education, all colleges being closed against her. . . .

He has created a false public sentiment by giving the world a different code of morals for men and women, by which moral delinquencies which exclude women from society, are not only tolerated, but deemed of little account in man. . . .

He has endeavored, in every way that he could, to destroy her confidence in her own powers, to lessen her self-respect and to make her willing to lead a dependent and abject life. . . .

Resolved, That all laws which prevent woman from occupying such a station in society as her conscience shall dictate, or which place her in a position inferior to that of man, are contrary to the great precept of nature, and therefore of no force or authority.

Resolved, That woman is man's equal—was intended to be so by the Creator, and the highest good of the race demands that she should be recognized as such. . . .

Resolved, That it is the duty of the women of this country to secure to themselves their sacred right to the elective franchise. . . .

Questions

1. Read the Declaration of Independence (see text pp. D-1–D-2) and consider the structural as well as ideological reasons why Stanton used it as a model.
2. In light of the tone and substance of Stanton's protest, why did so many male abolitionists fail to see these "self-evident" truths?
3. How are Stanton's arguments related to the interests and experiences of middle-class women (see text pp. 367–368)?

Questions for Further Thought

1. Fuller, Grimké, and Stanton were all concerned with women's rights (Documents 12-5–12-7). How did their respective concerns with transcendentalism, moral reform, and political reform shape their arguments?
2. Use Fuller's, Grimké's, and Stanton's arguments to describe the world they hoped to transform. By what logic were women traditionally considered subordinate to men?
3. In 1870 the Fifteenth Amendment to the U.S. Constitution prohibited states from denying the vote to black men; in 1920 the Nineteenth Amendment prohibited states from denying the vote to women. In your opinion, why did gender discrimination last fifty years longer in this arena than did racial discrimination?

The Antislavery Movement, to 1844

The moral crusade against slavery had its origin in the evangelical reforms of the Second Great Awakening. Since all people were understood to be individual units in the eyes of God, abolitionists argued that the relationship of master and slave fundamentally violated Christian morality (see text pp. 375–376). Animated by the millennial spirit of the age, abolitionists attacked slavery with a zeal that alarmed many northerners and embittered most southerners (Document 12-8). In the abolitionist view, slavery denied the essential humanity of the enslaved, a point they underscored by emphasizing the brutality of the system (Document 12-9).

12-8 "Commencement of *The Liberator*" (1831)

William Lloyd Garrison

In 1829 William Lloyd Garrison (1805–1879) broke with traditional abolitionist proposals for gradual emancipation to demand the immediate abolition of slavery in the United States (see text pp. 375–376). Later in that year he added his voice to those of

African-American freedmen in the North who denounced the American Colonization Society as a thinly disguised plot to remove free blacks, not slaves, from America. In 1830 Garrison prepared to launch the Boston *Liberator* to express his new views; the paper's first number appeared on January 1, 1831. The publication of *The Liberator* in January and the bloody slave rebellion led by Nat Turner in Southampton County, Virginia in August 1831 (see text p. 375) reinforced each other in ways that unsettled northern and southern whites and prompted the supporters of Andrew Jackson to attempt to silence the abolitionist "incendiaries." The following extracts are from Garrison's opening editorial, "Commencement of *The Liberator*," in the first issue.

Source: William Lloyd Garrison, "Commencement of *The Liberator*," *Liberator*, January 1, 1831. In *Selections from the Writings and Speeches of William Lloyd Garrison* (New York: New American Library, 1969), pp. 62–63.

In Park Street Church, on the Fourth of July, 1829, in an address on slavery, I unreflectingly assented to the popular but pernicious doctrine of gradual abolition. I seize this opportunity to make a full and unequivocal recantation, and thus publicly to ask pardon of my God, of my country, and of my brethren, the poor slaves, for having uttered a sentiment so full of timidity, injustice and absurdity. . . .

I am aware, that many object to the severity of my language; but is there not cause for severity? I will be as harsh as truth, and as uncompromising as justice. On this subject, I do not wish to think, or speak, or write, with moderation. No! no! Tell a man, whose house is on fire, to give a moderate alarm; tell him to moderately rescue his wife from the hands of the ravisher; tell the mother to gradually extricate her babe from the fire into which it has fallen; but urge me not to use moderation in a cause like the present! I am in earnest. I will not equivocate—I will not excuse—I will not retreat a single inch, AND I WILL BE HEARD. . . .

It is pretended, that I am retarding the cause of emancipation by the coarseness of my invective, and the precipitancy of my measures. The charge is not true. On this question, my influence, humble as it is, is felt at this moment to a considerable extent, and shall be felt in coming years—not perniciously, but beneficially—not as a curse, but as a blessing; and POSTERITY WILL BEAR TESTIMONY THAT I WAS RIGHT.

Questions

1. Why does Garrison describe the doctrine of gradual abolition as "pernicious"?
2. What reasons does Garrison give for rejecting moderation? Are they convincing?
3. What does Garrison express more effectively—his belief in himself or his belief in his cause? Do you think his tone worked for him or against him?

12-9 *American Slavery as It Is* (1839)

Theodore Dwight Weld

Converted to the evangelistic ministry by Charles Grandison Finney, Theodore Dwight Weld (1803–1895) moved beyond his mentor's interest in temperance to join the newly invigorated abolitionist crusade. A founding member of the American Anti-Slavery Society, Weld organized a group of antislavery ministers who toured the country preaching against the sin of slavery. Weld married Angelina Grimké (Document 12-5) in 1838 at the height of his reform career, a career that ended shortly after the abolitionist schism of 1840 (see text pp. 368–369, 376–377). Weld's aim in the 1830s was the aim of abolitionism generally, to convince all who would listen that slavery was morally wrong. Evangelical abolitionists, he believed, would launch a moral reformation across the land, and the slaves would be set free. His best-known effort to produce such a moral reformation, written in collaboration with Sarah and Angelina Grimké, was *American Slavery as It Is: Testimony of a Thousand Witnesses*, which compiled documentary information, especially from southern newspapers, to support the moral argument against slavery.

Source: Theodore Dwight Weld, *American Slavery as It Is: Testimony of a Thousand Witnesses* (New York, 1839; reprint, New York: Arno Press, 1968), pp. 60–63.

PUNISHMENTS.

I. Floggings.

The slaves are terribly lacerated with whips, paddles, etc.; red pepper and salt are rubbed into their mangled flesh; hot brine and turpentine are poured into their gashes; and innumerable other tortures inflicted upon them.

We will in the first place, prove by a cloud of witnesses, that the slaves are whipped with such inhuman severity, as to lacerate and mangle their flesh in the most shocking manner, leaving permanent scars and ridges; after establishing this, we will present a mass of testimony, concerning a great variety of other tortures. The testimony, for the most part, will be that of the slaveholders themselves, and in their own chosen words. A large portion of it will be taken from the advertisements, which they have published in their own newspapers, describing by the scars on their bodies made by the whip, their own runaway slaves. To copy these advertisements *entire* would require a great amount of space, and flood the reader with a vast mass of matter irrelevant to the *point* before us; we shall therefore insert only so much of each, as will intelligibly set forth the precise point under consideration. In the column under the word "witnesses," will be found the name of the individual, who signs the advertisement, or for whom it is signed, with his or her place of residence, and the name and date of the paper, in which it appeared, and generally the name of the place where it is published. Opposite the name of each witness, will be an extract, from the advertisement, containing his or her testimony.

WITNESSES.	TESTIMONY.
Mr. D. Judd, jailor, Davidson Co., Tennessee, in the "Nashville Banner," Dec. 10th, 1838.	"Committed to jail as a runaway, a negro woman named Martha, 17 or 18 years of age, has *numerous scars of the whip* on her back."
Mr. Robert Nicoll, Dauphin st. between Emmanuel and Conception st's, Mobile, Alabama, in the "Mobile Commercial Advertiser."	"Ten dollars reward for my woman Siby, *very much scarred about the neck and ears by whipping.*"
Mr. Bryant Johnson, Fort Valley, Houston Co., Georgia, in the "Standard of Union, Milledgeville Ga. Oct. 2, 1838.	"Ranaway [sic], a negro woman, named Maria, *some scars on her back occasioned by the whip.*"
Mr. James T. De Jarnett, Vernon, Autauga Co., Alabama, in the "Pensacola Gazette," July, 14, 1838.	"Stolen a negro woman, named Celia. On examining her back you will find *marks caused by the whip.*"
Maurice Y. Garcia, Sheriff of the County of Jefferson, La., in the "New Orleans Bee," August 14, 1838.	"Lodged in jail, a mulatto boy, *having large marks of the whip*, on his shoulders and other parts of his body."
R. J. Bland, Sheriff of Claiborne Co, Miss., in the "Charleston (S.C.) Courier," August, 28, 1838.	"Was committed a negro boy, named Tom, is *much marked with the whip.*"
Mr. James Noe, Red River Landing, La., in the "Sentinel," Vicksburg, Miss., August 22, 1837.	"Ranaway, a negro fellow named Dick—has *many scars* on his back from being *whipped.*"
William Craze, jailor, Alexandria, La. in the "Planter's Intelligencer," Sept. 26, 1838.	"Committed to jail, a negro slave—his back is *very badly scarred.*"

WITNESSES.	TESTIMONY.
John A. Rowland, jailor, Lumberton, North Carolina, in the "Fayetteville (N. C.) Observer," June 20, 1838.	"Committed, a mulatto fellow—his back shows *lasting impressions of the whip*, and leaves no doubt of his being a SLAVE."
J. K. Roberts, sheriff, Blount county, Ala., in the "Huntsville Democrat," Dec. 9, 1838.	"Committed to jail, a negro man—his back *much marked* by the whip."
Mr. H. Varillat, No. 23 Girod street, New Orleans—in the "Commercial Bulletin," August 27, 1838.	"Ranaway, the negro slave named Jupiter—has a *fresh mark* of a cowskin on one of his cheeks."
Mr. Cornelius D. Tolin, August, Ga., in the "Chronicle and Sentinel," Oct. 18, 1838.	"Ranaway, a negro man named Johnson—he has a *great many marks of the whip* on his back."
W. H. Brasseale, sheriff, Blount county, Ala., in the "Huntsville Democrat," June 9, 1838.	"Committed to jail, a negro slave named James—*much scarred* with a whip on his back."
Mr. Robert Beasley, Macon, Ga., in the "Georgia Messenger," July 27, 1837.	"Ranaway, my man Fountain—he is marked *on the back with the whip.*"
Mr. John Wotton, Rockville, Montgomery county, Maryland, in the "Baltimore Republican," Jan. 13, 1838.	"Ranaway, Bill—has *several LARGE SCARS* on his back from a *severe* whipping in *early* life."
D. S. Bennett, sheriff, Narchitoches, La., in the "Herald," July 21, 1838.	"Committed to jail, a negro boy who calls himself Joe—said negro bears *marks of the whip.*"
Messrs. C. C. Whitehead, and R. A. Evans, Marion, Georgia, in the Milledgeville (Ga.) "Standard of Union," June 26, 1838.	"Ranaway, negro fellow John—from being whipped, has *scars on his back, arms, and thighs.*"
Mr. Samuel Stewart, Greensboro, Ala., in the "Southern Advocate," Huntsville, Jan. 6, 1838.	"Ranaway, a boy named Jim—with the marks of the *whip* on the small of the back, reaching round to the flank."
Mr. John Walker, No. 6, Banks' Arcade, New Orleans, in the "Bulletin" August 11, 1838.	"Ranaway, the mulatto boy Quash—*considerably marked* on the back and other places with the lash."
Mr. Jesse Beene, Cahawba, Ala., in the "State Intelligencer," Tuskaloosa, Dec. 25, 1837.	"Ranaway, my negro man Billy—he has the *marks of the* whip."
Mr. John Turner, Thomaston, Upson county, Georgia—in the "Standard of Union," Milledgeville, June 26, 1838.	"Left, my negro man named George—has *marks of the whip very plain* on his thighs."
James Derrah, deputy sheriff, Claiborne county, Mi., in the "Port Gibson Correspondent," April 15, 1837.	"Committed to jail, negro man Toy—he has been *badly whipped.*"
S. B. Murphy, sheriff, Wilinson county, Georgia—in the Milledgeville "Journal," May 15, 1838.	"Brought to jail, a negro man named George—he has a *great many scars from the lash.*"
Mr. L. E. Cooner, Branchville Orangeburgh District, South Carolina—in the Macon "Messenger," May 25, 1837.	"One hundred dollars reward, for my negro Glasgow, and Kate, his wife. Glasgow is 24 years old—has *marks of the whip* on his back. Kate is 26—has a *scar* on her cheek, *and several marks of a whip.*"
John H. Hand, jailor, Parish of West Feliciana, La., in the St. "Francisville Journal," July 6, 1837.	"Committed to jail, a negro boy named John, about 17 years old—his back *badly marked* with the *whip*, his upper lip and chin *severely bruised.*"

CHAPTER *13*

Sections and Sectionalism 1840–1860

★　　　★　　　★

The Slave South: A Distinctive Society

Most southerners saw slavery primarily as a labor system—a means of getting crops planted and harvested and making sure that the large-scale agricultural enterprises known as plantations functioned effectively (Document 13-1). But the implications of slavery went far beyond agricultural labor. Slaves were property, "chattels personal" in the language of the law, and had a real monetary value to their owners (see text p. 388). Those who defended an economic system based on human property necessarily developed an ideological justification for it (see text p. 388). Proslavery ideology minimized the economic benefits enjoyed by slave owners and relied on the concept of race to justify the stark inequalities of the slave system (Document 13-2). Although owners legally defined and held their slaves as property, they could never entirely disregard the slaves' humanity, as when a slave defiantly fought back or evaded an unwelcome task (Document 13-3).

Proslavery ideology also emphasized the inequality and poverty produced by the Industrial Revolution in contrast to the slave system. The fact that slaves in the South enjoyed a standard of living equal to or higher than that of the laboring poor of the industrial North (see text p. 388) provided the defenders of slavery with a powerful argument: those who would reduce free white men to "wage slavery" should not criticize the South's paternalistic slave system (Document 13-4). But the trappings of paternalism could not obscure the fact that slavery remained first and foremost a system of coerced labor. The booming interstate slave trade (see text pp. 388–389) revealed the avarice and cruelty that pervaded, without fully defining, slave society (Document 13-5).

13-1   Slave Management on a Mississippi Plantation (1852)

Frederick Law Olmstead

In the two decades before the Civil War a number of journalists traveled through the South, reporting their observations on the lives and labors of slaves and their masters. The keenest of those observers was Frederick Law Olmsted, who first journeyed through the South in 1852 on a commission from the *New York Times*. In the following excerpt Olmsted describes an extremely large plantation in Mississippi. Contemporary management philosophy held that plantations employing more than a hundred slaves were difficult if not impossible to govern, and so the owners would often break up very large estates into smaller, more manageable entities. Each would have its own overseer, and either the owner or a manager would be in direct charge of the entire operation (see text p. 385).

Source: Frederick Law Olmsted, *A Journal in the Back Country* (New York: Mason Brothers, 1860; reprint, Williamstown, Mass.: Corner House Publishers, 1972), pp. 72–83.

SLAVE MANAGEMENT ON THE LARGEST SCALE

The estate I am now about to describe, was situated upon a tributary of the Mississippi, and accessible only by occasional steamboats; even this mode of communication being frequently interrupted at low stages of the rivers. The slaves upon it formed about one twentieth of the whole population of the county, in which the blacks considerably out-number the whites. . . .

The property consisted of four adjoining plantations, each with its own negro-cabins, stables and overseer, and each worked to a great extent independently of the others, but all contributing their crop to one [cotton] gin-house and warehouse, and all under the general superintendence of a bailiff or manager, who constantly resided upon the estate, and in the absence of the owner, had vice-regal power over the overseers, controlling, so far as he thought fit, the economy of all the plantations. . . .

. . . The overseers were superior to most of their class, and, with one exception, frank, honest, temperate and industrious, but their feelings toward negroes were such as naturally result from their occupation. They were all married, and lived with their families, each in a cabin or cottage, in the hamlet of the slaves of which he had especial charge. Their wages varied from $500 to $1,000 a year each. . . .

. . . Of course, to secure their own personal safety and to efficiently direct the labor of such a large number of ignorant, indolent, and vicious negroes, rules, or rather habits and customs, of discipline, were necessary, which would in particular cases be liable to operate unjustly and cruelly. It is apparent, also, that, as the testimony of negroes against them would not be received as evidence in court, that there was very little probability that any excessive severity would be restrained by fear of the law. A provision of the law intended to secure a certain privilege to

slaves, was indeed disregarded under my own observation, and such infraction of the law was confessedly customary with one of the overseers, and was permitted by the manager, for the reason that it seemed to him to be, in a certain degree, justifiable and expedient under the circumstances, and because he did not like to interfere unnecessarily in such matters.

In the main, the negroes appeared to be well taken care of and abundantly supplied with the necessaries of vigorous physical existence. A large part of them lived in commodious and well-built cottages, with broad galleries in front, so that each family of five had two rooms on the lower floor, and a loft. The remainder lived in log-huts, small and mean in appearance, but those of their overseers were little better, and preparations were being made to replace all of these by neat boarded cottages. Each family had a fowl-house and hog-sty (constructed by the negroes themselves), and kept fowls and swine, feeding the latter during the summer on weeds and fattening them in the autumn on corn *stolen* (this was mentioned to me by the overseers as if it were a matter of course) from their master's corn-fields. I several times saw gangs of them eating the dinner which they had brought, each for himself, to the field, and observed that they generally had plenty, often more than they could eat, of bacon, corn-bread, and molasses. The allowance of food is weighed and measured under the eye of the manager by the drivers, and distributed to the head of each family weekly: consisting of—for each person, 3 pounds of pork, 1 peck [8 quarts] of meal; and from January to July, 1 quart of molasses. Monthly, in addition, 1 pound tobacco, and 4 pints salt. No drink is ever served but water, except after unusual exposure, or to ditchers working in water, who get a glass of whisky at night. All hands cook for themselves after work at night, or whenever they please between nightfall and daybreak, each family in its own cabin. Each family had a garden, the products of which, together with eggs, fowls and bacon, they frequently sold, or used in addition to their regular allowance of food. Most of the families bought a barrel of flour every year. The manager endeavored to encourage this practice, and that they might spend their money for flour instead of liquor, he furnished it to them at rather less than what it cost him at wholesale. There were many poor whites within a few miles who would always sell liquor to the negroes, and encourage them to steal, to obtain the means to buy it of them. These poor whites were always spoken of with anger by the overseers, and they each had a standing offer of much more than the intrinsic value of their land, from the manager, to induce them to move away. . . .

Near the first quarters we visited there was a large blacksmith's and wheelwright's shop, in which a number of mechanics were at work. Most of them, as we rode up, were eating their breakfast, which they warmed at their fires. Within and around the shop there were some fifty plows which they were putting in order. The manager inspected the work, found some of it faulty, sharply reprimanded the workmen for not getting on faster, and threatened one of them with a whipping for not paying closer attention to the directions which had been given him. He told me that he once employed a white man from the North, who professed to be a first-class workman, but he soon found he could not do nearly as good work as the negro mechanics on the estate, and the latter despised him so much, and got such high opinions of themselves in consequence of his inferiority, that he had been obliged to discharge him in the midst of his engagement.

HOURS OF LABOR

Each overseer regulated the hours of work on his own plantation. I saw the negroes at work before sunrise and after sunset. At about eight o'clock they were allowed to stop for breakfast, and again about noon, to dine. The length of these rests was at the discretion of the overseer or drivers, usually, I should say, from half an hour to an hour. There was no rule.

OVERSEERS

The number of hands directed by each overseer was considerably over one hundred. The manager thought it would be better economy to have a white man over every fifty hands, but the difficulty of obtaining trustworthy overseers prevented it. Three of those he then had were the best he had ever known. He described the great majority as being passionate, careless, inefficient men, generally intemperate, and totally unfitted for the duties of the position. The best overseers, ordinarily, are young men, the sons of small planters, who take up the business temporarily, as a

means of acquiring a little capital with which to purchase negroes for themselves.

PLOW-GIRLS

The plowing, both with single and double mule teams, was generally performed by women, and very well performed, too. I watched with some interest for any indication that their sex unfitted them for the occupation. Twenty of them were plowing together, with double teams and heavy plows. They were superintended by a male negro driver, who carried a whip, which he frequently cracked at them, permitting no dawdling or delay at the turning; and they twitched their plows around on the head-land, jerking their reins, and yelling to their mules, with apparent ease, energy, and rapidity. Throughout the Southwest the negroes, as a rule, appear to be worked much harder than in the eastern and northern slave States. I do not think they accomplish as much daily, as agricultural laborers at the North usually do, but they certainly labor much harder, and more unremittingly. They are constantly and steadily driven up to their work, and the stupid, plodding, machine-like manner in which they labor, is painful to witness. This was especially the case with the hoe-gangs. One of them numbered nearly two hundred hands (for the force of two plantations was working together), moving across the field in parallel lines, with a considerable degree of precision. I repeatedly rode through the lines at a canter, with other horsemen, often coming upon them suddenly, without producing the smallest change or interruption in the dogged action of the laborers, or causing one of them to lift an eye from the ground. A very tall and powerful negro walked to and fro in the rear of the line, frequently cracking his whip, and calling out, in the surliest manner, to one and another, "Shove your hoe, there! shove your hoe!" But I never saw him strike any one with the whip.

DISCIPLINE

The whip was evidently in constant use, however. There were no rules on the subject, that I learned; the overseers and drivers punished the negroes whenever they deemed it necessary, and in such manner, and with such severity, as they thought fit. "If you do n't work faster," or "If you do n't work better," or "If you do n't recollect what I tell you, I will have you flogged," are threats which I have often heard. I said to one of the overseers, "It must be very disagreeable to have to punish them as much as you do?" "Yes, it would be to those who are not used to it—but it's my business, and I think nothing of it. Why, sir, I would n't mind killing a nigger more than I would a dog." I asked if he had ever killed a negro? "Not quite," he said, but overseers were often obliged to. Some negroes are determined never to let a white man whip them, and will resist you, when you attempt it; of course you must kill them in that case. Once a negro, whom he was about to whip in the field, struck at his head with a hoe. He parried the blow with his whip, and drawing a pistol tried to shoot him, but the pistol missing fire he rushed in and knocked him down with the butt of it. At another time a negro whom he was punishing, insulted and threatened him. He went to the house for his gun, and as he was returning, the negro, thinking he would be afraid of spoiling so valuable a piece of property by firing, broke for the woods. He fired at once, and put six buck-shot into his hips. He always carried a bowie-knife, but not a pistol.

Questions

1. Why were the slaves given such large food allowances?
2. From this description, how often do you think an overseer actually whipped a slave?
3. As a reporter, Olmsted tried to be neutral. Do you think he succeeded, or do you believe he had a personal opinion of the morality of slavery?

13-2   In Defense of Slavery (1831)

Thomas R. Dew

Although we normally think of abolition as a northern enterprise, the early debates on that issue took place south of the Mason-Dixon Line. Many southerners believed that in the long run slavery would work against the moral and economic interests of the region. Their problem lay in what to do with the slaves, because even those opposed to slavery believed that blacks were intellectually and morally inferior to whites. The debate, which began in the eighteenth century, lasted well into the nineteenth and ended only after the invention of the cotton gin made cotton king and made the slave economy very profitable (see text p. 386). The last major debate in the South over emancipation took place in the Virginia legislature in 1831; this commentary on that debate was written by Thomas R. Dew, president of the College of William and Mary and a staunch defender of the "peculiar institution." (Thomas Jefferson's thoughts on slavery, to which Dew refers, are excerpted in the special documents module on the American South.)

Source: Thomas R. Dew, "The Virtues of Slavery, The Impossibility of Emancipation," *Dew's Review* (1831).

We have now, we think, proved our position, that slave labor, in an economical point of view, is far superior to free negro labor; and have no doubt that if an immediate emancipation of negroes were to take place, the whole southern country would be visited with an immediate general famine, from which the productive resources of all the other States of the Union could not deliver them.

It is now easy for us to demonstrate the second point in our argument—that the slave is not only *economically* but *morally* unfit for freedom. And first, idleness and consequent want are, of themselves, sufficient to generate a catalogue of vices of the most mischievous and destructive character. . . .

The great evil, however, of these schemes of emancipation, remains yet to be told. They are admirably calculated to excite plots, murders and insurrections; whether gradual or rapid in their operation, this is the inevitable tendency. . . . Two totally different races, as we have before seen, cannot easily harmonize together, . . . and even when [the negro is] free, . . . idleness will produce want and worthlessness, and his very worthlessness and degradation will stimulate him to deeds of rapine and vengeance; he will oftener engage in plots and massacres, and thereby draw down on his devoted head, the vengeance of the provoked whites. . . . [L]iberate [our] slaves, and every year you would hear of insurrections and plots, and every day would perhaps record a murder. . . .

[Thomas Jefferson] has supposed the master in a continual passion—in the constant exercise of the most odious tyranny, and the child, a creature of imitation, looking on and learning. But is not this master sometimes kind and indulgent to his slaves? . . . We may rest assured, in this intercourse between a good master and his servant, more good than evil may be taught the child; the exalted principles of morality and religion may thereby be sometimes indelibly inculcated upon his mind. . . . Look to the slaveholding population of our country, and you every where find them characterized by noble and elevated sentiments, by humane and virtuous feelings. . . .

Let us now look a moment to the slave, and contemplate his position. Mr. Jefferson has described him as hating, rather than loving his master, and as losing, too, all that *amor patriae* [love of country] which characterizes the true patriot. We assert again, that Mr. Jefferson is not borne out by the fact. We are well convinced that there is nothing but the mere relations of husband and wife, parent and child, brother and sister, which produce a closer tie, than the relation of master and servant. We have no hesitation in affirming, that throughout the whole slaveholding country, the slaves of a good master are his warmest, most constant, and most devoted friends; they have been accustomed to look up to him as their supporter, director and defender. Everyone acquainted with southern states, knows that the slave rejoices in the elevation and prosperity of his master; and the heart of no one is more gladdened at the successful debut of young master or miss on the great theatre of the world, than that of either the young slave who has grown up with them, and shared in all their sports, and even partaken of all their delicacies—or the aged one who has looked on and watched them from birth to manhood, with the kindest and most affectionate solicitude, and has ever met from them all the kind treatment and generous sympathies of feeling, tender hearts. . . .

Questions

1. Why does Dew believe that slaves are *morally* unfit for freedom?
2. Why does Dew believe that emancipation would inevitably lead to violence?
3. Why would Dew think that a slave would "rejoice" in the elevation and prosperity of his or her master?

13-3 Memories of a Slave Childhood

Despite southern claims that slaves were happy and treated well, the evidence is overwhelming that those in bondage resented their condition and fought back whenever and however they could. Slave owners recognized this, and in order to keep their slaves in line often resorted to harsh disciplinary measures or sold slaves who were difficult to handle to planters west of the Mississippi (see text p. 388).

The following excerpt displays not only the anger felt by slaves over their treatment, but also the subtle interplay that took place among slaves as well as between slave and master. The source is an oral history interview from the 1930s with an elderly woman who had spent her youth as a slave.

Source: O. S. Egypt, J. Masuoka and C. S. Johnson, "Unwritten History of Slaves: Autobiographical Accounts of Negro Ex-Slaves," Social Science Source Documents No. 1 (Nashville, Tenn.: Fisk University, Social Science Institute, 1946), pp. 113–117, 276–279; In Gerda Lerner, ed., *The Female Experience: An American Documentary* (Indianapolis: Bobbs-Merrill, 1977), pp. 11–14.

[The] overseer . . . went to my father one morning and said, "Bob, I'm gonna whip you this morning." Daddy said, "I ain't done nothing," and he said, "I know it, I'm gonna whip you to keep you from doing nothing," and he hit him with that cowhide—you know it would cut the blood out of you with every lick if they hit you hard—and daddy was chopping cotton, so he just took up his hoe and chopped right down on that man's head and knocked his brains out. Yes'm, it killed him, but they didn't put colored folks in jail then, so when old Charlie Merrill, the nigger trader, come along they sold my daddy to him, and he carried him way down in Mississippi. Ole Merrill would buy all the time, buy and sell niggers just like hogs. They sold him Aunt Phoebe's little baby that was just toddling long, and Uncle Dick—that was my mammy's brother.

The way they would whip you was like they done my oldest sister. They tied her, and they had a place just like they're gonna barbecue a hog, and they would strip you and tie you and lay you down. . . . Old Aunt Fanny had told marster that my sister wouldn't keep her dress clean, and that's what they was whipping her 'bout. So they had her down in the cellar whipping her, and I was real little. I couldn't say "Big Sis," but I went and told Mammy. "Old

Marster's got 'Big Jim' down there in the cellar beating her," and mammy got out of bed and went in there and throwed Aunt Fan out the kitchen door, and they had to stop whipping Big Sis and come and see about Aunt Fan. You see, she would tell things on the others, trying to keep from getting whipped herself. I seed mistress crack her many a time over the head with a broom, and I'd be so scared she was gonna crack me, but she never did hit me, 'cept slap me when I'd turn the babies over. I'd get tired and make like I was sleep, and would ease the cradle over and throw the baby out. I never would throw mammy's out, though. Old Miss would be setting there just knitting and watching the babies; they had a horn and every woman could tell when it was time to come and nurse her baby by the way they would blow the horn. The white folks was crazy 'bout their nigger babies, 'cause that's where they got their profit. . . . When I'd get tired, I would just ease that baby over and Mistress would slap me so hard; I didn't know a hand could hurt so bad, but I'd take the slap and get to go out to play. She would slap me hard and say, "Git on out of here and stay till you wake up," and that was just what I wanted, 'cause I'd play then. . . .

Questions

1. Why do you think Bob wasn't prosecuted for murdering the overseer?
2. Do you think that slaves normally stood up to their masters the way that Bob did? Why or why not?
3. Why would whites take such a great interest in slave babies?

13-4   Slavery as It Exists in America; Slavery as It Exists in England (1850)

As slavery in the United States came under attack from the champions of progress in the industrializing North, the institution's defenders emphasized the material well-being of southern slaves in contrast to factory operatives, particularly the pauper laborers of Great Britain (see text p. 388). This argument gained adherents among proslavery Whigs as well as Democrats and directly influenced American foreign policy toward Great Britain during John Tyler's presidency (see Document 13-10). The text in the balloons is reprinted on p. 244.

Source: Lithograph published by J. Haven, Boston, from Library of Congress. In Elizabeth Johns, *American Genre Painting: The Politics of Everyday Life* (New Haven: Yale University Press, 1991), p. 129.

Questions

1. In the lithograph, which conditions of labor are emphasized and which conditions are ignored?
2. According to the argument presented in the lithograph, how could the growing sectional conflict be eased?
3. Do you agree with the argument presented in the lithograph that factory labor reduced workers to a slavery more cruel than chattel slavery in the South? Explain why or why not.

The words in the balloons are as follows:

America

First gentleman: "It this the way that Slaves are treated at the South?"

Second gentleman: "Is it possible that we of the North have been so deceived by false Reports? Why did we not visit the South before we caused this trouble between North and South, and so much hard feeling amongst our friends at home?"

Third gentleman: "It is as a general thing, some few exceptions, after mine have done a certain amount of labor which they finish by 4 or 5 P.M. I allow them to enjoy themselves in any reasonable way."

Fourth gentleman: "I think our Visitors will tell a different Story when they return to the North, the thoughts of this Union being dissolved is to[o] dreadful a thing to be contemplated, but we must stand up for our rights let the consequence be as it may."

England

Poor man: "Ah! Farmer we operatives are <u>fast men</u>, and generally die of old age at Forty."

Farmer: "Why my Dear Friend, how is it that you look so old? You know we were playmates when boys."

Poor woman: "Oh Dear! what wretched Slaves this Factory Life makes me & my children."

First ragged worker: "I say Bill, I am going to run away from the Factory and go to the Coal Mines where they have to work only 14 hours a Day instead of 17 as you do here."

Second ragged worker: "Oh! how I would like to have such a comfortable place. Wont you speak a good word for me Tom?"

In the background, a church warden carries a ledger book for "Tythes"; his companion, an equally stout politician, carries a ledger book for "Taxes."

Seated figure: "Thank God my Factory Slavery will soon be over."

"[George] Thompson The English Anti-Slavery Agitator. 'I am proud to boast that Slavery does not breathe in England.' (See his speech at the African Church in Belknap St. [Boston])"

13-5   The Enslavement of Solomon Northup (1841)

Solomon Northup, a free person of color, lived peacefully with his wife in upstate New York. A musician of local prominence, Northup supported himself in part by playing the violin at dances and parties. In 1841 he took the word of two strangers that they would find work for him in a traveling circus. Lured by the money they offered and undoubtedly by a desire for adventure, Northup accompanied his new friends to New York and then to Washington, D.C., a center of the interstate slave trade (see text pp. 388–389). Evidently drugged, Northup awoke to find himself the slave of James H. Birch, Washington's leading slave trader. Birch sold Northup to a New Orleans slave trader, who in turn sold him to a planter in the developing Red River district of Louisiana. For twelve years Northup lived and labored as a slave in Louisiana. Finally, placing his trust in an itinerant white workingman (a native of Canada who had expressed hostility toward slavery), Northup managed to get a letter delivered to his former employers in New York, who secured his freedom in 1853. Following Northup's narrative of his enslavement is an advertisement placed in 1834 in the Washington, D.C., *Globe* by the slave trader Birch.

Source: Solomon Northup, *Twelve Years a Slave. Narrative of Solomon Northup, a Citizen of New-York, Kidnapped in Washington City in 1841, and Rescued in 1853, From a Cotton Plantation Near the Red River, in Louisiana* (Auburn, N.Y.: Derby and Miller, 1853; reprint, edited by Sue Eakin and Joseph Logsdon, Baton Rouge: Louisiana State University Press, 1968), pp. 12–26. Advertisement "Cash for Negroes," appeared in *The Globe* (Washington, D.C.), June 10, 1834.

One morning, towards the latter part of the month of March, 1841, having at that time no particular business to engage my attention, I was walking about the village of Saratoga Springs. . . . I was met by two gentlemen of respectable appearance . . . introduced to me by some of my acquaintances . . . with the remark that I was an expert player on the violin. . . . [T]hey immediately entered into conversation on that subject, making numerous inquiries touching my proficiency in that respect. My responses being to all appearances satisfactory, they proposed to engage my services for a short period, stating, at the same time, I was just such a person as their business required. . . . They were connected, as they informed me, with a circus company, then in the city of Washington; that they were on their way thither to rejoin it. . . . They also remarked that they had found much difficulty in procuring music for their entertainments, and that if I would accompany them as far as New-York, they would give me one dollar for each day's service, and three dollars in addition for every night I played at their performances, besides sufficient to pay the expenses of my return from New-York to Saratoga.

I at once accepted the tempting offer, both for the reward it promised, and from a desire to visit the metropolis. They were anxious to leave immediately. . . . [I]n due course . . . we reached New-York [and] . . . I supposed my journey was at an end. . . . [H]owever [they] began to importune me to continue with them to Washington. . . .

They promised me a situation and high wages if I would accompany them. . . . I finally concluded to accept the offer. . . . All the way from New-York, their anxiety to reach the circus seemed to grow more and more intense. We . . . proceeded to Washington, at which place we arrived just at nightfall, the evening previous to the funeral of [President] General Harrison. . . .

My friends, several times during the [next] afternoon, entered drinking saloons, and called for liquor . . . after serving themselves, they would pour out a glass and hand it to me. . . . Towards evening, and soon after partaking of one of these potations, I began to experience most unpleasant sensations. . . . I only remember, with any degree of distinctness that I was told it was necessary to go to a physician and procure medicine. . . . From that moment I was insensible. How long I remained in that condition—whether only that night, or many days and nights—I do not know; but when consciousness returned, I found myself alone, in utter darkness, and in chains. . . . A key rattled in the lock—a strong door swung back upon its hinges, admitting a flood of light, two men entered and stood before me. One of them was a large powerful man, forty years of age. . . . His name was James H. Burch [Birch], as I learned afterwards—a well-known slave-dealer in Washington. . . .

"Well, my boy, how do you feel now?" said Burch, as he entered through the open door. I replied that I was sick, and inquired the cause of my imprisonment. He answered that I was his slave—that he had bought me, and that he was about to send me to New-Orleans. I asserted, aloud and boldly, that I was a free man—a resident of Saratoga, where I had a wife and children, who were also free, and that my name was Northup. . . . He denied that I was free, and with an emphatic oath, declared that I came from Georgia. Again and again I asserted I was no man's slave. . . . With blasphemous oaths, he called me a black liar, a runaway from Georgia, and every other profane and vulgar epithet that the most indecent fancy could conceive. . . . Burch ordered the paddle and cat-o'-ninetails to be brought in. . . .

As soon as these formidable whips appeared, I was seized by both of them and roughly divested of my clothing. . . . With the paddle, Burch commenced beating me. . . . When his unrelenting arm grew tired, he stopped and asked if I still insisted I was a free man, I did insist upon it, and then the blows were renewed. . . . When again tired, he would repeat the same question, and receiving the same answer, continued his cruel labor. . . . At length the paddle broke. . . . Casting madly on the floor the handle of the broken paddle, he seized the rope. This was far more painful than the other. I struggled with all my power, but it was in vain. I prayed for mercy, but my prayer was only answered with imprecations and with stripes. I thought I must die beneath the lashes of the accursed brute. Even now the flesh crawls upon my bones, as I recall the scene. . . .

At last I became silent to his repeated questions. I would make no reply. In fact, I was becoming almost unable to speak. Still he plied the lash without stint upon my poor body, until it seemed that the lacerated flesh was stripped from my bones at every stroke. . . . He swore that he would either conquer or kill me. . . . I was left in darkness as before.

CASH FOR NEGROES.

We will pay the highest cash price for any number of likely Negroes, from 12 to 25 years of age. As we are at this time permanently settled in the market, we can at all times be found at Mr. Isaac Beers's Tavern, a few doors below Lloyd's Tavern, opposite to the Centre Market, in Washington, D. C., or at Mr. McCandless's Tavern, corner of Bridge and High Street, Georgetown. Persons having servants to dispose of, will find it to their advantage to give us a call.

June 10—dw&swtf   BIRCH & JONES.

Questions

1. What does the kidnapping of Solomon Northup suggest about the profitability of the interstate slave trade?
2. What does the kidnapping of Northup suggest about the status of free blacks in slave territories? How could Northup prove he was a free man?
3. Comment on the significance of coercion in the slave system as you consider what purpose Birch had in mind in committing this act of ruthless violence.

Questions for Further Thought

1. As the Industrial Revolution advanced, why did northerners become increasingly sensitive to and repulsed by the violence associated with slavery (Document 13-1).
2. Comment on the importance of race in the defense of slavery (Document 13-2).
3. Abolitionists argued that slavery corrupted masters as it debased slaves. How would a defender of slavery respond to that charge?

The Northeast and the Midwest: The Industrial Revolution Accelerates

The Industrial Revolution, along with burgeoning western expansion and economic and political turmoil in Europe, led to a major influx of immigrants to the United States. The newcomers did not shed their emotional attachment to their old homes overnight, but the opportunities available in the United States soon helped many become ardent Americans (Document 13-6). As part of the broad social upheaval in industrializing America, immigrants became the objects of the hostility of native-born Americans who wanted to defend their older way of life from increasing competition in the labor market (see text pp. 394–396 and Document 13-7). A more positive response to that social instability and uncertainty came in the form of middle-class support for compulsory and broadly inclusive public education. Through education (see text pp. 402–403) the state could instill the values that would make good citizens of immigrants and the restless wage-earning class (Document 13-8).

One of the principal arguments of proslavery ideologues contrasted the concern and care of paternalistic slave owners with the cruel indifference of market-directed factory owners (see Document 13-4). In the enormously popular novel *Uncle Tom's Cabin* (see text p. 402) Harriet Beecher Stowe turned this proslavery argument against itself. A good master could not save Uncle Tom from the evil Simon Legree. Instead, a good master elicited from Uncle Tom the most refined sentiments of human nature, sentiments that breached the racial border. This demonstration denied any moral standing to the racial defense of slavery (Document 13-9).

13-6 A German Immigrant in Philadelphia (1855)

Carl Schurz (1829–1906) was part of the great tide of German immigrants who came to the United States in the two decades before the Civil War (see text p. 394). A participant in the liberal German revolution of 1848, Schurz had to flee to Switzerland when that movement collapsed. He arrived in Philadelphia in 1852 and four years later moved to Watertown, Wisconsin, where he became the leader of the large community of German immigrants in the Old Northwest. In 1855 he returned to Europe for a visit. In this letter to a German-American acquaintance he reflects on his new and old homes. Schurz went on to a distinguished career as a Union general in the Civil War, a newspaper editor, and a United States senator.

Source: Carl Schurz to Gottfried Kinkel, March 25, 1855. In Frederic Bancroft, ed., *Speeches, Correspondence, and Political Papers of Carl Schurz* (New York, 1913), vol. 1, pp. 17–20.

Philadelphia, March 25, 1855.

To Gottfried Kinkel

You seem to surmise that my visit to Europe means that I am returning there for good, and I see that many of my friends have the same idea. It is my intention that this visit shall be a mere interlude in my American life. As long as there is no upheaval of affairs in Europe it is my firm resolve to regard this country not as a transient or accidental abode, but as the field for my usefulness. I love America and I am vitally interested in the things about me—they no longer seem strange. I find that the question of liberty is in its essence the same everywhere, however different its form. Although I do not regard the public affairs of this country with the same devotion as those of our old home, it is not mere ambition nor eagerness for distinction that impels me to activity. My interest in the political contests of this country is so strong, so spontaneous, that I am profoundly stirred. More self-control is required for me to keep aloof than to participate in them. These are the years of my best strength. Shall I devote myself wholly to the struggle for existence while I have hopes that I may soon be independent in that respect? I venture to say that I am neither avaricious nor self-indulgent.

If I now seek material prosperity, it is only that I may be free to follow my natural aspirations. Or shall I again subject myself to that dreary condition of waiting, which must undermine the strongest constitution when it is the only occupation? We have both tasted its bitterness; and I am burning with the desire to be employed with visible, tangible things and no longer to be bound to dreams and theories. I have a holy horror of the illusory fussiness which characterizes the life of the professional refugees. My devotion to the cause of the old Fatherland has not abated but my expectations have somewhat cooled; I have only faint hopes for the next few years. Even if the revolution should come sooner than I expect, I do not see why I should not utilize the intervening time. I feel that here I can accomplish something. I am convinced of it when I consider the qualities of the men who are now conspicuous. This inspires me, and even if the prospects of success did not correspond with my natural impulses, I should suddenly find that I had involuntarily entered into the thick of the fight. In these circumstances, why should I wish to return to Europe? I am happy that I have a firm foothold and good opportunities.

After my return from Europe I expect to go to Wisconsin. I transferred some of my business interests there when on my last trip to the West. The German element is powerful in that State, the immigrants being so numerous, and they are striving for political recognition. They only lack leaders that are not bound by the restraints of money-getting. There is the place where I can find a sure, gradually expanding field for my work without truckling to the nativistic elements, and there, I hope, in time, to gain influence that may also become useful to our cause. . . .

Questions

1. What seems to attract Schurz most to the United States?
2. What can you discern about Schurz's politics from this letter?
3. How does Schurz deal with his conflicting loyalties to Germany and the United States?

13-7   The American ("Know-Nothing") Party Platform (1856)

Although America has been a nation of immigrants since 1607, there has been a continuous pattern in which those whose ancestors came earlier display hostility and prejudice toward those who came later, especially in the case of newcomers from a different part of the world. Many of the newcomers entering the United States in the mid-nineteenth century from Germany and Ireland were Catholic, a fact that fed Protestant fears that the papacy intended to take over the government of the United States (see text pp. 396–397). Out of those prejudices emerged a number of nativist societies to combat the "alien menace." In 1850 several of them combined to form the Order of the Star-Spangled Banner, which adopted a pledge of secrecy; if people asked them about their program, they responded, "I know nothing." The Know-Nothings (as they came to be called) and other nativist groups created the American party and in 1856 nominated the former president Millard Fillmore as their presidential candidate; the party polled almost 900,000 votes in the election that year.

Source: In Donald Bruce Johnson and Kirk H. Porter, *National Party Platforms, 1840–1976* (Urbana: University of Illinois Press, 1978), pp. 22–23.

I. An humble acknowledgment to the Supreme Being who rules one universe, for His protecting care vouchsafed to our fathers in their revolutionary struggle, and hitherto manifested to us, their descendants, in the preservation of the liberties, the independence and the union of these states.

II. The perpetuation of the Federal Union, as the palladium of our civil and religious liberties, and the only sure bulwark of American independence.

III. *Americans must rule America;* and to this end, *native*-born citizens should be selected for all state, federal, or municipal offices of government employment, in preference to naturalized citizens—*nevertheless,*

IV. Persons born of American parents residing temporarily abroad, shall be entitled to all the rights of native-born citizens; but

V. No person should be selected for political station (whether of native or foreign birth), who recognizes any alliance or obligation of any description to any foreign prince, potentate or power, who refuses to recognize the federal and state constitutions (each within its own sphere), as paramount to all other laws, as rules of particular [political] action.

VI. The unequalled recognition and maintenance of the reserved rights of the several states, and the cultivation of harmony and fraternal good-will between the citizens of the several states, and to this end, non-interference by Congress with questions appertaining solely to the individual states, and non-intervention by each state with the affairs of any other state.

VII. The recognition of the right of the native-born and naturalized citizens of the United States, permanently residing in any territory thereof, to frame their constitutions and laws, and to regulate their domestic and social affairs in their own mode, subject only to the provisions of the federal Constitution, with the right of admission into the Union whenever they have the requisite population for one representative in Congress. *Provided, always,* That none but those who are citizens of the United States, under the Constitution and laws thereof, and who have a fixed residence in any such territory, are to participate in the formation of the constitution, or in the enactment of laws for said territory or state.

VIII. An enforcement of the principles that no state or territory can admit other than native-born citizens to the right of suffrage, or of holding political office unless such persons shall have been naturalized according to the laws of the United States.

IX. A change in the laws of naturalization, making a continued residence of twenty-one years, of all not heretofore provided for, an indispensable requisite for citizenship hereafter, and excluding all paupers or persons convicted of crime from landing upon our shores; but no interference with the vested rights of foreigners.

X. Opposition to any union between Church and State; no interference with religious faith or worship, and no test oaths for office, except those indicated in the 5th section of this platform.

XI. Free and thorough investigation into any and all alleged abuses of public functionaries, and a strict economy in public expenditures.

XII. The maintenance and enforcement of all laws until said laws shall be repealed, or shall be declared null and void by competent judicial authority. . . .

XIV. Therefore, to remedy existing evils, and prevent the disastrous consequences otherwise resulting therefrom, we would build up the "American Party" upon the principles herein-before stated eschewing all sectional questions, and uniting upon those purely national, and admitting into said party all American citizens (referred to in the 3rd, 4th, and 5th sections) who openly avow the principles and opinions heretofore expressed, and who will subscribe their names to this platform.—*Provided nevertheless,* that a majority of those members present at any meeting of a local council where an applicant applies for membership in the American party, may, for any reason by them deemed sufficient, deny admission to such applicant.

XV. A free and open discussion of all political principles embraced in our platform.

Questions

1. Is there any rationale in this document that explains why the Know-Nothings believed that only native-born Americans should rule the country?
2. Who controlled matters of citizenship and voting at that time—the states or the federal government? Why?
3. Why would a naturalization period of twenty-one years satisfy the Know-Nothings?

13-8 Democracy, Social Change, and the Schools (1848)

Horace Mann

Horace Mann (1796–1859) was the preeminent champion of public education in the United States (see text pp. 402–403). Abandoning a promising political career, Mann became the first secretary of the Massachusetts Board of Education in 1837 and spent the next decade advocating and securing educational reforms in that state. His accomplishments, which included increased funding for schools, higher standards for teaching and curricula, and longer school terms, became models for the rest of the country. But most important, in a time beset by social change, Mann preached that the education of the masses was a substantial safeguard to equitable economic distribution and security of property in a democratic republic.

Source: Horace Mann, "Twelfth Annual Report to the Massachusetts Board of Education (1848)." In Lawrence A. Cremin, ed., *The Republic and the School: Horace Mann on the Education of Free Men* (New York: Teachers College Press, 1957), pp. 84–89.

I suppose it to be the universal sentiment of all those who mingle any ingredient of benevolence with their notions on Political Economy, that vast and overshadowing private fortunes are among the greatest dangers to which the happiness of the people in a republic can be subjected. . . . Not one in five thousand of English [factory] operatives, or farm laborers, is able to build or own even a hovel; and therefore they must accept such shelter as Capital offers them. . . . By its industrial condition, and its business operations, [Massachusetts] is exposed, far beyond any other state in the Union, to the fatal extremes of overgrown wealth and desperate poverty. . . . are we not in danger of naturalizing and domesticating among ourselves those hideous evils which are always engendered between Capital and Labor, when all the capital is in the hands of one class, and all the labor is thrown upon another?

Now, surely, nothing but Universal Education can counterwork this tendency to the domination of capital and the servility of labor. If one class possesses all the wealth and the education, while the residue of society is ignorant and poor, it matters not by what name the relation between them may be called; the latter, in fact and in truth, will be the servile dependents and subjects of the former. But if education be equally diffused, it will draw property after it, by the strongest of all attractions; for such a thing never did happen, and never can happen, as that an intelligent and practical body of men would be permanently poor. Property and labor, in different classes, are essentially antagonistic; but property and labor, in the same class, are essentially fraternal. . . .

Education, then, beyond all other devises of human origin, is the great equalizer of the conditions of men—the balance-wheel of the social machinery. . . . I mean that it gives each man the independence and the means, by which

he can resist the selfishness of other men. It does better than to disarm the poor of their hostility towards the rich; it prevents being poor. . . . The spread of education, by enlarging the cultivated class or caste, will open a wider area over which the social feelings will expand; and, if this education should be universal and complete, it would do more than all things else to obliterate factitious distinctions in society.

The main idea set forth in the creeds of some political reformers, or revolutionaries, is, that some people are poor *because* others are rich. This idea supposes a fixed amount of property in the community, which, by fraud or force, or arbitrary law, is unequally divided among men; and the problem presented for solution is, how to transfer a portion of this property from those who are supposed to have too much, to those who feel and know that they have too little. At this point, both their theory and their expectation of reform stop. But the beneficent power of education would not be exhausted, even though it should peaceably abolish all the miseries that spring from the coexistence, side by side, of enormous wealth and squalid want. It has a higher function. Beyond the power of diffusing old wealth, it has the prerogative of creating new . . . education creates or develops new treasures . . . . That Political Economy, therefore, which busies itself about capital and labor, supply and demand, interest and rents, favorable and unfavorable balances of trade; but leaves out of account the element of a wide-spread mental development, is nought but stupendous folly. The greatest of all the arts in political economy is, to change a consumer into a producer; and the next greatest is to increase the producer's producing power;—an end to be directly attained, by increasing his intelligence.

Questions

1. Summarize Mann's argument linking education and wealth.
2. In Mann's view, how did education ameliorate class divisions?
3. In what ways did Mann expect the diffusion of education and wealth to secure property? Compare his views on this issue with those of Seth Luther (Document 11-7).

13-9 *Uncle Tom's Cabin* (1852)

Harriet Beecher Stowe

Harriet Beecher Stowe (1811–1896), a native of Litchfield, Connecticut, was the daughter of Lyman Beecher and the sister of Henry Ward Beecher (see text p. 402 and *American Lives*, text pp. 400–401). She lived with her father in Cincinnati while he served as the president of Lane Seminary. The seminary was the site of a lively debate over slavery, and Cincinnati, separated by the Ohio River from the slave state of Kentucky, was a center of the turmoil associated with abolitionist agitation and efforts to aid fugitive slaves. After marrying Calvin E. Stowe, Harriet Beecher Stowe returned to New England, where her husband began teaching biblical literature at Bowdoin College in 1850. There, with the images of Kentucky slavery and Cincinnati abolitionism fresh in her mind, Stowe wrote *Uncle Tom's Cabin*, telling the story of a loyal slave separated from his family in Kentucky by the interstate slave trade. Much of the story focuses on the kindness of little Eva and her father, St. Clare, before their deaths lead to Uncle Tom's sale to the murderous and insane Simon Legree. Stowe muted the abolitionists' moral repugnance for slavery with a sentimentality that offered her readers emotional release as the social tensions of the sectional crisis increased. The death of little Eva was the sentimental climax of the novel, and it became embedded in northern popular culture as the central focus of stage productions and the subject of popular songs.

Source: Harriet Beecher Stowe, *Uncle Tom's Cabin; or, Life among the Lowly* (Boston: John P. Jewett & Company, 1852; reprinit, New York: Bantam Books edition, 1981), pp. 283–294.

The deceitful strength which had buoyed Eva up for a while was fast passing away. . . . Eva lay back on her pillows; her hair hanging loosely about her face, her crimson cheeks contrasting painfully with the intense whiteness of her complexion and the thin contour of her limbs and features. . . .

Uncle Tom was much in Eva's room. The child suffered much from nervous restlessness, and it was a relief to her to be carried; and it was Tom's greatest delight to carry her little frail form in his arms, resting on a pillow, now up and down her room, now out into the verandah; and when the fresh sea-breezes blew from the lake . . . he would sometimes . . . sing to her their favorite old hymns. . . .

The child felt no pain,—only a tranquil, soft weakness, daily and almost insensibly increasing; and she was so beautiful, so loving, so trustful, so happy, that one could not resist the soothing influence of that air of innocence and peace which seemed to breathe around her. . . .

The friend who knew most of Eva's own imaginings and foreshadowings was her faithful bearer, Tom. To him she said what she would not disturb her father by saying. To him she imparted those mysterious intimations which the soul feels; as the cords begin to unbind, ere it leaves its clay forever.

Tom, at last, would not sleep in his room, but lay all night in the outer verandah, ready to rouse to every call.

. . .

"Hush!" said St. Clare, hoarsely; "*she is dying!*"

The large blue eyes unclosed,—a smile passed over her face;—she tried to raise her head, and to speak.

"Do you know me, Eva?"

"Dear papa," said the child, with a last effort throwing her arms about his neck. In a moment they dropped again. . . .

Tom had his master's hands between his own; and, with tears streaming down his dark cheeks, looked up for help where he had always been used to look. . . .

"O, bless the Lord! It's over,—it's over, dear Master!" said Tom; "look at her."

The child lay panting on her pillows, as one exhausted,—the large clear eyes rolled up and fixed. Ah, what said those eyes, that spoke so much of heaven? Earth was past, and earthly pain; but so solemn, so mysterious, was the triumphant brightness of that face, that it checked even the sobs of sorrow. They pressed around her, in breathless stillness.

"Eva," said St. Clare, gently.

She did not hear.

"O Eva, tell us what you see! What is it?" said her father.

A bright, a glorious smile passed over her face, and she said, brokenly,—"O! Love,—joy,—peace!" gave one sigh, and passed from death into life!

Questions

1. What sentiments does Stowe develop to create an emotional release at little Eva's death?
2. What relationship does Uncle Tom bear to those sentiments?
3. Does this passage suggest why *Uncle Tom* became a term of disparagement in the twentieth century?

Questions for Further Thought

1. Read the passage from Carl Schurz's letter (Document 13-6) from the perspective of a member of the Know-Nothing party (Document 13-7). Why did the foreign-born seem dangerous?
2. The power of public education to solve society's problems has been a powerful theme in American history, but never more so than in the 1830s and 1840s. Why do you think Horace Mann's ideas (Document 13-8) were so popular with the middle class at that time?
3. Examine the passage from *Uncle Tom's Cabin* (Document 13-9) to determine how sentimentalism helped turn the northern middle class against slavery.

Conflict over the Trans-Mississippi West, 1844–1846

By the time of the Civil War half the nation's 31.4 million people lived west of the Appalachian Mountains. This situation represented America's expansion from the crowded East and South to the open lands across the mountains, but it also involved Manifest Destiny, the conviction that God had given this great expanse of land to the American people, who had an obligation to conquer and settle it (see text p. 407). However, the confrontation of Manifest Destiny and slavery emerged as the central contradiction in the American perception of national purpose. Although Americans broadly agreed that their westward march to the Pacific represented the progress of civilization, they could not agree about the relationship between slavery and progress (see text p. 410). For growing numbers of northerners it seemed clear that slavery and progress were contradictions. Slavery might be the proper status of Africans in America, but slaves and their masters should remain where they were, in the existing slave states; the West should be reserved for free white men. Increasingly on the defensive, southern slaveholders insisted that their property in slaves be treated in the same manner as all other forms of property. In their view efforts to close the West to slavery constituted a direct assault on the South's social order and prosperity.

After the Louisiana Purchase Congress settled the question of slavery in the Missouri Compromise. In 1844–1845 the Texas crisis raised the slavery issue anew, and agreement was more difficult to reach. During the presidency of John Tyler of Virginia (1841–1845) slave owners received strong support from the federal government and vigorously pressed the argument that hostility to slavery was part of a British plan to weaken the United States, limit its control of the West, and degrade free white men to the status of pauper laborers (see text p. 410 and Document 13-10). Although nominally a Whig, Tyler sided with the proannexation Democrats who nominated James K. Polk in 1844 (see text p. 411). Caught between the broad popular appeal of territorial expansion and the growing sectional conflict over slavery, the Whig candidate, Henry Clay, unsuccessfully attempted to steer a middle course by putting aside the Texas issue until the dispute between Texas and Mexico could be resolved (Document 13-11).

13-10   The American Secretary of State Defends Slavery to the British Minister in Washington (1844)

In 1833 John C. Calhoun (1782–1850) resigned as vice-president in Andrew Jackson's first administration to return to South Carolina, which he soon represented in the U.S. Senate. In 1844–1845 Calhoun briefly served as secretary of state during the Texas crisis (see text p. 411). A conflict developed in the Mexican province of Texas when American settlers declared their independence in 1836. Great Britain offered to mediate peace during the Texas-Mexico war that followed. The 1844–1845 Texas crisis in the United States centered on the issue of slavery in the West and the advisability of admitting Texas as a slaveholding state. The crisis also involved what Calhoun and Tyler believed to be a British plot to secure emancipation in Texas. Calhoun's attention was focused on Lord Aberdeen, the British foreign minister, and Richard Pakenham, the British minister in Washington. Aberdeen had written to Pakenham to complain that the Tyler administration was distorting his government's views on slavery in North America. Pakenham then wrote to the State Department, acknowledging that in general Great Britain opposed slavery but insisting that the British government was not plotting to undermine slavery in Texas or the United States. The following document is an excerpt from Calhoun's reply to Pakenham.

Source: John C. Calhoun to Richard Pakenham, 18th April, 1844. In Clyde N. Wilson, ed., *The Papers of John C. Calhoun* (Columbia: University of South Carolina Press, 1989), vol. 18, pp. 273–278.

The Undersigned, Secretary of State of the United States, has laid before the President the note of the Right Honorable Mr. Pakenham, Envoy Extraordinaire and Minister Plenipotentiary of Her Britannic Majesty, addressed to this Department on the 26th of February last, together with the accompanying copy of a despatch [*sic*] of Her Majesty's Principal Secretary of State for Foreign Affairs to Mr. Pakenham.

In reply, the Undersigned is directed by the President to inform the Right Honorable Mr. Pakenham that, while he regards with pleasure the disavowal of Lord Aberdeen of any intention on the part of Her Majesty's Government "to resort to any measures, either openly or secretly, which can tend to disturb the internal tranquillity of the slaveholding States, and thereby affect the tranquillity of the Union," he, at the same time, regards with deep concern, the avowal, for the first time made to this Government,

"that Great Britain desires, and is constantly exerting herself to procure the general abolition of slavery throughout the world."

So long as Great Britain confined her policy to the abolition of slavery in her own possessions and colonies, no other country had a right to complain. . . . But when she goes beyond, and avows it as her settled policy, and the object of her constant exertions, to abolish it throughout the world, she makes it the duty of all other countries, whose safety or prosperity may be endangered by her policy, to adopt such measures as they may deem necessary for their protection.

It is with still deeper concern the President regards the avowal of Lord Aberdeen of the desire of Great Britain to see slavery abolished in Texas; and, as he infers, is endeavoring, through her diplomacy, to accomplish it, by making abolition of slavery one of the conditions on which Mexico should acknowledge her independence. . . . Under this conviction, it is felt to be the . . . duty of the Federal Government . . . to adopt, in self-defence, the most effectual measures to defeat it. . . .

It is well know that Texas has long desired to be annexed to this Union; that her People, at the time of the adoption of her constitution, expressed by an almost unanimous vote, her desire to that effect. . . . While they conceded to Great Britain the right of adopting whatever policy she might deem best, in reference to the African race, within her own possessions, they, on their part, claim the same right for themselves. . . . With us, it is a question to be decided, not by the Federal Government, but by each member of this Union for itself. . . . A large number of the States has [sic] decided, that it is neither wise nor humane to change the relation, which has existed from their first settlement, between the two races; while others, where the African is less numerous, have adopted the opposite policy. . . . The census and other authentic documents show that, in all instances in which the States have changed the former relation between the two races, the condition of the African, instead of being improved, has become worse. They have invariably sunk into vice and pauperism, accompanied by the bodily and mental inflictions incident thereto—deafness, blindness, insanity and idiocy, to a degree without example; while, in all other States which have retained the ancient relation between them [slavery], they have improved greatly in every respect. . . .

If such be the wretched condition of the race in their changed relation, where their number is comparatively few, and where so much interest is manifested for their improvement, what would it be in those States where the two races are nearly equal in numbers, and where, in consequence, would necessarily spring up mutual fear, jealousy, and hatred, between them. It may, in truth, be assumed as a maxim, that two races differing so greatly, and in so many respects, cannot possibly exist together in the same country. . . . Experience has proved, that the existing relation in which the one is subjected to the other in the slaveholding States, is consistent with the peace and safety of both, with great improvement to the inferior; while the same experience proves, that the relation which it is the desire and object of Great Britain to substitute in its stead, in this and all other countries, under the plausible name of the abolition of slavery, would, (if it did not destroy the inferior by conflicts to which it would lead) reduce it to the extremes of vice and wretchedness. In this view of the subject, it may be asserted that what is called Slavery, is, in reality, a political institution, essential to the peace, safety, and prosperity of those States of the Union in which it exists.

Questions

1. In Calhoun's argument, what has been the effect of emancipation in the northern states?
2. Why is this "experience" relevant to the question of Texas?
3. Consider the motivation behind Calhoun's argument. Why did he attach to an argument for state sovereignty the issue of the well-being of Africans in America?

13-11　Texas and Politics

Common wisdom held that Henry Clay would be the Whig candidate for president in 1844 and Martin Van Buren would be the Democratic nominee. The two men, realizing how the Texas question might inflame passions in the campaign, agreed to eliminate the issue and issued letters to that effect. One such letter by Clay, published in a Washington newspaper, is excerpted here. Clay and Van Buren's action seemed a statesmanlike decision, but it cost Van Buren the Democratic nomination and Clay the election (see text pp. 410–411).

Source: Daily National Intelligencer (Washington, D.C.), April 27, 1844. In Melba Porter Hay, ed., The Papers of Henry Clay (Lexington: University Press of Kentucky, 1991), vol. 10, pp. 41–46.

Subsequent to my departure from Ashland, in December last, I received various communications from popular assemblages and private individuals, requesting an expression of my opinion upon the question of the Annexation of Texas to the United States. I have forborne to reply to them, because it was not very convenient, during the progress of my journey, to do so, and for other reasons. I did not think it proper, unnecessarily, to introduce at present a new element among the other exciting subjects which agitate and engross the public mind. The rejection of the overture of Texas, some years ago, to become annexed to the United States, had met with general acquiescence. Nothing had since occurred materially to vary the question. I had seen no evidence of a desire being entertained, on the part of any considerable portion of the American people, that Texas should become an integral part of the United States. . . . To the astonishment of the whole nation, we are now informed that a treaty of annexation has been actually concluded, and is to be submitted to the Senate for its consideration. The motives for my silence, therefore, no longer remain, and I feel it to be my duty to present an exposition to the public consideration. . . .

I regret that I have not the advantage of a view of the treaty itself, so as to enable me to adapt an expression of my opinion to the actual conditions and stipulations which it contains. Not possessing that opportunity, I am constrained to treat the question according to what I presume to be the terms of the treaty. If, without the loss of national character, without the hazard of foreign war, with the general concurrence of the nation, without any danger to the integrity of the Union, and without giving an unreasonable price for Texas, the question of annexation were presented, it would appear in quite a different light from that in which, I apprehend, it is now to be regarded. . . .

The events which have since transpired in Texas are well known. She revolted against the Government of Mexico, flew to arms, and finally fought and won the memorable battle of San Jacinto, annihilating a Mexican army and making a captive of the Mexican President. The signal success of that Revolution was greatly aided, if not wholly achieved, by citizens of the United States who had migrated to Texas. These succors, if they could not always be prevented by the Government of the United States, were furnished in a manner and to an extent which brought upon us some national reproach in the eyes of an impartial world. And, in my opinion, they impose on us the obligation of scrupulously avoiding the imputation of having instigated and aided the Revolution with the ultimate view of territorial aggrandizement. After the battle of San Jacinto, the United States recognised the independence of Texas, in conformity with the principle and practice which have always prevailed in their councils of recognising the Government "*de facto* ["in fact"]," without regarding the question *de jure* ["by law"]. That recognition did not affect or impair the rights of Mexico, or change the relations which existed between her and Texas. She, on the contrary, has preserved all her rights, and has continued to assert, and so far as I know yet asserts, her right to reduce Texas to obedience, as a part of the Republic of Mexico. According to late intelligence, it is probable that she has agreed upon a temporary suspension of hostilities; but, if that has been done, I presume it is with the purpose, upon the termination of the armistice, of renewing the war and enforcing her rights, as she considers them.

This narrative shows the present actual condition of Texas, so far as I have information about it. If it be correct, Mexico has not abandoned, but perseveres in the assertion of her rights by actual force of arms, which, if suspended, are intended to be renewed. Under these circumstances, if the Government of the United States were to acquire Texas, it would acquire along with it all the incumbrances which Texas is under, and among them the actual or suspended war between Mexico and Texas. Of that consequence there cannot be a doubt. Annexation and war with Mexico are identical. Now, for one, I certainly am not willing to involve this country in a foreign war for the object of acquiring Texas. I know there are those who regard such a war with indifference and as a trifling affair, on account of the weakness of Mexico, and her inability to inflict serious injury upon this country. But I do not look upon it thus lightly. I regard all wars as great calamities, to be avoided, if possible, and honorable peace as the wisest and truest policy of this country. What the United States most need are union, peace, and patience. Nor do I think that the weakness of a Power should form a motive, in any case, for inducing us to engage in or to depreciate the evils of war. Honor and good faith and justice are equally due from this country towards the weak as towards the strong. And, if an act of injustice were to be perpetrated towards any Power, it would be more compatible with the dignity of the nation, and, in my judgment, less dishonorable, to inflict it upon a powerful instead of a weak foreign nation. But are we perfectly sure that we should be free from injury in a state of war with Mexico? Have we any security that countless numbers of foreign vessels, under the authority and flag of Mexico, would not prey upon our defenceless commerce in the Mexican gulf, on the Pacific ocean, and on every other sea and ocean? What commerce, on the other hand, does Mexico offer, as an indemnity for our losses, to the gallantry and enterprise of our countrymen? This view of the subject supposes that the war would be confined to the United States and Mexico as the only belligerents. But have we any certain guaranty that Mexico would obtain no allies among the great European Powers? Suppose any such Powers, jealous of our increasing greatness, and disposed to check our growth and cripple us, were to take part in behalf of Mexico in the war, how would the different belligerents present themselves to Christendom and the enlightened world? We have been seriously charged with an inordinate spirit of territorial aggrandizement; and, without admitting the justice of the charge, it must be owned that we have made vast acquisitions of territory within the last forty years. . . .

Assuming that the annexation of Texas is war with Mexico, is it competent to the treaty-making power to plunge this country into war, not only without the concurrence of, but without deigning to consult Congress, to which, by the Constitution, belongs exclusively the power of declaring war?

I have hitherto considered the question upon the supposition that the annexation is attempted without the assent of Mexico. If she yields her consent, that would materially affect the foreign aspect of the question, if it did not remove all foreign difficulties. On the assumption of that assent, the question would be confined to the domestic considerations which belong to it, embracing the terms and conditions upon which annexation is proposed. I do not think that Texas ought to be received into the Union, as an integral part of it, in decided opposition to the wishes of a considerable and respectable portion of the Confederacy. I think it far more wise and important to compose and harmonize the present Confederacy, as it now exists, than to introduce a new element of discord and distraction into it. In my humble opinion, it should be the constant and earnest endeavor of American statesmen to eradicate prejudices, to cultivate and foster concord, and to produce general contentment among all parts of our Confederacy. And true wisdom, it seems to me, points to the duty of rendering its present members happy, prosperous, and satisfied with each other, rather than to attempt to introduce alien members, against the common consent and with the certainty of deep dissatisfaction. Mr. [Thomas] Jefferson expressed the opinion, and others believed, that it was never in the contemplation of the framers of the Constitution to add foreign territory to the confederacy, out of which new States were to be formed. The acquisitions of Louisiana and Florida may be defended upon the peculiar ground of the relation in which they stood to the States of the Union. After they were admitted, we might well pause awhile, people our vast wastes, develop our resources, prepare the means of defending what we possess, and augment our strength, power, and greatness. If thereafter further territory should be wanted for an increased population, we need entertain no apprehensions but that it will be acquired by means, it is to be hoped, fair, honorable, and constitutional.

It is useless to disguise that there are those who espouse and those who oppose the annexation of Texas upon the ground of the influence which it would exert, in the balance of political power, between two great sections of the Union. I conceive that no motive for the acquisition of foreign territory would be more unfortunate, or pregnant with more fatal consequences, than that of obtaining it for the purpose of strengthening one part against another part of the common Confederacy. Such a principle, put into practical operation, would menace the existence, if it did not certainly sow the seeds of a dissolution of the Union. It would be to proclaim to the world an insatiable and unquenchable thirst for foreign conquest or acquisition of territory. For if to-day Texas be acquired to strengthen one part of the Confederacy, tomorrow Canada may be required to add strength to another. And, after that might have been obtained, still other and further acquisitions would become necessary to equalize and adjust the balance of political power. Finally, in the progress of this spirit of universal dominion, the part of the Confederacy which is now weakest, would find itself still weaker from the impossibility of securing new theatres for those peculiar institutions which it is charged with being desirous to extend.

But would Texas, ultimately, really add strength to that which is now considered the weakest part of the Confederacy? If my information be correct, it would not. According to that, the territory of Texas is susceptible of a division into five States of convenient size and form. Of these, two only would be adapted to those peculiar institutions to which I have referred, and the other three, lying west and north of San Antonio, being only adapted to farming and grazing purposes, from the nature of their soil, climate, and productions, would not admit of those institutions. In the end, therefore, there would be two slave and three free States probably added to the Union. If this view of the soil and geography of Texas be correct, it might serve to diminish the zeal both of those who oppose and those who are urging annexation. . . .

In the future progress of events, it is probable that there will be a voluntary or forcible separation of the British North American possessions from the parent country. I am strongly inclined to think that it will be best for the happiness of all parties that, in that event, they should be erected into a separate and independent Republic. With the Canadian Republic on one side, that of Texas on the other, and the United States, the friend of both, between them, each could advance its own happiness by such constitutions, laws, and measures, as were best adapted to its peculiar condition. They would be natural allies, ready, by co-operation, to repel any European or foreign attack upon either. Each would afford a secure refuge to the persecuted and oppressed driven into exile by either of the others. They would emulate each other in improvements, in free institutions, and in the science of self-government. Whilst Texas has adopted our Constitution as the model of hers, she has, in several important particulars, greatly improved upon it. . . .

Questions

1. What was it about Texas that Clay feared would inflame passions in the campaign?
2. Was Clay totally and permanently opposed to the annexation of Texas or opposed to it only for the moment?
3. Why did Clay believe that annexation of Texas and war with Mexico were identical?

Questions for Further Thought

1. Discuss the factors that made Texas a divisive issue in the presidential election of 1844.
2. How might Calhoun (Document 13-10) have extended his argument to claim that the annexation of Texas was in the best interests of the United States?
3. Do you find Clay's argument (Document 13-11) appealing or persuasive? Explain why or why not.

CHAPTER 14

Disrupting the Union 1846–1860

★   ★   ★

The Mexican War and Its Aftermath, 1846–1850

In the early 1840s President John Tyler and Secretary of State John C. Calhoun worked aggressively for the annexation of the Texas Republic (see text pp. 416–417). However, the treaty of annexation did not receive the required two-thirds majority in the Senate. In the presidential election of 1844 the Texas question dominated political discourse. The Democratic party's candidate, James K. Polk, campaigned on an expansionist platform, while the more timorous Whig candidate, Henry Clay, advocated a diplomatic approach. Polk won handily in the electoral college, although he received less than 50 percent of the popular vote. Declaring the Democratic victory a mandate for annexation, Tyler accepted a joint resolution of Congress (passed by a majority of the House) and declared Texas part of the United States.

The annexation of Texas was only the first step for Polk, who succeeded during his single term in expanding the western border of the United States from the Sabine River to the Rio Grande and from the Great Divide to the Pacific Ocean. That expansion required a war with Mexico. The Mexican government had recognized neither the Republic of Texas nor American claims to sovereignty over Texas. To assert American control Polk sent an army commanded by Zachary Taylor to the Rio Grande, the new border claimed by the United States (see text pp. 418–420). Any act of hostility by Mexico would be deemed an act of war. Polk also pursued a diplomatic course by sending an envoy to Mexico City to seek recognition of American sovereignty in Texas and offer to purchase California and the territory of New Mexico, linking California to Texas. An outraged Mexican government ignored the envoy, and Polk prepared his war message to Congress (Document 14-1). After news arrived that Mexican troops had crossed the Rio Grande and killed sixteen American soldiers in a skirmish with Taylor's army, Polk delivered the message on May 11, 1846.

Despite increasingly bitter divisions over slavery in the West, most Americans enthusiastically supported the war with Mexico. The war offered adventure to a new generation and valuable military experience for a youthful cadre of army officers, including Ulysses S. Grant, who would emerge as major military figures in the American Civil War (see text p. 417) (Document 14-2). Despite the popularity of the war, Polk's aggressive expansionism set off a political reaction that propelled the slaveholding states toward secession and the United States toward civil war. Northern opponents of the expansion of slavery embraced the doctrine laid down by the Democratic representative David Wilmot that any territory won from Mexico should be free of slavery. The Wilmot Proviso (see text p. 420) became the central idea of a new party, the Free Soil party, that was composed of antislavery Democrats and Whigs and won 10 percent of the popular vote in the presidential election of 1848. More important, the Free Soil party held the balance of power in a number of states and successfully formed coalitions—sometimes with Democrats and sometimes with Whigs—to send antislavery men to the House and the Senate. One of the new antislavery senators, Salmon P. Chase of Ohio, spoke at length in opposition to the Compromise of 1850 (see text pp. 428–429) and articulated in the process an interpretation of the laws on slavery that limited that institution to existing slave states (Document 14-3). This interpretation of the constitutional limits of slavery became the organizing principle of the Republican party.

14-1 James Polk Decides for War (1846)

A native of North Carolina, James K. Polk (1795–1849) joined the stream of migration to the trans-Appalachian West and settled in Tennessee. Polk was an ardent Jacksonian Democrat whose political career carried him from the state legislature to seven consecutive terms in Congress, where he served twice as Speaker of the House. Elected governor of Tennessee three times, Polk won the Democratic party's nomination for president in 1844 and had the distinction, as the eleventh president of the United States, of adding more territory to the country than any president except Thomas Jefferson (see text pp. 416–417). Polk made it the goal of his administration to fulfill his vision of the United States as a continental empire extending from sea to sea and as far north and south as he could manage through war with Mexico and the threat of war with Great Britain.

Source: "The Steps Leading to War" is in Allen Nevins, ed., *Polk: The Diary of a President, 1845–1849* (New York: Capricorn, 1968), pp. 80–91; "President Polk's War Message to Congress (Sent to Congress May 11, 1846)" is in James D. Richardson, ed., *A Compilation of the Messages and Papers of the Presidents* (Washington, D.C.: U.S. Government Printing Office, 1896–1899), vol. 5, pp. 2287–2293.

THE STEPS LEADING TO WAR

Saturday, 9th May, 1846.—The Cabinet held a regular meeting today; all the members present. I brought up the Mexican question, and the question of what was the duty of the administration in the present state of our relations with that country. The subject was very fully discussed. All agreed that if the Mexican forces at Matamoras [Matamoros] committed any act of hostility on General Taylor's forces I should immediately send a message to Congress recommending an immediate declaration of war. I stated to

the Cabinet that up to this time, as we knew, we had heard of no open act of aggression by the Mexican army, but that the danger was imminent that such acts would be committed. I said that in my opinion we had ample cause of war, and that it was impossible that we could stand in *statu quo* [in the same state], or that I could remain silent much longer; that I thought it was my duty to send a message to Congress very soon and recommend definite measures. . . . I then propounded the distinct question to the Cabinet, and took their opinions individually, whether I should make a message to Congress on Tuesday, and whether in that message I should recommend a declaration of war against Mexico. All except the Secretary of the Navy gave their advice in the affirmative. . . . [Secretary of State James] Buchanan said he would feel better satisfied in his course if the Mexican forces had or should commit any act of hostility, but that as matters stood we had ample cause of war against Mexico, and he gave his assent to the measure. It was agreed that the message should be prepared and submitted to the Cabinet in their meeting on Tuesday. . . .

About six o'clock P.M. General R. Jones, the Adjutant-General of the army, called and handed to me despatches received from General Taylor by the Southern mail which had just arrived, giving information that a part of the Mexican army had crossed the Del Norte [Rio Grande] and attacked and killed and captured two companies of dragoons of General Taylor's army consisting of 63 officers and men. . . . I immediately summoned the Cabinet. . . . The Cabinet were unanimously of opinion, and it was so agreed, that a message should be sent to Congress on Monday laying all the information in my possession before them and recommending vigorous and prompt measures to enable the executive to prosecute the war. . . .

Sunday, 10th May, 1846.—As the public excitement in and out of Congress was very naturally very great, and as there was a great public necessity to have the prompt action of Congress on the Mexican question, and therefore an absolute necessity for sending my message to Congress on tomorrow, I resumed this morning the preparation of my message. . . .

Monday, 11th May, 1846.— . . . The Secretaries of War and State called a few minutes before eight o'clock but before I had consulted the former in relation to Col. Benton's note, Col. Benton came in. . . . Col. Benton said that the House of Representatives had passed a bill today declaring war in two hours, and that one and a half hours of that time had been occupied in reading the documents which accompanied my message, and that in his opinion in the nineteenth century war should not be declared without full discussion and much more consideration than had been given to it in the House of Representatives. Mr. Buchanan then remarked that war already existed by the act of Mexico herself and therefore it did not require much deliberation to satisfy all that we ought promptly and vigorously to meet it. . . .

Wednesday, 13th May, 1846.— . . . Among other things Mr. Buchanan had stated that our object was not to dismember Mexico or to make conquests, and that the Del Norte was the boundary to which we claimed; or rather that in going to war we did not do so with a view to acquire either California or New Mexico or any other portion of the Mexican territory. I told Mr. Buchanan that I thought such a declaration to foreign governments unnecessary and improper; that the causes of the war as set forth in my message to Congress and the accompanying documents were altogether satisfactory. I told him that though we had not gone to war for conquest, yet it was clear that in making peace we would if practicable obtain California and such other portion of the Mexican territory as would be sufficient to indemnify our claimants on Mexico, and to defray the expense of the war which that power by her long continued wrongs and injuries had forced us to wage. I told him it was well known that the Mexican Government had no other means of indemnifying us. . . .

PRESIDENT POLK'S WAR MESSAGE TO CONGRESS
(sent to Congress on May 11, 1846)

. . . An envoy of the United States repaired to Mexico, with full powers to adjust every existing difference. But though present on the Mexican soil, by agreement between the two governments, invested with full powers, and bearing evidence of the most friendly dispositions, his mission has been unavailing. The Mexican government not only refused to receive him, or listen to his propositions, but, after a long continued series of menaces, have at last invaded our territory, and shed the blood of our fellow-citizens on our own soil. . . .

In my message at the commencement of the present session, I informed you that, upon the earnest appeal both of the congress and convention of Texas, I had ordered an efficient military force to take a position "between the Nueces and the Del Norte." This had become necessary, to meet a threatened invasion of Texas by the Mexican forces, for which extensive military preparations had been made. The invasion was threatened solely because Texas had determined, in accordance with a solemn resolution of the Congress of the United States, to annex herself to our Union; and, under these circumstances, it was plainly our duty to extend our protection over her citizens and soil. . . .

Meantime Texas, by the final action of our Congress, had become an integral part of our Union. The Congress of Texas, by its act of December 19, 1836, had declared the Rio del Norte to be the boundary of that republic. Its jurisdiction had been extended and exercised beyond the Nueces. The country between that river and the Del Norte had been represented in the congress and in the convention of Texas; had thus taken part in the act of annexation itself; and is now included within one of our congressional districts. . . . It became, therefore, of urgent necessity to provide for the defence of that portion of our country. Accordingly, on the 13th of January last, instructions were issued to the general in command of these troops to occupy the left bank of the Del Norte. This river, which is the south-western boundary of the State of Texas, is an exposed frontier; from this quarter invasion was threatened; upon it, and in its immediate vicinity, in the judgment of high military experience, are the proper stations for the protecting forces of the government. . . .

The Mexican forces at Matamoras assumed a belligerent attitude, and, on the twelfth of April, General Ampudia, then in command, notified General Taylor to break up his camp within twenty-four hours, and to retire beyond the Nueces river, and, in the event of his failure to comply with these demands, announced that arms, and arms alone, must decide the question. . . . A party of dragoons . . . were . . . despatched from the American camp . . . to ascertain whether the Mexican troops had crossed, or were preparing to cross, the river, [and] "became engaged

with a large body of these troops, and, after a short affair, in which some sixteen were killed and wounded, appear to have been surrounded and compelled to surrender." . . .

In the meantime, we have tried every effort at reconciliation. The cup of forebearance had been exhausted, even before the recent information from the frontier of the Del Norte. But now, after reiterated menaces, Mexico has passed the boundary of the United States, has invaded our territory, and shed American blood upon the American soil. She has proclaimed that hostilities have commenced, and that the two nations are now at war.

As war exists, and, notwithstanding all our efforts to avoid it, exists by the act of Mexico herself, we are called upon by every consideration of duty and patriotism to vindicate with decision and honor, the rights, and the interests of our country. . . .

Questions

1. The notion of Manifest Destiny played a major role in American expansionism. What evidence do you find of this sentiment in Polk's diary and war message?
2. If the Mexicans had not acted against General Taylor's forces, would that have made any difference to Polk? What evidence is there in the documents to support your answer?
3. How was Polk being less than straightforward with Congress?

14-2 Ulysses S. Grant Commands Troops in Mexican War (1847)

Born in Point Pleasant, Ohio, near Cincinnati, Ulysses S. Grant (1822–1885) was the son of a farmer and tanner of modest means. Self-educated and a frequent contributor to western newspapers, the elder Grant secured the best formal education he could obtain for his children. As a result of his father's ambition, Grant received an appointment to West Point, from which he graduated in 1843. Although Grant resigned his commission in 1854 (he would return to the army as a colonel in 1861), the first decade of his military career went well. Grant served with distinction during the Mexican War under General Winfield Scott and General Zachary Taylor and rose to the rank of captain in 1852. In his memoirs, published shortly before his death and widely praised as a distinguished work of military history, Grant recounted his experiences in the capture of Veracruz and the battle Cerro Gordo (see text pp. 417, 419).

Source: [Ulysses S. Grant], *Personal Memoirs of U. S. Grant* (New York: Charles L. Webster & Company, 1885), vol. 1, pp. 119–134.

The Mexican war was a political war, and the administration conducting it desired to make party capital out of it. General Scott . . . was a Whig and the administration was democratic. . . . Scott had estimated the men and material that would be required to capture Vera Cruz and to march on the capital of the country, two hundred and sixty miles

in the interior. He was promised all he asked and seemed to have not only the confidence of the President, but his sincere good wishes. The promises were all broken. Only about half the troops were furnished that had been pledged, other war material was withheld . . . Scott remained in command: but every general appointed to serve under him was politically opposed to the chief, and several were personally hostile. . . .

The army lay in camp upon the sand-beach in the neighborhood of the Rio Grande for several weeks, awaiting the arrival of transports to carry it to its new field of operation. The transports were all sailing vessels. The passage was a tedious one, and many of the troops were on shipboard over thirty days from the embarkation at the mouth of the Rio Grande to the time of debarkation south of Vera Cruz. . . . With the fleet there was a little steam propeller dispatch-boat—the first vessel of the kind ever seen by any one then with the army. At that day ocean steamers were rare, and what there were were side-wheelers. This little vessel, going through the fleet so fast, so noiselessly and with its propeller under water out of view, attracted a great deal of attention. . . .

Finally on the 7th of March, 1847, the little army of ten or twelve thousand men, given Scott to invade a country with a population of seven or eight millions, a mountainous country affording the greatest possible natural advantages for defence, was all assembled and ready to commence the perilous task of landing from vessels lying in the open sea.

The debarkation took place inside of the little island of Sacrificious, some three miles south of Vera Cruz. . . . The Mexicans were very kind to us, however, and threw no obstacles in the way of our landing except an occasional shot from their nearest fort. During the debarkation one shot took off the head of Major Albertis. . . . Vera Cruz, at the time of which I write and up to 1880, was a walled city. The wall extended from the water's edge south of the town to the water again on the north. There were fortifications at intervals along the line and at the angles. . . . The siege continued with brisk firing on our side till the 27th of March, by which time a considerable breach had been made in the wall surrounding the city. . . . On the 29th, Vera Cruz [was] occupied by Scott's army. About five thousand prisoners . . . fell into the hands of the victorious force. The casualties on our side during the siege amounted to sixty-four officers and men, killed and wounded. . . .

It was very important to get the army away from Vera Cruz as soon as possible, in order to avoid the yellow fever, or vomito, which usually visits that city early in the year, and is very fatal to persons not acclimated. . . . The leading division ran against the enemy at Cerro Gordo, some fifty miles west, on the road to Jalapa, and went into camp at Plan del Rio, about three miles from the [enemy] fortifications. . . . General Scott . . . at once commenced his preparations for the capture of the position held by Santa Anna. . . .

Cerro Gordo is one of the highest spurs of the mountains some twelve to fifteen miles east of Jalapa, and Santa Anna had selected this point as the easiest to defend against an invading army. The road, said to have been built by Cortez, zigzags around the mountain-side and was defended at every turn by artillery. On either side were deep chasms or mountain walls. A direct attack along the road was an impossibility. A flank movement seemed equally impossible. After the arrival of the commanding-general upon the scene, reconnoissances [sic] were sent out . . . under the supervision of Captain Robert E. Lee, assisted by Lieutenants P. G. T. Beauregard . . . [and] George B. McClellan . . . of the corps of engineers. . . . The reconnoisance [sic] was completed, and the labor of cutting out and making roads by the flank was . . . accomplished without the knowledge of Santa Anna or his army, and over ground where he supposed it impossible. . . . The engineers, who had directed the opening, led the way and the troops followed. Artillery was let down the steep slopes by hand. . . . In like manner the guns were drawn by hand up the opposite slopes. In this way Scott's troops reached their assigned position in rear of most of the entrenchments of the enemy, unobserved. The attack was made. . . . The surprise of the enemy was complete, the victory overwhelming; some three thousand prisoners fell into Scott's hands. . . . Santa Anna['s] . . . attack on Taylor [at Buena Vista] was disastrous to the Mexican army, but, notwithstanding this, he marched his army to Cerro Gordo, a distance not much short of one thousand miles . . . in time to intrench himself well before Scott got there. If he [Santa Anna] had been successful at Buena Vista his troops would no doubt have made a more stubborn resistance at Cerro Gordo. Had the battle of Buena Vista not been fought Santa Anna would have had time to move leisurely to meet the invader further south and with an army not demoralized nor depleted by defeat.

Questions

1. According to Grant, the American force at Veracruz was numerically small for the task it faced. What advantages did it enjoy at Veracruz and Cerro Gordo?
2. According to Grant, what was General Santa Anna's greatest disadvantage at Cerro Gordo?
3. What military experiences from this campaign would be particularly useful to Grant, Lee, Beauregard, and McClellan in the Civil War?

14-3   Salmon P. Chase Defines the Constitutional Limits of Slavery (1850)

Born in New Hampshire and educated at Dartmouth College, Salmon P. Chase (1808–1873) studied law with President John Quincy Adams's attorney general, William Wirt, before moving west to establish himself as a successful young lawyer in Cincinnati, Ohio. Chase voted for William Henry Harrison in 1840 but soon afterward joined the fledgling abolitionist Liberty party (see text p. 422). Chase volunteered to be the defense attorney in a celebrated 1836 fugitive slave case involving a woman named Matilda and James G. Birney (the Liberty party presidential candidate in 1840 and 1844), who employed her in his home. Chase lost the case, but the state supreme court ordered his argument printed, securing for Chase the title "attorney general of the fugitive slave" in antislavery circles. Chase took a leading role in the formation of the Free Soil party in 1848 and forged a Free Soil–Democratic coalition in Ohio that elected him to the United States Senate (see text p. 428). In the Senate Chase opposed the compromise measures crafted by Henry Clay, Daniel Webster, and Stephen Douglas. The argument he developed became the central tenet of the Republican party.

Source: Salmon P. Chase, *Union and Freedom, without Compromise. Speech of Mr. Chase of Ohio, On Mr. Clay's Compromise Resolutions* (Washington, D.C.: Buell and Blanchard, 1850).

I think, Mr. President, that two facts may now be regarded as established: First that in 1787 the national policy in respect to slavery was one of restriction, limitation, and discouragement. Second that it was generally expected that under the action of the State Governments slavery would gradually disappear from the States.

Such was the state of the country when the Convention met to frame the Constitution of the United States. . . . The framers of the Constitution acted under the influence of the general sentiment of the country. Some of them had contributed in no small measure to form that sentiment. Let us examine the instrument [the Constitution] in its light, and ascertain the original import of its language.

What, then, shall we find in it? The guaranties so much talked of? Recognition of property in men? Stipulated protection for that property in national territories and by national law? No, sir: nothing like it.

We find, on the contrary, extreme care to exclude these ideas from the Constitution. Neither the word "slave" nor "slavery" is to be found in any provision. There is not a single expression which charges the National Government with any responsibility in regard to slavery. No power is conferred on Congress either to establish or sustain it. The framers of the Constitution left it where they found it, exclusively within and under the jurisdiction of the States. Wherever slaves are referred to at all in the Constitution, whether in the clause providing for the apportionment of representation and direct taxation [Article I, section 2], or in that stipulating for the extradition of fugitive from service [the "fugitive slave" clause, Article IV,

section 2], or in that restricting Congress as to the prohibition of importation or migration [Article I, section 9], they are spoken of, not as persons held as property, but as persons held to service, or having their condition determined, under State laws. We learn, indeed from the debates in the Constitutional Convention that the idea of property in men was excluded with special solicitude. . . .

Unhappily . . . the original policy of the Government and the original principles of the Government in respect to slavery did not permanently control its action. A change occurred—almost imperceptible at first but becoming more and more marked and decided until nearly total. . . . It was natural, though it does [not] seem to have been anticipated, that the unity of the slave interest strengthened by this accession of political power, should gradually weaken the public sentiment and modify the national policy against slavery. . . . Mr. President, I have spoken freely of slave State ascendency in the affairs of this Government, but I desire not to be misunderstood. I take no sectional position. The supporters of slavery are the sectionalists. . . . Freedom is national; slavery only is local and sectional. . . .

What have been the results . . . of the subversion of the original policy of slavery restriction and discouragement . . . instead of slavery being regarded as a curse, a reproach, a blight, an evil, a wrong, a sin, we are now told that it is the most stable foundation of our institutions; the happiest relation that labor can sustain to capital; a blessing to both races . . . this is a great change, and a sad change. If it goes on, the spirit of liberty must at length become extinct, and a despotism will be established under the forms of free institutions. . . . There can be no foundation whatever for the doctrine advanced . . . that an equilibrium between the slaveholding and non-slaveholding sections of our country has been, is, and ought to be, an approved feature of our political system. . . . I shall feel myself supported by the precepts of the sages of the Revolutionary era, by the example of the founders of the Republic, by the original policy of the Government, and by the principles of the Constitution.

Questions

1. Why is Chase concerned with the history of the slavery issue? What difference did it make?
2. Locate in the Constitution (see text pp. D-7–D-15) the passages cited by Chase as referring to slaves. Do you agree with Chase that these passages were part of an original policy of "slavery restriction and discouragement"? Explain why.
3. What are the implications of Chase's conclusion that "Freedom is national; slavery . . . is . . . local"?

Questions for Further Thought

1. Compare Polk's diary excerpts and message to Congress (Document 14-1) in terms of both tone and content. Which is more reliable as a source on his decision-making process? Is there any evidence that he was less than candid in private as well as public pronouncements?
2. Was General Scott foolhardy to think that he could take Mexico City with an army of fewer than 12,000 men (Document 14-2)? Explain why.
3. Consider Chase's slavery restriction argument (Document 14-3) from the perspective of the South. Why were southerners not content with the tenets of states' rights in their defense of slavery? Did the slaveholding interest need the protection of the federal government? Explain why.

Sectional Strife and the Third Party System, 1850–1858

An essential component of the Compromise of 1850 was the passage of a new and much more stringent Fugitive Slave Act (see text p. 429). The new law replaced a 1793 act that relied on state authorities to capture and return fugitive slaves in compliance with the "fugitive clause" of the Constitution. In *Prigg v. Pennsylvania* (1842) the U.S. Supreme Court placed the full burden of enforcing the fugitive clause on the federal government. The new Fugitive Slave Act of 1850 set out the procedures by which fugitives could be captured in free states and returned to slavery in the South (Document 14-4). The Fugitive Slave Act angered many northerners, not only ardent abolitionists (see text pp. 429–430). To abolitionists, however, the new law seemed to place the federal government squarely on the side of slavery. Under these circumstances obedience to the law of the land meant the enforcement of slavery; civil disobedience was the only morally acceptable response (Document 14-5) and efforts to rescue slaves increased (Document 14-6).

As sectional tensions mounted, violence erupted between free-soil and proslavery settlers in Kansas (see text pp. 435–437). Massachusetts's new antislavery senator, Charles Sumner, eloquently championed the cause of freedom in Kansas. Sumner had been elected to replace Daniel Webster, an author of the Compromise of 1850 who left the Senate to become secretary of state under Millard Fillmore. A few days after Sumner's speech on the "Crime against Kansas" (Document 14-7) Representative Preston Brooks of South Carolina entered the Senate chamber and assaulted the unsuspecting senator, caning him into unconsciousness. In 1857 Chief Justice Roger B. Taney's decision in the case of *Dred Scott v. Sandford* (see text pp. 438–439) added to the developing sectional crisis. A Marylander appointed to the court by President Andrew Jackson to replace John Marshall, Taney drafted his opinion in the *Dred Scott* case with the intention of extending constitutional protection to slaveholders (Document 14-8). The Republican party—a party of northern principles—had organized in opposition to the Kansas-Nebraska Act. "Bleeding Kansas," the caning of Sumner, and Taney's decision in the *Dred Scott* case provided the new party with powerful arguments against the "Slave Power" conspiracy.

14-4 The Fugitive Slave Act of 1850

Under the Constitution (Article IV, section 2), states were obligated to surrender escaped slaves back to their owners. Growing antislavery sentiment in the North had led most states to ignore that provision, and as tensions rose, the South insisted that the northern states live up to their constitutional obligation. As part of the Compromise of 1850 Congress enacted a tougher fugitive slave statute to satisfy southern demands (see text p. 429).

Source: United States, *Statutes at Large*, vol. 9, pp. 462ff.

Be it enacted by the Senate and House of Representatives of the United States of America in congress assembled, . . .

SEC. 6. *And be it further enacted,* That when a person held to service or labor in any State or Territory of the United States, has heretofore or shall hereafter escape into another State or Territory of the United States, the person or persons to whom such service or labor may be due, or his, her, or their agent or attorney, duly authorized, by power of attorney, in writing, acknowledged and certified under the seal of some legal officer or court of the State or Territory in which the same may be executed, may pursue and reclaim such fugitive person, either by procuring a warrant from some one of the courts, judges, or commissioners aforesaid, of the proper circuit, district, or county, for the apprehension of such fugitive from service or labor, or by seizing and arresting such fugitive, where the same can be done without process, and by taking, or causing such person to be taken, forthwith before such court, judge, or commissioner, whose duty it shall be to hear and determine the case of such claimant in a summary manner. . . . In no trial or hearing under this act shall the testimony of such alleged fugitive be admitted in evidence; and the certifi-

cates in this and the first [fourth] section be mentioned, shall be conclusive of the right of the person or persons in whose favor granted, to remove such fugitive to the State or Territory from which he escaped, and shall prevent all molestation of such person or persons by any process issued by any court, judge, magistrate, or other person whomsoever.

SEC. 7. *And be it further enacted,* That any person who shall knowingly and willingly obstruct, hinder, or prevent such claimant, his agent or attorney, or any person or persons lawfully assisting him, her, or them, from arresting such a fugitive from service or labor, either with or without process as aforesaid, or shall rescue, or attempt to rescue, such fugitive from service or labor, from the custody of such claimant, his or her agent or attorney, or other person or persons lawfully assisting as aforesaid, when so arrested, pursuant to the authority herein given and declared; or shall aid, abet, or assist such person so owing service or labor as aforesaid, directly or indirectly, to escape from such claimant, his agent or attorney, or other person or persons legally authorized as aforesaid; or shall harbor or conceal such fugitive, so as to prevent the discovery and arrest of such person, after notice or knowledge of the fact that such person was a fugitive from service or labor as aforesaid, shall, for either of said offences, be subject to a fine not exceeding one thousand dollars, and imprisonment not exceeding six months . . . and shall moreover forfeit and pay, by way of civil damages to the party injured by such illegal conduct, the sum of one thousand dollars, for each fugitive so lost as aforesaid. . . .

SEC. 9. *And be it further enacted,* That, upon affidavit made by the claimant of such fugitive, his agent or attorney, after such certificate has been issued, that he has reason to apprehend that such fugitive will be rescued by force from his or their possession before he can be taken beyond the limits of the State in which the arrest is made, it shall be the duty of the officer making the arrest to retain such fugitive in his custody, and to remove him to the State whence he fled, and there to deliver him to said claimant, his agent, or attorney. And to this end, the officer aforesaid is hereby authorized and required to employ so many persons as he may deem necessary to overcome such force, and to retain them in his service so long as circumstances may require. The said officer and his assistants, while so employed, to receive the same compensation, and to be allowed the same expenses, as are now allowed by law for transportation of criminals, to be certified by the judge of the district within which the arrest is made, and paid out of the treasury of the United States.

Questions

1. How does the act discourage people from helping fugitive slaves?
2. The Constitution called for the states to surrender runaways. Which people were specifically charged in the act with the enforcement of this law?
3. According to the act, whose responsibility is it to pay the expenses of slave catchers? Why was this provision included?

14-5 "A Sabbath Scene" (1850)

John Greenleaf Whittier

Born in Haverhill, Massachusetts, the son of Quaker parents, John Greenleaf Whittier (1807–1892) published his first poem in a newspaper edited by the abolitionist William Lloyd Garrison. Whittier became part of the close-knit group of Garrisonian abolitionists. Unlike Garrison, however, Whittier supported the Liberty and Free Soil parties (see text p. 431). By the 1850s Whittier had become one of the nation's best-known poets. "The Barefoot Boy" (1855)—"Blessings on thee, little man, /Barefoot boy, with cheek of tan"—celebrated his rural youth. In the twentieth century Whittier's literary reputation declined steadily, and he is probably best remembered as the principal poet of the antislavery cause. Whittier responded to the passage of the Fugitive Slave Act of 1850 with a moral outrage that was further inflamed by the willingness of most northerners to accept the measure as the law of the land, necessary for the preservation of the Union. Whittier was particularly distressed by the acquiescence of northern ministers, who, he believed, had a moral obligation to denounce the law. In his poem "A Sabbath Scene" Whittier attacked the conventional morality of his day with all the irony and sarcasm he could muster, and he justified his lack of civility with a quote from Garrison: "it is a waste of *politeness* to be courteous to the devil." In the poem, "Polyglott" refers to a large volume containing the scriptures in several languages. In the Bible, "Onesimus" is the runaway slave of Philemon. In "The Epistle of Paul to Philemon," Paul appeals to Philemon as a Christian to accept Onesimus's return.

Source: [John Greenleaf Whittier], *The Complete Poetical Works of John Greenleaf Whittier,* Cambridge ed. (Boston and New York: Houghton Mifflin Company, 1894), pp. 312–313.

Scarce had the solemn Sabbath-bell
   Ceased quivering in the steeple,
Scarce had the parson to his desk
   Walked stately through his people,

When down the summer-shaded street
   A wasted female figure,
With dusky brow and naked feet,
   Came rushing wild and eager.

She saw the white spire through the trees,
   She heard the sweet hymn swelling:
O pitying Christ! a refuge give
   That poor one in Thy dwelling!

Like a scared fawn before the hounds,
   Right up the aisle she glided,
While close behind her, whip in hand,
   A lank-haired hunter strided.

She raised a keen and bitter cry,
   To Heaven and Earth appealing;
Were manhood's generous pulses dead?
   Had woman's heart no feeling?

A score of stout hands rose between
   The hunter and the flying:
Age clenched his staff, and maiden eyes
   Flashed tearful, yet defying.

"Who dares profane this house and day?"
   Cried out the angry pastor.
"Why, bless your soul, the wench's a
     slave,
   And I'm her lord and master!

"I've law and gospel on my side,
   And who shall dare refuse me?"
Down came the parson, bowing low,
   "My good sir, pray excuse me!

"Of course I know your right divine
   To own and work and whip her;
Quick, deacon, throw that Polyglott
   Before the wench, and trip her!"

Plump dropped the holy tome, and o'er
   Its sacred pages stumbling,
Bound hand and foot, a slave once more,
   The hapless wretch lay trembling.

I saw the parson tie the knots,
   The while his flock addressing,
The Scriptural claims of slavery
   With text on text impressing.

"Although," said he, "on Sabbath day
   All secular occupations
Are deadly sins, we must fulfil
   Our moral obligations:

"And this commends itself as one
   To every conscience tender;
As Paul sent back Onesimus,
   My Christian friends, we send her!"

Shriek rose on shriek,—the Sabbath air
   Her wild cries tore asunder;
I listened, with hushed breath, to hear
   God answering with his thunder!

All still! the very altar's cloth
   Had smothered down her shrieking,
And, dumb, she turned from face to face,
   For human pity seeking!

I saw her dragged along the aisle,
   Her shackles harshly clanking;
I heard the parson, over all,
   The Lord devoutly thanking!

My brain took fire: "Is this," I cried,
   "The end of prayer and preaching?
Then down with pulpit, down with priest,
   And give us Nature's teaching!

"Foul shame and scorn be on ye all
   Who turn the good to evil,
And steal the Bible from the Lord,
   To give it to the Devil!

"Than garbled text or parchment law
   I own a statute higher;
And God is true, though every book
   And every man's a liar!"

Just then I felt the deacon's hand
   In wrath my coat-tail seize on;
I heard the priest cry, "Infidel!"
   The lawyer mutter, "Treason!"

I started up, — where now were church,
   Slave, master, priest, and people?
I only heard the supper-bell,
   Instead of clanging steeple.

But, on the open window's sill,
   O'er which the white blooms drifted,
The pages of a good old Book
   The wind of summer lifted,

And flower and vine, like angel wings
    Around the Holy Mother,
Waved softly there, as if God's truth
    And Mercy kissed each other.

And freely from the cherry-bough
    Above the casement swinging,
With golden bosom to the sun,
    The oriole was singing.

As bird and flower made plain of old
    The lesson of the Teacher,
So now I heard the written Word
    Interpreted by Nature!

For to my ear methought the breeze
    Bore Freedom's blessed word on;
Thus saith the Lord: Break every yoke,
    Undo the heavy burden!

Questions

1. In the poem the first response of the minister and parishioners was to protect the fugitive. What sentiments initially motivated them? What changed their perspective?
2. In what ways did Whittier believe that the Fugitive Slave Act violated the Christian conscience?
3. Do you agree with Whittier that one has a moral obligation on such occasions to obey God's "higher law" and disobey human law? Explain why or why not.

14-6   The Rescue of a Slave

The South's demand for a stronger fugitive slave law grew out of increased efforts by northern abolitionists to help slaves escape and to assist runaway slaves in reaching safe havens in the North and in Canada. After passage of the Fugitive Slave Act, such rescue attempts increased. In 1855 Colonel John Wheeler, the American minister to Nicaragua, was traveling by boat to New York with three slaves. At a stopover in Philadelphia, a member of the Vigilance Committee came aboard and informed Wheeler's slave, Jane Johnson, that under Pennsylvania law she was free. Johnson left the boat with her children, while Wheeler unsuccessfully tried to secure her return. Following is the affidavit Jane Johnson filed with a New York magistrate.

Source: William Still, *The Underground Railroad* (Philadelphia, 1872), pp. 86–97, *passim.*

Jane Johnson being sworn, makes oath and says—

My name is Jane—Jane Johnson: I was the slave of Mr. Wheeler of Washington; he bought me and my two children, about two years ago, from Mr. Cornelius Crew, of Richmond, Va.; my youngest child is between six and seven years old, the other between ten and eleven; I have one other child only, and he is in Richmond; I have not seen him for about two years; never expect to see him again; Mr. Wheeler brought me and my two children to Philadelphia, on the way to Nicaragua, to wait on his wife; I didn't want to go without my two children, and he consented to take them; we came to Philadelphia by the cars; stopped at Mr. Sully's, Mr. Wheeler's father-in-law, a few

moments; then went to the steamboat for New York at 2 o'clock, but were too late; we went into Bloodgood's Hotel; Mr. Wheeler went to dinner; Mr. Wheeler had told me in Washington to have nothing to say to colored persons, and if any of them spoke to me, to say I was a free woman traveling with a minister; we staid at Bloodgood's till 5 o'clock; Mr. Wheeler kept his eye on me all the time except when he was at dinner; he left his dinner to come and see if I was safe, and then went back again; while he was at dinner, I saw a colored woman and told her I was a slave woman, that my master had told me not to speak to colored people, and that if any of them spoke to me to say that I was free; but I am not free; but I want to be free; she said: 'poor thing, I pity you;' after that I saw a colored man and said the same thing to him, he said he would telegraph to New York, and two men would meet me at 9 o'clock and take me with them; after that we went on board the boat, Mr. Wheeler sat beside me on the deck; I saw a colored gentleman come on board, he beckoned to me; I nodded my head, and could not go; Mr. Wheeler was beside me and I was afraid; a white gentleman then came and said to Mr. Wheeler, 'I want to speak to your servant, and tell her of her rights;' Mr. Wheeler rose and said, 'If you have anything to say, say it to me—she knows her rights;' the white gentleman asked me if I wanted to be free; I said 'I do, but I belong to this gentleman and I can't have it;' he replied, 'Yes, you can, come with us, you are as free [as] your master, if you want your freedom come now; if you go back to Washington you may never get it;' I rose to go, Mr. Wheeler spoke, and said, 'I will give you your freedom,' but he had never promised it before, and I knew he would never give it to me; the white gentleman held out his hand and I went toward him; I was ready for the word before it was given me; I took the children by the hands, who both cried, for they were frightened, but both stopped when they got on shore; a colored man carried the little one, I led the other by the hand. We walked down the street till we got to a hack; nobody forced me away; nobody pulled me, and nobody led me; I went away of my own free will; I always wished to be free and meant to be free when I came North; I hardly expected it in Philadelphia, but I thought I should get free in New York; I have been comfortable and happy since I left Mr. Wheeler, and so are the children; I don't want to go back; I could have gone in Philadelphia if I had wanted to; I could go now; but I had rather die than go back. I wish to make this statement before a magistrate, because I understand that Mr. Williamson is in prison on my account, and I hope the truth may be of benefit to him.

her
Jane × Johnson
mark

Questions

1. What did Wheeler specifically instruct Johnson to tell others about herself? Why?
2. What evidence is there that the meeting between Johnson and the member of the Vigilance Committee had been prearranged?
3. Under what provisions of the fugitive slave law would Mr. Williamson be jailed?

14-7   "The Crime against Kansas" (1856)

Charles Sumner

Born in Boston and educated at Harvard, Charles Sumner (1811–1874) entered the world of New England social reform in the 1840s and moved quickly into antislavery political activity after the organization of the Free Soil party in 1848. A political coalition of Free-Soilers and Democrats in Massachusetts sent Sumner to the U.S. Senate in 1851, replacing Daniel Webster, whose authorship of and support for the Compromise of 1850 and the Fugitive Slave Act outraged the growing antislavery sentiment in Massachusetts. Sumner's purpose in the Senate was first and foremost to fight the "Slave Power," which he blamed for the outbreak of violence in Kansas (see text pp. 435–437). Sumner took the floor of the Senate over two days (May 19 and 20, 1856) to defend the free-soil settlers and denounce as barbarians the proslavery forces that were attempting to seize control of the territory. In the course of that speech, "The Crime against Kansas," Sumner made derogatory personal references to South Carolina's elderly senator, Andrew Butler, who had recently suffered a stroke. Two days later Senator Butler's nephew, Representative Preston S. Brooks of South Carolina, severely beat Sumner with a cane. Brooks became a hero in South Carolina (see text p. 437). Sumner, revered as a martyr to the cause of freedom, won reelection to the Senate until he died.

Source: Charles Sumner: His Complete Works (Lee and Shepard, 1900; reprint, New York: Negro Universities Press edition, 1969), vol. 5, pp. 125–126.

Mr. President,—You are now called to redress a great wrong. Seldom in the history of nations is such a question presented. Tariffs, army bills, navy bills, land bills, are important, and justly occupy your care; but these all belong to the course of ordinary legislation. . . . Far otherwise is it with the eminent question now before you, involving, as it does, Liberty in a broad Territory, and also involving the peace of the whole country, with our good name in history forevermore. . . .

The wickedness which I now begin to expose is immeasurably aggravated by the motive which prompted it. Not in any common lust for power did this uncommon tragedy have its origin. It is the rape of a virgin Territory, compelling it to the hateful embrace of Slavery; and it may be clearly traced to a depraved desire for a new Slave State, hideous offspring of such a crime, in the hope of adding to the power of Slavery in the National Government. Yes, Sir, when the whole world alike . . . is rising up to condemn this wrong . . . here in our Republic, *force*—ay, Sir, FORCE—is openly employed in compelling Kansas to this pollution, and all for the sake of political power. . . .

Before entering upon the argument, I must say something of a general character, particularly in response to what has fallen from Senators who have raised themselves to eminence on this floor in championship of human wrong: I mean the Senator from South Carolina [Mr. Butler]. . . . The Senator from South Carolina had read many books of chivalry, and believes himself a chivalrous knight, with sentiments of honor and courage. Of course he has chosen a mistress to whom he has made his vows, and who, though ugly to others, is always lovely to him,—though polluted in the sight of the world, is chaste in his sight: I mean the harlot Slavery. For her his tongue is always profuse with words. Let her be impeached in character, or any proposition be made to shut her out from the extension of her wantonness, and no extravagance of manner or hardihood of assertion is then too great for this Senator. . . .

I undertake, in the first place, to expose the CRIME AGAINST KANSAS, in origin and extent. . . . The debate [over the Kansas-Nebraska bill], which convulsed Congress, stirred the whole country. From all sides attention was directed upon Kansas, which at once became the favorite goal of emigration. The bill loudly declares that its object is "to leave the people perfectly free to form and regulate their domestic institutions in their own way"; and its supporters everywhere challenge the determination of the question between Freedom and Slavery by a competition of emigration. . . . The populous North, stung by sense of outrage, and inspired by a noble cause, are pouring into the debatable land, and promise soon to establish a supremacy of Freedom.

Then was conceived the consummation of the Crime against Kansas. What could not be accomplished peaceably was to be accomplished forcibly. . . . The violence, for some time threatened, broke forth on the 29th of November, 1854, at the first election of a Delegate to Congress, when companies from Missouri, amounting to upwards of one thousand, crossed into Kansas, and with force and arms proceeded to vote for . . . the candidate of Slavery. . . . Five . . . times and more have these invaders entered Kansas in armed array, and thus five . . . times and more have they trampled upon the organic law of the Territory. These extraordinary expeditions are simply the extraordinary witnesses to successive, uninterrupted violence. . . . Border incursions, which in barbarous ages or barbarous lands fretted and harried an exposed people, are here renewed, with this peculiarity, that our border robbers do not simply levy blackmail and drive off a few cattle . . . they commit a succession of deeds in which . . . the whole Territory is enslaved.

Private griefs mingle their poignancy with public wrongs. I do not dwell on the anxieties of families exposed to sudden assault, and lying down to rest with the alarms of war ringing in the ears, not knowing that another day may be spared to them. . . . Our souls are wrung by individual instances. . . .

Thus was the Crime consummated. Slavery stands erect, clanking its chains on the Territory of Kansas, surrounded by a code of death, and trampling upon all cherished liberties. . . . Emerging from all the blackness of this Crime . . . I come now to the APOLOGIES which the Crime has found. . . .

With regret I come again upon the Senator from South Carolina [Butler. His speech slurred by a stroke, Butler had interjected critical comments on more than thirty occasions while Sumner spoke] who, omnipresent in this debate, overflows with rage at the simple suggestion that Kansas has applied for admission as a State, and, with incoherent phrase, discharges the loose expectoration of his speech, now upon her representative, and then upon her people. . . . [I]t is against the [free-soil majority in] . . . Kansas that sensibilities of the Senator are particularly aroused. . . .

The contest, which, beginning in Kansas, reaches us will be transferred soon from Congress to that broader stage, where every citizen is not only spectator, but actor; and to their judgment I confidently turn. To the people, about to exercise the electoral franchise, in choosing a Chief Magistrate of the Republic, I appeal, to vindicate the electoral franchise in Kansas. Let the ballot-box of the Union . . . protect the ballot-box in that Territory.

Questions

1. According to Sumner, why did the Slave Power no longer support the "popular sovereignty" solution to the question of the extension of slavery?
2. Read Sumner's comments about Senator Butler from the perspective of Representative Preston Brooks. How had Sumner challenged the honor of his uncle?
3. What is the political intent of Sumner's speech? Who does he expect to agitate with his heated remarks? To what purpose?

14-8   The *Dred Scott* Decision

In his inaugural address on March 4, 1857, President James Buchanan announced that the constitutional issues associated with the struggle between proslavery and antislavery forces in Kansas would soon be "speedily and finally settled" by the judicial branch of the federal government. Two days later the Supreme Court announced its decision in the case of *Dred Scott v. Sandford*, which the Court had accepted for review in 1854. Scott had been the slave of Dr. John Emerson, a surgeon in the U.S. Army. While on active duty, Emerson had taken Scott to Illinois in 1834 and to the upper Louisiana Purchase territory in 1836 and then had returned to Missouri. Slavery had been excluded in Illinois by the Northwest Ordinance of 1787 and from the upper Louisiana Purchase territory by the Missouri Compromise of 1820. In his suit Scott claimed to have been freed by reason of his residence in free territory (see text pp. 438–439). The Supreme Court's decision came in nine separate decisions, two in dissent. But it was the wideranging opinion of Chief Justice Roger B. Taney that was popularly considered the decision of the Court. Taney had been in correspondence with Buchanan before his inaugural address. In his decision Taney endeavored to provide a final settlement to the question of slavery.

Source: Dred Scott v. Sandford, 19 How. 393 (1857).

Chief Justice Taney delivered the opinion of the Court.

The question is simply this: Can a negro, whose ancestors were imported into this country, and sold as slaves, become a member of the political community formed and brought into existence by the constitution of the United States, and as such become entitled to all the rights, and privileges, and immunities, guaranteed by that instrument to the citizen? One of which rights is the privilege of suing in a court of the United States in the cases specified in the constitution. . . .

The words "people of the United States" and "citizens" are synonymous terms, and mean the same thing. They both describe the political body who, according to our republican institutions, form the sovereignty, and who hold the power and conduct the government through their representatives. They are what we familiarly call the "sovereign people," and every citizen is one of this people, and a constituent member of this sovereignty. The question before us is, whether the class of persons described in the plea in abatement compose a portion of this people, and are constituent members of this sovereignty? We think they are not, and that they are not included, and were not intended to be included, under the word "citizens" in the constitution, and can therefore claim none of the rights and privileges which that instrument provides for and secures to citizens of the United States. On the contrary, they were at that time considered as a subordinate and inferior class of beings, who had been subjugated by the dominant race, and, whether emancipated or not, yet remained subject to their authority, and had no rights or privileges but such as those who held the power and the government might choose to grant them. . . .

In discussing this question, we must not confound the rights of citizenship which a State may confer within its own limits, and the rights of citizenship as a member of the Union. It does not by any means follow, because he [Scott] has all the rights and privileges of a citizen of a State, that he must be a citizen of the United States. He may have all of the rights and privileges of the citizen of a State, and yet not be entitled to the rights and privileges of a citizen in any other State. For, previous to the adoption of the constitution of the United States, every State had the undoubted right to confer on whomsoever it pleased the character of citizen, and to endow him with all its rights. But this character of course was confined to the boundaries of the State, and gave him no rights or privileges in other States beyond those secured to him by the laws of nations and the comity of States. Nor have the several States surrendered the power of conferring these rights and privileges by adopting the constitution of the United States. . . .

It is very clear, therefore, that no State can, by any act or law of its own, passed since the adoption of the constitution, introduce a new member into the political community created by the constitution of the United States. It cannot make him a member of this community by making him a member of its own. And for the same reason it cannot introduce any person, or description of persons, who were not intended to be embraced in this new political family, which the constitution brought into existence, but were intended to be excluded from it.

The question then arises, whether the provisions of the constitution, in relation to the personal rights and privileges to which the citizen of a State should be entitled, embraced the negro African race, at that time in this country, or who might afterwards be imported, who had then or should afterwards be made free in any State; and to put it in the power of a single State to make him a citizen of the United States, and endue him with the full rights of citizenship in every other State without their consent? Does the constitution of the United States act upon him whenever he shall be made free under the laws of a State, and raised there to the rank of a citizen, and immediately clothe him with all the privileges of a citizen in every other State, and in its own courts?

In the opinion of the court, the legislation and histories of the times, and the language used in the declaration of independence, show, that neither the class of persons who had been imported as slaves, nor their descendants, whether they had become free or not, were then acknowledged as a part of the people, nor intended to be included in the general words used in that memorable instrument. . . .

It is too clear for dispute, that the enslaved African race were not intended to be included, and formed no part of the people who framed and adopted this declaration; for if the language, as understood in that day, would embrace them, the conduct of the distinguished men who framed the declaration of independence would have been utterly and flagrantly inconsistent with the principles they asserted; and instead of the sympathy of mankind, to which they so confidently appealed, they would have deserved and received universal rebuke and reprobation.

We proceed . . . to inquire whether the facts relied on by the plaintiff entitled him to his freedom. . . .

The act of Congress, upon which the plaintiff relies, declares that slavery and involuntary servitude, except as a punishment for crime, shall be forever prohibited in all that part of the territory ceded by France, under the name of Louisiana, which lies north of thirty-six degrees thirty minutes north latitude and not included within the limits of Missouri. And the difficulty which meets us at the threshold of this part of the inquiry is whether Congress was authorized to pass this law under any of the powers granted to it by the Constitution; for, if the authority is not given by that instrument, it is the duty of this Court to declare it void and inoperative and incapable of conferring freedom upon anyone who is held as a slave under the laws of any one of the states.

The counsel for the plaintiff has laid much stress upon that article in the Constitution which confers on Congress the power "to dispose of and make all needful rules and regulations respecting the territory or other property belonging to the United States"; but, in the judgment of the Court, that provision has no bearing on the present controversy, and the power there given, whatever it may be, is confined, and was intended to be confined, to the territory which at that time belonged to, or was claimed by, the United States and was within their boundaries as settled by the [1783] treaty with Great Britain and can have no influence upon a territory afterward acquired from a foreign government. It was a special provision for a known and particular territory, and to meet a present emergency, and nothing more. . . .

. . . It may be safely assumed that citizens of the United States who migrate to a territory belonging to the people of the United States cannot be ruled as mere colonists, dependent upon the will of the general government, and to be governed by any laws it may think proper to impose. The principle upon which our governments rest, and upon which alone they continue to exist, is the union of states, sovereign and independent within their own limits in their internal and domestic concerns, and bound together as one people by a general government, possessing certain enumerated and restricted powers, delegated to it by the people of the several states, and exercising supreme authority within the scope of the powers granted to it, throughout the dominion of the United States. A power, therefore, in the general government to obtain and hold colonies and dependent territories, over which they might legislate without restriction, would be inconsistent with its own existence in its present form. Whatever it acquires, it acquires for the benefit of the people of the several states who created it. It is their trustee acting for them and charged with the duty of promoting the interests of the whole people of the Union in the exercise of the powers specifically granted. . . .

But the power of Congress over the person or property of a citizen can never be a mere discretionary power under our Constitution and form of government. The powers of the government and the rights and privileges of the citizen are regulated and plainly defined by the Constitution itself. And, when the territory becomes a part of the United States, the federal government enters into possession in the character impressed upon it by those who created it. It enters upon it with its powers over the citizen strictly defined and limited by the Constitution, from which it derives its own existence, and by virtue of which alone it continues to exist and act as a government and sovereignty. . . .

Upon these considerations it is the opinion of the Court that the act of Congress which prohibited a citizen from holding and owning property of this kind in the territory of the United States north of the line therein mentioned is not warranted by the Constitution and is therefore void; and that neither Dred Scott himself, nor any of his family, were made free by being carried into this territory; even if they had been carried there by the owner with the intention of becoming a permanent resident.

Questions

1. What did the Court decide about whether a slave had standing to sue in a federal court?
2. If the Court lacked jurisdiction, why do you think Chief Justice Taney went ahead and dealt with the merits? Why did he not just say: "This Court lacks jurisdiction; case dismissed"?
3. What status does Tancy say slaves enjoyed at the time the Constitution was adopted?

Questions for Further Thought

1. What were the fundamental constitutional conflicts concerning slavery that increasingly divided the North and the South?
2. In what ways did the question of fugitive slaves interject moral issues in matters of constitutional law? Could morality and law be disengaged? Why or why not?
3. Consider why moderate efforts to settle the issue of slavery failed.

Abraham Lincoln and the Breaking of Union, 1858–1860

With the death of Henry Clay and the disintegration of the Whig party, Stephen Douglas, a Democrat from Illinois, had emerged as the leading political figure in the North. The "Little Giant" had shepherded the Kansas-Nebraska Act through Congress to facilitate the building of the transcontinental railroad. But to achieve this Douglas had been forced to permit southerners to bring slaves into the part of the Louisiana Territory that had been closed to slavery by the Missouri Compromise of 1820 (see text p. 433).

To calm angry northerners, Douglas had put forth the notion of popular sovereignty (see text pp. 441–442), which on the surface seemed an ideal solution. Let the people of the territory involved decide for themselves whether they wanted to have slavery. If they did, that was their democratic choice; if not, that also expressed the people's will.

But the *Dred Scott* decision undercut the notion of popular sovereignty, since Chief Justice Taney's opinion seemed to say that it did not matter what the people wanted: slaves were property, and therefore their owners had rights that could not be diminished by either Congressional action or the decision of a local majority.

The Republican party gained in strength in response to the Kansas-Nebraska Act and the *Dred Scott* decision, and various politicians began jockeying for the Republican presidential nomination of 1860 (see text pp. 444–445). One of the leading candidates was the former Illinois congressman Abraham Lincoln, who had run against Stephen Douglas for the Senate in 1858. In that campaign Douglas had debated Lincoln in several Illinois towns, and at Freeport they had discussed the question of under what circumstances slavery could be allowed into the territories (Document 14-9).

By 1860 time was running out, and when a messianical fanatic named John Brown attempted to instigate a rebellion to free the slaves (see text pp. 443–444 and Document 14-10), the Union seemed doomed.

14-9　The Lincoln-Douglas Debates (1858)

Stephen Douglas had tried to finesse the issue of slavery in the territories with his theory of popular sovereignty, by which the people could decide. But the *Dred Scott* decision seemed to cut the ground from under his argument. When Lincoln and Douglas ran for the Senate in 1858, they engaged in a series of debates (see text pp. 443–444). At Freeport, Lincoln put the issue to him squarely, and Douglas attempted to resolve the seeming inconsistencies between the Court's ruling and his own political views.

Source: In Alonzo T. Jones, ed., *Political Speeches and Debates of Abraham Lincoln and Stephen A. Douglas, 1854–1861* (Battle Creek, Mich., 1895).

LINCOLN'S OPENING SPEECH

As to the first one, in regard to the fugitive slave law, I have never hesitated to say, and I do not now hesitate to say, that I think, under the Constitution of the United States, the people of the southern states are entitled to a congressional fugitive slave law. Having said that, I have had nothing to say in regard to the existing fugitive slave law further than that I think it should have been framed so as to be free from some of the objections that pertain to it, without lessening its efficiency. And inasmuch as we are not not now in an agitation in regard to an alteration or modification of that law, I would not be the man to introduce it as a new subject of agitation upon the general question of slavery.

In regard to the other question of whether I am pledged to the admission of any more slave states into the Union, I state to you very frankly that I would be exceedingly sorry ever to be put in a position of having to pass upon that question. I should be exceedingly glad to know that there would never be another slave state admitted into the Union; . . . but I must add, that if slavery shall be kept out of the territories during the territorial existence of any one given territory, and then the people shall, having a fair chance and a clear field, when they come to adopt the constitution, do such an extraordinary thing as to adopt a slave constitution, uninfluenced by the actual presence of the institution among them, I see no alternative, if we own the country, but to admit them into the Union. . . .

The fourth one is in regard to the abolition of slavery in the District of Columbia. In relation to that, I have my mind very distinctly made up. I should be exceedingly glad to see slavery abolished in the District of Columbia. . . . I believe that Congress possesses the constitutional power to abolish it. Yet as a member of Congress, I should not with my present views, be in favor of *endeavoring* to abolish slavery in the District of Columbia, unless it would be upon these conditions. *First,* that the abolition should be gradual. *Second,* that it should be on a vote of the majority of qualified voters in the District, and *third,* that compensation should be made to unwilling owners. With these three conditions, I confess I would be exceedingly glad to see Congress abolish slavery in the District of Columbia, and, in the language of Henry Clay, "sweep from our Capital that foul blot upon our nation." . . .

My answer as to whether I desire that slavery should be prohibited in all the territories of the United States is full and explicit within itself, and cannot be made clearer by any comments of mine. So I suppose in regard to the question of whether I am opposed to the acquisition of any more territory unless slavery is first prohibited therein, my answer is such that I could add nothing by way of illustration, or making myself better understood, than the answer which I have placed in writing. . . .

I now proceed to propound to the Judge the interrogatories, as far as I have framed them. . . . The first one is—

Question 1. If the people of Kansas shall, by means entirely unobjectionable in all other respects, adopt a state constitution, and ask admission into the Union under it, *before* they have the requisite number of inhabitants according to the English Bill—some ninety-three thousand—will you vote to admit them? . . .

Q. 2. Can the people of a United States territory, in any lawful way, against the wish of any citizen of the United States, exclude slavery from its limits prior to the formation of a state constitution? . . .

Q. 3. If the Supreme Court of the United States shall decide that states can not exclude slavery from their limits, are you in favor of acquiescing in, adopting and following such decision as a rule of political action? . . .

Q. 4. Are you in favor of acquiring additional territory, in disregard of how such acquisition may affect the nation on the slavery question? . . .

DOUGLAS'S REPLY

In a few moments I will proceed to review the answers which he has given to these interrogatories; but in order to relieve his anxiety I will first respond to those which he has presented to me. . . .

First, he desires to know if the people of Kansas shall form a constitution by means entirely proper and unobjectionable and ask admission into the Union as a state, before they have the requisite population for a member of Congress, whether I will vote for that admission. . . . In reference to Kansas; it is my opinion, that as she has population enough to constitute a slave state, she has people enough for a free state. . . . I will not make Kansas an exceptional case to the other states of the Union. ("Sound," and "hear, hear.") I hold it to be a sound rule of universal application to require a territory to contain the requisite population for a member of Congress, before it is admitted as a state into the Union. I made that proposition in the Senate in 1856, and I renewed it during the last session, in a bill providing that no territory of the United States should form a constitution and apply for admission until it had the requisite population. . . .

The next question propounded to me by Mr. Lincoln is, can the people of a territory in any lawful way against the wishes of any citizen of the United States; [*sic*] exclude slavery from their limits prior to the formation of a state constitution? I answer emphatically, as Mr. Lincoln has heard me answer a hundred times from every stump in Illinois, that in my opinion the people of a territory can, by lawful means, exclude slavery from their limits prior to the formation of a state constitution. . . . Mr. Lincoln knew that I had answered that question over and over again. He heard me argue the Nebraska Bill on that principle all over the state in 1854, in 1855 and in 1856, and he has no ex-

cuse for pretending to be in doubt as to my position on that question. It matters not what way the Supreme Court may hereafter decide as to the abstract question whether slavery may or may not go into a territory under the Constitution, the people have the lawful means to introduce it or exclude it as they please, for the reason that slavery cannot exist a day or an hour anywhere, unless it is supported by local police regulations. . . . Those police regulations can only be established by the local legislature, and if the people are opposed to slavery they will elect representatives to that body who will by unfriendly legislation effectually prevent the introduction of it into their midst. If, on the contrary, they are for it, their legislation will favor its extension. Hence, no matter what the decision of the Supreme Court may be on that abstract question, still the right of the people to make a slave territory or a free territory is perfect and complete under the Nebraska Bill. I hope Mr. Lincoln deems my answer satisfactory on that point. . . .

The third question which Mr. Lincoln presented is, if the Supreme Court of the United States shall decide that a state of this Union cannot exclude slavery from its own limits will I submit to it? I am amazed that Lincoln should ask such a question. . . . Yes, a school boy does know better. Mr. Lincoln's object is to cast an imputation upon the Supreme Court. He knows that there never was but one man in America, claiming any degree of intelligence or decency, who ever for a moment pretended such a thing. It is true that the Washington *Union*, in an article published on the 17th of last December, did put forth that doctrine, and I denounced the article on the floor of the Senate. . . .

The fourth question of Mr. Lincoln is, are you in favor of acquiring additional territory in disregard as to how such acquisition may affect the Union on the slavery question. This question is very ingeniously and cunningly put. . . .

The Black Republican creed lays it down expressly, that under no circumstances shall we acquire any more territory unless slavery is first prohibited in the country. I ask Mr. Lincoln whether he is in favor of that proposition. Are you (addressing Mr. Lincoln) opposed to the acquisition of any more territory, under any circumstances, unless slavery is prohibited in it? That he does not like to answer. When I ask him whether he stands up to that article in the platform of his party, he turns, Yankee-fashion, and without answering it, asks me whether I am in favor of acquiring territory without regard to how it may affect the Union on the slavery question. . . . I answer that whenever it becomes necessary, in our growth and progress to acquire more territory, that I am in favor of it, without reference to the question of slavery, and when we have acquired it, I will leave the people free to do as they please, either to make it slave or free territory, as they prefer. . . . It is idle to tell me or you that we have territory enough. Our fathers supposed that we had enough when our territory extended to the Mississippi River, but a few years' growth and expansion satisfied them that we needed more, and the Louisiana territory, from the west branch of the Mississippi, to the British possessions, was acquired. Then we acquired Oregon, then California and New Mexico. We have enough now for the present, but this is a young and a growing nation. It swarms as often as a hive of bees, and as new swarms are turned out each year, there must be hives in which they can gather and make their honey.

Questions

1. Which speaker in this exchange do you think is more consistent in his arguments? Why?
2. Does it seem that Lincoln is speaking primarily to one part of the country, and Douglas to the other? Explain.
3. Does Lincoln oppose slavery completely? If not, what is his position?

14-10   The Trial of John Brown

Lincoln and the Republicans tried to reassure the South that they did not want to disturb slavery where it existed but only to halt its spread. Then came John Brown's attempt to raid the government arsenal at Harpers Ferry and trigger a massive slave rebellion (see text pp. 443–444). Although Republican leaders disavowed his action, private letters showed that he had had support from prominent abolitionists. Brown was tried and convicted of treason, and his statement before sentencing has become a classic (see text p. 414). He was hanged on December 2, 1859, and abolitionists, as Emerson said, now had a "new saint." Slaveholders blamed Republican ideas for the raid and more than ever feared a Republican presidential victory.

Source: The Life, Trial and Execution of Captain John Brown . . . (New York: R. M. DeWitt, 1859), pp. 94–95.

The clerk then asked Mr. Brown whether he had anything to say why sentence should not be pronounced upon him.

Mr. Brown immediately rose, and in a clear, distinct voice, said:

I have, may it please the Court, a few words to say. In the first place, I deny everything but what I have all along admitted, of a design on my part to free slaves. I intended certainly to have made a clean thing of that matter, as I did last winter when I went into Missouri, and there took slaves without the snapping of a gun on either side, moving them through the country, and finally leaving them in Canada. I designed to have done the same thing again on a larger scale. That was all I intended to do. I never did intend murder or treason, or the destruction of property, or to excite or incite the slaves to rebellion, or to make insurrection. I have another objection, and that is that it is unjust that I should suffer such a penalty. Had I interfered in the manner which I admit, and which I admit has been fairly proved—for I admire the truthfulness and candor of the greater portion of the witnesses who have testified in this case—had I so interfered in behalf of the rich, the powerful, the intelligent, the so-called great, or in behalf of any of their friends, either father, mother, brother, sister, wife, or children, or any of that class, and suffered and sacrificed what I have in this interference, it would have been all right, and every man in this Court would have deemed it an act worthy of reward rather than punishment. This Court acknowledges, too, as I suppose, the validity of the law of God. I see a book kissed, which I suppose to be the Bible, or at least the New Testament, which teaches me that all things whatsoever I would that men should do to me, I should do even so to them. It teaches me further to remember them that are in bonds as bound with them. I endeavored to act up to that instruction. I say I am yet too young to understand that God is any respecter of persons. I believe that to have interfered as I have done, as I have always freely admitted I have done in behalf of His despised poor, is no wrong, but right. Now, if it is deemed necessary that I should forfeit my life for the furtherance of the ends of justice, and mingle my blood further with the blood of my children and with the blood of millions in this slave country whose rights are disregarded by wicked, cruel, and unjust enactments, I say let it be done. Let me say one word further. I feel entirely satisfied with the treatment I have received on my trial. Considering all the circumstances, it has been more generous than I expected. But I feel no consciousness of guilt. I have stated from the first what was my intention, and what was not. I never had any design against the liberty of any person, nor any disposition to commit treason or excite slaves to rebel or make any general insurrection. I never encouraged any man to do so, but always discouraged any idea of that kind. Let me say also in regard to statements made by some of those who were connected with me, I fear it has been stated by some of them that I have induced them to join me, but the contrary is true. I do not say this to injure them, but as regretting their weakness. Not one but joined me of his own accord, and the greater part at their own expense. A number of them I never saw, and never had a word of conversation with till the day they came to me, and that was for the purpose I have stated. Now, I am done.

While Mr. Brown was speaking, perfect quiet prevailed, and when he had finished the Judge proceeded to pronounce sentence upon him. After a few primary remarks, he said, that no reasonable doubt could exist of the guilt of the prisoner, and sentenced him to be hung in public, on Friday, the 2d of December next.

Mr. Brown received his sentence with composure.

Questions

1. Do you think Brown really meant to free so many slaves without firing a shot? If so, why did he seize the arsenal?
2. Was Brown making a legal argument, or was he appealing to a "higher authority"?
3. Does it appear to you that Brown was seeking martyrdom? Why or why not?

Questions for Further Thought

1. Do you think that the Douglas formula for popular sovereignty (Document 14-9) was enough to satisfy slave owners by 1858? Why or why not?
2. Why did the *Dred Scott* decision (Document 14-8) mean so much politically to Lincoln and Doug-las?
3. It has been argued that John Brown's raid in 1859 (Document 14-10) and the election of Abraham Lincoln a year later were key events in the South's decision to secede. What in these two men's actions and utterances so alarmed the South? Do you think the southern reaction was justified or overblown?

CHAPTER 15

Two Societies at War
1861–1865

★   ★   ★

Choosing Sides, 1861 and War Machines, North and South

The election of Abraham Lincoln in 1860 signaled the end of southern planters' hopes of a federal guarantee of their right to hold property in slaves (see text p. 449). The best slave owners could expect under Republican party rule was the confinement of slavery to existing slave states. But many Republicans spoke of ending the interstate slave trade, repealing the Fugitive Slave Act, and, through judicial appointments, reversing the *Dred Scott* decision. The future stability of southern slavery, if not its immediate existence, seemed threatened.

South Carolina, long a hotbed of secessionist sentiment, led the way in leaving the Union and was quickly followed by the rest of the Lower South: Georgia, Florida, Alabama, Mississippi, Louisiana, and Texas. In February 1861 the seven seceded states joined together as the new Confederate States of America. The new union of states elected Jefferson Davis as its president and Alexander Stephens as its vice-president (Document 15-1).

Lincoln took office on March 4, 1861, determined to resist secession but uncertain how to proceed in a manner that would assert federal resolve but minimize further defections among the states of the Upper South (see text p. 452). The status of Fort Sumter in Charleston harbor tested the will of Confederates and federals alike. When Lincoln announced his decision to resupply the federal garrison, Confederate forces began an artillery bombardment that forced the garrison's surrender (see text p. 451). The firing on Fort Sumter, as both sides understood, marked the beginning of a civil war (Document 15-2).

In mobilizing for war, Abraham Lincoln and Jefferson Davis faced similar challenges: recruiting troops, suppressing dissent, and paying the enormous costs of the conflict. The Union had significant advantages in human and material resources—if its citizens were willing to fight a total war. But many in the North opposed the war, especially after the Enrollment Act imposed conscription in 1863. The suppression of the

New York City draft riots in July 1863 (see text pp. 456–457) demonstrated the depth of the war's unpopularity as well as the extraordinary measures the federal government was willing to adopt to preserve the Union (Document 15-3). The federal government could crush dissent because a sizable majority in the North supported the Union's military cause and served in public and private capacities to achieve victory. The Civil War left in its wake a significantly larger and stronger central government (see text p. 459), but much of the work of maintaining home-front morale and mobilizing the civilian population had been done by private voluntary organizations, most notably the United States Sanitary Commission, which brought the energies of northern women to bear on the war effort (see text pp. 459–460 and Document 15-4).

15-1 Alexander Stephens's "Cornerstone" Speech (March 1861)

Southern secessionists were deeply concerned about the support of non-slaveholding whites for their cause. Secessionists claimed that they were fighting for liberty and justice, but what stake did southern yeomen have in the concerns of slaveholders? At the heart of southern society was the paradoxical notion that slavery was the basis for the liberty of whites. Without slavery, secessionists argued, poor whites would assume the menial status of inferior blacks because they would no longer belong to the "aristocracy" of the white race. In March 1861 the Confederate vice-president, Alexander Stephens, attempted to outline the basis of the southern cause to a friendly audience in Savannah, Georgia (see text p. 453). (The text of the speech is taken from a newspaper report published the following day.)

Source: Henry Cleveland, *Alexander H. Stephens in Public and Private* (Philadelphia: National Publishing Company, 1866), pp. 717–729.

. . . The new constitution [of the Confederacy] has put at rest, *forever*, all the agitating questions relating to our peculiar institution—African slavery as it exists amongst us—the proper *status* of the negro in our form of civilization. This was the immediate cause of the late rupture and present revolution. Jefferson in his forecast, had anticipated this, as the "rock upon which the old Union would split." He was right. What was conjecture with him, is now a realized fact. But whether he fully comprehended the great truth upon which that rock *stood* and *stands*, may be doubted. The prevailing ideas entertained by him and most of the leading statesmen at the time of the formation of the old constitution, were that the enslavement of the African was in violation of the laws of nature; that it was wrong in *principle*, socially, morally, and politically. It was an evil they knew not well how to deal with, but the general opinion of the men of that day was that, somehow or other in the order of Providence, the institution would be evanescent and pass away. This idea, though not incorporated in the constitution, was the prevailing idea at that time. The constitution, it is true, secured every essential guarantee to the institution while it should last, and hence no argument can be justly urged against the constitutional guarantees thus secured, because of the common sentiment of the day. Those ideas, however, were fundamentally wrong. They rested upon the assumption of the equality of races. This was an error. It was a sandy foundation, and the government built upon it fell when the "storm came and the wind blew."

Our new government is founded upon exactly the opposite idea; its foundations are laid, its corner-stone rests upon the great truth, that the negro is not equal to the white man; that slavery—subordination to the superior race—is his natural and normal condition. [Applause.] . . .

It is the first government ever instituted upon the principles in strict conformity to nature, and the ordination of Providence, in furnishing the materials of human society. Many governments have been founded upon the principle of the subordination and serfdom of certain classes of the same race; such were and are in violation of the laws of nature. Our system commits no such violation of nature's laws. With us, all of the white race, however high or low, rich or poor, are equal in the eye of the law. Not so with the negro. Subordination is his place. He, by nature, or by the curse against Canaan, is fitted for that condition which he occupies in our system. The architect, in the construction of buildings, lays the foundation with the proper material—the granite; then comes the brick or the marble. The substratum of our society is made of the material fitted by nature for it, and by experience we know that it is best, not only for the superior, but for the inferior race, that it should be so. It is, indeed, in conformity with the ordinance of the Creator. It is not for us to inquire into the wisdom of his ordinances, or to question them. For his own purposes, he has made one race to differ from another, as he has made "one star to differ from another star in glory."

The great objects of humanity are best attained when there is conformity to his laws and decrees, in the formation of governments as well as in all things else. Our confederacy is founded upon principles in strict conformity with these laws. This stone which was rejected by the first builders "is become the chief of the corner"—the real "corner-stone"—in our new edifice. [Applause.] . . .

Questions

1. Which ideas held by Jefferson and the other Founders does Stephens condemn as "fundamentally wrong"?
2. In Stephens's view, what is the cornerstone of the Confederate government? Of southern society?
3. Why did Stephens think it was necessary for the Confederacy to repudiate the principles of the Founders?

15-2 The Crisis at Fort Sumter (April 1861)

When South Carolina seceded from the United States on December 20, 1860, the construction of Fort Sumter, on an island in Charleston harbor, was not complete and the fort had not yet been occupied by federal troops. On December 26, however, the federal commander in Charleston, Major Robert Anderson, consolidated his forces (fewer than a hundred men) at the new fort. Anderson's force could not be easily defeated, but it also could not be easily reenforced or resupplied. On March 1, 1861, General P. G. T. Beauregard assumed command of Confederate forces at Charleston; on March 4 Lincoln became president of the United States. Throughout the month of March the crisis at Fort Sumter grew increasingly tense (see text p. 451). On April 6 Lincoln announced a "humanitarian" effort to resupply the fort. On April 9 the Confederate president, Jefferson Davis, ordered Beauregard to capture the fort. The Confederate bombardment began on April 12 at 4:30 A.M. Anderson surrendered on April 14, and on April 15 Lincoln called on the states to send 75,000 troops to suppress the insurrection. The Civil War had begun.

The wife of James C. Chesnut, a wealthy planter and prominent southern politician, Mary Chesnut (see American Voices in Chapter 13 of the textbook, p. 387), began her diary as the war clouds gathered and ended it when the Confederacy collapsed under the pressure of the advancing Union armies. Surrounded by the leaders of the Confederate cause, Mary Chesnut epitomized the aristocratic southern lady: charming in manners, clever in conversation, and modest in deferring to the public life of the men around her. In her diary, however, she revealed her independent cast of mind and deep misgivings about the Confederate cause.

Source: Excerpted from C. Vann Woodward, ed., *Mary Chesnut's Civil War* (New Haven and London: Yale University Press, 1981), pp. 35–53.

March 26, 1861. Charleston. Yesterday we came down here by rail, as the English say. . . .

March 31, 1861 . . . At church today, saw one of the peculiar local traits—old Negro maumeys going up to the communion in their white turbans.

Being the Lord's table—so-called. Even there—black, white, and brown, separate according to caste. . . .

No war yet, thank God. . . .

There stands Fort Sumter . . . and thereby hangs peace or war. . . .

April 6, 1861. The plot thickens. The air is red-hot with rumors. The mystery is to find out where these utterly groundless tales originate. . . .

April 7, 1861 . . . [Former] Governor [John Laurence] Manning walked in, bowed gravely, and seated himself by me.

Again he bowed low, in mock heroic style and, with a grand wave of his hand said, "Madame, your country is invaded."

When I had breath to speak, I asked, "What does he mean?"

"He means this. There are six men-of-war outside of the bar. . . . Governor [Francis Wilkinson] Pickens and [General P. G. T.] Beauregard are holding a council of war."

Mr. [James C.] Chesnut then came in. He confirmed the story.

[Louis Trezevant] Wigfall next entered in boisterous spirits. . . .

In any stir or confusion, my heart is apt to beat so painfully. Now the agony was so stifling—I could hardly see or hear. The men went off almost immediately. And I crept silently to my room, where I sat down to a good cry.

Mrs. Wigfall came in, and we had it out on the subject of civil war. We solaced ourselves with dwelling on all its known horrors, and then we added what we had a right to expect, with Yankees in front and negroes in the rear.

"The slave-owners must expect a servile insurrection, of course," said Mrs. Wigfall, to make sure that we were unhappy enough. . . . Ammunition wagons rumbling along the streets all night. Anderson burning blue lights—signs and signals for the fleet outside, I suppose.

Today at dinner there was no allusion to things as they

stand in Charleston Harbor. There was an undercurrent of intense excitement. . . . In earnest, [former] Governor Means rummaged a sword and red sash from somewhere and brought it for Colonel Chesnut, who has gone to demand the surrender of Fort Sumter.

And now, patience—we must wait.

Why did that green goose Anderson go into Fort Sumter? Then everything began to go wrong. . . .

April 12, 1861. Anderson will not capitulate. . . .

I do not pretend to go to sleep. How can I? If Anderson does not accept terms—at four—the orders are—he shall be fired upon.

I count four—St. Michael chimes. I begin to hope. At half-past four, the heavy booming of a cannon.

I sprang out of bed. And on my knees—prostrate—I prayed as I never prayed before.

There was a sound of stir all over the house—pattering of feet in the corridor—all seemed hurrying one way. I put on my double gown and a shawl and went, too. It was to the housetop.

The shells were bursting. In the dark I heard a man say "waste of ammunition."

I knew my husband was rowing about in a boat somewhere in that dark bay. And that the shells were roofing it over—bursting toward the fort. If Anderson was obstinate—he [Chesnut] was to order the forts on our side to open fire. Certainly fire had begun. The regular roar of the cannon—there it was. And who could tell what each volley accomplished of death and destruction. . . .

April 13, 1861 . . . Not by one word or look can we detect any change in the demeanor of these negro servants. Laurence sits at our door, as sleepy and as respectful and as profoundly indifferent. So are they all. They carry it too far. You could not tell that they hear even the awful row that is going on in the bay, though it is dinning in their ears night and day. And people talk before them as if they were chairs and tables. And they make no sign. Are they stolidly stupid or wiser than we are, silent and strong, biding their time? . . .

April 15, 1861. I did not know that one could live such days of excitement. . . .

And so we took Fort Sumter.

Questions

1. Unlike the men around her, Chesnut appears to be fearful of war. Why?
2. Does Chesnut seem confident and comfortable as part of the slave-holding elite? Explain why or why not.
3. Why are the slaves quiet and subdued during the bombardment of Fort Sumter?

15-3 The New York City Draft Riots (July 1863)

Anna Elizabeth Dickinson

When the Union instituted conscription in 1863, it allowed men to avoid the draft if they could provide a substitute or pay a $300 fee—over half an average worker's annual income. Democratic opponents of Lincoln exploited resentment over the high fee to win support from recent immigrants and the urban poor. In July 1863 riots against the draft exploded in New York City (see text pp. 456–457). The following description of the riots is by Anna Dickinson, who was involved in the antislavery and women's rights movements. Her account is no exaggeration; the rioting was finally suppressed on the fourth day by troops from the Army of the Potomac.

Source: Anna Elizabeth Dickinson, *What Answer?* (Boston, 1868), pp. 242–259.

On the morning of Monday, the thirteenth of July, began this outbreak, unparalleled in atrocities by anything in American history, and equalled only by the horrors of the worst days of the French Revolution. Gangs of men and boys, composed of railroad *employees*, workers in machine-shops, and a vast crowd of those who lived by preying upon others, thieves, pimps, professional ruffians,—the scum of the city,—jail-birds, or those who were running with swift feet to enter the prison-doors, began to gather on the corners, and in streets and alleys where they lived; from thence issuing forth they visited the great establishments on the line of their advance, commanding their instant clos[ing] and the companionship of the workmen,—many of them peaceful and orderly men,—on pain of the destruction of one and a murderous assault upon the other, did not their orders meet with instant compliance.

A body of these, five or six hundred strong, gathered about one of the enrolling-offices in the upper part of the city, where the draft was quietly proceeding, and opened the assault upon it by a shower of clubs, bricks, and paving-stones torn from the streets, following it up by a furious rush into the office. Lists, records, books, the drafting-wheel, every article of furniture or work in the room was rent in pieces, and strewn about the floor or flung into the street; while the law officers, the newspaper reporters,—who are expected to be everywhere,—and the few peaceable spectators, were compelled to make a hasty retreat through an opportune rear exit, accelerated by the curses and blows of the assailants.

A safe in the room, which contained some of the hated records, was fallen upon by the men, who strove to wrench open its impregnable lock with their naked hands, and, baffled, beat them on its iron doors and sides till they were stained with blood, in a mad frenzy of senseless hate and fury. And then, finding every portable article destroyed,—their thirst for ruin growing by the little drink it had had,—and believing, or rather hoping, that the officers had taken refuge in the upper rooms, set fire to the house, and stood watching the slow and steady lift of the flames, filling the air with demoniac shrieks and yells, while they waited for the prey to escape from some door or window, from the merciless fire to their merciless hands. One of these, who was on the other side of the street, courageously stepped forward, and, telling them that they had utterly demolished all they came to seek, informed them that helpless women and little children were in the house, and besought them to extinguish the flames and leave the ruined premises; to disperse, or at least to seek some other scene.

By his dress recognizing in him a government official, so far from hearing or heeding his humane appeal, they set upon him with sticks and clubs, and beat him till his eyes were blind with blood, and he—bruised and mangled—succeeded in escaping to the handful of police who stood helpless before this howling crew, now increased to thousands. With difficulty and pain the inoffensive tenants escaped from the rapidly spreading fire, which, having devoured the house originally lighted, swept across the neighboring buildings till the whole block stood a mass of burning flames. The firemen came up tardily and reluctantly, many of them of the same class as the miscreants who surrounded them, and who cheered at their approach, but either made no attempt to perform their duty, or so feeble and farcical a one, as to bring disgrace upon a service they so generally honor and ennoble.

At last, when there was nothing more to accomplish, the mob, swollen to a frightful size, including myriads of wretched, drunken women, and the half-grown, vagabond boys of the pavements, rushed through the intervening streets, stopping cars and insulting peaceable citizens on their way, to an armory where were manufactured and stored carbines and guns for the government. In anticipation of the attack, this, earlier in the day, had been fortified by a police squad capable of coping with an ordinary crowd of ruffians, but as chaff before fire in the presence of these murderous thousands. Here, as before, the attack was begun by a rain of missiles gathered from the streets;

less fatal, doubtless, than more civilized arms, but frightful in the ghastly wounds and injuries they inflicted. Of this no notice was taken by those who were stationed within; it was repeated. At last, finding they were treated with contemptuous silence, and that no sign of surrender was offered, the crowd swayed back,—then forward,—in a combined attempt to force the wide entrance-doors. Heavy hammers and sledges, which had been brought from forges and workshops, caught up hastily as they gathered the mechanics into their ranks, were used with frightful violence to beat them in,—at last successfully. The foremost assailants began to climb the stairs, but were checked, and for the moment driven back by the fire of the officers, who at last had been commanded to resort to their revolvers. A half-score fell wounded; and one, who had been acting in some sort as their leader,—a big, brutal, Irish ruffian,— dropped dead. . . .

Late in the afternoon a crowd which could have numbered not less than ten thousand, the majority of whom were ragged, frowzy, drunken women, gathered about the Orphan Asylum for Colored Children,—a large and beautiful building, and one of the most admirable and noble charities of the city. When it became evident, from the menacing cries and groans of the multitude, that danger, if not destruction, was meditated to the harmless and inoffensive inmates, a flag of truce appeared, and an appeal was made in their behalf, by the principal, to every sentiment of humanity which these beings might possess,—a vain appeal! Whatever human feeling had ever, if ever, filled these souls was utterly drowned and washed away in the tide of rapine and blood in which they had been steeping themselves. The few officers who stood guard over the doors, and manfully faced these demoniac legions, were beaten down and flung to one side, helpless and stunned,

whilst the vast crowd rushed in. All the articles upon which they could seize—beds, bedding, carpets, furniture,—the very garments of the fleeing inmates, some of these torn from their persons as they sped by—were carried into the streets, and hurried off by the women and children who stood ready to receive the goods which their husbands, sons, and fathers flung to their care. The little ones, many of them, assailed and beaten; all,—orphans and care-takers,—exposed to every indignity and every danger, driven on to the street,—the building was fired. This had been attempted whilst the helpless children— some of them scarce more than babies—were still in their rooms. . . .

By far the most infamous part of these cruelties was that which wreaked every species of torture and lingering death upon the colored people of the city,—men, women, and children, old and young, strong and feeble alike. Hundreds of these fell victims to the prejudice fostered by public opinion, incorporated in our statute-books, sanctioned by our laws, which here and thus found legitimate outgrowth and action. . . .

It was absurd and futile to characterize this new Reign of Terror as anything but an effort on the part of Northern rebels to help Southern ones, at the most critical moment of the war,—with the State militia and available troops absent in a neighboring Commonwealth,—and the loyal people unprepared. These editors [of Democratic newspapers] and their coadjutors, men of brains and ability, were of that most poisonous growth,—traitors to the Government and the flag of their country,—renegade Americans. Let it, however, be written plainly and graven deeply, that the tribes of savages—the hordes of ruffians—found ready to do their loathsome bidding, were not of native growth, nor American born. . . .

Questions

1. According to Dickinson, what kinds of people made up the mobs?
2. Why did the mob attack blacks, including black children?
3. Why were the police and firemen so ineffective in stopping the riots and arson?

15-4 The Work of the United States Sanitary Commission (1864)

The United States Sanitary Commission represented the largest and most successful volunteer wartime activity in the North (see text pp. 459–460). The commission's founders intended to bring modern methods of sanitation to the treatment of sick and wounded soldiers and thereby avoid the devastating health problems that had plagued British and French troops during the Crimean War (1854–1856). In June 1861 the United States Sanitary Commission received official recognition from the War Department as a civilian agency supporting the Army Medical Bureau.

Sharply critical of traditional army methods, Sanitary Commission inspectors visited military encampments to direct latrine construction, food preparation, and the design of hospitals. Sanitary Commission activities dominated the home-front activities of northern women. Hundreds of volunteers organized "sanitary fairs" in northern cities to raise funds to supply soldiers with medical supplies, fresh fruits and vegetables, and nurses and doctors to assist in the care and evacuation of the wounded. Although the intrusion of civilians into military matters disturbed some commanders, the commission's popularity among the troops and its influence with Congress assured the success of its efforts.

Source: [Linus P. Brockett], *The Philanthropic Results of the War in America: Collected from Official and Other Authentic Sources, by an American Citizen* (New York: Sheldon & Co., 1864), pp. 32–42, 89–91.

The proclamation of the President [following the fall of Fort Sumter] . . . evoked the patriotic and earnest sympathies of the women of the nation, as well as those of the sterner sex. Everywhere fair hands were at work, and fair brows grew grave with thought, of what could be done for those who were going forth to fight the nation's battles. With the characteristic national fondness for organization, Ladies' Aid and Relief Societies were formed everywhere. One, "The Soldiers' Aid Society," at Cleveland, Ohio, bearing the date April 20, 1861, only five days after the President's proclamation; another at Philadelphia, "The Ladies' Aid Society," adopting its constitution on the 26th of April, and a third, "The Woman's Central Association of Relief, of New York," on the 30th of the same month. By the middle of May there were hundreds of these associations formed. As yet, however, they hardly knew what was to be done, or how, when, and where to do it. . . . The Woman's Central Association of Relief had among its officers some gentlemen of large experience in sanitary science, and of considerable knowledge of military hygiene, and they wisely gave a practical turn to its labors from the first. . . . Other organizations of gentlemen were attempting by . . . similar measures, to render assistance to the Government. . . . Fraternizing with each other . . . these associations resolved to send a joint delegation to Washington. . . .

On the 18th of May, 1861 . . . representatives of these . . . associations drew up and forwarded to the Secretary of War a communication setting forth the propriety of creating an organization which should unite the duties and labors of [these] associations, and co-operate with the Medical Bureau of the War Department . . . in securing the welfare of the army. For this purpose they asked that a mixed commission of civilians, military officers, and medical men, might be appointed by the Government, charged with the duty of methodizing and reducing to practical service the already active but undirected benevolence of the people. . . .

The President and Secretary of War were not at first disposed to look with any great favor upon this plan, which they regarded rather as a sentimental scheme concocted by women, clergymen, and humane physicians, than as one whose practical workings would prove of incalculable benefit to the army. . . . [But] when the Acting Surgeon-General asked for it, as a needed adjuvant to the Medical Bureau, likely soon to be overwhelmed by its new duties, they finally decided, though reluctantly, to permit its organization.

Accordingly the Secretary of War, on the 9th of June, decided on the creation of . . . "The United States Sanitary Commission." . . . After the Government had established its own permanent hospitals . . . a considerable number of the supplies were furnished by the Sanitary Commission. The value of these supplies furnished by private hands . . . has been carefully ascertained . . . [and] could not have been less in value than $2,200,000.

One of these hospitals, now under the charge of the Government, originated in the philanthropic spirit of the citizens of . . . Philadelphia. . . . After the great battles before Washington, in the summer of 1862 [the Second Battle of Bull Run], trains, freighted with the wounded, poured into Philadelphia, and no provisions having been made for their quiet and speedy transfer to the hospitals, most of which were at considerable distance, they were temporarily placed in churches. . . . The citizens of the vicinity, a large portion of them mechanics, laboring by day in the busy manufactories of that vicinity, were greatly distressed at witnessing this suffering, and resolved . . . to erect near the station-house a hospital for the temporary accommodation of sick and wounded soldiers. A landowner generously gave them the use of some vacant lots . . . others contributed lumber, furniture, heating apparatus, bath-tubs, and some, money. One poor Irishman wheeled a half-worn stove to the new hospital. "He had nothing else to give," he said, "and must do something for the sogers." The hospital was erected, and furnished with five hundred beds in fifteen days. . . .

The feeling of sympathy and patriotism which has actuated the masses of the people, manifested itself in numberless instances of thoughtfulness and tenderness, even from classes, among whom it was hardly to be looked for.

Questions

1. Why do you think the president and the secretary of war were initially leery of civilian involvement in aiding sick and wounded soldiers?
2. Even if these volunteer activities were not absolutely necessary to the Union cause, were they important in maintaining home-front morale? Explain why or why not.
3. What class of people did the writer of this document expect to respond to the Sanitary Commission's philanthropic appeal? Why?

Questions for Further Thought

1. Consider the options available to Major Robert Anderson in Charleston in the secession crisis and to President Lincoln after his inauguration. Were there alternatives that might have averted war?
2. If the only alternative to war was the federal government's acceptance of peaceful secession, should that have been permitted? Explain why or why not.
3. In a "total war" an entire society is involved in the outcome of a military struggle and the distinction between military and civilian spheres is blurred. In what ways did the New York City draft riots (Document 15-3) and the United States Sanitary Commission (Document 15-4) reveal that the North was engaged in a total war?
4. The home-front activities described in Documents 15-3 and 15-4 occurred in cities. In what ways was the urbanization of the North a military asset; in what ways was it a military liability?

Military Deadlock, 1861–1863

In 1861 and 1862 the Confederacy successfully prosecuted its limited, defensive war (see text p. 460). Its war aims were clear and constant—to turn back northern invasion and secure southern independence. The Confederacy's war aims were particularly successful in the East, where less than 150 miles separated the U.S. capital at Washington, D.C., from the new Confederate capital at Richmond, Virginia. The devastating defeat of federal forces near Washington, at the First Battle of Bull Run in July 1861 (see text pp. 460–461 and Document 15-5), buoyed Confederate hopes and caused northerners to reconsider their expectations for a swift victory.

As the war continued, Lincoln gradually assented to the advice of antislavery leaders and some of his generals and redefined northern war aims. The slaves of the South could not be ignored: wherever northern armies penetrated the Confederacy they encountered large numbers of slaves eager to support their masters' enemies. At the very least, these "contrabands" (see text p. 465) required the protection of federal forces. Eager to prepare downtrodden slaves for freedom, northern reformers followed Union armies into the South to aid and educate blacks behind Union lines (Document 15-6).

From the outset of the struggle the social consequences of defeat were clear to Confederates (Document 15-7). Most northerners were much slower to perceive the social consequences (and responsibilities) of victory. A full year of warfare preceded

Lincoln's announcement, on September 22, 1862, that he intended to end slavery in portions of the Confederacy on January 1, 1863 (see text pp. 465–466). The decisive Union victory at the battle of Gettysburg (July 1863) marked the military turning point of the war (see text pp. 467–470); Lincoln acknowledged the moment somberly but sternly in his brief Gettysburg Address (Document 15-8). The war to preserve the Union had become a war to expand liberty, equality, and democratic government.

15-5 A British Reporter Witnesses the First Battle of Bull Run (July 1861)

William Howard Russell

William Howard Russell, a special correspondent for the London *Times*, began his career in journalism in the early 1840s when he began publishing reports on events in Ireland. Russell wrote in a style that appeared to be unbiased, objective, and illuminating. When he covered the Crimean War, many of his letters to the London *Times* were also published in American newspapers. As civil war loomed on the horizon in the United States, Russell—now well known to Americans as a war correspondent—arrived in New York in March 1861. In April and June he toured the South, arriving in Charleston shortly after the fall of Fort Sumter. His southern tour ended in Washington, D.C., in July as the North and the South prepared for the first battle of the war. Russell's coverage of the Union defeat at Bull Run (see text pp. 460–461) angered many in the North, and the pro-Confederate sympathies of the London *Times* caused President Lincoln to deny Russell any special privileges. Without the ability to write the firsthand reports that had made him famous, Russell soon returned to England, where he published the diary of his American journey.

Source: William Howard Russell, *My Diary North and South* (London, 1863; reprinted, edited by Eugene H. Berwanger, New York: Knopf, 1988), pp. 257–277.

July 20th. The great battle which is to arrest rebellion, or to make it a power in the land, is no longer distant or doubtful. [General Irvin] McDowell has completed his reconnaissance of the country in front of the enemy and General [Winfield] Scott anticipates that he will be in possession of Manassas tomorrow night. All the statements of officers concur in describing the Confederates as strongly entrenched along the line of Bull's Run covering the railroad. . . . July 21st. . . . I swallowed a cup of tea and a morsel of bread . . . got a flask of light Bordeaux, a bottle of water, a paper of sandwiches, and having replenished my small flask with brandy, stowed them all away in the bottom of the gig . . . and thus through the deserted city we proceeded [across the Potomac into Virginia]. . . . [About] nine o'clock . . . I thought I heard . . . the well-known boom of a gun, followed by two or three in rapid succession. . . . "They are at it! We shall be late! Drive on as fast as you can!" . . . the sounds which came upon the breeze, and the fights which met our eyes, were in terrible variance with the tranquil character of the landscape. The woods far and near echoed to the roar of cannon, and then frayed

lines of blue smoke marked the spots whence came the muttering sound of rolling musketry; the white puffs of smoke burst high above the tree tops, and the gunners' rings from shell and howitzer marked the fire of the artillery. . . .

On the hill beside me there was a crowed of civilians on horseback and in all sorts of vehicles, with a few of the fairer, if not gentler sex. A few officers and some soldiers . . . from the regiments in reserve, moved about among the spectators and pretended to explain the movements of the troops below, of which they were profoundly ignorant. . . .

Loud cheers suddenly burst from the spectators as a man dressed in the uniform of an officer . . . galloped along the front . . . shouting at the top of his voice. . . . "We've whipped them on all points," he cried. "We have taken all their batteries. They are retreating as fast as they can, and we are after them". . . . I had ridden between three and a half and four miles [further] . . . when my attention was attracted by loud shouts in advance. . . . My first impression was that the wagons were returning for fresh supplies of ammunition. But every moment the crowd increased, drivers and men cried out with the most vehement gestures, "Turn back! Turn back! We are whipped".... A[n] ... officer ... confirmed the report that the whole army was in retreat and that the Federals were beaten on all points.... All these things took place in a few seconds. I got up out of the road into a cornfield, through which men were hastily walking or running, their faces streaming with perspiration, and generally without arms, and worked my way for about half a mile or so ... against an increasing stream of fugitives, the ground being strewed with coats, blankets, firelocks, cooking tins, caps, belts, bayonets.... [Then] the dreaded cry, "The cavalry! cavalry are coming!" rang through the crowd, and looking back to Centreville I perceived coming down the hill, between me and the sky, a number of mounted men, who might at a hasty glance be taken for horsemen in the act of sabering the fugitives. In reality they were soldiers and civilians with, I regret to say, some officers among them.... [To a] fellow who shouting out, "Run! run!" as loud as he could beside me ... I said, "What on earth are you running for? What are you afraid of?" He was in the roadside below me, and at once turning on me exclaimed, "I'm not afraid of you," presented his piece and pulled the trigger so instantaneously, that had it gone off I could not have swerved from the ball. As the scoundrel deliberately drew up to examine the [gun] ... I judged it best not to give him another chance and spurred on through the crowd....

And I continued through the wood till I got a clear space in front on the road, along which a regiment of infantry was advancing towards me. They halted ere I came up, and with leveled firelocks arrested the men on horses and the carts and wagons galloping towards them, and blocked the road to stop their progress.... [A] soldier pointed his firelock at my head from the higher ground on which he stood ... and sung out, "Halt! Stop—or I fire!" ... Bowing to the officer who was near me, I said ... "I am a civilian going to Washington; will you be kind enough to look at this pass, specially given to me by General Scott." The officer looked at it ... [a]nd with a cry of "Pass that man!" ... I ... very leisurely ... got out on the road.... July 22nd. I awoke from a deep sleep this morning, about six o'clock. The rain was falling in torrents ... but louder than all came a strange sound ... I saw a steady stream of men covered with mud, soaked through with rain, who were pouring irregularly, without any semblance of order up Pennsylvania Avenue towards the Capitol. A dense steam of vapour rose from the multitude.... Many of them were without knapsacks, crossbelts, and firelocks. Some had neither greatcoats nor shoes, others were covered with blankets.... I ran down stairs and asked an "officer" ... where the men were coming from. "Where from? Well, sir, I guess we're all coming out of Verginny as far as we can, and pretty well whipped too."

Questions

1. In what ways would an orderly retreat from Bull Run have differed from the scenes described by Russell?
2. How did the inexperience of the troops contribute to the confusion of the retreat?
3. What do you think the federal forces learned from the defeat at Bull Run?

15-6 A Northern Black Woman Teaches Contrabands in South Carolina (1862)

Charlotte Forten

In November 1861 federal gunboats forced the evacuation of the Confederate defenders of the Sea Islands region of South Carolina (between Charleston and Savannah on the Atlantic coast). The Sea Islands became a federal base in the Atlantic blockade of southern commerce. Confederate soldiers left the islands, as did the wealthy planters and their families. The slaves remained, sensing that the enemies of their masters would be their friends. With the federal government now in control of about 10,000 "contrabands" (see text p. 465) and some of the most productive cotton land in the South, the future development of the plantations and the fate of the laborers attracted immediate attention. The Treasury Department took control of the plantations and appointed superintendents to direct their operations. Northern abolitionists sent teachers into the region to educate the former slaves and prove them worthy of emancipation. One of the teachers was Charlotte Forten (1838–1914) of Philadelphia. For generations the Fortens had been abolitionist leaders in the black community. Charlotte Forten had taught in the nonsegregated public schools of Salem, Massachusetts, before visiting the Sea Islands. Her light complexion and northern ways raised suspicions at first, but she deemed her labors on the islands a success. From her journal she drafted a narrative of her experience to share with her friends. One friend, the poet John Greenleaf Whittier (see Document 14-5), arranged to have the piece published in the *Atlantic Monthly* in May and June 1864.

Source: Charlotte Forten, "Life on the Sea Islands," *Atlantic Monthly* 13 (May 1864 and June 1864), pp. 587–596, 666–676. In *Two Black Teachers during the Civil War* (New York: Arno Press and New York Times, 1969).

It was on the afternoon of a warm, murky day late in October that our steamer, the United States, touched the landing at Hilton head. A motley assemblage had collected on the wharf,—officers, soldiers, and "contrabands" of every size and hue: black was, however, the prevailing color. . . . It is wonderful with what ease they carry all sorts of things on their heads,—heavy bundles of wood, hoes and rakes, everything, heavy or light, that can be carried in the hands; and I have seen a woman, with a bucketful of water on her head, stoop down to take up another in her hand, without spilling a drop from either. We noticed that the people had much better taste in selecting materials for dresses than we had supposed. They do not generally like gaudy colors, but prefer neat, quiet patterns. They are, however, very fond of all kinds of jewelry. I once asked the children in school what their ears were for. "To put rings in," promptly replied one of the little girls.

These people are exceedingly polite in their manner towards each other, each new arrival bowing, scraping his feet, and shaking hands with the others, while there are constant greetings, such as, "Huddy? How's yer lady?" ("How d' ye do? How's your wife?"). The hand-shaking is performed with the greatest possible solemnity. There is never the faintest shadow of a smile on anybody's face during this performance. The children, too, are taught to be very polite to their elders, and it is the rarest thing to hear a disrespectful word from a child to his parent, or to any grown persons. They have really what the New-Englanders call "beautiful manners" . . . .

In the evenings, the children frequently come in to sing and shout for us. These "shouts" are very strange,—in truth, almost indescribable. It is necessary to hear and see in order to have any clear idea of them. The children form a ring, and move around in a kind of shuffling dance, singing all the time. Four or five stand apart, and sing very energetically, clapping their hands, stamping their feet and rocking their bodies to and fro. These are the musicians, to whose performance the shouters keep perfect time. . . . We cannot determine whether it has a religious character or not. Some of the people tell us that it has, others, that it has not. But as the shouts of the grown people are always in connection with their religious meetings, it is probable that they are the barbarous expression of religion, handed down to them from their African ancestors, and destined to pass away under the influence of Christian teachings. . . . Prince, a large black boy from a neighboring plantation, was the principal shouter among the children. . . . His performances were most amusing specimens of Ethiopian gymnastics. Amaretta . . . a cunning, kittenish little creature of only six years old, had a remarkably sweet voice. . . .

Daily the long-oppressed people of these islands are demonstrating their capacity for improvement in learning and labor. What they have accomplished in one short year exceeds our utmost expectations. . . . An old freedman said to me one day, "De Lord make me suffer long time, Miss. 'Peared like we nebber was gwine to get troo. But now we's free. He bring us all out right at las'." In their darkest hours they have clung to Him, and we know He will not forsake them.

Questions

1. What does Forten find most surprising about the people of the Sea Islands?
2. What strengths and weaknesses does she discern in the culture she encounters?
3. At the very moment of emancipation why does Forten feel the need to demonstrate the African-Americans' "capacity for improvement in learning and labor"?

15-7 A Soldier's Letter to His Wife (1862)

James B. Griffin

In 1861 James B. Griffin rode off to Virginia from Edgefield, South Carolina, in a style befitting a southern gentleman: on a fine blooded horse, with two slaves to wait on him, two trunks, and his favorite hunting dog. He joined the Army of Northern Virginia, where he served under P. G. T. Beauregard and Joseph E. Johnson. He was thirty-five years old, a wealthy planter, and the owner of sixty-one slaves when he joined Wade Hampton's elite legion as a major of cavalry. He left behind seven children, the eldest only twelve, and a wife who was eight and a half months pregnant. ("Little Jimmie," referred to in the letter, was born while Griffin was away at war.) This letter home was written from the Virginia front and refers to the surrender of Fort Donelson (see text p. 461) by General Simon Bolivar Buckner to Ulysses S. Grant. It is one of eighty-seven letters Griffin wrote to his wife between June 1861 and February 1865.

Source: Papers of James B. Griffin, Center for American History, University of Texas at Austin. In Orville Vernon Burton and Judith N. McArthur, eds., *"A Gentleman and an Officer": A Social and Military History of James B. Griffin's Civil War* (New York: Oxford University Press, 1996).

Camp of the Legion
February 26th 1862

My Darling Leila

I am delighted, my Darling to learn by your last letter that Minnie has at last "Come through". And I am also pleased, and tender my congratulations that she has another Boy. Notwithstanding you all were anxious for her to have a daughter. I really think she should be proud that she has another Boy. This is the time, above all others, that *men* should be raised. And this too, is the time above all others when females deserve sympathy. I assure you, I feel, far more anxiety about my dear little daughters, than I do about my Boys. For while men can manage to work for themselves, and can fight the battles of their Country if necessary, Females are very dependent. True, they too can do a great deal, and, 'tis true that our Southern Ladies have done and are still acting a conspicuous part in this war[.] In many instances (to the same of our Sex be it said) a much bolder and more *manly* part than many men. But still, when it comes to the physical test, of course, they are helpless. It is on this account, that I think the Parents should congratulate themselves on the birth of a son rather than a daughter. We cannot see, My Darling, into the future, but I trust & have confidence in our people to believe, that if the unprincipled North shall persist in her policy of Subjugating the South, that we, who are able to resist them, will continue to do so, until we grow old and worn out in the service, and that then, our Sons will take the arms from our hands, and spend their lives, if necessary, in battling for Liberty and independence. As for my part, If this trouble should not be settled satisfactorily to us sooner—I would be proud of the thought that our

youngest Boy—Yes Darling little Jimmie, will after awhile be able and I trust willing to take his Father's place in the field, and fight until he dies, rather than, be a Slave, *Yea* worse than a Slave to Yankee Masters—Have you ever anticipated, My Darling, what would be our probable condition, if we should be conquered in this war? The picture is really too horrible to contemplate. In the first place, the tremendous war tax, which will have accumulated, on the northern Government, would be paid entirely and exclusively by the property belonging to the Southerners. And more than this we would be an humbled, down trodden and disgraced, people. Not entitled to the respect of any body, and have no respect for ourselves. In fact we would be the most wretched and abject people on the face of the Earth. Just be what our Northern Masters say we may be. Would you, My Darling, desire to live, if this was the case? would you be willing to leave your Children under such a government? No—I know you would sacrifice every comfort on earth, rather than submit to it. Excuse me, My Darling, I didn't intend to, run off in this strain. You might think, from my painting this horrid picture to you, that I had some doubts as to whether we might not have to experience it. But No, I havent the most remote idea that we will. I think our people will arouse themselves, shake off the lethargy, which seems now to have possession of them, and will meet the issue like *men*. We must see that we have *all*—Yes our all—staked upon the result—And we are obliged to succeed and we will do it. Just at this time the Enemy appears to have advantage of us. But this is no more than we have, all along, had of him, until lately. He did not succombe and give up for it—and shall we, Who have so much more to fight for than he has, do so? I am completely surprised and mortified at the feeling manifested by our people at this time. But they will soon rally and come with redoubled energy. Our Soldiers too, or rather our Generals have got to learn to fight better. The idea, of a Genl surrendering with 12000 men under his command, is a species of bravery and Generalship, which I do not understand. I wish Congress would pass a law breaking an officer of his commission who surrenders. I received a letter last night from your Uncle Billy—was very glad to hear from him. If you havent sent my holsters and boot legs—you neednt send them as I dont now need them. I also received a letter last night from Sue, will write to her soon. My Darling tell Spradley, not to commence planting corn early[.] My land will not admit of early planting, of either corn or cotton. I generally, commence planting corn from the 15th to the 20th of March, and cotton about the same time in april. I see that Congress is about passing a bill, to impose a heavy tax on cotton raised this year. If they pass it—I wish no land planted in cotton except the new ground, and the field next to the overseers house, all the ballance planted in corn. I will write you, however in time. My Darling, Now is the time to bring out all your courage—Do not become despondent—Dont matter what *alarmists* and Croakers may say—take advice from him whom you *know* will advise you for the best. Keep up your spirits and your courage, and the clouds will soon pass away, and sun shine will return—My sheet is full—and I will close by begging to be remembered to all—My love to My Children and My Darling Leila

from Your Husband

I enclose a few Virginia Cabbage seed—and a sprig of spruce pine. It grows here beautifully. G—Tell Willie to write often

---

Questions

1. Which appears to be more important to Griffin, his family or the Confederacy?
2. What does Griffin's letter reveal about white planters' views of men and women?
3. Griffin warned that if the South surrendered, southern whites would become slaves to the "Yankee Masters." What did he mean, and what was the basis of his understanding of slavery?
4. How does military defeat seem to have affected the resolve of an aristocratic soldier such as Griffin?

15-8   The Gettysburg Address (1863)

Abraham Lincoln

The Battle of Gettysburg in July 1863 was the bloodiest of the Civil War. But the costly Union victory strengthened northern resolve and ended any hopes the Confederacy had of winning foreign recognition (see text pp. 467–470). Later that year, in a speech dedicating a cemetery at Gettysburg, Abraham Lincoln helped define the modern concept of the American nation.

Source: In Roy P. Basler et al., eds., *The Collected Works of Abraham Lincoln* (New Brunswick, N.J.: Rutgers University Press, 1953), vol. 7, p. 23.

Four score and seven years ago our fathers brought forth on this continent, a new nation, conceived in Liberty, and dedicated to the proposition that all men are created equal.

Now we are engaged in a great civil war, testing whether that nation, or any nation so conceived and so dedicated, can long endure. We are met on a great battlefield of that war. We have come to dedicate a portion of that field, as a final resting place for those who here gave their lives that that nation might live. It is altogether fitting and proper that we should do this.

But, in a larger sense, we can not dedicate—we can not consecrate—we can not hallow—this ground. The brave men, living and dead, who struggled here, have consecrated it, far above our poor power to add or detract. The world will little note, nor long remember what we say here, but it can never forget what they did here. It is for us the living, rather, to be dedicated here to the unfinished work which they who fought here have thus far so nobly advanced. It is rather for us to be here dedicated to the great task remaining before us—that from these honored dead we take increased devotion to that cause for which they gave the last full measure of devotion—that we here highly resolve that these dead shall not have died in vain—that this nation, under God, shall have a new birth of freedom—and that government of the people, by the people, for the people, shall not perish from the earth.

Questions

1. Why did Lincoln say in 1863 that the United States had been founded on the "proposition that all men are created equal"?
2. Why did Lincoln want to tie the Union's cause so closely to that of the Founders? Was Lincoln attempting to redefine the Union cause with the Gettysburg Address? If so, in what way?
3. Lincoln concluded his address with the thought "that this nation, under God, shall have a new birth of freedom." What type of freedom did he mean?

Questions for Further Thought

1. When the Civil War began, President Lincoln pursued the limited war aim of the restoration of the Union. What aspects of the war encouraged him to pursue emancipation as well?
2. Was an emancipation policy likely to weaken southern resolve? Was it likely to strengthen northern resolve? Explain why or why not.
3. Critically analyze Lincoln's Gettysburg Address from the perspective of a Confederate patriot.

The Union Victorious, 1864–1865

In 1864 and 1865 the Union prosecuted a total war against the Confederacy (see text pp. 472–474). The Union armies were now led by energetic, relentless generals—Grant, Sherman, Sheridan—and their ranks were reinforced by almost 200,000 African-American troops who secured freedom for themselves and their families as they fought down their former owners (Document 15-9).

Sherman's march across Georgia (see text pp. 476–478) and Lincoln's reelection in 1864 insured that the Union's war effort would continue until the South surrendered unconditionally. Union victory meant triumph for the Republican party's vision of America and the fulfillment of the Yankee sense of moral and material destiny. Lincoln recognized that the defeat of the Confederacy also meant demoralization and humiliation for white southerners. In his Second Inaugural Address, only slightly longer than his Gettysburg Address, Lincoln summarized the northern view of the war's causes and purposes and offered conciliation to former enemies. As the president prayed for peace and reconciliation, however, he also employed his harshest language of the war, promising a total victory over southern rebellion (Document 15-10).

15-9   Black Soldiers in Missouri Bring Families to Freedom (May 1864)

When President Abraham Lincoln issued the final Emancipation Proclamation on January 1, 1863, he exempted areas in eastern and western Virginia and lower Louisiana as well as the states of Delaware, Maryland, Kentucky, Tennessee, and Missouri. But Lincoln had also decided to end his long-standing opposition to the recruitment of black soldiers (see text pp. 471–472). Now the federal army admitted blacks and offered freedom to those who still remained slaves. Despite desultory recruitment efforts in Missouri, nearly 40 percent of the black men of military age, well over 8,000, joined the federal army, for the most part in late 1863 and early 1864. Although the status of freedom was not automatically passed on to the wives and children of black soldiers, the protection of the federal government was. In a striking reversal of social relationships, former slaves, now Union soldiers, intervened against former masters.

Source: Assistant Provost Marshal J. P. Lewis, telegram to Assistant Adjutant General J. Rainsford, 6 March 1864; and Sam Bowmen to Dear Wife, 10 May 1864, National Archives, Washington, D.C. In Ira Berlin et al., eds., *Freedom: A Documentary History of Emancipation, 1861–1867* (Cambridge, England: Cambridge University Press, 1985), series I, vol. 1, pp. 479, 483–485.

Glasgow, March 6, '64

Some negroes who were enlisted in this county and sent to St. Louis, have come back to Booneville and crossed into Howard County with some white soldiers and are hauling off tobacco from their former masters and owners and taking their wives and children.

Is this to be allowed.

(Signed) J. P. Lewis
Asst Prov. Ml.

Benton Barracks Post Hospital Mo St. Louis
May the 10, 1864

Dear Wife It is with pleasure that I am allowed this morning to write to you and inform you that by the tender mercies of that God who has been my Protector and keeper thus far and still watches over me with paternal care & Love—and it is my prayer that when this comes to you it may find You in the enjoyment of good health and in the Love of God. . . . General Piles [William A. Pile] has given orders if I want you to come here that it shall be granted & determined by the Provost at Tipton. So it lays to your own choice to stay or come. . . . If You do not want to stay tell Mr. Wilson in a decent manner . . . and General Pile says if You Mr Wilson is . . . a good . . . Union man . . . you will let her come on good terms and give her a piece of writing to shew that You are what you profess to be, and if you do not . . . we will shew You what we intend to do.— We are not expecting that this will insult a Union man. . . . I will find out whether this has been read to her . . . or not, and if I should find out that she has never heard her deliverance I will undoubtedly punish you. . . . [R]ecollect I am writing to Your interest if You look at it right. You can See I have power and You know that on the 10 day of May I write to You with this determination that by the 20th day of May this matter must & will be closed so you can rest till Then or do it sooner as it will be better for You. . . . I want you to understand that we have labourd in the field to Subdue Slavery and now we mean to protect them. . . .

P.S. please read this to my wife and then if you please answer it Immediately so I may know what Steps to take. Your Friend Sam Bowmen

Questions

1. How did the enlistment of black troops undermine slavery in Missouri?
2. How do you think Mr. Wilson reacted to Bowmen's letter?
3. What changes will Mr. Wilson have to make in the future if he wishes to employ the labor of his former slaves?

15-10   Abraham Lincoln, Second Inaugural Address (1865)

Abraham Lincoln's reelection in 1864 demonstrated the desire of northerners to continue the war until the Confederacy was totally defeated and had yielded to all northern war aims (see text p. 476). In his Second Inaugural Address in March 1865 Lincoln presented the "causes" of a war that was in its fourth year and suggested that the Almighty had imposed "this terrible war" on the nation as punishment for the evils of slavery.

Source: In James D. Richardson, ed., *A Compilation of the Messages and Papers of the Presidents* (Washington, D.C.: U.S. Government Printing Office, 1896–1899), vol. 6, pp. 276ff.

At this second appearing to take the oath of the presidential office, there is less occasion for an extended address than there was at the first. Then a statement, somewhat in detail, of a course to be pursued, seemed fitting and proper. Now, at the expiration of four years, during which public declarations have been constantly called forth on every point and phase of the great contest which still absorbs the attention, and engrosses the energies of the nation, little that is new could be presented. The progress of our arms, upon which all else chiefly depends, is as well known to the public as to myself; and it is, I trust, reasonably satisfactory and encouraging to all. With high hope for the future, no prediction in regard to it is ventured.

On the occasion corresponding to this four years ago, all thoughts were anxiously directed to an impending civil-war. All dreaded it—all sought to avert it. While the inaugural address was being delivered from this place, devoted altogether to *saving* the Union without war, insurgent agents were in the city seeking to *destroy* it without war—seeking to dissolve the Union, and divide effects, by negotiation. Both parties deprecated war; but one of them would *make* war rather than let the nation survive; and the other would *accept* war rather than let it perish. And the war came.

One eighth of the whole population were colored slaves, not distributed generally over the Union, but localized in the Southern part of it. These slaves constituted a peculiar and powerful interest. All knew that this interest was, somehow, the cause of the war. To strengthen, perpetuate, and extend this interest was the object for which the insurgents would rend the Union, even by war; while the government claimed no right to do more than to restrict the territorial enlargement of it. Neither party expected for the war, the magnitude, or the duration, which it has already attained. Neither anticipated that the *cause* of the conflict might cease with, or even before, the conflict itself should cease. Each looked for an easier triumph, and a result less fundamental and astounding. Both read the same Bible, and pray to the same God; and each invokes His aid against the other. It may seem strange that any men should dare to ask a just God's assistance in wringing their bread from the sweat of other men's faces; but let us judge not that we be not judged. The prayers of both could not be answered; that of neither has been answered fully. The Almighty has His own purposes. "Woe unto the world because of offences! for it must needs be that offences come; but woe to that man by whom the offence cometh!" If we shall suppose that American Slavery is one of those offences which, in the providence of God, must needs come, but which, having continued through His appointed time, He now wills to remove, and that He gives to both North and South, this terrible war, as the woe due to those by whom the offence came, shall we discern therein any departure from those divine attributes which the believers in a Living God always ascribe to Him? Fondly do we hope—fervently do we pray—that this mighty scourge of war may speedily pass away. Yet, if God wills that it continue, until all the wealth piled by the bond-man's two hundred and fifty years of unrequited toil shall be sunk, and until every drop of blood drawn with the lash, shall be paid by another drawn with the sword, as was said three thousand years ago, so still it must be said "the judgments of the Lord, are true and righteous altogether."

With malice toward none; with charity for all; with firmness in the right, as God gives us to see the right, let us strive on to finish the work we are in; to bind up the nation's wounds; to care for him who shall have borne the battle, and for his widow, and his orphan—to do all which may achieve and cherish a just, and a lasting peace, among ourselves, and with all nations.

Questions

1. What is Lincoln saying about the treatment of African-Americans in the United States?

2. In this speech, does Lincoln view the Civil War and slavery as a tragedy, a sin, or a crime?

3. Which do you think Lincoln is emphasizing in this speech, the extraordinarily radical statement about race relations in America or the "with malice toward none" passage?

Questions for Further Thought

1. How did the Civil War change the status of African-Americans, slave and free, in the United States?

2. Why did the hope for racial inequality remain unfulfilled?

3. After four years of the nation's most bloody and terrible war, how did Lincoln come to view the meaning and purpose of the conflict?

CHAPTER 16

The Union Reconstructed 1865–1877

★   ★   ★

Presidential Restoration

Planning for Reconstruction began to take shape in December 1863 (see text p. 486), when President Lincoln laid out his ideas in a presidential proclamation. His pronouncement opened a debate that became the central issue in American politics for more than a decade (see text pp. 486–494). The power struggle that followed led to a collision between the executive and legislative branches of government, the displacement of presidential Reconstruction by Congressional Reconstruction, and the first impeachment of a president of the United States, a process that nearly resulted in the removal of President Andrew Johnson, Lincoln's successor (Document 16-1).

Reconstruction involved fundamental questions: Who had the primary responsibility for Reconstruction: the president or Congress? What should the basic aims of Reconstruction be: reunion of the nation as quickly as possible or reunion only after ensuring that the South would remain loyal (Document 16-2)? Congress made its views known in the Wade-Davis bill of July 2, 1864, and then in its strongly negative reaction to Lincoln's veto of the bill (see text p. 487). Lincoln realized that he had to strike a compromise with Congress on Reconstruction, but Johnson did not, setting the stage for a dramatic confrontation with Congress (see text pp. 488–489).

Other fundamental questions about Reconstruction involved determining the place African-Americans would have in the United States (Documents 16-3 and 16-4), especially in the former slave states, and deciding whether the federal government should take measures to prevent the restoration of slavery or a facsimile of slavery. What about the place and role of Unionists in the South?

A number of factors were critical to the way these questions were answered. The first was the Constitution, which set the ground rules by which Americans governed themselves and therefore guided the way in which they dealt with Reconstruction. The second factor was the deep commitment of Americans to private property and their belief that the government should play only a limited role in daily life. The third was the profoundly held idea of self-government, or the belief that the only legitimate governments were those chosen freely by the governed. The fourth was the critical role racism played in both the South and the North. The fifth factor was the strong emotions that followed four years of bloody and expensive war, emotions that were compounded by this country's long history of sectionalism.

16-1   Andrew Johnson's Plan of Reconstruction (1865)

As the Civil War came to an end, Lincoln's successor, Andrew Johnson, moved quickly to implement his plan for Reconstruction, which differed little from Lincoln's plan (see text p. 486). Johnson acted largely on his own, without much consultation with Congress. In particular, he ignored Congress's demand for a harsher policy toward the former Confederate states (see text pp. 488–489).

On May 29, 1865, President Johnson set forth his plan in two presidential proclamations. In the first he promised amnesty to all rebels who would swear an oath of future loyalty, except for certain high-ranking officials and officers of the Confederacy, who had to petition for a presidential pardon.

In the second proclamation, which appears below, Johnson announced the creation of a provisional government for North Carolina. After appointing William W. Holden, a North Carolina Unionist who had opposed secession, as the provisional governor, Johnson described the means by which that state could be restored to the Union. Johnson intended this plan to serve as a model for the other seceded states, hoping that all could be restored before Congress reconvened in December.

Johnson's approach to Reconstruction was very different from that proposed by the Wade-Davis bill (see text p. 487), which stipulated that more than 50 percent of the voters who were qualified in 1860 in each southern state had to be able to prove their past loyalty and swear future loyalty to the Union. Johnson and Congress also differed about allowing former Confederate leaders to participate in Reconstruction and in government. Presidents Lincoln and Johnson envisioned temporary disqualification; Congress favored permanent disqualification (see text pp. 486–487).

Source: In James D. Richardson, ed., *A Compilation of the Messages and Papers of the Presidents* (Washington, D.C.: U.S. Government Printing Office, 1896–1899), vol. 6, pp. 312–313.

Whereas the fourth section of the fourth article of the Constitution of the United States declares that the United States shall guarantee to every State in the Union a republican form of government and shall protect each of them against invasion and domestic violence; and

Whereas the President of the United States is by the Constitution made Commander in Chief of the Army and Navy, as well as chief civil executive officer of the United States, and is bound by solemn oath faithfully to execute the office of President of the United States and to take care that the laws be faithfully executed; and

Whereas the rebellion which has been waged by a portion of the people of the United States against the properly constituted authorities of the Government . . . and

Whereas it becomes necessary and proper to carry out and enforce the obligations of the United States to the people of North Carolina in securing them in the enjoyment of a republican form of government:

Now, therefore, in obedience to the high and solemn duties imposed upon me by the Constitution of the United States and for the purpose of enabling the loyal people of said State to organize a State government whereby justice may be established, domestic tranquillity insured, and loyal citizens protected in all their rights of life, liberty, and property, I, Andrew Johnson, President of the United States and Commander in Chief of the Army and Navy of the United States, do hereby appoint William W. Holden provisional governor of the State of North Carolina, whose duty it shall be, at the earliest practicable period, to prescribe such rules and regulations as may be necessary and proper for convening a convention composed of delegates to be chosen by that portion of the people of said State who are loyal to the United States, and no others, for the purpose of altering or amending the constitution thereof, and with authority to exercise within the limits of said State all the powers necessary and proper to enable such loyal people of the State of North Carolina to restore said State to its constitutional relations to the Federal Government and to present such a republican form of State government as will entitle the State to the guaranty of the United States therefor and its people to protection by the United States against invasion, insurrection, and domestic violence: *Provided*, That in any election that may be hereafter held for choosing delegates to any State convention as aforesaid no person shall be qualified as an elector or shall be eligible as a member of such convention unless he shall have previously taken and subscribed the oath of amnesty as set forth in the President's proclamation of May 29, A. D. 1865, and is a voter qualified as prescribed by the constitution and laws of the State of North Carolina in force immediately before the 20th day of May, A. D. 1861, the date of the so-called ordinance of secession; and the said convention, when convened, or the legislature that may be thereafter assembled, will prescribe the qualification of electors and the eligibility of persons to hold office under the constitution and laws of the State—a power the people of the several States composing the Federal Union have rightfully exercised from the origin of the Government to the present time.

And I do hereby direct—

. . . That the military commander of the department and all officers and persons in the military and naval service aid and assist the said provisional governor in carrying into effect this proclamation; and they are enjoined to abstain from in any way hindering, impeding, or discouraging the loyal people from the organization of a State government as herein authorized. . . .

Questions

1. According to President Johnson, what was his authority for this proclamation? Who was to be in charge of the process?
2. What steps did Johnson prescribe for restoring civil government in North Carolina?
3. Under Johnson's plan, would freedmen be able to vote? (*Hint:* See the section starting "*Provided.*")

16-2   Report on Conditions in the South (1865)

Carl Schurz

By December 1865, when Congress was gathering in Washington for a new session, Johnson had declared that all the Confederate states but Texas had met his requirements for restoration. Newly elected senators and congressmen from the former Confederacy had arrived to take seats in Congress (see text pp. 488–489).

Johnson's efforts to restore the South stalled. Congress exercised its constitutional authority to deny seats to delegations from the South and launched an investigation into conditions there (see text pp. 488–492). In response to a Senate resolution requesting "information in relation to the States of the Union lately in rebellion," Johnson painted a rosy picture: "In 'that portion of the Union lately in rebellion' the aspect of affairs is more promising than, in view of all the circumstances, could well have been expected. The people throughout the entire south evince a laudable desire to renew their allegiance to the government, and to repair the devastations of war by a prompt and cheerful return to peaceful pursuits. An abiding faith is entertained that their actions will conform to their professions, and that, in acknowledging the supremacy of the Constitution and the laws of the United States, their loyalty will be unreservedly given to the government, whose leniency they cannot fail to appreciate, and whose fostering care will soon restore them to a condition of prosperity. It is true, that in some of the States the demoralizing effects of war are to be seen in occasional disorders, but these are local in character, not frequent in occurrence, and are rapidly disappearing as the authority of civil law is extended and sustained."

Johnson's message to the Senate was accompanied by a report from Major General Carl Schurz (see also Document 13-6). Among the subjects on which Schurz reported were whether southern whites had accepted defeat and emancipation, and whether ex-slaves and southern Unionists were safe in the South and were receiving fair treatment. Schurz's report was apparently largely ignored by President Johnson, who had assigned him to make the report but was not happy with what he said.

Schurz went to considerable lengths to get an accurate reading of attitudes in the South. He tried to get a representative sample of people to interview in his three-month tour of portions of South Carolina, Georgia, Alabama, Mississippi, and Louisiana and gathered documentary evidence as well as interviews. Then he tried to analyze his findings carefully and make recommendations on the basis of those findings. Clearly, he believed that Reconstruction in the South involved more than the restoration of civil government.

Source: U.S. Congress, Senate, 39th Cong., 1st sess., 1865, Ex. Doc. No. 2, pp. 1–5, 8, 36–39, 41–44.

SIR: . . . You informed me that your "policy of reconstruction" was merely experimental, and that you would change it if the experiment did not lead to satisfactory results. To aid you in forming your conclusions upon this point I understood to be the object of my mission, . . .

CONDITION OF THINGS IMMEDIATELY AFTER THE CLOSE OF THE WAR

In the development of the popular spirit in the south since the close of the war two well-marked periods can be distinguished. The first commences with the sudden collapse of the confederacy and the dispersion of its armies, and the second with the first proclamation indicating the "reconstruction policy" of the government. . . . When the news of Lee's and Johnston's surrenders burst upon the southern country the general consternation was extreme. People held their breath, indulging in the wildest apprehensions as to what was now to come. . . . Prominent Unionists told me that persons who for four years had scorned to recognize them on the street approached them with smiling faces and both hands extended. Men of standing in the political world expressed serious doubts as to whether the rebel States would ever again occupy their position as States in the Union, or be governed as conquered provinces. The public mind was so despondent that if readmission at some future time under whatever conditions had been promised, it would then have been looked upon as a favor. The most uncompromising rebels prepared for leaving the country. The masses remained in a state of fearful expectancy. . . .

Such was, according to the accounts I received, the

character of that first period. The worst apprehensions were gradually relieved as day after day went by without bringing the disasters and inflictions which had been vaguely anticipated, until at last the appearance of the North Carolina proclamation substituted new hopes for them. The development of this second period I was called upon to observe on the spot, and it forms the main subject of this report.

RETURNING LOYALTY

. . . [T]he white people at large being, under certain conditions, charged with taking the preliminaries of "reconstruction" into their hands, the success of the experiment depends upon the spirit and attitude of those who either attached themselves to the secession cause from the beginning, or, entertaining originally opposite views, at least followed its fortunes from the time that their States had declared their separation from the Union. . . .

I may group the southern people into four classes, each of which exercises an influence upon the development of things in that section:

1. Those who, although having yielded submission to the national government only when obliged to do so, have a clear perception of the irreversible changes produced by the war, and honestly endeavor to accommodate themselves to the new order of things. Many of them are not free from traditional prejudice but open to conviction, and may be expected to act in good faith whatever they do. This class is composed, in its majority, of persons of mature age—planters, merchants, and professional men; some

of them are active in the reconstruction movement, but boldness and energy are, with a few individual exceptions, not among their distinguishing qualities.

2. Those whose principal object is to have the States without delay restored to their position and influence in the Union and the people of the States to the absolute control of their home concerns. They are ready, in order to attain that object, to make any ostensible concession that will not prevent them from arranging things to suit their taste as soon as that object is attained. This class comprises a considerable number, probably a large majority, of the professional politicians who are extremely active in the reconstruction movement. They are loud in their praise of the President's reconstruction policy, and clamorous for the withdrawal of the federal troops and the abolition of the Freedmen's Bureau.

3. The incorrigibles, who still indulge in the swagger which was so customary before and during the war, and still hope for a time when the southern confederacy will achieve its independence. This class consists mostly of young men, and comprises the loiterers of the towns and the idlers of the country. They persecute Union men and negroes whenever they can do so with impunity, insist clamorously upon their "rights," and are extremely impatient of the presence of the federal soldiers. A good many of them have taken the oaths of allegiance and amnesty, and associated themselves with the second class in their political operations. This element is by no means unimportant; it is strong in numbers, deals in brave talk, addresses itself directly and incessantly to the passions and prejudices of the masses, and commands the admiration of the women.

4. The multitude of people who have no definite ideas about the circumstances under which they live and about the course they have to follow; whose intellects are weak, but whose prejudices and impulses are strong, and who are apt to be carried along by those who know how to appeal to the latter. . . .

FEELING TOWARDS THE SOLDIERS AND THE PEOPLE OF THE NORTH

. . . [U]pon the whole, the soldier of the Union is still looked upon as a stranger, an intruder—as the "Yankee," "the enemy." . . .

It is by no means surprising that prejudices and resentments, which for years were so assiduously cultivated and so violently inflamed, should not have been turned into affection by a defeat; nor are they likely to disappear as long as the southern people continue to brood over their losses and misfortunes. They will gradually subside when those who entertain them cut resolutely loose from the past and embark in a career of new activity on a common field with those whom they have so long considered their enemies. . . . [A]s long as these feelings exist in their

present strength, they will hinder the growth of that reliable kind of loyalty which springs from the heart and clings to the country in good and evil fortune.

SITUATION OF UNIONISTS

. . . It struck me soon after my arrival in the south that the known Unionists—I mean those who during the war had been to a certain extent identified with the national cause—were not in communion with the leading social and political circles; and the further my observations extended the clearer it became to me that their existence in the south was of a rather precarious nature. . . . Even Governor [William L.] Sharkey, in the course of a conversation I had with him in the presence of Major General Osterhaus, admitted that, if our troops were then withdrawn, the lives of northern men in Mississippi would not be safe. . . . [General Osterhaus said]: "There is no doubt whatever that the state of affairs would be intolerable for all Union men, all recent immigrants from the north, and all negroes, the moment the protection of the United States troops were withdrawn." . . .

NEGRO INSURRECTIONS AND ANARCHY

. . . [I do] not deem a negro insurrection probable as long as the freedmen were assured of the direct protection of the national government. Whenever they are in trouble, they raise their eyes up to that power, and although they may suffer, yet, as long as that power is visibly present, they continue to hope. But when State authority in the south is fully restored, the federal forces withdrawn, and the Freedmen's Bureau abolished, the colored man will find himself turned over to the mercies of those whom he does not trust. If then an attempt is made to strip him again of those rights which he justly thought he possessed, he will be apt to feel that he can hope for no redress unless he procure it himself. If ever the negro is capable of rising, he will rise then. . . .

There is probably at the present moment no country in the civilized world which contains such an accumulation of anarchical elements as the south. The strife of the antagonistic tendencies here described is aggravated by the passions inflamed and the general impoverishment brought about by a long and exhaustive war, and the south will have to suffer the evils of anarchical disorder until means are found to effect a final settlement of the labor question in accordance with the logic of the great revolution.

THE TRUE PROBLEM—DIFFICULTIES AND REMEDIES

In seeking remedies for such disorders, we ought to keep in view, above all, the nature of the problem which is to be solved. As to what is commonly termed "reconstruction," it is not only the political machinery of the States and their constitutional relations to the general government, but the whole organism of southern society that must be reconstructed, or rather constructed anew, so as to bring it in harmony with the rest of American society. The difficulties of this task are not to be considered overcome when the people of the south take the oath of allegiance and elect governors and legislatures and members of Congress, and militia captains. That this would be done had become certain as soon as the surrenders of the southern armies had made further resistance impossible, and nothing in the world was left, even to the most uncompromising rebel, but to submit or to emigrate. It was also natural that they should avail themselves of every chance offered them to resume control of their home affairs and to regain their influence in the Union. But this can hardly be called the first step towards the solution of the true problem, and it is a fair question to ask, whether the hasty gratification of their desire to resume such control would not create new embarrassments.

The true nature of the difficulties of the situation is this: The general government of the republic has, by proclaiming the emancipation of the slaves, commenced a great social revolution in the south, but has, as yet, not completed it. Only the negative part of it is accomplished. The slaves are emancipated in point of form, but free labor has not yet been put in the place of slavery in point of fact. And now, in the midst of this critical period of transition, the power which originated the revolution is expected to turn over its whole future development to another power which from the beginning was hostile to it and has never yet entered into its spirit, leaving the class in whose favor it was made completely without power to protect itself and to take an influential part in that development. The history of the world will be searched in vain for a proceeding similar to this which did not lead either to a rapid and violent reaction, or to the most serious trouble and civil disorder. It cannot be said that the conduct of the southern people since the close of the war has exhibited such extraordinary wisdom and self-abnegation as to make them an exception to the rule.

In my despatches from the south I repeatedly expressed the opinion that the people were not yet in a frame of mind to legislate calmly and understandingly upon the subject of free negro labor. And this I reported to be the opinion of some of our most prominent military commanders and other observing men. It is, indeed, difficult to imagine circumstances more unfavorable for the development of a calm and unprejudiced public opinion than those under which the southern people are at present laboring. The war has not only defeated their political aspirations, but it has broken up their whole social organization. . . .

In which direction will these people be most apt to turn their eyes? Leaving the prejudice of race out of the question, from early youth they have been acquainted with but one system of labor, and with that one system they have been in the habit of identifying all their interests. They know of no way to help themselves but the one they are accustomed to. . . .

It is certain that every success of free negro labor will augment the number of its friends, and disarm some of the prejudices and assumptions of its opponents. I am convinced one good harvest made by unadulterated free labor in the south would have a far better effect than all the oaths that have been taken, and all the ordinances that have as yet been passed by southern conventions. But how can such a result be attained? The facts enumerated in this report, as well as the news we receive from the south from day to day, must make it evident to every unbiased observer that unadulterated free labor cannot be had at present, unless the national government holds its protective and controlling hand over it. . . . One reason why the southern people are so slow in accommodating themselves to the new order of things is, that they confidently expect soon to be permitted to regulate matters according to their own notions. Every concession made to them by the government has been taken as an encouragement to persevere in this hope, and, unfortunately for them, this hope is nourished by influences from other parts of the country. Hence their anxiety to have their State governments restored *at once*, to have the troops withdrawn, and the Freedmen's Bureau abolished, although a good many discerning men know well that, in view of the lawless spirit still prevailing, it would be far better for them to have the general order of society firmly maintained by the federal power until things have arrived at a final settlement. Had, from the beginning, the conviction been forced upon them that the adulteration of the new order of things by the admixture of elements belonging to the system of slavery would under no circumstances be permitted, a much larger number would have launched their energies into the new channel, and, seeing that they could do "no better," faithfully co-operated with the government. It is hope which fixes them in their perverse notions. That hope nourished or fully gratified, they will persevere in the same direction. That hope destroyed, a great many will, by the force of necessity, at once accommodate themselves to the logic of the change. If, therefore, the national government firmly and unequivocally announces its policy not to give up the control of the free-labor reform until it is finally accomplished, the progress of that reform will undoubtedly be far more rapid and far less difficult than it will be if the attitude of the government is such as to permit contrary hopes to be indulged in. . . .

IMMIGRATION [AND CAPITAL]

[The south would benefit] from immigration of northern people and Europeans. . . . The south needs capital. But capital is notoriously timid and averse to risk. . . . Capitalists will be apt to consider—and they are by no means wrong in doing so—that no safe investments can be made in the south as long as southern society is liable to be convulsed by anarchical disorders. No greater encouragement can, therefore, be given to capital to transfer itself to the south than the assurance that the government will continue to control the development of the new social system in the late rebel States until such dangers are averted by a final settlement of things upon a thorough free-labor basis.

How long the national government should continue that control depends upon contingencies. It ought to cease as soon as its objects are attained; and its objects will be attained sooner and with less difficulty if nobody is permitted to indulge in the delusion that it will cease *before* they are attained. This is one of the cases in which a determined policy can accomplish much, while a half-way policy is liable to spoil things already accomplished. . . .

NEGRO SUFFRAGE

It would seem that the interference of the national authority in the home concerns of the southern States would be rendered less necessary, and the whole problem of political and social reconstruction be much simplified, if, while the masses lately arrayed against the government are permitted to vote, the large majority of those who were always loyal, and are naturally anxious to see the free labor problem successfully solved, were not excluded from all influence upon legislation. In all questions concerning the Union, the national debt, and the future social organization of the south, the feelings of the colored man are naturally in sympathy with the views and aims of the national government. While the southern white fought against the Union, the negro did all he could to aid it; while the southern white sees in the national government his conqueror, the negro sees in it his protector; while the white owes to the national debt his defeat, the negro owes to it his deliverance; while the white considers himself robbed and ruined by the emancipation of the slaves, the negro finds in it the assurance of future prosperity and happiness. In all the important issues the negro would be led by natural impulse to forward the ends of the government, and by making his influence, as part of the voting body, tell upon the legislation of the States, render the interference of the national authority less necessary.

As the most difficult of the pending questions are intimately connected with the status of the negro in southern society, it is obvious that a correct solution can be more easily obtained if he has a voice in the matter. In the right to vote he would find the best permanent protection against oppressive class-legislation, as well as against individual persecution. The relations between the white and black races, even if improved by the gradual wearing off of the present animosities, are likely to remain long under the troubling influence of prejudice. It is a notorious fact that the rights of a man of some political power are far less exposed to violation than those of one who is, in matters of public interest, completely subject to the will of others. . . .

In discussing the matter of negro suffrage I deemed it my duty to confine myself strictly to the practical aspects of the subject. I have, therefore, not touched its moral merits nor discussed the question whether the national government is competent to enlarge the elective franchise in the States lately in rebellion by its own act; I deem it proper, however, to offer a few remarks on the assertion frequently put forth, that the franchise is likely to be extended to the colored man by the voluntary action of the southern whites themselves. My observation leads me to a contrary opinion. Aside from a very few enlightened men, I found but one class of people in favor of the enfranchisement of the blacks: it was the class of Unionists who found themselves politically ostracised and looked upon the enfranchisement of the loyal negroes as the salvation of the whole loyal element. But their numbers and influence are sadly insufficient to secure such a result. The masses are strongly opposed to colored suffrage; anybody that dares to advocate it is stigmatized as a dangerous fanatic; nor do I deem it probable that in the ordinary course of things prejudices will wear off to such an extent as to make it a popular measure. . . .

DEPORTATION OF THE FREEDMEN

. . . [T]he true problem remains, not how to remove the colored man from his present field of labor, but how to make him, where he is, a true freeman and an intelligent and useful citizen. The means are simple: protection by the government until his political and social status enables him to protect himself, offering to his legitimate ambition the stimulant of a perfectly fair chance in life, and granting to him the rights which in every just organization of society are coupled with corresponding duties.

CONCLUSION

I may sum up all I have said in a few words. If nothing were necessary but to restore the machinery of government in the States lately in rebellion in point of form, the movements made to that end by the people of the south might be considered satisfactory. But if it is required that the southern people should also accommodate themselves to the results of the war in point of spirit, those movements fall far short of what must be insisted upon. . . .

Questions

1. Why did Schurz recommend keeping the Freedmen's Bureau and the army in the South? How did that differ from what Johnson wanted?
2. Why did Schurz suggest that it might be wise to give African-Americans in the South the vote?
3. What does Schurz say about the Unionists in the South? About the emergence of a free labor system?

16-3   The Mississippi Black Codes (1865)

As Carl Schurz reported, after the Civil War whites in the South sought a system of race relations in which African-Americans would be clearly subordinate to whites and would constitute a readily accessible and controllable work force (see text p. 491).

Immediately after the Civil War southern whites wrote or revised vagrancy laws and the old slave codes as a means of establishing the system of race relations they wanted (see text p. 492). Below is one of their most famous attempts to codify race relations, the Black Codes passed by the Mississippi legislature.

The Mississippi codes gave blacks rights they had not had before and clearly acknowledged that chattel slavery had ended. The codes recognized the right of African-Americans to own property, though not in incorporated towns or cities. (Before the Civil War there were black property owners in Mississippi and even a few black slaveholders, but their legal standing was not clear.) The 1865 codes also recognized marriages among blacks as legal.

Not all the southern states passed comprehensive Black Codes, and some codes were much less stringent than those of Mississippi. South Carolina's codes differed in that they restricted blacks to buying property in cities or towns.

The creators of the codes drew their ideas from the world in which they lived. Slavery had just ended very abruptly, and the ravages of war were ever present. The men who drafted these codes used the old slave codes from the South, vagrancy laws from the North and the South, laws for ex-slaves in the British West Indies, and antebellum laws for free blacks. They were also aware that most northern states had laws that discriminated against African-Americans and that very few northern states allowed African-Americans to vote.

Most of these codes and similar measures were declared void by the Union army officials who were stationed in the former Confederate states. Subsequently, during Reconstruction, the rights of African-Americans were greatly expanded (see text pp. 492–493).

Source: Laws of Mississippi, 1865, pp. 82ff.

1. CIVIL RIGHTS OF FREEDMEN IN MISSISSIPPI

. . . That all freedmen, free negroes, and mulattoes may sue and be sued . . . may acquire personal property . . . and may dispose of the same in the same manner and to the same extent that white persons may: [but no] freedman, free negro, or mulatto . . . [shall] rent or lease any lands or tenements except in incorporated cities or towns, in which places the corporate authorities shall control the same. . . .

All freedmen, free negroes, or mulattoes who do now and have heretofore lived and cohabited together as husband and wife shall be taken and held in law as legally married, and the issue shall be taken and held as legitimate for all purposes; that it shall not be lawful for any freedman, free negro, or mulatto to intermarry with any white person; nor for any white person to intermarry with any freedman, free negro, or mulatto; and any person who shall so intermarry, shall be deemed guilty of felony, and on conviction thereof shall be confined in the State penitentiary for life; and those shall be deemed freedmen, free negroes, and mulattoes who are of pure negro blood, and those descended from a negro to the third generation, inclusive, though one ancestor in each generation may have been a white person. . . .

[F]reedmen, free negroes, and mulattoes are now by law competent witnesses . . . in civil cases [and in criminal cases where they are the victims]. . . .

All contracts for labor made with freedmen, free negroes, and mulattoes for a longer period than one month shall be in writing, and in duplicate. . . . and said contracts shall be taken and held as entire contracts, and if the laborer shall quit the service of the employer before the expiration of his term of service, without good cause, he shall forfeit his wages for that year up to the time of quitting.

. . . Every civil officer shall, and every person may, arrest and carry back to his or her legal employer any freedman, free negro, or mulatto who shall have quit the service of his or her employer before the expiration of his or her term of service without good cause; and said officer and person shall be entitled to receive for arresting and carrying back every deserting employe aforesaid the sum of five dollars. . . .

. . . If any person shall persuade or attempt to persuade, entice, or cause any freedman, free negro, or mulatto to desert from the legal employment of any person before the expiration of his or her term of service, or shall knowingly employ any such deserting freedman, free negro, or mulatto, or shall knowingly give or sell to any such deserting freedman, free negro, or mulatto, any food, raiment, or other thing, he or she shall be guilty of a misdemeanor. . . .

2. MISSISSIPPI APPRENTICE LAW

. . . It shall be the duty of all sheriffs, justices of the peace, and other civil officers of the several counties in this State, to report to the probate courts of their respective counties semi-annually, at the January and July terms of said courts, all freedmen, free negroes, and mulattoes, under the age of eighteen, in their respective counties, beats or districts, who are orphans, or whose parent or parents have not the means or who refuse to provide for and support said minors; . . . the clerk of said court to apprentice said minors

to some competent and suitable person, on such terms as the court may direct, having a particular care to the interest of said minor: *Provided*, that the former owner of said minors shall have the preference when, in the opinion of the court, he or she shall be a suitable person for that purpose. . . .

. . . In the management and control of said apprentice, said master or mistress shall have the power to inflict such moderate corporal chastisement as a father or guardian is allowed to inflict on his or her child or ward at common law: *Provided*, that in no case shall cruel or inhuman punishment be inflicted. . . .

3. MISSISSIPPI VAGRANT LAW

. . . That all rogues and vagabonds, idle and dissipated persons, beggars, jugglers, or persons practicing unlawful games or plays, runaways, common drunkards, common night-walkers, pilferers, lewd, wanton, or lascivious persons, in speech or behavior, common railers and brawlers, persons who neglect their calling or employment, misspend what they earn, or do not provide for the support of themselves or their families, or dependents, and all other idle and disorderly persons, including all who neglect all lawful business, habitually misspend their time by frequenting houses of ill-fame, gaming-houses, or tippling shops, shall be deemed and considered vagrants, under the provisions of this act, and upon conviction thereof shall be fined not exceeding one hundred dollars . . . and be imprisoned at the discretion of the court, not exceeding ten days.

. . . All freedmen, free negroes and mulattoes in this State, over the age of eighteen years, found on the second Monday in January, 1866, or thereafter, with no lawful employment or business, or found unlawfully assembling themselves together, either in the day or night time, and all white persons so assembling themselves with freedmen, free negroes or mulattoes, or usually associating with freedmen, free negroes or mulattoes, on terms of equality, or living in adultery or fornication with a freed woman, free negro or mulatto, shall be deemed vagrants, and on conviction thereof shall be fined in a sum not exceeding, in the case of a freedman, free negro or mulatto, fifty dollars, and a white man two hundred dollars, and imprisoned at the discretion of the court, the free negro not exceeding ten days, and the white man not exceeding six months. . . .

4. PENAL LAWS OF MISSISSIPPI

. . . That no freedman, free negro or mulatto, not in the military service of the United States government, and not licensed so to do by the board of police of his or her county, shall keep or carry fire-arms of any kind, or any ammunition, dirk or bowie knife. . . .

. . . Any freedman, free negro, or mulatto committing

riots, routs, affrays, trespasses, malicious mischief, cruel treatment to animals, seditious speeches, insulting gestures, language, or acts, or assaults on any person, disturbance of the peace, exercising the function of a minister of the Gospel without a license from some regularly organized church, vending spirituous or intoxicating liquors, or committing any other misdemeanor, the punishment of which is not specifically provided for by law, shall, upon conviction thereof in the county court, be fined not less than ten dollars, and not more than one hundred dollars,

and may be imprisoned at the discretion of the court, not exceeding thirty days. . . .

. . . If any freedman, free negro, or mulatto, convicted of any of the misdemeanors provided against in this act, shall fail or refuse for the space of five days, after conviction, to pay the fine and costs imposed, such person shall be hired out by the sheriff or other officer, at public outcry, to any white person who will pay said fine and all costs, and take said convict for the shortest time.

Questions

1. What was the intent of these laws?
2. Who was charged with enforcing them? ("Every civil officer shall, and every person may, arrest and carry back to his or her legal employer. . . .") Who was considered a "person"? Who was not a "person"?
3. How were vagrants defined? Were these laws based on the assumption that the only vagrants were African-Americans? What restrictions were placed on the freedom of expression of African-Americans? What restrictions were placed on their freedom of association? On whites in Mississippi?

16-4   The Civil Rights Act of 1866

When Congress reconvened in December 1865, it blocked President Johnson's attempts to restore the South quickly. It extended the life of the Freedmen's Bureau over the president's veto and passed another landmark law, the Civil Rights Act of 1866, again over the president's veto (see text pp. 492–493). This act made African-Americans citizens and countered the *Dred Scott* decision of 1857, in which the Supreme Court had declared that no African-American who was descended from a slave was or could ever be a citizen.

Doubts about the constitutionality and permanence of the Civil Rights Act of 1866 prompted Congress to pass the Fourteenth Amendment (see text pp. 493 and D-13). Ratified in 1868, this amendment for the first time constitutionally defined citizenship and some of the basic rights of citizenship; it also embraced the Republican program for Reconstruction.

Source: United States, *Statutes at Large*, vol.14, pp. 27ff.

An Act to protect all Persons in the United States in their Civil Rights, and furnish the Means of their Vindication.

Be it enacted, That all persons born in the United States and not subject to any foreign power, excluding Indians not taxed, are hereby declared to be citizens of the United States; and such citizens, of every race and color, without regard to any previous condition of slavery or involuntary servitude, except as a punishment for crime whereof the party shall have been duly convicted, shall

have the same right, in every State and Territory in the United States, to make and enforce contracts, to sue, be parties, and give evidence, to inherit, purchase, lease, sell, hold, and convey real and personal property, and to full and equal benefit of all laws and proceedings for the security of person and property, as is enjoyed by white citizens, and shall be subject to like punishment, pains, and penalties, and to none other, any law, statute, ordinance, regulation, or custom, to the contrary notwithstanding.

SEC. 2. *And be it further enacted,* That any person who, under color of any law, statute, ordinance, regulation, or custom, shall subject, or cause to be subjected, any inhabitant of any State or Territory to the deprivation of any right secured or protected by this act, or to different punishment, pains, or penalties on account of such person having at any time been held in a condition of slavery or involuntary servitude, except as a punishment for crime whereof the party shall have been duly convicted, or by reason of his color or race, than is prescribed for the punishment of white persons, shall be deemed guilty of a misdemeanor, and, on conviction, shall be punished by fine not exceeding one thousand dollars, or imprisonment not exceeding one year, or both, in the discretion of the court.

SEC. 3. *And be it further enacted,* That the district courts of the United States, . . . shall have, exclusively of the courts of the several States, cognizance of all crimes and offences committed against the provisions of this act, and also, concurrently with the circuit courts of the United States, of all causes, civil and criminal, affecting persons who are denied or cannot enforce in the courts or judicial tribunals of the State or locality where they may be any of the rights secured to them by the first section of this act. . . .

SEC. 4. *And be it further enacted,* That the district attorneys, marshals, and deputy marshals of the United States, the commissioners appointed by the circuit and territorial courts of the United States, with powers of arresting, imprisoning, or bailing offenders against the laws of the United States, the officers and agents of the Freedmen's Bureau, and every other officer who may be specially em-

powered by the President of the United States, shall be, and they are hereby, specially authorized and required, at the expense of the United States, to institute proceedings against all and every person who shall violate the provisions of this act, and cause him or them to be arrested and imprisoned, or bailed, as the case may be, for trial before such court of the United States or territorial court as by this act has cognizance of the offence. . . .

SEC. 8. *And be it further enacted,* That whenever the President of the United States shall have reason to believe that offences have been or are likely to be committed against the provisions of this act within any judicial district, it shall be lawful for him, in his discretion, to direct the judge, marshal, and district attorney of such district to attend at such place within the district, and for such time as he may designate, for the purpose of the more speedy arrest and trial of persons charged with a violation of this act; and it shall be the duty of every judge or other officer, when any such requisition shall be received by him, to attend at the place and for the time therein designated.

SEC. 9. *And be it further enacted,* That it shall be lawful for the President of the United States, or such person as he may empower for that purpose, to employ such part of the land or naval forces of the United States, or of the militia, as shall be necessary to prevent the violation and enforce the due execution of this act.

SEC. 10. *And be it further enacted,* That upon all questions of law arising in any cause under the provisions of this act a final appeal may be taken to the Supreme Court of the United States.

Questions

1. What was the intent of the Civil Rights Act?
2. Who was responsible for enforcing this law, and what powers might they use? Was it necessary to wait until the law was violated before officers of the law could act?
3. According to the Fourteenth Amendment, who is a citizen of the United States? What rights does the amendment say citizens have? What does "equal protection of the laws" mean?

Questions for Further Thought

1. Compare and contrast President Johnson's description of conditions in the South (Document 16-1) with that of General Schurz (Document 16-2). Which do you find to be more accurate? Why?
2. What did Johnson and Schurz say about relations between blacks and whites?
3. Compare the Mississippi Black Codes (Document 16-3) with the Civil Rights Act of 1866 (Document 16-4). Why do you think Congress believed that it had to pass the Civil Rights Act and then adopt the Fourteenth Amendment?

Radical Reconstruction

When only Tennessee ratified the Fourteenth Amendment (and was readmitted to the Union), Congressional Republicans, strengthened by their victories in the 1866 Congressional elections, passed the Reconstruction Acts (see text p. 494). These laws forced unreconstructed Confederate states to meet Republican conditions for readmission, including granting African-American men the vote (Document 16-5). Although labeled as "radical," these measures actually fell short of what some in Congress called for (see text p. 496).

Northern support for Reconstruction fluctuated (Document 16-6). Forced to choose between presidential Reconstruction and the Reconstruction programs proposed by Congress, most northerners preferred the latter. However, northern support for Reconstruction faded after 1868 and virtually disappeared in the 1870s (see text p. 503).

Most southern whites had opposed Republican Reconstruction from the outset, though the intensity of the opposition fluctuated (see text pp. 497–498). The animosity of southern whites toward Reconstruction, Republicans, and African-Americans intensified during election campaigns and whenever a sensitive issue was put before the public (Document 16-6). The Ku Klux Klan was especially active during such times (Document 16-7), despite legislation enacted against it.

During Reconstruction African-Americans obtained a number of civil and political rights, most of which were lost in the years that followed Reconstruction (see text pp. 498–500 and American Voices, text p. 502). Blacks made other gains which they were able to keep even after Reconstruction: formalizing their marriages, stabilizing their families, distancing themselves from slavery, creating institutions such as the black church, pursuing educational opportunities, and acquiring property (Document 16-8). Over the years, increasing (though still small) numbers of African-Americans became property holders.

16-5   Thaddeus Stevens on Black Suffrage and Land Redistribution (1867)

The Radical Republicans, including Congressman Thaddeus Stevens of Pennsylvania, believed that besides the vote, freedmen would need an economic basis for controlling their lives (see text pp. 486–487). Below are excerpts from the remarks of Thaddeus Stevens and from a bill in which he proposed to alter the South drastically.

Source: Congressional Globe, January 3, 1867, p. 252; March 19, 1867, p. 203.

ON BLACK SUFFRAGE

Unless the rebel States, before admission, should be made republican in spirit, and placed under the guardianship of loyal men, all our blood and treasure will have been spent in vain. I waive now the question of punishment which, if we are wise, will still be inflicted by moderate confiscations. . . . Impartial suffrage, both in electing the delegates and ratifying their proceedings, is now the fixed rule. There is more reason why colored voters should be admit- ted in the rebel States than in the Territories. In the States they form the great mass of the loyal men. Possibly with their aid loyal governments may be established in most of those States. Without it all are sure to be ruled by traitors; and loyal men, black and white, will be oppressed, exiled, or murdered. There are several good reasons for the passage of this bill. In the first place, it is just. I am now confining my argument to negro suffrage in the rebel States. Have not loyal blacks quite as good a right to choose rulers and make laws as rebel whites? In the second place, it is a necessity in order to protect the loyal white men in the seceded States. The white Union men are in a great minority in each of those States. With them the blacks would act in a body; and it is believed that in each of said States, except one, the two united would form a majority, control the States, and protect themselves. Now they are the victims of daily murder. . . .

Another good reason is, it would insure the ascendency of the Union party. . . . I believe . . . that on the continued ascendency of that party depends the safety of this great nation. If impartial suffrage is excluded in the rebel States, then every one of them is sure to send a solid rebel representative delegation to Congress, and cast a solid rebel electoral vote. They, with their kindred Copperheads of the North, would always elect the President and control Congress. While slavery sat upon her defiant throne, and insulted and intimidated the trembling North, the South frequently divided on questions of policy between Whigs and Democrats, and gave victory alternately to the sections. Now, you must divide them between loyalists, without regard to color, and disloyalists, or you will be the perpetual vassals of the free-trade, irritated, revengeful South. . . . I am for negro suffrage in every rebel State. If it be just, it should not be denied; if it be necessary, it should be adopted; if it be a punishment to traitors, they deserve it.

BILL ON LAND REDISTRIBUTION

Whereas it is due to justice, as an example to future times, that some proper punishment should be inflicted on the people who constituted the "confederate States of America," both because they, declaring an unjust war against the United States for the purpose of destroying republican liberty and permanently establishing slavery, as well as for the cruel and barbarous manner in which they conducted said war, in violation of all the laws of civilized warfare, and also to compel them to make some compensation for the damages and expenditures caused by said war: Therefore,

Be it enacted by the Senate and House of Representatives of the United States of America in Congress assembled, That all the public lands belonging to the ten States that formed the government of the so-called "confederate States of America" shall be forfeited by said States and become forthwith vested in the United States. . . .

That out of the lands thus seized and confiscated the slaves who have been liberated by the operations of the war and the amendment to the Constitution or otherwise, who resided in said "confederate States" on the 4th day of March, A.D. 1861, or since, shall have distributed to them as follows, namely: to each male person who is the head of a family, forty acres; to each adult male, whether the head of a family or not, forty acres; to each widow who is the head of a family, forty acres—to be held by them in fee-simple, but to be inalienable for the next ten years after they become seized thereof. . . .

That out of the balance of the property thus seized and confiscated there shall be raised, in the manner hereinafter provided, a sum equal to fifty dollars, for each homestead, to be applied by the trustees hereinafter mentioned toward the erection of buildings on the said homesteads for the use of said slaves; and the further sum of $500,000,000, which shall be appropriated as follows, to wit: $200,000,000 shall be invested in United States six per cent securities; and the interest thereof shall be semi-annually added to the pensions allowed by law to pensioners who have become so by reason of the late war; $300,000,000, or so much thereof as may be needed, shall be appropriated to pay damages done to loyal citizens by the civil or military operations of the government lately called the "confederate States of America." . . .

That in order that just discrimination may be made, the property of no one shall be seized whose whole estate on the 4th day of March, A.D. 1865, was not worth more than $5,000, to be valued by the said commission, unless he shall have voluntarily become an officer or employé in the military or civil service of the "confederate States of America," or in the civil or military service of some one of said States. . . .

Questions

1. On what grounds did Stevens justify granting African-American men the vote?
2. What did Stevens want to do with land confiscated in the South?
3. Why do you think Congress rejected Stevens's land confiscation and redistribution proposal? Do you think that if Congress had adopted the proposal, it would have made a difference in the history of the South or the United States? Why or why not?

16-6   The Rise and Fall of Northern Support for Reconstruction (1868, 1874)

Evidence of broad northern support for the Republican program could be found in many places other than the ballot box. Illustrations from *Harper's Weekly* such as the one in the text (p. 497) and the one from 1868 titled "This Is a White Man's Government" reflected popular attitudes in the North in the 1860s.

However, northern support for Reconstruction began to erode as early as 1868. For various reasons Republican state governments in the South got a very bad reputation in the North. Northern willingness to use force to keep Republican governments in office in the South, even when threatened by violence, intimidation, and fraud, was exhausted by 1874 (see text p. 503), the year the second *Harper's Weekly* illustration appeared. Both cartoons shown here are by Thomas Nast.

The first cartoon is packed with specific allusions. On the left is a caricature of an Irishman; note the cross and clay pipe in his hatband, which reads "5 POINTS." Five Points, in lower Manhattan, was reputed to be the most dangerous slum in the United States; even police officers did not go there except in groups. Note the liquor bottle in his pocket; his shillelagh reads "A VOTE." Just visible behind him are a black man who has been lynched from a lamppost and the burning Colored Orphan Asylum (references to the 1863 New York City draft riots; see text p. 456 and Document 15-3).

The center figure is Nathan Bedford Forrest (see text pp. 504–505), identifiable from the initials on his hatband. His upraised dagger reads "THE LOST CAUSE"; note also his whip and pistol. His belt buckle carries the initials CSA (for Confederate States of America). Forrest's lapel button—a skull with the words "FORT PILLOW"—recalls the 1864 massacre of African-American soldiers by Forrest's troops (see text p. 501). Behind Forrest a building labeled "SOUTHERN SCHOOL" is burning.

At right a figure representing Big Business holds aloft a bundle of money labeled "CAPITAL FOR VOTES." His lapel button reads "5TH AVENUE," home for many of the wealthy in New York City.

Together, the three figures are crushing an African-American Civil War veteran; note his Union jacket and cap, as well as the saber and the American flag.

Source: Thomas Nast, "This Is a White Man's Government," *Harper's Weekly,* September 5, 1868; Thomas Nast, "Colored Rule in a Reconstructed State," *Harper's Weekly,* March 14, 1874. Art courtesy the Research Libraries, New York Public Library.

Questions

1. Note the picture of African-Americans presented here and in the illustration on text p. 497. Contrast that with the portrayal of government by southern whites.
2. Compare the portrayal of African-Americans in the last illustration with that in the earlier illustrations.
3. What do you think accounts for the change?

COLORED RULE IN A RECONSTRUCTED(?) STATE.—[See Page 242.]

(THE MEMBERS CALL EACH OTHER THIEVES, LIARS, RASCALS, AND COWARDS.)

COLUMBIA. "You are Aping the lowest Whites. If you disgrace your Race in this way you had better take Back Seats."

16-7 *"A Fool's Errand. By One of the Fools"* (1879)

A native of Ohio, Albion Winegar Tourgee (1838–1905) was working as a school-teacher in New York when the Civil War began. In April 1861 he joined the 27th New York Regiment and was wounded at the first battle of Bull Run. He returned to the army in July 1862 as a lieutenant in the 105th Ohio Regiment. Captured in 1863 at Murfreesboro, he returned to Ohio through a prisoner exchange and then rejoined his regiment to fight at Chickamauga, Lookout Mountain, and Missionary Ridge. Twice charged with insubordination, Tourgee resigned his commission in December 1863 and returned to Ohio to study law. By the fall of 1865 he had relocated, as a "carpet-bagger" (see text p. 498), in Greensboro, North Carolina. In 1868, under the electoral rule imposed under radical Reconstruction (see text p. 494), Tourgee won election as a judge on the state superior court. He served there for six years, finding ample opportunity to defend the rights of freedmen and denounce the atrocities of the Ku Klux Klan. When his tenure on the court ended, President Grant appointed him pension agent at Raleigh, from which office he continued his battle with the Klan and with redeemer Democrats (see text pp. 501–503). By the summer of 1879 he had had enough and moved north with his family, making Mayville, New York, his home by 1881. In the novel *A Fool's Errand*, published in the year of his departure from North Carolina, Tourgee described his experiences during Reconstruction through the character Colonel Comfort Servosse, whom he depicted as "the Fool."

Source: [Albion W. Tourgee], *A Fool's Errand. By One of the Fools* (New York: Fords, Howard, & Hulbert, 1878), pp. 182–192.

It was in the winter of 1868-69 . . . when it was said that already Reconstruction had been an approved success, [and] the traces of the war been blotted out . . . a little company of colored men came to the Fool one day; and one of them, who acted as spokesman said,—

"What's dis we hear, Mars Kunnel [Master Colonel], bout de Klux?"

"The what?" he asked.

"De Klux—de Ku-Kluckers dey calls demselves."

"Oh! The Ku-Klux, Ku-Klux-Klan . . . you mean."

"Yes: dem folks what rides about at night a-pesterin' pore colored people, an' pretendin' tu be jes from hell, or some of de battle-fields ob ole Virginny."

"Oh, that's all gammon [humbug]! There is nothing in the world in it,—nothing at all. . . ."

"You don't think dey's ghostses, nor nothing' ob dat sort?" asked another.

"Think! I know they are not."

"So do I," growled one of their number who had not spoken before, in a tone . . . that . . . drew the eyes of the Fool upon him at once.

"So your mind's made up on that point too, is it Bob?" he asked laughingly.

"I know dey's not ghosts, Kunnel. I wish ter God dey was!" was the reply.

"Why, what do you mean, Bob?" asked the colonel in surprise.

"Will you jes help me take off my shirt, Jim?" said Bob . . . as he turned to one of those with him. . . .

"What d'ye tink ob dat, Kunnel?"

"My God!" exclaimed the Fool, starting back in surprise and horror. "What does this mean, Bob?"

"Seen de Kluckers, sah," was the grimly-laconic answer.

The sight which presented itself to the Fool's eyes was truly terrible. . . . The whole back was livid and swollen, bruised as if it had been brayed in a mortar. Apparently, after having cut the flesh with closely-laid welts and furrows, sloping downward from the left side towards the right, with the peculiar skill . . . which could only be obtained through the abundant opportunity for severe . . . flagellation which prevailed under . . . slavery, the operator had changed his position, and scientifically cross-checked the whole. . . . "Nobody but an ole oberseer ebber dun dat, Kunnel." . . . When his clothing had been resumed, he sat down and poured into the wondering ears of the Fool this story:—

BOB'S EXPERIENCE.

"Yer see, I'se a blacksmith at Burke's Cross-Roads. I've been thar ever since a few days arter I heer ob de surrender. I rented an ole house dar, an' put up a sort of shop . . . an' went to work. . . .

"Long a while back—p'raps five er six month—I refused ter du some work fer Michael Anson or his boy, 'cause they'd run up quite a score at de shop, an' allers put me off when I wanted pay. . . . Folks said I waz gettin' too smart fer a nigger, an' sech like; but I kep right on; tole em I waz a free man . . . an' I didn't propose ter do any man's work fer noffin'. Most everybody hed somefin' ter say about it; but it didn't seem ter hurt my trade very much. . . . When ther come an election, I sed my say, did my own votin', an' tole de other colored people dey waz free, an' hed a right ter du de same. Thet's bad doctrine up in our country. . . . Dey don't mind 'bout . . . our votin', so long ez we votes ez day tell us. Dat' dare idea uv liberty fer a nigger.

"Well, here a few weeks ago, I foun' a board stuck up on my shop one mornin', wid dese words on it:—

"'BOB MARTIN,—You're gettin' too dam smart! The white folks round Burke's Cross-Roads don't want any sech smart niggers round thar. You'd better git, er you'll hev a call from the

"'K.K.K.'

. . . [Y]esterday . . . my ole 'ooman . . . tuk part ob de chillen into bed wid her; an' de rest crawled in wid me. . . . I kinder remember hearin' de dog bark, but I didn't mind it; an', de fust ting I knew, de do' was bust in. . . . Dar was 'bout tirty of 'em standin' dar in de moonlight, all dressed in black gowns thet come down to ther boots, an' some sort of high hat on, dat come down ober der faces. . . . Den dey tied me tu a tree, an' done what you've seen. Dey tuk my wife an' oldes' gal out of de house, tore de close right about off 'em, an' abused 'em shockin' afore my eyes. After tarin' tings up a heap in de house, dey rode off, tellin' me dey reckoned I's larn to be 'spectful to white folks here-arter. . . .

"Why have you not complained of this outrage to the authorities?" . . . asked [the Fool] after a moment.

"I tole Squire Haskins an' Judge Thompson what I hev tole you," answered Bob.

"And what did they say?"

"Dat dey couldn't do noffin' unless I could sw'ar to the parties." . . .

There was a moment's silence. Then the colored man asked,—

"Isn't dere no one else, Kunnel, dat could do any ting? Can't de President or Congress do somefin'? De gov'ment sot us free, an' it 'pears like it oughtn't to let our old mas-ters impose on us in no sech way now. . . . We ain't cow-ards. We showed dat in de wah. I'se seen darkeys go whar de white troops wa'n't anxious to foller 'em, mor'n once."

"Where was that, Bob?"

"Wal, at Fo't Wagner, for one."

"How did you know about that?"

"How did I know 'bout dat? Bress yer soul, Kunnel, I was dar!"

Questions

1. Tourgee, thinly disguised as Comfort Servosse in the novel, depicted himself as "the Fool." Why?
2. Could the president or Congress have acted in ways that they did not to suppress the Ku Klux Klan? Describe the measures you think would have been necessary.
3. Were equal rights for blacks and the restoration of civil government in the South compatible? Explain why or why not.

16-8   Black Farm Owners in the South (1870–1910); Black Homeowners in the South (1870–1910)

During Reconstruction the lives of African-Americans improved significantly, largely as a result of their own efforts. When Reconstruction ended, many of those gains were lost, particularly in the areas of civil and political rights (see text pp. 503, 506). Still, African-Americans continued to improve themselves. As the statistics below indicate, African-Americans after 1870 increasingly joined the ranks of farm owners and home-owners (see text pp. 506–507).

Source: Loren Schweninger, *Black Property Owners in the South, 1790–1915*, pp. 164, 170, 174, 180. Copyright 1990 by the Board of Trustees of the University of Illinois. Used with per-mission of the University of Illinois Press.

Black Farm Owners in the South, 1870–1910: Total Number and Percentage of Owners (Black and White)

State	1870		1890		Percentage of increase, 1870–1890	1900		Percentage of increase, 1890–1900	1910		Percentage of increase, 1900–1910
	Total	Percentage	Total	Percentage		Total	Percentage		Total	Percentage	
Alabama	1,152	1.3	8,847	13	668	14,110	15	59	17,047	15	21
Arkansas	1,203	5.2	8,004	24	565	11,941	25	49	14,660	23	23
Florida	596	3.5	4,940	38	729	6,551	48	33	7,286	50	11
Georgia	1,367	1.4	8,131	13	495	11,375	14	40	15,698	13	38
Louisiana	1,107	1.8	6,685	18	504	9,378	16	40	10,681	19	14
Mississippi	1,600	1.9	11,526	13	620	20,973	16	82	24,949	15	19
North Carolina	1,628	2.2	10,494	26	545	16,834	31	60	20,707	32	23
South Carolina	3,062	4.0	13,075	21	327	18,970	22	45	20,356	21	7
Tennessee	1,301	2.2	6,378	23	390	9,414	28	48	10,698	28	14
Texas	839	1.8	12,513	26	1,391	20,139	31	61	21,182	30	5
Virginia	860	1.0	13,678	43	1,490	26,527	59	94	32,168	67	21

Black Homeowners* in the South, 1870–1910: Total Number and Percentage of Owners (Black and White)

State	1870		1890		1910	
	Total	Percentage	Total	Percentage	Total	Percentage
Alabama	215	4.3	6,898	11	16,714	17
Arkansas	56	5.3	3,840	17	9,802	27
Florida	46	3.7	5,709	28	13,581	22
Georgia	232	2.9	11,874	12	22,544	16
Louisiana	639	5.7	7,917	11	16,160	16
Mississippi	138	4.5	5,430	11	13,783	20
North Carolina	199	5.6	9,516	15	19,627	26
South Carolina	312	4.8	8,026	11	12,730	15
Tennessee	187	3.0	8,285	16	16,070	23
Texas	27	1.0	8,367	22	20,443	26
Virginia	409	3.3	16,210	20	24,405	27

*Excludes farm homes

Questions

1. Which state(s) had the greatest increase in black farm owners? In black homeowners?
2. What do the tables reveal about African-Americans in the South in an era when they were systematically oppressed by whites?
3. How can you explain this evidence of the success of African-Americans in the South in the late nineteenth century?

Questions for Further Thought

1. What were the principal obstacles faced by radical Republicans as they passed the Civil Rights Acts of 1866 and 1875 as well as the Fourteenth and Fifteenth amendments? Did they successfully overcome those obstacles? Explain why or why not.
2. Do you agree with Tourgee (Document 16-7) that northern Reconstruction efforts were a "Fool's Errand"? Why do you think Tourgee came to that conclusion?
3. Clearly, emancipation and Reconstruction did not bring about equal rights for blacks. But what did change?

The North during Reconstruction

After the Civil War the Republican party remained firmly entrenched in power in the North and, with the implementation of radical Reconstruction, throughout the South as well. The war had offered Republicans an occasion to consolidate a great deal of power in the federal government (see text p. 508), a tendency that left many Americans ill at ease. The Democrats, traditionally the party of limited government, endeavored to free themselves of their proslavery past by presenting themselves as the party of reform. "Stalwart" Republicans remained solidly behind President Grant even as rumors of scandal in his first administration were proved to be true in his second (text pp. 509–511). But "Liberal" Republicans took a more critical look at their party and its leadership. Grant's efforts to push through the annexation of Santo Domingo precipitated a break with Senator Charles Sumner that provided a prominent example of a widening breach in Republican ranks (Document 16-9).

Northerners also grew increasingly uncertain about the future of federally directed Reconstruction in the southern states. Northerners did demand evidence that the South had accepted its defeat. Most northerners found that evidence in the ratification of the Fourteenth and Fifteenth amendments to the Constitution. The question then became a mater of what was to be accomplished by continued federal occupation of southern states. Democrats and Liberal Republicans argued that universal (manhood) suffrage should be accompanied by universal amnesty, that a republican form of government required the participation of all citizens, and that the perpetual disfranchisement of former rebels simply transformed them into an outlaw caste. The willingness of Liberal Republicans to join with Democrats to support Horace Greeley in 1872 (see text p. 510) marked the first significant break in Republican ranks and offered to the Democrats political issues that were free of association with the Civil War. The nomination of Samuel J. Tilden as the Democratic presidential candidate in 1876 changed the dynamics of party politics. Few doubted that Tilden had won the election, but there were enough disputed electoral votes to prevent his inauguration (see text pp. 511–512). Republican efforts to maintain control of the presidency led to the Compromise of 1877 (see text pp. 512–513) and to a new era of two-party politics (Document 16-10).

16-9 "Republicanism vs. Grantism" (1872)

Charles Sumner   Charles Sumner had come to the U.S. Senate during the first wave of antislavery political insurgency across the North (see Document 14-7). Throughout the Civil War and Reconstruction he had been among the most vehement and politically powerful radical Republicans (see text p. 509). During the Grant administration, however, Sumner frequently opposed the president, most openly by denouncing Grant's efforts to acquire Santo Domingo (the present-day Dominican Republic) as a territory of the United States. Grant loyalists retaliated by deposing Sumner as chairman of the Foreign Relations Committee in 1872. With a remarkable number of former radical Republicans (George Washington Julian among them), Sumner cast his lot with the Liberal Republicans, strongly opposing Grant's reelection and supporting the candidacy of Horace Greeley (see text p. 510). This break in the ranks of the Republicans, specifically the defection of radical Republicans to the Liberal Republican platform of sectional reconciliation, marked the beginning of the end of Reconstruction. Here Sumner denounces "Grantism" (see text p. 510) on the Senate floor.

Source: Charles Sumner: His Complete Works (Lee and Shepard, 1900; reprint, New York: Negro Universities Press, 1969), vol. 20, pp. 83–171.

Mr. President,—I have no hesitation in declaring myself a member of the Republican Party, and one of the straitest of the sect. I doubt if any Senator can point to earlier or more constant service in its behalf. I began at the beginning, and from that early day have never failed to sustain its candidates and to advance its principles. . . .

Turning back to its birth, I recall a speech of my own at a State Convention in Massachusetts, as early as September 7, 1854, where I vindicated its principles and announced its name in these words: "as *Republicans* we go forth to encounter the *Oligarches* of Slavery." . . . The Republican Party was necessary and permanent, and always on an ascending plane. For such a party there was no death, but higher life and nobler aims; and this was the party to which I gave my vows. But, alas, how changed! Once country was the object, and not a man; once principle was inscribed on the victorious banners, and not a name only.

THE REPUBLICAN PARTY SEIZED BY THE PRESIDENT

It is not difficult to indicate when this disastrous change . . . became not merely manifest, but painfully conspicuous . . . suddenly and without any warning through the public press or any expression from public opinion, the President elected by the Republican Party precipitated upon the country an ill-considered and ill-omened scheme for the annexaton of a portion of the island of San Domingo. . . .

PRESIDENTIAL PRETENSIONS

. . . [t]he Presidential office has been used to advance his own family on a scale of nepotism dwarfing everything of

the kind in our history . . . and . . . all these assumptions have matured in a *personal government*, semi-military in character and breathing the military spirit,—being a species of Caesarism or *personalism*, abhorrent to republican institutions. . . . [T]he chosen head of the Republic is known chiefly for Presidential pretensions, utterly indefensible in character, derogatory to the country, and of evil influence, making personal objects a primary pursuit, so that . . . he is a bad example, through whom republican institutions suffer and the people learn to do wrong. . . .

PERSONAL GOVERNMENT UNREPUBLICAN

Personal Government is autocratic. It is the One-Man Power elevated above all else, and is therefore in direct conflict with republican government, whose consummate form is tripartite . . . each independent and coequal. . . .

A government of laws and not of men is the object of republican government; nay, more, it is the distinctive essence without which it becomes a tyranny. Therefore personal government in all its forms, and especially when it seeks to sway the action of any other branch or overturn its constitutional negative, is hostile to the first principles of republican institutions, and an unquestionable outrage. That our President has offended in this way is unhappily too apparent.

THE PRESIDENT AS CIVILIAN

To comprehend the personal government that has been installed over us we must know its author. His picture is the necessary frontispiece,—not as soldier, let it be borne in mind, but as civilian. . . .

To appreciate his peculiar character as a civilian it is

important to know his triumphs as a soldier, for the one is the natural complement of the other. The successful soldier is rarely changed to the successful civilian. There seems to be an incompatibility between the two. . . . One always a soldier cannot late in life become a statesman. . . . Washington and Jackson were civilians as well as soldiers. . . .

THE GREAT PRESIDENTIAL QUARRELER

Any presentment of the President would be imperfect which did not show how this ungovernable personality breaks forth in quarrel, making him the great Presidential quarreler of our history. . . . With the arrogance of arms he resents any impediment in his path,—as when, in the spring of 1870, without allusion to himself, I felt it my duty to oppose his San Domingo contrivance. . . .

DUTY OF THE REPUBLICAN PARTY

And now the question of Duty is distinctly presented to the Republican Party. . . . Do the Presidential pretensions merit the sanction of the party? Can Republicans, without departing from all obligations, whether of party or patriotism, recognize our ambitious Caesar as a proper representative? . . . Therefore with unspeakable interest will the country watch the National Convention at Philadelphia. It may be an assembly (and such is my hope) where ideas and principles are above all personal pretensions, and the unity of the party is symbolized in the candidate; or it may add another to Presidential rings, being an expansion of the military ring at the Executive Mansion, the senatorial ring in the [Senate] Chamber, and the political ring in the customhouses of New York and New Orleans. A National Convention which is a Republican ring cannot represent the Republican Party. . . . I wait the determination of the National Convention. . . . Not without anxiety do I wait, but with the earnest hope that the Convention will bring the Republican Party into ancient harmony, saving it especially from the suicidal folly of an issue on the personal pretensions of one man.

Questions

1. What does Sumner mean when he denounces "personal government"? Why is such a government "unrepublican"?

2. In Sumner's view, why did Grant's military career make him unsuitable for the presidency?

3. Sumner contrasts a party of "principle" with a party of "rings." What does he mean by making this distinction?

16-10 Montgomery Blair on the Compromise of 1877

Like his father, Andrew Jackson's close adviser Francis P. Blair, Montgomery Blair (1813–1883) left the Democratic party for the Republican party in the 1850s. Abraham Lincoln appointed the younger Blair postmaster general, and during the early years of the Civil War Montgomery Blair promoted conservative policies in the Lincoln administration to preserve the loyalties of border state slave owners like himself. After Lincoln settled on a policy of emancipation, Blair's vocal aversion to radical Republicans became a political liability, and Lincoln forced his resignation before the 1864 election. Blair returned to the Democratic party and urged its leaders to leave the "sham" proslavery democracy behind and present the Democratic party to the public as the party of reform. In the following correspondence with Gideon Welles, a fellow conservative (and former Democrat) in Lincoln's cabinet, Blair suggested a new course for the Democrats, reported on the electoral crisis of the 1850s, and analyzed its resolution in the Compromise of 1877 (see text pp. 512–513).

Source: Excerpted from letters of Montgomery Blair to Gideon Welles about the Compromise of 1877, Montgomery Blair Papers, Missouri Historical Society, St. Louis.

M. Blair to G. Welles, 25 December 1875
Slave Democracy . . . Sham Democracy . . . sacrificed the peace of the country & the blood of [our] . . . countrymen. . . . [T]he Greeley movement got rid of the nasty sectional quarrel which blocked the way to the consideration of any other question. . . . The people see that they are in fact the victims of the monopolies created by the radicals['] abuses in possession of the Govt & that it is their great monied corporations that put Grant in power.

M. Blair to G. Welles, 8 June 1876
The [Democratic] party will have to return to its proper principles & to their proper leaders before we can ever hope to see it installed in power. . . . [I]t is absolutely necessary that the country should see that these followers have turned back to the men of the right school of Democracy. . . . Going to Greeley was not enough. It was not going as far as going to Tilden. . . . It will . . . end the dominance of Radicalism. . . .

M. Blair to G. Welles, 19 June 1876
I have great doubt I confess whether [Tilden] . . . can ever be elected President. But there is a chance now. The Govt. has become so corrupt in the hands of the Radicals that there is a deep & wide [mood] in favor of reform. . . . The time will come when Radicalism will become synonymous in the minds of the people with every thing detestable in Govt. Nothing but power makes our present rulers respectable. . . .

   If we put up Tilden he can make an aggressive war upon the Rascality which is now the essence of Radicalism. Being sound in finance and having also sustained the war by contributions of money and speeches, he can fend off on the side issues the rads will try to make—and thus be able to focus on the reform issue & . . . the chaos of Govt. in the hands of the Rad party.

M. Blair to G. Welles, 15 January 1877
The situation here is very complicated, & it is not easy to predict the result. Every day . . . makes it plainer that Tilden is Elected & the enemy will find it difficult to prevent his inauguration. . . . But notwithstanding this there is a . . . class of politicians who are operating with great skill & industry to prevent the inauguration of Tilden. . . . Hayes['] . . . men turn to the southern leaders offering to reconstruct the old whig party at the South & to give up the negro and carpet bag govt. . . . I have no doubt . . . that the Rads are letting S.C. and La slide having already given up Fla.

M. Blair to G. Welles, 19 February 1877
The [electoral] commission is no mystery to me. It resulted from the demoralization of our forces. . . . Besides, I do not think the members of Congress really wanted Tilden here. His advent would put a stop to the system of expenditures which has made it profitable to be in congress. If the result is . . . to infuse a sterner policy on the Democracy we shall have lost nothing by defeat.

M. Blair to G. Welles, 3 March 1877
There never was any intention of inaugurating Tilden.

M. Blair to G. Welles, 20 July 1877
I am afraid the compromise bill will pass notwithstanding its objectionable character. I fear that some of our people do not want Tilden here. Reform after all is not exactly the thing some of them want. . . . But in making these men directly responsible for the defeat of Tilden[,] if he is defeated[,] we open the way for a better understanding of the real nature of the struggle in the future, & get rid of the treacherous leaders. . . .

Questions

1. In Blair's view, what aspects of the Democratic party had to change before it could elect a president?
2. Why does Blair think the "Radicals" are vulnerable in 1876?
3. How did the Republicans gain the support of southern Democrats to secure the inauguration of Hayes over Tilden

Questions for Further Thought

1. How did the Civil War reshape the two-party system?
2. As Grant began his second term, what were the great weaknesses of the Republican and Democratic parties?
3. The Compromise of 1877 achieved sectional reconciliation and ended Reconstruction. Do you view it as smart politics or as a corrupt bargain? Explain why.

Credits and Acknowledgments

Please note that most credits and acknowledgments appear together with their respective documents.

Document 12-3, p. 224 (The Shakers: Rebecca Cox Jackson) excerpted from Jean McMahon Humez, ed., *Gifts of Power: The Writings of Rebecca Jackson, Black Visionary, Shaker Eldress* (Amherst: University of Massachusetts Press, 1981), pp. 220–221. Courtesy: The Western Reserve Historical Society, Cleveland, Ohio.

Document 15-2, p. 281 (The Crisis at Fort Sumter [April 1861]) excerpted from C. Vann Woodward, *Mary Chesnut's Civil War* (New Haven and London: Yale University Press, 1981) pp. 35–53. Copyright © 1981 by Yale University Press. Reprinted by permission.

Document 15-7, p. 290 (A Soldier's Letter to His Wife [1862]) reprinted by permisson from the Papers of James B. Griffin, Center for American History, University of Texas at Austin. In Orville Vernon Burton and Judith N. McArthur, eds., *"A Gentleman and an Officer": A Social and Military History of James B. Griffin's Civil War* (New York: Oxford University Press, 1996).